Macromedia®
Flash® Professional 8

UNLEASHED

David Vogeleer
Eddie Wilson
Lou Barber

800 East 96th Street, Indianapolis, Indiana 46240 USA

Macromedia® Flash® Professional 8 Unleashed

Copyright © 2006 by Sams Publishing

International Standard Book Number: 0-672-32761-9

Library of Congress Catalog Card Number: 2004097936

Printed in the United States of America

First Printing: October 2005

08   07   06   05   4   3   2   1

Trademarks

Warning and Disclaimer

Bulk Sales

Sams Publishing offers excellent discounts on this book when ordered in quantity for bulk purchases or special sales. For more information, please contact

> U.S. Corporate and Government Sales
> 1-800-382-3419
> corpsales@pearsontechgroup.com

For sales outside of the U.S., please contact

> International Sales
> international@pearsoned.com

Senior Acquisitions Editor
Linda Bump Harrison

Development Editor
Damon Jordan

Managing Editor
Charlotte Clapp

Project Editor
George E. Nedeff

Copy Editor
Barbara Hacha

Indexer
Erika Millen

Proofreader
Leslie Joseph

Technical Editors
Jonathan Duran
Aria Danika

Publishing Coordinator
Vanessa Evans

Book Designer
Gary Adair

Page Layout
Michelle Mitchell

Contents at a Glance

Table of Contents

About the Author

David Vogeleer has been working in Flash since version 4, focusing mainly on ActionScript. He has been certified as a Flash developer and instructor and now works as a Media Specialist for Ocean Systems Engineering focusing on web-based training. David also has contributed articles to FlashMagazine.com as well as the *MX Developers Journal*. He also co-founded EMLlabs.com with Eddie Wilson as a tutorial based site for intermediate to advanced Flash usage. David is also a very devoted supporter of snowboarding whenever free time and cold weather present themselves.

About the Contributing Authors

Eddie Wilson, a graphic designer by profession, directed his interests toward Flash design with the release of v4. Continually educating himself in interactive design, he strives to develop Flash applications that are visually appealing, intuitive, and useable. Eddie has utilized his talent and experience on projects for such companies as American Family Fitness, Dunmar Moving Companies, *Time Magazine*, Overnite Shipping, Freddie Mac, and The Switch Beverage Company to name a few. Previously a partner in a Richmond-based design firm, Eddie has branched out on his own and provides his services on a contract basis. Eddie is also a cofounder of EMLlabs (along with David Vogeleer), an online resource for advanced Macromedia Flash techniques.

Lou Barber is manager and founder of FDUG (Flash Development User Group, www.fdug.org) in Richmond, VA. Lou, a Certified Macromedia Flash instructor, enjoys teaching and sharing his knowledge of Flash with anyone willing to learn. He is also owner and creative director of Silhouette Multimedia, LLC, a company specializing in Flash web development and Flash applications. He has been the driving force behind some very impressive and unique websites and continues to introduce the advantages and strengths of Flash to prospective clients.

Dedication

This book is dedicated to my parents, David and Rita Vogeleer,
two of the best things that ever happened to me.

Acknowledgments

I would like to start by thanking Sams Publishing for another opportunity to work on *Flash Unleashed*. I would also like to thank all the editors who were more than a major part of this book including, and in no particular order, Linda Harrison, Damon Jordan, George "Georgius" Nedeff, Barbara Hacha, Jonathan Duran, and Aria Danika. Also, thanks go to Eddie Wilson and Lou Barber for their outstanding contributions to the middle ware chapters. Thanks also go to Jeremy for all the shortcut hints, Jason for the use of his server for a couple of the middle ware chapters, and Donna for letting me have some time off when I needed to make deadlines. Of course, thanks to all my family and friends who have no idea what I do for a living, but encourage me anyway. And special thanks to God for Jolt Cola, a viable substitute for sleep.

We Want to Hear from You!

As the reader of this book, *you* are our most important critic and commentator. We value your opinion and want to know what we're doing right, what we could do better, what areas you'd like to see us publish in, and any other words of wisdom you're willing to pass our way.

You can email or write me directly to let me know what you did or didn't like about this book—as well as what we can do to make our books stronger.

Please note that I cannot help you with technical problems related to the topic of this book, and that due to the high volume of mail I receive, I might not be able to reply to every message.

When you write, please be sure to include this book's title and author as well as your name and phone or email address. I will carefully review your comments and share them with the author and editors who worked on the book.

Email: webdev@samspublishing.com

Mail: Mark Taber
          Associate Publisher
          Sams Publishing
          800 East 96th Street
          Indianapolis, IN 46240 USA

Reader Services

For more information about this book or another Sams Publishing title, visit our website at www.samspublishing.com. Type the ISBN (excluding hyphens) or the title of a book in the Search field to find the page you're looking for.

Introduction

Macromedia Flash 8 is the latest in the Flash family of software. Flash was originally just a vector animation tool but is now one of the most advanced programs for creating rich Internet applications to provide powerful user experiences. Not only is the player that plays Flash content one of the most downloaded pieces of software—surpassing both Internet Explorer and Netscape as well as nearly all media players—but the content is so small in file size that anyone can create great user experiences for dial-up users.

This new version of Flash continues its hard-to-follow tradition of bringing new and exciting features for developers and designers who have been begging for dynamic PNG, GIF, and progressive JPEG support. New features include file upload and download right from the SWF, alpha channel support in video, and real-time dynamic filters and effects. And Macromedia didn't stop with content features—they streamlined panel management, bringing back tabs in panels as well as more robust preference controls, and brought back Normal mode (now Script Assist) in the Actions panel. This new version of Flash is definitely one to take notice of.

Along with the newest version of Flash comes the new edition of *Macromedia Flash Professional 8 Unleashed*. Throughout this book, you will find countless examples and explanations of some of the newest and most powerful tools Flash has to offer, including a complete overview of ActionScript 2.0, the new version of Flash's programming language. Also included in this book is a handy reference guide for ActionScript to help with faster workflow.

Macromedia Flash Professional 8 Unleashed was created with the reader's needs in mind. Please don't hesitate to email me your experiences with this book as well as with Flash 8 at missing-link@mllabs.com.

PART I

Getting Started

IN THIS PART

What's New?

If you are new to Flash, everything in this book will be somewhat new to you, but if you have worked in previous versions of Flash, this chapter will introduce you to some of the new features, both in what can be done in Flash and how it is done inside the Flash IDE.

The Interface

There have been a lot of upgrades to the Flash authoring environment, and one in particular is a "catch-up" feature added to the Mac.

Tabs on the Mac

One of the best productivity features in the previous version of Flash was the document tabs at the top of the screen. This allowed users working in the interface to quickly switch between files, including FLAs, ActionScript files, and JSFL files. But in the previous version of Flash, this feature was PC only. Now, as you can see in Figure 1.1, document tabs have indeed been included in the Mac interface. However, if you prefer the old way of having several floating file windows, you can easily switch back to it on the Mac platform.

Tabs in Panels Are Back

Those who worked in Flash as early as Flash 5 will remember when you could group panels together into a single panel with a tab for each individual section. When Flash MX came out, this feature was removed in favor of dockable/collapsible panels. Now this feature is back, and dockable/collapsible panels are still here as well. To group panels together, select the panel options drop-down (in the top right of the panel) and select Group "PANEL NAME" with, and then select the panel or group of panels you want to group the current panel with. You can also choose New Panel Group to remove the selected panel from the group it is currently in. Figure 1.2 shows the Transform tab among other tabs inside the same panel window.

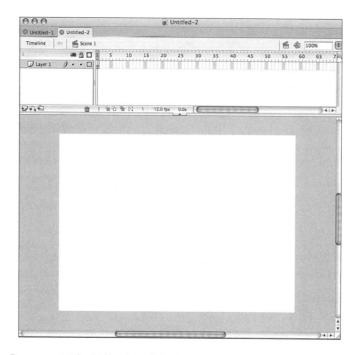

FIGURE 1.1   Document tabs in the Mac interface.

FIGURE 1.2   Grouping panels is a welcome feature returned to the Flash authoring environment.

One Library to Rule Them All

In previous versions of Flash, when you had multiple documents open, and you wanted to grab elements from one library and place them in another file, you would have a separate library for each document. The new library has a drop-down menu, as shown in Figure 1.3, that enables you to switch among different document libraries. You can also "pin" the current library so that when you switch documents, it stays as the current library. This new feature is similar to the feature added in the previous version of Flash that enabled you to pin ActionScript in the Actions panel. If you want to have several libraries floating around instead of the one, you can do this as well by clicking the New Library panel to the right of the Pin Current Library button.

FIGURE 1.3   A single Library panel will help you keep as much screen real estate as possible.

Bigger Pasteboard

Sometimes, you will want to have content available, but not necessarily on the stage where it is visible to end users. Most Flash users will put these elements off the stage in what's called the *pasteboard*. This area will not be viewable by end users viewing your Flash content, but you can manipulate it with ActionScript or tweening. In Flash 8, the pasteboard has been expanded to allow the storage of even more elements.

Two Levels of Undo

With Flash 8, you now have two options for undoing mistakes:

- **Document-level Undo**—A huge list of every action you have taken from anywhere in your Flash document. This is the default selection.

- **Object-level Undo**—Keeps separate lists for the different objects you are working with in Flash so that undoing several things within an object will not affect any changes to others.

You can set which type of undo you want to use by going to Edit, Preferences, and opening the Preferences window, which has also been updated, as you can see in Figure 1.4.

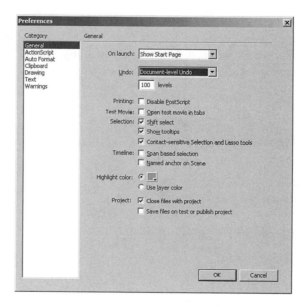

FIGURE 1.4   The new and improved Preferences window.

Object Drawing—The New Grouping

When dealing with raw shapes on the stage, if you place one shape over top of the other (in the same layer) and then move that shape, the shape in the background will have lost the area the foreground shape was overlaying. You can group shapes so that this will not happen, but then you lose the ability to directly edit them. Drawing Objects, however, have the best of both worlds. Drawing Objects can be placed over other Drawing Objects or raw shapes on the same level, and they will not affect one another. In addition, Drawing Objects can have changes applied to them just as if they were a raw shape.

You can create Drawing Objects as you draw the shape with the Rectangle and Oval tool by selecting the Object Drawing option in the Options section of the toolbar. You can also convert raw shapes to Drawing Objects by selecting the shape and going to Modify, Combine Objects, Union.

You can see in Figure 1.5 that when a Drawing Object is selected, the Properties Inspector will still show the same options as if it were a raw shape.

FIGURE 1.5   Drawing Objects have the capability to be edited like raw shapes, but do not affect other elements like groups.

Content on the Go

With the capability to publish to both Flash Lite 1.0 and 1.1, you might be using Flash to create a great deal of mobile content. Macromedia has included several templates and panels to help you.

After you set your publish settings to publish to Flash Lite, the device settings become available, as shown in Figure 1.6. Here you can select the content type your application will be, and as you do, all the available devices for that content type become available. Then you can select the individual devices that you want to test on and click OK.

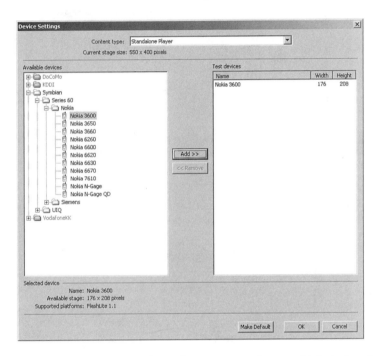

FIGURE 1.6   The Device Settings window where you can choose which devices to test for.

When you have your Flash app ready for testing, you can test the movie as you would normally by going to Control, Test Movie, but this time a different window will appear, as in Figure 1.7. In this test window, you can choose the different devices to test and output information about your application. You can also adjust the magnification level and rotation of the device in the test environment.

Hide and Seek Is Over

One of the major complaints about Flash content on the web (.swf files) is that their content cannot be searched by search engines such as Google. But now in Flash 8, you can actually embed data directly into your published content instead of just having comments and text within the HTML that many search engines do not fully index. To create the metadata necessary for search engines to see SWFs, fill out two fields in the Document Properties dialog box, as shown in Figure 1.8.

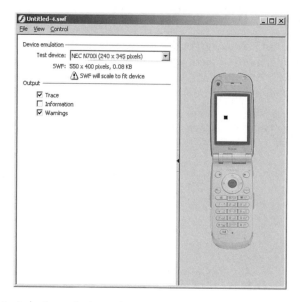

FIGURE 1.7   The test devices window where you can test your Flash content in emulators of your selected devices.

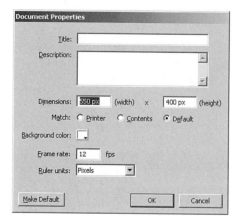

FIGURE 1.8   You can now embed metadata directly into your SWF file through Document Properties.

Following are descriptions of the two fields:

- **Title**—The title of your projects; this does not have to match the title tag in your html document.

- **Description**—This field can contain anything from searchable keywords for your project to copyright information.

There are even more new features in the interface, and you will find them scattered throughout the book. But the interface is not the only part of Flash to receive upgrades.

Welcome Back, Normal Mode

If you have worked in Flash MX or earlier, you might remember an optional way to enter ActionScript that did not require a great deal of typing, but instead allowed you to choose certain options for certain scripts. This was called Normal mode, and it was removed from Flash MX 2004. However, it has returned to Flash as Script Assist.

Script Assist will help you if you are unfamiliar with ActionScript or are concerned that you might be missing some options of a given script. To activate Script Assist, click the Script Assist button in the Actions panel (Window, Actions) and you will see something like Figure 1.9.

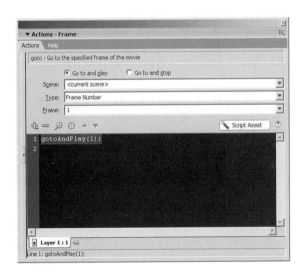

FIGURE 1.9   The Actions panel with Script Assist turned on and the `gotoAndPlay` action selected.

The Fastest Flash Player Ever

Major improvements have been made to increase not only the speed of the player in both data parsing and animation, but the player has received a new text-rendering engine that allows it to show much sharper text.

FlashType

FlashType is a new text-rendering technology that has been included in the Flash Player 8. It uses adaptively sampled distance fields (ADFs) to improve the anti-aliasing quality of text for static, dynamic, and input text fields. This will be especially noticeable when you are dealing with small point text. These ADFs create outlines that determine glyphs in a different way than most text-rendering engines do. They can also use subpixel rendering on LCDs in much the same way that ClearType works. You should notice in the Properties Inspector several new anti-aliasing options, which are covered in great detail in Chapter 15, "Working with Text."

But the rendering engine is not the only thing new to text in Flash. Flash now has a much better WYSIWYG for dealing with text on the stage; you can now select it with the arrow tool, and sizing handles will appear that, if used, affect the dimensions of the text field without scaling the text itself.

Also assisting the Flash player in speed is bitmap caching.

Cache as Bitmap

You can now cache movie clips and buttons as bitmaps to increase the level of performance because the Flash player actually caches a copy of the vector data into the player itself. When you set this option on a button, the player will cache all four states of the button.

To set this property manually, select a movie clip on the stage and check the Use Runtime Bitmap Caching option. This can also be set with ActionScript, as you will see later in Chapter 13, "The Movie Clip Objects."

In the following cases, however, even if this option is selected, it will not work:

- The computer is out of memory, and the bitmap cannot allocate more.
- The object you are trying to set is larger than 2,880 pixels in either height or width.

There are also new visual features of Flash that many designers will enjoy working with, as discussed in the following sections.

Blending

Blending will not be new to people who have worked in applications such as Photoshop, but it is new to Flash. Basically, *blending* controls how colors interact when overlaid. You can set the Blend mode manually from the Property Inspector (Flash Professional 8 only) or in ActionScript, as you will see in Chapter 13.

Following are the available options in the Blend drop-down from the Properties Inspector:

- **normal**—This default option signifies that the pixel values of the blend image will override the pixel values of the base image.

- **layer**—This option creates a temporary buffer for precomposition. This option is done automatically when there is more than one child in a movie clip, and Normal is not selected.

- **darken**—This option compares pixel colors of the overlapping images and displays the darker of the two.

- **multiply**—This option multiplies the color values of the corresponding movie clips where they overlap, usually creating a darker color.

- **lighten**—This option compares pixel colors of the overlapping images and displays the lighter of the two.

- **screen**—The exact opposite of the Multiply option, this option takes the complementing colors of the overlapping movie clips and creates a lighter color.

- **overlay**—This option multiplies the colors of the overlapping movie clips while preserving both highlights and shadows.

- **hardlight**—This option, similar to the Overlay option, will multiply or screen the two movie clips depending on their source color value. If it is darker than .5, it is multiplied. Otherwise, it is screened, or lightened.

- **add**—This option adds the overlapping pixel colors of the two movie clips and sets a maximum color of 0×ff.

- **subtract**—This option subtracts the overlapping pixel colors of the two movie clips and sets a minimum color of 0×00.

- **difference**—This option compares pixel colors of the overlapping images and subtracts the darker color from the lighter color.

- **invert**—This option inverts the background.

- **alpha**—This option applies the alpha of the foreground onto the background, but only if the parent movie clip has a blend mode of Layer set.

- **erase**—This option will "cut out" part of the background with the foreground's alpha, but only if the parent movie clip has a blend mode of Layer set.

Follow these steps to see blending at work:

1. Create a new Flash document.

2. Draw a red rectangle on the stage about 100×150 in size.

3. Convert it to a movie clip called **rec1MC**.

4. Draw a blue rectangle on the stage about 100×150 in size.

5. Convert it to a movie clip called **rec2MC** and slide it over the red rectangle so they overlap somewhat.

6. With the blue rectangle selected, go to the Properties Inspector and set Multiply as the Blend option.

Notice that the part where both rectangles overlap is darker, as if the top rectangle were semitransparent. But this is not that case, as you would see if you put a text field with some text in it under the blue rectangle; the text will be completely obscured.

Another new visual effect includes a list of a few visual filters.

Filters

Much like blend modes, filters will not be new to Photoshop users, but they are new to Flash. Filters allow things such as drop shadow, blur, and beveling to be applied directly to a movie clip, a button, or a text field right from the Filters panel, which is held in Properties Inspector (Flash Professional 8 only). You can also have multiple filters applied to a single object and stack them in different orders to get different effects.

You can see the Filter panel options for the Drop Shadow filter in Figure 1.10. Notice that you can not only adjust the filter, but also how the object interacts with the filter. For instance, you can check the Knockout option, and the filter will remain, but the object on the stage will have vanished.

Following is a list of all available filters:

- **DropShadow**—Adds a drop shadow to an object, inner or outer.
- **Blur**—Adds a blur effect to an object.
- **Glow**—Adds a glow to an object, inner or outer.
- **Bevel**—Adds a simple bevel to an object.
- **GradientGlow**—Adds a gradient glow to an object, inner or outer.
- **GradientBevel**—Adds a gradient bevel to an object.
- **AdjustColor**—Allows you to adjust the Brightness, Contrast, Saturation, and Hue of an object.

Even more options are available when you apply filters to objects with ActionScript, as you will see in Chapter 13.

FIGURE 1.10   The Filters panel, for applying visual effects to objects on the stage.

Stroke Improvements

There has also been a great deal of improvement made to creating lines in Flash. You can now have gradients on lines, whether they are drawn manually or created with ActionScript.

Another improvement for lines is their ends. You can now set the line ends (caps) to either None, Round, or Square. You can also set how lines embedded into movie clips will scale with the following options:

- **Normal**—Always scale the thickness of the line. This is the default choice.

- **Horizontal**—Do not scale the thickness of the line when the line is horizontally scaled.

- **Vertical**—Do not scale the thickness of the line when the line is vertically scaled.

- **None**—Never scale the thickness of the line.

Video in Flash

Although video is discussed on more than one occasion throughout this book, it is important to note a major improvement for video in Flash—the alpha channel.

Now Flash can import, convert to FLV, and play back video with an alpha channel, allowing developers and designers to quickly add video to their Flash content and still be able to see what is behind the video.

As you can see in Figures 1.11 and 1.12, both use the same video, yet have different backgrounds. This was easily done because the video itself has the background taken out.

FIGURE 1.11   You can see the woman walking in front of platform 9 3/4.

Again, video is covered in more detail in Chapter 6, "Working with Sound and Video," and Chapter 26, "Streaming Media."

FIGURE 1.12   This time, the woman is walking in front of a text field, with highlighted text, which means the user is interacting with it as the video plays.

Do not think ActionScript was forgotten; there are several new Object classes, and we will go over a few of them. But for more information on the new objects, check out the reference section at the end of the book.

New Dynamic Content

In previous versions of Flash, the only visuals that could be loaded in at runtime were nonprogressive JPEGs and SWF files. Now you can import GIFs, PNGs, and progressive JPEGs in the same manner as in previous versions of Flash. When you import any of these image types with transparency, the transparency will be maintained.

Following is an example of loading a progressive JPEG as a background image and then loading a PNG image over top of it.

You can use any images you like, or grab the ones from the website.

1. Create a new Flash document.

2. In the first frame, open the Actions panel (Window, Actions) and place this code in it:

```
//create the two movieclips to hold the images
var image1:MovieClip = this.createEmptyMovieClip("image1_mc",1);
var image2:MovieClip = this.createEmptyMovieClip("image2_mc",2);
//now load the first image
image1.loadMovie("mountains.jpg");
//then, when the user clicks the stage, the second image will load
this.onMouseDown = function(){
    image2.loadMovie("atSign.png");
}
```

The preceding code first creates two empty movie clips to house the images you are loading. Then you load the background image into the first movie clip. After that, you create an event so that when a user clicks the mouse on the stage, the second image will load.

Test this movie, and you should see something like Figure 1.13. Notice that the transparency of the second image is maintained.

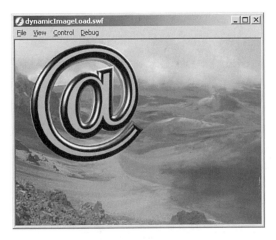

FIGURE 1.13   Flash can load in transparent PNGs at runtime.

BitmapData

The BitmapData class allows the creation and manipulation of bitmaps during runtime. This means you can create complex images without some of the performance problems associated with bitmaps on the timeline. You can also perform certain visual effects that would have been impossible in previous versions of Flash.

Another nice feature of the BitmapData class is that it can also retrieve information about bitmaps, as you will see in this next example:

1. Create a new Flash document.

2. Import an image 400×300 in size (or use the one from the website) by going to File, Import, Import to Library.

3. Open the library by going to Window, Library, and you will see the image you just imported. Select it, then right-click it (Mac:Ctrl+click) and select Linkage.

4. Check the Export for ActionScript check box, give it an identifier of **bridge**, and click OK.

5. On the stage, draw a rectangle 50×300 in size and place it at 400,0.

6. While the rectangle is selected, choose Modify, Convert to Symbol.

7. Give it a symbol name of **recMC**, set the behavior to Movie Clip, and then click OK.

8. Back on the main stage, give the rectangle an instance name of **rec_mc**.

9. Create a second layer called **actions** and place the following code in the first frame of that layer:

```
import flash.display.BitmapData;
//get the image we need
var img:BitmapData = BitmapData.loadBitmap("bridge");
//create a movie clip to hold the image
var target_mc:MovieClip = this.createEmptyMovieClip("target_mc",1);
//attach the movie
target_mc.attachBitmap(img,1);
//set up the color object
var pix_color:Color = new Color(rec_mc);
//monitor mouse movement
this.onMouseMove = function(){
    //make sure the mouse is over the image
    if(target_mc.hitTest(_xmouse,_ymouse)){
        pix_color.setRGB(img.getPixel(_xmouse,_ymouse));
    }
}
```

The preceding code does a lot of things. First, it imports the necessary class file. Then it creates an instance of the BitmapData object and loads the bitmap directly from the library. Next, the code creates an empty movie clip to hold the bitmap. After that, you instantiate a Color object, which you use inside the onMouseMove event. Then you create the event to trigger whenever the user moves the mouse, and you make sure that the mouse cursor is over the image. If the mouse is over the image, you pass the color of that pixel through the Color object you created to change the color of the rectangle.

Test the movie and you will see that the rectangle changes to the color of the pixel the mouse is hovering over, as shown in Figure 1.14.

FIGURE 1.14   The BitmapData is an object with a great deal of potential for image manipulation.

File Upload

One of the most exciting new features of Flash is the capability to download and upload files directly from your SWF. Flash accomplishes this by means of the `FileReference` object.

The `FileReference` object allows you to browse for files with the `browse()` method. You can even tell Flash what types of files you want the end user to be able to select. And when a user selects a file, the `FileReference` will have these available properties:

- **creationDate**—A `Date` object representing the creation date of the file on the users computer.

- **creator**—The Mac creator type of the file on the user's computer.

- **modificationDate**—A `Date` object representing the last modified date of the file.

- **name**—The name of the file.

- **size**—The size of the file in bytes.

- **type**—The file type of the file.

Following is an example that will allow you to select a file and then display all the information in the Output panel.

1. Create a new Flash document.

2. Drag an instance of the Button component onto the stage and give it an instance name of **browse_butn** and set the label to **browse**.

3. Now create a second layer called **actions** and place the following code in the first frame of that layer:

```
//import the FileReference Object
import flash.net.FileReference;

//the file reference object
var file_fr:FileReference = new FileReference();
//object for listening to for FileRefernce events
var list_obj:Object = new Object();
//the event for when a user selects a file and hits open
list_obj.onSelect = function(){
    trace("name: "+file_fr.name);
    trace("creation date: "+file_fr.creationDate);
    trace("modification date: "+file_fr.modificationDate);
    trace("type: "+file_fr.type);
    trace("size in bytes: "+file_fr.size);
    trace("creator: "+file_fr.creator);
}
//add the listener to the FileReference object
```

```
file_fr.addListener(list_obj);
//event for the Button component
browse_butn.clickHandler = function(){
    file_fr.browse();
}
```

This code does quite a few things. First, it imports the necessary class file for the FileReference object. Then it creates a generic object to use as a listener for the onSelect event that is triggered when a user selects a file and clicks Open. Then we create the actual event callback for the listener object. Next the listener object is added to our FileReference. And finally, we create the event for the Button component, so that when the button is clicked, the File Browse window will appear.

Test this movie, and when you select a file and click Open, you should see some information about the file in the Output panel, as shown in Figure 1.15.

If you want to see the FileReference object working with a server-side script to actually be able to upload images, check out Chapter 22, "PHP and Flash."

FIGURE 1.15   One of the best new features in Flash is the capability to select files for upload and download.

Summary

This chapter briefly introduced you to several of the new features in Flash Professional 8. And as mentioned earlier, many of these features will be revisited throughout the book.

The next chapter introduces you to the interface and shows how you can create and maintain a workspace that will be conducive to how you like to work.

CHAPTER 2

Getting Started with Flash Professional 8

This chapter covers some of the basics of Flash: where it came from, what it is, and the general interface features. The first question about Flash is, What are its roots?

Humble Beginnings—Where Flash Came From

In 1996, a small company called FutureWave Software was selling a product called FutureSplash Animator. This product was designed to do vector-based drawing and animation.

Vector-Based Graphics

For those not familiar with vector-based graphics, here is an explanation:

Most graphics are pixel-based, which means that there are thousands of tiny blocks of color making up a picture. This becomes a problem when resizing images because, for instance, if you increase the size of a JPEG, you are not redrawing it. Instead, you are increasing the size of those tiny blocks of color, and the larger you make them, the more fuzzy and unclear the picture becomes.

Vector-based graphics are made with mathematical vector points so that in the case of a resize, they can redraw themselves to maintain quality. This and their generally smaller file size make them not only perfect for animation, but perfect for the web as well.

Figure 2.1 shows four circles; two are vector-based and two are pixel-based JPEGs.

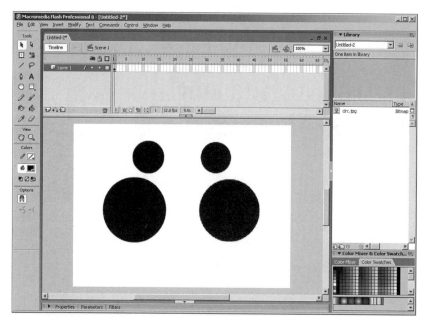

FIGURE 2.1   The difference between vector- and pixel-based graphics is obvious, especially in curves.

As FutureSplash Animator gained in popularity throughout the year, another software company began to notice—Macromedia. So in December of that same year, FutureSplash Animator was purchased by Macromedia and became Flash 1.0.

As Flash progressed, it transformed from a simple drawing and animation tool to a multi-media tool and now into a full-blown web application development tool. It has its own object-oriented programming language, it can tie to nearly all middleware systems, and it has one of the most downloaded pieces of software in the world as its player.

Now that you know where Flash started and where it is heading, let's take a look at how to use it.

The Interface

This version of Flash includes a few upgrades to the interface, such as a better panel system and in particular, a better Library panel. But there is one feature that PC users enjoyed with Flash 2004 that Mac users can now enjoy as well—the tabbed file system (see Figure 2.2).

The tabbed file system makes it very easy to move from file to file without ever having to minimize a window, which is a major impro1vement for Mac developers and designers alike.

Beyond the new tab system, the first part of the interface you will notice is the large white rectangle in the middle of the screen, called the stage.

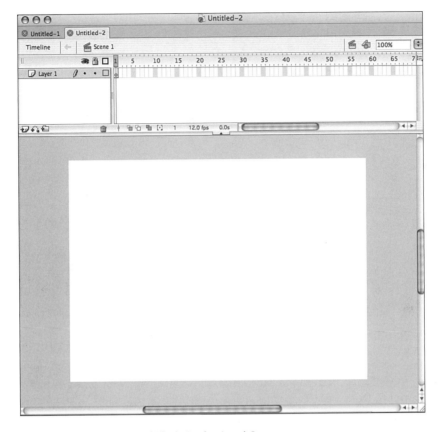

FIGURE 2.2   The Mac version of Flash Professional 8.

The Stage

This space represents the visible area of the file you create, and it is where you place all your visual elements. You can see the stage in Figure 2.2 and Figure 2.3. Figure 2.3 shows the PC version of Flash.

Some default settings for the stage are as follows:

- **Dimensions**—550×400

- **Match**—Default

- **Background Color**—#FFFFFF (White)

- **Frame Rate**—12

- **Ruler Units**—Pixel

You can change these settings by choosing Modify, Document (PC—Ctrl+J, Mac—Open Apple+J). This opens the Document Properties window shown in Figure 2.4, where you can change the settings mentioned in the preceding list as well as two others.

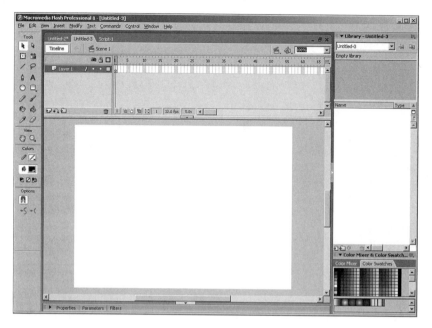

FIGURE 2.3   The PC version of Flash Professional 8.

New to Flash 8 is the capability to embed metadata in your SWF file so that search engines on the web can better index your files. The following two properties can be adjusted from the Document Properties dialog box:

- **Title**—The title of your projects, which does not have to match the `title` tag in your HTML document.

- **Description**—This field can contain anything from searchable keywords for your project to copyright information.

> **NOTE**
>
> At any time, you can click the Make Default button in the Document Properties dialog box to make your current document properties the default. However, the Title and Description fields must be set for each individual file.

You can also use the Properties Inspector to open the Document Properties dialog box.

The Properties Inspector Panel

This interface panel can be found by default at the bottom of the screen (but can be moved, as you will see soon) and is used for almost everything.

The Properties Inspector panel was one of the best additions back in Flash MX because it changes based on what you are doing. For instance, if you use the Arrow tool and select the stage, the Properties Inspector will look like Figure 2.5, but if you choose the Text tool, the Properties Inspector will look like Figure 2.6. And if you choose a keyframe in the timeline, the Properties Inspector will look like Figure 2.7. The Properties Inspector was designed to be the central area for changing settings and properties of all visual elements on the stage, including the stage itself. And, if you are running the Professional Edition of Flash 8, you will also notice the Filters tab as part of the Properties Inspector. Remember from the previous chapter that filters are new to Flash 8. Although these filters can be set with ActionScript in the standard version as well as the pro version, only the pro version has the capability to manually set them at authoring time.

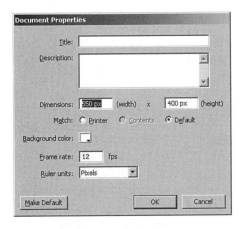

FIGURE 2.4   The Document Properties dialog box for setting certain stage properties.

FIGURE 2.5   The Properties Inspector for the stage.

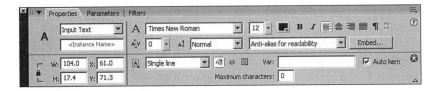

FIGURE 2.6   The Properties Inspector for the Text tool.

FIGURE 2.7   The Properties Inspector for a keyframe.

The Properties Inspector is one of many dockable panels in Flash. The next section covers a few other useful ones.

Flash Panels

In Flash, if you want to change settings such as size, rotation, or color or add ActionScript, you will have to use one of the panels. By default, most panels are on the right side of the screen. To drag and dock a panel, click and drag the top left part of the panel's title bar where it appears perforated. Then release it when you see a darkened black border around the panel. You can also group panels by either right-clicking (Ctrl+clicking on a Mac) the title bar of the panel or selecting the panel's drop-down options in the upper-right corner of the panel. Then select Group "Panel Name" With and select the group you want to assign that panel to. In Figure 2.8, you can see that both the Color Mixer and Color Swatches panels are grouped together.

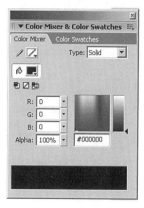

FIGURE 2.8   Grouping panels has been brought back from Flash 5, and it is a welcomed return.

There are three basic categories of panels; all are found under Window in the menu system. The following list should help you navigate them with ease:

- **Design Panels**—These panels are used mostly for visual aspects of objects:
  - **Align** (PC—Ctrl+K, Mac—Open Apple+K) —This panel is used to assist in aligning objects either to the stage or to one another.

- **Color Mixer** (Shift+F9)—This panel is used to refine colors and gradients for shapes.

- **Color Swatches** (PC—Ctrl+F9, Mac—Open Apple+F9)—This panel is for choosing colors from a set of color swatches.

- **Info** (PC—Ctrl+I, Mac—Open Apple+I)—This panel is used to get information, such as size and position, about selected objects. It also keeps track of the mouse position in the authoring environment.

- **Transform** (PC—Ctrl+T, Mac—Open Apple+T) —This panel is used to manipulate the size, rotation, and skew of selected objects.

- **Development Panels**—These panels focus more on the functionality side of Flash.

  - **Actions** (F9)—This panel is for entering and editing ActionScripts associated with frames and objects.

  - **Behaviors** (Shift+F3)—This panel is for applying certain actions directly to objects; it replaces the normal mode of the Actions panel.

  - **Components** (PC—Ctrl+F7, Mac—Open Apple+F7) —This panel holds all components used in Flash; select them and drag them directly onto the stage.

  - **Components Inspector** (Alt+F7)—This panel is used to adjust certain parameters and properties of selected components.

  - **Debugger** (Shift+F4)—This panel is used for debugging your application or Flash movie.

  - **Output** (F2)—This panel displays errors in ActionScript or messages sent directly to it by use of the `trace` command.

  - **Web Services** (PC—Ctrl+Shift+F10, Mac—Open Apple+Shift+F10)—This panel keeps track of all the web services that you have added at any point as well as what web methods are available in each of them.

- **Other Panels**—The name is self-explanatory; these are the panels that are left over.

  - **Scene** (Shift+F2)—This panel is used to keep track of scenes as well as to add or remove scenes.

  - **Accessibility** (Alt+F2)—This panel is used to control the accessibility features of Flash.

  - **History** (Alt+F10)—This panel keeps track of everything you do on the stage, and you can use it to create reuseable commands.

  - **Movie Explorer** (Alt+F3)—Use this panel to search your entire Flash document for anything including ActionScript, text, and objects.

  - **Strings** (Alt+F11)—This panel is used for translating Unicode text into other languages.

  - **Common Libraries**—This isn't really a panel; it's a library that holds a lot of premade objects you can use in your own documents.

2

The great thing about these panels is that even though there are quite a few of them, they can all be docked and grouped in different sections of your screen. Not only can you dock them in place, but you can also expand and collapse them to save screen space. Figures 2.9 and 2.10 show some of the panels. To expand and collapse a panel, you just click the black arrow on the panel's title bar.

FIGURE 2.9   Several panels docked and all collapsed.

Now that you have seen how to control the panels, we are going to go over three of the most commonly used panels: the Align, Transform, and Info panels.

> **NOTE**
>
> Many other panels are covered in later chapters, such as Chapter 8, "Welcome to ActionScript 2.0," and Chapter 16, "Components."

The Align Panel

The Align panel, as mentioned earlier, is used either to align and/or size objects to themselves or to the stage. It accomplishes this by means of five sets of buttons (see Figure 2.11):

FIGURE 2.10 Several panels with two of them expanded.

- **Align**—This set is used to control the x and y coordinate of object(s) selected.
- **Distribute**—This set is used for distributing objects and spacing them out based on the objects' dimensions.
- **Match Size**—This set is used to create the same dimensions for at least two different objects.
- **Space**—This set is also for spacing out objects, but unlike the Distribute set, which spaces out items based on dimensions, Space makes sure that the items selected are evenly spaced.
- **To Stage**—This single button, when selected, will make all the previously listed features align selected objects using the boundaries of the stage as the reference.

FIGURE 2.11 The Align panel.

Here is an example of how to use the Align panel:

1. Create a new Flash document.

2. Draw three separate rectangles on the stage at random spots and at different sizes.

3. Choose Edit, Select All.

4. Open the Align panel, make sure the To Stage button is selected, and choose the Align Horizontal Center button (second from the left). The rectangles should look like those in Figure 2.12.

5. While the rectangles are still selected, unselect the To Stage button and choose the Match Width and Height button from the Align panel. Now the rectangles should all be the same size and appear similar to Figure 2.13.

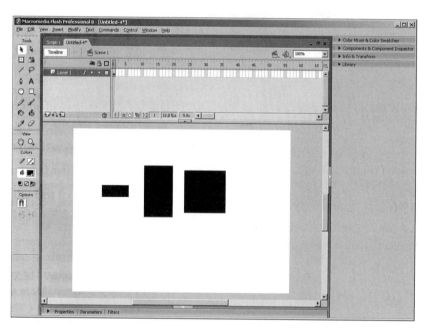

FIGURE 2.12   Aligning the rectangles horizontally.

The Transform Panel

The Transform panel allows users to manipulate the size, rotation, and skew of an object, as you can see in Figure 2.14. Following are the Transform panel options and their uses:

- **Sizing Options**—Two text boxes enable you to put in a percentage for vertical and horizontal sizing. If you always want them to be the same proportions, check the Constrain check box.

- **Rotate**—In the Rotate text box, put a positive or negative integer showing, in degrees, how much you want the object to rotate.

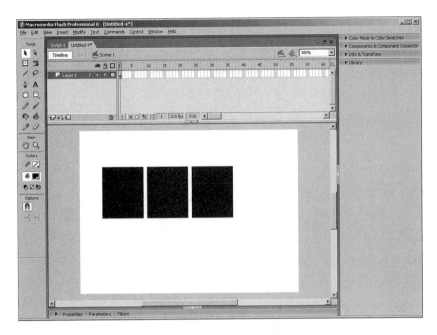

FIGURE 2.13   Using the Align panel, you can also match dimensions.

- **Skew**—There are two text boxes that accept positive or negative integers for controlling both the vertical and horizontal skew of the selected object.

- **Copy and Apply Transform**—This button, on the left in the lower-right corner, takes the transform selected as well as the object and creates a copy on the stage.

- **Reset**—This button, the one on the right in the lower-right corner, resets an object's transform to its original state.

FIGURE 2.14   The Transform panel.

The Info Panel

The last panel we will discuss in this chapter is the Info panel. This panel can be very useful when you are trying to align objects in certain positions. It can also get the RGB settings of a given object, as you can see in Figure 2.15.

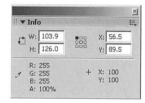

FIGURE 2.15   The Info panel.

Check Your Spelling

A much-needed feature that was added in Flash2004 is spell checking. You can start spell checking right out of the box, but you might want to set your spelling-check settings first. To do that, choose Text, Spelling Setup; the Spelling Setup window will appear as shown in Figure 2.16. You have to have it check something, or it will not work at all; instead you will get a pop-up error message as shown in Figure 2.17.

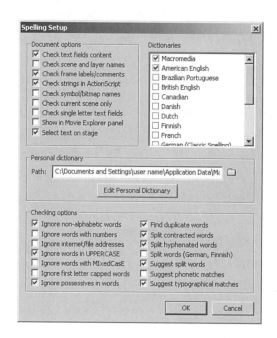

FIGURE 2.16   Choose what you want the spell checker to look at.

FIGURE 2.17   Pop-up error message if the Spelling Setup has not been completed.

When you have set the options you want, whenever you want to check spelling, just select Text, Check Spelling. The Check Spelling window will appear as shown in Figure 2.18.

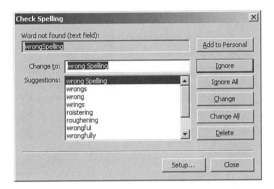

FIGURE 2.18 The Check Spelling window.

Now that you have seen a lot of the interface elements and how to use them, the next step to familiarizing yourself with Flash is to see how to customize your preferences, and the view of the stage.

Preferences

One of the nice things that you can do with the authoring environment is customize it. To do this on the PC, go to Edit, Preferences. On the Mac, go to the Application menu and select Preferences. You will see one of two screens, depending on your operating system, as shown in Figures 2.19 and 2.20.

The Preferences window has seven categories: General, ActionScript, Auto Format, Clipboard, Drawing, Text, and Warnings.

The General Category

This section covers the options available in the General category, as shown in Figure 2.21.

- **On Launch**—This is a new preference in Flash, which allows you to select what you want to happen when Flash starts up. It has the following options:

  - **No Document**—This will make it so when Flash launches, it will still require some user interaction to either create a new file, or open a recent document.

  - **New Document**—This option automatically starts a new Flash document when Flash launches.

  - **Last Document Open**—This option automatically opens the most recent document you worked in.

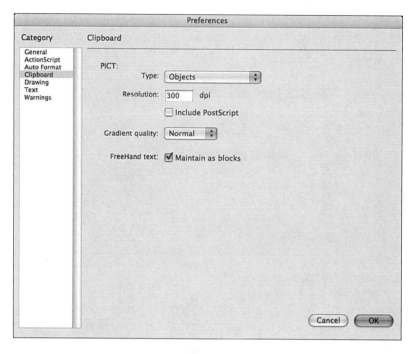

FIGURE 2.19   Clipboard preferences for the Mac.

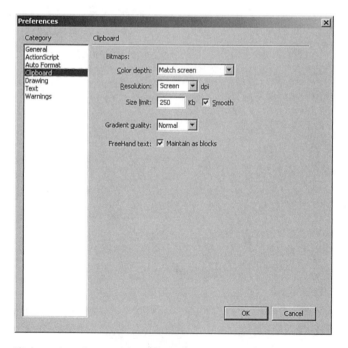

FIGURE 2.20   Clipboard preferences for Windows.

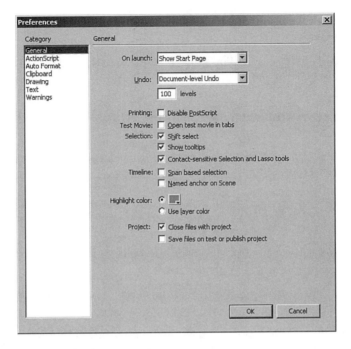

FIGURE 2.21   The General category.

- **Show Start Page**—This shows the start page, which contains links to your most recent files (up to 10), new document options, and templates. This is the default selection.

- **Undo**—This option enables you to set the type of undo to use in your Flash files. Following are the available choices:

  - **Document-level Undo**—A huge list of every action you have taken from anywhere in your Flash document. This is the default selection.

  - **Object-level Undo**—Keeps separate lists for the different objects you are working with in Flash so that undoing several things within an object will not affect any changes to other objects that may also have been changed.

- **Undo Levels**—This number represents the number of steps that are recorded and undoable. This number must be between 2 and 300, but the higher the number, the more memory it will take up.

- **Printing** (PC only)—You can enable or disable PostScript printing; however, if it is enabled, it will slow down printing from Flash. The default value is disabled.

- **Document** (Mac only)—This has a single option that will either open documents in tabs or in separate windows. The default value is to open documents in tabs.

- **Test Movie**—This option controls how the test movie screen will open, either in a new window or in another tab. The default value is in a new window.

- **Selection**—This set of options has several suboptions for controlling how selections work:

  - **Shift Select**—This option allows the Shift select method to be active, meaning that to select multiple objects, you must hold down the Shift key. By default, this option is already on.

  - **Show ToolTips**—This option controls whether ToolTips appear during authoring.

  - **Contact-Sensitive Selection and Lasso Tools**—This option controls how much of an object must be within a selection rectangle before it is considered selected. If this option is set to false, the entire object must be selected. The default value is set to true.

- **Timeline**—This set has several suboptions for controlling certain aspects of the timeline:

  - **Span-based Selection**—This option enables you to select frames in the timeline like a span, in contrast to frame by frame.

  - **Named Anchor on Scene**—This option makes Flash make the first frame in every Scene a named anchor.

- **Highlight Color**—This option controls the highlighting color on layers. You can either choose a color from the palette or use the layer color.

- **Project**—This set has two suboptions for controlling aspects of Flash projects:

  - **Close files with Project**—If selected, this option makes it so that when a project is closed, all associated files in Flash close as well.

  - **Save Files on Test or Publish Project**—This option makes it so that when you either test or publish the project, all associated files in Flash are saved.

The ActionScript and Auto Format Categories

The ActionScript and Auto Format categories control the settings for the Actions panel, which is discussed further in Chapter 8. Figures 2.22 and 2.23 show these two category tabs.

The Clipboard Category

This section covers the options available in the Clipboard category, as shown earlier in Figures 2.19 and 2.20.

- **Bitmaps**—This section has several suboptions.

  - **Color Depth**—The default setting is Match Screen, which means it will use enough colors to match the screen. You can increase or decrease this value.

  - **Resolution**—Setting for the Dots per Inch (dpi) for copying a graphic.

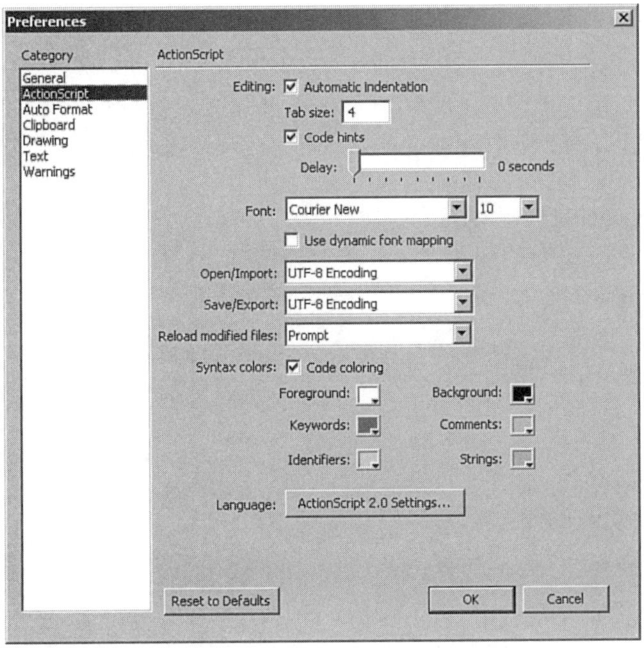

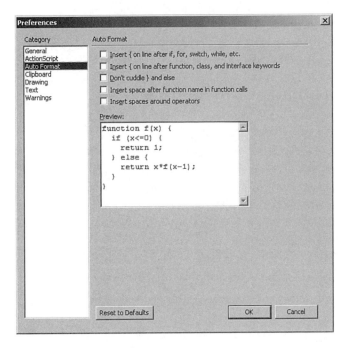

FIGURE 2.22   The ActionScript category.

FIGURE 2.23   The Auto Format category.

- **Size Limit**—This setting uses a positive integer to determine how much available space to use for copying graphics to the Clipboard from Flash.

- **Gradients**—This option controls the quality of the gradient being used.

- **FreeHand Text**—This option keeps text as text when taking it over to FreeHand.

The preceding settings are for Windows. The Mac has a slightly different-looking Clipboard tab, as you can see in Figure 2.19, and it has these options:

- **PICT Settings**—This section has several suboptions:

  - **Type**—This option allows you to choose what format to use for copying graphics to the Clipboard. The Objects format is best because it maintains the vector format.

  - **Resolution**—This option determines the Dots per Inch setting when copying graphics to the Clipboard. You can also keep PostScript data by checking the Include PostScript check box.

  - **Gradient**—This option controls the quality of the gradient being used.

- **FreeHand Text**—This option keeps text as text when taking it over to FreeHand.

The Drawing Category

This section covers the options available in the Drawing category, as shown in Figure 2.24.

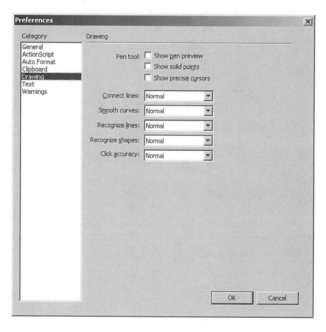

FIGURE 2.24   The Drawing category.

- **Pen Tool**—This section controls the visualizations of the pen tool as you are using it and has the following suboptions:
  - **Show Pen Preview**—When checked, this option shows a preview of the line being drawn. When unchecked, the line is shown only after the mouse button has been released.
  - **Show Solid Points**—When checked, this option shows selected anchor points as hollow squares and unselected anchor points as solid squares. When unchecked, it shows the reverse.
  - **Show Precise Cursors**—This option shows the cursor as a crosshair instead of the default pen cursor.
- **Connect Lines**—This option connects a line to another line for you when you are within a certain range of the other line and Snap to Objects is turned on.
- **Smooth Curves**—This option sets how smooth a curve should appear.
- **Recognize Lines**—This option sets how straight a line has to be before Flash will make it a perfectly straight line.
- **Recognize Shapes**—This option is similar to the Recognize Lines option. It tells Flash at what level to determine whether a shape is perfect.
- **Click Accuracy**—This determines how close you have to be to an object for Flash to recognize that you are touching the object.

The Text Category

This section covers the options available in the Text category, as shown in Figure 2.25.

- **Font Mapping Default**—This option sets the default font if the selected font is not available on a user's computer.
- **Vertical Text**—This has several suboptions:
  - **Default Text Orientation**—This option makes the default way you create text fields vertical, which is good in the case of some languages.
  - **Right to Left Text Flow**—This reverses the default way that text flows.
  - **No Kerning**—This option turns off kerning for vertical text, which can help save space.
- **Input Method**—Enables you to select the appropriate language.

The Warnings Category

The Warnings categorycategory (see Figure 2.26) contains check boxes for when warnings should appear; they are easy to understand and follow.

FIGURE 2.25   The Text category.

FIGURE 2.26   The Warnings category.

Shortcuts

When working in Flash, you will begin to notice that the abundant tools, commands, panels, and options take up time when you have to search for them and click options in a certain order. That's why I love shortcuts. When you get comfortable using them, your design and development time will begin to shorten.

To see the available shortcuts, choose Edit, Keyboard Shortcuts and you will see a screen pop up, as shown in Figure 2.27.

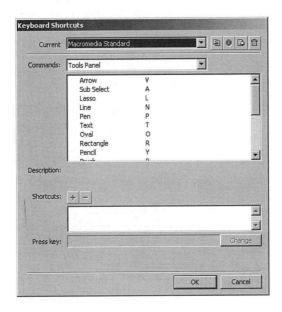

FIGURE 2.27   The Keyboard Shortcuts dialog box.

The options in this menu are the following:

- **Current**—This allows you to choose which type of built-in shortcuts you prefer, including Macromedia Standard, Fireworks 4, Flash 5, FreeHand 10, Illustrator 10, or Photoshop 6.

- **Commands**—This holds the groups of commands that have shortcuts, including Drawing Menu Commands, Drawing Tools, Test Movie Menu Commands, Workspace Accessibility Commands, and Actions Panel Commands. In the large list box under Commands, you can see the subsets of groups.

- **Description**—Gives a description of the command when you choose one. (This is not an option that can be adjusted.)

- **Shortcuts** (+/-)—Allows you to add or remove shortcuts from the selected command.

- **Press Key**—Retrieves the set of keys when you press them for the shortcut and lets you know if they are available.

- **Change Button**—Sets the focus into the Press Key box.

- **Duplicate Set Button**—Duplicates the current set of shortcuts you are viewing so that you can make changes.

- **Rename Set Button**—Allows you to rename the current set of shortcuts.

- **Export Set as HTML**—Allows you to export the selected list of shortcuts to an HTML file that can be viewed at any time as a reference. You can see an example in Figure 2.28.

- **Delete Set Button**—Allows you to delete the current set of shortcuts. (You cannot delete any of the built-in sets of shortcuts that come with Flash.)

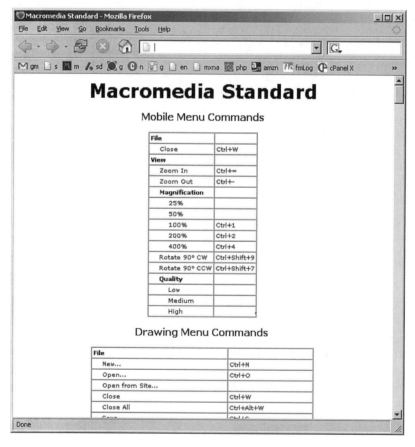

FIGURE 2.28   The exported Macromedia Standard shortcuts.

You can also create your own set of shortcuts, as this next walkthrough will show you:

1. In the Keyboard Shortcuts dialog box, select Macromedia Standard in the Current drop-down box.

2. Click the Duplicate Set button, name the new set **mySet**, and click OK.

3. If you decide you do not like the name **mySet**, at any time you can choose to rename the set by selecting it in the Current drop-down box and clicking the Rename Set button. Then name it anything you like.

4. To continue to change the shortcuts, choose a set you like, such as the Tools panel for this example.

5. Select the Arrow selection in the list box.

6. Click the plus sign beside Shortcuts.

7. The word <empty> will appear in the Press Key box as well as in the list box under Shortcuts.

8. Press the "D" key and then click Change.

9. Click OK. Now you can select the Arrow tool by pressing "V" or "D."

Making a Better Workspace

Sometimes, when you're drawing graphics or working with animations, it is a lot easier to draw with rulers or grids. Flash offers you both.

To turn on rulers, go to View, Rulers, and your screen should now look similar to Figure 2.29.

You can also use gridlines. Gridlines are great for animation as well as application layout so that you can see exactly where to place visual objects on the stage.

To turn gridlines on, go to View, Grid, Show Grid. Now your stage should look similar to Figure 2.30.

You can also edit the grid to better fit your needs by choosing View, Grid, Edit Grid, and the Grid settings dialog box will appear as shown in Figure 2.31. Some of the options for the grid are as follows:

- **Color**—This is the actual color of the gridlines.
- **Show Grid**—Toggles the grid between visible and invisible.
- **Snap to Grid**—This option allows objects to snap to cross sections in the grid.
- **Horizontal Space**—The horizontal space between gridlines in pixels.
- **Vertical Space**—The vertical space between gridlines in pixels.
- **Snap Accuracy**—This option tells Flash how close you need to be to a cross section in the grid for the object to snap to it.

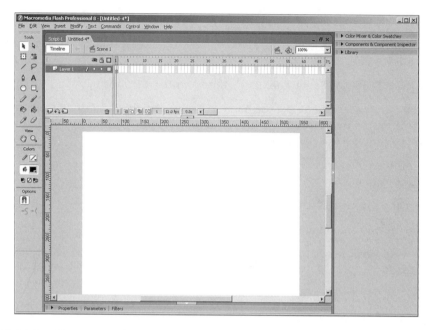

FIGURE 2.29 The stage with rulers turned on.

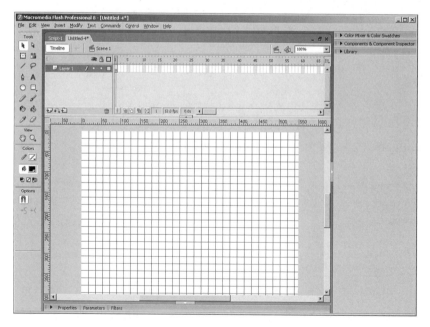

FIGURE 2.30 The stage with the grid turned on.

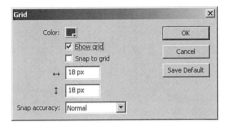

FIGURE 2.31   The Grid settings dialog box.

If you want something a little more customizable, you can turn on guidelines.

Guidelines are lines you create yourself during authoring. To turn them on, choose View, Guides, Show Guides. For them to work, you must have Rulers turned on as well.

If you have both guides and rulers turned on, you can click in the ruler at a set point and drag a line out to the stage. After you release it, you can still move it by clicking it and dragging it again. By choosing View, Guides, Lock Guides, you can also lock the guides down so that you do not accidentally move them. Figure 2.32 is an example of a stage that has guides.

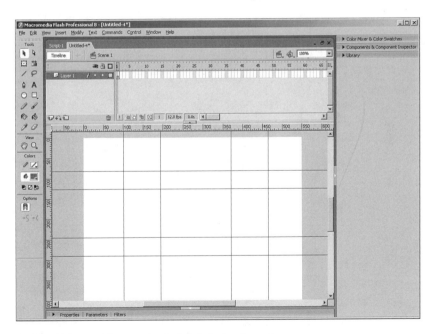

FIGURE 2.32   Using guides can be helpful during layout.

You can also customize the guidelines by choosing View, Guides, Edit Guides. The Guides settings dialog box will pop up as shown in Figure 2.33.

The settings are the same basic settings as the grid.

FIGURE 2.33   The Guides settings dialog box.

Finally, if you want to clear the guides and start over, you can select View, Guides, Clear Guides, or drag them individually back over to the rulers.

Summary

This chapter introduced you to the world of Flash and its interface. You learned how to customize it to your personal working experience as well as how to create your own keyboard shortcuts. Throughout the remainder of this book, we will continue to go more in depth into the many features of Flash, and you will also learn how to expand it.

CHAPTER **3**

Creating Graphics in Flash

In the later part of this book we will go over how to manipulate objects on the stage using ActionScript, but before that can be done, you need to know how to create these objects on the stage. If you have used other drawing tools in the past, such as Freehand or Illustrator, you will be somewhat familiar with most of the tools that Flash offers for drawing. This chapter will go over each tool individually, including how they work and ways to speed up and refine the process. We will also go over how to import bitmaps to your Flash project and work with them.

The Toolbar

As mentioned in the previous paragraph, many of the drawing tools found in Flash may be somewhat familiar, as you can see in Figure 3.1. As we move through the tools, special note will be made of options that are available to each specific tool, as well as shortcuts that can be used in conjunction with the tool.

As you can see from the preceding figure, the toolbar has four major sections:

- **Tools**—This group is the set of tools that enable you to draw and manipulate shapes and objects on the stage.
- **View**—This group assists you in controlling the view of the stage, including the stage position and magnification level.
- **Colors**—This group helps you control both the color of the stroke (line) and fill of shapes.

FIGURE 3.1   The Flash 8 toolbar.

- **Options**—This group will change as you select different tools to reveal more options for those tools. Because technically this really is not a group, but more of a section, each set of options will be gone over with its associated tool.

Now that you are familiar with the sections, let's go over what is in each section, from bottom to top, starting with the colors section.

The Colors Section

As previously mentioned, this section of the toolbar is one of the many places where you can control the color of both the stroke and fill. Although colors and gradients will be discussed in more detail later in this chapter, it's important that you understand how to use this section of the toolbar before you begin creating shapes.

In addition to the two-color drop downs for both stroke and fill, there are also three little buttons along the bottom of this section, as shown in Figure 3.1. Here is what they do:

- **Black and White**—Instantly change the stroke color to white (#ffffff) and the fill color to black (#000000).

- **No Color**—Set the selected color (either fill or stroke) to not be created when drawn.

- **Swap Colors**—Swap the current colors of the fill and stroke.

Also, more options for choosing colors can be found by clicking the color wheel in the color drop-down of either the fill or the stroke. The color pop-up window will appear as shown in Figure 3.2.

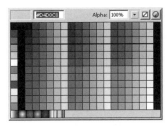

FIGURE 3.2   In the color pop-up, you choose from an assortment of colors; you can change the lightness and darkness and even set RGB values.

When you select a fill or stroke color from the Colors section, you can either select any color or gradient from the color palette or type the color in #rrggbb form into the input box. You can also adjust the alpha of the color or turn off the color completely with the No Color button.

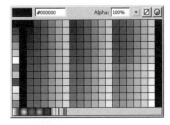

FIGURE 3.3   The stroke color section: Notice how gradients and alpha control are now available to both the fill and the stroke color section.

The View Section

This section in the toolbar contains tools to help control the view of the stage.

The Hand Tool
Shortcut: PC and Mac—H

Use the Hand tool to drag the entire stage around to be able to see certain sections more clearly, especially while you're zoomed in. Also, holding down the Shift key while dragging the stage will make it so the stage can be dragged at only 45-degree angles from its original position.

> **TIP**
>
> You can also double-click the Hand Tool icon in the toolbar to make the stage go as large as possible while still being able to see it in its entirety. (Shortcut: PC—Ctrl+2, Mac—Open Apple+2.)

The Zoom Tool (or Magnification Tool)
Shortcut: PC and Mac—Z or M

The Zoom tool controls the magnification at which you are viewing the stage. This tool is very helpful when you need to create very detailed drawings. It has two options in the options section of the toolbar, as you can see in Figure 3.4. The options switch the direction of magnification when you click the stage. Besides being able to click the stage and have the stage zoom in or out, you can also click and draw a rectangle around a particular section of the stage to zoom into.

FIGURE 3.4   The two options for the Zoom tool.

As with many things in Flash, there is more than one way to control the magnification level of the stage. Following is a short list of shortcuts:

- (CTRL + -)—Zoom Out

- (CTRL + +)—Zoom In

- (CTRL + 1)—Zoom to 100%

- (CTRL + 2)—Zoom in as far as possible while showing everything on the stage and center

- (CTRL + 4)—Zoom to 400%

- (CTRL + 8)—Zoom to 800%

> **NOTE**
>
> These shortcuts are all PC shortcuts. For Macs, simply replace Ctrl with Open Apple.

The Tools Section

This section contains all the tools for drawing shapes, manipulating objects, and creating text on the stage. Make special note of the options for each tool that can be found in the Options section of the toolbar; as previously mentioned, these change with each tool. As we go through the tools, they will be covered from top to bottom, and left to right on the toolbar.

The Arrow Tool
Shortcut: PC and MAC—V

The Arrow tool is Flash's basic selection tool. It can be used to select objects by clicking them or by clicking outside and dragging a rectangle around what you want to select. Remember, when selecting shapes on the stage, you must double-click to select both the fill and the stroke.

The Arrow tool has three options: the first is the Snap to Objects option. This option, when selected, helps snap objects to one another, depending on how close they get to each other. This option is helpful when you're doing precise layouts. The other two options, which may appear grayed out, as in Figure 3.5, are for adjusting line segments on the stage and will not become active until a line is selected. Here are the other two options:

- **Smooth**—This option smooths out ragged edges of the selected line each time it is selected.

- **Straighten**—This option attempts to sharpen the curves of the selected line each time it is selected.

FIGURE 3.5   The options for the Arrow tool. If a line is selected on the stage, the bottom two options become available.

> **TIP**
>
> - While moving an object with the Arrow tool, you can hold down the Shift key to make the object draggable only at degree increments of 45 (0, 45, 90, 135, 180, and so on) from its original position.
>
> - Holding down the Alt key while dragging a selection will make a copy of the selection where you release the mouse instead of simply moving the selection.

> **NOTE**
>
> You can also use the arrow keys to move a selected object around the stage. The object will move more quickly if the Shift key is depressed while you use the arrow keys.

The Subselection Tool
Shortcut: PC and Mac—A

This works similarly to the Arrow tool, except the Subselection tool is designed to specifically select vector points. Unlike the Arrow tool, the Subselection tool has no options.

The Free Transform Tool
Shortcut: PC and Mac—Q

This tool is used to manipulate objects on the stage through the use of several small boxes, called *handles*, which appear around the object when it is selected with the Free Transform tool. It can be used to size, rotate, and skew the selected object by clicking and dragging.

The Free Transform tool has the following options:

- Snap to Objects—This option, when selected, will snap the scaling handles to other objects on the stage.

- Rotate and Skew—This option makes the corner handles become rotate handles, and the center handles become skewing handles.

- Scale—This option turns all handles into sizing handles.

- Distort—This option turns the corners into independent distortion handles where you can drag one corner at a time (or use the Shift key to control two adjacent points at the same time to make a tapering effect).

- Envelope—This option creates more handles than the other options, including handles with the capability to curve segments of the selected object.

> **NOTE**
>
> The final two options of the Free Transform tool can be used on primitive shapes, but not on graphics or movie clips.

The Gradient Transform Tool
Shortcut: PC and MAC—F

The Gradient Transform tool is used to adjust gradients or bitmap fills in shapes on the stage. Depending on which kind of gradient the selection has, a different set of handles will appear to adjust such things as center point, size, and rotation of the gradient, as you can see in Figure 3.6. This tool has one option, Snap to Objects. When selected, this option allows the sizing handle to snap to other objects on the stage.

The Line Tool
Shortcut: PC and Mac—N

The Line tool is used to draw straight lines from point to point on the stage. Simply select the tool, click where you want the start point to be, and then drag and release where the end point should be.

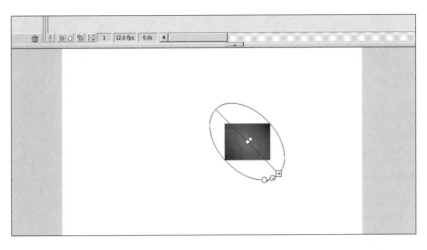

FIGURE 3.6   Using the handles to adjust the gradient is an easy way to make precise gradient fills.

The Line tool has the following two options in the toolbar:

- **Snap to Objects**—Similar to the Arrow tool, when selected, this option snaps the end point of the line to objects, depending on how close they are being drawn.

- **Object Drawing**—This option, which is discussed in more detail later in this chapter, allows you to draw Drawing Objects directly on the stage (Shortcut: PC and Mac—J).

> **TIP**
>
> - While using the Line tool, you can hold down the Shift key to draw lines at degree increments of 45 (0, 45, 90, 135, 180,and so on).
> - Holding down the Alt key while drawing a line will draw the line in both directions from the start point.

There are more options available for the Line tool in the Properties Inspector, as seen in Figure 3.7. The option available is actually the options for the stroke settings, which are used by the Line tool. The options available for the stroke settings are as follows:

- **Stroke Color**—The color or gradient setting for the stroke. This is the same as in the Colors section of the toolbar.

- **Stroke Height**—This is the weight of the stroke, which can range from .25 to 200, with 200 being thickest.

- **Stroke Style**—This has several prebuilt styles for how the stroke can look. Following is a list of the prebuilt styles:

FIGURE 3.7   You can adjust stroke settings from the Properties Inspector.

- **Hairline**—The hairline stroke style will remain one pixel in size no matter how much it is scaled. This is the only stroke style that will not scale.

- **Solid**—The default stroke style that has only size, color, and sharp corners as options.

- **Dashed**—This stroke style creates a dashed line. You can change the length of the dash and gap between them in the Stroke Style pop-up by clicking the Custom button in the Properties Inspector. You can also adjust the other stroke attributes such as size, color, and sharp corners.

- **Dotted**—This stroke style creates a line with evenly spaced dots along it. You can adjust the distance between the dots as well as the normal stroke attributes.

- **Ragged**—This stroke style creates a line with "ragged" edges created by wavy lines and small dots. You can adjust the pattern of the wave as well as the wave's length and height.

- **Stipple**—This stroke style creates a line that resembles a ballpoint pen line. It is made up of tiny little dots, which can be adjusted in size, variation, and density.

- **Hatched**—This stroke style creates a line made up of several short lines to resemble a hatched line. You can adjust thickness (which is different than the stroke size), space, jiggle, rotate, curve, and length, as well as the other normal stroke properties.

- **Custom**—This enables you to create your own line styles in a small pop-up, as shown in Figure 3.8.

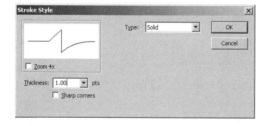

FIGURE 3.8   In the Stroke Style pop-up, you can change most of the stroke properties and see a preview.

- **Cap**—This option controls the ends of a line. You can set None to make the line flush with the end point, or you can set either Round or Square to extend the stroke height beyond the end point.

- **Stroke Hinting**—When selected, this option makes subtle adjustments to the curve and line anchor points to help prevent blurring.

- **Scale**—This controls how the stroke will act during scaling. It has these options:

    - **Normal**—Always scale the thickness of the line. This is the default choice.

    - **None**—Never scale the thickness of the line.

    - **Vertical**—Do not scale the thickness of the line when the line is vertically scaled.

    - **Horizontal**—Do not scale the thickness of the line when the line is horizontally scaled.

- **Join**—The option controls the corners where lines intersect. You can set Normal, Miter, or Bevel (see Figure 3.9). When Miter is selected, you can set a Miter Limit to help prevent beveling. In a Miter Limit, lines that exceed the set value will be cut off instead of being sharpened to a point.

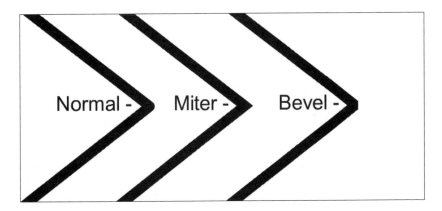

FIGURE 3.9   The three Join options for a line.

The Lasso Tool
Shortcut: PC and Mac—L

The Lasso tool is another selection tool that can be used to select more precisely than the Arrow tool. Simply draw a shape as you would with any other drawing tool; make sure you close the shape before releasing the mouse or odd selections may be made.

This tool does have a few options that can make it easier to make a desired selection starting with the Magic Wand. The Magic Wand will select areas based on where the tolerance level is set. To set this tolerance level, click the option to the right of the Magic Wand and you will see something similar to Figure 3.10. You will also be able to adjust the smoothing as well, which determines how smooth the selection should be. Here are those options:

- **Smooth**—The selection will be rounded.

- **Pixels**—The selection will wrap around pixel edges of similar color.

- **Rough**—The selection will have more jagged edges than with the pixel selection.

- **Normal**—This selection will have the smoothness between the smooth selection and the pixel selection.

The final option for the Lasso tool is the Polygon Mode option. This option, when selected, enables you to draw point-to-point lines to make selections in the shape of a polygon.

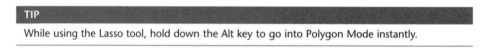

TIP

While using the Lasso tool, hold down the Alt key to go into Polygon Mode instantly.

FIGURE 3.10   The options for the Magic Wand.

The Pen Tool
Shortcut: PC and Mac—P

The Pen tool is another drawing tool used to draw both straight and curved lines. Drawing with the Pen tool is a little different from using the Line tool. As you move and click the mouse, a new line will be drawn that is connected to the previous one. And to draw curved lines, drag the mouse cursor away from the selected point.

Although there is only one option for this tool, the Object Drawing option, its preferences can be found in the Preferences window by going to Edit, Preferences, Editing Tab (Shortcut Ctrl+U).

Also, after you have drawn the shape or line you desire, you can use the Subselection tool to control the curves by selecting the handles. If you need more handles, use the Pen tool again to add them anywhere along the lines.

- **Show Pen Preview**—This option, when selected, will show a preview of the next stroke before it's drawn, based on the mouse position.

- **Show Solid Points**—This option, when selected, will show the reverse of the default settings in that selected points will appear hollow and unselected points will appear filled.

- **Show Precise Cursors**—When selected, this option will show a crosshair cursor instead of a pen cursor. You can also switch between these two views by toggling the Caps Lock key.

Besides these options, special smaller icons also appear with the Pen tool while it is in use to help refine the drawing you are making. Following is a list of those special icons and how to use them:

- (-)—Shown when a vector point can be deleted by clicking it.

- (+)—Shown where a vector point can be added to an existing line.

- (^)—Shown when a vector point can be converted to a right angle.

- (o)—This icon appears when you hover over the initial point of the shape you are drawing, allowing you to completely close the shape if clicked.

- (x)—Shown when there is no available line to edit.

- **(arrow with filled box)**—Shown when the Shift key is down and the cursor is over a line.

- **(arrow with hollow box)**—Shown when the Shift key is down and the cursor is over a vector point.

The Text Tool
Shortcut: PC and Mac—T

This tool is used to manually create text fields on the stage. Although text fields will be gone over in extensive detail in Chapter 15, "Working with Text," it is important to go over some of the major points of the Text tool here.

When you're drawing a text field, click approximately where you want the top-left corner of the text field to be, and then drag down and to the right (doing the opposite will have unexpected results). After the text field is drawn, you can manually type text into the field and use some of the basic text options, such as color, bold, and italic, as found in the Properties Inspector (see Figure 3.11).

TIP

New to Flash 8, you can now adjust the size of a text field by selecting it with the Arrow tool and using the blue handles that appear. Do not use the Free Transform tool to change the size of a text field unless you want the text within the field to scale as well.

FIGURE 3.11   The Properties Inspector for the Text tool.

There are three basic types of text fields:

- **Static**—This type of text field can be edited at authoring time only.

- **Dynamic**—This type of text field can be edited at authoring time or at runtime by using either the text property or the var property.

- **Input**—This type of text field, like the dynamic text field, can be edited either at authoring time or at runtime. The user can also type into this type of text field at runtime.

As previously mentioned, this tool is covered in more detail in Chapter 15.

The Oval Tool
Shortcut: PC and Mac—O

The Oval tool is used to draw circular shapes. This tool has two options; the first is the Object Drawing option, which is discussed later in more detail. The other option is the Snap to Objects option, which if selected, enables you to draw perfect circles if drawn at a 45-degree angle. You can also hold down the Shift key while drawing to accomplish the same task of drawing a perfect circle.

New to Flash 8 is yet another way to create ovals on the stage. Simply hold down the Alt key and click the stage to reveal the Oval Settings dialog box, as shown in Figure 3.12. With this, you can set the width, height, and whether to draw from the center of the point you clicked on or have that point be the upper-left coordinate of the oval.

FIGURE 3.12   The Oval Settings dialog box for creating ovals with numbers.

TIP

While drawing an oval, you can hold down the Alt key to make the circle draw in both directions, so it will increase in size twice as fast.

The Rectangle Tool

Shortcut: PC and Mac—R

The Rectangle tool is used to draw rectangular shapes. The Rectangle tool has three options; the first is the Object Drawing option. The second option is the Snap to Objects option, which when selected, enables you to draw perfect squares when drawing at 45-degree angles. Again, you can accomplish the same thing by holding down the Shift key when you draw a rectangle. The third option is the Round Rectangle Radius option. When this option is selected (or you double-click the Rectangle tool in the toolbar), the Rectangle Settings pop-up appears, allowing you to set the roundness of the corners of the rectangle between 0 and 999.

Like the Oval tool, you can now create rectangles on the stage without having to draw them by hand. Just hold down the Alt key and click the stage to reveal the Rectangle Settings dialog box, as shown in Figure 3.13. With this, you can set the width, height, corner radius, and whether to draw from the center of the point you clicked or have that point be the upper-left coordinate of the rectangle.

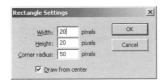

FIGURE 3.13   The Rectangle Settings dialog box for creating rectangles with numbers.

TIP

- It may be difficult to know how round you want the corners to be on your rectangle, so hold down the down-arrow key to increase the roundness, or hold down the up-arrow key to decrease the roundness.

- While drawing a rectangle, hold down the Alt key to make the rectangle draw in both directions; that way, it will increase in size twice as fast.

The PolyStar Tool

Shortcut: none

The PolyStar tool is used to draw multisided polygons or multipoint stars. To select this tool, click and hold down the Rectangle tool in the toolbar. A submenu appears, as shown in Figure 3.14. Select the PolyStar tool from there. There is no shortcut key for this tool on the Mac or the PC.

When you select the PolyStar tool, the same options for the Rectangle and Oval tools appear—Object Drawing and Snap to Objects. Also notice another option, called Options, in the Properties Inspector, as shown in Figure 3.15. Clicking this brings up the Tool Settings dialog box where you can choose either polygon or star, the number of sides (or points when drawing a star), and the star point size (which affects only stars).

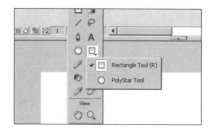

FIGURE 3.14   Choose the PolyStar tool.

FIGURE 3.15   Click the Options button to open the Tool Settings dialog box.

> **NOTE**
>
> The maximum value of sides is 32, and the minimum is 3. The maximum value for point size is 1, and the minimum value is 0.

Drawing polystars can be a bit tricky at first because unlike the other shape drawing tools, while you are drawing the size of the shape, you can also control the rotation of the shape.

> **TIP**
>
> Holding down the Shift key while drawing polystars will make it so they are drawn only at a rotation of 45-degree increments.

The Pencil Tool
Shortcut: PC and Mac—Y

The Pencil tool is used to draw lines, but unlike the Line tool, which draws point to point, the Pencil tool can be used like a normal pencil. It does have some options to make drawing much easier, as you can see in Figure 3.16, as well as the Object Drawing option found in all the drawing tools.

Here is a list of those options and what they mean:

- **Straighten**—This is the default setting of the Pencil tool and helps to draw perfect shapes such as rectangles or circles. You can adjust how well it recognizes shapes and specify smoothing options in the Preferences panel.

- **Smooth**—This option attempts to smooth out ragged edges of the drawn line.

> **NOTE**
>
> When this option is selected, the Smoothing option in the Properties Inspector becomes active and can be adjusted from 0 to 10 to control how smooth to draw the line.

- **Ink**—This option makes the Pencil tool act as close to a real pencil as possible and will not attempt to alter the drawn line.

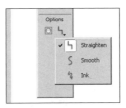

FIGURE 3.16   The options for the Pencil tool.

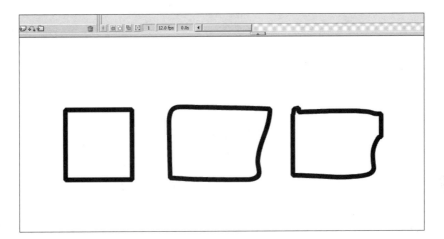

FIGURE 3.17   You can see the difference in drawing a similar shape with each of the three pencil options.

The Brush Tool

Shortcut: PC and Mac—B

The Brush tool is used to paint the stage, much like a normal paintbrush would be used. Unlike the Pencil tool, the Brush tool's color options are controlled with the fill settings. There are also several options for the Brush tool that make a difference in how the brush works, as well as the Object Drawing option. The first is the mode of the Brush tool, which has these options:

- **Paint Normal**—The default option that will allow you to paint fill anywhere you use the brush.

- **Paint Fills**—This option is similar to the Paint Normal option, except that it will not affect any line on the stage.

- **Paint Behind**—This option paints behind any previously drawn shape or object on the stage.

- **Paint Selection**—This option allows you to paint fill only in shapes that are selected.

- **Paint Inside**—This option will paint fill only in the interior of the object where you begin to paint. For instance, if you start painting inside a rectangle, it will paint only within that rectangle; however, if you start painting outside the rectangle, it paints on the stage.

Other options that affect the fill being painted are the size of the brush (from approximately 2.5 pixels to 30 pixels wide) and the style of the brush, as shown in Figure 3.18.

FIGURE 3.18   The different choices of brush styles for the Brush tool.

TIP

When you use the Brush tool, note that the size of the brush is not relative—the more you magnify the stage and use the Brush tool, the larger the painted fill will be.

The final option for the Brush tool is the Lock Fill option. This option, when selected, will make a gradient or bitmap fill (discussed later in this chapter) more consistent over several items.

The Ink Bottle Tool
Shortcut: PC and Mac—S

The Ink Bottle tool is designed to help make adjustments to line segments on the stage through stroke properties. Although it has no options in the options section of the toolbar, you can make stroke settings in the Properties Inspector. Then you can apply these settings by clicking line segments with the tip of the Ink Bottle.

The Paint Bucket Tool

Shortcut: PC and Mac—K

The Paint Bucket tool is used to change fill settings of shapes on the stage. Select the color or gradient you want to use and click the fill you want to change.

The Paint Bucket tool does have a couple options:

- Gap Closing—This option has a drop–down, as you can see in Figure 3.19, which shows the different gap sizes to fill in shapes that do not have connecting line segments.

- Lock Fill—This option will assist in making gradients consistent over different shapes.

FIGURE 3.19   The gap fill selections for the Paint Bucket tool.

The Eyedropper Tool

Shortcut: PC and Mac—I

The Eyedropper tool is used to snag properties of either strokes or fills. As you hover over a line or fill of a shape, a small icon will appear with an eyedropper to indicate which you are working with. When you've made your selection, the tool will automatically change to either the Paint Bucket (for fills) or the Ink Bottle tool (for strokes).

> **TIP**
>
> While using the Eyedropper tool, hold down the Shift key when you make a selection, and both the fill and stroke color will be changed to that selection.

The Eraser Tool

Shortcut: PC and Mac—E

The Eraser tool is used to erase both fills and strokes. Besides the size and shape drop-down (see Figure 3.20), the Eraser tool has a couple more options, including how to erase the following:

- **Erase Normal**—The default setting, which when selected will make the Eraser tool erase both lines and fills from the stage.

- **Erase Fills**—While erasing with this option selected, lines will not be affected, only fills.

- **Erase Lines**—The exact opposite of the previous option, this option affects only lines and will not erase fills.

- **Erase Selected Fills**—With this option selected, the eraser will affect only the fills you have selected.

- **Erase Inside**—This option will make the eraser erase fills only from a shape where you initially begin to erase from.

The final option of the Eraser tool is the Faucet option. This option, when selected, turns the Eraser tool into a one-click wonder. Just click the line or fill you want to get rid of, and the entire selection will be erased.

FIGURE 3.20   The different settings for how the Eraser tool will erase.

TIP

While using the Eraser tool (not in Faucet mode), hold down the Shift key to erase in straight lines.

NOTE

Although the Eraser tool will make quick work of getting rid of shapes and lines on the stage, it will not affect any nonprimitive object such as groups, graphics, movie clips, or text fields, but it will affect Drawing Objects.

Colors and Gradients

We have briefly gone over how colors work, but this section will delve into more detail and introduce you to gradients, how they work, and how to create them.

The easiest way to adjust color is to use the Color Swatches panel and the Color Mixer panel.

The Color Swatches Panel

Windows, Color Swatches (Ctrl+F9)

As you can see in Figure 3.21, the Color Swatches panel has the default web 256 colors in it as well as a few gradients at the bottom from which you can select. You can sort these colors to group by color or leave them in the standard layout. You can add colors from color files (.clr), which can be found at C:\Program Files\Macromedia\Flash8\en\First Run\Color Sets. You can also add colors from graphics by going through the following steps:

1. Open the Color Swatches panel.

2. Select Add Colors from the submenu in the panel.

3. Choose any GIF file (or use image_1.gif, which can be found on the website).

That's it. You now have all the colors from that GIF file. If you do not see any change in the colors in the panel, the GIF you chose did not have any new colors. Try a higher-quality GIF file (nature pictures are great for this).

After you have the new colors in your swatches, you can save them back out as a .clr file or even set them as your default from the same submenu.

FIGURE 3.21   The Color Swatches panel.

The Color Mixer Panel

Windows, Color Mixer (Shift+F9)

The Color Mixer panel can create and edit colors and gradients. As you can see from Figure 3.22, the Color Mixer panel is a bit different than the Color Swatches panel; however, they work together to create and store colors and gradients.

This walkthrough will go over how to edit and save a gradient using the Color Mixer panel.

1. Draw an oval on the stage with a solid color.

2. With the Color Mixer panel open, select Radial from the fill type drop-down. (It will now look similar to Figure 3.22.)

3. You can select either of the handles, slide them along the color bar, or change their color completely using the color drop-down. You can also add colors to the color bar by clicking when you see a white plus sign.

4. When you're satisfied with your new gradient, select the submenu drop-down from the Color Mixer panel and choose Add Swatch.

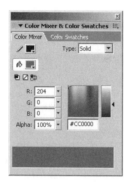

FIGURE 3.22   The Color Mixer panel.

TIP

Gradients can handle up to 15 different colors.

Grouping and Drawing Objects

Throughout this chapter, we have gone over how to draw, modify, and erase shapes from the stage. Following are a few helpful tips about grouping them.

Groupies

In the next chapter, you will see how to convert primitive objects to a Graphic symbol, but they are a more permanent solution for grouping shapes. Actually, grouping shapes together is a much less permanent solution because you can quickly group and ungroup them.

To group a few selections together, select Modify, Group (Ctrl+G). To Ungroup them, select Modify, Ungroup (Ctrl+Shift+G or Ctrl+B).

Drawing Objects

New to Flash 8, Drawing Objects are a special kind of group. You can draw your shapes within Drawing Objects automatically if the tool has the Object Drawing option turned on (Shortcut: J). They can also be created by selecting raw shapes (and other Drawing Objects) and selecting Modify, Combine Objects, Union.

What is unique about Drawing Objects is that even though they do not act like raw shapes, you can still modify them the same way with the Arrow tool, the Paint Bucket, the Eraser, and the other drawing tools without having to double-click them to go into Edit mode. You can also adjust them with the Properties Inspector, unlike groups, as shown in Figure 3.23. And like groups, you can stack Drawing Objects over top of one another in the same layer without having to worry about them affecting each other or raw shapes.

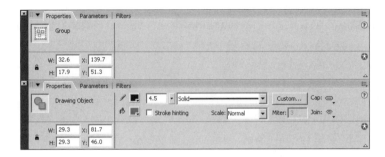

FIGURE 3.23   You can see the difference in the Property Inspector from selecting a group to selecting a Drawing Object.

You can, however, have them affect one another by overlaying them and selecting the other options under Modify, Combine Objects:

- **Intersect**—Leaves only the part of the shape where all shapes overlaid.

- **Punch**—Removes the section of all shapes beneath top shape where the top shape overlaid.

- **Crop**—Leaves sections of all shapes beneath top shape where top shape overlaid. Exact opposite of punch option.

See Figure 3.24 to see what these options mean.

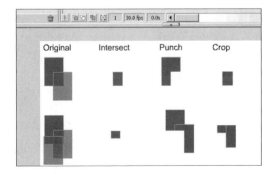

FIGURE 3.24   The effects of the different Combine Objects options.

Stacking Groups

As you get more familiar with grouping shapes as groups or Drawing Objects, you will notice that as you group them, they tend to stack on top of one another. Controls found under Modify, Arrange can help this, including:

- **Bring to Front**—Brings the selection to the top viewing level in the layer. (Ctrl+Shift+Up)

- **Bring Forward**—Moves the selection up one viewing level. (Ctrl+Up)

- **Send Backward**—Moves the selection down one viewing level. (Ctrl+Down)

- **Send to Back**—Sends the selection to the bottom-most viewing level. (Ctrl+Shift+Down)

You can also lock shapes within a layer so that they cannot be selected and then unlock shapes to reselect them.

Now that you have seen how to work with shapes, groups, and Drawing Objects, you'll learn about bitmaps.

Importing and Working with Bitmaps

Even though vector graphics are usually smaller in file size, oftentimes you will still need bitmap graphics. After these bitmaps are in Flash, they will become a symbol in the Library (more on the Library and Symbols in Chapter 5). This means that you can manipulate them much the same as a group or other symbol, such as sizing and rotating.

To import a bitmap into Flash, follow these steps:

1. Select File, Import, Import to Stage (Ctrl+R).

2. Select the bitmap you want to bring in and click Open.

After the bitmap is on the stage, you can take several courses of action.

Creating a Bitmap Fill

A bitmap fill is similar to a gradient. When one is selected, you can use the Paint Bucket tool to fill in shapes with it.

Here are the steps to create a bitmap fill after the bitmap has been imported:

1. With the bitmap selected, choose Modify, Break Apart (Ctrl+B).

2. With the Eyedropper tool, select the newly broken-apart bitmap.

3. Now select the Rectangle tool and draw a rectangle on the stage. You will see it is filled with the bitmap.

Tracing Bitmaps

Modify, Bitmap, Trace Bitmap

Although we converted the bitmap to a fill, we really could not grab sections of it as pieces. This is because the entire bitmap is currently seen as a single fill. To fix this, you can trace bitmap by going to Modify, Bitmap, Trace Bitmap. This will produce a pop-up, such as Figure 3.25, with the following options:

- **Color Threshold**—This option looks at the color of adjacent pixels. If the color value is less than this option, the pixels will be combined into one color. The value range is between 1 and 500.

- **Minimum Area**—This option controls how many pixels to evaluate at a time. The value range is between 1 and 1,000.

- **Curve Fit**—This option controls the smoothness of the vector edges being created.

- **Corner Threshold**—This option controls the amount of corners that are preserved in the process.

By setting smaller threshold Minimum area settings, you will create a higher resolution image, but the file size will increase as well. Setting many corners will also help in creating a higher resolution image. For an example of what a bitmap next to a traced bitmap looks like, see Figure 3.26.

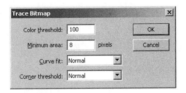

FIGURE 3.25   The Trace Bitmap pop-up window.

FIGURE 3.26   Before and after shot of a bitmap tracing. Notice the stylized look on the right.

Swap Bitmap

Modify, Bitmap, Swap Bitmap

The Swap Bitmap feature allows you to swap out bitmaps on the stage with any other bitmap in the library. After importing another bitmap and deleting it from the stage, select the bitmap still on the stage and choose Modify, Bitmap, Swap Bitmap, which will allow you to grab another bitmap from the library and replace the selected one on the stage (see Figure 3.27).

FIGURE 3.27   The Swap Bitmap pop-up.

Summary

This chapter was a good introduction to the toolbar, how to draw shapes, and how to work with them on the stage. Like nearly everything else Flash related, the more you work with them, the more comfortable they will become.

In the next chapter, we will go over how to animate some of the drawings we create and a few best practices for that process.

CHAPTER **4**

Flash Animation

Although Flash has evolved into a full-featured development platform, it has not forgotten its roots as a vector animation tool. So far we have covered most of the interface, including drawing and stage manipulation tools. This chapter expands on the previous chapter in that we will be taking some of these drawings and animating them in different ways.

But before we jump into animating shapes on the stage, it's important to know where they are going to be animated.

Welcome to the Timeline

Often seen by animators, but rarely seen by developers and web designers, the timeline is where animation takes place. Each frame of the timeline represents a frame of the movie, so as objects are placed at different positions as the frames progress, it gives the appearance of movement through time. You can see what the timeline looks like in Figure 4.1.

The timeline contains two basic sections: the layers section and the frames section.

The Layers Section

If you have worked with PhotoShop or Freehand before, layers will not be a new concept. However, if layers are new to you, the basic idea is that you can put objects on different layers, which will stack over top of each other through the layer order. Layers work from top to bottom, so anything on the uppermost layer will be above objects placed on all layers beneath it.

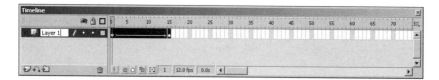

FIGURE 4.1   The timeline in Flash, where animation takes place.

The different layer options for the timeline are outlined next and shown in Figure 4.2:

- **Insert Layer**—Creates a new layer on top of the selected layer.

- **Add Motion Guide**—Creates a motion guide above the selected layer and automatically associates itself with the selected layer. (You'll learn more about motion guides in Chapter 5, "Symbols and the Library.")

- **Insert Layer Folder**—Creates a folder to hold layers in. It can be collapsed and expanded for a more organized timeline.

- **Remove Layer**—Removes selected layer(s) or layer folder(s).

FIGURE 4.2   The layers section of the timeline.

You can also choose from three more options to control some visual aspects of layers and the capability for them to be edited.

- **Show/Hide Layers**—Turns everything in the layer invisible.

- **Lock Layers**—Makes the layer uneditable, but objects are still visible.

- **Show Layer as Outline**—Creates an outline around all objects in the layer and turns the objects themselves invisible. Objects are still editable.

You can see the icons for the preceding options at the top of the layers section. If you click these, it affects all layers. However, if you click the dots under the icon (in each layer), it affects only that layer.

> **TIP**
>
> When you click the individual layer controls, hold down the Alt key, and all layers but the selected layer will be affected.

That covers the layers side of the timeline, but remember that there are two sections, and the frames section is the most important when it comes to animation.

The Frames Section

As mentioned previously, the frames section is where all the animation takes place. The layers section is more for stacking shapes and objects. As you go through the chapter, you will use different types of frames, so here is a quick rundown of what they are:

- **Keyframe**—A keyframe indicates change on that layer. For instance, in a movie, where action takes place, each movement is in its own keyframe. To insert a keyframe, go to Insert, Timeline, Keyframe (PC—F6).

- **Blank Keyframe**—Just like a normal keyframe, these frames show change in the timeline. The difference is that with blank keyframes, the change is that nothing is there anymore. To insert a blank keyframe, go to Insert, Timeline, Blank Keyframe (PC—F7).

- **Frame**—A frame also has data in it, but there has been no change to it from the previous frame. Frames must always follow keyframes. To insert a frame, select Insert, Timeline, Frame (PC—F5).

- **Unpopulated Frame**—Unpopulated frames are frames that have no changes in them from the previous frame, and the frame does not have any content in it. Unpopulated frames must follow a blank keyframe. You insert an unpopulated frame the same way you would a normal frame: Insert, Timeline, Frame (PC—F5).

Also, when moving through frames, you will use the play head, which can be seen in Figure 4.3. The play head is visual representation of where in the movie you are, and the stage will change accordingly to what is in the frames where the play head is.

You can control the play head by dragging it along the timeline, or you can open the controller window by going to Window, Toolbars, Controller. It is shown in Figure 4.4 and works like a VCR would.

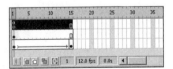

FIGURE 4.3   The frames section of the timeline.

FIGURE 4.4   Use the controller window to play, pause, and move through the timeline.

More options are available that will greatly help when you're animating. They can be found at the bottom left of the frames section and are marked in Figure 4.3. Here are what those options are, followed by a description of what they do:

- **Center Frame**—Use this option to center the timeline in the view so that the selected frame will be the center.

- **Onion Skin**—This option allows you to see several frames at once. Onion skinning will show previous and future frames as shadows on the stage. You can adjust how many frames forward and backward to display at once by grabbing the onion skin brackets and dragging them. As you adjust the play head, the onion skins will automatically adjust. To see what onion skinning looks like, see Figure 4.5.

- **Onion Skin Outlines**—Similar to normal onion skinning, onion skin outlines show content on previous and future frames, but only in outline form.

- **Edit Multiple Frames**—This option enables you to edit any frame within the onion skin; otherwise, although you can see other frames, you can edit only the current frame.

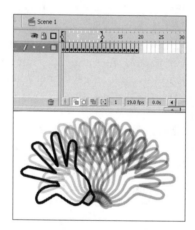

FIGURE 4.5   Using onion skins allows you to see more than one frame as shadows on the stage.

- **Modify Onion Markers**—Clicking this option will reveal a drop-down menu with several options for the onion-skinning technique. Following is a short list of those options:

  - **Always Show Markers**—This option makes it so the onion skin brackets are always visible.

  - **Anchor Onion**—This option locks the onion skin set in its current position; however, you can still adjust its beginning and ending frame.

  - **Onion 2**—This option sets the brackets of the onion skin exactly two frames from the current frame, in both directions.

- **Onion 5**—This option sets the brackets of the onion skin exactly five frames from the current frame, in both directions.

- **Onion All**—This option will onion skin from the first frame all the way to the last frame.

Just past the Modify Onion Markers option are a few fields with some information about the movie and the play head's position within it:

- **Current Frame**—This is the current frame the play head resides on.

- **Frame Rate**—This is the current frames-per-second (FPS) that your Flash movie is set for. The default value is 12 FPS. You can adjust this setting in the Properties Inspector. (Tip: you can also adjust this setting by double-clicking the field itself.)

- **Elapsed Time**—This is the number of seconds from frame 1 to the selected frame. Because this is time based on a frame number, if you adjust the FPS setting, it will also adjust.

The final set of options can be seen in the top right of the timeline, the HH button, where the view options are. Following is a list of those options:

- **Tiny, Small, Normal, Medium, and Large**—These options control the width of the frames.

- **Short**—This option adjust the height of the frames and subsequently the height of the layers.

- **Tinted Frames**—This option makes frames that have content in them a shade of gray. By default, this option is on.

- **Preview**—This option shows a thumbnail of the content from that frame in the frame itself. You can see an example in Figure 4.6.

- **Preview in Context**—This option also shows a small thumbnail of the content in the frame, but it shows the content in context with the stage, as you can see in Figure 4.7.

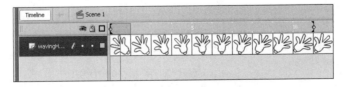

FIGURE 4.6   This is what the frames look like in Preview mode.

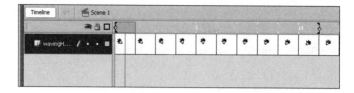

FIGURE 4.7   These are the same frames, but in Preview in Context mode.

That wraps up the options for the timeline, so now let's get into some actual animation. But before we get into the ways Flash can help you animate, let's go over how real cartoonists do animations.

Frame by Frame

Although it is a tedious process, frame-by-frame animation has been done for quite some time and does give the animator the most control of his or her animation. Some of the best cartoons have been done using the process of creating a separate frame for each and every piece of animation.

Your First Animation

In the following exercise, you are going to create a frame-by-frame animation of a hand waving.

1. Create a new Flash document by going to File, New (Ctrl+N), and then select Flash Document and save it as **wavingHand.fla**.

2. Double-click Layer 1 and rename it **wavingHand**.

3. In wavingHand, draw a small hand like the one shown in Figure 4.8.

4. Select the second frame of the same layer, and then choose Insert, Timeline Keyframe (PC—F6). This creates an identical copy of the previous frame, so select the hand on the stage and then open up the Transform panel (Window, Design Panels, Transform, or Ctrl+F7 for PC users).

5. While the hand is still selected, in the Transform panel, set the Rotate field to 10 and press Enter.

6. Follow the previous two steps for frames 3 through 10 until you have completed frame 10 (at which point, the hand will have rotated 90 degrees).

7. If you test the movie right now (Control, Test Movie, or use Ctrl+Enter), the hand will wave from left to right and then jump back to the first frame. We could go through the process we just did and use –10 as the rotation, but there is an easier way to do it.

8. After closing the test movie screen, select frames 1–9.

The easiest way to select frames is to select the first frame you want, then hold down the Shift key and select the last frame you want.

9. After the frames are selected, right-click (Ctrl+click on MAC) and choose Copy Frames from the menu. (Ctrl+Alt+C)

10. Select frame 11, right-click, and choose Paste Frames. At this point, if you tested the movie again, it would show the hand waving twice and then starting over. What we want to do is make the hand wave one direction and then go back the other direction in a smooth manner.

11. Now select frames 11–19; then select Modify, Timeline, Reverse Frames.

Now you're done. Test the movie again and you will see the hand waving back and forth continuously.

4

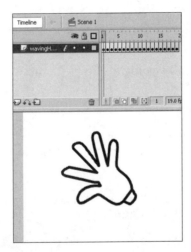

FIGURE 4.8   Using keyframe animation is a powerful way of controlling every aspect of your animation.

You can definitely see some of the benefits of using keyframe animation with the capability to control every aspect of the stage in each frame. The downside is that you have to make adjustments for each frame. The previous example was not too complicated because it was just a hand waving, but imagine if it was an entire person that was walking and waving—that would take a lot of keyframes to accomplish. This is where tweening comes in.

Tweening

Tweening is used in animation when you know what the first frame should look like, when you know what the last frame should look like, but you don't want to manually draw all the frames in the middle. Tweening will draw what it believes to be the frames be-"tween" the first and last keyframe. There are two types of tweening: Shape Tweening and Motion Tweening. We will be going over only Shape Tweening in this chapter, but the next chapter covers Motion Tweening.

> **NOTE**
>
> As you learned from the last chapter, you can also draw raw shapes as Drawing Objects. This will not affect the shape tween, and in some cases may assist in creating it.

Your First Tween

Although the waving hand would be a good example to show the benefits of tweening, we will use a simpler animation so that we can go over all the tweening options.

In this example, we will move a circle from one side of the stage to the other. It is an easy task for frame-by-frame animation, but even easier using a tween:

1. Create a new Flash movie by going to File, New and select Flash Document. Save the file as **moveCircle.fla**.

2. Rename Layer 1 **circle**.

3. In the first frame of circle, draw a small circle on the left side of the stage about 75×75 pixels with a black fill color, as shown in Figure 4.9.

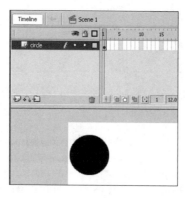

FIGURE 4.9   Shape tweens can be used to speed up the process of animating.

4. Select frame 20 of circle and choose Insert, Timeline, Keyframe (PC—F6).

5. In frame 20, move the circle to the right side of the stage.

6. Now select frame 1 again, and in the Properties Inspector under the tween drop-down, choose Shape. (Your Properties Inspector should now look similar to Figure 4.10). Also notice that the frames between 1 and 20 are now green and have an arrow pointing to frame 20. This means that the tween was successful. If the tween had not been successful, you would have seen a dashed line there instead.

You can now test the movie (Control, Test Movie, or Ctrl+Enter), and you will see the circle move from left to right over and over. The next step is to make the circle slow down as it reaches its destination point using easing.

FIGURE 4.10   The Properties Inspector for a Shape tween.

7. Close the test movie screen and select frame 1 again.

8. In the Properties Inspector, set the Ease field to 100.

> **NOTE**
>
> Easing set at positive numbers is easing out (at the end of the tween). Easing set to negative numbers is easing in (at the beginning of the tween).

Test the movie again, and this time you will see that as the circle moves from the left of the screen to the right of the screen, it begins to slow down. This is another great example of why sometimes tweening is better than frame-by-frame animation, because changes can be made quickly.

But shape tweens can do a lot more than simply move a shape around on the stage; it can also morph the shape into another shape, as you will see in the next few steps:

1. Close the test movie screen again, and select frame 20.

2. Delete the circle in this keyframe. The tween will go from an arrow to a dashed line, like Figure 4.11, because the tween is no longer valid.

3. Approximately where the circle was, draw a square with 100×100 pixels with a fill color of red. At that point, the tween should be valid again, and the arrow will have reappeared.

Test the movie one more time, and this time you will see that shape tweens not only can change position of a shape, but the shape itself as well as color.

FIGURE 4.11   A dashed line in a tween means that the tween will not work.

> **NOTE**
>
> Although you can change the fill color, and the tween will fade to it, gradients don't work as well. You cannot fade to a gradient, however, if the shape in the last keyframe has a gradient fill; the tween will move through the gradient itself. For instance, if you have a radial gradient set, the shape will move into it, and the gradient itself never moves.

That tween was not too difficult, but sometimes, when changing shapes in the tween, it does not act exactly as you would expect. In come shape hints.

Shape Hints

Shape hints are how you override Flash's tweening algorithms for better control. When you add shape hints (as you will in the next example), a small circle with a letter in it is created in the first frame of the tween. You place it at any point on the shape you like. Then in the final frame of the tween, there will be another circle with the same letter that you place where you want that point to end up.

Shape hints are easier to understand when you use them, so in this example you will create a morphing shape tween that inherently will not do exactly what you want, until you add shape hints.

1. Create a new Flash document and save it as **shapeHint1.fla**.

2. Rename Layer 1 as **xMorph**.

3. In the first frame of xMorph, select the text tool and create an uppercase "X" on the stage.

4. Now you want to convert the letter to a shape by using the Arrow tool to first select this X; then choose Modify, Break Apart (Ctrl+B).

5. Now that the X is a shape on the stage, select it with the Free Transform tool and stretch it to about 100×100 pixels so that it looks like Figure 4.12.

6. Select frame 20 and insert a blank keyframe by going to Insert, Timeline, Blank Keyframe (Ctrl+F7).

7. Draw a rectangle on the stage about 100×100 in frame 20.

8. Select frame 1 again, and in the Properties Inspector, set the tween to Shape.

   Now you can test the movie here and see that as the X morphs into the square, it rotates. In general, that might not be bad, but for this example, we do not want it to rotate.

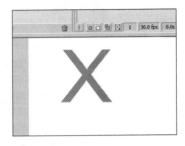

FIGURE 4.12   Create an X on the stage; then break it apart and size it to 100×100.

9. After closing the test movie screen, select frame 1 again and choose Modify, Shape, Add Shape Hint (Ctrl+Shift+H), and a little red circle with the letter "a" will appear on the stage.

10. Add three more shape hints.

11. Place the letter "a" shape hint on the inner side of the top-left part of the X.

12. The "b" goes on the bottom left, the "c" on the top right, and the "d" on the bottom right. Just make sure they are on the inside shape corner, as shown in Figure 4.13.

13. Now select frame 20 and you will see yellow versions of the same circles. (They will probably be stacked on top of one another, with "d" being on top.)

14. Put the associated letters in the corners matching the X, as in Figure 4.14.

15. Test the movie again, and you will see that this time, as the morph progresses, it does not rotate.

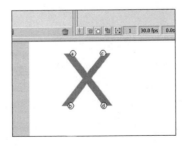

FIGURE 4.13   Place the shape hints on the inside corners of the X.

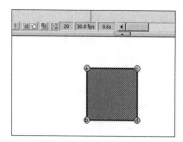

FIGURE 4.14   Place the shape hints in their associated corners to match the X.

So you can see how to use shape hints to better control your tween, but there is still no substitute for control that is stronger than frame-by-frame.

> **TIP**
>
> If you want to quickly make an animation, but still use frame-by-frame, create a normal tween animation, then highlight all the frames in the tween and select Insert, Timeline, Keyframe, and they will all be converted to keyframes. Just remember to turn each frames tween option back to None.

Summary

This chapter was a good introduction to animation, showing a few different techniques and how to use them. However, this chapter was not the end of animation; we covered only how to animate primitive shapes. The next chapter will come back to animation using the motion tween, and you'll learn about the three basic symbols Flash has as well as the Library panel.

CHAPTER **5**

Symbols, Instances, and the Library

So far we have been dealing with primitive objects on the stage, such as shapes, groups, and Drawing Objects (which are just groups of shapes).

In this chapter, we move on to more advanced objects on the stage, including the three basic symbol types: Graphics, Buttons, and Movie Clips. We also discuss instances of these symbols as well as the library where all symbols are kept. And finally, we return to the timeline for some more animation techniques.

What Is a Symbol?

A *symbol* is an item stored in the library to be used once or multiple times throughout your Flash file. This is a benefit of symbols, not only because of file size, but also because of ease of changes. If you edit a symbol, all copies of that symbol will reflect the changes of the original. All symbols are kept in the library (which we discuss later in this chapter) and can be accessed through the library at any time during authoring. When you drag a symbol from the library onto the stage, you create an instance of that symbol.

What Is an Instance?

An *instance* is nothing more than a copy of a library symbol that has been placed on the stage. When a symbol has been changed, all instances of that symbol will change accordingly. Also, because you are using an instance of the symbol, that again is no more than just a copy of the original, you can adjust certain settings of that instance, such as size, coloring, and alpha, without altering other instances of the symbol or the symbol itself. When we get into ActionScript later in this chapter, you will see the importance of instances because they will have unique names, and that is how to control them with ActionScript.

Remember that symbols are items held in the library and instances are copies of symbols that have been placed on the stage.

The Graphic Symbol

Graphic symbols are the first symbol we will discuss because it is the most basic. Things to note about Graphic symbols are that they have a synced timeline. This means that when a graphic is rendered on the main timeline, if the graphic has several frames of animation, it will play ahead only if the timeline it is residing on moves ahead as well. ActionScript (which is discussed later in this book) will not work within Graphic symbols either on their timeline or within them as Object Actions. Also, you cannot apply filters or blending options to graphics.

TIP

Although the timeline of a graphic is synced, you can control which frame to start on by selecting the graphic, going to the Properties Inspector, and adjusting the First: field, which defaults to 1.

When Should You Use a Graphic?

Going back to what we have already covered, when you draw on the stage, you are creating primitive objects that will have to be rendered at runtime by Flash. Even groups and Drawing Objects are just several shapes grouped together that will also have to be rendered at runtime.

In comes the Graphic symbol. Because shapes on the stage are rendered in each frame of the Flash player, sometimes they take up more resources and processor cycles than what are necessary. Using an instance of a graphic symbol, because it is a copy of a symbol in the library, will take up fewer resources because in each frame, the Flash player refers back to the original and makes the necessary changes.

Because of the inherent simple nature of Graphic symbols, they are best used for static imagery or simple animations. (Complex animations are usually more suited for the Movie Clip symbol, which is discussed later in this chapter.)

But enough about what Graphic symbols are; following is a step-by-step list showing how to create them:

1. Create a new Flash document by going to File, New (PC—Ctrl+N, Mac—Open Apple+N), and choosing Flash Document.

2. Now choose Insert, New Symbol (PC—Ctrl+F8, Mac—Open Apple+F8), which will bring up the Create New Symbol dialog box, as shown in Figure 5.1.

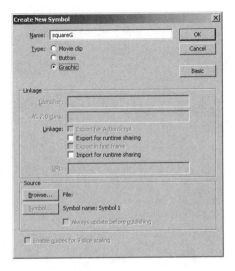

FIGURE 5.1 The Create New Symbol dialog box.

3. In this dialog box, you will choose several options concerning your symbol. If however, your dialog box does not look like Figure 5.1, click the Basic button. This will hide the other options that are discussed later in this book.

4. The first choice you will make is the name of your symbol. So name it **squareG**.

> **TIP**
>
> Although the symbol name is used only in the library and not used anywhere in ActionScript, it is still important to give it a name that somewhat describes what the symbol will be. In this walkthrough, we name it squareG because we will draw a square shape in it. Also, as a personal preference, I tend to put a capitol "G" at the end of graphics to symbolize that they are graphics, but it is not necessary to do so.

5. The next choice to make is the Behavior of the symbol, which in this case is Graphic. Choose that and click OK.

6. Notice that your screen has changed to Figure 5.2, a blank stage with a tiny crosshair in the center. Draw a square using the rectangle tool (R) so that it is roughly centered over the crosshair.

> **TIP**
>
> Aligning shapes inside a symbol is more important than it may appear here. When you begin to work with symbols on the stage, you will see that rotation and certain sizing techniques depend on the center of the symbol, so keep it in mind. But don't worry if you put shapes in the wrong place at first because you can always edit the symbol and change it later.

7. After the square is drawn, go back to the main timeline by clicking Scene 1 at the top left of the timeline.

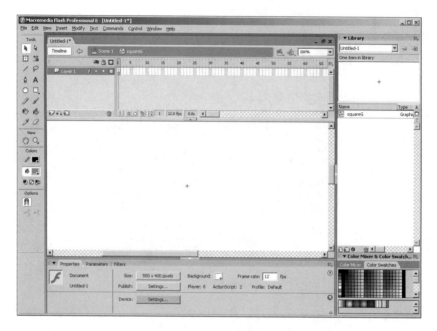

FIGURE 5.2   The empty graphic symbol before you draw anything in it.

8. On returning to the main timeline, you will notice that the stage is again empty, but your work was not in vain because the symbol, like all symbols, is held in the library.

9. To open the library, choose Window, Library (PC—Ctrl+L, Mac—Open Apple+L). The library should look like Figure 5.3, where you will also see the symbol we just created, squareG.

10. To add an instance of this symbol to the stage, select it in the library and drag it out to the stage.

FIGURE 5.3   The library containing the squareG symbol.

This example shows how to create a symbol from scratch and then create an instance of it on the stage, but many times you will already have a shape or other object on the stage that you want to make into a symbol.

Converting to a Symbol

Converting to a symbol is a slightly different process from creating one from scratch. To convert a selection to a symbol, choose Modify, Convert to Symbol (F8). This will produce the Convert to Symbol dialog box (see Figure 5.4), which looks similar to the Create New Symbol dialog box except for the Registration option. The Registration option enables you to select the alignment of your selection within the symbol.

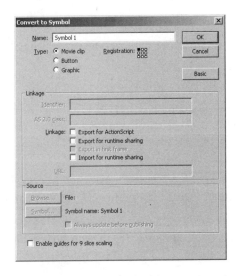

FIGURE 5.4   The Convert to Symbol dialog box. Notice the Registration option.

> **TIP**
>
> You can also convert selections to a new symbol by dragging them directly into the library.

That covers the graphic symbol. Next up is the Button symbol, a much more interactive symbol, as you will see.

The Button Symbol

The Button symbol is different from the other two major symbols because it has a unique timeline, as you will see, and cannot have ActionScript within this timeline. However, buttons are very important to a Flash document because they provide a quick and easy way to enable the user to interact with your movie.

Buttons have four distinct states on their unique timeline, as shown in Figure 5.5:

- **Up**—When the mouse cursor is not over the button.
- **Over**—When the mouse cursor is over the button, but the mouse button is not pressed.
- **Down**—When the user presses the mouse button over the button itself.
- **Hit**—This is a nonvisual state that enables you to define the area that will activate the buttons other states.

Follow these steps to create your first button:

1. Create a new Flash document and save it as **button1.fla**.

2. On the stage, draw a small square about 100×100 in size with a red fill color (0xff0000).

3. Select the square (both stroke and fill) and choose Modify, Convert to Symbol (F8).

4. In the Convert to Symbol dialog box, give it the symbol name **squareB** and choose Button as the behavior. Because this example is not concerned with rotation or resizing of the button, the registration point is not important, so leave it at the default.

5. Click OK; now the shape has become a button symbol on the stage. If you tested right now, whenever you moved the mouse over the square, the cursor would turn to a pointing hand.

6. Now you want to edit the different states of your button. Select the button on the main stage and choose Edit, Edit Selected (or you can double-click it).

7. You should see something similar to Figure 5.5 with the four button states that are unique to the Button symbol. As you can see, the Up state is already done for you, so select the Over frame and choose Insert, Timeline, Keyframe (F6).

8. A copy of the Up frame is made, so all you have to do is change the fill color to green (0x00ff00).

9. Repeat the preceding step for the Down frame and change its fill color to blue (0x0000ff).

10. The final frame is the Hit frame, which defines the area of the button that interacts with the user. It does not have to be the same shape as the other states, but in this case it will be. Select the Hit frame and choose Insert, Timeline, Frame (F5).

Test again and you will see that as you move the mouse over the button, the color changes to green, and if you click the button, the color changes to blue.

> **TIP**
>
> One thing you should remember when building buttons with text in them is to never use the text in the Hit state. This will cause unpredictable interactions with the user. Always use a shape for the Hit state.

FIGURE 5.5   The four states of the Button timeline.

You can also test buttons on the main stage by choosing Control, Enable Simple Buttons (PC—Ctrl+Alt+B, Mac—Option+Open Apple+B).

The next step, after learning how to create a button, is to learn how to use a button.

An Interactive Button

Although the button you just created is somewhat interactive with the mouse cursor, true interaction with the user requires some coding. And all code associated with a button must be placed in the object actions of the button, or must reference the button (by its instance name) in a movie clip's timeline (which is discussed in more detail later in this book).

For right now, you will add code to the object actions of the button itself. Within the object actions of a button, all ActionScript must fall within one or more of an event like this:

```
on(release){
 _root.stop();
}
```

With the preceding code, if the button is pressed at runtime, the root timeline will stop playing.

Following is a list of all button events:

- **press**—When the user clicks down on the button.
- **release**—When the user releases the mouse click while still hovering over the button itself after the button has been pressed.
- **releaseOutside**—When the user releases the mouse click while no longer hovering over the button itself after the button has been pressed.

- **rollOver**—When the user moves the mouse cursor over the button without the mouse being clicked.

- **rollOut**—When the user moves the mouse cursor off the button without the mouse button being pressed.

- **dragOver**—When the user moves the mouse cursor over the button with the mouse being clicked. Can occur only after a dragOut event.

- **dragOut**—When the user moves the mouse cursor off the button with the mouse still being clicked.

- **keyPress "key"**—When the user presses a defined key that is surrounded by quotes. An example is if you wanted to capture the lower case "a."

```
on(keyPress "a"){
  trace("a");
}
```

Now that you see the basic events for the button, you can add some code to the one you have previously created to see how it interacts.

1. Continuing from the previous example, select the button on the main timeline and open the Actions panel by going to Window, Actions (F9).

2. Put these actions within the panel:

```
on(release){
  //fade the button out
  _alpha -= 5;
}
```

(handwritten annotation: -alpha -= 5;)

(handwritten annotation: not a fullstop)

Now you can test the movie and see that the more you click the button, the more transparent it becomes. Of course, you can put the code that does the fading in any one of the other events of the button as well.

So far you have learned how to create a visual button and how to add ActionScript to it for a more interactive button. But sometimes you will want the functionality of a button without the visual aspect of it. This is where the invisible button comes in.

Memoirs of an Invisible Button

Many times, when you're working with graphics on the web, you might want to make certain sections of a single graphic "hot spots" so that the user can click them for interaction. This is a perfect opportunity for invisible buttons.

An invisible button is nothing more than a button with all but the Hit state left empty. It is invisible only at runtime; during authoring it looks like Figure 5.6, a semitransparent turquoise shape. But even though it is invisible at runtime, it will act as a normal button would, including having the capability to place ActionScript within it to increase interactivity.

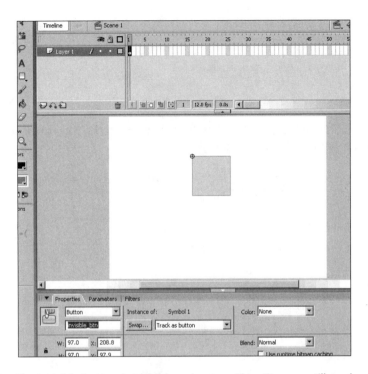

FIGURE 5.6 The invisible button is invisible only at runtime. You can still work with it in Flash as you would any other button.

Follow this walkthrough to see how to make and use invisible buttons:

1. Create a new Flash document and save it as **invisibleButton.fla**.

2. Draw a square in the top-left portion of the stage about 50×50 in size.

3. Double-click just the stroke of that square and delete it.

4. Select the square itself now, and choose Modify, Convert to Symbol (F8).

5. Set the symbol name to **invisibleB**, choose Button as the behavior, and click OK.

6. Select the square on the stage and choose Edit, Edit Symbol (Ctrl+E).

7. The first frame (Up) should already be selected, but if not, select it.

8. Drag this frame to the *Hit* frame. This should make the previous frames empty, like Figure 5.7.

9. Go back to the main stage and you should see that the square is still there, but it is semitransparent and the color turquoise, like Figure 5.6.

10. Select the button and open the Actions panel.

11. Place these actions within it:

```
on(release){
 //send a message to the output panel
 trace("I'm invisible");
}
```

Test the movie, and when you click the invisible button (after you locate it in the top left), a message is sent to the output panel.

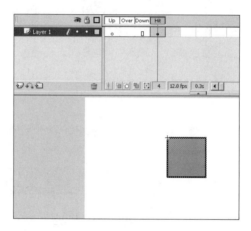

FIGURE 5.7   Invisible buttons are simple to make because they have content only in the Hit frame.

Now you have seen a lot of what buttons have to offer. Next up is the final symbol covered in this chapter, the Movie Clip symbol.

The Movie Clip Symbol

We have saved the best for last in this chapter because the movie clip has it all. Movie clips have an independent timeline in that their timeline is not dependent on the main timeline; therefore, their play head can move in sync or out of sync with the main play head. Also, movie clips can have ActionScript within their own timeline and/or have ActionScript in their object actions. The main timeline itself is a movie clip, although you won't find it in the Library panel with the others. Movie clips are so powerful, in fact, that an entire chapter, Chapter 13, "The Movie Clip Objects," has been devoted to them. But we will still run through the major points in this chapter.

Making a Movie Clip symbol is the same as making the other symbols, but you choose a different behavior.

1. Create a new Flash document and save it as **myFirstMovieClip.fla**.

2. Draw a circle in the center of the stage about 75×75 and give it a red fill color (0xff0000) like Figure 5.8.

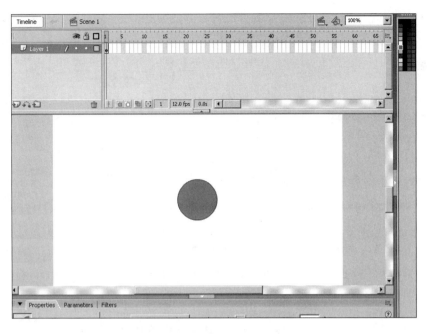

FIGURE 5.8   Movie Clip symbols are the most reusable symbol Flash has to offer.

3. Select the circle, both stroke and fill, and choose Modify, Convert to Symbol (F8).

4. In the Convert to Symbol dialog box, give it a symbol name of **circleMC**, choose Movie Clip for the behavior, and click OK.

   If you tested the movie right now, the square would be there. But if that was all you were going to do, you could have used a graphic. Instead, you will go back into the movie clip and add some ActionScript to make the circle interactive.

5. Back on the main timeline, select the circle movie and open the Actions panel by choosing Window, Actions (F9).

6. In the object actions of the circle, place the following code:

```
onClipEvent(mouseDown){
  //if the user clicks the circle
  if(hitTest(_root._xmouse,_root._ymouse)){
    //drag the circle
    this.startDrag(false);
  }
}
//when the user lets go
onClipEvent(mouseUp){
  //stop dragging the circle
  stopDrag();
}
```

Do not worry if the code is new to you, it will be covered in later chapters, but the code is necessary so that you can see the power of movie clips.

Test the movie at this point, and you will see that if you click the circle and move the mouse, the circle will drag. Let go and the movie will stop dragging.

That covers the basics of movie clips, as well as the other two symbols. The next step is to see where they are stored.

The Library

The Library is a specific panel that keeps track of every symbol in a Flash document. It also keeps track of all bitmaps, sound files, video files, and embedded fonts. The library can also help organize all these symbols into folders and can even sort items.

To open the library, select Window, Library (PC—Ctrl+L, Mac—Open Apple+L). You can see it in Figure 5.9, which has the following options:

- **Total Items**—Keeps track of the total number of items in the library, including all items in folders.

- **Preview Window**—This section shows a preview of a selected item if applicable and will also provide Play/Stop buttons to further enhance the preview.

- **Sorting Options**—These are the different properties that items in the library can be sorted by:

    - **Name**—The symbol name of the item.

    - **Kind**—The behavior or item type.

    - **Use Count**—The number of times an item is used in the Flash document.

> **NOTE**
>
> Although the use count keeps track of items used in the Flash document, if an item is supposed to be brought in at runtime through ActionScript, the library does not make note of it and will say the item has 0 uses—so be careful if you delete it.

    - **Linkage**—An identifier used in conjunction with ActionScript to add items from the library to the stage at runtime.

    - **Date Modified**—Shows the date and time the last modification to the item had been made.

- **Sort Toggle**—This option reverses the order of the items in the library based on your sorting selection.

- **Wide View**—This option widens the Library panel so all sorting fields are visible.

- **Narrow View**—This option narrows the Library panel back to its original size.

- **New Symbol**—This option enables you to add a new symbol to the library the same as selecting Insert, New Symbol.

- **New Folder**—This option adds a folder to the library so that you can drag items directly into it; it also can be collapsed so that you can see more items. You can have subfolders, as well.

- **Properties**—This button opens the Properties dialog box for the selected item, as in Figure 5.10.

- **Delete**—This button deletes the selection in the library, including folders.

FIGURE 5.9   The Library panel.

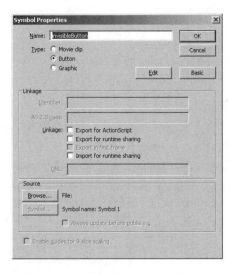

FIGURE 5.10   The Symbol Properties dialog box.

To add an item to a document from the library, drag and drop it onto the stage.

TIP

You can quickly get rid of unused items from the library to both clean up the library itself and save in file size of the Flash document. Select the options drop-down menu in the Library panel and choose Select Unused Items. This highlights every item that is not on the stage, either by itself or embedded into another object on the stage. Then delete those selections. But remember, if the item has a linkage, it may be added at runtime, so be cautious when deleting it.

That covers the library, so now we can go back and cover a few things in the timeline.

Back to the Timeline

As mentioned in the previous chapter, there are two types of tweens: the Shape tween, which was covered last chapter, and the Motion tween.

Your First Motion Tween

Motion tweening works just like Shape tweening does, except it works with symbol instances instead of primitive shapes, and you have more control over it with the Custom Ease In/Ease Out window (covered in more detail later in this section).

Follow these steps to create a Motion tween:

1. Create a new Flash document and save it as `motionTween1.fla`.

2. Draw a circle on the left side of the stage, about 75×75 with a red fill color (0xff0000).

3. Select both the stroke and fill of the circle and choose Modify, Convert to Symbol (F8).

4. Give it a symbol name of `circleMC`, set its behavior to Movie Clip, and click OK.

5. Back on the main timeline, select frame 20 and choose Insert, Timeline, Keyframe (F6).

6. In frame 20, move the circle to the right side of the stage.

7. Select frame 1, and in the Properties Inspector panel, select Motion from the Tween drop-down. *← select symbol + stroke by dragging around it*

8. You can test inside the authoring environment using the controller, or you can test the movie all together by going to Control, Test Movie (PC—Ctrl+Enter, Mac—Open Apple+Enter).

You can go a step further thanks to a new tween editor in Flash 8.

The Tween Editor

The Custom Ease In/Ease Out window (or tween editor) is a new tool that enables you to control the easing of your Motion tweens. To launch it, select the first frame of your

Motion tween; you will see an Edit button in the Properties Inspector, below the tween type drop-down. Click that, and the tween editor will appear, as shown in Figure 5.11.

This panel enables you to control the easing of your Motion tween by adjusting the tween curve. Along the bottom of the curve are the frames, so you can see where in the tween your settings will take place. Also on the left of the tween curve, you will see the tween percentage.

You can select either of the two end handles, and a new handle will appear, allowing you to bend the curve. You can also add new handles anywhere on the curve as well to create different effects. You can adjust all the properties that are being tweened (position, rotation, transparency, and so on) or you can tween them individually by unselecting the Use One Setting for All Properties check box. Then the Property drop-down will become available. At any time during your tween customization, you can preview the tween by clicking the Play button at the bottom, or reset the tween by clicking the Reset button.

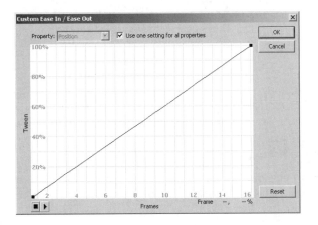

FIGURE 5.11   The tween editor.

> **TIP**
>
> If you want a good starting point for creating your custom tween, use the tween slider first to get the basic tween you want, then open the tween editor. It will have the easing already calculated into the curve.

Now that you know how to create a Motion tween and how to customize the easing, it's time to move on to the real power of Motion tweening—nested animations.

Nested Animation

Because movie clips have their own independent timeline, you can embed movie clips in other movie clips and have them animate independent of one another.

Continuing from the previous example, follow these steps to see the capability of nested animations:

1. Select the first frame in the main timeline.

2. Select the circle Movie clip on the stage and choose Edit, Edit Symbol (PC—Ctrl+E, Mac—Open Apple + E).

3. While in Edit mode of the circle, select the circle shape on the stage and choose Modify, Convert to Symbol (F8).

4. In the Convert to Symbol dialog box, set the symbol name to `circle2MC` and the behavior should already be set for Movie Clip. Then click OK.

5. Still in Edit mode of the original symbol, select frame 20 of the timeline and choose Insert, Timeline, Keyframe (F6).

6. While in frame 20, move the circle down near the bottom of the stage, but to roughly the same horizontal position.

7. Still in Edit mode, go back to frame 1 and in the Properties Inspector, set the tween to Motion.

Test the movie again, and you will see this time that the circle moves diagonally from the top left to roughly the bottom right. This is because two animations are taking place at the same time. One animation is moving the circle down while the other is moving the circle to the right. It's true that this could have been done in a single tween, but you can still see the benefit of having nested animations.

So far, all of your animations have taken a very linear path, but sometimes you may want your animation to take a less-straight path. This is where Motion Guides come in handy.

Motion Guides

Motion Guides are a special type of layer that you can draw lines in to create a path for your animations. Because movie clips will snap to these Motion Guides, they will follow it throughout the tween. And even though you are drawing directly into the Motion Guide layer, it will not be visible at runtime.

Following is an example of creating and using a Motion Guide:

1. Create a new Flash document and save it as `motionTween2.fla`.

2. Rename layer 1 to `animation`.

3. Draw a square in the upper left of the stage with 50×50 dimensions.

4. Select the square, both stroke and fill, and choose Modify, Convert to Symbol.

5. Give it a symbol name of `squareMC`, set the behavior to Movie Clip, set the registration to Center, and click OK.

6. Select frame 20 of the main timeline and choose Insert, Timeline, Keyframe (F6).

7. Create a Motion Guide layer by clicking the Add Motion guide button, as shown in Figure 5.12, and name it **Path**.

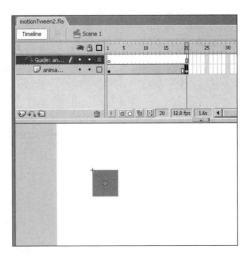

FIGURE 5.12   Motion guides help a great deal when moving objects in a curved manner.

8. In the Motion Guide, draw a curved line, as in Figure 5.13, using the Pencil tool.

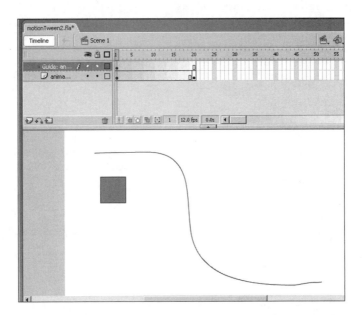

FIGURE 5.13   Use the Pencil tool to create your path in the Motion Guide.

9. Select frame 20 of the Motion Guide and choose Insert, Timeline, Frame (F5).

10. Select frame 1 of the Animation layer, and set the tween to Motion in the Properties Inspector panel.

11. While still in frame 1 of the Animation layer, select the square Movie Clip and drag it onto the top left of the line in the Motion Guide until it snaps. (If it does not snap, make sure snapping is turned on.)

12. Select frame 20 of the Animation layer, and drag the square Movie Clip until it snaps to the bottom right of the line in the Motion Guide.

You can test the movie now, and you will see that the square moves from the top left to the bottom right in a curved path. Plus, the Motion Guide is not visible. If you went back in and removed the Motion Guide, the square would then revert back and move in a straight fashion.

The final piece to add to this animation is a mask.

The Mask Layer

Masks are used to show only sections of masked layers. For example, suppose you have an image on one layer, and you want to display only a small section. You would draw a shape to define the area you want to display in its own layer. Then set that layer as a mask and make sure the layer with the image in it is set to be masked.

Continuing from the previous example, we will create a mask in the center of the stage, so the animation will be visible only when the square movie clip moves into the same area where the mask presides.

1. Continuing from the previous example, return to the main timeline.

2. Select the Motion Guide layer and click the Delete Layer icon. (Motion Guides and masks don't mix well.)

3. Then select the Animation layer.

4. Click the Add Layer button so it adds a layer right above the Animation layer. (If it adds the layer anywhere else, don't worry; just drag the layer so it is directly above the Animation layer and right below the Motion Guide.)

5. Name this new layer **mask**.

6. In the Mask layer, draw a large circle in the center of the stage, about 200×200 in size. The fill color does not matter as long as it has a fill.

7. Right-click (Mac—Ctrl+click) the Mask layer and select Mask.

Notice that Flash locks both the Mask layer and the Animation layer as well as puts new icons on the left side of the layer names, as shown in Figure 5.14. If the Animation layer is not affected, right-click (Mac—Ctrl+click) it and select Properties to reveal the Layer Properties dialog box (see Figure 5.15) where you can select Masked to force the layer to be masked by the Mask layer.

Test the movie and you will see the square animate the same as before, but it will be visible only as it moves through the mask.

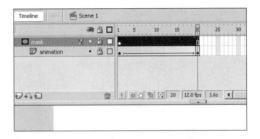

FIGURE 5.14   When converting a layer to a mask, the changes are obvious.

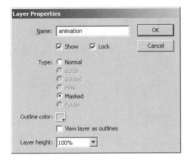

FIGURE 5.15   The Layer Properties dialog box.

You can also do masks dynamically, which is discussed later in Chapter 13, "The Move Clip Objects."

Summary

This chapter covered all the basics with regard to symbols and instances. Concepts to take away from this chapter are that instances are copies of the original symbol, and making changes to symbols affects all instances, but changes made directly to instances affect only that one instance.

Other things to take away from this chapter are the fundamental differences in the three main symbols:

- Graphic:
  - Synced Timeline
  - No ActionScript anywhere

- Button:
  - Unique timeline
  - No ActionScript within its timeline, only object actions
- Movie Clip:
  - Independent timeline
  - ActionScript in the timeline and/or in object actions

We also went over some new techniques and options for animating content in Flash, including how to use the tween editor, Motion Guides, and masks.

In the next chapter, you'll learn how to add video and sound to your projects.

CHAPTER **6**

Working with Sound and Video

This chapter covers two topics that are important for enhancing a user's experience when viewing your Flash content: sound and video. Both offer a little more than the basic web viewing experience you still find in conventional websites. We start off with sound.

Why Sound?

Developing web content with Flash can be tricky sometimes. You walk a fine line where on one side you must conform to good usability standards, design, and form, which many standard HTML websites accomplish. But what separates them from Flash content is Flash's inherent capability to engage the end user in a way that is not possible through standard HTML, even with the aid of JavaScript. And adding sound to your websites or applications is one of the quickest and easiest ways to engage the user.

Because sound is practically all around us, it is almost unnatural when we go to interactive places on the web for them not to have sound. This is not to say that in certain cases, adding sound can be both intrusive and obnoxious, but when it is done well, sound can add to the experience a user gets when viewing your work.

A great example of well-thought-out audio for a site is a site designed to teach young children about different animals in their various environments. For instance, if they were learning about animals in the rain forest, some subtle noises in the background would add a great deal of immersion to the learning environment.

As you go through this section, you will learn how to add sound to your movie, as well as some ways in which to manipulate it within Flash. As you are building your own projects, you will have to decide when and where sounds will be appropriate, but here are a few good general rules:

- If you add music tracks or add ambient sound to be audible throughout your entire site, always give the user the option to turn it off.

- For accessibility, sometimes narration is a great way to add the sense of someone being there with you, especially when working in e-learning situations.

- Know your end user. If you are building a site for the new rave club downtown, classical music is probably not your best choice.

- Add subtle sounds to your interaction that go with the overall design. If you are building a site to view used cars, you might have the sound of an engine starting or a car door opening.

- Use original sound. There are so many great free programs out there that can help you build your own tracks or sounds, you should have plenty to choose from.

    And it will make your site that much more original.

Some great places to find free sounds are

- http://www.findsounds.com/
- http://www.flashkit.com/soundfx/

And to find some free or almost-free software to work with sound, try here:

- http://www.download.com/

Adding Sound

When adding sound to your Flash document timeline, you must add the sound to a keyframe. (See Chapter 4, "Flash Animation," for more information on keyframes.) That is also true for adding to both a Movie Clip timeline and a Button timeline. Go through the following steps to see how it's done:

In this walkthrough, you will be adding a sound to the Down frame of a button so that when a user clicks it, a sound occurs.

1. Create a new Flash document and save it as `buttonSound.fla`.

2. You can either create your own button from scratch, or grab one from the common libraries included with Flash by going to Window, Common Libraries, Buttons, which will open up similar to Figure 6.1.

For this walkthrough, I chose the Arcade button style because it will go well with the sound we are going to add to it. Remember, adding the right sound to your interaction is key; you want to make users believe that they are actually experiencing the interactions on your website—as if they were there. For this example, you want users to feel like they are actually pressing an arcade button instead of clicking a graphic.

3. Whether you created a button from scratch or are using one from the common libraries, drag an instance of it onto the stage.

4. We are going to use a click sound called **click.wav**. You can grab it from the companion website of this book. After you have it somewhere on your system, choose File, Import, Import to Library; then map to the sound file and click Open. This will add the sound to your library, as shown in Figure 6.2. You can also test the sound at this point by selecting it in the library and clicking the Play button in the Preview pane.

5. Select the button on the main stage and choose Edit, Edit Selected (or double-click it) to take you into Edit mode of the button.

6. Insert a new layer at the top of the button and name it **click**.

7. In the Down frame of the Click layer, insert a keyframe by selecting it and choosing Insert, Timeline, Keyframe (or use F6).

8. While still in that frame, and with the library open, select click.wav and drag it onto the stage. You will see a squiggly line appear in the frame itself, as shown in Figure 6.3, indicating that a sound file is in there.

9. Test the movie now, and you will hear a click sound when you click the button.

FIGURE 6.1   The Button library in Common Libraries.

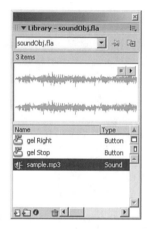

FIGURE 6.2   You can see the sound file in the library and, if selected, can also test it right there.

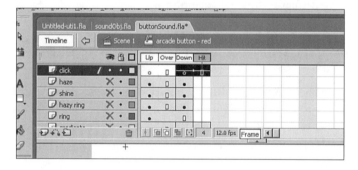

FIGURE 6.3   The timeline after a sound file has been placed on the stage.

TIP

When placing sound in the timeline of a Movie Clip, never put it in the first frame. This will cause difficulty when fixing issues with the sound, such as not being able to make it stop playing when you move through the timeline. It can be even worse in older versions of the Flash player. So remember to put the sound at frame 2 or later.

Now that you have seen how to add sound to your Flash documents, let's go over how to control them after they are there.

Sound in the Properties Inspector

After you have dropped the sound on the stage and can see it in the timeline, you can access its properties by selecting the frame, opening the Properties Inspector, and choosing Window, Properties. The Properties Inspector will look similar to Figure 6.4.

FIGURE 6.4   The Sound section of the Properties Inspector.

The first thing you will notice is the Sound drop-down list. This list contains every available sound file in the library, making it easy to switch to another sound or to remove the sound completely by choosing None.

Sound Effects

The next available option in the Sound section of the Properties Inspector is the Effect list. This allows you to apply different premade effects to your sound. Following are the available options in the list:

- **None**—Resets the sound effect for the selected sound to Normal.

- **Left Channel**—Plays the sound only in the left speaker.

- **Right Channel**—Plays the sound only in the right speaker.

- **Fade Left to Right**—Slowly fades the left speaker out at the same time the right speaker fades in.

- **Fade Right to Left**—Slowly fades the right speaker out at the same time the left speaker fades in.

- **Fade In**—The sound gradually fades in on both speakers in the beginning of the sound.

- **Fade Out**—The sound gradually fades out on both speakers at the end of the sound.

- **Custom**—Signifies that you have created your own custom sound effect to use with the selected sound.

Creating a Custom Effect

Creating custom effects can help give a sense of a three-dimensional environment. You can, for instance, create effects that change the sound from the left speaker to right speaker and back again to give a sense that something is moving back and forth in front of the user.

To create a custom effect, select the Edit button in the Properties Inspector when you have a sound selected on the timeline. This launches the Edit Envelope window, as shown in Figure 6.5.

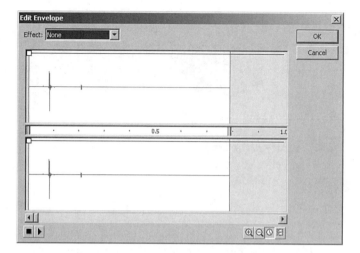

FIGURE 6.5   The Edit Envelope window for creating custom sound effects.

Looking at the interface, you will see several things—the first being another Effect drop-down. Here you can choose some of the premade effects to give you a good place to start from when building your own effect.

The next thing you will notice are the two windows on top of each other with a visual representation of your sound in them. The top window is the left channel, and the bottom window is the right channel. Each window has a white square in it that represents that channel's volume at that point in the sound. You can click directly in the windows with the sound to add more volume handles, and the volume handles can be dragged around for better control over the sound. Notice that as you add volume handles in one window, they are added in the other window as well.

At the bottom of the Edit Envelope window are several buttons to help you test and work with the effect.

- **Stop**—This button will stop the preview play of the sound with the effect.

- **Play**—This button plays the selected sound with the effect you have created in Preview mode.

- **Zoom In**—This option will "zoom in" on the sound, actually making the visual representation of the sound wider for more precise editing.

- **Zoom Out**—This option will "zoom out" on the sound, actually making the visual representation of the sound thinner to be able to view more of the sound at once.

- **Set to Seconds**—This option will convert the scale to seconds.

- **Set to Frames**—This option will convert the scale to frames.

Play around with the settings to get used to them, but they make it quite easy to quickly create your own custom sound effect.

Now let's go back to the Properties Inspector to see the syncing and looping actions.

Syncing and Looping

Back in the Properties Inspector, the final set of options involve syncing and looping your sound. The first of the two options is Sync, which controls how your sound file will play in the Flash document. Here are the syncing choices:

- **Event**—This choice makes the sound play independent of the timeline. This also means that with this choice, it is possible to have overlapping sounds from the same file because each time the event is triggered, it starts a new sound playing regardless of whether it was already playing.

- **Start**—This choice also plays independent of the timeline, but it will not overlap itself.

- **Stop**—This choice stops the selected sound when it reaches the ending keyframe.

- **Stream**—This choice is the easiest way to keep your soundtrack and the timeline synced. Setting the Sync option to this choice will tell the Flash player to keep up no matter what, and if a user's system cannot keep up because of processor limitations, frames will be skipped as well as the corresponding sound.

When you are deciding which of these options to use, make sure you test the movie to listen to the sound, because these options can sometimes have an effect on the quality of the sound itself.

After syncing, you can choose from the looping options. Looping is the best way to make a short sound loop appear longer than it actually is. Because the longer the original sound file is, the more file size it will create, looping is a great alternative to longer tracks. The two options for looping are the following:

- **Repeat**—This choice will loop through the sound a set number of times. The default value is 1, and if you put 0 in its place, the same result will occur.

- **Loop**—This choice will loop the sound infinitely. There are no secondary settings for this option.

After you set a looping preference greater than 1, the Edit Envelope window for the Effect option will look something like Figure 6.6.

That concludes editing the sound as far as syncing and effects are concerned, but you can also edit the compression of the sound file itself from the library.

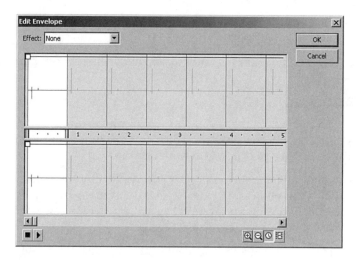

FIGURE 6.6   The Edit Envelope window after a looping option of 10.

Compressing Sound

When publishing a Flash Movie (SWF) with sound embedded in it, Flash will compress the sound for better file size and try to retain the highest quality possible in the process. You can compress all the sounds in your file at once from the Flash tab in the Publish Settings, as shown in Figure 6.7. You can adjust both Event and Stream sounds by clicking their associated Set button.

The best way to compress sound, especially if you have multiple tracks, is to compress them individually from the library. Compressing each sound individually gives you better control over both size and sound quality for each sound track.

To open the Sound Properties window from the library, select the sound file, then right-click (Ctrl+click on a Mac) and select Export Settings. You will see a window similar to Figure 6.8. Select the Compression drop-down for the different options of compression.

- **Default**—This choice will use the Publish Settings of the file.

- **ADPCM (Advanced Differential Pulse Code Modulation)**—This compression is here for one reason only: to be used in the Flash 3 or older players. This option has become obsolete because with the Flash 4 player or later, you can use MP3 compression. However, if you are creating content for older players, you may want to try this one out.

- **MP3**—This choice produces sounds of good quality and good compression and can be used in the Flash 4 player or later.

- **Raw**—This is a great setting for CD media because of the high quality of the sound. But because it uses no compression, the size of your movie will increase a great deal as well.

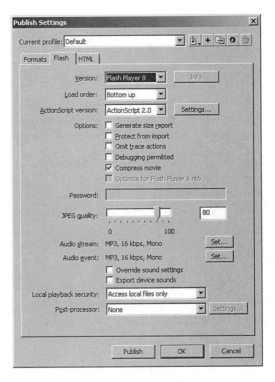

FIGURE 6.7 In the Flash tab of the Publish Settings, you can control overall sound compression of your Flash file.

- **Speech**—This is a great choice for audio narration of your Flash file. Because this choice is designed for straight speech audio, it can often produce a better quality of compression and sound for narrations than MP3 compression.

FIGURE 6.8 The Sound Settings dialog box.

These settings can also be adjusted from the Sound Properties dialog box. To access this window, select the sound in the library and click the Properties button at the bottom of the library. You can test the sound from within the Sound Properties dialog box, as well as quickly and easily swap out instances of your sound track throughout your entire Flash file. To change the sound file, click the Import button and map to the replacement sound. After this is done, all instances of the sound will be replaced by your new sound. Following are the available formats to import:

- **AIFF**—Similar to the WAV file, but created on Macs. Many Windows machines may have problems with these files.

- **MP3**—One of the most popular, and therefore readily available, sound file formats on the web. Excelling in both sound quality and small file size, MP3s work well within Flash. This format is also the only sound format that can be loaded into the Flash movie (SWF) at runtime.

- **WAV**—WAV files, although larger than MP3s in file size, still maintain good sound quality and are a Windows sound format standard.

You have seen how to work with audio manually on the stage, but in the next section you learn how to work with sound in ActionScript.

Sound with ActionScript

Although we have not covered ActionScript much thus far, it is important to understand some of the basic ideas and uses of the Sound object, one of the many native objects in ActionScript, which will be covered in more detail later in Chapter 8 and beyond.

Before you can use the Sound object, it must be initialized in the Actions panel, like this:

```
var mySound_sound:Sound = new Sound();
```

After you have a Sound object initialized, several methods and properties can be called to manipulate this sound. But the first thing you want to do with a new Sound object is to get the sound into it. There are two methods for doing this, the `loadSound()` method and the `attachSound()` method. Because ActionScript is still new in the book, we will focus on the simpler method, the `attachSound()` method, which will grab the sound file from the library after it has been imported and you have set the linkage property.

In the following example, you are going to import an MP3 song, set its linkage property, and use ActionScript to start and stop it.

1. Start by creating a new Flash document.

2. Select File, Import, Import to Library, and then choose your favorite MP3 song or use the one from the accompanying website.

3. After it is imported, go to the library, select the song you just imported, choose the panel Properties button from the top right of the library and select Linkage from the drop-down.

4. Select the Export for ActionScript check box, and give it a linkage name of **sample**.

5. Next, you'll want to add Start and Stop buttons to the stage. You can get them from the Common Libraries or create your own; just make sure they each have the instance property names of `play_btn` and `stop_btn`, respectively.

6. Create a new layer and name it **actions**; then open the Actions panel in the first frame of this new layer (F9) and place the following actions in it:

```
//create the new sound object
var mySound_sound:Sound = new Sound();
//attach the song we want to this sound object
mySound_sound.attachSound("sample");
//when released, the song will play
play_btn.onRelease=function(){
    mySound_sound.start(0,0);
}
//when released, the sound will stop
stop_btn.onRelease=function(){
    mySound_sound.stop();
}
```

Now you can test the movie, and when you click the Play button, the song will begin to play. When you click the Stop button, the song will stop.

That was a simple way to make Start and Stop buttons with sound. Another great thing you can do with the sound object is to control the volume and pan of the sound itself. Pan is the left and right speaker control; basically, you can use the pan controls to make a sound appear to be coming more from the left or right speaker.

Building on the last example, you are going to make the sound automatically play, but this time, as it starts playing, it will fade out and to the left (if you have stereo speakers).

Simply replace the code in the Actions layer with this code:

```
//create the new sound object
var mySound_sound:Sound = new Sound();
//attach the song we want to this sound object
mySound_sound.attachSound("sample");
//start the sound
mySound_sound.start(0,0);
//set the initial pan
mySound_sound.setPan(100);
//this function will fade it from the left to the right, and the volume to zero
this.onEnterFrame=function(){
    if(mySound_sound.getVolume()>0){
        mySound_sound.setVolume(mySound_sound.getVolume()-.5);
        mySound_sound.setPan(mySound_sound.getPan()-3);
    }
}
```

Now when you test the movie, the sound automatically plays, and as it does, it fades out gradually from left to right.

You can do more things with the Sound object, such as get the current position in a song, as well as ID3 information about a song, which is included in most MP3s. You can also capture the event when the sound has completely finished playing. Just add the following code to the previous example, and you will see something in the Output panel when the song is done.

```
mySound_sound.onSoundComplete = function(){
    trace("All Done");
}
```

But sound is not the only way to add a better experience to your website—there is also video.

Video in Flash

Video on the web is one of the most exciting (and high bandwidth) kinds of content out there. And Flash has not forgotten this in Flash Professional 8. With a streamlined import wizard and the capability to cut segments from imported videos, Flash has never looked better when it comes to video integration—especially now that Flash has full support for the alpha channel in video, allowing you to completely remove the background.

Importing Video into Flash

Video can play natively inside the Flash 8 player or can be brought in at runtime as either a stream (if you have a streaming server) or progressive download (see Chapter 26, "Streaming Media," for more details). The video formats Flash supports are as follows: DV, MPEG, WMV, MOV, AVI, and Flash Video FLV.

Chapter 26 will focus more on keeping video external to your Flash file, but this section covers how to work with video in the authoring environment. After the video is inside the authoring environment, you can scale, skew, distort, mask, rotate, and make it interactive using ActionScript.

To import a video, follow these steps:

1. Select File, Import, Import Video.

2. When the Video Import Wizard pops up (see Figure 6.9), click Browse and choose any video you want (or use one from the companion site). Notice, however, that you can also map to videos that are out on the web.

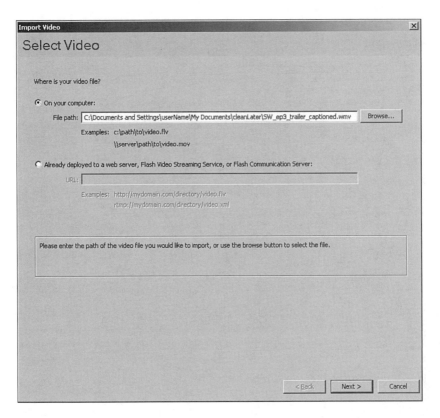

FIGURE 6.9   The Import Video Wizard.

3. Click Next and the next screen asks you how you want to deploy video (see Figure 6.10). For this chapter, choose Embed Video in SWF and Play in Timeline. Chapter 26 talks a bit more about having the video be external.

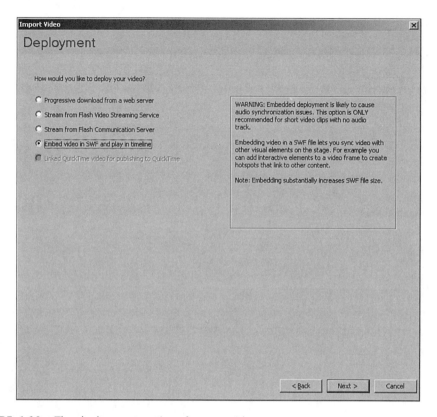

FIGURE 6.10   The deployment options for your video.

4. The Embedding window (see Figure 6.11) enables you to choose different options for the symbol type. Set this to Movie Clip so it will work with a later example. You can also choose whether you want the audio either integrated into the video or as a separate file. And you can choose to place an instance of it on the stage and stretch the timeline. Finally, in this section, you can choose to edit your video before you import it, so choose that option and click Next.

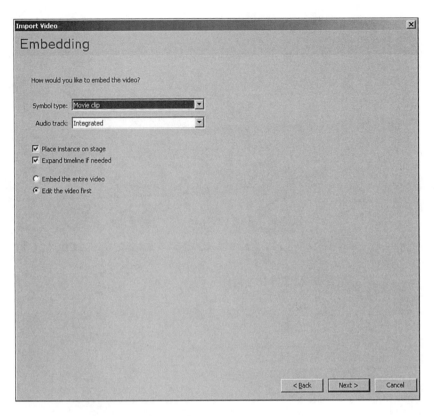

FIGURE 6.11   The embedding options for your video.

5. Now the screen should look similar to Figure 6.12. In the video's progression bar, the top arrow represents the position in the video you are viewing, and the bottom two bars represent the starting and ending points of the segment of the video you would like to create. You can use the controls to go through and preview your selection, and then use the Create a New Clip in the List button (the plus sign in the top left) to make the video slice, which will then appear in the video list box.

FIGURE 6.12   The editing video interface.

6. After you have made the slice you want, click Next to get to the Encoding section.
   This section enables you to select the type of encoding, including quality and
   player, because the Flash 8 player has a different video codec than the Flash 7
   player. This means that if your intended audience has the Flash 7 player, and you
   choose the Flash 8 player, errors will occur, and users with the older player will not
   be able to view all your content. Also in this section are some more options. If you
   click the Show Advanced Settings button, you will see something similar to Figure
   6.13. This is where you can set it to encode the alpha channel, so keep that in
   mind. Click Next when you have the settings you like.

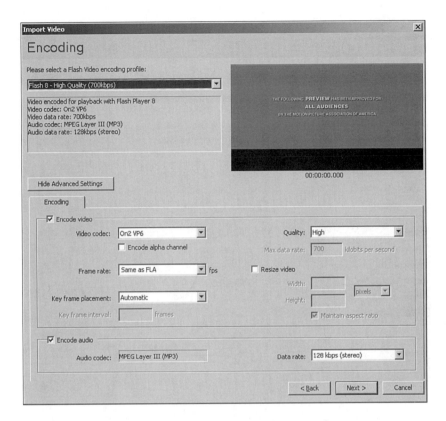

FIGURE 6.13   The Encoding section with the advanced options shown.

7. Now your screen will look like Figure 6.14, where the only option is whether you want video help files to pop open when the video is done encoding. Go ahead and click Finish.

Play around with different video settings until you find the right settings for you and your audience, especially when it comes to quality versus file size.

When the video is done importing, a movie clip will appear on the stage with the video embedded into it. And in the library, you will see both the movie clip and the video object. If you test now, the video will play right through, so the next example will take it a step further by showing how easy it is to add controls.

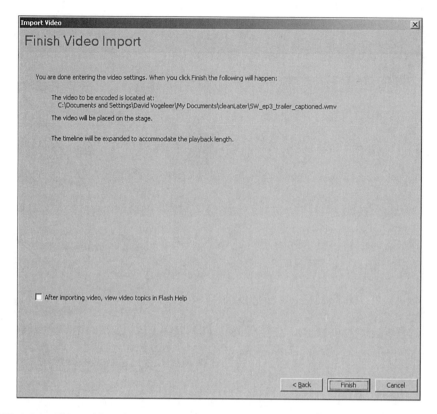

FIGURE 6.14   The Finish Video Import section.

CREATING CONTROLS TO PLAY AND STOP VIDEO

In this exercise, we will be working from the previous example:

1. If your video is very short, you might want to reimport the entire video so that the controls will make more of an impact.

2. Back on the stage, name the layer the video resides in **video** and add two more layers, **actions** and **buttons**.

3. Give the movie clip with your video in it an instance name of **video_mc**.

4. Now you're going to set up the controls to stop and play the movie. Select the Button layer, then open the Buttons Common Library by choosing Window, Common Libraries, and choose Buttons. Choose a play and stop button you want (or you can create your own) and drag out an instance of each onto the stage in the Buttons layer and give them instance names of play_btn and stop_btn, respectively, as shown in Figure 6.15.

5. Next, double-click the movie clip with your video in it to go inside for editing. Inside the movie clip, create another layer and call it **actions**. Then highlight the first frame in that layer and open up the Actions panel by choosing Window, Actions, and put these actions within it, which will keep the movie from automatically playing:

```
stop();
```

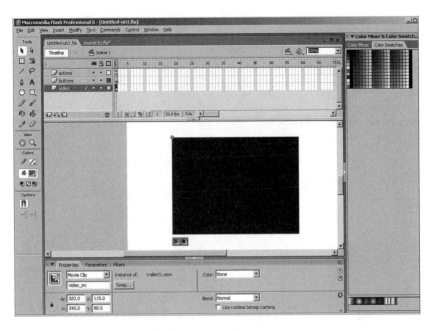

FIGURE 6.15   The Play and Stop buttons under the video clip.

6. Now go back to the main timeline and select the Actions layer. Then in the first frame of that layer, open the Actions panel (if it is not still open) and place these actions in it:

```
//this is for the play button
play_btn.onRelease=function(){
     video_mc.play();
}
//this is for the stop button
stop_btn.onRelease=function(){
     video_mc.stop();
}
```

Test your movie. Notice that it takes a second to export. In a real-world situation, you would create a preloader to overcome the blank space while waiting for content to load. Preloaders are discussed later in Chapter 13, "The Movie Clip Object."

You can also add fast-forward and rewind buttons using the goto action. This should give you a good understanding of how video is handled in Flash. Remember, you always have the options of animating, scaling, and rotating the video, just to name a few. In fact, if you're not satisfied with the quality of the video, you might consider taking down the alpha of the video, which seems to take away some of the compression artifacts.

Summary

This chapter covered two areas of Flash that help enrich your users' experience. Things to keep in mind with both video and sound is that the lower the quality, the lower the file size, and generally the better the performance.

Another thing to note is that you should change and play with the settings on the examples in the chapter to better understand the capabilities that Flash is offering in both sound and video.

The next chapter will take all you have learned so far and show you how to publish so you can begin posting your content on the web.

CHAPTER **7**

Publishing

W e have covered a great deal of content so far, including drawing, animating, and adding sound and video to your Flash file. Now it is time to publish your work.

Publishing can be as easy as going to File, Publish (F12). This will create the basic HTML and SWF file necessary to put your Flash work on the web. However, to take total control of publishing your Flash content, you need to dive into the publish settings.

The Publish Settings

To get to the publish settings, choose File, Publish Settings (Ctrl+Shift+F12). As you can see in Figure 7.1, Flash can save to many formats. We will go over each of them individually throughout this chapter, but first we should go over what publishing profiles are and how to use them.

Publishing Profiles

When working on projects with guidelines on formats, and rules for those formats, sometimes it can become tedious to set those publishing settings every time. This is where publishing profiles come in handy. They offer the capability to create new profiles based on project requirements. You can save those profiles so the next time you need to use those settings, you just choose the profile from the drop-down. You can create, duplicate, edit, and remove publishing profiles.

To create a new publishing profile, follow these steps:

1. Click the Create New Profile Button.

2. Give your profile a name, as shown in Figure 7.2.

3. Make all the changes you like to the options, and you're done.

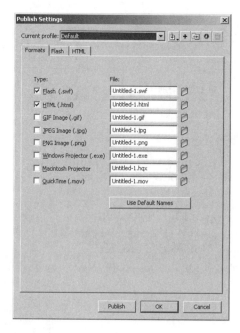

FIGURE 7.1   The publish settings.

You can return the settings whenever you like, select the profile you created, and all your settings will be made.

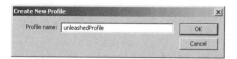

FIGURE 7.2   The Create New Profile pop-up.

Creating multiple publishing profiles in conjunction with large-scale projects will save you time in the long run. Now that you have seen how to create publish profiles, let's go over some of the different formats you can publish to.

The Formats Tab

The Formats tab is the first tab that appears when you open the Publish Settings dialog box. This tab controls all the different formats that you will be creating when you publish your finished work. By default, there are already two choices selected: Flash (.swf) and HTML (.html). Also in this tab, you can set each file to its own name and individual file location. Returning the filenames to their original names is as easy as clicking the Use Default Names button.

Here is a rundown of the publishing formats:

For the Web

The two formats for the web are the default choices: Flash and HTML. The Flash extension, .swf, stands for Shockwave Flash (or Small Web Format if you are a web history buff). The HTML embeds the Flash content to be viewable through a browser, but is itself not a format containing your Flash work. (You'll learn more on embedding Flash in HTML later in this chapter.) This means that, although you can publish just the Flash content, you cannot publish just the HTML. Even if you could publish just the HTML, it would not display anything; it would merely have the necessary HTML tags to contain the published Flash file (SWF).

Graphics

Because of Flash's built-in and easy-to-use drawing tools, you may also want to use the Flash authoring environment to create graphics to use in conjunction with other programs. Flash makes it as simple as checking a box to be able to publish JPEG, PNG, and GIF images. Also, as you will see later in this chapter, you can adjust properties of the publish formats for better control.

Projectors and QuickTime

Projector formats are very useful for projects such as CD media, where you can't be sure if the end user will have the necessary Flash Player installed on his or her system. For both PC and Mac, Projector files include their own run-time Flash Player so that the end user does not need it. This makes Projector files (.exe) much larger than Flash files (.swf), so choose wisely when it is appropriate to use them.

You can also publish your Flash content into a QuickTime movie (.mov). This is a great format to publish your animations in because it has good video quality and is one of the most popular video formats on the web.

Those are the different formats that Flash can create. Before we go into greater detail about each of these formats and their associated tab, it is important to understand the relationship between your Flash content and the Flash Player.

Flash Player 8 and SWFs

Although in Flash, you generally publish both the Flash content (SWF) and the HTML to embed the content, Flash content can be viewed in other ways as well:

- Through a Flash Player equipped browser with HTML tags embedding it. (Some browsers can open SWFs automatically without HTML embedding them, but it is good practice to embed the SWF.)

- With an ActiveX control, Flash content can be viewable in many office documents, such as Power Point (PPT or PPS), as well as other software supporting ActiveX.

- Macromedia Director and Authorware.

- QuickTime Player, although depending on what version of the QuickTime player you are using, certain functionality will be lost. (Note: this is not the same as publishing to a QuickTime movie.)

The first bullet point is the one to focus on because not all users will have the most current version of the Flash plug-in for the browser. This means that content created in the current player version may not be able to be viewed by all users. Also, any content created in a player version greater than the one on a user's system will not be displayed. You can get the latest Flash player penetration statistics here:

http://www.macromedia.com/software/player_census/flashplayer/version_penetration.html

And you can get the most recent player here:

http://www.macromedia.com/shockwave/download/download.cgi?P1_Prod_Version= ShockwaveFlash.

Not only do you need to be concerned with the player version, but you also need to consider the player's subversion. In the Flash 6 player, there were several releases fixing security holes, adding features and increasing performance.

Fortunately, many features in Flash 8 are backward compatible (if not, an error message will appear in the output panel to let you know, such as the message shown in Figure 7.3).

FIGURE 7.3   When you attempt to use a script that is not supported by your selected player version, you will receive an error like this.

To tell whether an ActionScript action is supported by a given player, you can use the ActionScript dictionary in the Help panel to check the player availability, as shown in Figure 7.4.

No need to worry—Flash 8 has a way of helping you out by creating an automatic Flash Player detection (which is discussed later in the section covering the HTML tab of the Publish Settings dialog box.)

But before you start to worry about having to detect which version of the Flash Player the end user is using, you first have to set which version you are going to publish your content into.

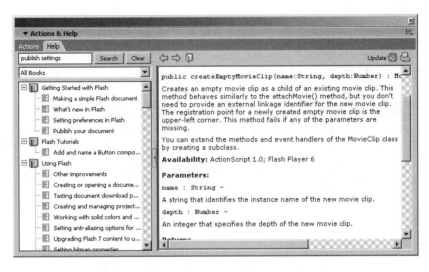

FIGURE 7.4   Checking the player availability for an ActionScript action in the Help panel.

The Flash Tab

The first format tab we will go over is the Flash tab (see Figure 7.5). In this tab are all the controls for the published version of your Flash project (SWF).

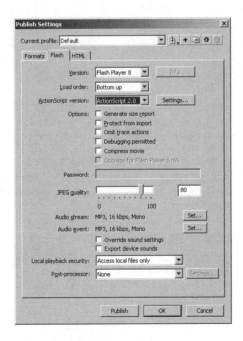

FIGURE 7.5   The Flash tab in publish settings.

The Version Field

Flash has the capability to publish in more than a single Flash Player version. You can publish your Flash work in every Flash version created from 1 to 8, as well as the "lite" versions for mobile devices.

> **NOTE**
>
> Choosing the right player version is an important step; you should do this at the beginning of a project to avoid duplicating work later. The best way to choose your player version is to know the intended user. If the intended user is a more tech-savvy person, you can opt for the higher version. As a general rule, I tend to wait until the statistics say it's at or close to 70% of the web using the player before I will do most projects in it.

The Sound Settings

Although the sound settings are at the bottom, there is a lot more to them than meets the eye. These options will allow you to set certain compressions for all audio files in your file. Although it is the best practice to adjust the compression of audio files individually for best quality, following are the steps required to adjust them all from the Flash tab:

1. At the bottom of the Flash tab, you will see two Set buttons for audio settings: one for Audio Stream and the other for Audio Event. The difference between these two settings is that events must be fully downloaded before they can be played, but streams can start playing immediately. So click the Set button for either of these two options.

2. A window like the one shown in Figure 7.6 will pop up. The first option is the compression type (refer back to Chapter 6 for more information on compression types). Select the compression type you want, or choose Disable to be able to set the audio files individually.

3. After that, depending on what you chose, you can now select the Bite rate, Sampling rate, ADPCM bits and Quality. After those are chosen, click OK.

4. Back in the Flash tab, you can also choose Override Sound Settings to use the publish settings and ignore any settings you have in the library. You can also select Export Device Sounds to export sounds specifically for devices such as mobile devices and handhelds.

FIGURE 7.6   The Sound Settings pop-up from the Flash tab.

Play around with the sound settings until you get the right mix of quality and compression. Those were the two major settings in the Flash tab, and here are the rest of them:

- **Load Order**—This option controls the order in which layers are loaded. The choices are Bottom Up (the default) and Top Down. This may not seem all that important, but if you have content on one layer that accesses a variable in another layer, the order in which they are loaded becomes very important. Keep that in mind when you're putting variables in layers.

- **ActionScript Version**—This option controls which version of ActionScript you are compiling to. The choices are ActionScript 2.0 (the default) and ActionScript 1.0. This is another decision that should be made early on in your project to avoid errors later. If you select ActionScript 2.0, you can use the Settings button beside the option to map to class paths for use within your file, as shown in Figure 7.7.

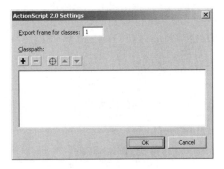

FIGURE 7.7   Class path settings for ActionScript 2.0.

- **Generate Size Report**—This option generates a size report for frame-by-frame analysis of your file to see which frames are the bottlenecks in the project. The report is generated in the Output panel as well as a text file in the same directory as the Flash file.

- **Protect from Import**—This option makes it difficult for other users to import your work (SWF) into one of their files. When this option is selected, the Password field becomes active, allowing you to set a password so that certain users with the password will be able to import the file.

- **Omit Trace Actions**—Trace actions are used for debugging in the authoring environment only. They send text to the Output panel during testing and are very useful during the development process. This option disallows them to output information; therefore, this option should be checked only when the project is complete.

- **Debugging Permitted**—This option allows your movie (SWF) to be debugged over the web. It also enables the password field to give you some security over who can remotely debug your file.

- **Compress Movie**—This option, which is available only on Flash Player 6 and later, attempts to compress your finished file (SWF) as much as possible. The default setting is checked.

- **Optimize for Flash Player 6 r65**—This option is available only when choosing the Flash Player 6. It is used to improve performance for the Flash Player 6 only.

- **JPEG Quality**—This option controls the quality of the JPEG images in your file. The values range from 0–100, with 0 being the lowest quality/best compression and 100 being the highest quality/lowest compression. The default value is 80, but I tend to move it up to about 90 for better quality. Play with this setting to get the right mix.

The HTML Tab

Even though it is possible to publish your finished file (SWF), most people will not be able to view it except through a browser. And not all browsers support the capability to view SWF files without them being embedded in an HTML page. For this reason, you will usually have to publish the HTML along with the SWF, and the HTML tab (shown in Figure 7.8) will help you fine-tune it.

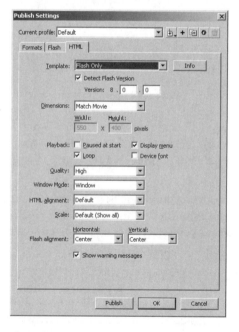

FIGURE 7.8   The HTML tab in the publish settings.

The option in the HTML tab is the Template option. This sets the basic format of your HTML. The default choice for this option is Flash Only, which will produce HTML similar to the following:

```
<!DOCTYPE html PUBLIC "-//W3C//DTD XHTML 1.0 Transitional//EN"
 "http://www.w3.org/TR/xhtml1/DTD/xhtml1-transitional.dtd">
<html xmlns="http://www.w3.org/1999/xhtml" xml:lang="en" lang="en">
<head>
<meta http-equiv="Content-Type" content="text/html; charset=iso-8859-1" />
<title>Example</title>
</head>
<body bgcolor="#ffffff">
<!—url's used in the movie—>
<!—text used in the movie—>
<object classid="clsid:d27cdb6e-ae6d-11cf-96b8-444553540000"
codebase="http://fpdownload.macromedia.com/pub/shockwave/cabs/
flash/swflash.cab#version=8,0,0,0" width="600" height="500"
➥id="Example" align="middle">
<param name="allowScriptAccess" value="sameDomain" />
<param name="movie" value="Example.swf" />
<param name="quality" value="high" />
<param name="bgcolor" value="#ffffff" />
<embed src="Example.swf" quality="high" bgcolor="#ffffff" width="600"
height="500" name="Example" align="middle" allowScriptAccess="sameDomain"
type="application/x-shockwave-flash" pluginspage="http://www.macromedia.com/go/get-
flashplayer" />
</object>
</body>
</html>
```

Note that the SWF name is in bold type so that you can easily see where it would go. This is the basic template for embedding Flash content in an HTML page. The other available templates are the following:

- **Flash for Pocket PC 2003**—Displays Flash content in HTML with Pocket PC-specific alignment.

- **Flash HTTPS**—Displays Flash content just like Flash Only; however, if users do not have the Flash player, they are directed to an HTTPS (HTTP secure) server to get the player.

- **Flash with AICC Tracking**—Displays Flash content like normal, but also includes support for AICC tracking.

- **Flash with FS Commands**—Displays Flash content like normal, but adds code to further assist the interaction between the page and FS Commands and JavaScript.

- **Flash with Named Anchors**—Displays Flash content like normal, but includes code and HTML anchors to enable bookmarking for Flash 6 content and later.

- **Flash with SCORM Tracking**—Displays Flash content like normal, but includes code for ADL/SCORM (www.adlnet.org) communication. The additional code in the

HTML page is created to support learning interactions. The HTML also includes JavaScript to find and initialize an associated ADL API object, as well as code to allow FSCommands to interact more easily with LMS functions.

- **Image Map**—This sets up image maps to be used with either PNGs, JPEGs, or GIFs. (You must have either GIF or PNG selected to publish for this option to fully work.)

- **QuickTime**—This option will embed a QuickTime movie in the HTML document. (You must have QuickTime selected to publish for this option to fully work.)

Most of the time, the Flash Only template combined with altering the other options will suffice for your project. Here are the rest of those options for the HTML tab.

Detect Flash Version

As mentioned earlier, knowing your intended audience for your project is the best practice for choosing the correct Flash player, but even within your intended audience, not everyone will have the player, especially if you choose a newer version. This is why detecting what the latest version of the player the user is running is so important, and Flash has an easy way to do this.

In the HTML tab, there is a check box that enables you to set up the required version and subversions of the Flash player for your content. And when you publish the file, included in the HTML will be some client-side code verifying the current Flash player on the end user's computer.

You can also use the $version variable in your ActionScript to verify the player version. This variable is available to you at runtime, as the following example shows:

```
trace($version);
//output: MAC 8,0,0,450
```

The preceding code shows that the current Flash player is the 8 player.

But, even if you are using an older version of the Flash player, it is still a good idea to include some type of Flash detection to make sure the user never sees the infamous "white page."

The rest of the options in the HTML tab have to do with how the Flash content will appear in the HTML itself:

- **Dimensions**—This option enables you to set the dimensions that your Flash movie will display in. These are the options:

  - **Match Movie**—This choice sets the dimensions of the movie (SWF) to the same dimensions as the stage.

  - **Pixels**—This choice allows you to hard-code the dimensions of your movie in pixels. Notice that when this choice is selected, the Width and Height fields become active.

- **Percent**—This choice allows you to set your Flash movie dynamically based on the window size of the browser that opens it. You can hard-code the percentage of both the width and height of your movie, and it will adjust itself as the browser adjusts. Be careful, however, if you are using bitmaps in your Flash movie, because they may not scale well. Notice that when this choice is selected, the Width and Height fields become active.

- **Paused at Start**—This is an option that has stuck around since early on in Flash. It gives you the capability to automatically pause the playback head in the first frame of your movie and wait until it's told to play again. This can easily be accomplished with a single line of code in ActionScript; the default is unselected.

- **Display Menu**—This option, when selected, displays a full featured list of options when an end user right-clicks your Flash content. This gives them the ability to control how they move through your movie as well as other key features. Most developers will turn this option off, keeping the control within the movie itself. When this option is deselected, the context menu will only display a link to their Flash Player settings (Flash Player 6 and later) and a link to information about the Flash Player. You can also disable and edit the menu from ActionScript. By default, this option is selected.

- **Loop**—This option is another option left over from previous versions of Flash. If selected, when the user gets to the final frame of your movie, the user is taken back to frame 1. If this option is not selected, the playback head will stop at the last frame. By default, this option is selected.

- **Device Font**—When selected, this option tells Flash to display system fonts when text fields in your movie are using a font that is not installed on an end user's system. By default, this option is not selected.

- **Quality**—This option is used to decide what is more important—visual quality or performance. If Quality is set to Best, the visual quality will be high. If you choose Low, the visual quality will be lower, but performance will improve. This is a decision that should be based on your intended audience.

- **Window Mode**—This option controls the window mode of the Flash Player in your HTML. In certain versions of browsers, you can use Opaque Windowless to hide objects behind the Flash player, or use Transparent Windowless to show items behind the Flash player. The default value is Window and unless a change is necessary, it is suggested that this option stay at its default.

- **HTML Alignment**—This option aligns your Flash movie in the HTML document itself. This option is essential when you are attempting to have your Flash movie as close to the edge of the browser as possible.

- **Scale**—This option determines how your Flash movie will scale if the dimensions of the browser are not exactly the same as your Flash movie. And almost all the time, they will not be exactly the same. This option has the following choices:

7

- **Default (Show all)**—The default value will display the entire movie without having to change its proportions.

- **No Border**—This choice scales the movie to the specified area, but it may also crop your movie to keep its proportions.

- **Exact Fit**—This choice displays the entire movie to the exact size and may distort your movie depending on which Dimensions choice you made.

- **No Scale**—This option will prevent your Flash movie from scaling at all when the browser resizes.

- **Flash Alignment**—This option will attempt to align and/or crop your Flash movie based on the other options selected.

- **Show Warning Messages**—This option, when selected, displays information about your options if they conflict with each other, or if there are errors in your code that conflict with your player settings. By default, this option is selected, which is recommended.

That concludes the options for the basic Publish Settings setup. Now let's look at some of the other publishing format options.

The GIF Tab

GIF files are great for low- to medium-quality images because of their small file size. This makes GIFs excellent for web usage when the intended audience has a slow connection.

There are several rules and labels used in conjunction with publishing GIF files:

- When publishing a GIF in Flash, unless otherwise labeled, the first frame will be published for static GIFs.

- To set the frame you want to publish as a GIF, give it a frame label of `#Static`.

- By default, if you are publishing an animated GIF, all frames will be published.

- To publish a range of frames in an animated GIF, give the first frame you want to publish the frame label of `#First` and the last frame you want to publish `#Last`.

- To export an image map, give the frame you want to publish the frame label of `#Map`.

Those are the different ways in which you can publish a GIF. Now let's take a look at its settings under the GIF tab (see Figure 7.9):

- **Dimensions**—This option enables you to set the size of your GIF. The default value is Match Movie, which will keep the size of your stage, or you can uncheck that box and set your own dimensions in pixels.

- **Playback**—These options signify which kind of GIF you are creating. The default Static will create a single frame image. If you choose to create an animated GIF, the following options become available:

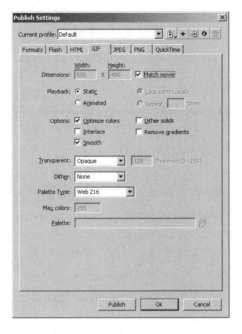

FIGURE 7.9   The GIF tab in publish settings.

- **Loop Continuously**—This choice makes it so that the animated GIF continues to animate.

- **Repeat __ Times**—This choice enables you to set the number of loops for the animated GIF to iterate through.

- **Optimize Colors**—This option gets rid of any unused colors from the color table. This means it will include only the colors the image is actually using.

- **Dither Solids**—This option applies dithering to both solids and gradients, which is how GIFs handle colors not found in their color palette.

- **Interlace**—This option makes it so the GIF will load incrementally, similar to how JPEGs can be progressive. Do not use this when publishing an animated GIF.

- **Remove gradients**—This option turns all gradient fills to a solid color (the first color in the gradient), which decreases the file size.

- **Smooth**—This option applies antialiasing to both text and bitmap images in the published GIF.

- **Transparent**—This option controls the transparency of your GIF image with the following choices:

  - **Opaque**—This choice keeps the image's background.

  - **Transparent**—This choice completely removes the background of your GIF image.

- **Alpha**—This choice enables you to set the transparency of the background from 0–255, with 0 being completely transparent.

- **Dither**—This option controls how colors that are not present in your palette will appear. This option usually increases both the quality of the GIF image and the file size. It has the following choices:

  - **None**—This choice estimates the color in question to the closest color in the palette.

  - **Ordered**—This choice balances file size and color quality while choosing colors.

  - **Diffusion**—This choice gives you the best quality for your GIF image.

- **Palette Type**—This option controls which palette of colors to use to create your GIF image, and it has the following choices:

  - **Web 216**—This default choice uses the 216 colors, which is accepted in most web browsers.

  - **Adaptive**—This choice analyzes the colors of your image and creates a palette for the best possible quality.

  - **Web Snap Adaptive**—This choice combines both Web 216 and Adaptive by choosing to use the Web 216 whenever possible.

  - **Custom**—This choice enables you to map to a color palette of your choice. This option will usually take more patience but can have surprisingly better results in both quality and file size.

- **Max Colors**—This option enables you to set a maximum number of colors to use in your palette for both Adaptive and Web Snap Adaptive Palette Types.

- **Palette**—This option is used with the Custom Palette Type for mapping to the palette you want to use.

The PNG Tab

PNG images have similar options to the GIF image, so we will go over only the differences. First is the Bit Depth (see Figure 7.10). Because PNG images are built on a bit-depth system, they can have transparency in the image itself. This is very useful when doing "cutout" images and shapes. The only way to get transparency in the PNG is to set its Bit Depth to 24-bit with Alpha (the default choice). If you do not need your image to have transparency in it, choose either 24-bit or 8-bit for a smaller file size.

The other major difference in the GIF tab and the PNG tab is the capability to use filters with PNGs. This option attempts to compress the file further by going line by line through the image to see where it can make adjustments. Like many of the settings, you will have to play with them to get the desired result. Here are the choices for this option:

- **None**—This default choice does not apply any filter.

- **Sub**—This choice evaluates the following and preceding pixel of each pixel to create a set value.

- **Up**—This choice evaluates the current pixel and the one above it to gain a pixel value.

- **Average**—This choice evaluates the pixel to the left and the one above to gain a pixel value.

- **Path**—This choice creates a function to evaluate the top, top-left, and left pixels to gain a pixel value.

- **Adaptive**—This choice evaluates all the colors necessary to create the highest quality image.

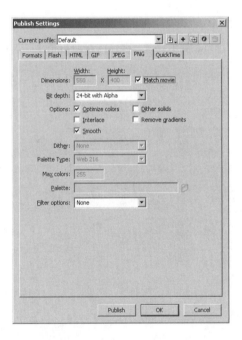

FIGURE 7.10   The PNG tab in publish settings.

The JPEG Tab

JPEG images (.jpg) are useful on the web because they provide a medium between quality and file size. To publish JPEG images in Flash, move the playback head to the frame you want to publish, and all other frames will be ignored.

The JPEG tab has a couple of options that we have not covered yet with the other image tabs:

- **Quality**—This option controls the visual quality of the JPEG image you are publishing. It can range from 0–100, with 100 being the highest quality and file size. The default value is 80.

- **Progressive**—This option allows the JPEG to incrementally download to the browser. This is great for people with slow connections.

> **TIP**
>
> If you are creating a JPEG image to later load back into your Flash project dynamically, do not set the Progressive option, because Flash has problems loading progressive JPEGs.

This ends the section covering the Image tabs. The final tab to go over is the QuickTime tab.

The QuickTime Tab

The final tab in publish settings is the QuickTime tab, as shown in Figure 7.11. Publishing into a QuickTime movie (.mov) can sometimes be beneficial, especially when you have complicated animations that take up a lot of processor power. Going to a QuickTime movie can often fix those problems as well as a few others, such as audio syncing.

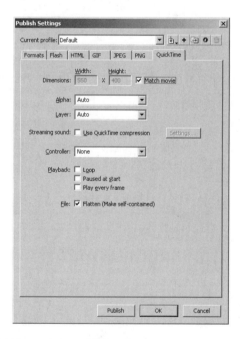

FIGURE 7.11   The QuickTime tab in publish settings.

If you want to publish into QuickTime, here are the settings you can adjust:

- **Dimensions**—Much like the other publishing formats, you can set the dimensions of your QuickTime movie with this option.

- **Alpha**—This option decides the transparency of the Flash content in your QuickTime movie.

  - **Auto**—This default choice sets the Flash background to opaque if there are no other tracks in the movie. If there is content behind the Flash track, it sets the background to transparent.

  - **Alpha-transparent**—This choice automatically sets the background to transparent.

  - **Copy**—This choice automatically sets the background to opaque.

- **Layer**—This option sets where in the stacking order your Flash movie will be.

  - **Auto**—This default choice will decide if there is other content in front. If so, it puts your Flash movie in the back; otherwise, it puts it on the top.

  - **Top**—This choice automatically sets the Flash movie at the top track.

  - **Bottom**—This choice automatically sets the Flash movie to the bottom track.

- **Streaming Sound**—If you have audio in your Flash file, you can compress it even more by selecting this option and setting the QuickTime audio settings in the pop-up, as shown in Figure 7.12.

FIGURE 7.12   The QuickTime streaming sound settings.

- **Controller**—This option sets the interface controller for your QuickTime movie. It has the following choices:

  - **None**—This default choice creates the QuickTime move with no controls.

  - **Standard**—This choice sets up your QuickTime movie with the standard movie interface controller.

  - **QuickTime VR**—This choice gives the end user all the controls from the QuickTime VR controller interface.

- **Playback**—This option is similar to the GIF animation options. You can set your QuickTime movie to loop when it gets to the end, to pause at the beginning, and even force it to play every single frame.

- **File**—If this option is selected (it is by default), it will create a single QuickTime movie at the end of publishing. If you deselect this option, it will still have to reference all your content.

That concludes all the tabs in publish settings. Both Windows and Mac projectors do not have a tab because their options are controlled from the Flash tab. You can also have some control over them using FS Commands. See the reference section for more information on FS Commands.

Summary

This chapter covered a great deal about publishing, not only formats, but the ins and outs of how those formats work and how they can be altered through the publish settings. This chapter also finishes up the introductory section of this book. You have learned how to create new Flash files, how to draw and animate, as well as how to add sound to your files. The next section will go over how to add ActionScript to your files for better interactivity and data structuring.

PART II

ActionScript

IN THIS PART

CHAPTER **8**

Welcome to ActionScript 2.0

So far in this book, you've learned how to create different things in Flash manually, how to publish Flash documents, and how to do basic animation and interactivity. This chapter begins a new world of understanding for Flash. In this chapter we cover ActionScript, the native language of Flash. We go over the basic principles of programming in Flash as well as some of the key features in ActionScript 2.0.

Before we start talking about the fundamentals of programming, it is important to understand what the language itself is.

What Is ActionScript?

ActionScript is the programming language of Flash. It is based on the European Computer Manufacturers' Association (ECMA) scripting language model. Other languages such as Java and JavaScript are based on the same model. ActionScript has been around since early versions of Flash, but it really began to take form in Flash 5. Then in Flash MX, ActionScript really stepped into the object-oriented programming (OOP) arena (don't worry, we go over what OOP means in the next section). Then came ActionScript 2.0 in Flash MX 2004 with more objects, stricter syntax, and stronger OOP especially in the class construction model.

The next section will help you become familiar with the object-oriented programming model.

Object-Oriented Programming

Object-oriented programming is more than a type of programming language; it is how you approach a problem in the context of programming.

Back in the early days of programming, everything ran in a straight line with hundreds of conditionals to check to see if something should happen or not. For instance, let's say driving is the program; the program would start by going to the car, opening the door, putting the key in the ignition, and turning the key (which would start the car). It then would go through a series of conditional statements checking to see if the user wants their headlights on or not, if they want the radio on or not, and if the emergency brake is on or not (see Figure 8.1). Already this program is long and painstakingly slow, and we haven't even begun to drive yet.

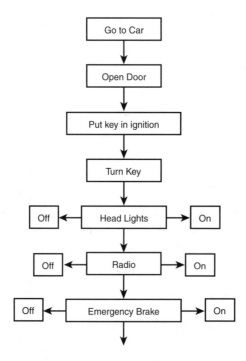

FIGURE 8.1   The old way of programming.

This is where object-oriented programming can come in handy. Instead of having all of these steps and conditional checks, you could have a single object on which all the code could be based.

What Is an Object?

An *object*, as it relates to programming, is a self-contained chunk of code containing the three very important elements that all objects contain: properties, methods, and events.

These three elements of objects are what makes them so powerful and gives them the ability to be self-contained.

Properties of an Object

A *property* of an object is raw data. Basically, each property of an object holds information about that specific instance of an object. Some properties can be read and changed, but others are read-only.

Here are some examples of built-in object properties in Flash:

- `movieClip._x`—The horizontal position of a movie clip object, read and write editable.

- `array.length`—A read-only property of the `Array` object that holds the number of elements in a given array.

- `textField.text`—A read-write property for getting and setting the text of a text field object.

- `Math.PI`—A constant property of the `Math` object, which is read-only; it translates to 3.14159265358979 roughly.

- `textformat.bold`—A read-write property of the `TextFormat` object, and can be set to either `true` or `false`.

These are just a few of the many properties already built into Flash and its objects.

Going back to the driving program, if we were to build an object for it, the object would be a `Car` object.

Some of its properties might be the following:

- `Car.type`—The type of car being driven; Mustang, Liberty, or 911 Carerra Twin Turbo.

- `Car.color`—The exterior color of the car; red, blue, or green.

- `Car.speed`—This property would constantly change depending on how fast the car is being driven.

- `Car.passengers`—This property could be either the number of passengers in a car or an array with the names of each passenger in the car.

Of course, the `Car` object could have literally hundreds more properties.

But that's just the information about the car. What about what the car does?

Methods of an Object

If properties are the "adjectives" of objects, then methods are the "verbs." Methods make things happen. A *method*, when it comes down to it, is nothing more than a function that is associated with a specific object.

Here are a few built-in methods for objects in Flash:

- `movieClip.stop()`—This method stops the play head for a specific movie clip's timeline.
- `array.reverse()`—This method reverses the order of elements in a given array.
- `textField.getDepth()`—This method returns the depth number of a specific text field.
- `Math.random()`—This method returns a random number between 0 and 1.
- `color.getRGB()`—This method returns information on a `Color` object's color.

Again, methods are what make objects do things.

With the `Car` object, you could have many methods to make the car do things:

- `Car.start()`—This method would start the car.
- `Car.brake()`—This method would apply the brakes.
- `Car.honkHorn()`—This method would let the person in front of you know you don't appreciate them cutting you off.
- `Car.accelerate()`—This method would accelerate the car.

Of course, these methods do a specific thing, no variance whatsoever. When the `Car.start()` method is called, the car starts; when the `Car.honkHorn()` method is called, the car honks. But that is not the limit of methods: They can have parameters in which you pass information to them that can dictate what will happen and to what degree.

For instance, the movie clip object has a method called the `gotoAndStop()` method. By itself, it can do nothing, but if you pass it information, it can run that specific task.

Here are some examples of this method with parameters:

- `movieClip.gotoAndStop(2)`—This method will take the play head to frame 2 and stop.
- `movieClip.gotoAndStop("end")`—This method will take the play head to the frame labeled "end" and stop.

With this in mind, we could make our methods for the `Car` object more reusable. For instance, we could make the `accelerate()` method accelerate to a certain speed like this:

`Car.accelerate(55);`

Now the car will accelerate to 55 miles per hour and hold that speed.

So now you see the power of methods, the code that makes things work. The last element that objects are made of is events.

Events of an Object

Properties are information about objects. Methods do things with objects. *Events* tell Flash when certain things have occurred with objects. This is the most difficult aspect of objects to understand, which is why a whole chapter is devoted to events (Chapter 14, "Events"). Events usually have code associated with them that will function when triggered through either a callback or a listener. This makes it easy to call code at only certain points.

For example, here are some built-in events of Flash objects:

- `movieClip.onEnterFrame`—This event fires as close to the frame rate of a given movie clip as possible, for instance, if the frame rate is 12 frames per second (the default setting), the event will fire approximately 12 times per second.

- `textField.onChanged`—This event fires when a user changes the content in a specific text field.

- `button.onRelease`—This event fires when a user releases a button after it has been clicked.

- `XML.onLoad`—This event is triggered when an XML document has completely loaded into Flash.

- `click`—This is an event for the `Button` component.

You can see why these events are very important to objects. If events did not exist, you would have to use looping conditional statements to check to see if something has occurred, but with events, you can have code ready whenever the event fires.

Here is an example of loading content into Flash and checking to see if it has loaded without events:

```
//there is a property coming in called "done"
var sample:LoadVars = new LoadVars();
//load the file in
sample.load("test.txt");
//use a loop to see if "done" has been received
this.onEnterFrame = function(){
    if(sample.done == "true"){
        //do something
        //get rid of the loop
        delete this.onEnterFrame;
    }else{
        //continue to wait
    }
}
```

The preceding block of code uses a movie clip event to continuously check to see if the variable done has been loaded into the LoadVars object we created. If it has been loaded, the code executes on the information, placing it either in a component or a text field, and then it destroys the looping statement.

Now here is the code with the onLoad event:

```
//create the LoadVars object
var sample:LoadVars = new LoadVars();
//the event for the LoadVars object
sample.onLoad = function(){
    //do something
}
//load the file in
sample.load("test.txt");
```

This block of code, besides being much shorter, is more efficient. Instead of having a looping statement look to see if the content has loaded, an event triggers and lets Flash know when the content is loaded.

Now that you see the benefit of events, let's take that approach back to the Car object. Although it's hard to imagine because we take them for granted, a car has a great many events. Here are a few of them:

- Car.onStart—Lets Flash know when the car starts.
- Car.onDoorOpen—This event triggers when any of the doors open.
- Car.onBrake—Lets Flash know the brake has been applied so that it knows to turn on the brake lights.
- Car.onCrash—This event could trigger the air bag to be released and notify other "emergency objects" to come see if everyone is okay.

Events have a high priority when writing object-oriented code.

Now that we've discussed the three major features of objects, we're going to learn how objects are created.

Where Do Objects Come From?

When two objects have known each other for a long time, and are very much in love, they.... Wait a minute, that's something else. Objects come from classes.

A *class* acts as a blueprint from which object instances of that class can be created. It states what properties that object has and what things that object can do (methods).

There are two ways of building objects: One is the old way that can still be done in the Flash authoring environment. The other way must be done in an external ActionScript file written in ActionScript 2.0. It is beyond the scope of this chapter to go into great detail about building classes, but it is covered in Chapter 18, "External ActionScript." Our main examples will be in ActionScript 2.0, but there will also be the ActionScript 1.0 counterparts so you can see the difference.

To create an object class in Flash, you first have to create an external ActionScript file (*.as) with the same name as your class (in our examples, "Car"). Although it is not a necessity, it is good coding practice to capitalize object class names. To begin the object class, you use the keyword `class` then the class name followed by an open curly bracket. And you will need the constructor function, which is basically just a function inside the class file that has the same name as the class itself as you can see below. Then a closing curly bracket to close the class.

ActionScript 2.0

```
//create the class
class Car{
    function Car(){
        //stuff
    }
}
```

ActionScript 1.0

```
//create the class
Car = function(){
//stuff
}
```

Now, this example doesn't have any properties, methods, or events. Nor are there any instantiated properties. The instantiated properties are passed to the object by means of parameters in the constructor function. So now we will add some properties to the class and some parameters to the function. Then we will instantiate the properties from within the constructor function.

ActionScript 2.0

```
//create the class
class Car{
    public var speed:Number;
    private var speedLimit:Number;
    private var color:String;
    function Car(theColor:String, theSpeed:Number, theSpeedLimit:Number){
        this.color = theColor;
        this.speed = theSpeed;
        this.speedLimit = theSpeedLimit;
    }
}
```

ActionScript 1.0

```
//create the object class constructor
Car = function(theColor:String, theSpeed:Number, theSpeedLimit:Number) {
    //instantiate a few properties
```

```
      this.color = theColor;
      this.speedLimit = theSpeedLimit;
      this.speed = theSpeed;
}
```

This block of code is a little more advanced than the previous. We pass three parameters into the constructor function and then instantiate them to the object within the function. Of course, there could be several more properties, but for now we are just sticking with three; the color of the car, its current speed, and its maximum allowable speed.

We now have an object class. From this we can create several `Car` objects, which are called *instances*, and set their individual properties.

This next block of code would be written in a frame action of a Flash movie that has access to our class file (i.e. in the same directory):

```
//create a mustang
var mustang:Car = new Car("red", 35, 170);
//create a jeep
var liberty:Car = new Car("silver", 45, 130);
//create a 86 pinto
var lemon:Car = new Car("yellow", 10, 45);
//now get the current speed of the jeep
trace(liberty.speed);
//Output: 45
```

As you can see, we created three individual instances of the `Car` object. We gave them each individual properties and even retrieved the current speed of the Jeep instance we made.

So far, our object just has properties. Of course, we want any car we make to be able to do things, so now let's add a method to the class:

ActionScript 2.0

```
//create the class
class Car{
   public var speed:Number;
   private var speedLimit:Number;
   private var color:String;
   function Car(theColor:String, theSpeed:Number, theSpeedLimit:Number){
      this.color = theColor;
      this.speed = theSpeed;
      this.speedLimit = theSpeedLimit;
   }
   //create a method for the Car class
   public function accelerate(amount:Number):Number{
      //increase the speed
```

```
        this.speed += amount;
        //return the current speed
        return this.speed;
    }
}
```

ActionScript 1.0

```
//create the object class constructor
Car = function(theColor:String, theSpeed:Number, theSpeedLimit:Number) {
    //instantiate a few properties
    this.color = theColor;
    this.speedLimit = theSpeedLimit;
    this.speed = theSpeed;
    //create a method for the Car class
    this.accelerate = function(amount:Number):Number{
        //increase the speed
        this.speed += amount;
        //return the current speed
        return this.speed;
    }
}
```

In this block of code, we take our object class a bit further by creating a method that has one parameter, the amount to increase the speed by. Notice that after we increase the speed, we also return the current speed of the object calling the method.

Now we can create a car, call the method, and see what happens. Again, the next block of code is after the Car constructor:

```
//create a mustang
var mustang:Car = new Car("red", 35, 170);
//get the current speed
trace(mustang.speed);
//call the accelerate method
mustang.accelerate(10);
//now get the current speed
trace(mustang.speed);
//call the accelerate method, and get the new speed
trace(mustang.accelerate(15));
//Output: 35
//        45
//        60
```

This time, we create a single instance of the Car object. We then send the current speed to the Output panel. After that, we call the accelerate method, and then send the current speed again to the Output panel. Finally, we call the accelerate method and send the new speed to the Output panel at the same time; this is where the `return` action comes in handy.

Now we can create cars and increase their speed, but what if they go over their designated speed limit? This is where the events come in.

This time, we create a blank method that will act as a callback (more on callbacks in Chapter 13). Then in the `accelerate` method, we will put a conditional to check if the car has gone over its designated speed limit. If it has, the blank method will be called.

ActionScript 2.0

```
//create the class
class Car{
   public var speed:Number;
   private var speedLimit:Number;
   private var color:String;
   function Car(theColor:String, theSpeed:Number, theSpeedLimit:Number){
      this.color = theColor;
      this.speed = theSpeed;
      this.speedLimit = theSpeedLimit;
   }
   //event callback
   public function onSpeedLimitBreak():Void{};

   public function accelerate(amount:Number):Number{
      //increase the speed
      this.speed += amount;
      //if the car is going to fast, call the event
      if(this.speed > this.speedLimit){
         this.onSpeedLimitBreak();
      }
      //return the current speed
      return this.speed;
   }
}
```

ActionScript 1.0

```
//create the object class constructor
Car = function(theColor:String, theSpeed:Number, theSpeedLimit:Number) {
    //instantiate a few properties
    this.color = theColor;
    this.speedLimit = theSpeedLimit;
    this.speed = theSpeed;
    //here is the event
```

```
    this.onSpeedLimitBreak = function(){};
    //create a method for the Car class
    this.accelerate = function(amount){
        //increase the speed
        this.speed += amount;
        //check to see if the car is going to fast
        if(this.speed > this.speedLimit){
            //trigger the event
            this.onSpeedLimitBreak();
        }
        //return the current speed
        return this.speed;
    }
}
```

This time, we create what looks like a normal method, but it is in fact our event callback for when the cars speed is beyond its speedLimit. You can tell it is meant to be an event because it starts with "on". Then in the accelerate method, we still increase the car's speed, but then we check to see if the speed is above the speedLimit. If so, we call the empty event. Then the current speed is returned.

So now let's create an instance of the Car object. Create a callback event method (again, events are covered in greater detail in Chapter 14). Then use the accelerate method to push the car's speed past its speed limit.

```
//create a mustang
var mustang:Car = new Car("red", 55, 170);
//create the event callback for this Car
mustang.onSpeedLimitBreak=function(){
    //send a message to the output panel
    trace("slow down lead foot");
}
//call the accelerate method
trace(mustang.accelerate(120));
//Output: slow down lead foot
//          175
```

As just mentioned, we create the instance of the Car object. Then we create a callback method that will send a message to the Output panel in the event that the car goes beyond its speedLimit property. Finally, we call the accelerate method to increase the car's speed.

Now you have created your own object class with properties, methods, and events. You have created an instance of that object and used its methods and events. There is one more way to add information to an object class without having to place it in the class file.

Prototyping an Object

Most of the time when you hear the word "prototype," it means a first working draft of a project. And in Flash, that can be true as well, but it can also mean the prototype chain.

The prototype chain in Flash starts with the `Object` object. All other objects are based on this supreme parent object. This means that if you add a property or method to the `Object` object, all other objects in Flash will then have the ability to use this property or method. But the `Object` object is already instantiated, so how do you add things to its constructor class after the fact? By using the `prototype` property.

The `prototype` property is designed to be able to add methods and properties to any and all object classes after the object class has already been instantiated. It's easy to use; you just call the object class's name, add the `prototype` property, and then add the new property or method name.

Here is an example of adding a method to the `Array` class that will, when called, send back a message saying hello:

```
//add the method to the Array class
Array.prototype.hello = function(){
    return "Hello world!";
}
//now create a new Array
var myArray:Array = new Array();
//send the message to the output panel
trace(myArray.hello());
//Output: Hello world!
```

The preceding code adds a new method to the `Array` class that will send a message back using the `return` action. We then create a new array and use the `trace` action to send the message to the Output panel.

But now let's say we want all object classes to able to instantly know what kind of object they are. We could add a new method to the `Object` object like this:

```
//add a method to the Object object
Object.prototype.whatAmI = function(){
    return typeof this;
}
//now create a new Array
var myArray:Array = new Array()
//now using the new Object method
//trace what kind of object the array and the _root timeline are
trace(this.whatAmI());
trace(myArray.whatAmI());
//Output: movieclip
//        object
```

The preceding code adds a method to the Object object. Then we create an array. After that, we call the new method on the array we created as well as the root timeline and send the results to the Output panel.

TIP

Even though you can add methods and properties to the core objects in Flash using the prototype property, you cannot do the same with your own classes because Flash's classes are precompiled and our custom class is not. But because it is your own class, you do not need to add methods or properties at runtime, you can just add them directly to the class file unlike the core classes of ActionScript.

Now that you have an understanding of how the object-oriented programming model works and the benefits it has, we can go over some of the differences in ActionScript 2.0 from ActionScript 1.0.

Introduction to ActionScript 2.0

Those of you who have been coding with earlier versions of Flash such as Flash MX or before will find this section very useful; it covers some of the differences and advantages in ActionScript 2.0.

But not to worry—those of you still wanting to code in ActionScript 1.0 (Flash MX style coding) still have this option as you can see in Figure 8.2. Go to the publish settings; choose File>Publish Settings (Ctrl+Shift+F12), choose the Flash tab, and choose ActionScript 1.0. Be warned, it's not only possible, but likely that you will run into conflicts using ActionScript 1.0 with ActionScript 2.0 anywhere in the file. You can also see which version of ActionScript you are running in your file by selecting the stage and viewing the Properties Inspector as in Figure 8.3.

But the first feature we will discuss in ActionScript 2.0 is the case-sensitive structure.

Back in ActionScript 1.0, you could easily declare a variable myVariable and then call it by using MYVARIABLE; they both would have been considered the same variable. But now, all internal and external ActionScript is case sensitive.

For example, in ActionScript 1.0, you would write this:

```
var myVariable = "test";
trace(MYVARIABLE);
//Output: test
```

In ActionScript 2.0, you would write this:

```
var myVariable = "test";
trace(MYVARIABLE);
//Output: undefined
```

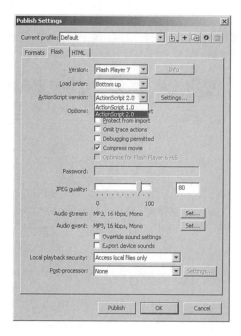

FIGURE 8.2   Use the Publish Settings dialog box to set which version of ActionScript you would like your file to support.

FIGURE 8.3   Use the Properties Inspector to quickly see which version of ActionScript you are using.

It is the same when passing parameters into functions:

```
//create the function
function myFunction(sample){
    trace(SAMPLE);
}
//call the function
myFunction("testing");
//Output: undefined
```

As you can see, in ActionScript 2.0, the preceding code would return undefined. So remember to always check your letter casing.

Declaring Variables and Instance Names

Other features of ActionScript 2.0 that bring it more in line with ECMA standards are shown in Table 8.1.

TABLE 8.1   New Features of ActionScript 2.0

	ActionScript 2.0	ActionScript 1.0
Undefined numbers	Resolve to NaN.	Resolve to 0.
Undefined strings	Resolve to undefined.	Resolve to empty strings, "".
When converting strings to Boolean values	Resolve to true if the string has a length greater than 0, false if the string is empty.	The string is first converted to a number, and the Boolean value is true if the number is a non-zero number, false if it is zero.

Strict Data Typing Variables

Another great feature in ActionScript 2.0 is strict data typing. *Strict data typing* is the ability to declare the data type of a variable when that variable is initialized. This helps a great deal in debugging large applications. For instance, if you have a login variable that will hold the user's login name as a string, you do not want it accidentally changing to a number or hexadecimal color by accident later in the code.

In ActionScript 1.0, it was possible to have a variable change data types constantly through an application. This is not good coding practice.

This was allowed in ActionScript 1.0:

```
var myName = "David";      //declares the variable myName with a String
myName = 12;               //places a number in myName
myName = 0xff0000;         //changes myName to a hexadecimal color of red
myName=function(){}        //changes myName to a function
```

And, truth be told, this is still allowed in ActionScript 2.0, but that is because we have not used the strict data typing features yet.

To use the new strict data typing features when declaring variables, first use the keyword var and then the name of the variable followed by a colon. At this point a pop-up list of all the available data types including component data types appears, as you can see in Figure 8.4.

You can also see the list of allowable data types by choosing the Add a New Item to the Script button in the Actions panel, and going down to Types.

Here is a correct declaration of a variable in ActionScript 2.0:

```
  var myName:String = "David";
//declares the myName variable as type String
  var myAge:Number = 25;
//declares the myAge variable as type number
  var myObject:Object = new Object();     //declares a new object type Object
```

8

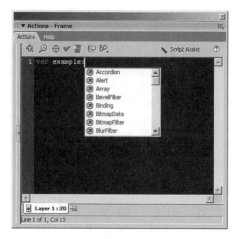

FIGURE 8.4   The pop-up list of all available data types in the Actions panel.

Now that these variables are declared, if at any time within the code, we attempt to change the variable's data type, when we either test the movie or check the syntax, we will receive an error.

To see this error, try this code:

```
var myName:String = "David";
myName = 25;
```

Now test this code, and you should see an error in the Output panel as shown in Figure 8.5.

FIGURE 8.5   The error seen when a strict data type of a variable is changed.

Strict data typing is not limited to variables, however; they can also be very useful in functions.

Strict Data Typing with Functions

A common problem in ActionScript 1.0 is building a function that is supposed to return a certain data type, a number for example, but, somehow it sends out a Boolean value instead. Or worse yet, you have parameters set to receive a certain data type, but another developer passes it a different data type, and then that developer cannot figure out where the error is. (More on functions in Chapter 12.)

Strict data typing in functions comes to the rescue. You cannot only data type the result of a function, but also all parameters in that function.

To data type the parameters of a function, you simply place a colon after each parameter name, and the data type pop-up list appears where you can choose which data type this parameter is meant to be.

To data type the return value of a function, you place a colon after the closing parenthesis of the parameters, and then choose which data type the return value is to be in.

Here is an example of data typing a function:

```
//create the function
function square(num:Number):Number{
    return num*num;
}
//call the function
trace(square(3));
//Output: 9
```

The preceding code creates the function with a single parameter, num. Both num and the result are set to the Number data type.

If the result does not match the strict data type, as in the following case, a similar error message will appear in the Output panel as in the earlier example.

```
//create the function
function square(num:Number):Number{
    return "num*num";
}
//call the function
trace(square(3));
```

And what if the parameters placed in a calling function do not match the strict data types they were assigned, like this?

```
//create the function
function square(num:Number):Number{
    return num*num;
}
//call the function
trace(square("3"));
```

This time the function is declared correctly, but when invoked, we use a string instead of a number.

Another error will appear, as shown in Figure 8.6.

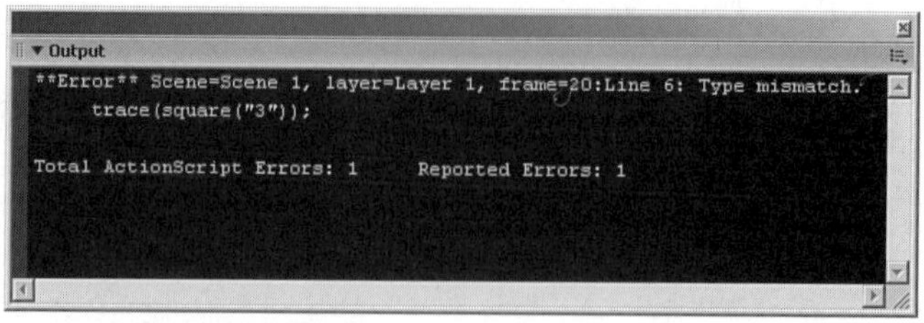

FIGURE 8.6   Strict data typing can even make sure parameters match the correct data type declared.

And because you can have strict data typing in both functions and variables, there is increased debugging help when combining them, as in the following example:

```
//create the function
function square(num:Number):Number{
    return num*num;
}
//call the function
var myName:String = square(3);
```

This code creates the function we have been using, and this time sets the result to a variable that has a different data type from the one declared as the result returned from the function.

Run this code, and again you will receive another error message like Figure 8.6.

That concludes the discussion on the differences and features of ActionScript 2.0 for this chapter. Again, there is more on class construction in Chapter 18.

You have seen a lot of ActionScript already in this chapter, but what about all the features of the Actions panel?

The Actions Panel

The Actions panel is where you can manually type in ActionScript. To access the Actions panel, choose Window>Actions (F9).

The Actions panel, as seen in Figure 8.7, has three main sections:

- **The Actions window**. This is where you will type in your ActionScript code.

- **The quick reference**. This holds all the snippets of code in a categorized hierarchical format. To choose a code, find the one you want and double-click it, or click and drag it into the Actions window.

- **Go to Action window**. This window acts like a small Windows Explorer panel for finding actions anywhere in the Flash movie. To go to one, simply map to it and click on it, and the Actions window will go to that frame of object.

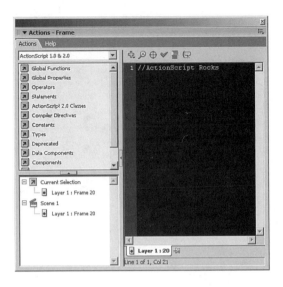

FIGURE 8.7   The Actions panel.

Those are the three main sections of the Actions panel. You can close and resize them with the small arrows on their sides.

The main Actions window of the Actions panel is where all of your actions will be. It has several buttons across the top, and their functions are as follows:

- **Add Script**. This button, when clicked, will show a drop-down menu with the same categories as the quick reference. You can map to a specific action, and select it for it to appear in the Actions window.

- **Find**. This button, when clicked, will open the Find dialog box, as shown in Figure 8.8, for finding specific sections or words in your ActionScript and replacing them if necessary.

FIGURE 8.8   The Find dialog box for finding words in ActionScript.

- **Insert Target Path**. This opens the Insert Target Path dialog box, shown in Figure 8.9, which is used to map to individual objects on the stage from within ActionScript.

- **Check Syntax**. This will quickly check your code for basic errors.

FIGURE 8.9   The Insert Target Path dialog box for helping to map to specific objects on the stage in ActionScript.

- **Auto Format**. This button will turn on and off the Auto Format features of the Actions panel.

- **Show Code Hints**. This button will turn on and off the code-hinting features of the Actions panel.

- **Debug Options**. Used in debugging ActionScript (for more on debugging, see Chapter 17, "Debugging").

- **Script Assist**. For those who worked in "Normal Mode" back in Flash MX or before, this button might be a welcome feature return. When clicked, this button will activate the Script Assist area in the Actions panel like Figure 8.10. The Script Assist section will help you with some of your code by giving fields and options for methods and functions so you don't have to memorize as much or look things up as often.

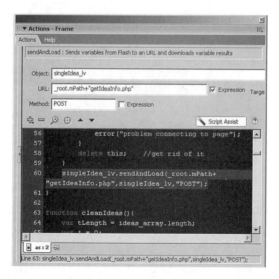

FIGURE 8.10   The Script Assist section of the Actions panel is there to help users by simply filling in field elements instead of typing them in the Actions panel directly.

- **Reference**. This button will launch the Help Panel and map to highlighted code for easy search.

> **NOTE**
>
> The Script Assist will be a helpful feature to those who are new to code, or do not like to type the code in directly, however, when activated, the Script Assist will not allow you to type in the Actions panel at all, you will have to turn it off to return to full Expert Mode.

A nice feature in the Actions panel is the ability to pin multiple scripts. This is very useful in that you can select multiple frames and objects containing ActionScript at once and simply choose the corresponding tab at the bottom of the Actions panel to move between them. To pin a script, follow these steps:

1. Choose a frame or object containing ActionScript so that the code will display in the Actions panel.

2. Select the icon of a pushpin in the bottom left corner of the Actions panel or go to the Actions panel Options menu and chose Pin Script.

3. Now you will see a corresponding tab at the bottom of the Actions panel that you can select at any time to return to the actions of that specific frame or object.

There are several options that you can change with the Actions panel to help developers program better. The first is the Auto Format Options found in the Preferences window (Edit, Preferences), as seen in Figure 8.11. This will help in setting rules for things such as line spacing with brackets, spacing with operators, and other visual aspects of coding. You can select each of the options to see what it would look like in the Preview window. And you can always select the Reset to Defaults button to return to default settings.

There are also a few options in the Options drop down in the top right of the Actions panel:

- **Escape-Shortcut Keys**. Shortcut keys are used to shorten the number of keystrokes necessary to place an action in the Actions panel.

- **Hidden Characters**. A new feature to Flash 8, when activated, this option will turn on hidden characters to appear in ActionScript like spaces. You can see an example in Figure 8.12.

- **Line Numbers**. This will display line numbers on the left side of the Actions window, which makes it easier to track down malfunctioning code.

- **Word Wrap**. A new feature to Flash MX 2004; you can now wrap your code to the next line without errors occurring. This is a very useful feature if you do not have a lot of screen room.

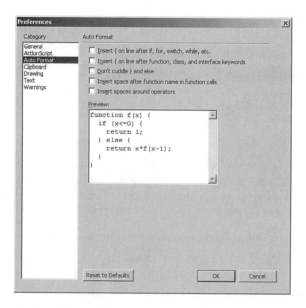

FIGURE 8.11   Use the Auto Format Options to make changes in the layout of auto formatted code.

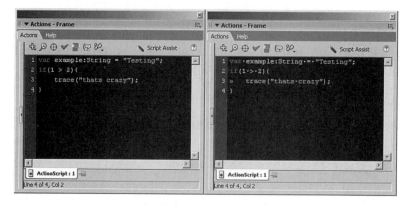

FIGURE 8.12   You can see the difference in these two images of the Actions panel. The one on the right has hidden characters turned on.

Another place where you can make changes to the layout of the Actions panel is the preferences for the Actions panel.

Actions Panel Preferences

If you don't like the default settings of the Actions panel, you can change them. You can get to the preferences by choosing the Options drop-down for the Actions panel and selecting Preferences. A window will pop up as shown in Figure 8.13.

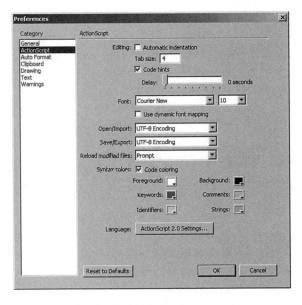

FIGURE 8.13   The preferences for the Actions panel.

The preferences for the Actions panel have three main sections for settings; Editing, ActionScript appearance options, and ActionScript 2.0 settings.

The Editing section allows you to select options and settings to control the flow of writing ActionScript, and it has these options:

- **Automatic Indentation**. This allows automatic spacing for lines following brackets.

- **Tab Size**. This sets the amount of space each press of the tab key (used in spacing) will take.

- **Code Hints**. This turns on or off the code-hinting features of the Actions panel.

- **Delay**. The number of seconds before a code hint appears.

- **Open/Import**. This sets the encoding of ActionScript files being opened or imported.

- **Save/Export**. This sets the encoding of ActionScript files being saved or exported.

- **Reload modified files**. This option sets which reload action to take place when a linked file has been modified.

The ActionScript appearance options section of the Actions panel preferences is used to control the color, size, and font of every piece of ActionScript code in the Actions panel. It has these options:

- **Font**. This controls the font of the ActionScript in the Actions panel.

- **Size**. This controls the font size of the ActionScript in the Actions panel.

- **Syntax Coloring**. This turns on or off the ability to distinguish certain keywords in ActionScript from the rest; you should leave this option on.

- **Syntax Color Settings**. This section allows you to choose the color of every aspect of ActionScript as well as the background of the Actions panel.

- **Use dynamic font mapping**. This option, when checked, will verify the necessary glyphs for the selected font, and if they are not present will substitute a different font.

> **NOTE**
>
> By personal preference, many developers choose the background to be a dark color or black, and all of the code itself to be a lighter color. This makes the code easier to see from farther away from the screen.

The last section of the preferences for the Actions panel is the ActionScript 2.0 settings. This button will open the Class Path dialog box, which is used to map to external ActionScript files. This option is covered in more detail in Chapter 18. And of course, you can always hit the *Reset to Defaults* button to return to the default settings.

There are over a thousand different commands and actions that can be placed in ActionScript. It is nearly impossible to remember all of them and their parameters. This is where the Reference button comes in.

Reference/Help Panel

You can open the Help panel by either selecting the reference button in the Actions panel, or choosing Help, Help (see Figure 8.14).

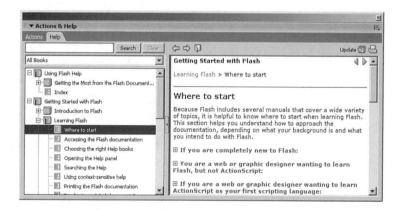

FIGURE 8.14   The Help panel and the reference panel all in one.

The Help panel has a drop down that lists the different sections of the help panel including: Tutorials and Samples, ActionScript 2.0, Features and Flash Lite.

The Help panel allows you to go through tutorials, or you can search for what you are looking for. The search option will return results based in different categories including the ActionScript reference. You can also print right from the Help panel and run the update from there as well.

Behaviors and the Behaviors Panel

Behaviors are small pieces of code that can be placed in frames or within objects themselves. When a behavior is selected, an interface will pop up for certain parameters of the behavior to be chosen or filled in. When placing actions within objects, behaviors have events associated with them that can be adjusted directly from the Behaviors panel. Flash comes with a certain number of built-in behaviors, and you can download more from select vendors or from Macromedia. You can also create your own behaviors, which is covered in Chapter 27, "Extending Flash."

You can open the Behaviors panel by selecting Window> Behaviors. You can see the Behaviors panel in Figure 8.15.

FIGURE 8.15   The Behaviors panel.

Follow these steps to place a behavior in a button:

1. Create a new Flash document.

2. Choose Window> Common Libraries>Buttons, and choose your favorite button to drag out onto the stage.

3. Give this button the instance name of button_btn.

4. Open the Behaviors panel by selecting Window>Behaviors.

5. With the button selected, click the Add Behavior button in the Behaviors panel and choose Web, Go to Web Page. The Go to URL dialog box will pop up as shown in Figure 8.16.

6. Type **http://www.samspublishing.com** in the URL field, choose "_blank" as the Open In choice, and click OK.

7. Now the Behaviors panel will show the behavior you just placed in the button, and under the Event column, it will say On Release, which is fine.

8. Now open up the Actions panel and select the button on the stage. You should see the following code:

```
on (release) {
    //Goto Webpage Behavior
    getURL("http://www.samspublishing.com","_blank");
    //End Behavior
}
```

Now test the movie by going to Control, Test Movie and then clicking the button. It should take you to something like Figure 8.17 if you are connected to the Internet.

FIGURE 8.16   The interface for the Go to Web Page behavior.

FIGURE 8.17   Use behaviors to quickly add ActionScript to your files.

That was an easy and fast way to add some interactivity to the Flash file. Now we will begin to delve into the fundamental aspects of ActionScript itself including some of the built-in objects and good practices.

ActionScript Fundamentals

ActionScript, as mentioned throughout this chapter, is the programming language of Flash, but do not let that intimidate you. Unlike many other languages, ActionScript allows its programmers to write minimal amounts of code and still see results.

You can type in this simple line of code, test the movie, and something will happen:

```
trace("something happened");
```

Now granted, it is not doing much—just simply sending a message to the Output panel, but it is still doing something. You can see the results of your hard work in writing that line instantly, and that's what ActionScript is about. Of course, the more ActionScript you put in, the more results you will get out of it. And that is what this section is for.

In this section, we will briefly go over many pieces of ActionScript that are covered in more detail as you continue through this book. But this section will show the simple uses of these pieces to get simple results.

Looking back at that one line of code we just used, if I hadn't mentioned what it was going to do, the only way you might have known is by testing the movie. When you see the results, you know what the trace function does; it sends messages to the Output panel. Of course, there was only one line of code, so it was easy to see which line sent the message, but what if you had 500 lines of code instead? It would be that much more difficult to figure out which line of code sent the message to the Output panel. This is why developers use comments.

Comments

Comments are lines of code the ActionScript reader skips over, but they are visible to people who open the file in the authoring environment. Comments are used to tell the story of ActionScript to the next person who looks at your code, (or to tell yourself later if you have to go back into the file). They are placed with variables to tell what those variables are used for. Comments are placed with functions to tell what the parameters are and what should go in them. And they are used to help narrow down bugs in code by commenting out specific lines.

To make a comment, you simply put two forward slashes (//) in front of your comment like this:

```
//this is a comment
```

You can put comments on their own line like the preceding one, or you can put them at the end of a line after some code, like these:

```
this.stop(); //this stops the movie clip
var name:String = "David" //declares a variable
function myFunction (){ //start of a function
    this.stop();    //the guts of a function
}               //the end of a function
```

You can even comment out several lines at once using /* at the beginning and */ at the end of the comment like this:

```
/*
this entire section is commented
I know, because I commented it
ok, that's enough...
*/
```

And as mentioned, they are used to tell someone looking at your ActionScript (including yourself) what the code is doing and why.

You can also comment out lines of code for debugging as previously mentioned, like this:

```
this.stop();
function myFunction(){
    this.gotoAndStop(2);
    myVariable = 15;
//    myNumber = myVariable/Math.PI;
}
```

Notice that when you put the comment in front of the line of code, it changes the entire line's color, meaning that the ActionScript reader will skip it because it is now a comment.

Another very important point is naming conventions.

Code Hints and Naming Conventions

Even though commenting is very helpful, and is good coding practice, sometimes you take a variable for granted and think that anyone will be able to tell what that variable is with or without a comment. And that may be true if you practice good naming conventions.

When naming variables, instances, functions, methods, and events, it is important to use names that can be easily understood. For instance, if you have a variable that represents the beginning horizontal position of an object on the stage, which of the following would you be more apt to recognize as what it is?

```
var startX = myMovie_mc._x;          or

var s1 = myMovie_mc._x;
```

Obviously the first variable is named something appropriate to what it is holding, whereas the second variable, even though it is holding the same information, does not give you a clue about what it holds. As its creator, you will remember (at least for a short time) what the variable is, but the next person to look at your code will have no idea what the variable is for.

Some rules to follow when naming instances and variables:

- They must start with either a letter or an underscore (_).

- They may not have any spaces within them.

- They cannot be one of the reserved keywords such as `var` or `this`.

- Although this is not a rule, but more of a warning, you should also not give variables the same name as object classes such as `Color` or `Date`, which can cause errors in your coding in certain situations.

Also, when creating instances of objects, there are special suffixes that can be added to the ends of the names to make the code hints pop up. Code hints are used to assist developers when working with objects. When the Actions panel knows what object type you are working with, it can give you a list of all the available methods, properties, and events of that object so that you don't have to remember them all.

To see an example of code hints, follow these steps:

1. Create a new Flash document.

2. Open the Actions panel in the first frame of the main timeline and create a string like this:

```
var myString_str = "test";
```

3. Now, after that line of code, begin typing the string's name (`myString_str`) and then type a period after the last character of the name. The code hints will pop up.

If the code hints do not appear, make sure they are turned on by going to the Show Code Hint button in the Actions panel.

What controls these code hints?

ActionsPanel.xml

The code hints for objects are controlled in an XML file at `C:\Program Files\Macromedia\Flash 8\en\First Run\ \ActionsPanel\ActionScript_1_2\ActionsPanel.xml` for Windows users and `Applications\Macromedia\Flash 8\en\First Run\ActionsPanel\ActionScript_1_2\ActionsPanel.xml` for Mac users. You can view all of the suffixes as well as other hinting tools at the bottom of those files. Or you can use this list to see the available suffixes:

- MovieClip—_mc
- Array—_array
- String—_str
- Button—_btn
- Text Field—_txt
- Text Format—_fmt
- Date—_date
- Sound—_sound
- XML—_xml
- XML Node—_xmlnode
- XML Socket—_xmlsocket
- Color—_color
- Context Menu—_cm
- Context Menu Item—_cmi
- Print Job—_pj
- Movie Clip Loader—_mcl
- Error—_err
- Camera—_cam
- LoadVars—_lv
- LocalConnection—_lc
- Microphone—_mic
- NetConnection—_nc
- NetStream—_ns
- Shared Object—_so
- Video—_video

Of course, using suffixes is not the only way to trigger code hints. You can also declare the data type in comments.

Triggering Code Hints with Comments

You do not have to use the suffixes with object names to get code hints to work; you can also declare the object's data type in a commented line. After that, the object's name will pop open the code hints for that object.

To declare a data type of an object on a commented line, you first put the two forward slash marks (//), followed by the object class name (i.e., `Array`, `String`, `Color`), then a space followed by the object's instance name, and finally a semicolon to end the line.

For example, place this code in the first frame of the main timeline in the Actions panel:

```
//Color myColor;
```

Now whenever `myColor` is used, it will pop open the code hints for the `Color` object.

There is one final way to trigger the code hints, and we have already used it: strict data typing.

Strict Data Typing to Trigger Code Hints

You can trigger code hints by declaring the object's data type in a commented line because you are declaring the object's data type. Strict data typing does the same thing without the commented line.

Place this line of code in the first frame of the main timeline in the Actions panel:

```
var myString:String = "test";
```

Now when you use the `myString` string, when you place a period after its name in the Actions panel, the code hints for the `String` object will appear.

Dot Syntax

With every programming language, there are rules and guidelines to using it correctly also known as its syntax. ActionScript is no exception to this; it has its own syntax called *dot syntax*.

The idea behind dot syntax is simple. When using properties, methods, or events with objects, the name of the property, method, or event must be separated from the object by a dot (period), like the following:

```
myMovie_mc.stop();      //Stops the play head for the movie clip
myString_str.length;    //this is the read only length property of a string
myText_txt.text="test";    //sets the text of a text field
myStuff_lv.onLoad=function(){};//declares the onLoad event for a LoadVars object
```

As you can see, each time a property, method, or event is associated with an object, a dot is used to separate them. Also, if you are going to use a target path to a child movie clip, you must use dot syntax to separate the movie clip's instance names, like this:

```
parentMovie.childMovie.gotoAndPlay(10);
```

```
//tell the child movie clip to go to frame 10 and play
```

Another thing to notice about the preceding line of code is the use of the semicolon (;). In ActionScript, semicolons tell the ActionScript reader that the line is done. They are not necessary, but it is good practice to include them.

Another piece of the ActionScript language to mention is the use of parentheses () and curly brackets {}.

Parentheses are used for the following reasons:

- To group segments of math together so that they are calculated first:

```
trace(5+4*3);     //returns 17
trace((5+4)*3);    //returns 27
```

- To enclose parameters when creating or calling functions:

```
function addNumbers(num1:Number,num2:Number):Number{
    return num1+num2;
}
trace(addNumbers(1,3));     //returns 4
```

- To enclose a conditional:

```
if(5 < 10){
    trace("5 is less than 10");
}
```

Curly brackets are used for the following reason:

- To enclose ActionScript to run as a block of code:

```
// with a conditional
if(5 < 10){
    trace("5 is less than 10");
}
//with a loop
while(i<10){
    trace(i);
    i++;
}
//with an event
button.onPress=function(){
    trace("the button was pressed");
}
```

Those are some of the basic pieces that are used in ActionScript. Now we will begin to cover some of the basic objects and actions of ActionScript starting with the movie clip.

The Movie Clip Object

The movie clip object is unique among all other objects because it can be created manually or with ActionScript. It also has a timeline that is independent from the main timeline. This means that you can have content on a movie clip's timeline that runs on its own, unconnected from its parent timeline.

The movie clip object also has an extensive list of properties, methods, and events. It can also handle button events, so you can see why it is the most popular object to use in Flash.

In this example, we will create a movie clip manually, and then control it with ActionScript.

1. Create a new Flash document.

2. Draw a circle on the stage about 100 pixels in width and height.

3. Highlight the circle by using both stroke and fill, and choose Modify>Convert to Symbol.

4. Give it a symbol name of `circleMC` and make sure the behavior is set for Movie clip.

5. Back in the main timeline, give the instance of the circle an instance name of `circle_mc` in the properties inspector.

6. Create a new layer called **actions**.

7. In the first frame of the actions layer, open up the Actions panel, and place this code in it:

```
//create the speed variable
var speed:Number = 10;
//the event to move the circle
circle_mc.onEnterFrame=function(){
    //get the distance between the mouse and the circle
    var xDist = _xmouse-this._x;
    var yDist = _ymouse-this._y;
    //set the circles position
    this._x+=xDist/speed;
    this._y+=yDist/speed;
}
```

The preceding code first creates a variable to control the speed of the circle. Then it simply creates a callback function that continually fires. In this callback, we get the distance between the circle and the mouse on both the horizontal and vertical plane. We then set the circle's position based on that distance.

Now test the movie and move the mouse around on the screen. You will see that the `circle_mc` movie clip follows the mouse wherever it goes while still on the screen.

You can find more information on the movie clip object in Chapter 13, "The Movie Clip Objects."

Functions

Functions are an important part of programming. The basic idea behind a function is to create one when you have repetitive blocks of code. For instance, if you are constantly getting the area of a rectangle, that is a perfect opportunity for a function.

You create a function with the keyword `function` and then the name of the function followed by an opening parenthesis, which will hold any parameters you may want to put in the function, followed by a closing parenthesis. Then an opening curly bracket ({), after that, any code that you want to run, and then a `return` statement to send information back out of the function, followed, finally, by a closing curly bracket (}) on its own line.

> **NOTE**
>
> Not all functions need `return` statements, as you will see in Chapter 12, "Functions."

Here is an example of creating and using a function to get the area of a rectangle:

```
//create the function
function getArea(width:Number, height:Number):Number{
    //return the area in pixels
    return width * height;
}
//now call the function, and send the results to the output panel
trace(getArea(20,31));
//Output: 620
```

The preceding code creates the function `getArea`, which has two parameters, `width` and `height`. In the function, it returns the width times the height. Then we call the function and send the result to the Output panel.

You can clearly see the benefit of using functions. Now we can get the area of any rectangle on which we use the function. We could even send it information about a movie clip's width and height, and it will send back its area.

For more on functions, see Chapter 12.

Conditionals

Conditionals are what make programming smart. Conditionals ask questions, and based on the answer, they either do or do not execute code associated with them. The type of question they ask is a simple yes or no, or rather a true or false question such as whether one number is greater than another.

When building a conditional, such as the `if` statement, you put a condition within parenthesis that the conditional looks at. If the condition is met, in other words, if it is true, then the code associated with the `if` statement is run. If it is not met, or is false, the entire code within is skipped over.

Programmers use conditionals to set boundaries, verify information, and make logical decisions. For instance, if we had a simple login for a page, we would want to verify if the user's name and password were correct. The code for that might look something like this:

```
if(userName == correctUserName){
    if(userPass == password){
        trace("welcome");
    }else{
        trace("password incorrect");
    }
}else{
    trace("no user found");
)
```

The preceding code checks to see if the userName given is the correct user. If so, it then checks to see if the password is correct as well. If both are correct, a welcome message is sent to the Output panel. If the userName is correct, but the password is not, another message is sent to the Output panel. And if the user has not entered the correct user name, a different message is sent to the Output panel for that as well.

You can see how conditionals follow a path of logic and can be used in many circumstances, as you will see as you work through the other chapters.

You can find more information on conditionals in Chapter 11, "Statements and Expressions."

Loop Statements

Conditionals are used to check something once, and then move on. *Loop statements* are used to continually run a piece of code until the condition is no longer true.

Loop statements are often used with numerical values to see if a certain number of objects are present, or if a certain object has reached a designated spot on the stage. For instance, if we have an array of information, and we want to know each element in that array, we could use a loop statement to cycle through each element in an array until there are no more, like this:

```
//create an array
var myArray_array:Array = new Array("David","Ben","Lesley","Missy","Jen");
//now loop through the entire array and display each element in the output panel
for(var i:Number = 0; i<myArray_array.length; i++){
    trace(myArray_array[i]);
}
//Output: David
//        Ben
//        Lesley
//        Missy
//        Jen
```

The preceding code creates an array full of names. Then a loop statement is created that will loop through the entire array and display each element in the Output panel.

Loop statements can be very powerful, but also very processor-intensive, so make sure the loop does not continue forever.

For more on loop statements, see Chapter 11.

Summary

This chapter covered a lot of information on ActionScript. Do not feel alarmed if some concepts were difficult—they are covered in more detail as you continue through the following chapters.

A few key points to remember are

- Objects have three features:

  - **Properties**. Information about the object

  - **Methods**. What the object does

  - **Events**. Let Flash know when something happens with the object

- Use strict data typing to help debug applications early in development.

- Comment your code. If you're in doubt whether or not it's important enough to comment, comment it.

- Set the preferences of the Actions panel to your liking. You are going to be using it a lot from here on out, and it should be just the way you want it.

- Use code hints to help keep track of individual objects' code.

CHAPTER **9**

Strings, Numbers and Variables—In Depth

In this chapter we discuss different types of data and variables that store data.

Data, simply put, is anything and everything you want it to be, including text, numbers, and logical representations (known as Boolean data). In its most raw form (binary code), data is represented as a bunch of zeros and ones, which comprise the basic data computers use as their primitive language. For instance, this next excerpt is the binary translation of "Flash Professional 8":

```
01000110 01101100 01100001 01110011 01101000 00100000
00111000 00100000 01010000 01110010 01101111 01100110
01100101 01110011 01110011 01101001 01101111 01101110
01100001 01101100
```

Types of Data Types

Before we get into any major details about any of the data types, let's briefly look at a few of the different data types in Flash:

- String. Any piece of data to be listed as basic text (for example, "This is a string data type"). Notice the quotation marks, which signify that this is a string.

- Number. Any piece of data to be listed as an integer, or floating-point with a numeric value (for example, 1, 44, -10, 21.7, and -0.8 are all legal number data types).

- Boolean. This is a logical representation used for conditions and results of certain functions (true and false are the only two Boolean data types).

- `Null`. This data type is used to show the absence of data or having a value of `null`.

- `Undefined`. This data type is used to show the absence of value in a variable; its value is undefined.

- `Array`. This is used for lists of data (it is its own data type); the data itself can be any type such as String, or Number, or it can also be mixed within the array.

The two most commonly used data types are strings and numbers. We will go into greater detail on these two and discuss the different parts of both data types.

First, let's take a look at these data types and see how easily they can be misinterpreted:

```
"My name is David."      // this is a string datatype
1234                     // this is a number datatype
"1234"                   // this is a string datatype
1+2+3                    // this is an expression that evaluates to a number
datatype
"My name "+"is David"    // this is an expression that evaluates to a string
datatype
'Single quote marks'     // this is a string datatype with single quote marks
```

These are the basic forms of the string and number data types. The text to the right with the double forward slashes (//) just represents comments in the code (as mentioned in the previous chapter, the interpreter skips comments completely).

The `String` Data Type

The `string` data type can be categorized as any amount of text between quotes. This includes characters, numbers, and certain properties of object instances such as the _name property of the movie clip object.

Creating a String

To create a string, place some text between quotation marks, as shown here:

```
"this is a string literal";
"this is also a string";
//that was simple enough
```

Another way of creating a string using the `string` data type is to declare a new string with the `new` constructor, which will make an instance of an object, in this case the `String` object:

```
new String("this is a string literal");
```

Also, you can set a variable equal to a string (which we will discuss later in this chapter):

```
var myString_str:String = new String("this is a string literal");
```

And you don't even need to use the new constructor; you can set a string to a variable like this:

```
var myString_str:String = "another string";
```

Empty Strings

You do not have to put anything between the quotes for it to be a string literal. You can just place an opening and closing set of quotes to create an empty string, as shown here:

```
""      // an empty string with double quotes
''      // an empty string with single quotes
```

Although this is an empty string, it is not equal to the null or undefined data types. In the following example, we first start a new file by going to File in the menu bar, choosing New (PC–Ctrl+N, Mac–Open Apple+N), and then choosing Flash Document. Then we use an if statement in the actions of the first frame in the main timeline and test it by going to Control in the menu bar and selecting Test Movie (if statements are discussed in Chapter 11, "Statements and Expressions"). Below is the ActionScript for the first frame.

```
if ("" != null) {
        trace ("An empty string is not equal to null");
}
// output: An empty string is not equal to null
```

Notice that we use a trace function that, when the movie is tested, displays our output in the Output panel. You'll see how to use this empty string, like the one found in the if statement, at the end of this chapter.

Quotes

As you have seen, all string literals must be surrounded by quotes. These quotes can be single quotation marks (') or double quotation marks ("), but you must close with the same type of quotation mark you started with. Here are some examples:

```
"double quotes"      //legal string
'single quotes'      //legal string
"double to single'   //illegal string
'single to double"   //illegal string
```

If you do not close with the same quotation mark you opened with, you will receive this error:

```
String literal was not properly terminated
```

However, you can put quotation marks inside quotation marks, as shown here:

```
'Then David said: "These are quotes inside a string"'
//this is a legal string containing a quote within it
```

You do need to be careful though, because a single quotation mark can also be used as an apostrophe. This can cause errors if you are not paying attention. Here's an example:

```
'He wasn't going to go'
//the interpreter reads this as 'He wasn' and throws an error message
```

If we had used opening and closing double quotation marks instead of single quotation marks here, the interpreter would not have thrown the error. However, let's say we want to use single quotation marks anyway. In this case, there is a workaround: the escape sequence.

Escape Sequences

Escape sequences are string literals used with a backslash (\). This tells the interpreter to consider the following character or character representation as a character and not part of an action.

Here are some basic escape sequences:

```
\"      double quote escape sequence
\'      single quote escape sequence
\\      backslash escape sequence using the backslash not as an escape sequence
```

Let's take a look at our example again, but this time using the escape sequence:

```
'He wasn't going to go'
//as before, this will cause errors and not display the proper text
'He wasn\'t going to go'
//now using an escape sequence, the problem is solved, and the
//interpreter reads it correctly
```

Now the interpreter reads the string correctly. Remember, you only have to use the quote escape sequences when you have quotation marks (double or single) that you want to display in between the opening and closing quotation marks of a string.

Now you have the basics of creating a string, let's go over how to manipulate them.

Manipulating Strings

String manipulation includes creating new strings, joining strings, and much more. In this section, we'll start with the easy tasks and work our way up.

Joining Strings

Joining strings is as simple as putting a plus operator (+) between two string literals. Here's an example:

```
"This is " + "a string literal"
// the interpreter translates this as "This is a string literal"
```

Notice the space after "is" in the preceding example. This space is necessary in strings; otherwise, the string would appear like this: `"This isa string literal"`. Alternatively, we could use a space string to make the code look cleaner, as shown here:

```
"This is" + " " + "a string literal"
// the interpreter translates this as "This is a string literal"
```

Note that the space string is not equal to the empty string we discussed earlier:

```
if (" " != '') {
        trace ("A space string is not equal to an empty string")
}
// output: A space string is not equal to an empty string
```

You can also add strings by setting them to variables:

```
var fName_str:String = "David";
var lName_str:String = "Vogeleer";
var space_str:String = " ";
trace (fName_str + space_str + lName_str);
// output: David Vogeleer
```

Here, all we did was set each string to a variable and then add the variables.

Another way to add strings with variables is to set the same variable to an additional string with an assignment operator. Here's an example:

```
var myName_str:String = "David ";
myName_str += "Vogeleer";
trace (myName_str);
// output: David Vogeleer
```

Notice that we added the string to the variable, but you cannot add the variable from within a string. The following example shows this:

```
var fName_str:String = "David ";
var lName_str:String = "Vogeleer";
```

6

```
var fullName_str:String = "fName_str + lName_str";
trace (fullName_str);
// output: fName_str + lName_str
```

So keep in mind that you cannot use variables from within a string.

You can, however, create a new string by adding a string to a variable that contains a string, as shown here:

```
var fName_str:String = "David ";
var fullName_str:String = fName_str + "Vogeleer";
trace (fullName_str);
// output: David Vogeleer
```

The concat Function

Using dot syntax, the concat function acts similarly to the assignment variable (+=) we looked at earlier. Simply attach it to a string with another string in the parenthesis:

```
var name_str:String = "David ".concat("Vogeleer");
trace (name_str);
// output: David Vogeleer
```

And, of course, you can attach the concat function to a variable:

```
var fName_str:String = "David ";
var fullName_str:String = fName_str.concat("Vogeleer");
trace (fullName_str);
// output: David Vogeleer
```

Now let's put a variable in the parentheses instead of a string literal:

```
var fName_str:String = "David ";
var lName_str:String = "Vogeleer";
var fullName_str:String = fName_str.concat(lName_str);
trace (fullName_str);
// output: David Vogeleer
```

This technique can even handle multiple expressions:

```
var myString_str:String = "This is ".concat("a"+" ".concat("string " + "literal"));
trace (myString_str);
// output: This is a string literal
```

Not only can you use multiple joining expressions, but you can also embed concat functions within concat functions.

You can use the concat() method in place of the plus sign (+) in order to add strings together, but it is not necessary. As you can see in the previous examples, even though the end result is the same, using the plus sign to add strings reads better when you are looking over your code.

Indexing Characters in Strings

Characters inside of strings can be indexed, stored, and displayed. Each character in a string has a specific index, starting with the first character at the index zero (0). The indexing of strings always starts with 0 instead of 1 in Flash; therefore, the second character has an index of 1 and the third character has an index of 2, and so on (see Figure 9.1).

FIGURE 9.1   Indexing strings start with index 0 for the first character.

The charAt Method

You can use the charAt method with strings to see characters at a defined index. Just attach the method to a string and place a number in the parentheses that represents the index you want to grab. Here's an example:

```
trace("David".charAt(2));
// output: v
```

This function can also be attached to a variable holding a string:

```
var name_str:String = "David";
trace (name_str.charAt(2));
// output: v
```

What's more, you can use a variable in place of the number in the parentheses:

```
var place:Number = 2;
var name_str:String = "David";
trace (name_str.charAt(place));
// output: v
```

The length Property

The length property provides a way to determine the number of characters in a given string. Simply attach it to a string, and it will return a numeric value. Here's an example:

```
trace ("Unleashed".length);
// output: 9
```

TIP

The index of the last character in a string will always be *string*.length minus one.

9

Of course, this property can also be attached to a variable holding a string, as shown here:

```
var myTitle_str:String= "Unleashed";
trace (myTitle_str.length);
// output: 9
```

Even though you might not consider a space to be a character, ActionScript does:

```
var myTitle_str:String = "Flash Unleashed";
trace (myTitle_str.length);
// output: 15
```

In this example, the output is 15 instead of 14 because the space is counted as a character.

Using the `length` property combined with the `charAt` method, we can identify every character in a word based on a defined function (more on functions in Chapter 12). Here's an example:

```
//first create the function
list = function (myString:String):Void {
   //use a loop statement to cycle through
   //all the characters in the string
   for(var i:Number = 0; i < myString.length; i++){
        trace (myString.charAt(i));
   }
}
//create our string
var myTitle_str:String = "Unleashed";
//run the function on our string
list(myTitle_str);
// output: U
//          n
//          l
//          e
//          a
//          s
//          h
//          e
//          d
```

The `indexOf` Method

The `indexOf` method takes a given character, looks for the first instance of it in a string, and returns that character's index. As before, you can attach it directly to a string or a variable holding a string. Place the character you are looking for in the parentheses as a string literal, like this:

```
//attach the function directly to a string
trace ("Flash".indexOf("a"));
```

```
// now create a variable and attach the function to the variable
var myTitle_str:String = "Unleashed";
trace (myTitle_str.indexOf("e"));
// output: 2
//         3
```

In the second part of the preceding example, the indexOf method found the first index of *e*, but let's say we now want to find the next one. To do this, we just place a starting index in the function after the character we are looking for and separate them with a comma:

```
var myTitle_str:String = "Unleashed";
trace (myTitle_str.indexOf("e",4));
// output: 7
```

In this case, we put in the index of the character following the first *e* and the indexOf method found the next one with no problem.

You can also look for certain strings of characters with the indexOf method. Just place the string in quotes as you would a single character. The indexOf method will return the first index of the first character in the string you are looking for:

```
var myTitle_str:String = "Unleashed";
trace (myTitle_str.indexOf("she"));
// output: 5
```

The Output panel displays the index of the first character in the string you're looking for (in this case, *s*).

Here's another nice feature of the indexOf method: If it does not find the character or characters in the string, it will return -1 in the Output window when you trace it:

```
var myTitle_str:String = "Unleashed";
trace (myTitle_str.indexOf("o"));
// output: -1
```

Let's take a look at what happens when we look for the letter *u* in the same string:

```
var myTitle_str:String = "Unleashed";
trace (myTitle_str.indexOf("u"));
// output: -1
```

The indexOf method could not find *u* in this case because Flash reads upper- and lower-case letters as completely different characters.

This can be useful when you're using forms in Flash. For example, let's say your company is willing to pay for in-state shipping to its customers, but if the recipient is outside the state, he or she must pay the shipping. Therefore, when users enter another state in the

6

shipping form, they are greeted with a message reminding them to include shipping costs (otherwise, a thank-you message appears):

```
//first create the variables
var homeState_str:String = "VA";
var thankYou_str:String = "Thank you for your order";
var reminder_str:String = "Please remember to include shipping";
//now create the if statement
if (enteredState.indexOf(homeState_str) == -1) {
     message = reminder_str;
} else {
     message = thankYou_str;
}
```

This code determines whether the variable `homeState_str` is in `enteredState` and sends the appropriate message.

The `lastIndexOf` Method

Like the `indexOf` method, the `lastIndexOf` method searches a string for a character or group of characters. However, unlike the `indexOf` method, which starts at the beginning of the string and moves toward the end, the `lastIndexOf` method starts at the end and works toward the beginning.

Also, this method works the same as the `indexOf` method in that you simply attach it to a string or variable holding a string and place the desired character or characters in parentheses, followed by a comma with a starting index. If no starting index is defined, the starting index automatically becomes the last character in the string. Here's an example:

```
var myTitle_str:String = "Unleashed";
trace (myTitle_str.lastIndexOf("e"));
// output: 7
```

Although this method may not seem like much, consider that the following code is what it would take to do the same thing without the built-in `lastIndexOf` method:

```
theLastIndexOf=function(myString:String,searchFor:String){
     for (var i:Number = 0; i < myString.length; i++){
          if (myString.charAt(i) == searchFor) {
               found = i;
          }
     }
     trace (found);
}
var myTitle_str:String = "Unleashed";
theLastIndexOf(myTitle_str,"e");
// output: 7
```

The substring Method

Many times, it is necessary to pull more than one character from a string. Flash has a few built-in methods for this task. One of them is the substring method.

The substring method attaches to strings and variables like other methods. However, in the parentheses, you put the starting and ending index, separated by a comma. Here's an example:

```
trace("Unleashed".substring(2,7))
// output: leash
```

Now let's attach it to a variable and leave out the ending index:

```
var myTitle_str:String = "Unleashed";
trace (myTitle_str.substring(2));
// output: leashed
```

As you can see, without an ending index, the substring method grabs all the characters from the starting index onward.

So far we have put in numbers representing the starting and ending indexes. Now let's use a variable instead of a number. This will make the function more dynamic. For example, let's say you would like to pull the ZIP Code out of the last line of an address:

```
var line3_str:String = "Richmond, VA 23866";
var finalSpace:Number = line3_str.lastIndexOf(" ");
var zip_str:String = line3_str.substring(finalSpace+1);
trace (zip_str);
// output: 23866
```

This takes the last space in the third line and makes it the starting point. It then grabs everything after that, which in this case is the ZIP Code.

And, if by mistake, you place the ending index first and the starting index second, the interpreter will switch them for you:

```
var myTitle_str:String = "Unleashed";
trace (myTitle_str.substring(7,2));
// output: leash
```

Even though the numbers were reversed, the interpreter still retrieves the correct information.

The substr Method

The substr method acts similarly to the substring method. However, in place of an ending index, you put the desired number of characters to be returned. The substr method still uses a starting index like the substring method. Here's an example:

```
var myTitle_str:String = "Unleashed";
trace (myTitle_str.substr(2,5));
// output: leash
```

If you have a starting index but not a designated number of characters to pull, the substr method will begin at the starting point and pull all the following characters:

```
var myTitle_str:String = "Unleashed";
trace (myTitle_str.substr(2));
// output: leashed
```

You can also place a negative number in the starting index, and the substr method will start counting from the end toward the beginning using the specified number of spaces:

```
var myTitle_str:String = "Unleashed";
trace (myTitle_str.substr(-4,2));
// output: sh
```

The slice Method

The slice method acts similarly to the substring method, except you can use negative numbers in the starting and ending indexes, as shown here:

```
var myTitle_str:String = "Unleashed";
trace (myTitle_str.slice(-7,-2));
// output: leash
```

The split Method

The split method is a unique method when it comes to manipulating strings. It divides a string into separate strings that can be stored in an array (more on arrays in Chapter 10, "Arrays").

Attach the split method to a string or variable and in the parentheses place the delimiting character. Here's an example:

```
var myTitle_str:String = "Unleashed";
trace (myTitle_str.split("e"));
// output: Unl,ash,d
```

The preceding example separates the original string based on the letter *e*. This is very powerful because you can take apart a sentence and store each individual word as its own variable or within an array as elements. Let's take a look:

```
//first, create a variable holding the string
var myTitle_str:String = "Flash 8 Unleashed";
// then set an array equal to the string with the function attached
var myArray_array:Array = myTitle_str.split(" ");
//display the entire array
trace (myArray_array);
```

```
//display just the first element in the array
trace (myArray_array[0]);
// output: Flash,8,Unleashed
//          Flash
```

Now you can see some of the capabilities this method has. You can sort, store, and send all this data in a nice, clean format thanks to the split method.

The toLowerCase Method

Earlier, we ran into a problem when trying to find a lowercase *u* in the word *Unleashed* because Flash does not treat lowercase characters the same as uppercase characters. This problem can be overcome with either the toLowerCase method or the toUpperCase method. Both work the same, except one converts characters to lowercase and the other to uppercase.

Let's go over toLowerCase first. When you want to find a letter in lowercase format in a string with uppercase letters, you must first convert all the uppercase letters to lowercase so that Flash will be able to find the lowercase version of the letter you are looking for. This can be done on an individual basis with a lot of tedious coding, or you can simply attach the toLowerCase method directly to the string. Here's an example:

```
var myTitle_str:String = "Unleashed";
myTitle_str = myTitle_str.toLowerCase();
trace (myTitle_str);
// output: unleashed
```

In this case, we converted the uppercase *U* to a lowercase *u*. Now we can run the indexOf method as before and view the results:

```
var myTitle_str:String = "Unleashed";
myTitle_str = myTitle_str.toLowerCase();
trace (myTitle_str.indexOf("u"));
// output: 0
```

The toUpperCase Method

The toUpperCase method is identical to the toLowerCase method, except instead of lower-casing a value in a string, it uppercases it. Attach this method as you would any other method with nothing in the parentheses:

```
var myTitle_str:String = "Unleashed";
myTitle_str = myTitle_str.toUpperCase();
trace (myTitle_str);
// output: UNLEASHED
```

Like the toLowerCase method, the toUpperCase method affects the entire string.

The charCodeAt **Method**

We've talked about how Flash reads upper- and lowercase letters as different letters. This is because Flash doesn't see them as letters at all but rather as code points. The String object has two built-in methods for dealing with code points: the charCodeAt method and the fromCharCode method.

The first method, charCodeAt, takes characters at defined indexes of strings and returns the code point value in a numeric form. Attach this method as you would any other, and in the parentheses put the index of the character you're interested in. Here's an example:

```
var myTitle_str:String = "Unleashed";
trace (myTitle_str.charCodeAt(2));
// output: 108 (the code point for the letter "l")
```

The following code goes through any string and displays each character's code point in the Output window:

```
//create the function
listCodePoints = function (myString:String):Void{
//set the loop statement to run through each character
    for(var i:Number=0; i < myString.length; i++){
    //trace each character's code point
        trace (myString.charCodeAt(i));
    }
}
//create the variable to hold the string
var myTitle_str:String = "Unleashed";
//run the function
listCodePoints(myTitle_str);
// output: 85
//          110
//          108
//          101
//          97
//          115
//          104
//          101
//          100
```

Putting a negative value in the index place will always return the value NaN (Not a Number, covered later in this chapter in the "NaN" section):

```
var myTitle_str:String = "Unleashed";
trace (myTitle_str.charCodeAt(-2));
// output: NaN
```

The `fromCharCode` **Method**

Unlike the `charCodeAt` method, the `fromCharCode` method allows you to put code points in parentheses, and it translates them back to their string characters. Attach this method to a String identifier and put the code points you would like to see in parentheses, separated by commas:

```
//create the variable to hold our string
var myTitle_str:String ;
myTitle_str = String.fromCharCode(85,110,108,101,97,115,104,101,100);
trace (myTitle_str);
// output: Unleashed
```

> **TIP**
>
> The `fromCharCode` method must be attached to a `String` identifier when it is run because it is a static method; otherwise, it will return Undefined.

Unicode-Style Strings

Another way to create a string is by using Unicode-style escape sequences. Because Flash does not completely support the Unicode style, it emulates this style instead. The basic form of a Unicode escape sequence starts with a backslash character, then a lowercase u, followed by a four-digit number:

```
var myTitle_str:String = "\u0055\u006e\u006c\u0065\u0061\u0073\u0068\u0065\u0064"
trace (myTitle_str);
// output: Unleashed
```

Now you can type data in Unicode format into strings. The only real reason you would want to do this is to get those characters you can't simply type from the keyboard, such as the copyright symbol (©), which in Unicode is \u00A9.

You can also type Unicode in shorthand format by replacing the \u00 with \x, as shown here:

```
trace ("\u0068");
trace ("\x68");
// output: h
//         h
```

That ends the string data type section. Up next is the other most popular data type in Flash.

6

The Number **Data Type**

The next data type we'll discuss is the Number data type. Numbers come in all sorts of forms and are used for lots of different reasons, ranging from counting, to mathematical properties of movie clips, to expressions. Let's look at a few examples:

```
1                    //legal number
4.998                //legal number
3+4                  //legal number
_x                   //legal number representing a horizontal position
string.length        //legal number representing the length of a string
0123                 //legal number representing an octal number
10e2                 //legal number using exponents
0x000000             //legal hexadecimal number
"1234"               //not a legal number, but a string literal
```

The two basic types of numbers supported by Flash are integers and floating-point numbers. Integers are whole numbers (positive or negative). Floating-point numbers are also positive or negative, but they include decimal points as well as fractional values (which are converted to decimal values).

Integers have two basic rules:

- They cannot contain decimals or fractional values.

- They cannot go below Number.MIN_VALUE or above Number.MAX_VALUE.

Some of the basic integers are raw numbers, such as 15 and 4400. These numbers are plain and simple. However, another example of an integer is a hexadecimal number, which is often used in color-coding (e.g., 0x6F9AB1). Yet another form of integer is an octal number, such as 0123, which translates to the following:

```
(1*64) + (2*8) + (3*1)
```

Floating-point numbers include decimal values, fractional values, and exponents. Exponents are defined by using the letter *e* followed by a number. This number represents the number of zeros to be added to the preceding number. Here's an example:

```
trace (10e2);
// output: 1000
```

Creating a Number

One way to create a number is to simply type it:

You can also use the Number data type in conjunction with the new constructor to create a number:

```
new Number(4);
```

Now you can set it equal to a variable:

```
var myNumber:Number = new Number(4);
trace (myNumber);
// output: 4
```

You can also create numbers without the new constructor like this:

```
var myNumber:Number = 4;
trace(myNumber);
//output:    4
```

Solving the Problem of Repeating Decimal Points

Because computers have difficulties with defining repeating decimal places and can sometimes misrepresent a number with multiple decimal places, it's a good idea to round or drop the decimal places with the built-in methods Math.round and Math.floor.

When using the Math.round method, simply place the number or variable holding the number in parentheses, and the method will round it to its nearest whole value, thus creating an integer:

```
trace (Math.round(1.23333));
trace (Math.round(1.566666));
// output: 1
//         2
```

The Math.floor method, on the other hand, completely drops the decimal places from the number and returns an integer. Its use is the same as the Math.round method:

```
trace (Math.floor(1.23333));
trace (Math.floor(1.566666));
// output: 1
//         1
```

Predefined Values for Numbers

Even though you can create almost any number manually, Flash has a few values for numbers built into it. Ironically, the first predefined value for a number is Not a Number (NaN).

NaN

Rarely would you set a number equal to NaN, but occasionally you might see this value in the Output panel when the number you are trying to use is not a number. A NaN value can be the result of placing text inside a `Number` data type or trying to divide zero by zero. Here's an example:

```
var seatsAvailable:Number = new Number("lots");
trace (seatsAvailable);
// output: NaN
```

Because NaN is not a number, variables with this value cannot be equal to each other:

```
//create our variables
var seatsAvailable:Number = new Number("lots");
var seatsTaken:Number = new Number ("a few");
//create the if statement to see if it is not equal
if (seatsAvailable != seatsTaken) {
        trace("These two are not equal");
}
```

You can also test to see if a number is NaN by using the `isNaN` function as in the following example:

```
var myNum:Number = new Number("not a number");
if(isNaN(myNum)){
    trace("the number is NaN");
}
//output: the number is NaN
```

But this does not mean that NaN is a string. For instance, you cannot do this:

```
var myNum:Number = new Number("not a number");
if(myNum == "NaN"){
    trace("the number is NaN");
}
//output: (nothing)
```

MAX_VALUE and MIN_VALUE

Flash has limitations as to what a number can be. Two of these limitations are `MAX_VALUE` and `MIN_VALUE`. Currently, the maximum allowable value for a number is 1.79769313486231e+308, and the minimum allowable value is 4.94065645841247e-324.

This doesn't mean a number has to be between these two values. For example, a number can be lower than `MIN_VALUE`, as shown here:

```
//create our variable
var myNumber:Number = -1;
//create an if statement to see if myNumber
```

```
//is lower than the MIN_VALUE
if (myNumber < Number.MIN_VALUE) {
     trace ("myNumber is lower than MIN_VALUE");
}
// output: myNumber is lower than MIN_VALUE
```

This is because `MIN_VALUE` is the minimum value a number can be in Flash, not the largest negative number. To see the largest negative number, set `MAX_VALUE`, the largest number Flash can handle, to negative and run the same code:

```
//create our variable
var myNumber:Number = -1;
//create an if statement to see if myNumber
//is lower than the -MAX_VALUE
if (myNumber < -Number.MAX_VALUE) {
     trace ("myNumber is lower than -MAX_VALUE");
}
// output: (nothing because -1 is not smaller than -MAX_VALUE)
```

POSITIVE_INFINITY **and** NEGATIVE_INFINITY

If, by some chance, you create a number greater than `Number.MAX_VALUE`, the value will be `Infinity`. Likewise, if you create a negative number larger than `-Number.MAX_VALUE`, the value will be `-Infinity`.

Predefined values are built into Flash that represent `Infinity` and `-Infinity`. They are `Number.POSITIVE_INFINITY` and `Number.NEGATIVE_INFINITY`.

Using these predefined values, we can test whether a number is infinite in the code:

```
//create our variable
var myNumber:Number = Number.MAX_VALUE * Number.MAX_VALUE;
//create the if statement
if (myNumber == Number.POSITIVE_INFINITY){
     trace ("myNumber is infinite");
}
// output: myNumber is infinite
```

Bonus Numbers

Here's a list of more predefined `Math` constants:

- `Math.E`. The natural base for a logarithm. The approximate value is 2.71828.

- `Math.LN2`. The natural logarithm of 2. The approximate value is 0.69314718055994528623.

- `Math.LN10`. The natural logarithm of 10. The approximate value is 2.3025850929940459011.

- `Math.LOG2E`. The base-2 logarithm of `MATH.E`. The approximate value is 1.442695040888963387.

- `Math.LOG10E`. The base-10 logarithm of `MATH.E`. The approximate value is 0.43429448190325181667.

- `Math.PI`. The ratio of the circumference of a circle to its diameter, expressed as pi. The approximate value is 3.14159265358979.

- `Math.SQRT1_2`. The reciprocal of the square root of one half. The approximate value is 0.707106781186.

- `Math.SQRT2`. The square root of 2. The approximate value is 1.414213562373.

Numbers are the basis of almost all object-oriented programming. In Chapter 13, you'll see a lot of ActionScript that involves using numbers.

Boolean **Data Type**

The next data type we'll discuss is `Boolean`. Boolean data types are logical answers in the form of `true` or `false`. Also notice that these words cannot be used as variable names or identifiers in ActionScript because they are strictly Boolean data types. Let's take a look at a use of `Boolean`:

```
var alarm:Boolean = true;
if (alarm == true) {
      trace ("Wake me up!");
}else{
      trace ("Let me sleep in.");
}
// output: Wake me up!
```

Because `alarm` is set to `true`, the `if` statement evaluates to `true` and traces the appropriate message. If the alarm had been set to `false`, the `else` statement would have taken effect.

Also note, Boolean values can be written numerically as well. The number zero represents `false`, and all nonzero numbers, including negative numbers, are `true` like the following examples.

```
trace(Boolean(0));      //false
trace(Boolean(1));      //true
trace(Boolean(-1));     //true
```

Null **Data Type**

The `null` data type is a representation that a variable has no data or definable data (`string`, `number`, `boolean`, and so on). `Null` will not show up in the Output panel unless assigned in the code.

Because null is a representation of no data, it is only equal to itself and the undefined data type. Here's an example:

```
if (null == undefined) {
     trace ("no data equals no data");
}
// output: no data equals no data
```

Undefined **Data Type**

Much like null, undefined represents the absence of data. However, unlike null, undefined can be assigned in several ways:

- It can be manually assigned in the Actions panel.
- The interpreter will assign it if a variable does not exist.
- The interpreter will assign it if a variable has no value.

Let's take a look at the undefined data type in action.

```
var myTitle_str:String;
trace (typeof(myTitle_str));
// output: undefined
```

Like null, because undefined represents the absence of data, it is only equal to itself and null.

Array **Data Type**

Arrays are used to hold lists of data and sometimes even lists of lists. Here's an example of an array:

```
var myArray_array:Array = new Array("David","Mike","Bart");
```

For more on arrays, see Chapter 10.

Variables

Now that we have covered data, let's take a look at what holds this data, variables.

Data without variables only lives for a second; once the interpreter has passed it, its lifespan is over. Variables are like Tupperware: They can hold data for long periods of time, and whenever you want that data, you just go to the variable and it's still there. A variable can hold any type of data, including strings, numbers, Boolean values, and even other variables.

A downside to variables is that they can only hold one piece of data. Arrays, on the other hand, can hold multiple pieces of data (see Chapter 10 for more information).

Making a Variable

A variable can be created in several different ways. Let's start with the easiest method, which is the one we will be using most often. You simply use the keyword var to start the process, name the variable, and finally assign it a type. You close the line with a semicolon so that the interpreter knows the line has finished. Here's an example:

```
var myVariable_str:String;
```

That's easy enough. Now let's do the same thing, but this time assign it some data:

```
var myVariable_str:String = "Unleashed";
//we set myVariable_str to the string literal "Unleashed"
```

Although it is possible to create variables without setting the data type, it is good practice to assign the data type when the variable is created. Also, after you declare the data type, you cannot change the type of data being held within the variable without receiving an error.

You do not actually need the keyword var to declare a variable (although the code is easier to follow when you're looking through it, and you cannot declare a data type without the keyword var); the interpreter will recognize that a variable has been declared when data is assigned. Here's an example:

```
myVariable_str = "Unleashed";
//we still declared a variable, but without the keyword var
```

Another way to declare a variable is by using the set action. In the parentheses, you declare the variable's name with a string literal and then set its value after a comma:

```
set ( "myVariable", 6 );
trace (myVariable);
// output: 6
```

We have looked at assigning variables with single pieces of data; now let's look at one assigned with an expression:

```
var myVariable:Number = 2+4;
trace (myVariable);
// output: 6
```

This time, we are going to assign the value of a variable to another variable:

```
var myVariable_str:String = "Unleashed";
var variable2_str:String = myVariable_str;
trace (variable2_str);
// output: Unleashed
```

You can create multiple variables with the same data using equality marks to separate them, as shown here:

```
var myVariable_str:String = variable2_str = variable3_str = "Unleashed";
trace (myVariable_str);
trace (variable2_str);
trace (variable3_str);
// output: Unleashed
//         Unleashed
//         Unleashed
```

Even though each variable has the same value, the last two variables are not bound by the data type, and can be changed without an error popping up, but it is good practice to not change the data type of variables during runtime.

You can even assign a variable to an expression using other variables:

```
var myVariable:Number = 4;
var myVariable2:Number = 2;
var addedVariables:Number = myVariable + myVariable2;
trace (addedVariables);
// output: 6
```

Changing Data in Variables

Now that you have seen how to create variables and add data to them, let's see how to change the data in them.

The process is as simple as reassigning data to the variables:

```
var myVariable_str:String = "Unleashed";
trace (myVariable_str);
myVariable_str = "Flash";
trace (myVariable_str);
// output: Unleashed
//         Flash
```

Another way to change a variable is to add to it. Here's an example:

```
var myVariable_str:String = "Flash";
trace (myVariable_str);
myVariable_str = myVariable_str + " Unleashed";
```

```
trace (myVariable_str);
// output: Flash
//          Flash Unleashed
```

Here, all we did was set the variable equal to itself plus another string. There is an easier way of doing this—by using an assignment operator, called the *addition assignment operator* (+=).

We'll use the same code as before but replace the long, written method of adding additional text with this new way:

```
var myVariable_str:String = "Flash";
trace (myVariable_str);
myVariable_str +=  " Unleashed";
trace (myVariable_str);
// output: Flash
//          Flash Unleashed
```

Now let's look at another variable that uses an incremental operator to increase its value.

Incrementing and Decrementing Variables

As you have just seen, you can add to already created strings. Now let's look at how to do it with numbers.

First, create a new Flash document, and then open the Actions panel on the first frame of the main timeline and place the following code in it:

```
//let's create our variable
var i:Number = 0;
//this event will continue to run
this.onEnterFrame=function(){
//let's increase our variable one at a time
    i = i + 1;
    trace (i);
}
// output: (it will start with 1, and increase by 1 constantly)
```

That was the old way of adding to variables; now let's do it the new way:

```
//let's create our variable
var i:Number = 0;
//this event will continue to run
this.onEnterFrame=function(){
//let's increase our variable one at a time
    i += 1;
    trace (i);
}
// output: (it will start with 1, and increase by 1 constantly)
```

That looks better, but there's still an easier way to increase a variable by one each time, and that's by using the increment operator (++):

```
//let's create our variable
var i:Number = 0;
//this event will continue to run
this.onEnterFrame=function(){
//let's increase our variable one at a time
    i++;
    trace (i);
}
// output: (it will start with 1, and increase by 1 constantly)
```

That was great! However, if we want to increase our variable by more than one at a time, we'll have to go back to the addition assignment operator because the increment operator only increases at a rate of one at a time.

Now that we have these numbers, let's make them move a movie clip to the right. So now create a small circle on the left of the stage and convert it to a movie clip symbol by selecting the fill and the stroke and going to Modify > Convert to Symbol. When the Convert to Symbol window pops up, set Movie clip as the behavior and leave everything else at the default settings and hit OK. Then back on the stage, give the circle an instance name of circle_mc in the properties inspector, and finally, make this change to the actions: (More on movie clips in Chapter 13.)

```
//let's create our variable
var i:Number = 0;
//this event will continue to run
this.onEnterFrame=function(){
//let's increase our variable one at a time
    i = i + 1;
    circle_mc._x = i;
}
// output: (it will start with 1, and increase by 1 constantly)
```

Now when you test the movie, the little circle will move to the right one pixel at a time.

Technically, you could have written the preceding code like this:

```
this.onEnterFrame=function(){
        circle_mc._x++;
}
```

We've covered increment variables, so now let's review decrement variables. These variables are the exact opposite of increment variables because they take away one at a time.

Let's look at our previous code with the circle move clip. Using the same code, replace instances of ++ with --, which will cause the variable to decrease:

```
//let's create our variable
var i:Number = 0;
//this event will continue to run
this.onEnterFrame=function(){
//let's decrease our variable one at a time
    i—;
    circle_mc._x = i;
}
```

Now the circle moves to the left one pixel at a time.

Empty Variables

As you know from previous sections, an empty variable has a value of `undefined`. We can use this to test whether a variable is being used. We use an `if` statement to test whether a variable is equal to `undefined`; if it is, the variable needs to be filled. Let's take a look at an example:

```
var title_str:String;
if (title_str == undefined) {
        trace ("This variable is empty");
}else{
        trace ("This variable has information in it");
}
// output: This variable is empty
```

Because the variable we created has yet to be assigned any data, it is automatically valued as `undefined` and the `if` statement value is `true`.

Comparing Variables

Often, when using variables, you'll want to compare one against another (for password verification, memory games, and high score validation, for example).

When you're comparing variables, it's important that they are the same data type. Keep that in mind until we get to the next section.

Let's start with a password-verification example. We'll use a predefined password and a user input password and compare them. If they are equal, we'll run some specific code; if they are not equal, we'll run different code. Here are the steps to follow:

1. Start a new file by going to File, New and then choosing Flash Document.

2. Create two more layers on the main timeline and label the layers Actions, Input, and Validate, respectively top to bottom.

3. Now create a movie clip symbol called "validate" that has a rectangle in it with the text "Validate" over top of it. Place this movie on the Validate layer of the main timeline and label its instance name `validate_mc`.

4. In the Input layer, choose the Text tool and draw a text box. Change the type in the properties inspector to Input Text and choose Show Border Around Text so you can easily see the text box when we test the movie. Then choose Password for the line type instead of Single Line (this will place asterisks instead of characters in the text box). Finally, give the text field an instance name of password_txt. The settings should look like Figure 9.2.

5. Now for the actions. In the first keyframe of the Actions layer, place this code:

```
//We first create the password
var password_str:String ="flash";
//Now we set the button actions for the validate movie
validate_mc.onRelease = function (){
//this will check to see if the password and the input match
    if(password_txt.text == password_str){
        trace("You may enter");
    }else{
        trace("You do not have clearance");
//This clears the input field
        password_txt.text="";
    }
}
```

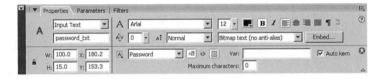

FIGURE 9.2   The stage for the validate example.

When you test the movie, note that if you enter the correct password, it issues a welcome message in the Output panel; otherwise, the Output panel displays a different message and clears the user input field.

As another example of using variables, let's try to determine whether a new score is the high score.

Create a new file as before in previous examples (PC–Ctrl+N, Mac–Open Apple+N) and put the following code in the first frame of the main timeline:

```
//first create the current high score
var highScore:Number = 1200;
//then create a new score to rival the high score
var newScore:Number = 1300;
//now create the if statement that will determine and adjust the high score
if (newScore > highScore){
    highScore = newScore;
    trace ("congratulations, the new high score is " + highScore);
```

```
}else if (newScore == highScore) {
    trace ("You are now tied for 1st at " + highScore);
}else{
    trace ("Your score of " + newScore + " was not good enough");
}
// output: congratulations, the new high score is 1300
```

Test the movie. Then go back and change the variables to see different results.

Combining Types of Values in Variables

You may have noticed in the preceding high-score example that we were adding two different types of values into one statement. So, what does that make the value of the statement? That depends on what was combined and how. Because in the preceding example we added a string with text in it to a number, the interpreter automatically converted the entire thing to a string.

Now let's take a look at using the typeof function to check the value of a given variable:

```
var name_str:String = "Kevin ";
var age:Number = 35;
var combined_str:String = name_str + age;
trace (typeof(combined_str));
// output: string
```

Let's suppose we have two variables (one a number and the other a string containing numbers):

```
var year_str:String = "1967"
var age:Number = 35;
var combined_str:String = year_str + age;
trace (typeof(combined_str));
// output: string
```

This still comes back as string. However, if we subtract them, the result changes, as shown here:

```
var year_str:String = "1967"
var age:Number = 35;
var combined:Number = year_str - age;
trace (typeof(combined));
// output: number
```

When the variables are subtracted, the interpreter converts the combination to a number.

Although the conversion has taken place in the combined variable, it has not affected the original values. Automatic conversion only works when evaluating an expression.

When using a Boolean in an expression involving a number, the conversion will always be to a number, as shown here:

```
var answer:Boolean = true;
var age:Number = 35;
var combined:Number = answer + age;
trace (typeof(combined));
// output: number
```

The same goes for a Boolean and a string. Both data types will always convert to a string:

```
var answer:Boolean = true;
var age_str:String = "35";
var combined_str:String = answer + age_str;
trace (typeof(combined_str));
// output: string
```

As far as conversion goes, what does the interpreter convert each element to? To find out, let's take a look at the next few lists.

These rules apply to string conversions:

- A number converts to a string literal equal to that number (for example, 123 to "123").
- A Boolean converts to `true` if true and `false` if false.
- `Undefined` converts to `undefined`.
- `Null` converts to `null`.
- NaN converts to NaN.
- An array converts to a list of elements separated by commas.

These guidelines apply to number conversions:

- A string containing numbers converts to a numeric value represented in those numbers.
- A string not containing numbers converts to NaN.
- `Undefined` converts to NaN.
- `Null` converts to NaN.
- A Boolean converts to `1` if true and `0` if false.
- NaN converts to NaN.
- An array converts to NaN.

These are the rules for Boolean conversions:

- A string with a length greater than 0 converts to `true`.

- An empty string converts to `false`.

- A number converts to `true` if it's a nonzero number and `false` if it's zero.

- `Undefined` converts to `false`.

- `Null` converts to `false`.

- NaN converts to `false`.

- An array converts to `true`.

Converting Variables Using Functions and Methods

Now that you know what values convert to, let's see how to convert them. We will start the conversions by using the `toString` method. Remember, you are only converting the data type within the variable to another data type, not the variable itself.

The `toString` Method

This method acts like any of the previous methods we've discussed. Simply attach it directly to a data type you would like to convert to a string or attach it to a variable you would like to convert. There are no arguments in the parentheses. Here's an example:

```
var age:Number = 35
var myString_str:String = age.toString();
//Converts the variable age to a string
var myString_str:String = false.toString();
 //Converts the boolean datatype false to a string
var myString_str:String = (50).toString();
//Converts the number 50 to a string
// the parentheses are there so as not to
// confuse the interpreter into
//thinking it was a decimal point
```

The `String` Function

To use the `String` function, simply place the variable or data type you would like to convert in the parentheses, and the function will convert it to a string:

```
var myString_str:String = String(myVariable);
var myString_str:String = String(123);
var myString_str:String = String(null);
// the String function converts all of these datatypes to a string datatype
```

Using Operators

You have already seen that using a plus sign (+) will convert numbers and variables to a string, as shown here:

```
var myString_str:String = 500 + "string";
//Converted to a string
var myString_str:String = myVariable + "";
//Using an empty string to convert variables to a string
```

The Number Function

This function acts nearly identically to the String function. Place the variable or data you want to convert in between the parentheses, and the function will convert it to a number:

```
var myNum:Number = Number(myVariable);
//Converts value of myVariable to a number
var myNum:Number = Number("Unleashed");     //Becomes NaN
var myNum:Number = Number("1234");          //Becomes the number 1234
```

This function is great for converting input fields that are string literals such as ZIP codes or age.

The parseInt and parseFloat Methods

These methods convert strings to numbers much like the Number function. However, unlike the Number function, these two methods can pull numbers out of text, as long as the first nonspace character is a number.

Let's take a look at the parseInt function, which is for pulling whole integers (remember from earlier, integers have no decimals or fractional values). Just call this function as you would any other function and place the variable or string you want to convert in the parentheses:

```
var idNumber_str:String = "123abc";
trace (parseInt(idNumber_str));
// output: 123
```

The parseFloat function works in much the same manner, but it pulls floating numbers instead of integers:

```
var idNumber_str:String = "123.487abc";
trace (parseFloat(idNumber_str));
// output: 123.487
```

If the first nonspace character is anything but a numeric value, the function returns NaN:

```
var idNumber_str:String = "abd123.487";
trace (parseInt(idNumber_str));
// output: NaN
```

In case you're wondering what happens when you use `parseInt` on a floating number, the following example shows that the function will return everything up to the decimal point:

```
var idNumber_str:String = "123.487abc";
trace (parseInt(idNumber_str));
// output: 123
```

However, if you use the `parseFloat` function on an integer, it will return the same value as the `parseInt` function:

```
var idNumber_str:String = "123abc";
trace (parseFloat(idNumber_str));
// output: 123
```

The `Boolean` Function

Converting to a Boolean is as easy as using the `String` or `Number` function. Place the variable or data type in the parentheses, and the `Boolean` function converts it to a Boolean:

```
var mySample:Boolean = Boolean(myVariable);
//Converts the value of myVariable to Boolean
var mySample:Boolean = Boolean(123);          //Converts to true
var mySample:Boolean = Boolean(0);            //Converts to false
```

The Scope of a Variable

So far, we have placed variables on the main timeline and in a movie on the main time-line. It's now time for you to learn about the scope of variables and how to overcome the shortcomings of the local scope of variables.

Timeline Variables

Whenever a variable is created or defined on a timeline, it is available to every frame on that timeline as well as any buttons that have been placed on the stage associated with that timeline.

Any code placed in the object actions of a movie clip instance can access variables on the timeline of that movie, but not the timeline the movie is in. Here's an exercise to make this clear:

1. Start a new file as you did before.

2. On the main timeline, place the following code:

    ```
    var myVariable_str:String = "Success";
    ```

    In the second frame of the main timeline, place this code:

    ```
    //this will stop the movie from looping
    stop();
    trace (myVariable_str);
    ```

3. Now create a new layer called rectangle and place a rectangle on that layer. Highlight the rectangle and press F8 on your keyboard to convert it to symbol (or select Modify>Convert to Symbol). Then choose Button as the behavior. And give this button an instance name of myButton_btn.

4. Go back into the actions of the first frame, and place these actions in:

```
myButton_btn.onRelease=function(){
    trace(myVariable_str);
}
```

You're done, so test it.

You should see the word *Success* pop up in the Output window, and when you click the rectangle button, the variable should appear again (see Figure 9.3).

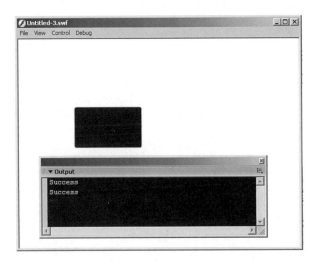

FIGURE 9.3   A successful implementation of a timeline variable.

Dot Syntax

Dot syntax enables code to see from one timeline to the next, either by direct route with the use of instance names or with special predefined identifiers such as _root and _parent. Just remember that each level must be separated by a dot, hence *dot syntax*.

The _root and _parent identifiers are constants: _root is always the main timeline and will never change (however, you can define the _root of a movie clip using the _lockroot property of a movie clip), but _parent is relative to where you are using it, and it always goes up one level in hierarchy.

Another part of dot syntax involves using the instance names of symbols. For example, if you want to know the horizontal position of myMovie_mc on the main timeline, you would type the following:

```
_root.myMovie_mc._x;
```

If you need to know the value of `myVariable` in the movie `myMovie_mc`, which is embedded in `theMovie_mc`, which in turn is on the main timeline, you would use this:

```
_root.theMovie_mc.myMovie_mc.myVariable
```

The _root Identifier

The _root identifier represents the main timeline; everything on it can be accessed like so:

```
_root.whatever
```

Let's look at an example of this:

Create a new Flash file like before.

Create a second layer, and name the layers Actions and Content.

On the main timeline, in the Content layer, create a movie clip with these actions on its timeline:

```
trace (theVariable_str);
trace (_root.theVariable_str);
```

   2. On the main timeline in the first frame of the Actions layer, place this code:

```
var theVariable_str:String = "theRoot";
```

Now test the movie again. Here's the output:

```
// output: undefined
//         theRoot
```

The movie came back with undefined because the variable could not be found in its local scope, but using _root, it found the variable with ease.

The _parent Identifier

The _parent identifier is used in dot syntax to refer to one step up. Parents can be overlapped like this:

```
_parent._parent
```

Now go back into the actions of the movie you created earlier and replace its code with the following:

```
trace (_parent.theVariable);
```

Now test again:

```
// output: theRoot
```

This time, the _parent part of the dot syntax looks up one level and finds the variable.

Although this may seem tedious and difficult to understand, thanks to the _global identifier, many of these problems can be solved.

The _global Identifier

Introduced back in Flash MX, the _global identifier creates data types that can be seen from all parts of the Flash movie without the use of dot syntax and target pathing.

Just attach the _global identifier to what you would like to make global; then you can access it from anywhere in the Flash movie.

1. Start a new Flash movie. Then on the main timeline, in the first frame, place this code:

```
_global.myVariable = "Omnipotent";
```

2. On the stage, draw a rectangle and convert it to a movie clip symbol (F8) with the symbol name draw1.

3. Convert it again, this time with the symbol name draw2.

4. Convert it for a third time, with the symbol name draw3.

5. Open up your library (PC–Ctrl+L, Mac–Open Apple+L) and go into draw1. In the first frame of the timeline, place the following code:

```
trace (myVariable);
```

Now test the movie:

```
// output: Omnipotent
```

Is that powerful or what? You have just traced a variable on the main timeline from another timeline that is embedded into three separate movies.

If you happen to create a local variable with the same name, only ActionScript attempting to access it locally will be affected; it will not affect the global variable.

The this Identifier

The this identifier is used to refer to the current timeline, or object it is being placed in. It acts in the same way the understood "you" does in English. To better understand the this identifier, here is an example:

1. Create a new Flash document.

2. Draw a circle about 50×50 in size on the left side of the stage.

3. Convert it to a movie clip with the symbol name circleMC.

4. Back on the stage, give the circle an instance name of circle_mc in the properties inspector.

6

5. Add a new layer called actions and place this code in the first frame of that layer:

```
//this variable is placed on the main timeline
this.myTime = getTimer();
//this event is for a movie clip on the main timeline
circle_mc.onEnterFrame=function(){
    //this variable refers to the timeline of circle_mc
    this._x += 1;
}
```

The this identifier is not necessary in most cases, but it is good practice to use it to make it easy when going back over code to see which timeline or object it is referring to.

An Applied Example

You have learned a lot of fun stuff in this chapter (and some not-so-fun stuff). Let's end with an easily applied example of how to use variables. Follow these steps:

1. Start a new Flash movie and make its dimensions 400×400 in the stage properties.

2. Now draw a circle on the main stage, but not too big—about 50×50 should do. Convert this circle to a movie clip symbol. Then give it an instance name of circle_mc.

3. Create a new layer called actions, open the Actions panel in the first frame of that layer, and then put these actions in:

```
//create all our variables
var friction:Number = .5;
var pointX:Number = Math.round(Math.random()*400)
var pointY:Number = Math.round(Math.random()*400);
//create the event
this.onEnterFrame=function(){
//set our if statements to move at different speeds
//based on distance, and to pick a new spot once the
//designated spot has been reached
    if (Math.round(circle_mc._x) != pointX){
        circle_mc._x+=(pointX-circle_mc._x)*friction;
    }else if (Math.round(circle_mc._x) == pointX){
        pointX = Math.round(Math.random()*400);
    }
    if (Math.round(circle_mc._y) != pointY) {
        circle_mc._y+=(pointY-circle_mc._y)*friction;
    }else if (Math.round(circle_mc._y) == pointY){
        pointY = Math.round(Math.random()*400);
    }
}
```

Now test the movie.

In this example, the `if` statements are saying that if the object is not at its designated spot yet, adjust its position based on the distance it is from the designated spot. Then, once it has reached the spot, pick a new spot and keep moving the circle.

Note that you can adjust the friction to achieve some interesting effects.

Summary

This chapter covered all the basics of the major data types and variables. Remember that variables are used as containers for data, and when creating them, even if they are left empty, it is good practice to give them a data type.

Also, use caution when changing the data type of variables. It is better to create a separate variable to hold the value as a different data type than to keep swapping the data type throughout your code.

In the next chapter, we go over the Array data type in more detail to show the benefits of using sequential data.

CHAPTER **10**

Arrays

What Is an Array and How Does It Work?

Back in Chapter 9, "Strings, Numbers and Variables," we discussed different data types, including variables. Variables can hold one piece of data or another data type, including another variable. Like variables, arrays can hold any type of data, including strings, integers, and Booleans. They can also hold other data types, including variables and other arrays (called *nested arrays*), which we will discuss later in this chapter.

In this chapter, we will go over what an array is, how to create one, and how to retrieve, manipulate, and delete data from arrays with an applied example at the end.

So let's jump right in and see what makes up an array.

Deconstructing an Array

As stated earlier, an array is a data type that can hold multiple pieces of information. Here's an easy way to imagine this: A variable is like a chair, and it can hold one person (one piece of data). On the other hand, an array is more like a bench, it can hold multiple people (multiple pieces of data).

Each piece of data in an array is called an *element*. Each element is automatically assigned the name of the array and a unique number called its *index*, which is enclosed in brackets. However, the first element in an array is not assigned the number 1; it is instead assigned the number 0 because arrays are zero-indexed meaning that they start counting at zero instead of one.

Therefore, the first element in the array my_array is labeled my_array[0]. Likewise, for the seventh element in the same array, you would use my_array[6].

This indexing is great for holding and retrieving sequential information.

The number of elements in an array is known as its *length*, and we will cover this topic in greater detail later in the chapter when the properties of an array are discussed.

Creating an Array

Now that you know what an array is and what it does, let's discuss how to create one. There are several different ways to create an array; however, we will be dealing mainly with the new operator and the Array constructor to build our sample array.

When creating arrays using the new operator and the Array constructor, start by setting a variable. Then make the variable equal to the new operator combined with the Array constructor, followed by a set of parentheses and then a semicolon (to end the line of code). Here's an example:

Open a new movie, click the first frame of the main timeline, and open the Actions panel (F9).

Place the following code in your actions:

```
var my_array:Array = new Array();
```

You're done! You just created your first array, so let's take a look at it. Add the following trace function to your code:

```
trace(my_array);
```

Now test your movie by going to the toolbar and choosing Control > Test Movie. When you test your movie, an output window will open because of the trace function in the code. However, nothing appears in the window, as shown in Figure 10.1. That's because there is nothing in our array. Let's go back and add some data to the array.

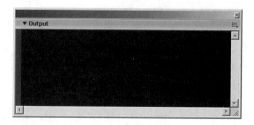

FIGURE 10.1   An empty output window for your movie.

As mentioned earlier, each element in an array is labeled with the array's name and an integer that represents its position inside of the array. The first element in an array will always have an index of 0, followed by 1, and so on. Because you have already created the array, you will label the new elements manually. Under where you created the array, type the array name and then **0** in brackets, like this:

```
var my_array:Array = new Array();
my_array [0] = "fName";
my_array [1] = "lName";
trace(my_array);
//output: fName, lName
```

Now that you have data in the array, you can continue to add elements. However, it's much easier to create the elements right in the beginning, so let's do that next. Also, notice this time that the output of the code is preceded by comment marks (//). As in previous chapters, these marks are merely to show the output of the code from within the ActionScript itself.

You will still be using the original code, but when you create the array this time, you will create it with data inside. Elements in an array can be of any data type, as discussed earlier. Let's use a couple strings to start with. When putting elements in an array when it is created, place them in the parentheses and separate them with commas, like this:

```
var my_array:Array = new Array("fName","lName");
trace(my_array);
//output: fName, lName
```

Another way of creating an array with information doesn't involve the new operator or the Array constructor. You can simply set a variable equal to the elements you want in the array, but instead of putting them inside parentheses, place them between brackets, as shown here:

```
var my_array:Array = ["fName","lName"];
trace(my_array);
//output: fName, lName
```

This code outputs the same as the other examples. However, just remember that when you do not use the new operator and the Array constructor, you must place the elements in brackets.

You can even put just one piece of data in the array when you create it, but make sure it is not an integer. Otherwise, some surprising results will happen. Let's take a look.

Use the same code as before but replace what is in the parentheses with the number 5 (note that the output of the code is shown within the code using comment marks):

```
var my_array:Array = new Array(5);
trace(my_array);
//output: undefined,undefined,undefined,undefined,undefined
```

When you test the movie, notice that it doesn't display the number 5 but instead displays 5 elements as undefined. This is because when you place only an integer in an array, it creates that many *blank* elements.

You can also store variables in arrays just like any other type of data, and the data stored in the variables will display in the array:

```
var myName:String = "David";
var myAge:Number = 25;
var my_array:Array = new Array(myName, myAge);
trace(my_array);
//output: David, 25
```

But make note, when storing a variable in an array, it actually stores the data from that variable, and not the reference to the variable. Here is an example of this:

```
var myName:String = "David";
var myAge:Number = 25;
var my_array:Array = new Array(myName, myAge);
trace(my_array);
myAge = 35;
trace(my_array);
//output: David, 25
//        David, 25
```

You can see that although we changed the value of *myAge*, when we traced the array for the second time, the data was the same.

Besides variables, arrays can also hold other arrays (called *nested arrays*). Nested arrays are useful for holding multiple lists in one place. Just place the name of the array as an element, as you would a variable:

```
var myNames:Array = new Array("fName","lName");
var my_array:Array = new Array("age",myNames);
trace(my_array);
//output: age, fName, lName
```

The second array simply encompasses the first array. However, if you trace the last element in my_array, you will see that it doesn't separate the elements from myNames. Let's take a look at this:

```
var myNames:Array = new Array("fName","lName");
var my_array:Array = new Array("age",myNames);
trace(my_array [1]);
//output: fName, lName
```

As you can see, even though it appears that when we added myNames to my_array, the elements from myNames came over as one element. Just keep this in mind when you add arrays to arrays.

Retrieving Information from an Array

When retrieving information from an array, use the index of the array element to pull that specific piece of data, as shown here:

```
var my_array:Array = new Array("fName","lName","age");
trace(my_array [1]);
//output: lName
```

In this example, we simply call the second element in `my_array`, which has the index of 1 because arrays start counting at 0.

There is a way to count the number of elements within an array—using the `length` property. It is the only property that an array has. Just attach the `length` property to any array with a period, and it will return the length. Here's an example:

```
var my_array:Array = new Array("fName","lName","age","location");
trace(my_array.length);
//output: 4
```

> **TIP**
>
> Remember, the last element in any array will always be the value of `array.length` minus 1.

When combined with loop statements, the `length` property can be used to retrieve sequential information.

This example lists each element vertically in the output window, as opposed to all in one line. Place this code in the first frame of the main timeline actions of the movie:

```
var my_array:Array = new Array("fName","lName","age","location");
//the loop statement to cycle through the Array
for(var i:Number = 0; i < my_array.length; i++){
   trace(my_array[i]);
}
//output: fName
//        lName
//        age
//        location
```

This is just a simple example of how to use a loop statement and the `length` property.

Adding Elements to Arrays

So far we have created an array and placed elements in the array; now lets add elements to an array. There are a couple ways of accomplishing this. Let's start with the simple methods and move into the more dynamic methods.

You can start by setting the `length` property of an array. Setting the `length` property of an array will add as many blank elements to that array as you specify—but again, the last *blank* element will have the index of the length minus 1. Here's an example:

```
var my_array:Array = new Array();
my_array.length = 5;
trace(my_array);
//output: undefined,undefined,undefined,undefined,undefined
```

Using the `length` property to add elements will only add undefined elements to the beginning.

Now we will add elements that actually have data in them. Start by creating an array and adding elements using the index of the elements, as shown here:

```
var my_array:Array = new Array("fName","lName");
trace(my_array);
my_array [2] = "age";
my_array [3] = "location";
trace(my_array);
//output: fName, lName
//        fName, lName, age, location
```

That was pretty easy. All we did was add elements manually by looking at the next index of the array and assigning an element to it.

Now we will make it more dynamic. Create a button and place it on the main stage. Give it an instance name of "myButton_btn". Then add these actions to the first frame of the main movie:

```
var my_array:Array = new Array();
var i:Number = 0;
myButton_btn.onPress = function(){
        var thisLength:Number = my_array.length;
        my_array[thisLength] = i;
        i++;
        trace(my_array);
}
//output: (depending on how many times you click the button, increasing
//output continued: numbers starting at 0)
```

Let's take a look at what we did. First, we created an empty array and a variable that equals zero. Then, we added actions to a button on the main timeline that, when pressed, will set the element with the index of the array's length to the variable i. The variable i will be increased by 1 each time the button is clicked. Finally, we traced the array.

Well, that was pretty dynamic, but we had to write some code that lets us know what the next index of the array should be. Now we're going to talk about an array method that will do the checking for us: the push method.

The push Method

The push method is great when you want to add elements to the end of an array without checking the length. Just call the method on the array using a period and put what you want to add in parentheses following the push. Take a look at the following example:

Start a new Flash document and add these actions to the first frame of the main timeline

```
var my_array:Array = new Array();
//create the object to listen for the event
var keyListen:Object = new Object();
//create the event
keyListen.onKeyDown=function(){
        var theKey:String = String.fromCharCode(Key.getAscii());
        my_array.push(theKey);
        trace(my_array);
}
//Add the listener
Key.addListener(keyListen);
//output: (every key you press depending on how many
// and which key(s) you press)
```

This example is a simple keystroke recorder to show how easily the push method works. It simply "pushes" the keystroke to the end of the array.

> **NOTE**
>
> If, at first, when pressing keys in the test screen, you do not see anything, click the mouse on the stage inside the Flash movie. Even though a keyDown event is occurring, sometimes the mouse must be clicked inside at least once for the event to take place because Flash movies do not always initially receive focus.

You can also push more than one element at a time into an array. In the next example, we will add two pieces of data at the end of the array using the push method:

```
var my_array:Array = new Array("fName","lName");
trace(my_array);
my_array.push("age","location")
trace(my_array);
//output: fName, lName
//         fName, lName, age, location
```

10

Here, we just added two elements, separated by a comma, to my_array simultaneously using the push method.

You can add any kind of data type using the push method, as shown in the following example:

```
var my_array:Array = new Array("fName","lName");
trace(my_array);
var x:Number = 10;
var another_array:Array = new Array("age","location");
var y:Number = 5 + x;
my_array.push(x,y,another_array);
trace(my_array);
//output: fName, lName
//        fName, lName, 10, 15, age, location
```

Here, we've added a variable, an expression, and even another array to our original array using the push method.

As an interesting side note to what the push method for arrays can do, you can also check the new length of an array while using the push method to add elements, as shown here:

```
var my_array:Array = new Array("fName","lName");
trace(my_array.push("age","location"));
trace(my_array);
//output: 4
//        fName, lName, age, location
```

You can even substitute this method of returning the length for the length property in some cases. Here's an example:

```
var my_array:Array = new Array("fName","lName");
trace(my_array.push(my_array.push()));
trace(my_array);
//output: 3
//        fName, lName, 2
```

Because this method adds the number before it checks the length using the push method, it adds the number 2, representing the length of the array, instead of 3.

The push method is great for gathering repetitive information for retrieval. Some examples might be providing back and forward control inside the Flash movie and recording users' information for the next time they visit.

Another example is a search function that searches inside an array and returns the frequency and position of the element you are looking for:

```
//First, create the function and label your variables
searchArray = function(theArray:Array,lookFor:String) {
```

```
//Then create an array to hold the positions
        var position:Array = new Array();
    //Use a for loop statement to check through each element
        for (var i:Number = 0; i <=theArray.length-1; i++) {
    //Use an if statement to compare each element to what you're looking for
            if (theArray[i] == lookFor) {
    //If the element matches, add to the position array
                position.push([i]);
            }
        }
    //Lastly, trace the results
        trace("The frequency is " + position.length);
        trace("In position(s) " + position);
}
var my_array:Array = new Array("fName","lName","age","location","age");
searchArray(my_array,"age");
//output: The frequency is 2
//        In position(s) 2, 4
```

This is just another example of how to use the push method and the length property to retrieve elements from an array.

Another method you can use to add elements to an array is the unshift method.

The unshift **Method**

The unshift method works identically to the push method, except, instead of adding elements to the end, it adds them to the beginning. Here's an example:

```
var my_array:Array = new Array("fName","lName");
trace(my_array);
my_array.unshift("age");
trace(my_array);
//output: fname, lName
//        age, fName, lName
```

Again, the unshift method adds elements to the beginning of an array. Therefore, each of the original elements' indexes are increased. For instance, fName will go from my_array[0] to my_array[1], and age will become my_array[0].

Also, like the push method, the unshift method can be used to show the length of an array:

```
var my_array:Array = new Array("fName","lName");
trace(my_array.unshift("age","location"));
trace(my_array);
//output: 4
//        age, location, fName, lName
```

10

Like the push method, `unshift` traces the new length and adds elements to the array, but unlike push, it adds them to the front of the array.

The `splice` Method

The `splice` method is one of the more powerful methods of arrays. Not only can it add elements to an array, but it can also delete elements and place elements in the middle of arrays. Its syntax is very similar to the other methods we have talked about, except it has multiple parameters:

```
my_array.splice(startingIndex,deleteNumber,itemsToAdd);
```

Let's take a look at the first part, the part that will delete items from the starting point forward. Attach the method like you would any other, and in the parentheses, place the index of where you want to start deleting items from the array:

```
var my_array:Array = new Array("fName","lName","age","location","phone");
my_array.splice(2);
trace(my_array);
//output: fName, lName
```

The method started with the second index, which was age, and deleted all remaining elements. The elements were permanently removed. As a matter of fact, if you check the length of my_array after the splice, the value will be 2.

Now that you know how to delete from one index to the end, let's see how to remove a certain number of elements from a starting point. Use the same code, only this time, in the parentheses place a comma after the starting point and put in however many elements to remove. Here's an example:

```
var my_array:Array = new Array("fName","lName","age","location","phone");
my_array.splice(2,2);
trace(my_array);
//output: fName, lName, phone
```

This time the method removed elements from the starting index we assigned and permanently removed the number of elements we assigned. If you check the length, it will return the value 3.

The last step of the `splice` method is to add elements in the middle of the array, beginning with the starting point. Again, we will be using the same code as before. This time after the number representing the number of elements to remove, we'll place another comma and then add the elements in while separating them with commas:

```
var my_array:Array = new Array("fName","lName","age","location","phone");
my_array.splice(2,2,"fax","email");
trace(my_array);
//output: fName, lName, fax, email, phone
```

This time, the `splice` method removed the number of assigned elements at the assigned starting point and added elements at the starting point. Again, when adding elements, you can add any type of data, including variables and other arrays.

Now let's add elements to the middle of an array without deleting any elements. This time, we'll use the same syntax but set the number of items we want to delete to zero:

```
var my_array:Array = new Array("fName","lName","age","location","phone");
my_array.splice(2,0,"fax","email");
trace(my_array);
//output: fName,lName,fax,email,age,location,phone
```

Because we set the number of items to delete to zero, the method simply adds the elements in at the index we listed and slides the other elements over.

The `splice` method has yet another great use. It can return the values of the items removed. Here's an example:

```
var my_array:Array = new Array("fName","lName","age","location","phone");
trace(my_array.splice(2,2));
//output: age,location
```

In this case, instead of showing what the array looks like after the splice, the method shows what elements were removed. At this point, if you trace the array, it will show the new array with these elements removed. This is really useful if you want to remove certain information from one array and place that information in another array. Here's an example:

```
var my_array:Array = new Array("fName","lName","age","location","phone");
var another_array:Array = my_array.splice(2,2);
trace(another_array);
trace(my_array);
//output: age, location
//        fName, lName, phone
```

This time, we removed items from an array and placed them in a new array called `another_array`.

You can even add elements to the original array while removing elements from it and placing them into a new array. Using the same code as before, this time we'll add an element to the original array:

```
var my_array:Array = new Array("fName","lName","age","location","phone");
var another_array:Array = my_array.splice(2,2,"fax");
trace(another_array);
trace(my_array);
//output: age, location
//        fName,lName,fax,phone
```

That was simple enough. We removed two elements and placed them in a new array while adding an element to the original array.

To summarize, the `splice` method can almost do it all. You can use it to add, remove, and change the elements inside an array. It can even be used to create new arrays.

Another method used for adding elements to arrays is the `concat` method.

The `concat` Method

The `concat` method works similarly to the `push` method in that it adds elements to the end of an array. However, it does not affect the original array. Instead, it creates a new array with the new elements.

To demonstrate the `concat` method, let's use our sample array. Now we can create another array by adding elements to the original with the `concat` method:

```
var my_array:Array = new Array("fName","lName","age");
var another_array:Array = my_array.concat("phone","fax");
trace(another_array);
//output: fName, lName, age, phone, fax
```

The new array, `another_array`, has both the elements from the original array, `my_array`, and the new elements we add to the end. If you trace `my_array`, nothing changes because the `concat` method only affects the new array it creates.

One nice thing about the `concat` method is that when adding an array to another array, it separates the elements and adds them as singular elements. Let's take a look at two examples: one using the `push` method and the other using the `concat` method.

Here's the example that uses the `push()` method:

```
var my_array:Array = new Array("fName","lName");
var another_array:Array = new Array("age","location");
my_array.push(another_array);
trace(my_array [2]);
//output: age, location
```

And here's the example that uses the `concat()` method:

```
var my_array:Array = new Array("fName","lName");
var another_array:Array = new Array("age","location");
my_array = my_array.concat(another_array);
trace(my_array[2]);
//output: age
```

In the first example, we used the `push` method to add the second array to `my_array`. Notice that it doesn't separate the elements into their own individual elements. Instead, it places the entire array in `my_array[2]`. In the second example, we used the `concat` method to add the second array to `my_array`. When the `concat` method is used, array elements are separated into individual elements.

> **NOTE**
>
> Unless you set the array equal to itself, the `concat` method will not permanently affect the original array.

Even though `concat` will separate the elements in an array into individual elements, it will not separate nested arrays. Here's an example:

```
var my_array:Array = new Array(["fName","lName"],["age","location"]);
var another_array:Array = my_array.concat(my_array);
trace(another_array[0]);
//output: fName, lName
```

Naming Array Elements

Most array elements are numbered, but they can also be named. Naming array elements is an easy way to keep information organized within an array. None of these named elements can be manipulated by array methods, nor can they be seen when the array is traced.

There are two ways to create named array elements. The first uses dot syntax, and the second uses brackets and string literals. Here's an example of both methods:

> **NOTE**
>
> When you use dot syntax with any other object in Flash, the word that follows the dot is referred to as a property. But because the Array is a unique class of Object, when you use dot syntax, the elements are called Named Array Elements.

```
var my_array:Array = new Array();
my_array.fName = "David";
my_array ["age"] = 25;
trace(my_array);
//output: (nothing)
```

We first created an empty array to hold the named elements and then we attached the first element using dot syntax and set it equal to a string. Then we attached the next named element using brackets and a string to name it, and we set its value to a number. Finally, we traced the array, but there were no results. This is because, as previously stated, when you trace an array, named elements will not appear. You have to call the named elements individually. Therefore, using the same code as before, we will trace both named elements individually when tracing the array:

10

```
var my_array:Array = new Array();
my_array.fName = "David";
my_array ["age"] = 25;
trace(my_array ["fName"]);
trace(my_array.age);
//output: David
//         25
```

This time, when we traced the elements individually, the trace was successful.

Named array elements will also not show up in the array's length. Here's an example:

```
var my_array:Array = new Array();
my_array.fName = "David";
trace(my_array.length);
//output: 0
```

Now that you know how to add elements to an array, let's cover how to remove them.

Removing Array Elements

Just like adding elements, removing them has several different options. We will start with the simple options and then move into using the array methods.

The first option for removing elements from an array is using the delete operator.

The delete Operator

The delete operator is misleading. It does not actually delete the element in the array; it merely sets the element to undefined. To use this operator, type **delete** then use a space to separate the array element you want to "delete" by using its index. Here's an example:

```
var my_array:Array = new Array("fName","lName");
trace(my_array [0]);
delete my_array [0];
trace(my_array [0]);
//output: fName
//        undefined
```

As you can see, when we traced the first element in my_array before we used the delete operator, it displayed fName. Then after we used the delete operator, the output of the first element became undefined. Also note that the length of an array after the use of the delete operator will stay the same—even though the operator removes the data in the element, it does not remove the element itself.

The delete operator can also be used on named array elements, as shown here:

```
var my_array:Array = new Array();
my_array.fName = "David";
```

```
trace(my_array.fName);
delete my_array.fName;
trace(my_array.fName);
//output: David
//         undefined
```

Just like indexed array elements, the delete operator simply removes the value of the named element, but the element is still in the array.

To remove the element itself, we have a few choices. The first involves using the length property. Then there are the pop, shift, and splice methods.

Removing Elements Using the length Property

Using the length property to remove elements in an array is very similar to using it to add elements. Just create an array and set its length, like so:

```
var my_array:Array = new Array("fName","lName","age","location");
trace(my_array);
my_array.length = 2;
trace(my_array);
//output: fName, lName, age, location
//         fName, lName
```

Using the length property to remove elements is a very simple way to get rid of everything that comes after the desired length of the array.

The splice Method Revisited

The splice method was already covered earlier in this chapter. This time, however, we'll use it strictly for the removal of elements in an array.

You can use the splice method in two different ways when removing elements. The first way removes all elements beginning with the starting index you define. The second way sets the number of elements to remove at the starting index. Here's an example:

```
var my_array:Array = new Array
("fName","lName","age","location","phone","fax","email");
trace(my_array);
my_array.splice(5);
trace(my_array);
my_array.splice(2,2);
trace(my_array);
//output: fName, lName, age, location, phone, fax, email
//         fName,lName, age, location, phone
//         fName, lName, phone
```

10

The first `splice` sets the starting index and removes all elements at and beyond that point. The second `splice` sets the starting index and the number of elements to remove and then actually removes those elements. Another method used for removing array elements is the `pop` method.

The `pop` Method

The pop method can be thought of as being the "archenemy" of the `push` method. Whereas the `push` method adds elements to the end of an array, the pop method removes singular elements from the end of the array. Its syntax is the same as the other methods—just attach the method to the array you want to remove elements from, as shown here:

```
var my_array:Array = new Array("fName","lName","age","location");
my_array.pop();
trace(my_array);
//output: fName, lName, age
```

In this example, the pop method simply dropped the last element in the array completely and changed the length of the array.

The pop method can also return the value of the element it removes. Here's an example:

```
var my_array:Array = new Array("fName","lName","age","location");
trace(my_array.pop());
//output: location
```

The next method for removing array elements is the shift method.

The `shift` Method

If the pop method is the archenemy of the `push` method, then the `shift` method is the archenemy of the `unshift` method. The `shift` method removes one element from the beginning of an array and decreases its length by one:

```
var my_array:Array = new Array("fName","lName","age","location");
my_array.shift();
trace(my_array);
//output: lName, age, location
```

Also like the pop method, the shift method returns the value of the element it removes:

```
var my_array:Array = new Array("fName","lName","age","location");
trace(my_array.shift());
//output: fName
```

But what if we don't want to get rid of the elements in an array and instead just want to change them?

Changing Elements in Arrays

Now that you know how to add and remove elements, let's discuss how to change them. We will create an array, trace it to see the original, change the first element to something else by using the index, and then trace it again to see the difference as shown in the following code:

```
var my_array:Array = new Array("fName","lName");
trace(my_array);
my_array [0] = "age";
trace(my_array);
//output: fName, lName
//        age, lName
```

That was pretty simple. We just renamed the first element, just like renaming a variable. What's more, changing named array elements is just as easy, as shown here:

```
var my_array:Array = new Array();
my_array.age = 24;
trace(my_array.age);
my_array.age = 25;
trace(my_array.age);
//output: 24
//        25
```

The next section covers in greater detail nested arrays and how they can be used and manipulated.

Advanced Nested Arrays

Earlier in this chapter, we briefly discussed nested arrays (arrays held within other arrays). Now we are going to discuss some advantages to using these nested arrays. First, let's go over again how to create one. The example we'll use here involves the starting five of a basketball team by position. This example shows the following information:

- Points scored
- Shots taken
- Total rebounds

We will start with just the first two positions and combine them, as shown here:

```
var pG:Array = new Array(12,15,4);
var sG:Array = new Array(20,22,5);
var team:Array = new Array(pG,sG);
trace(team);
//output: 12,15,4,20,22,5
```

Now that we have the data entered in, we could get the point guard's rebounds from the team array, without showing the other elements. To do this, we call the index of an indexed element. This may sound complicated, but it's not. We want to know how many rebounds the point guard has (the third element in the first element of the team array). Here's the code we'll use:

```
var pG:Array = new Array(12,15,4);
var sG:Array = new Array(20,22,5);
var team:Array = new Array(pG,sG);
trace(team[0][2]);
//output: 4
```

Success! We retrieved an individual element from a nested array. This is a very powerful tool when you have massive arrays with many nested arrays. Now let's take this a step further. We'll add the rest of the team and this time get the total for each category and place this information in an array called totals. We'll also divide the totals, as they are being calculated, by the main array's length property to get the averages for the players and then place that information into another array called averages. Here's the code:

```
//First, get all the players ready with their stats in their own array
var pG:Array = new Array(12,15,4);
var sG:Array = new Array(20,22,5);
var sF:Array = new Array(11,13,8);
var pF:Array = new Array(18,14,16);
var c:Array = new Array(20,17,21);
//Now combine all the players arrays into one array called "team"
var team:Array = new Array(pG,sG,sF,pF,c);
var totals:Array = new Array();
var averages:Array = new Array();
//Now lets create the loop statement that will perform all the necessary
//tasks we want
for(var i:Number = 0; i<team[0].length; i++){
    //reset the holders
    var tempTotal:Number = 0;
    var tempAvg:Number = 0;
    for(var j:Number = 0; j<team.length; j++){
        tempTotal += team[j][i];
//Place the total of each tempElement into the totals array
        totals[i]=tempTotal;
//Divide the total of each sub-element by
//the main array's length to get the //average
        tempAvg +=(team[j][i])/team.length;
        averages[i] = tempAvg;
    }
}
trace(totals);
```

```
trace(averages);
//output: 81, 81, 54
//         16.2,16.2,10.8
```

In this example, we drew information in sequence from the nested arrays, totaled each column, and placed the totals in another array. We also successfully got the averages for all the players and placed them in another array. This is just one of the many possibilities for using this method.

Additional Array Methods

So far we have gone over methods for adding and removing elements. Now we will go over some other array methods for manipulating elements within an array.

The toString Method

Oftentimes, you might want to set an array equal to a variable, but when you set a variable equal directly to an array, the script simply copies the array over to that variable and stores each element as its own element. We'll use the toString method, which you saw before in Chapter 9, to convert an entire array to one string, with each element separated by commas:

```
var my_array:Array = new Array("fName","lName");
var another_array:Array = my_array;
var myVariable:String = my_array.toString();
trace(another_array[0]);
trace(myVariable[0]);
//output: fName
//         undefined
```

This example shows that when we copied my_array into another_array, an exact copy of the original array was created. Then we copied the same array to myVariable, but attached the toString method to it. When we tried to trace a singular element out of myVariable, undefined was returned. So now let's drop the index of myVariable and see what happens:

```
var my_array:Array = new Array("fName","lName");
var another_array:Array = my_array;
var myVariable:String = my_array.toString();
trace(another_array[0]);
trace(myVariable);
//output: fName
//         fName,lName
```

Notice that the elements are separated with commas when the array becomes a string. But what if you want to separate each element with some other character? The join method can accomplish this.

10

The `join` Method

Similar to the `toString` method, the `join` method converts all elements in an array to one string to place in a variable. Unlike the `toString` method, the `join` method separates each element the way you want it to. Again, just call this method on an array like you would any other method and then place whatever string you want to separate the elements with between the parentheses. Here's an example:

```
var my_array:Array = new Array("fName","lName","age","location");
var myVariable:String = my_array.join(" — ");
trace(myVariable);
//output: fName — lName — age — location
```

Alternatively, you can leave the parentheses blank, which causes `join` to act just like the `toString` method:

```
var my_array:Array = new Array("fName","lName","age","location");
var myVariable:String = my_array.join();
trace(myVariable);
//output: fName,lName,age,location
```

You can even put in an expression, as shown here:

```
var my_array:Array = new Array("fName","lName","age","location");
var myVariable:String = my_array.join(2+2);
trace(myVariable);
//output: fName4lName4age4location
```

Now let's look at another method for arrays—the `slice` method.

The `slice` Method

Like the `splice` method, the `slice` method can grab elements from an array and place them into a new array. Unlike the `splice` method, however, the `slice` method does not affect the original array. Here's an easy way to think of these methods: The `splice` method is like cutting, and the `slice` method is like copying.

The syntax for the `slice` method is the same as the `splice` method—you can set the starting point and how many elements you want to copy. Here's an example:

```
var my_array:Array = new Array("fName","lName","age","location");
var another_array:Array = my_array.slice(2);
trace(another_array);
trace(my_array);
//output: age, location
//        fName, lName, age, location
```

The `slice` method copies the elements, starting with the declared index, to the last element of the original array and places them in a new array without affecting the original array.

You can also set the ending index of the elements you wish to copy:

```
var my_array:Array = new Array("fName","lName","age","location");
var another_array:Array = my_array.slice(2,3);
trace(another_array);
//output: age
```

So far, these methods have removed, added, and shifted elements. Now let's change the order of them with the reverse method.

The reverse Method

The reverse method is exactly what it sounds like—it's a method for reversing the order of all the elements in an array. Once an array is created, you can call the reverse method on it, like so:

```
var my_array:Array = new Array("fName","lName","age","location");
my_array.reverse();
trace(my_array);
//output: location, age, lName, fName
```

The reverse method is used mainly for reversing already sorted arrays. The next section shows you how sorting is accomplished.

Sorting Arrays

Sorting plays an important role in using arrays. With sorting, you can put names in alphabetical order, put prices from greatest to least, and even see who has the highest score so far in a video game.

There are two types of sorting: One involves a general sort on the elements in an array, and the other involves the sorting of nested arrays.

Let's go over the general sort method. Just call this method like you would any other method, and it sorts somewhat alphabetically. Here's an example:

```
var fName:Array = new Array("David","Shelley","Linda","Jonathan","Kim");
fName.sort();
trace(fName);
//output: David,Jonathan,Kim,Linda,Shelley
```

The sort worked fine. So why did I mention it will sort "somewhat" alphabetically? As you'll notice, all the strings in the fName array start with a capital letter. However, change the first letter in "David" to a lowercase *d* and see the results:

```
var fName:Array = new Array("david","Shelley","Linda","Jonathan","Kim");
fName.sort();
trace(fName);
//output: Jonathan,Kim,Linda,Shelley,david
```

This time, "david" is moved to the back, even though it's the same name. The `sort` method does not recognize "david" as being the same as "David" because it doesn't look at the letters themselves; instead, it looks at their keycodes (discussed in Chapter 9), in which capital letters come before lowercase letters. There are solutions to this, however, and that is where the arguments to the `sort` method come in. You can pass arguments to control how the `sort` method will sort. There are three arguments you can pass:

- 1—for when A appears after B in the sorted sequence
- -1—for when A appears before B in the sorted sequence
- 0—if A is equal to B

Lets see what each does to our example we have been using.

```
var fName:Array = new Array("david","Shelley","Linda","Jonathan","Kim");
fName.sort(1);
trace(fName);
fName.sort(-1);
trace(fName);
fName.sort(0);
trace(fName);
//output: david,Jonathan,Kim,Linda,Shelley
//        david,Jonathan,Kim,Linda,Shelley
//        Jonathan,Kim,Linda,Shelley,david
```

In this example, we created an array filled with peoples first names, except one of them was not capitalized confusing the sort method. We passed it three different arguments to see which way we wanted it sorted.

> **NOTE**
>
> If you pass the sort method 0 as an argument, it is the same as leaving it blank.

The `sortOn` Method

The `sortOn` method is an extremely tricky method to use. This method sorts nested arrays by the value of a specific named element in each array. The syntax is similar to other methods covered so far, but in the parentheses, you put the named field you want to sort all the nested arrays by. Each of the nested arrays you want to sort must have that named field in it. Let's take a look at an example:

```
var one:Array = new Array();
one.a = "a";
one.b = "b";
one.c = "c";
var two:Array = new Array();
two.a = "b";
```

```
two.b = "c";
two.c = "a";
var three:Array = new Array();
three.a = "c";
three.b = "a";
three.c = "b";
var my_array:Array = new Array(one,two,three)
trace(my_array [0].a);
my_array.sortOn("b");
trace(my_array [0].a);
//output: a
//        c
```

In this example, we first created the three arrays we are going to put in our main array. In each of the nested arrays, we created three named array elements: one, two, and three. Then we set each of the three named elements to three different string literal letters: a, b, or c. Then, we placed each of these three arrays in my_array. After that, we traced the named element a in the first nested array of my_array. Then we ran the sort based on the named element b in all the nested arrays. After the sort, we traced my_array again based on the named element a in the first array element, and this time it was c. Therefore, the sort was successful.

Applied Example

We have gone over a lot of code and different examples of how to use some of the methods of arrays. Now let's look at an applied example of arrays at work. We are going to create a mouse recorder that, after a certain length of recording, will replay the recorded positions of the mouse.

First, we must create the necessary symbols for the movie:

1. Create a movie symbol with an arrow graphic that's centered at the point of the arrow. Name this symbol **arrowMC** (see Figure 10.2).

2. Create a button symbol to move from frame to frame (I used one from the common libraries under Window > Other Panels > Common Libraries > Buttons). Name this symbol **button** (see Figure 10.3).

Next, on the main stage, create four layers with the following labels:

- Actions
- Labels
- Arrow
- Button

10

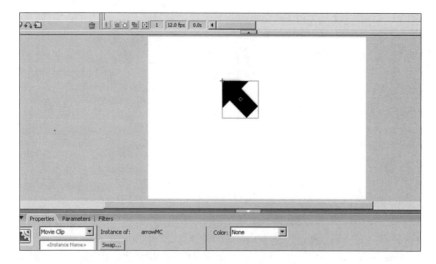

FIGURE 10.2   The "arrowMC" symbol.

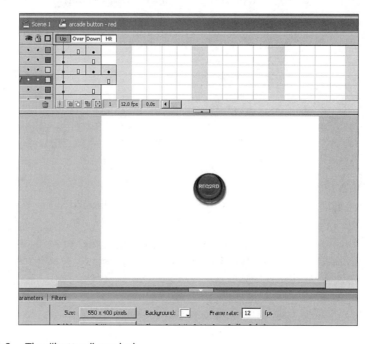

FIGURE 10.3   The "button" symbol.

The movie will consist of three keyframes. In the Labels layer, label the frames like this:

- frame 1—start
- frame 10—record
- frame 20—playRecord

In the Button layer, place a copy of the button we created and give it an instance name of "record_btn".

Now we will move to the Actions layer. In the first frame, place this code:

```
stop();
//Create our arrays to hold our data
var mouseX:Array = new Array();
var mouseY:Array = new Array();

//this is the event for the button
record_btn.onRelease = function()
      gotoAndStop("record");
}
```

Next, create a second keyframe in frame 10 of the Actions layer. Place the following code within that frame:

```
//Create a variable to adjust the length of the recording
var time:Number = 10;  //seconds

this.onEnterFrame=function(){
//Then use a loop statement to check if time is up
      if(time >= Math.floor(getTimer()/1000)){
//Record the positions of the mouse and place them
//in the associated arrays
            mouseX.push(_xmouse);
            mouseY.push(_ymouse);
      }else {
//When time is up
            gotoAndStop("playRecord");
            delete this.onEnterFrame;
      }
}
```

Then, on the Arrow layer, place an arrow instance on the main stage with an instance name of "arrow_mc" in the third keyframe (frame 20) as well as create another keyframe in the actions layer, and place these actions in it:

```
//create the incramental variable
var i:Number=0;
this.onEnterFrame=function(){
//as long as the you are not at the end of the array
//keep playing
      if(i<mouseX.length){
//Set the positions of the arrow equal to positions
```

```
//held in the arrays
            arrow_mc._x = mouseX[i];
            arrow_mc._y = mouseY[i];
            i++;
    }else {
//When it's over, go to the beginning
            gotoAndStop("start");
    }
}
```

That's it! Now test the movie and have some fun coming up with your own experiments using arrays. Also note that the higher the frame rate, the smoother the animation will play.

Summary

We have gone over all the basics of arrays including how to create them. We have also covered the methods used in Flash to control arrays including adding and removing data as well as re-sorting data on command. Also covered in this chapter is the only property of an array, the length property. Remember that the last element in an array is the array's length minus 1.

After going over the fundamentals and theories behind the structure of arrays and when to use them, we then applied them in a real-world example.

CHAPTER 11

Statements and Expressions

This chapter covers statements and expressions. Even though we have not formally gone over statements, you have already used them. A *statement* is simply a small piece of code made up of keywords, operators, and identifiers. Statements can be in one of six categories:

- **Declaration statements**—These statements involve declaring variables, creating functions, setting properties, declaring arrays, and so on. Here's an example:

```
var myVariable:String;          // declares a
variable
myObject._x = 235;              //setting the hori-
zontal position
var my_array:Array = new Array ();//creating an
array
function myFunction (){         //creates a func-
tion
```

- **Expressions**—These include any type of legal expression. Here's an example:

```
i++;                    //increase a variable
lName + space + fName;  //combining variables
```

- **Flow modifiers**—These include any statement that disrupts the natural flow of the interpreter reading the ActionScript. There are two subtypes of flow modifiers: conditional statements and loop statements.

Conditional statements use Boolean answers to determine what to do next or what *not* to do next. Here's an example:

```
if (inputName == userName){
      if (inputPassword == password){
            gotoAndPlay("startPage");
      }else {
                  displayMessage = "Double check your password";
      }
}else if (inputName != userName){
            if (inputPassword == password){
                  displayMessage = "Double check your user name";
            }
}else{
      displayMessage = "Double check your all your information";
}
```

Loop statements run until a defined condition has been met. Here's an example where the trace function will be run while *i* is less than 30:

```
for (var i:Number=0; i<30; i++) {
      trace (i);
}
//output: (numbers 0-29)
```

- **Predefined functions**—Functions that are predefined in ActionScript. Here's an example:

```
trace ("function");            //a simple trace function
gotoAndStop (2);               //a playback function
getProperty( myMovie, _x );    //gets the horizontal position
```

- **Object statements**—Statements that deal with and manipulate objects. Here's an example:

```
var myGrades:Object = { tests: 85, quizzes: 88, homework: 72 };
for (name in myGrades) {
      trace ("myGrades." + name + " = " + myGrades[name]);
}
//output: myGrades.tests = 85
//        myGrades.quizzes = 88
//        myGrades.homework = 72
```

- **Comments**—This last category is one of a kind. It includes comments used in code merely as information for the user while in the Actions panel. The interpreter will skip over these comments. Here's an example:

```
//this is a comment used in ActionScript;

/*this
is
a
comment
block
*/
```

Breaking up statements into these simple categories is done only to help you understand the different types and uses of statements. We will go over a few of these categories in more detail later in this chapter.

Now let's look at some of the basics of building these statements.

Statement Syntax

As you've seen, statements are keywords, operators, and identifiers joined together to accomplish certain tasks. For instance, in the following code, var and new are the keywords, Array () is the identifier, :Array is the data type, and the equal sign is the operator:

```
var my_array:Array = new Array();
```

As you'll notice, a semicolon has been placed at the end of this statement. This semicolon tells the interpreter that the statement is complete and to move on to the next one. The semicolon is not required, and the interpreter will move on without it. However, it is good coding etiquette to place one there.

Also, it is good etiquette to place each new statement on its own line. Again, this is not necessary, but it is a good practice to follow. You can see this for yourself by examining the following two segments of code. Which code section is easier to read?

```
var myVariable:String = "Flash";
myVariable += " Unleashed";
trace (myVariable);
//output: Flash Unleashed
```

```
myVariable = "Flash"; myVariable += " Unleashed"; trace (myVariable);
//output: Flash Unleashed
```

Although the output is the same, the first section of code is much easier to read than the second. Note the spacing between each part of the statement. Often, this is a necessity for the interpreter to correctly identify each part. However, even if this spacing is not always required, it is *always* a good rule to follow.

Statement Block

Some statements have multiple statements associated with them, particularly *flow modifiers*. These statements have statements within them that appear between brackets. Let's take a look at an example:

```
if (book == "Flash Unleashed") {
    trace ("Your on the right track");
}
```

The first statement is an `if` statement (`if` statements are discussed in greater detail later in this chapter) that contains a function statement. Notice that not only is the `trace` function held between brackets, but it is indented as well. This indentation is not a requirement but is used for improved readability. You can, however, turn on the option to have statements indent automatically: Choose Auto Format under the ActionScript preferences or press Ctrl+Shift+F. You can even adjust the settings of the automatic formatting under Auto Format preferences.

Also, note that the lines with curly brackets do not have semicolons. You can put semicolons on closing curly brackets, but it is not necessary. What's more, the closing bracket is aligned with the beginning of the line that the opening bracket is on. Again, this is not a requirement; it's just placed this way for ease of readability.

The closing bracket is required if an opening bracket is used; otherwise, the interpreter will send an error message like this one:

```
Statement block must be terminated by '}'
```

Even though the earlier code is in brackets, because only one statement is held within the `if` statement, the use of brackets is not required. Instead, the code can be written like this:

```
if (book == "Flash Unleashed") trace ("You're on the right track");
```

As a personal preference, I use brackets in conditional statements, even if they are not required, just for consistency.

Another type of statement that uses brackets is a user-defined function. Here's an example:

```
function myFunction (myVariable:String):Void{
    trace (myVariable);
}
var name:String = "David";
myFunction (name);
//output: David
```

Again, the statement held within the function appears between brackets and is also indented for easy reading and consistency.

Now that we have gone over some of the basic syntax of statements, let's cover some of the statement categories in more detail.

Object Statements

This section covers a couple of the statements associated directly with objects. These include the with statement and the for in statement.

The with Statement

The with statement is for controlling multiple properties or methods of an object without the hassle of retyping the object over and over. Just place the object's name in the parentheses, and the properties and methods listed between the brackets are the ones affected for that object. Here's an example:

```
//first create an object
var myObject:Object = new Object();
with (myObject){
    //set 2 properites
      height = 50;
      width = 100;
    //call a method
      setName("Rectangle");
}
```

Another use of the with statement involves associating it with a movie clip and using some of the drawing API features available in Flash.

In this example, you create an empty movie clip on the main stage; then, using the onEnterFrame event, you'll make it possible for a line to be drawn wherever the mouse goes. You will also use a simple Math.random() method to make the line change color constantly to add a little style.

```
//create the empty movie clip
this.createEmptyMovieClip("line_mc",1);
//now the event that will allow a line to follow the mouse
line_mc.onEnterFrame=function(){
    with(line_mc){
        lineStyle(5,Math.random()*0x10000000,100);
        lineTo(_xmouse,_ymouse);
    }
}
```

As you can see, using with allows you to associate the drawing actions with a single movie at once, instead of having to associate each action individually, like this:

```
//create the empty movie clip
this.createEmptyMovieClip("line_mc",1);
```

```
//now the event that will allow a line to follow the mouse
line_mc.onEnterFrame=function(){
    line_mc.lineStyle(5,Math.random()*0x10000000,100);
    line_mc.lineTo(_xmouse,_ymouse);
}
```

As you have seen, the with statement can be very powerful, especially if it's used in conjunction with a function, as in the following example:

```
function myFunction (myMovie:MovieClip){
    with (myMovie){
        _x=50;
        _y=20;
        trace (myMovie._name);
    }
}
```

Now, all you have to do is call the function with any movie clip and all the properties and methods associated with the with statement will be applied to that clip.

The for in Statement

The for in statement is an advanced loop statement that's associated directly with objects. Unlike other loop statements, which run based on a defined condition, the for in statement runs until all properties of the assigned object are evaluated.

The syntax for this statement can be difficult, so it's important that you read this section carefully. Start with the for keyword; then add an opening parenthesis and the keyword var. Following that, name the variable that will hold each property name for the object; then add the keyword in. Next, place the name of the object you are using followed by a closing parenthesis and an opening bracket. Between the brackets is where you'll place the code that will use the properties of the object. Let's take a look at a generic template:

```
for (var myProp in myObject){
    //the code to use the properties;
}
```

This seems simple enough, so now let's go over how to use the properties. There are two types of property calls: one calls the property's name, and the other calls the property's value.

The first type of property call uses the variable you created to hold the property names. An example will help make this clearer.

First, let's create an object we can use for the rest of the exercise; then we'll use the for in statement to call each property's name in this object:

```
var contact:Object = new Object();
contact.name = "David";
```

```
contact.age = 25;
contact.state = "VA";
for (var myProp in contact){
    trace (myProp);
}
//output: state
//        age
//        name
```

In the preceding example, we traced the variable we created to hold each property in our object. As you'll notice, it does not start at the beginning, but rather at the end, and it moves toward the beginning.

Now that you know how to pull the names of the properties, let's go over how to pull the values of each property. To get the value of each property, use the object's name (in this case, contact) and connect it to the variable you created inside of brackets. Here is the example:

```
var contact:Object = new Object();
contact.name = "David";
contact.age = 25;
contact.state = "VA";
for (var myProp in contact){
    trace (contact[myProp]);
}
//output: VA
//        25
//        David
```

You know how to get the names of the properties, and you just saw how to get the values. Now let's combine the two:

```
var space:String = " "
var contact:Object = new Object();
contact.name = "David";
contact.age = 25;
contact.state = "VA";
for (var myProp in contact){
    trace (myProp + ":" + space + contact[myProp]);
}
//output: state: VA
//        age: 25
//        name: David
```

Let's not stop there; let's take a big step forward and set the for in statement to a function. Then you'll place all the properties of the object in an array as named elements (see Chapter 10, "Arrays," for more on arrays):

```
var contact:Object = new Object();
contact.name = "David";
contact.age = 25;
contact.state = "VA";
var my_array:Array = new Array();
function makeArray (myObject:Object, arr:Array):Void{
    for (var myProp in myObject){
        arr[myProp] = myObject[myProp];
    }
}
makeArray(contact, my_array); //call the function
trace (my_array.name);
//output: David
```

While we are on the subject of arrays, note that you can also pull each element out of an array using the for in statement, as if it were a property of an object. Here's an example:

```
var my_array:Array = new Array ("David",25,"VA");
var space:String = " ";
for (var element in my_array){
    trace (element + ":" + space + my_array[element]);
}
//output: 2: VA
//        1: 25
//        0: David
```

The for in statement also works on named array elements, as you can see here:

```
var my_array:Array = new Array ("David",25,"VA");
my_array.city = "Richmond";
var space:String = " ";
for (var element in my_array){
    trace (element + ":" + space + my_array[element]);
}
//output: city: Richmond
//        2: VA
//        1: 25
//        0: David
```

Now that we have discussed object statements, let's move on to flow modifiers.

Flow Modifiers

So far, we have gone over ActionScript as a language that executes code, one line after the other, without stopping. Now we are going to go over some statements that redefine how ActionScript functions.

Flow modifiers are statements that adjust the natural order the interpreter takes when reading ActionScript. When the interpreter hits a flow modifier, it doesn't just run the statement and move on. Instead, it runs the statement to see whether a condition has been met. If the condition hasn't been met, sometimes the interpreter will move on, but other times it will stay at that spot until the condition has been met. In most cases, this condition is user defined.

The first category of the flow modifiers we'll cover is the conditional statement.

Conditional Statements

Conditional statements are statements that are executed only when their conditions have been met. These conditions are based on Boolean values (either `true` or `false`). Here's an example of how a conditional statement acts:

```
if (true){
    //do something;
}
```

You'll often use conditional statements in situations where you want to test whether to run certain code. Without these condition statements, every piece of ActionScript you place in the Actions panel would run without being checked for whether it is necessary or even correct.

An example is a game where, after the user has finished, the ActionScript checks whether this user's score is higher than the present high score. If it is, the user's score becomes the new high score. However, if the user's score is not higher than the present high score, the new score will not replace the present one.

The code for this might look something like the following:

```
if (userScore > highScore) {
    highScore = userScore;
}
```

Everything between the parentheses is the *condition*, and the symbol between the two variables is the *comparison operator*. Before going on with more examples of conditional statements, we should go over each of the comparison operators and their uses.

Comparison Operators

If everything between the parentheses in a conditional statement is the condition, the comparison operator is the type of condition. This operator tells the conditional statement how to evaluate the data in the condition. Here's a list of the comparison operators:

- Equality (==)
- Inequality (!=)
- Less than (<)

- Less than or equal to (<=)
- Greater than (>)
- Greater than or equal to (>=)
- Strict equality (===)
- Strict inequality (!==)

Equality Operator (==)

This operator determines whether two pieces of data are equal to one another. Here are some examples:

```
var title:String = "Unleashed";        //creates our variable

if (title == "Unleashed"){        //evaluates to true

if (title == "Not Unleashed"){    //evaluates to false
```

Inequality Operator (!=)

This operator determines whether two pieces of data are not equal (note the exclamation point before the equal sign). Here are three examples:

```
var title:String = "Unleashed";        //creates our variable

if (title != "Unleashed"){        //evaluates to false

if (title != "Not Unleashed"){    //evaluates to true
```

Less-Than Operator (<)

This operator determines whether the variable on the left has a lower value than the variable on the right. Here are three examples:

```
var myAge:Number = 25;
var yourAge:Number = 26;
var myName:String = "David";
var yourName:String = "Jeremy";    //create all the variables we need

if (yourAge < myAge){        //evaluates to false

if (myName < yourName){        //evaluates to true
```

> **NOTE**
>
> Keep in mind that strings are evaluated based on their ASCII code point, not the letter itself.
>
> Therefore the upper- and lowercase versions of the same letter will not be equal to each other.

Less Than or Equal To Operator (<=)

This operator evaluates whether the data on the left is less than the data on the right. If this is true, or if they are equal, the condition will evaluate to true. Here are a few more examples:

```
var myAge:Number = 25;
var yourAge:Number = 26;
var myName:String = "David";    //create all the variables we need


if (myAge <= yourAge){    //evaluates to true


if ("David" <= myName){    //evaluates to true
```

Greater-Than Operator (>)

This operator determines whether the data on the left is greater than the data on the right. Following are three examples:

```
var myAge:Number = 25;
var yourAge = 24;
var myName = "David";
var yourName = "Ben";    //create all the variables we need


if (myAge > yourAge){    //evaluates to true


if (yourName > myName){    //evaluates to false
```

Greater Than or Equal To Operator (>=)

This operator determines whether the data on the left is greater than or equal to the data on the right. Either would evaluate this condition to true. Following are three examples:

```
var myAge:Number = 22;
var yourAge:Number = 24;
var myName:String = "David";    //create all the variables we need


if (myAge >= yourAge){    //evaluates to false


if ("David" >= myName){    //evaluates to true
```

Strict Equality (===)

This operator not only determines whether the values are equal, but also whether they are the same type of value. Notice the triple equal sign, in contrast to the double equal sign for the regular equality operator. Here are four examples:

```
if (5 == 5){    //evaluates to true


if (5 == "5"){    //evaluates to true
```

```
if (5 === 5){       //evaluates to true

if (5 === "5"){   //evaluates to false
```

Notice how that with an equality sign, the string value "5" is evaluated as being equal to the number 5, but with strict equality, they are not equal.

Strict Inequality (!==)

This operator not only determines whether the values are not equal but also determines whether the values are not the same type (note the exclamation point in front of the double equal signs). Here are four examples:

```
if (5 != 5){        //evaluates to false

if (5 != "5"){      //evaluates to false

if (5 !== 5){       //evaluates to false

if (5 !== "5"){    //evaluates to true
```

Strict equality and strict inequality are very useful, not only for determining whether two values are the same, but also whether they are being used the same.

Now that we have gone over the comparison operators, let's get back into the conditional statements, starting with the if statement.

The if Statement

You have been using the if statement for some time without a formal introduction, so let's start with the basics of how this statement works.

The if statement works like a simple "yes or no" questionnaire: If true, then run the code in the curly brackets; if false, skip the code in the curly brackets and move on.

The if statement starts out with the keyword if and is followed by a condition, which is any comparison expression held within parentheses. This is followed by an opening curly bracket, which is followed by all the ActionScript that is to run if the condition evaluates to true. Finally, a closing curly bracket finishes the statement.

The simplest of if statements involves actually placing a Boolean value right into the condition, as shown here:

```
if (true){
    trace ("True");
}
if(false){
    trace ("False");
}
//output: True
```

In this case, only "True" will be traced because it is within the only condition that evaluates to true. The condition that was set to false is skipped after it is evaluated.

You can also use the numeric equivalent to the Boolean representation to accomplish the same effect:

```
if (1){
      trace ("True");
}
if(0){
      trace ("False");
}
//output: True
```

Again, only "True" is traced because 0 is equal to the Boolean value false. This is a good tool for evaluating numbers, because any nonzero number will be considered true. Here's an example that checks to see whether there is any change between two test scores:

```
var myScore:Number = 80;
var previousScore:Number = 86;
if (myScore-previousScore){
      trace ("Something's changed");
}
//output: Something's changed
```

You can also use variables in if statements that hold values that translate to Boolean values or are Boolean values themselves:

```
var myVariable:Number = 1;
if (myVariable){
      trace ("True");
}
//output: True
```

Another great feature of the if statement is that it can check whether a movie clip instance exists. Place the name of the instance in the condition, and if this instance exists, the if statement will evaluate to true; otherwise, it will evaluate to false.

Let's look at an example. First, create a shape on the main stage and then convert it to a symbol by going to the toolbar and selecting Modify, Convert to Symbol (F8). Then name the instance **myMovie_mc**.

Next, create a new layer and call the layer **actions**.

Then place the following code in the first frame on the main timeline in the Actions layer:

```
if (myMovie_mc){
      trace ("myMovie_mc exists");
```

```
}
//output: myMovie_mc exists
```

This is great, but if you want to check for a certain movie on the go, set it to a function, as shown here:

```
function findMovie (movie:MovieClip):Void{
     if (movie){
          trace (movie +" exists");
     }
}
findMovie(myMovie_mc);    //call the function
//output: myMovie_mc exists
```

Now, whenever the movie exists on the same timeline as the function when the function is invoked with the proper name, the phrase will be displayed in the output window.

You can also test a single variable to see whether it is "not true" in a conditional statement using the logical NOT operator.

The Logical NOT Operator (!)

The logical NOT operator is used to show inequality or to test whether something is false. Place an exclamation point in front of the variable or expression you want to evaluate as "not true," as shown here:

```
var myVariable:Boolean = false;
if (!myVariable) {
     trace ("myVariable is false");
}
//output: myVariable is false
```

This, when used in conjunction with the function we just created, can determine whether there is no instance of a specific movie on the stage:

```
function findMovie (movie:MovieClip):Void{
   if (!movie){
     trace ("the movie does not exist");
   }
}
findMovie(myMovie_mc);    //call the function
```

The function we created determines whether the movie does not exist, and if it doesn't, the trace function is run.

Now that you've seen the basic workings of the if statement, we'll cover nested if statements.

Nested `if` Statements

Nested `if` statements are `if` statements held by other `if` statements to check more than one condition. You simply put the nested statement in as if it were a regular statement held within the original `if` statement. Here's an example:

```
var bookTitle:String = "Unleashed";
var name:String = "David";
if (bookTitle == "Unleashed"){
    if (name == "David"){
        trace ("They both match");
    }
}
//output: They both match
```

If the nested `if` statement evaluates to `false`, even with the original `if` statement evaluating to `true`, the `trace` function will not be run. Here's an example:

```
var bookTitle:String = "Unleashed";
var name:String = "David";
if (bookTitle == "Unleashed"){
    if (name == "Kevin"){
        trace ("They both match");
    }
}
//output: (nothing)
```

If the original `if` statement evaluates to `false`, the nested `if` statement will not even be evaluated. Again, the `trace` function will not be run. Here's an example:

```
var bookTitle:String = "Unleashed";
var name:String = "David";
if (bookTitle == "Flash"){
    if (name == "David"){
        trace ("They both match");
    }
}
//output: (nothing)
```

Now that you have seen how to evaluate multiple conditional statements using nested `if` statements, let's do the same thing the easy way, using a logical operator.

The AND Operator (&&)

In the condition part of an `if` statement, you can place multiple conditions using the short-circuit AND operator. After the first condition, place a space, followed by two ampersands (&&) and then the second condition. Let's look at our previous example using this operator:

```
var bookTitle:String = "Unleashed";
var name:String = "David";
if (bookTitle == "Unleashed" && name == "David"){
     trace ("They both match");
}
//output: They both match
```

As with nested if statements, both conditions must evaluate to true for the entire condition to evaluate to true. Here's an example:

```
var bookTitle:String = "Unleashed";
var name:String = "David";
if (bookTitle == "Unleashed" && name == "Kevin"){
     trace ("They both match");
}
//output: (nothing)
```

You can place many of these operators in a single conditional statement for checking multiple conditions, as shown here:

```
var bookTitle:String = "Unleashed";
var name:String = "David";
if (bookTitle == "Unleashed" && name == "David" && true){
     trace ("Everything is working");
}
//output: Everything is working
```

> **NOTE**
>
> Although you can see the benefits of using the AND operator (&&) as far as readability versus using nested if statements, there is a benefit sometimes to using nested if statements. When using a nested if statement to check multiple conditionals at once, you can have code run from the first condition independent of the results of the second condition; however, with the AND operator, both conditions must be met.

Now that you know how to check multiple conditions to see whether each is true, let's see whether any of the conditions are true using another logical operator.

The OR Operator (¦¦)

Oftentimes you'll want to see whether any one of a set of conditions is correct. To do this without the logical OR operator requires multiple if statements with the same response over and over, if any of the conditional statements are met. Let's take a look at what this would look like:

```
var name:String = "David";
var age:Number = 25;
if (name == "David"){
```

```
        trace ("One of them is correct");
}
if (age == 35) {
        trace ("One of them is correct");
}
//output: One of them is correct
```

Because the first conditional statement evaluates to true, the trace function is run. But what if both the if statements evaluate to true?

```
var name:String = "David";
var age:Number = 25;
if (name == "David"){
        trace ("One of them is correct");
}
if (age == 25) {
        trace ("One of them is correct");
}
//output: One of them is correct
//        One of them is correct
```

The problem we encounter using multiple if statements to determine whether one of them evaluates to true is that if they are both correct, both sections of code are executed, thus creating duplication. We could overcome this by using a test variable to hold a value if the first conditional statement is met. Instead, however, we are going to use the logical OR operator. The syntax of this operator is ¦¦ (Shift+\). Place this operator between conditions in the condition statement, separating them with a space on both sides. Let's take a look at this using our previous example:

```
var name:String = "David";
var age:Number = 25;
if (name == "David" ¦¦ age == 25){
        trace ("One of them is correct");
}
//output: One of them is correct
```

Now the interpreter reads the statement and checks to see whether the first condition is met. If so, it skips the second condition because of the OR operator and runs the trace function. If the first condition is not met, the interpreter evaluates the second condition, and if this condition is met, the trace function is run. If neither condition is met, the interpreter simply moves on.

With the OR operator, you can check to see whether any one of multiple conditions will be met. Here's an example:

```
var name:String = "David";
var age:Number = 25;
```

```
if (name == "Kevin" || age == 35 || true){
     trace ("One of them is correct");
}
//output: One of them is correct
```

Because neither of the first two conditions evaluates to true, the third condition is evaluated to true and the trace function is run.

Another type of conditional statement is known as the conditional. We'll cover this type of conditional statement before moving on because it acts very similar to an if statement.

The Conditional (?:)

The conditional is more of an expression than a conditional statement, although it does have a conditional statement in it.

The syntax is a condition followed by a question mark, a value (which we'll call *value 1*), a colon, and then another value (which we'll call *value 2*). It looks like this:

```
(condition) ? value 1 : value2;
```

If the condition evaluates to true, the expression's value is equal to value 1. If the condition does not evaluate to true, the expression's value is equal to value 2.

This is nice if you want to run a simple conditional statement without typing a lot. Here's an example:

```
var myVariable:Number = 1;
var myVariable2:Number = 2;
//set myVariable3 to the smallest variable
var myVariable3 = (myVariable < myVariable2) ? myVariable : myvariable2;
trace (myVariable3);
//output: 1
```

Let's look at another applied example:

```
var myPassword:String = "flash";
var userPassword:String = "flash";
trace ((myPassword == userPassword) ? "Correct" : "Incorrect");
//output: Correct
```

As you'll notice, the previous conditional statement not only does something if the condition evaluates to true but also if it does not evaluate to true. You can also create a statement that will run if the conditional in an if statement does not evaluate to true. These statements are called else statements.

The else Statement

An else statement is used in conjunction with an if statement. If the if statement does not evaluate to true, the else statement runs its code.

The syntax for `else` statements is like the syntax for other conditional statements, except it has no condition. It runs when the evaluator reaches it. Here's an example:

```
var name:String = "David";
if (name == "Kevin"){
      trace ("The name is Kevin");
}else{
      trace ("The name is not Kevin");
}
//output: The name is not Kevin
```

Because the `if` statement does not evaluate to `true`, the `else` statement is run. If the `if` statement does evaluate to `true`, the `else` statement is not read by the interpreter. Here's another example:

```
var name:String = "David";
if (name == "David"){
      trace ("The name is David");
}else{
      trace ("The name is not David");
}
//output: The name is David
```

Now let's take a look at a more practical example of using the `else` statement, this time as an age-verification check:

```
//create a date object
var date:Date = new Date();
//get the year
var year:Number = date.getFullYear();
var inputYear:Number = 1984;
//see the difference in inputYear and year
var age:Number = year-inputYear;
//evaluate if they are old enough
if (age>=21) {
    gotoAndPlay("welcome");
} else {
    gotoAndPlay("tooYoung");
}
```

Now that you have seen what the `else` statement can do when joined with an `if` statement, let's look at the `else if` statement to see how it works in conjunction with the other two.

The else if Statement

The else if statement allows you to run through several conditional statements in your code, and each is read only if the preceding conditional statement does not evaluate to true.

The syntax for the else if statement is nearly identical to the if statement, except that it has a preceding keyword of else, as demonstrated here:

```
var bookTitle:String = "Unleashed";
if (bookTitle == "Flash") {
     trace ("The title is Flash");
}else if (bookTitle == "Unleashed") {
     trace ("The title is Unleashed");
}else {
     trace ("We don't know what the title is");
}
//output: The title is Unleashed
```

Now that you understand the significance of the else if statement, let's take a look at the same code but without the else if statement:

```
var bookTitle:String = "Unleashed";
if (bookTitle == "Flash"){
     trace ("The bookTitle is Flash");
}else{
     if (bookTitle == "Unleashed") {
          trace ("The title is Unleashed");
     }else{
          trace ("We don't know what the title is");
     }
}
//output: The title is Unleashed
```

Besides fewer lines being required, the code is much easier to read in the first example than it is in the second one.

So far we have covered the if statement, the else statement, and the else if statement. Now let's go over another type of conditional statement: switch. We'll also discuss some of its methods.

switch, case, default, and break

A switch statement is used much like an if statement: It evaluates a condition and runs the code associated with that condition if the condition evaluates to true.

The syntax is difficult to understand, so don't feel bad if you don't get it the first time around.

The statement starts with the keyword switch, followed by a value in a set of parentheses and then an opening curly bracket. The value in the parentheses is usually a variable that you are looking for in strict equality (===) in your set of cases.

After the opening curly bracket, you begin to use the keyword case, followed by a space and another value and a colon. After the colon, you can put in any code you want to execute if the case evaluates to true. The value before the colon is what the switch is searching on, and it can be any data type. After the code you want to execute, place the keyword break to stop the code from going on to the next case without evaluating it.

Then, after all your cases, place the keyword default and a colon and then the code to be executed if none of the cases evaluates to true (like the else statement works).

That's a lot to do, so before we look at an applied example, let's see what all this looks like:

```
switch (mainValue) {
    case value1:
        //code to be executed;
        break;
    case value2:
        //code to be executed
        break;
    case value3:
        //code to be executed
        break;
    default:
        //default code to be executed
}
```

The preceding is fairly generic. Now let's see it using real information:

```
var name:String = "David";
switch (name) {
case "Jonathan":
    trace ("Jonathan is the name");
    break;
case "Linda":
    trace ("Linda is the name");
    break;
case "David":
    trace ("David is the name");
    break;
```

```
case "Shelley":
      trace ("Shelley is the name");
      break;
default:
      trace ("There isn't a name");
}
//output: David is the name
```

As previously stated, the break keyword plays a big part in executing this code smoothly. To prove this point, let's see what happens without it:

```
var name:String = "David";
switch (name) {
case "Jonathan":
      trace ("Jonathan is the name");
case "Linda":
      trace ("Linda is the name");
case "David":
      trace ("David is the name");
case "Shelley":
      trace ("Shelley is the name");
default:
      trace ("There isn't a name");
}

//output: David is the name
//        Shelley is the name
//        There isn't a name
```

And of course, if the variable is not found, the default keyword will execute its code:

```
var name:String = "Jeremy";
switch (name) {
case "Jonathan":
      trace ("Jonathan is the name");
      break;
case "Linda":
      trace ("Linda is the name");
      break;
```

```
case "David":
      trace ("David is the name");
      break;
case "Shelley":
      trace ("Shelley is the name");
      break;
default:
      trace ("There isn't a name");
}
```

```
//output: There isn't a name
```

You can also pass expressions as case values to see if they evaluate to true (similar to having a condition for each case). Here is an example that looks to see which letter is in a word:

```
var name:String = "David";
switch (true) {
case (name.indexOf("z") != -1):
    trace ("There is a 'z' in the name.");
    break;
case (name.indexOf("x") != -1):
    trace ("There is an 'x' in the name.");
    break;
case (name.indexOf("v") != -1):
    trace ("There is a 'v' in the name.");
    break;
default:
    trace("I don't know what letters are in name.");
}
```

```
//output: There is a 'v' in the name.
```

The preceding example goes through a few letters to determine if they are present in the word. And because the value you are looking for is the Boolean true, you can set several expressions that evaluate to true or false for each case.

We have covered the basics of conditional statements. Now it's time to move to the next group of flow modifiers: loop statements.

Loop Statements

Much like conditional statements, loop statements use conditions to modify the flow of ActionScript. Unlike conditional statements, loop statements run continuously until the condition has been met (evaluates to `false`).

We have already seen one loop statement—the `for in` loop statement used with objects. This statement is specific to objects; the other loop statements we'll cover have a different syntax from the `for in` loop statement.

Let's jump right in with our first loop statement: the `while` loop.

The `while` Loop

The `while` loop runs similarly to an `if` statement: If the condition is true, the statement runs its code. Unlike an `if` statement, however, a `while` loop will start over and run again until the condition is no longer true.

The `while` loop's syntax is very similar to that of the `if` statement as well, except it uses the keyword `while`, followed by the condition and an opening curly bracket that encloses the ActionScript to be run while the condition is true, along with a closing curly bracket that ends the statement.

Because the statement will run until the condition is not true, you must make sure the loop will eventually end. Otherwise, processor power can be affected and errors can occur. Let's take a look at an example:

```
var i:Number = 0;
while (i < 4) {
     trace (i);
     i++;
}
//output: 0
//        1
//        2
//        3
```

Notice that we put an incremental variable in the code to be run while the condition is true. This incremental variable is what shuts down the loop. Let's see what would happen if we didn't have that incremental variable:

```
var i:Number = 0;
while (i < 4) {
     trace (i);
}
//output: (an error message that says that a script in the movie is causing
//the flash player to run slowly, and then it asks do you want to abort)
```

This is why ending a loop statement at some point is very important. Another way to cause the loop statement to end is to use a break script. We covered the keyword `break` in the earlier section on `switch` statements. Now we're going to use it to end loops.

The break **Keyword**

The break keyword is often used to end long-running loop statements. The syntax is simple: Place the keyword break at the end of the code you would like run while the condition is true and follow it with a semicolon to end the line.

Let's take another look at our previous unstopping loop statement, but this time with the break keyword added:

```
var i:Number = 0;
while (i < 4) {
        trace (i);
        break;
}
//output: 0
```

Because the condition is true, the loop statement is run until the point where the interpreter hits the break keyword. After reaching break, the interpreter moves as if the condition is no longer true.

The while loop can also be used to duplicate movie clips much easier than manually duplicating them, as you will see in the following example.

1. Create a new Flash document.

2. Draw a small rectangle (about 100×100) in the top-left corner of the stage, as shown in Figure 11.1.

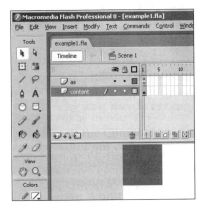

FIGURE 11.1 Draw a rectangle in the top-left corner.

3. Convert the rectangle to a movie clip symbol (F8) and then give it an instance name of **rec_mc**.

4. Now create a new layer, name it **actions**, and in the first frame, place the following code:

```
var i:Number = 0;
var amount:Number = 7;
while (i<=amount) {
        duplicateMovieClip("rec_mc", "rec_mc"+i, i)
        rec_mc._y =i * rec_mc._width;
        rec_mc._x =i * rec_mc._width;
        i++;
}
//this simply cleans the first duplicated movie
rec_mc0._visible = false;
```

Now test the movie by going to the toolbar and selecting Control, Test Movie (Ctrl+Enter).

Now you have steps (see Figure 11.2). Even if you want to duplicate each instance of the movie clip manually, you would have a line for each single time you create a new instance.

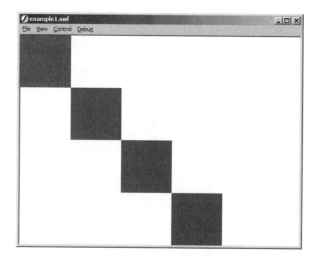

FIGURE 11.2   After the movie is tested, it should look similar to a staircase effect.

You can also set the condition to something a little more dynamic, such as the `length` property of a string or array. Let's take a look:

```
var date:Date = new Date();
var fullDate:Array = new Array();
fullDate.push(date.getDate());
fullDate.push(date.getMonth()+1);
fullDate.push(date.getFullYear());
var i:Number = 0;
var myDate:String = "";
```

```
while (i < fullDate.length){
     myDate +=fullDate[i];
     if (i < fullDate.length-1){
          myDate += "-";
     }
     i++;
}
trace (myDate);
//output: (the date from your system clock formatted like 25-6-2005)
```

Now you have a nice-looking full date that's dynamic! These are just a few of the hundreds of ways the while loop can be used. Other examples might include creating "bad guys" in a game while your character has enough energy, or while your screen still has room, fill it with text from an RSS feed.

Next, we'll take a look at another type of loop statement: the do while loop.

The do while Loop

The do while loop works identically to the while loop in that it runs its code while the set condition evaluates to true. The syntax, however, is completely different.

The syntax for the do while loop starts with the keyword do, followed by an opening curly bracket. Then comes the code to be executed while the condition evaluates to true. On the next line, following the last line of code to be executed, is a closing curly bracket followed by the keyword while, which is then followed by the condition inside a set of parentheses. Finally, a semicolon is used to end the line. Let's take a look at a generic template:

```
do {
     //code to be executed while true
}while (condition);
```

That's the basic format of the do while loop. Now let's revisit a couple of previous examples to see how they can be used with do while. Here's the first example:

```
var i:Number = 0;
do{
     trace (i);
     i++;
}while (i<4);
//output: 0
//        1
//        2
//        3
```

This is just a basic loop with an incremental variable. Now let's revisit the duplicate movie example and see how it would work with a do while loop:

```
var i:Number = 0;
var amount:Number = 7;
do{
        duplicateMovieClip("rec_mc", "rec_mc"+i, i)
        rec_mc._y =i * rec_mc._width;
        rec_mc._x =i * rec_mc._width;
        i++;
} while (i<=amount);
//this simply cleans the first duplicated movie
rec_mc0._visible = false;
```

Just like before, the staircase appears (see Figure 11.3).

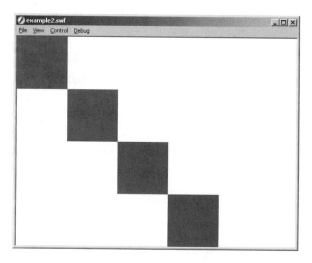

FIGURE 11.3   Here again is the staircase effect after you test the movie.

As you can see, the do while loop works identically to the while loop, just with different syntax.

Let's move on to our next loop statement: the for loop.

The for Loop

The for loop works like the other loop statements. It has a condition as well as code to be executed while the condition evaluates to true. The difference is that the condition and the incremental variable are both held in the same area.

The syntax of the for loop begins with the keyword for, followed by an opening parenthesis. However, instead of placing the condition first, you create an incremental variable and set a value to it. This variable is followed by a semicolon. After the first semicolon, you create your condition, which again is followed by a semicolon. After the second semi-colon, you adjust your incremental variable according to how you want it to work so that the loop will have an end. Then use a closing parenthesis and an opening curly bracket to end the line. The code to be executed begins on the following line, and the statement ends with a closing curly bracket. Here's the generic template of the for loop:

```
for (incremental variable; condition; adjustment of our variable){
//code to be executed
}
```

You may find this difficult to understand without real information, so let's put some in:

```
for (var i:Number = 0; i<4; i++){
    trace (i);
}
//output: 0
//        1
//        2
//        3
```

In this case, you created your incremental variable, i, and put a condition in i<4. Then you increased your variable so that the loop will end eventually.

This is all pretty basic, but you can put it to a function and make it more dynamic by attaching the function to whatever you want.

Next, you'll create a basic function using your for loop, and you'll separate each charac-ter in a string, place each character in an array that you create (more on arrays in Chapter 10), and then reverse the array and place it back into a variable as a string. Here's the code:

```
//create a function with just one variable
function reverseString(string:String):Void{
//create a blank array
    var my_array:Array = new Array();
//get each character and put it in the array
        for (var i:Number=0;i<string.length;i++){
            my_array[i] = string.charAt(i);
        }
//reverse the array
        my_array.reverse();
//use an empty string to join each character
//then set it equal to the original string
        var newString:String = my_array.join("");
        trace (newString);
}
//create a variable holding a string literal
var name:String = "David";
```

```
//call function
reverseString(name)
//output:divaD
```

In this function, you use the `for` loop to make sure you retrieve each character in your string.

You can also use nested `for` loops to pull even more information out of data types. This next example takes strings in an array and counts each one. Then it returns the string that appears most often (notice the use of nested `for` loops). Here's the code:

```
//create the function
function stringCount(theArray:Array):Void {
    //sort the array
    theArray.sort(1);
    //create the variables we need
    var preCount:Number = 1;
    var count:Number = 0;
    for (var i:Number = 0; i<=theArray.length-1; i++) {
        for (var j:Number = (i+1); j<=theArray.length-1; j++) {
            //change the element with the .toUpperCase () method when counting
            //because flash distinguishes between upper case and lower case letters
            if (theArray[i].toUpperCase() == theArray[j].toUpperCase()) {
                preCount += 1;
                //check to see if the new element
➥ has a higher frequency than the previous
                if (preCount>count) {
                    count = precount;
                    preCount = 1;
                    name = theArray[i];
                }
            }
        }
    }
    //then the answer is changed  to upper case and displayed in the output window
    trace(name.toUpperCase());
}
//example array
var myArray:Array = new Array("David", "eddie", "Lou",
➥"John", "Jeremy", "eddie", "jeremy", "Eddie");
//run the function
stringCount(myArray);
//output: EDDIE
```

You can also place multiple variables and conditions in loop statements, but this tends to produce surprising results.

Multiple Conditions in Loop Statements

Using multiple conditions in loop statements can serve a variety of purposes when you are dealing with multiple objects. For instance, we'll create two variables, i and j, and set them to 0 and 3, respectively. Then we'll increase each by 1 and test them both with a "less than 5" condition. First, we'll use the logical OR operator and test it; then we will use the short-circuit AND operator and test it. Finally, we'll discuss the results.

When placing multiple variables in for loops, separate them with commas, as shown here:

```
for (var i = 0, j = 3; i<5 || j<5;i++,j++){
      trace ("j="+j);
      trace ("i="+i);
}


//output j=3
//      i=0
//      j=4
//        i=1
//        j=5
//      i=2
//        j=6
//      i=3
//        j=7
//      i=4
```

Now we will use the short-circuit AND operator:

```
for (var i = 0, j = 3; i<5 && j<5;i++,j++){
      trace ("j="+j);
      trace ("i="+i);
}
//output j=3
//        i=0
//        j=4
//        i=1
```

This time, j counts up to 4 and i counts to 1.

This seems almost backward to what you learned about these two operators as they relate to conditional statements, because in loop statements, as long as a condition is true, the code will run. Therefore, in the case of the OR operator, as long as either of the conditions evaluates to true, the statement will run. When you used the AND operator, on the other hand, they both had to evaluate to true for the statement to continue to run.

That just about covers loop statements. However, you should know that using loop statements is not the only way to create loops in Flash. There are also event handler loops as well as timeline loops. Let's discuss them next.

Event Handler Loops

In Chapter 14, "Events," we will cover event handlers in more detail. For now, though, we're just going to cover one: the onEnterFrame event. This clip event is placed on the timeline of a movie clip instance (or the main timeline) and runs constantly. You can use conditional statements to create a mock loop, if you want.

For example, suppose you want to wait a little bit before moving on to the next frame of a movie. You could place the following on the main timeline in frame actions:

```
var i:Number = 0;
this.onEnterFrame=function(){
      if (i>=50){
            trace ("go to next frame");
            delete this.onEnterFrame;
      }else{
            trace ("not yet");
      }
      i++;
}
//output (a lot of "not yet"'s and "go to next frame")
```

Now, because of the onEnterFrame event, the movie will not move on until i is equal to 50.

Another type of loop is the timeline loop, which is covered next.

The Timeline Loop

A timeline loop uses a timeline and a set number of frames in that timeline to continuously play through a movie. Let's see one in action.

First, go to the second frame of the main timeline and insert a blank frame by going to the toolbar and choosing Insert, Timeline, Blank Key Frame (F7).

Now, in the first frame of the main timeline (on the same layer, because there should only be one layer), place the following code:

```
trace ("This is a loop");
```

Now when you test this code, you will see "This is a loop" a bunch of times, until you stop the movie from running.

You can also use goto functions to create a conditioned timeline loop. As an example, place three keyframes on the main timeline and use the following lines of code on the indicated frames.

Here's the code for frame 1:

```
var i:Number = 0;
```

Here's the code for frame 2:

```
i++;
```

Finally, here's the code for frame 3:

```
if (i<5){
      trace (i);
      gotoAndPlay (2);
}else {
      stop();
}
```

The output is the numbers 1–4.

Summary

In this chapter, we have covered expressions, including conditionals and enough loops to make anyone dizzy. One of the major points to remember about loops and conditionals is that they run on Boolean values or expressions that evaluate to Boolean values. Also, remember that any statement block you open with a curly bracket must be closed by a curly bracket as well. And lastly, remember when comparing strings, Flash will interpret a lowercase letter differently than the same letter in uppercase because Flash evaluates the ASCII code points of the character, not the character itself.

Continue to play with the structure and conditions of loops to really get a good feel for them and what can be accomplished using them.

CHAPTER 12

Functions

So far we have covered some of the basics of ActionScript, including variables, statements, and arrays. Now we'll get into functions.

A *function* is basically a reusable piece of code. After a function is created, it can be used over and over without your rewriting the code. This is very powerful, not only because it can save on file size, but also because it will make your code much more scalable and portable.

This chapter covers the topics of creating and using functions, as well as using functions as methods and objects. Instead of just talking about functions, let's jump right in and create one.

Creating a Function

Creating a function is as easy as using the keyword `function`, providing a name for the function, followed by a pair of parentheses for parameters (we discuss the topic of parameters in more depth later), then a colon, and the data type of the return value (return values are also discussed later in this chapter). After that, you can place whatever code you want between two curly brackets. It looks something like this:

```
function myFunction():ReturnType{
    //script to run in function
}
```

> **NOTE**
>
> ReturnTypes are not required, but it is good practice to have them for debugging purposes.

Now that you know what a function looks like, you can create one of your own. To begin, open a new Flash movie, click the first frame in the timeline, open the ActionScript panel (F2), and place the following code:

```
function myFunction ():Void{
    trace ("My first function");
}
```

Now you have your own function, with a simple `trace` statement placed within the curly brackets. However, if you tested your movie at this point, nothing would happen. This is because all you have done so far is create a function; now you need to run it.

> **NOTE**
>
> Notice the `Void` identifier after the parenthesis. Because we are not returning any value, `Void` is used.

Running the Function

Now that you have your function, let's make it work for you. To run this function (also called *invoking* or calling the function), you start with your function name, followed by a set of parentheses to hold your parameters, and you finish with a semicolon to end the line, as shown here:

```
function myFunction ():Void{
    trace ("My first function");
}
myFunction();
//output: My first function
```

That was easy. You created a function and then invoked it to see the statements run, and the message displayed in the Output panel.

Let's now look at another way of creating functions. This way starts with the function name that we set to the Function type. Then you set it equal to the keyword `function`, followed by a set of parentheses, a colon, and the return value type. Then the curly brackets for holding your code are added. Here's an example using a generic template:

```
var myFunction:Function = function():ReturnType{
    //script to run in function
}
```

Now let's put this into practice with the previous example:

```
var myFunction:Function = function():Void{
    trace("My second function");
}
```

```
myFunction();
//output: My second function
```

Now you have seen two basic ways of creating functions and running them. So far, all you have done is run a simple `trace` statement. Next, let's put some script in it that you can really use. We'll start with a function that fades out a movie:

```
function fadeOut():Void{
    myMovie_mc._alpha -= 5;
}
//now invoke the function
fadeOut();
```

Every time this function is invoked, the movie clip `myMovie_mc` will decrease its `alpha` value by 5. You would normally place this function within a looping event such as an `onEnterFrame` event. (For more on events, see Chapter 14.)

That was simple, but what if you only wanted to fade to a certain point? You can place conditional as well as loop statements within functions to perform a conditional test.

Here's the same example, but this time we're using an `if` statement to only allow `myMovie_mc` to fade to a certain point:

```
function fadeOut():Void{
    if(myMovie_mc._alpha >50){
        myMovie_mc._alpha-=5;
    }
}
//now invoke the function
fadeOut();
```

Now the function will check whether the movie clip has faded to the designated point yet. If it has reached the designated point, the function still runs, but the code in the `if` statement will not.

Suppose you want to set the point where the alpha will fade differently for two different functions that are invoked. This is where parameters come in.

Using Parameters in Functions

So far you have seen how to create functions and place scripts inside them. This is not very dynamic, though, in that after the information is in the function, it cannot be adjusted for different situations. Now we'll use parameters to change this limitation.

Parameters in a function act similarly to variables in ActionScript. They can be changed on-the-fly whenever the need arises. You place the parameters in parentheses following the name of the function, which looks something like this:

```
function myFunction(parameters:ParameterType):ReturnType{
    //script involving parameter;
}
```

You can also optionally set the type for the parameters, which is very helpful in debugging, as you will see in the next example.

The preceding code is simply a generic template, so let's look at some examples. The first example runs a simple trace statement:

```
//create a function with a string parameter
function myTrace(name:String):Void{
    trace(name);
}
//now we will run the function twice with two different parameters
myTrace("Eddie");
myTrace("Lou");
//output: Eddie
//        Lou
```

You can see we used the String data type to make sure that is the type of data being passed into the parameters. Notice that if you change one of the parameters to the number 15, you will receive this error in the Output panel when you test the movie or check your code:

```
**Error** Scene=Scene 1, layer=Layer 1, frame=1:Line 7: Type mismatch.
    myTrace(15);
```

The preceding example is a basic example of using parameters with functions, so let's return to the previous fading example and see how to use parameters with conditional statements.

As before, you will want to set a point that your movie clip will fade to, but this time you'll use three parameters—the instance name of the movie clip, the point to fade the movie to, and the amount to fade the movie by. In this example, you'll use a loop statement instead of a conditional statement:

```
function fade(movie:MovieClip, fadePoint:Number, amount:Number):Void{
    while(movie._alpha > fadePoint){
        movie._alpha -= amount;
    }
}
//now the function is made, let's run it on a couple movies
fade(myMovie,50,5);

function fade(movie:MovieClip, fadePoint:Number, amount:Number):Void{
    movie.onEnterFrame = function(){
        if(movie._alpha > fadePoint){
```

```
            movie._alpha -= amount;
        }
    }
}
//now the function is made, let's run it on a couple movies
fade(myMovie_mc,50,5);
fade(myMovie2_mc,20,2);


fade(myMovie2,20,2);
```

The preceding code would be placed in the timeline where both movies reside. Also note that because we are using a while statement, the fading effect will appear instantaneous to us, but you could also use an onEnterFrame event to actually be able to view the fading, like this:

```
function fade(movie:MovieClip, fadePoint:Number, amount:Number):Void{
    movie.onEnterFrame = function(){
        if(movie._alpha > fadePoint){
            movie._alpha -= amount;
        }
    }
}
//now the function is made, let's run it on a couple movies
fade(myMovie_mc,50,5);
fade(myMovie2_mc,20,2);
```

For more on scripted animation, see Chapter 13, "The Movie Clip Object."

So far we have used functions to perform basic repetitive tasks using code that we want to consolidate and use whenever we want without having to rewrite the entire script. In the next section, you'll learn how to make functions even more valuable by returning data.

Functions That Return Values

Currently we are using functions to run repetitive code using parameters, but all the functions are doing is running code. Now let's make them give back some information. To do this, we'll use the return statement.

The return statement does two things. First, when the interpreter reaches the return statement, it causes the function to end. Second, it returns the value of an expression assigned to it, but the expression is optional. Here is a generic template:

```
function functionName (parameter:ParameterType):ReturnType{
    //script to run when function is invoked
    return expression;
}
```

This is where the ReturnType option comes in handy—because you can use strict data typing on the return value for debugging purposes.

Now let's look at an example of using the `return` statement to end a function. This example contains a conditional statement, and if the condition is met, the function will end and will not run the remaining code:

```
function myFunction (num:Number):Void{
    if(num>5){
        return;
    }
    trace("Num is smaller than 5");
}
//Now we invoke the function twice
myFunction(6);
myFunction(3);
//output: Num is smaller than 5
```

Even though the function is run twice, because the conditional statement in the first function is met, the `return` statement is run and the function is ended. In the second function, the conditional statement is not met, and the `trace` statement is run.

This time, let's use the `return` statement to return a value back to us based on an expression we apply to the `return` statement:

```
function fullName (fName:String,lName:String):String{
    return fName+" "+lName;
}
//now we set a variable to the function
var myName:String = fullName("David", "Vogeleer");
trace(myName);
//output: David Vogeleer
```

All we did was set the function to a variable, and the `return` statement returned the value of the expression we assigned to it to the variable. Notice that we set the return value to the data type *String*, and if the return value is not that data type, you will get a type mismatch error.

Using `return` statements, you can nest functions within functions and even use them as parameters.

Nested Functions

Nested functions can be a great tool if you want to run a repetitive set of scripts within a function but use the result differently in each function. Let's take a look at a couple of functions—the first will square a user-defined number, and the second will combine two squared numbers by using the return value from the first function:

```
function square(num:Number):Number{
    return num*num;
}
//Now create the second function
function combineSquares():Number{
    var square1:Number = square(2);
    var square2:Number = square(3);
    return square1 + square2;
}
//Set the variable to the second function
myNum = combineSquares();
trace(myNum);
//output: 13
```

The preceding code uses the first function (square) and nests it within a second function (combineSquares) to return a value that uses the returned value of the square function.

Now let's create a function that uses another function as a parameter. We'll use the same example as before, but this time we'll set the square function as a parameter:

```
function square(num:Number):Number{
    return num*num;
}
//Now create the second function
function combineSquares(square1:Number, square2:Number):Number{
    return square1 + square2;
}
//Set the variable to the second function
myNum = combineSquares(square(2),square(3));
trace(myNum);
//output: 13
```

As stated, you can nest functions within themselves for repetitive use if you want to use the result differently in each function.

We have talked about creating and using functions in many ways; now let's see the scope of a function.

Function Scope

The scope of a function is like the scope of a variable; it is directly available (called by name, instead of dot syntax mapping to the function) only in the following ways:

- If the function is called on the same timeline the variable was created in.
- If the function is called from a button where the function resides on the same timeline as the button that called it.

In previous versions of Flash, if none of these criteria were met, you had to use dot syntax to map to the function you created. Since Flash MX, you can use the _global identifier to create a function that is available throughout the entire Flash movie and all its timelines. (We will discuss the _global identifier later in this chapter.)

First, let's go over how to map to functions using dot syntax.

Mapping to a Function

There are two basic ways of mapping to a function:

- **Using relative or absolute identifiers**—In this case, _root refers to the root time-line of the current level the script is run on, and _parent refers to the movie clip or object that contains the movie clip or object with the script. If a script using the _parent object is placed within a movie, the script looks to the movie containing itself. Also, _levelN refers to the *n*th level in the standalone Flash player or the Flash movie.

- **Using direct movie names**—An example is myMovie.myFunction();. Notice that every movie object or movie name used in dot syntax is separated by a period.

NOTE

Although it is possible to call functions created on other timelines, it is good practice to keep all functions on the main timeline, or in an external .as file so that you will always know where to find them.

Now that you have seen some generic ways for using dot syntax to map to functions, let's look at a few examples of using them:

```
_root.myFunction ()          //invokes the function in the _root timeline
_parent.myFunction()         //invokes the function in the _parent timeline
_parent._parent.myFunction() //invokes the function in the _parent of the
                             //_parent timeline
_root.myMovie.myFunction()   //invokes the function in myMovie which is
                             //located on the _root timeline
```

As mentioned before, using dot syntax is no longer a necessity when trying to reach a function from a timeline that's different from the one it was created on because of the _global identifier.

The _global Identifier

The *global* identifier, which was introduced back in Flash MX, has the power to allow functions and other data types to be reached from the entire movie. It can transform any variable, array, function, or object into a globally available data type. This way, you can create all the variables, functions, and whatever else you need to call upon in the main timeline and reuse them.

The generic template looks like this:

```
_global.datatype
```

We could go on for several pages talking about this object, but for this chapter, we'll use it in the context of functions. Therefore, let's look at the generic template:

```
_global.functionName = function(parameters:ParameterType):ReturnType{
    //script to be run
}
```

Now that you have seen the general form of a global function, let's jump right in and create one.

We'll start with a simple trace function, with no parameters this time, and place this script in the main timeline:

```
_global.myFunction = function():Void{
    trace("My first global function");
}
```

You can now call this function from anywhere within the entire Flash movie and on any timeline, provided there is not a local function with the same name, which will cause the interpreter to use the local function instead.

The preceding example was straightforward, and so is the next one. This time, we are going to use parameters with the function but still use a trace function as the script:

```
_global.myFunction = function(name:String):Void{
    trace(name);
}
```

Now whenever this function is invoked from anywhere, whatever string is passed as the parameter will be displayed in the output window when the movie is tested.

These two examples are great, but they do not show the true power of what the _global object can do. The next example requires a little more effort and understanding to see how the object works.

First, create a new Flash document. On the main stage, draw a circle and then convert it to a movie clip symbol (F8); then give it an instance name of **circle_mc** and place it on the far left side of the stage.

Now in the timeline that your circle resides in, create another layer and place the following actions in the first frame of the new layer:

> **NOTE**
>
> This layer should be blank. Technically, you can place code in layers where symbols reside, but this is not a good habit.

```
_global.frictionSlide = function(friction:Number,movie:MovieClip,
➥distance:Number,startX:Number):Void{
    var newX = startX + distance;
    if(movie._x <= newX){
        movie._x += (newX-movie._x)*friction;
    }
}
```

Now that this code is on the main timeline, you can put the function and a variable in your symbol. So, double-click circle_mc to edit it. Create a new layer called **actions**, and place these actions in the first frame of that layer:

```
var currentX = this._x;
//now invoke our function
this.onEnterFrame=function(){
    frictionSlide(.2,this,300,currentX);
//notice how the function can be invoked without a direct path to the function
}
```

When you test the movie, the circle will slide slightly to the right and then slow down. You can adjust the parameters for when you call the function to have it do different things. What we did in the actions of the circle_mc movie clip is to first get the current X position and store it in the variable. After that, we call our global function inside the onEnterFrame event so it will continually be called to make the circle appear like it is sliding, but it is really just changing its X position over and over. Of course, because this function is global, it can be called from anywhere, and the parameters can be changed for each movie clip.

Also note that, as shown in the preceding code, the global function calls a local variable. The next section covers some rules involved with calling variables with functions.

Variables and Functions

When using variables in conjunction with functions, you need to follow several rules to avoid errors and increase consistency.

First, you should be cautious when using a variable name that's the same as the name of a parameter in the function when they both reside in the same script. This should be common sense (if for no other reason than for the sake of organized code), but let's say it happens anyway.

Create a variable and call it myVariable; then create a function and have it trace myVariable:

```
var myVariable:String = "Flash";
//now create the function with no parameters
function myFunction ():Void{
    trace(myVariable);
```

```
}
//now run the function
myFunction();
//output: Flash
```

In this instance, the interpreter does not find `myVariable` anywhere in the function, so it begins to look outside the function, and it runs into the variable you created, which is named `myVariable`, and grabs the value of that variable.

Now let's see what happens when you use a parameter with the same name. Using the same code as before, add a parameter with the same name as the variable you created:

```
var myVariable:String = "Flash";
//now create the function
function myFunction (myVariable:String):Void{
    trace(myVariable);
}
//now run the function
myFunction("Unleashed");
//output: Unleashed
```

This time, the interpreter found `myVariable` within the function itself, as a parameter name, and ignored the variable that was created before the function was created.

Finally, let's add a variable inside the function with the same name as the parameter and the variable you created before the function (again, using the same code as before):

```
var myVariable:String = "Flash";
//Now create the function
function myFunction (myVariable:String):Void{
    var myVariable:String = "Professional";
    trace(myVariable);
}
//Now run the function
myFunction("Unleashed");
//output: Professional
```

This time, the interpreter found the variable `myVariable` inside the function and didn't bother with the parameter or the variable you created before you created the function.

So now you know how the interpreter looks for variables: First, it looks in the function itself; then it looks at the parameters, and finally it looks outside the function.

The variables available within the function are not available outside the function. Let's take a look at an example:

```
//First create the function
function myFunction (myVariable:String):Void{
```

```
    var myVariable:String = "Unleashed";
    trace(myVariable);
}
//call the function
myFunction();
//trace the variable
trace(myVariable);
//output: Unleashed
//        undefined
```

Notice how you cannot pull the variable name out of the function, even after the function has been invoked. This is important because that means that variables created inside of functions have a local scope to that function. After the function is run, the variable is no longer in existence, and you regain some (a small amount) of virtual memory back on a user's computer.

The next section will take functions a step further. As far as parameters are concerned, all we have covered involves using them to pass information to the script of a function. Now you'll see how to use them as objects.

The Arguments Class

Each time a function is invoked, an Arguments object is created automatically and can be referenced using the local variable arguments, which is automatically included within the scope of the function. Basically, arguments are the parameters you define when you invoke any function. The arguments variable of any function is more like an array (refer to Chapter 10, "Arrays," for more on arrays). As with an array, you can call specific elements as well as the number of total elements. The arguments variable can be used to get information about any and all of the parameters being passed to that function.

Let's start with the number of arguments in a given function. Gathering this information is as easy as using the length property of the arguments object.

The length Property

The length property of the arguments object found in all functions returns a value that represents the number of parameters a user has defined when a function is invoked. The generic template looks like this:

```
function functionName(parameters:ParameterType):Void{
    //code to be run in the function
    arguments.length;
}
```

As you'll notice, you must use the length property as well as the arguments object inside the function. (The length property is also a property of arrays as well as a property of strings and can be used outside a function only in that context.)

Now let's see this property in a real example. Create a function with two basic parameters and trace the length of the arguments, like so:

```
function myFunction (x:Number,y:Number):Void{
    trace (arguments.length);
}
//now run the function
myFunction(5,6);
//output: 2
```

The function runs, and the number of parameters are displayed in the output window. However, as mentioned before, the `length` property returns the number of arguments when the function is invoked, not created. To see what that means, here is an example:

```
//create a function with two parameters
function myFunction(x:Number,y:Number):Void{
    trace(arguments.length);
}
//now invoke the function, but add a parameter
myFunction (5,6,7);
//output: 3
```

Now that you have seen how to find the number of arguments, the next step is to pull individual arguments out of the entire set.

To call individual arguments, you use the `arguments` object and a numerical value held in brackets. The generic template looks like this:

```
function functionName(parameters:ParameterType):Void{
    //code to be run in the function
    arguments[N];
}
```

With this generic template, place a number (*N*) in the brackets that represent the argument in that position. However, note that arguments begin counting at 0 instead of at 1, like arrays, so the first element looks like this:

```
arguments[0];
```

Here is an example using this method of pulling individual arguments:

```
//create a function with three parameters
function myFunction(x:Number,y:Number,z:Number):Void{
    trace(arguments[1]);
}
//now invoke the function
myFunction(2,4,6);
//output: 4
```

Because arguments begin counting at 0 instead of at 1, the second argument is labeled [1] instead of [0].

Now, using this method combined with the length property, you can create some amazing code. Let's take a look at an example that creates a function that adds all numbers placed as parameters:

```
//first create a function with no parameters
function addArgs():Void{
//now use a loop statement to total the argument values
    var numTotal:Number = 0;
    for(var i:Number = 0; i<arguments.length; i++){
        numTotal += Number(arguments[i]);
    }
//display the total in the output window
    trace (numTotal);
}
//now invoke the function with as many
addArgs(1,2,3);


//This can also work with combining strings.
//first create a function with no parameters
function combineStrings():Void{
//create a variable that will hold a string literal space
    var space:String = " ";
    var total:String = "";
//now use a loop statement to combine the strings
    for(var i:Number = 0; i<arguments.length; i++){
//now convert each argument to a string for consistency
        total +=arguments[i].toString()+space;
    }
    trace (total);
}
//now invoke the function with as many
combineStrings("Flash","8 Professional","Unleashed");


//output: 6
// Flash 8 Professional Unleashed
```

Another great use of this technique involves creating an array that can hold the arguments outside of the function, because as previously stated, the arguments object cannot be used outside the function. Here's an example:

```
//first create a function with no parameters
function createArray():Array{
//create an array to hold the arguments
    var myArray:Array = new Array();
```

```
    for(var i = 0; i < arguments.length; i++){
        myArray.push(arguments[i]);
    }
    return myArray;
}
//set a variable equal to the returned array
var argsArray:Array = createArray(1,2,3,"One","Two");
//display new array in output window
trace(argsArray);
//output: 1,2,3,One,Two
```

These are just a few examples of using the length property combined with pulling individual arguments. There are two more properties of the Arguments object, and they are the callee function, which refers to the function being called, and the caller property that refers to the Arguments object of the calling function.

So far, you have seen functions used as easily repeatable code that can be changed, as needed, by using parameters. However, you can also use them for more than just actions because they can also be used as objects.

Functions as Objects

Using a function as an object may seem a bit unorthodox, but this actually greatly increases the usability of a function. To create a function object, you assign it without the parentheses and use it like an expression. Also, because the function is an object, you can move it around like any other type of data.

Following is an example using the built-in function trace() (built-in functions are discussed in the "Functions Built In to Flash" section, later in this chapter) to send a property of the object to the output window:

```
//First, create the function
function myInfo ():Void{
    trace(myInfo.name);
}
//Assign a property called name to the function
myInfo.name = "David";
//Run the function
myInfo();
//output: David
```

Assigning properties to functions is easy because of the built-in function object. You can even assign multiple properties to your functions. Now, suppose you would like to see a list of all the properties in a function. You can use the for in loop statement to pull properties of objects. (For more on loop statements, see Chapter 11, "Statements and Expressions.")

To use the `for in` loop statement, place the keyword `for` ahead of an opening parenthesis. Then place the keyword `var` followed by your variable's name (in this case, `functionProp`). Then place the keyword `in` followed by the name of the object (the function's name, in this case). Finally, place a closing parenthesis, then opening and closing curly brackets enclosing the script you want to run while the loop looks through the properties, and finally, a closing curly bracket. Here's what it looks like:

```
//First, create the function
function myInfo ():Void{
}
//Now assign properties to it
myInfo.fName = "David";
myInfo.lName = "Vogeleer";
myInfo.age = "25";
myInfo.location = "Virginia";
//now use the for in statement to look through our properties
for(var functionProp in myInfo){
    trace("The property "+functionProp+" equals "+myInfo[functionProp]);
}
//output: The property location equals Virginia
//          The property age equals 25
//          The property lName equals Vogeleer
//          The property fName equals David
```

Notice that, in this example, we not only called the name of the property but also the value by using the function's name and the property we wanted to call in brackets. Because we used a dynamic variable, we did not have to put it in quotes. However, to call a single property of a function using brackets, you must place the name of the property in quotes, as shown in the following code:

```
//First, create the function
function myInfo ():Void{
}
//Now assign the property to it
myInfo.age = "25";
trace(myInfo["age"]);
//output: 25
```

Let's take it another step forward by creating multiple functions with multiple properties. Then we'll store each function in an array. (As mentioned earlier, arrays are covered in greater detail in Chapter 10.) After that, we'll call all the properties of all the functions to be displayed in the output window, and because we stored the functions in the array as objects, we can invoke the functions by using the array.

First, we'll create the functions we need and, in the first one, store the `trace` function we'll use at the end of the code. After that, we'll assign the properties to the functions.

Then we'll create the array and store the functions in the array as objects. Finally, we'll run a script that looks through each element of the array as well as displays each property in each element.

After that, we'll invoke our first function using the array as a shortcut. Here's the code:

```
//First, create the functions
function myInfo ():Void{
//This script is for later use
    trace("Traced from myInfo");
}
function flashInfo ():Void{
}
//Create the properties for each function
myInfo.fName = "David";
myInfo.age = "25";
flashInfo.version = "8 Pro";
flashInfo.player = 8;
//Now create the array to hold the functions as objects
var functionArray:Array = new Array();
//Place the functions in the array
functionArray[0] = myInfo;
functionArray[1] = flashInfo;
/*
Finally we create the script to search through the array
and trace all of our properties with their values
*/
for (var myElement in functionArray){
    for (var functionProp in functionArray[myElement]){
        trace("Property "+functionProp);
    }
}
//and because the function is stored as an object in the array
//we can call it using the array
functionArray[0]();
//output: Property player
//        Property version
//        Property age
//        Property fName
```

In the preceding code, we used only two functions and two properties for each function. You can, however, increase both, and the script will still function properly.

Now that you have seen functions used as repeatable sets of code and as objects, let's move on to using them as methods to be used in conjunction with other objects.

Functions as Methods

Before we get into using functions as methods, we need to review what a method is. A method is a function used in conjunction with an object. A method can perform a desired task on an object or can be used to gather information from that object.

We call methods just like we call functions, using parentheses; however, methods are attached to objects using dot syntax. Here is a generic template for calling a method:

```
object.method();
```

The preceding template is just for calling a method; to assign a method, you drop the parentheses, like this:

```
object.method;
```

Now that you have the generic templates to go by, let's start creating a few methods. First, we'll place a simple trace function within a function we create. Then we'll create a generic object, called gObject, and assign a property of gObject to our function. Then we'll invoke it by using the entire name, including the property. Here's the code:

```
//First, the function
function myFunction():Void{
    trace("Flash 8 Professional Unleashed");
}
//Then the generic object
var gObject:Object = new Object();
//Now the property of the object
gObject.title = myFunction;
//Now invoke the method
gObject.title();
//output: Flash 8 Professional Unleashed
```

Using a method is stronger than using a function when dealing with an object in that the method can manipulate the object itself. Functions can also get information from objects when used as methods. Let's start by looking for a single property in an object and then have the function return its value instead of tracing it directly. Then we'll trace the method. Here's the code:

```
//Here, create the function, and have it look for the property
function getAge ():Number{
    return(this.age);
}
//create the object
var gObject:Object = new Object();
//Now add two properties to our object
gObject.age = 25;
gObject.ageVerify = getAge;
```

```
trace(gObject.ageVerify());
//output:25
```

You can also directly define the method of the object like this:

```
//create the object
var gObject:Object = new Object();
//Now add two properties to our object
gObject.age = 25;
//create the method
gObject.ageVerify = function():Number{
    return(this.age);
}
trace(gObject.ageVerify());
//output:25
```

That was a lot of work for not a big payoff. We could have simply traced the property itself. Therefore, let's build on the previous example and combine multiple properties in an expression that we may want to use again and again.

In this example, we'll create an object called myRec. Then we'll create a function that gets the area and the perimeter of the object. The idea is that no matter how often the properties we use change, the function will perform the same calculation on our object. Here's the code:

```
//First, create the object
var myRec:Object = new Object();
//Now add a property and two methods to our object
myRec.w = 5;
myRec.h = 10;
myRec.getArea = getRecArea;
myRec.getPerim = getRecPerim;
//Here, create the functions
function getRecArea():Number{
    return this.w * this.h;
}
function getRecPerim():Number{
    return (this.w * 2) + (this.h * 2);
}
//Finally, invoke the methods
trace(myRec.getArea());
trace(myRec.getPerim());
//output: 50
//         30
```

The preceding code shows that methods can be quite powerful when used in an expression. You can change the value of w or h to verify that the formula will still calculate correctly, or you can even apply the functions as methods to other objects for the same results.

Methods do exist in Flash without us creating them. As a matter of fact, it is difficult to write ActionScript without using methods. They are too numerous to have a full list here, because nearly each object has its own set of methods. You can review Chapter 8, "Welcome to ActionScript 2.0," for more on methods.

Here is a list of a few of the methods that are built in to Flash:

```
myArray.push();  //adds an element to an array
myMovie.stop();  //stops a movie clip's playhead
myXML.load();    //loads an XML document into an XML object
Math.sqrt();     //returns the square root of a number
```

Functions Built In to Flash

We have covered ways of creating and manipulating user-defined functions thus far. Now we'll focus on some of the built-in functions Flash has to offer. We'll briefly go over some basic built-in functions. Finally, we'll discuss some of the deprecated functions.

Because you know what functions look like, I'll only briefly label the parts:

```
stop();            //stops a movie clip from playing, and has no parameters
play();            //plays a movie clip, and has no parameters
gotoAndStop(5);    //goes to a specified frame (the parameter) and stops
trace("Flash");    //displays parameter in output window
```

This list goes on and on.

However, a couple functions deserve mentioning. One of them is the call function.

The call Function

The call function is an interesting function that's brought all the way from Flash 4. This function can run code from any given frame without moving to that frame. It is a deprecated function, and Macromedia recommends using the keyword function to make code available throughout the timeline, as we discussed earlier. However, it's still good to know how to use the call function in case you ever have the need to use it.

The generic template is straightforward. Use the keyword call, followed by a string representing the frame label or a number representing a frame number, enclosed in parentheses. Here is the generic template:

```
call(frame);
```

Now that you know what it looks like, let's use the call function in an example.

1. Start a new Flash document.

2. Then create a new layer. Name the top layer **labels** and the bottom layer **actions**. Then place two more keyframes in each layer (F6).

3. Open the Actions panel for the first frame on the Actions layer and place this code there:

```
stop();
```

This will stop the play head from moving past this frame.

4. Next, in frame 2 of the same layer, place this trace statement:

```
trace("This is code from frame two");
```

5. Then in the final frame of the Actions layer (frame 3), place this trace statement:

```
trace("This is code from the labeled frame");
```

6. Now we turn our attention to the label's layer. In the third frame of this layer, place the label "labeled." When you're done, your screen should look similar to Figure 12.1.

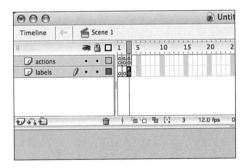

FIGURE 12.1   The project thus far.

7. If you were to test this movie right now, nothing would happen. This is because of the stop function in frame 1. If stop were removed, both trace statements would run repeatedly, over and over, while the movie loops through. However, when you place these next actions after stop, both statements will be run, but only once, and the frames will never be reached by the play head. So place the following code in the first frame of the Actions layer, and at the end, it will look like this:

```
stop();
call(2);
call("labeled");
```

```
//output: This is code from frame two
//         This is code from the labeled frame
```

Test the movie. There you have it—the code that was placed in frame 2 as well as the third frame, which was labeled "labeled," runs without the play head ever reaching these frames.

Now that we have covered this unique function, let's move on to some more built-in functions. Flash has predefined a couple of categories for functions in the Actions panel. One such category is the *conversion functions*.

Conversion Functions

Conversion functions perform a specific task on objects: they convert objects. Each of the five main data types has its own conversion script that will change it to another data type.

The generic template utilizes the keyword of the object you are trying to convert to, and the expression you are trying to convert follows, enclosed in parentheses, as shown here:

```
converter(expression);
```

We will use the following example to change some data from one type to another. After each step, we will use the `trace` function and the `typeof` operator to display the data type of each object following the conversion. Here's the code:

```
//Start off with a simple string
myString = "string";
trace (typeof myString);
//Now we begin converting the same object
//again and again while checking after each time
myString = Number(myString);
trace (typeof myString);
myString = Array(myString);
trace(typeof myString);
myString = Boolean(myString);
trace(typeof myString);
myString = Object(myString);
trace(typeof myString);
//Finally back to a string
myString = String(myString);
trace(typeof myString);
//output: string
//        number
//        object
//        boolean
//        object
//        string
```

> **NOTE**
>
> When converting to an array with the `Array` conversion function, whatever is being converted will be placed in the first element of the array and not separated into individual elements.

Converting data types is an important part of using ActionScript; however, the preceding code will not work with strict data typing, so keep that in mind if you want to change the data type of a variable over and over (which is bad practice). You can convert numbers from input text fields (all types of information from input text fields are strings; see Chapter 15, "Working with Text," for more information) into true number data types. You can convert Boolean data types into strings to use in sentences.

Let's now move on to the next category of functions: mathematical functions.

Mathematical Functions

Mathematical functions execute mathematical operations on expressions you assign to them. You may be thinking addition, subtraction, and so on, but these operations are much more advanced. Only four mathematical functions are listed in ActionScript:

> **NOTE**
>
> Although only four mathematical functions are in Flash, there is also the Math object, which has several methods for performing other mathematical calculations.

- `isFinite`
- `isNaN`
- `parseFloat`
- `parseInt`

The first two of the mathematical functions act more like conditionals. Let's see how they work individually.

The first, `isFinite`, checks to see whether the expression entered is a finite number. If the number is finite, the function returns `true`. If the expression is not finite (or *infinite*), the function returns `false`. Here is an example in which we test two numbers and trace the results:

```
trace(isFinite(15));
//evaluates to true
trace(isFinite(Number.NEGATIVE_INFINITY));
//evaluates to false
```

The second of these two functions, `isNaN`, works in the same manner. It checks to see whether the expression entered is not a real number. If the expression is not a real number, the function returns `true`. If the expression is a real number, the function returns `false`. Let's take a look:

```
trace(isNaN(15));
//evaluates to false
trace(isNaN("fifteen"));
//evaluates to true
trace(isNaN("15"));
//evaluates to false
```

Even though the last example is in fact a string, the interpreter converted it to a number when it was evaluated. Keep this in mind when evaluating numbers as strings.

The next mathematical function is `parseFloat`. This function takes numbers out of a string literal until it reaches a string character. Then it converts what it has removed into a true number data type. Here are a few examples:

```
trace(parseFloat("15"));
//output: 15
trace(parseFloat("fifteen"));
//output: NaN
trace(parseFloat("20dollars"));
//output: 20
```

As you can see in the preceding example, the function takes only the number and drops the rest of the string.

The last mathematical function is `parseInt`. This function can perform the same task as the `parseFloat` function, but it can also use a radix, which is useful when working with octal numbers. Here is an example:

```
trace(parseInt("15", 8));
//output: 13 (a representation of the octal number 15
//that has been parsed)
```

A few more functions are defined directly in ActionScript, including `getProperty()`, `getTimer()`, `targetPath()`, and `getVersion()`, all of which return information. There is also `eval`, `escape`, and `unescape`, which perform their desired tasks on expressions.

We have covered a great deal of information about functions; now let's look at some deprecated functions and alternatives to their use.

Deprecated Functions

If you have worked in Flash 4 or even Flash 5, you may notice that some of the functions are not where they used to be. No, they are not completely gone, but they are *deprecated*, which means that ActionScript provides new ways of performing the same tasks, and although these functions are still available for use, they might not be in the next release. Therefore, it is a good idea to get out of the habit of using them.

We'll go over each deprecated function briefly and discuss alternatives to their use.

chr

The chr function converts a numeric value to a character based on ASCII standards. It has been replaced by String.fromCharCode. Here are examples of both:

```
//The old way
trace(chr(64));
```

```
//The new way
trace(String.fromCharCode(64));
```

```
//output @
//       @
```

int

The int function takes a number with a decimal point and drops the decimal point. It has been replaced by Math.floor. Here are examples of both:

```
//the old way
trace(int(5.5));
```

```
//the new way
trace(Math.floor(5.5));
```

```
//output: 5
//        5
```

length

The length function returns the number of characters in a string or variable holding a string. It has been replaced by String.length. Here are examples of both:

```
//First create a variable holding a string
myString = "Flash";
```

```
//the old way
trace(length(myString));
```

```
//the new way
trace(myString.length);
```

```
//output: 5
//        5
```

mbchr

The mbchr function, like the chr function, converts a numeric value to a character based on ASCII standards. It has been replaced by String.fromCharCode. Here are examples of both:

```
//the old way
trace(mbchr(64));
```

```
//The new way
trace(String.fromCharCode(64));
```

```
//output @
//       @
```

mblength

The mblength function, like the length function, returns the number of characters in a string or variable holding a string. It has been replaced by String.length. Here are examples of both:

```
//First create a variable holding a string
myString = "Flash";
```

```
//the old way
trace(mblength(myString));
```

```
//the new way
trace(myString.length);
```

```
//output: 5
//        5
```

mbord

The mbord function converts a character to a number by using the ASCII standard. It has been replaced by String. CharCodeAt. Here are examples of both:

```
//the old way
trace(mbord("@"));
```

```
//the new way
trace(("@").charCodeAt(0));
```

```
//output: 64
//        64
```

mbsubstring

The mbsubstring function removes a set number of characters from a string. It has been replaced by String.substr. Here are examples of both:

```
//First, create a variable to hold a string
myVar = "Unleashed";

//the old way
trace(mbsubstring(myVar, 0, 2));

//the new way
trace(myVar.substr(0, 2));

//output: Un
//        Un
```

ord

The ord function, like the mbord function, converts a character to a number by using the ASCII standard. It has been replaced by String. CharCodeAt. Here are examples of both:

```
//the old way
trace(ord("@"));

//the new way
trace(("@").charCodeAt(0));

//output: 64
//        64
```

random

The random function returns a random number from a expression given. It has been replaced by Math.random. Here are examples of both:

```
//the old way
trace (random(5));

//the new way
trace (Math.floor(Math.random()*5));
//output: (2 random numbers between 0-4)
```

substring

The substring function, like the mbsubstring function, removes a set number of characters from a string. It has been replaced by String.substr. Here are examples of both:

```
//First, create a variable to hold a string
myVar = "Unleashed";
```

```
//the old way
trace(substring(myVar, 0, 2));

//the new way
trace(myVar.substr(0, 2));

//output: Un
//         Un
```

This is the last of the deprecated functions.

Summary

That's it for all the functions. We have gone over everything, from creating functions to using deprecated functions. We have even covered using functions as objects and methods.

Just remember that functions are mainly used as blocks of repetitive code, parameters are used to slightly modify functions for different uses, you can use the return statement to return a value from a function, and methods are functions attached directly to objects.

As you go through the rest of the book, you will begin to see where functions can come in handy.

CHAPTER **13**

The Movie Clip Object

The movie clip object is the most powerful object in Flash. Not only is it the only symbol that has its own timeline similar to, but independent of, the main timeline, but it is the only symbol that can have actions on its timeline.

But there is more to the movie clip object than its independent timeline. Movie clips have properties, methods, and events that set them apart from all other objects.

Throughout this chapter, we will be exploring many ways to use and manipulate movie clips, including using the Drawing API, Flash's way of drawing shapes and lines with ActionScript, as well as applying filters with ActionScript.

To start with, we'll discuss the different ways to create movie clips.

Creating Movie Clips

We covered how to create a movie clip manually back in Chapter 5, "Symbols and the Library," but we will review it quickly here.

Creating Movie Clips Manually

To create a Movie Clip symbol manually, follow these steps:

1. Choose Insert, New Symbol.

2. In the Create New Symbol dialog box, give the symbol a symbol name, choose Movie Clip as the behavior, and then click OK.

3. Now you are inside the newly created movie clip.

That was pretty simple; you just created a movie clip manually. Now if you want to use it, drag an instance of it from the library onto the stage and give it an instance name.

NOTE

Although technically you do not need to give every instance of a movie clip object an instance name unless you plan to refer to it with ActionScript, it is good practice to do so. Also remember that you cannot duplicate instance names in the same timeline or errors will occur.

Creating movie clips manually is not the only way to create them. You can also create them on-the-fly with ActionScript.

Creating Movie Clips with ActionScript

Since the MX version of Flash, users have been able to create movie clips with ActionScript. Before then, when you wanted an empty movie clip on the stage, you would have to create one manually, drag it onto the stage, and then give it an instance name.

To create empty movie clips in ActionScript, use the `createEmptyMovieClip()` method, which looks like this:

```
movieClip.createEmptyMovieClip(instanceName, depth);
```

The parameters of this method are as follows:

- `movieClip`—The instance name of the movie clip where the empty clip will be created.

- `instanceName`—This is a string literal that represents the instance name of the movie clip being created.

- `depth`—This is a numerical value that represents the stacking order of the movie clip being created (more on `depth` later in this chapter).

That is the basic layout of the `createEmptyMovieClip()` method. The next example shows how to implement it.

1. Create a new Flash document.

2. In the first frame of the main timeline, place these actions:

   ```
   //this refers the main timeline
   this.createEmptyMovieClip("sample_mc", 1);
   ```

3. Now test the movie by choosing Control, Test Movie.

4. Notice that when the movie runs, there isn't anything on the stage. This is because we created an empty movie clip; there is nothing inside it, but you can tell it's there.

When you're in the test movie screen, choose Debug, List Objects, and you should see in the Output panel something similar to Figure 13.1.

The movie is listed in the Output panel.

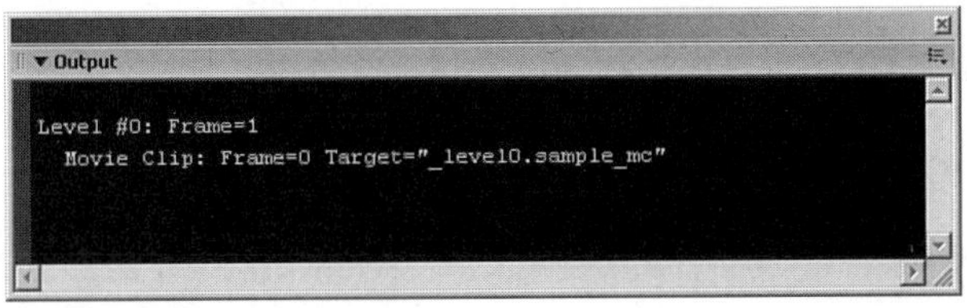

FIGURE 13.1   Using the List Objects option under Debug, you can see the movie clip you created via ActionScript.

Now that you have seen the different ways to create movie clips, continue on to see how to manipulate them.

Manipulating Movie Clips

Several properties of movie clips, such as color and alpha, can be manipulated to change the appearance of the movie clips. Other properties can be used to move the movie clip across the stage. There are even several properties of movie clips that control the visual aspects of the object, such as blend modes and filters.

Following is a short list of those properties with descriptions:

- _x—The horizontal position of a movie clip on the stage.

- _y—The vertical position of a movie clip on the stage.

- _xscale—The horizontal scale of a movie clip represented as a percentage; greater than 100% enlarges the clip, less than 100% shrinks the clip.

- _yscale—The vertical scale of a movie clip represented as a percentage; greater than 100% enlarges the clip, less than 100% shrinks the clip.

- _height—The height of a movie clip in pixels.

- _width—The width of a movie clip in pixels.

- _alpha—The transparent level of a movie clip from 0 to 100.

- _rotation—The rotation of a movie clip in degrees.

- _visible—A Boolean value representing whether a movie clip is visible (true) or not (false).

Now that you have a list of some of the basic visual properties of movie clips, we can begin using them to animate movie clips.

Animating Movie Clips with ActionScript

Animating movie clips with ActionScript has many benefits that manually animating them does not; file size reduction is one of the major benefits.

When you create tweens, such as in Chapters 4 and 5, you are requiring Flash to not only create the necessary animation between the two points, but to also remember it when the .swf file is compiled. This causes the file size to increase. Even if you use keyframe animation without any tweening, the file size will increase with each keyframe. Using ActionScript to control the movement of movie clips is an easy way to trim file size because Flash has to remember only the original position of the movie clip, and then ActionScript will execute the movement at runtime.

Here is a basic example of scripted movement:

1. Create a new Flash document.

2. Draw a small circle on the left side of the stage about 50 pixels wide.

3. Select the drawn circle (including the circle's stroke) and convert it to a symbol by choosing Modify, Convert to Symbol.

4. Give it a symbol name of **circleMC** and choose Movie Clip as the behavior.

5. Give the circle on the stage an instance name of **circle_mc**.

6. Create a new layer and name it **actions**.

7. In the first frame of the Actions layer, open the Actions panel and place these actions within it:

```
//this event will make the circle move
this.onEnterFrame = function(){
    //move the circle 5 pixels at a time
    circle_mc._x += 5;
}
```

You used the onEnterFrame event, which will continually trigger throughout the entire run of the movie at the same pace as the frames per second (fps). Within the onEnterFrame event, you are moving the circle_mc movie clip by 5 pixels each time the event fires.

8. Now test the movie and see the circle moving across the screen as shown in Figure 13.2.

That was a simple example of moving a movie clip from one side of the screen to the other, but the problem is that the circle_mc continues to move well past the end of the stage. So we will continue the example by adding a conditional statement to see if the circle_mc has moved far enough, and then it will stop moving. We are also adding a trace function, which we will discuss later.

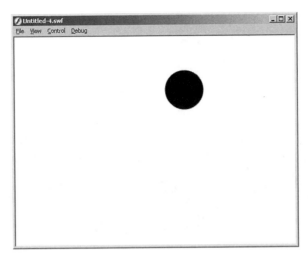

FIGURE 13.2 Using ActionScript, you can animate movie clips just as smoothly as using tweens, and the file size stays tiny.

Follow these steps to continue the example:

1. Close the test movie screen and return to the authoring environment.

2. In the first frame of the Actions layer, replace the actions in the Actions panel with these:

```
//this event will make the circle move
this.onEnterFrame = function(){
        //this trace function lets us know it is working
        trace("working");
        //if it hasn't gone too far, move the circle 5 pixels
        if(circle_mc._x < 550){
            circle_mc._x += 5;
        }
}
```

This code is taking the original code and placing a conditional statement to check whether circle_mc has passed 550 in its horizontal position (550 being the default width of the Flash stage). If it has not yet reached that point, the movie clip will continue moving to the right. Also, we put a trace function in the code, which will be discussed in the next section.

3. Now test the movie.

Notice that as before, the circle_mc movie clip moves across the screen, but this time, when it reaches a certain point it stops moving. Also, the trace function continues to run even after the circle has stopped moving, as you can see in Figure 13.3. This is because even though the circle has stopped moving, the onEnterFrame event is still being triggered.

Even though it's hard to tell, the onEnterFrame event is taking up valuable processor power that can be taken back. In the next extension of this example, we will remove the onEnterFrame event and regain the processor power.

FIGURE 13.3   Even though the circle_mc movie clip has stopped moving, the trace function continues to work while the onEnterFrame event fires.

The final step in this example is to remove the onEnterFrame event when we no longer need it, and regain the processor power. To do this, we will use the delete statement in conjunction with our conditional statement.

Follow these steps:

1. Close the test movie screen and return to the authoring environment.

2. In the first frame of the actions layer, replace the actions in the Actions panel with these:

```
//this event will make the circle move
this.onEnterFrame = function(){
    //this trace function lets us know it is working
    trace("working");
    //if it hasn't gone too far, move the circle 5 pixels
    if(circle_mc._x < 550){
        circle_mc._x += 5;
    }else{
        //destroy the onEnterFrame
        delete this.onEnterFrame;
    }
}
```

The changes were small; all we did was add an else statement to coincide with the if statement. When the circle_mc movie clip reaches the correct position, the else statement is triggered, the onEnterFrame event is destroyed, and the processor power is returned to other applications on the user's computer.

3. Test the movie.

When the movie is tested, the `circle_mc` acts exactly the same way it has been acting, moving from the left side of the stage to the right side. This time, however, when the `circle_mc` reaches the horizontal position of 550 or greater, the `circle_mc` movie clip stops moving and the `onEnterFrame` event is deleted, thereby stopping the `trace` function from occurring.

Even though this example was a little boring, it is very powerful. We moved a movie clip from one side of the screen to the other, stopped, and then destroyed the action that was moving it in the first place.

We are going to take the basic fundamentals from the preceding example and do a more advanced example of a movie clip moving from spot to spot on the stage. We will use some basic math to make it slow down and speed up. But before we do that, you need to learn about another feature new to Flash that will help a great deal with complex animations.

The `cacheAsBitmap` Property

The `cacheAsBitmap` property of a movie clip works in much the same manner as the Use Runtime Bitmap Caching option in the Properties Inspector. When this property of a movie clip is set to true, it will increase performance with regard to animations, especially in X,Y coordinate changes.

You set it in ActionScript as you would any other property:

```
myMovie.cacheAsBitmap = true;
```

Now for most of the animations in this chapter, this property will not make a substantial difference in performance. But in a later example, when there are multiple movie clips all being animated, you should notice a performance increase, especially if you increase the number of objects being animated.

> **NOTE**
>
> If you were to set a filter to a movie clip with ActionScript, the `cacheAsBitmap` property will automatically be set to `true`.

Using Math to Help Animate Movie Clips

So far we have just moved a movie clip using a static number. Using math, you can improve the appearance of animating movie clips. You can make them appear to have a bouncy momentum. You can make them appear to be bound by gravity. You can even make them appear to be easing in and out each time they move, and that is what we are going to cover in this next example, which extends the preceding example.

1. Close the test screen and return to the main timeline.

2. In the first frame of the Actions layer, open the Actions panel and replace the code with this:

```
//cache the circle for performance reasons
circle_mc.cacheAsBitmap = true;
//the easing control
var friction:Number = 0.5;
//the starting positions
var currentX:Number = circle_mc._x;
var currentY:Number = circle_mc._y;
//set the boundaries
var xBoundary:Number = 550;
var yBoundary:Number = 400;
//set some initial go to points
var newX:Number = Math.floor(Math.random()*xBoundary);
var newY:Number = Math.floor(Math.random()*yBoundary);
```

These actions first set the cacheAsBitmap property to true and then declare some variables we will be using in the event later on in the code. The friction variable controls the speed of the movie clip as it eases in and out of position. The currentX and currentY variables hold the current position of our movie clip. The boundary variables are used in setting the next position. The newX and the newY variables use the Math object to choose new positions at random, based on the boundaries, for the movie clip to move to. Now let's add the code to do the actual moving.

3. After the code is in the Actions panel, place this code:

```
//this is the event for the motion
this.onEnterFrame=function(){
    //continually get the current position
    currentX = Math.floor(circle_mc._x);
    currentY = Math.floor(circle_mc._y);
    //check the horizontal position
    if(currentX != newX){
        circle_mc._x += (newX-currentX)*friction;
    }else{
        newX = Math.floor(Math.random()*xBoundary);
    }
    //do the same with the horizontal position
    if(currentY != newY){
        circle_mc._y += (newY-currentY)*friction;
    }else{
        newY = Math.floor(Math.random()*yBoundary);
    }
}
```

This code constantly checks the current position of the movie clip and stores it in two of the variables we created earlier. It then checks to see whether the movie clip's current position is at the new position. If it is not, it moves it closer to the new position based on the friction that we declared earlier. If it is at the new position, it then creates another new position for the object to move to.

4. Test the movie.

Now when the test movie screen appears, you will see the `circle_mc` movie clip moving all over the stage from spot to spot, slowing down as it gets closer. Play with the friction variable to get some surprising results.

That example was not only powerful, but cool. You can try not only playing with the friction variable, but using other movie clip properties in conjunction with or without the _x and _y properties to see what else you can do. We will come back to this concept in later examples, but first we will cover another way you can manipulate movie clips. This time, we change their color.

Using the `Color` Object

The `Color` object is an object used to change the color or tint of a movie clip. It is unique among all other objects. Most objects, when created, have no association by default with other objects. The `Color` object, on the other hand, must be associated with a movie clip when the `Color` object is created.

Here is an example of creating a `Color` object:

```
var myColor_color:Color = new Color(myMovie);
```

The `myMovie` parameter is a reference to a movie clip that is either already on the stage or has been created with ActionScript.

The `Color` object has four basic methods, but we are going to focus on two of them, the `setRGB()` method and the `setTransform()` method. Both have unique attributes that make them suitable for different situations.

We will start with the `setRGB()` method because it is slightly easier to implement.

The `setRGB()` Method

The `setRGB()` method is used to set the RGB color of a movie clip. When called, it will change the color of the movie clip specified when the `Color` object was created to any legal hexadecimal color.

Here is the generic layout of the method:

```
colorObj_color.setRGB(hexColor);
```

The parameter it accepts, `hexColor`, can be any legal hexadecimal color such as `0x000000` (black), `0xffffff` (white), or `0xff0000` (red). It can also be a variable that is holding a legal hexadecimal color.

> **NOTE**
>
> Hexadecimal colors are represented in the form of 0xRRGGBB, where RR is the red amount, GG is the green amount, and BB is the blue amount. Each of these sections range from 00 to FF where 0x000000 is black and 0xFFFFFF is white.

Here is an example of using the setRGB() method:

1. Create a new Flash document.

2. Draw a square somewhere on the stage with the fill color some shade of red.

3. Highlight the square, including the stroke, and convert it to a movie clip symbol by choosing Modify, Convert to Symbol.

4. Give it a symbol name of **squareMC** and make sure the behavior is set to Movie Clip.

5. Give the instance of the square on the stage an instance name of **square_mc**.

6. Create a new layer and call it **actions**.

7. In the Actions layer, open the Actions panel in the first frame, and place these actions within it:

```
//create the color object, and pass it the square_mc
var myColor_color:Color = new Color(square_mc);
//set the color to a light shade of blue
myColor_color.setRGB(0x397dce);
```

The preceding code creates a color object and associates itself with the movie clip we already created. Then it calls the setRGB() method and passes it a hexadecimal color that translates to a light shade of blue.

When you test the movie, you will see that the square_mc movie clip has changed from its original red color to a light shade of blue. Notice that it did not just change the fill color, but the stroke color has also now become the same shade of blue. The setTransform() method, discussed in the following section, does something a bit different.

The setTransform() Method

The setTransform() method is slightly different in the way it changes the color of a movie clip from the setRGB() method. Instead of changing the entire movie clip to a flat color, the setTransform() method tints the movie clip.

Here is the generic layout of the setTransform() method:

```
myColor_color.setTransform(transformObject);
```

This method has only one parameter when called, the transformObject. The transformObject is an object you create prior to calling the method that has special properties set. Following is a list of the available properties you can set for the transformObject:

- ra—The percentage for the red coloring ranging from –100 to 100
- rb—The offset for the red coloring ranging from –255 to 255
- ga—The percentage for the green coloring ranging from –100 to 100
- gb—The offset for the green coloring ranging from –255 to 255
- ba—The percentage for the blue coloring ranging from –100 to 100
- bb—The offset for the blue coloring ranging from –255 to 255
- aa—The percentage for alpha ranging from –100 to 100
- ab—The offset for alpha ranging from –255 to 255

That might be a little confusing until you see how to create one of these transformObjects. As with most things in Flash, there is more than one way to accomplish this.

Here is the long way:

```
//first create the object
var transformObject:Object = new Object();
//now set some of the properties of that object
transformObject.rb = 200;
transformObject.gb = 100;
transformObject.bb = 50;
transformObject.ab = 50;
```

And here is the short way:

```
//first create the object
var transformObject:Object = {rb: '200', gb: '150', bb: '50', ab: '50'};
```

My personal preference is to use the long way, merely because it is easier to read and make corrections.

Now that you have seen the basic layout of not only the setTransform() method, but also the transformObject that we pass to the method, an example will bring it all together.

1. Create a new Flash document.
2. Draw a square somewhere on the stage with the fill color some shade of gray and the stroke color black.
3. Highlight the square, including the stroke, and convert it to a movie clip symbol by choosing Modify, Convert to Symbol.
4. Give it a symbol name of **squareMC** and make sure the behavior is set to Movie Clip.
5. Give the instance of the square on the stage an instance name of **square_mc**.
6. Create a new layer and call it **actions**.

7. In the Actions layer, open the Actions panel in the first frame, and place these actions within it:

```
//create the color object, and pass it the square_mc
var myColor_color:Color = new Color(square_mc);
//create the transformObject
var transformObject:Object = new Object();
//now set some of the properties of that object
transformObject.rb = 200;
transformObject.gb = 100;
transformObject.bb = 50;
//finally call the setTransform() method
myColor_color.setTransform(transformObject);
```

The preceding code creates a `Color` object and associates it with our movie clip. Then it creates an object that we will use as the `transformObject` in our method. After that, it sets a few basic properties of the `transformObject`. And finally, the code calls the `setTransform()` method using the `transformObject`.

Now when you test the movie, the `square_mc` movie clip appears with a pinkish tint. Notice that this time, the stroke is not the exact color as the fill, but it is the same tint.

> **NOTE**
>
> If the `setRGB()` method is called, it will override the settings of the `setTransform()` method.

That was another way movie clips can be manipulated. So far we have covered how to move and adjust movie clips using the built-in properties. We have also discussed how to change their color using the `Color` object. The next section covers a new property of the movie clip object, `blendMode`.

The `blendMode` Property

The `blendMode` property is new to Flash 8, and it controls how colors interact when overlaid. We went over this option briefly in Chapter 1, showing how to set it manually in the Properties Inspector, but this time we will accomplish the same thing with ActionScript.

Setting the `blendMode` is no different from setting any other property of a movie clip. This property can be set to either a numerical value or a string literal. Here are the available options:

- **1:normal**—This default option signifies that the pixel values of the blend image will override the pixel values of the base image.

- **2:layer**—This option creates a temporary buffer for precomposition. This option is done automatically when there is more than one child in a movie clip and Normal is not selected.

- **3:multiply**—This option multiplies the color values of the corresponding movie clips where they overlap, usually creating a darker color.

- **4:screen**—The exact opposite of the multiply option, this option takes the complementing colors of the overlapping movie clips and creates a lighter color.

- **5:lighten**—This option compares pixel colors of the overlapping images and displays the lighter of the two.

- **6:darken**—This option compares pixel colors of the overlapping images and displays the darker of the two.

- **7:difference**—This option compares pixel colors of the overlapping images and subtracts the darker color from the lighter color.

- **8:add**—This option adds the overlapping pixel colors of the two movie clips and sets a maximum color of 0xff.

- **9:subtract**—This option subtracts the overlapping pixel colors of the two movie clips and sets a minimum color of 0x00.

- **10:invert**—This option inverts the background.

- **11:alpha**—This option applies the alpha of the foreground onto the background, but only if the parent movie clip has a blend mode of `layer` set.

- **12:erase**—This option "cuts out" part of the background with the foreground's alpha, but only if the parent movie clip has a blend mode of `layer` set.

- **13:overlay**—This option multiplies the colors of the overlapping movie clips while preserving both highlights and shadows.

- **14:hardlight**—This option, similar to the `overlay` option, multiplies or screens the two movie clips depending on their source color value. If it is darker than .5, it is multiplied. Otherwise, it is screened, or lightened.

Now let's see these blend modes in action by going through the next example.

1. Create a new Flash document.

2. Draw a red rectangle on the stage about 100×150 in size.

3. Convert it to a movie clip called **rec1MC** with an instance name of **rec1_mc**.

4. Draw a blue rectangle on the stage about 100×150 in size.

5. Convert it to a movie clip called **rec2MC** with an instance name of **rec2_mc** and slide it over the red rectangle so that they overlap somewhat.

6. Create a new layer called **actions** and place the following code in its first frame:

```
//the blend mode variable
var bM = 1;
//each time the user clicks the mouse, go to the next mode
```

13

```
this.onMouseDown = function(){
    rec2_mc.blendMode = bM % 14 + 1;
    trace(rec2_mc.blendMode);
    bM++;
}
```

The preceding code first creates a variable that will hold the current blendMode. Then we use the onMouseDown event to iterate through each of the blend modes. And we use the trace function to show us which blend mode we are looking at.

Test the movie and each time you click, a new blend mode will be activated on the blue rectangle and the name of the blend mode will be displayed in the Output panel.

Another new way to manipulate the look and feel of a movie clip is using filters. We touched on them in Chapter 1, but we only went over how to control them manually. Now we will go over how to code them.

Filters

As mentioned in Chapter 1, filters are new to Flash 8, but if you have worked in applications such as Photoshop, they will not be new to you. Filters allow such things as drop shadow, blur, and a few other graphical effects to be applied to movie clips. Following is a full list of the available filters:

- **BevelFilter**—Creates a bevel effect on the movie clip.

- **BitmapFilter**—This is merely a base class for the other filters.

- **BlurFilter**—Creates a blur effect on the movie clip.

- **ColorMatrixFilter**—Allows the application of 4×5 transformation matrix with the RGBA for every pixel in the movie clip.

- **ConvolutionFilter**—Creates a matrix convolution effect.

- **DisplacementMapFilter**—This option allows you to displace specific pixels in the movie clip.

- **DropShadowFilter**—Creates a drop-shadow effect.

- **GlowFilter**—Creates a glow effect, both outer or inner.

- **GradientBevelFilter**—Creates gradient bevel effects.

- **GradientGlowFilter**—Creates a gradient glow effect, both outer and inner.

Follow these next steps to see how to create a dynamic drop-shadow effect on a movie clip:

1. Create a new Flash document.

2. Draw a rectangle in the middle of the stage about 200×200 in size.

3. Convert the rectangle to a movie clip with the symbol name **recMC** and set the registration point to center-center.

4. Back on the main stage, give the rectangle an instance name of **rec_mc**.

5. Create a new layer called **actions** and place the following code in the first frame of that layer:

```
//create an instance of the drop shadow effect
var myShadow = new flash.filters.DropShadowFilter();
//set a few properties
myShadow.blurX = 10;
myShadow.blurY = 10;
myShadow.distance = 10;
//while the mouse moves, move the shadow around like the mouse is the light
source
this.onMouseMove = function() {
  var yDist:Number = rec_mc._y - _ymouse;
  var xDist:Number = rec_mc._x - _xmouse;
  var degrees:Number = Math.atan2(yDist, xDist) / (Math.PI / 180);
  myShadow.angle = degrees;
  rec_mc.filters = [myShadow];
}
```

When you test this movie, you will see as you move the mouse around the stage, the drop shadow will move as if the mouse cursor is the light source. You can see how this works in Figure 13.4.

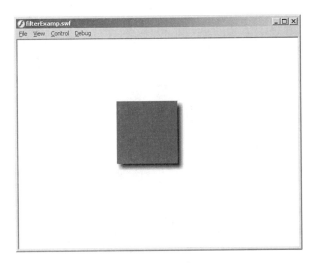

FIGURE 13.4   Filters enable you to add perspective and better visual effects to your movie clips.

Of course, this was just one filter, but for more on filters, check the reference at the end of the book.

Now that you have adjusted a lot of visual aspects of movie clips, next you'll learn how to adjust their stacking order.

Depth and the Stacking Order

We briefly mentioned depth earlier in this chapter when we were creating movie clips with ActionScript. To recap, depth is a numerical value representing the stacking order of objects on the stage during runtime. And because each object, whether created manually or dynamically, has its own depth, no two objects can exist at the same depth.

The first method for working with depth management is the getDepth() method.

The getDepth() Method

The getDepth() method will return a numerical value representing the depth of the object on which you call the method.

The generic layout is as follows:

```
myMovie.getDepth();
```

This method has no parameters; it just needs to be associated with an object on the stage.

In the following example, you will create a movie clip manually and then use the getDepth() method to see what depth it is residing on.

1. Start a new Flash document.

2. Draw a circle on the stage.

3. Convert the circle to a movie clip symbol by choosing Modify, Convert to Symbol.

4. Give it a symbol name of circleMC and make sure the behavior is set to Movie Clip.

5. Give the instance of the circle on the stage an instance name of **circle_mc**.

6. Create a new layer and name it **actions**.

7. In the first frame of the Actions layer, open the Actions panel and place this code in it:

   ```
   //send the depth of the movie clip to the output panel
   trace(circle_mc.getDepth());
   ```

The preceding code merely retrieves the depth of the circle_mc movie clip and sends it to the Output panel.

Test the movie and you should see the number –16383 in the Output panel. This is the first depth where objects created manually reside.

The getDepth() method retrieves information about an object's depth, but if you want to change an object's depth using ActionScript, you have to use the swapDepths() method.

The swapDepths() **Method**

The swapDepths() method, as mentioned, is used to change the depth of movie clips whether created manually or with ActionScript. This method has two ways of working. Here are both of them in generic layouts:

```
myMovie.swapDepths(depth);
myMovie.swapDepths(target);
```

Both uses have the myMovie in front of the method. This is the movie clip that you want to change the depth of.

Using the depth parameter, you will set a numerical value that will become the depth of myMovie. If there is already something on that depth, it will be moved to another available depth.

Using the target parameter, myMovie will change depths with the target movie clip. For the method to work correctly, both myMovie and target must reside within the same parent movie clip .

In this example, you will create two movie clips manually, align them slightly over one another, and then swap their depths so that at runtime, they will appear to have switched stacking orders.

1. Start a new Flash document.

2. Draw a circle on the stage.

3. Convert the circle to a movie clip symbol by choosing Modify, Convert to Symbol.

4. Give it a symbol name of **circleMC** and make sure the behavior is set to Movie Clip.

5. Give the instance of the circle on the stage an instance name of **circle_mc**.

6. While still in the same layer, draw a square shape (preferably with a different fill color, but that is not necessary).

7. Convert the square to a movie clip symbol by choosing Modify, Convert to Symbol.

8. Give it a symbol name of **squareMC** and make sure the behavior is set to Movie Clip.

9. Give the instance of the square on the stage an instance name of **square_mc** and align it so that it is partially covering up the circle_mc movie clip, as in Figure 13.5.

10. Create a new layer and name it **actions**.

11. In the Actions layer, open the Actions panel in the first frame and place these actions in it:

    ```
    //swap the two movie clips depths
    square_mc.swapDepths(circle_mc);
    ```

This code is simply swapping the two movie clips' depths with one another.

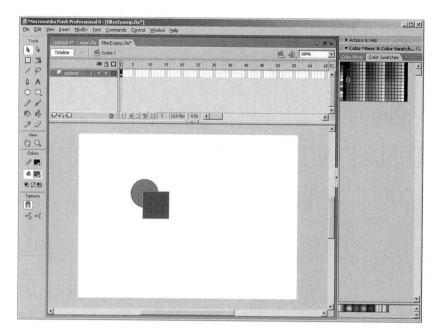

FIGURE 13.5   Place the square over the circle on the stage.

Test the movie, and you will see that now the circle movie clip appears above the square, as in Figure 13.6.

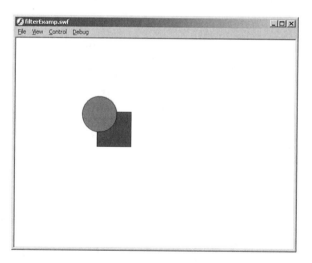

FIGURE 13.6   Now the circle appears above the square.

As you can see, it is important to know what depth movie clips are residing on, especially if you want to create them in ActionScript. Remember, two objects cannot reside on the same depth. Luckily, Flash has an easy way to find vacant depths, the `getNextHighestDepth()` method.

The `getNextHighestDepth()` Method

The `getNextHighestDepth()` method is used when creating movie clips in ActionScript. It returns the next available depth for a movie to be placed on as a numerical value starting with zero.

The generic layout is this:

```
myMovie.getNextHighestDepth();
```

The `myMovie` in the code represents the movie clip that you are checking for the next available depth.

Here is a short example:

1. Create a new Flash document.

2. In the first frame of the main timeline, open the Actions panel and place these actions in it:

```
//send the first available depth to the output panel
trace(this.getNextHighestDepth());
//create a movie clip on the first available depth
this.createEmptyMovieClip("test",this.getNextHighestDepth());
//send the next available depth to the output panel
trace(this.getNextHighestDepth());
//output: 0
//         1
```

The preceding code gets the first available depth and sends it to the Output panel. Then it creates a movie clip on the very same depth. Finally, it sends the next available depth to the Output panel.

Test the movie, and you should see an Output panel similar to Figure 13.7. Also, if you check the objects by clicking Debug, List Objects, you will see the movie clip we created in the Output panel as well.

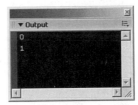

FIGURE 13.7   Using the `getNextHighestDepth()` method, you will never have to worry if you are overwriting another movie clip's depth.

Sometimes you know a movie clip is on a certain depth, but you just cannot remember which movie clipmovie clip. Flash has a method for that as well, the getInstanceAtDepth() method.

The getInstanceAtDepth() Method

The getInstanceAtDepth() method is used to find out what object is residing on a certain depth. It returns the instance name of the object residing in the depth specified.

Here is a generic layout of the getInstanceAtDepth() method:

```
myMovie.getInstanceAtDepth(depth);
```

The only parameter the getInstanceAtDepth() method has is the depth parameter. This is the numerical value representing the depth you would like to check. If there is no instance on that depth, undefined will be returned.

Following is an example of using the getInstanceAtDepth() method:

1. Create a new Flash document.

2. In the first frame of the main timeline, open the Actions panel and place these actions in it:

```
//create three movie clips on their own depth
this.createEmptyMovieClip("sample1_mc",this.getNextHighestDepth());
this.createEmptyMovieClip("sample2_mc",this.getNextHighestDepth());
this.createEmptyMovieClip("sample3_mc",this.getNextHighestDepth());
//now check to see what is on depth 1
trace(this.getInstanceAtDepth(1));
```

The foregoing code creates three instances of movie clips and then returns the instance of the movie clip on depth 1.

Test the movie, and you will see in the Output window the instance name of the second movie clip we created. Remember the getNextHighestDepth() method starts at zero, not one.

We have covered many ways to manipulate movie clips, including their visual properties, color, and now their depth. The next section goes in a different direction by talking about how to make copies of movie clips during runtime.

Duplicating Movie Clips

Duplicating movie clips can be useful and more file-size efficient than manually creating each new movie clip. When you manually duplicate movie clips, the .swf file increases in size because not only does it include each new movie clip, but also all the code each extra movie clip contains. Using ActionScript to duplicate movie clips is more efficient because it duplicates the movie clips at runtime. The method used in ActionScript for duplicating movie clips is the duplicateMovieClip() method.

The duplicateMovieClip() **Method**

The duplicateMovieClip() method was introduced back in Flash 5; it has the capability to take movie clips created manually or with ActionScript and make duplicate copies on the stage during runtime.

Its generic layout is this:

```
myMovie.duplicateMovieClip(instanceName, depth, initObject);
```

myMovie is the movie clip to be duplicated. As you can see, the duplicateMovieClip() method has three parameters:

- instanceName—A string literal representing the instance name given to the duplicated movie clip being created

- depth—The depth of the duplicated movie clip as a numerical value

- initObject—An optional parameter referring to an object that the duplicated movie clip will retain all actions from

The duplicateMovieClip() is usually used in conjunction with a loop statement so that several copies can be made with one instance of the method.

Here is an example using the duplicateMovieClip() method:

1. Create a new Flash document.

2. Draw a square in the upper-left corner of the stage, about 50 pixels wide.

3. Highlight the entire square, including the stroke, and convert it to a symbol by choosing Modify, Convert to Symbol.

4. Give it a symbol name of **squareMC** and make the behavior Movie Clip.

5. On the main stage, give the square an instance name of **square_mc**.

6. Create a new layer and give it the name **actions**.

7. In the first frame of the Actions layer, open the Actions panel and place these actions within it:

```
//create a loop statement to control the duplication
for(var i:Number = 0; i<10; i++){
    //duplicate the movie clip
    square_mc.duplicateMovieClip("square"+i+"_mc",i);
}
```

The preceding code uses a for loop statement to control the duplication of the movie clip. Then, in the duplicateMovieClip() method, we use the variable *i* that was created in the loop statement to give each instance of the duplicated movie clip a unique instance name and depth; two movie clips cannot have the same instance name or reside on the same depth.

Test the movie and notice that it appears that the duplication did not take place. But in fact it did work; select Debug, List Objects, and the Output panel will show all the duplicated movie clips, as you can see in Figure 13.8.

```
▼ Output
Movie Clip: Frame=1 Target="_level0.square_mc"
    Shape:
Movie Clip: Frame=1 Target="_level0.square0_mc"
    Shape:
Movie Clip: Frame=1 Target="_level0.square1_mc"
    Shape:
Movie Clip: Frame=1 Target="_level0.square2_mc"
    Shape:
Movie Clip: Frame=1 Target="_level0.square3_mc"
    Shape:
Movie Clip: Frame=1 Target="_level0.square4_mc"
    Shape:
```

FIGURE 13.8   The Output panel shows that the `duplicateMovieClip()` method was successful, even if the results on the stage appear otherwise.

Let's go back into the code to create a visual indicator that the `duplicateMovieClip()` method is working.

1. Close the test movie screen and go back to the main timeline.

2. Open the Actions panel in the first frame of the actions layer and change the code to this:

```
//create a loop statement to control the duplication
for(var i:Number = 0; i<10; i++){
    //duplicate the movie clip
    var ref:MovieClip = square_mc.duplicateMovieClip("square"+i+"_mc",i);
    //the following code will show visual appearance of the other movies
    ref._x += square_mc._width*i;
}
```

The preceding code is very similar to the code that was there before. The first difference you will notice is that we create a reference named `ref` so that we can access the duplicated movie clip's properties after it has been created. Then we move the square to the right by an amount equal to its own width, which will create a line of squares.

Test the movie again, and you should see that the `duplicateMovieClip()` method did in fact work, with each square being spaced out across the stage as shown in Figure 13.9.

The next example is going to take into consideration all that we have covered thus far. We will use the code that will make movie clips move around on the screen and we'll make use of the `Color` object and the `duplicateMovieClip()` object.

1. Create a new Flash document.

2. Draw a circle on the stage.

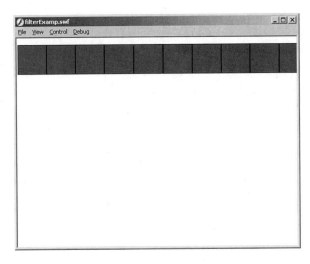

FIGURE 13.9   You can see that the `duplicateMovieClip()` method worked, because the squares are spaced along the stage.

3. Convert the circle to a Movie Clip symbol by choosing Modify, Convert to Symbol.

4. Give it a symbol name of **circleMC** and make sure the behavior is set to Movie Clip.

5. Give the circle on the stage an instance name of **circle_mc**.

6. Create a new layer and name it **actions**.

7. In the first frame of the Actions layer, open the Actions panel and place this code in it:

```
//set the cacheAsBitmap property
circle_mc.cacheAsBitmap = true;
//place some variables associated with circle_mc
circle_mc.friction = 0.3;
circle_mc.xBoundary = 550;
circle_mc.yBoundary = 400;
circle_mc.newX = Math.floor(Math.random()*circle_mc.xBoundary);
circle_mc.newY = Math.floor(Math.random()*circle_mc.yBoundary);
```

The preceding code creates variables associated with the `circle_mc` movie clip.

8. Next we will create a `Color` object, and use the `Math` object to select a random color. Place this code after the preceding code:

```
//this will color the circle_mc
circle_mc.newColor = new Color(this);
//set the RGB using the Math.random() method
circle_mc.newColor.setRGB(Math.random()*0x1000000);
```

This section of code creates a `Color` object within the `circle_mc` movie clip. You will see later why we are putting the variables and `Color` object in the `circle_mc`. After the `Color` object is created, we call the `setRGB()` method and pass it a random hexadecimal value by using the `Math.random()` method.

You can test the movie at this point if you like. Every time the movie is run, the color of the circle will change to a random color.

The next block of code will be used to move the circle around.

9. After the preceding block of code in the Actions panel, add these actions:

```
//this is the event for the motion
circle_mc.onEnterFrame=function(){
    //continually get the current position
    currentX = Math.floor(this._x);
    currentY = Math.floor(this._y);
    //check the horizontal position
    if(currentX != this.newX){
        this._x += (this.newX-currentX)*this.friction;
    }else{
        this.newX = Math.floor(Math.random()*this.xBoundary);
    }
    //do the same with the horizontal position
    if(currentY != this.newY){
        this._y += (this.newY-currentY)*this.friction;
    }else{
        this.newY = Math.floor(Math.random()*this.yBoundary);
    }
}
```

This code creates the function that will control the movement of the circles. You can test again here if you like to see that the `circle_mc` is moving around. Now all we have to do is make copies.

10. Now we'll create the final part of the code, the duplicating part. Add these actions to the bottom of the code we already have:

```
//this will duplicate the movie
for(var i=0; i<10; i++){
    circle_mc.duplicateMovieClip("circle"+i+"_mc",i, circle_mc);
}
```

This code duplicates the movie clip we have already built and uses the `circle_mc` as its initializing object, which means that each duplicate movie clip will take on the same characteristics as the object we place in there.

Now test the movie again, and you should see a bunch of circles flying around the screen, as shown in Figure 13.10. And each time you run this movie, their color will change.

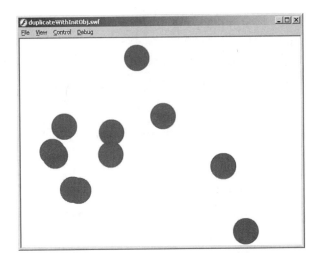

FIGURE 13.10   Using the duplicateMovieClip() method, you can create some cool effects.

We have seen how to create movie clips two different ways, as well as duplicate them. But what if we want to remove them?

Removing Movie Clips

Sometimes movie clips need to be removed from the stage because they are no longer necessary, and you prefer that your computer has its virtual memory and resources back for other objects on the stage to function more efficiently.

The method to use is the removeMovieClip() method.

The removeMovieClip() Method

The removeMovieClip() method is used to remove movie clips that have been created manually or with ActionScript.

It has two basic layouts:

```
myMovie.removeMovieClip(); //method
removeMovieClip(myMovie); //function
```

Both generic uses have myMovie either as a parameter or as the object the method is being called from. Both uses, when called, accomplish the same thing—removing myMovie from the stage.

Here is an example of removing movie clips from the stage:

1. Create a new Flash document.

2. Draw a square somewhere on the stage.

3. Highlight the entire square, including the stroke, and convert it to a symbol by choosing Modify, Convert to Symbol.

4. Give it a symbol name of **squareMC** and make the behavior Movie Clip.

5. On the main stage, give the square an instance name of **square_mc**.

6. Create a new layer and give it the name of **actions**.

7. In the first frame of the Actions layer, open the Actions panel and place these actions within it:

```
//create an empty movie clip
this.createEmptyMovieClip("test_mc",1);
//remove the square_mc movie clip
square_mc.removeMovieClip();
//remove the test_mc movie clip
removeMovieClip(test_mc);
//see if the test_mc movie clip is still available
trace(test_mc);
```

The preceding code creates an empty movie clip and then removes the square_mc movie clip we created manually. After that, it removes the test_mc movie clip we created with code, and finally it uses a trace action to check to see whether the test_mc movie clip is still available.

Test the movie and you should see nothing on the stage, and the Output window should say undefined, showing there isn't a test_mc movie clip available anymore.

So far in this chapter, we have covered how to create movie clips, manipulate movie clips, and remove movie clips. The final section will cover the Drawing API for movie clips.

The Drawing API

The Drawing API is Flash's way of drawing shapes and lines with ActionScript. The Drawing API can be used in conjunction with any movie clip including the _root timeline.

The following sections cover some of the methods used in the Drawing API, starting with the lineStyle() method.

The lineStyle() Method

The lineStyle() method is used to define the stroke size, color, and transparency of a line before you start drawing with the other methods.

Its generic layout is this:

```
movie.lineStyle(thickness, color, alpha, pixelHinting,
➡noScale, capsStyle, jointStyle, miterLimit);
```

This method has the following parameters:

- `thickness`—A numerical value used to declare the weight of the line.
- `color`—A hexadecimal value used to declare the color of the line.
- `alpha`—A numerical value representing the transparency level of the line.
- `pixelHinting`—An optional Flash 8 player parameter with a Boolean value stating whether to use pixel hinting, which affects anchors and position or curves.
- `noScale`—An optional Flash 8 player parameter with a string value stating how to scale the line:
  - `normal`—Always scale the thickness of the line. This is the default choice.
  - `none`—Never scale the thickness of the line.
  - `vertical`—Do not scale the thickness of the line when the line is vertically scaled.
  - `horizontal`—Do not scale the thickness of the line when the line is horizontally scaled.
- `capStyle`—An optional Flash 8 player parameter with a string value controlling the end caps of the line segment; it handles none, round, or square.
- `jointStyle`—An optional Flash 8 player parameter with a string value controlling the joint style of the line segments; it handles miter, round, or bevel.
- `miterLimit`—An optional Flash 8 player parameter with a string value controlling the level of miter on line segments, but only when the `jointStyle` parameter is set to "miter."

Although the `lineStyle()` method has many parameters, for the most part, you will need to work with the first three. And, this method alone will not show anything, so the example will have to wait until we draw a line.

The next method you would use with the Drawing API is the `moveTo()` method.

The `moveTo()` Method

The `moveTo()` method is used to create a starting point for the drawing API. It can also be used to move the drawing point without drawing a line. If the `moveTo()` method is skipped, the Drawing API begins drawing at points (0,0) of the movie clip it is being drawn in.

Here is the generic layout of the `moveTo` method:

```
myMovie.moveTo(X,Y);
```

This method has two parameters:

- X—A numerical value representing the horizontal position the drawing point is moved to without a line being drawn
- Y—A numerical value representing the vertical position the drawing point is moved to without a line being drawn

Like the `lineStyle()` method, the `moveTo()` method does not do anything that can be seen, so the example of its use can be seen in the following section covering the next method: the `lineTo()` method.

The `lineTo()` Method

The `lineTo()` method is used to draw a line from the preceding point created by either the `moveTo()` method or another `lineTo()` method to the next point. The line drawn will have the characteristics created by the `lineStyle()` method (or the `lineGradientStyle()` method, which we will discuss later).

The generic layout for this method is

```
myMovie.lineTo(X,Y);
```

The two parameters for this method are

- X—A numerical value representing the horizontal position to draw the line to
- Y—A numerical value representing the vertical position to draw the line to

Now that we have covered three of the basic methods for the drawing API, here is an example that will bring them together.

1. Create a new Flash document.

2. In the first frame of the main timeline, open the Actions panel and place these actions in it:

```
//create the line style
this.lineStyle(2,0x000000,100);
//move the starting point
this.moveTo(100,100);
//draw a line
this.lineTo(200,200);
```

The preceding code does three things. First, it creates the line style with a weight of 2 pixels, with black as its color, and a 100% alpha setting. After that, it moves the starting point to (100,100). Then it draws a diagonal line to point (200,200).

Test the movie and your screen should look similar to Figure 13.11 with a diagonal line. You can go back in and add more `lineTo()` methods to make the line go from point to point.

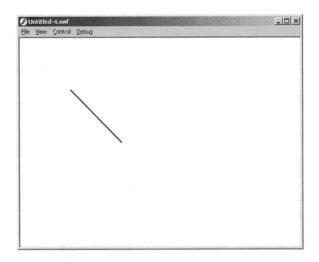

FIGURE 13.11 Use the Drawing API to draw lines right from ActionScript at runtime.

That was a simple enough example. Next is a more advanced example, which enables the user to draw lines during runtime all over the stage. To accomplish this, follow these steps:

1. Create a new Flash document.

2. In the first frame of the main timeline, open the Actions panel and place these actions in it:

```
//this event will trigger when the user presses the mouse button
this.onMouseDown = function(){
    //declare the line style
    this.lineStyle(4,Math.random()*0x1000000,100);
    //set the starting point
    this.moveTo(this._xmouse,this._ymouse);
    //this event will fire as the user moves the mouse
    this.onMouseMove=function(){
        //draw a line
        this.lineTo(this._xmouse,this._ymouse);
        //re-style the line
        this.lineStyle(4,Math.random()*0x1000000,100);
    }
}
//this event triggers when the user releases the mouse
this.onMouseUp = function(){
    //destroy the onMouseMove event
    delete this.onMouseMove;
}
```

The preceding code does many things. First, it creates an event for when the user clicks the mouse button, which in turn creates another event that triggers continuously while the user moves the mouse. While the user is moving the mouse, a line is drawn to where the mouse is, and the line continuously changes color. Finally, we create an event for when the user releases the mouse. When that event is triggered, the onMouseMove event is destroyed and the line will not follow the mouse any more.

Test the movie and you will see that when you click the mouse and move the mouse around, a constantly color-changing line will follow the mouse around.

There is also another way to set line properties, and that is to use the lineGradientStyle() method.

The lineGradientStyle() Method

New to Flash 8 is the capability to have gradients within strokes. This can also be accomplished in ActionScript using the lineGradientStyle() method like this:

```
myMovie.lineGradientStyle(fillType, colors, alphas, ratios, matrix,
➥spreadMethod, interpolationMethod, focalPointRatio);
```

The preceding method has the following parameters:

- **fillType**—This parameter controls the type of gradient, either "linear" or "radial."
- **colors**—This is an array of the different colors you want to use in the gradient.
- **alphas**—This is an array of the different levels of alpha you want to use in conjunction with the colors parameter.
- **ratios**—This is an array of the color distribution levels you want to use in conjunction with the colors parameter. Range from 0–255.
- **matrix**—This is the transformation matrix used in our gradient.
- **spreadMethod**—This controls the mode of gradient fill and will accept "pad," "reflect," or "repeat."
- **interpolationMethod**—This controls the type of interpolation of the colors and accepts "RGB" or "linearRGB."
- **focalPointRatio**—This numerical value controls the focal point of the gradient.

It is important to note that this method can be called only after calling the lineStyle() method to set the line size.

Revisiting our previous example, this next example will draw a line following the mouse, but use a predefined gradient.

1. Create a new Flash document.

2. In the first frame, place these actions:

```
//set up the properties of the gradient we are going to use
var colors:Array = [0x009900, 0x397dce];
var alphas:Array = [50, 100];
var ratios:Array = [0, 0xFF];
var matrix:Object = {a:200, b:0, c:0, d:0, e:200, f:0, g:200, h:200, i:1};
var sMethod:String = "repeat";
var iMethod:String = "RGB";
var fpRatio:Number = .5;

//set the line style and gradient
this.lineStyle(4);
this.lineGradientStyle("radial",colors,alphas,
➥ratios,matrix,sMethod,iMethod,fpRatio);

//this.lineGradientStyle(4,Math.random()*0x1000000,100);
//this event will trigger when the user presses the mouse button
this.onMouseDown = function() {
    //set the starting point
    this.moveTo(this._xmouse,this._ymouse);
    //this event will fire as the user moves the mouse
    this.onMouseMove = function() {
        //draw a line
        this.lineTo(this._xmouse,this._ymouse);
    }
}
//this event triggers when the user releases the mouse
this.onMouseUp = function() {
    //destroy the onMouseMove event
    delete this.onMouseMove;
}
```

The preceding code is very similar to the previous example, except this time we set the `lineStyle()` first and then set the new `lineGradientStyle()`. Test this movie, and after drawing for a little bit, you should see something similar to Figure 13.12.

> **NOTE**
>
> Note that the `lineGradientStyle()` method is available only in the Flash 8 player.

Now that you know how to draw a line, the next step is how to draw a shape and fill it with the `beginFill()` method.

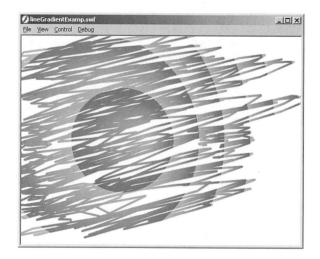

FIGURE 13.12   You can see the radial gradient being formed after drawing several lines.

The `beginFill()` Method

The `beginFill()` method is used to fill shapes drawn with drawing API. Whenever you use the `beginFill()` method, when you are done filling the shape, you should always have the `endFill()` method to tell the Drawing API you are done filling.

Here is the generic layout of the `beginFill()` method:

```
myMovie.beginFill(color,alpha);
```

This method has two parameters:

- `color`—A hexadecimal value used in declaring the color of the fill

- `alpha`—A numerical value representing the transparency of the fill

In the next example, we will draw a square and fill it with a light green color.

1. Create a new Flash document.

2. In the first frame of the main timeline, open the Actions panel and place these actions in it:

```
//create the line style
this.lineStyle(2,0x000000,100);
//move the starting point
this.moveTo(100,100);
//begin the fill
this.beginFill(0x00ff00,50);
//draw a line
this.lineTo(100,200);
```

```
this.lineTo(200,200);
this.lineTo(200,100);
this.lineTo(100,100);
//end the fill
this.endFill();
```

The preceding code started out similar to previous examples, but this time after we went to the starting point, we began to fill the shape. After that we drew the square. And finally, we ended the fill with the endFill() method.

Test the movie, and you should see a square with a light green color for the fill, as shown in Figure 13.13.

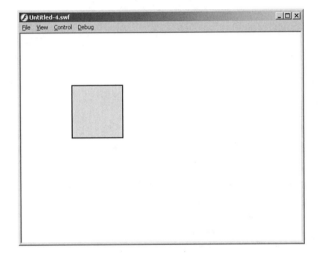

FIGURE 13.13   You can use the drawing API to draw shapes and color them in.

You can create gradient fills as well using the beginGradientFill() method.

The beginGradientFill() Method

The beginGradientFill() acts just like the beginFill() method, except it has these parameters:

```
myMovie.beginGradientFill(fillType, colors, alphas, ratios, matrix,
➥spreadMethod, interpolationMethod, focalPointRatio);
```

Following is a better explanation of those parameters:

- **fillType**—This parameter controls the type of gradient, either "linear" or "radial."
- **colors**—This is an array of the different colors you want to use in the gradient.

- **alphas**—This is an array of the different levels of alpha you want to use in conjunction with the *colors* parameter.

- **ratios**—This is an array of the color distribution levels you want to use in conjunction with the *colors* parameter. Range from 0–255.

- **matrix**—This is the transformation matrix used in our gradient.

- **spreadMethod**—This controls the mode of gradient fill and will accept "pad," "reflect," or "repeat."

- **interpolationMethod**—This controls the type of interpolation of the colors and accepts "RGB" or "linearRGB."

- **focalPointRatio**—This numerical value controls the focal point of the gradient.

Now let's see an example of this.

1. Create a new Flash document.

2. Place these actions in the first frame:

```
//properties for our gradient
var fillType:String = "radial";
var colors:Array = [0x009900, 0x397dce];
var alphas:Array = [50, 100];
var ratios:Array = [0x00, 0xFF];
var matrix:Object = {a:100, b:0, c:0, d:0, e:100, f:0, g:100, h:100, i:1};
var spreadMethod:String = "repeat";
//set the linestyle and gradient fill
this.lineStyle(2,0x000000,100);
this.beginGradientFill(fillType, colors, alphas,
➥ ratios, matrix, spreadMethod);
//draw a square
this.moveTo(0, 0);
this.lineTo(0, 200);
this.lineTo(200, 200);
this.lineTo(200, 0);
this.lineTo(0, 0);
this.endFill();
```

This code first creates some properties for our gradient and then sets the line style and gradient fill. Finally, the square is drawn, as you can see in Figure 13.14.

So far, we have drawn straight lines, but the next section will go over how to draw curved lines with the curveTo() method.

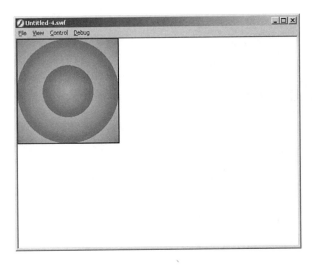

FIGURE 13.14   You can set gradients to the fill color for a more vibrant effect.

The `curveTo()` Method

The `curveTo()` method is used to draw curved lines with the Drawing API. It works similarly to the `lineTo()` method in that it starts from the previous point created by either a `moveTo()` method or a `lineTo()` method.

Its generic layout is as follows:

```
myMovie.curveTo(controlX,controlY,X,Y);
```

This method has four parameters:

- `controlX`—This represents the horizontal position toward which the line will curve.
- `controlY`—This represents the vertical position toward which the line will curve.
- `X`—This is the horizontal position where the curved line will end.
- `Y`—This is the vertical position where the curved line will end.

The generic layout is a little difficult to grasp without an example, so here is one:

1. Create a new Flash document.

2. In the first frame of the main timeline, open the Actions panel and place these actions in it:

   ```
   //declare the line style
   this.lineStyle(2,0x000000,100);
   //create the start point
   this.moveTo(100,100);
   //draw the curved line
   this.curveTo(200,100,200,200);
   ```

The preceding code creates the line style, then declares a starting point, and finally draws the curved line.

Test the movie and your screen should have a curved line on it similar to Figure 13.15.

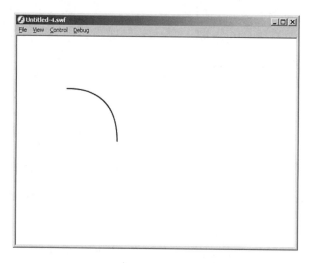

FIGURE 13.15 Use the curveTo() method to draw curved lines with the Drawing API.

That example was pretty simple. The following example shows off the curveTo() method a little further.

1. Create a new Flash document.

2. In the first frame of the main timeline, open the Actions panel and place these actions in it:

```
//declare the line style
this.lineStyle(3,0x000000,100);
//go to the start point
this.moveTo(300,260);
//start the fill
this.beginFill(0xff0000,100);
//start drawing the shape
this.curveTo(300,200,250,200);
this.curveTo(185,200,195,270);
this.curveTo(220,350,300,400);
this.curveTo(398,350,400,260);
this.curveTo(400,200,350,200);
this.curveTo(300,200,300,260);
//end the fill
this.endFill();
```

The preceding code doesn't really do anything special. It declares the line style we want to use. Then it sets a start point using the `moveTo()` method. After that, it begins the fill with a shade of red as its color. Then it begins to draw the shape using a few `curveTo()` methods. It finishes by ending the fill with the `endFill()` method (which is good practice).

Now test the movie, and you will see a shape on your screen similar to the one in Figure 13.16. Now that you see what can be accomplished with the Drawing API, you can start creating your own custom shapes entirely through ActionScript.

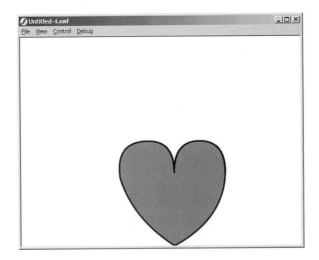

FIGURE 13.16   A heart is just one of the many shapes that can be drawn with a little math and the Drawing API.

Summary

This chapter covered a lot of information regarding the movie clip object. It started with how to create it manually (which was more review than new material) and also how to create it with ActionScript. Then it went on to show some of the many different ways movie clips can be manipulated. After that, you learned how to remove movie clips from the stage during runtime using the `removeMovieClip()` method. And finally, we went over some of the ways to use the Drawing API.

The next chapter covers events, which we have been using for a while but have not really explained.

CHAPTER **14**

Events

Back in Chapter 8, "Welcome to ActionScript 2.0," we went over the three basic elements that all objects in Flash have:

- **Properties**. Information about an object, held within the object.

- **Methods**. These are the "verbs" of objects; they are what the object does.

- **Events**. Events tell Flash when something has occurred with that object.

For instance, with a movie clip, here are the three elements:

- **Property**. _x

- **Method**. `gotoAndPlay(2)`

- **Event**. `onEnterFrame`

This chapter goes into more detail about the third thing that objects have, events.

An event, simply put, is when something happens. Every day you go through several hundred events. Every time you get email, that is an event. When you eat lunch, that's another event. And when you go home on Friday, you know that's an event.

So you see, events happen all the time in almost everything we do. So what's the big deal with events? Well, events in Flash are used to tell us when something occurs so that we can run a certain block of actions or go to a certain frame in the movie. To put it in real-world terms, sometimes people want to be notified when a certain event happens. For instance:

- "Let me know when she calls."
- "Let me know when lunch is here."
- "Let me know when the next meeting is."

These are just a few events that people want to be notified about in everyday life. When these events occur, the individual who is notified will do something about it. For instance, if someone is notified when lunch arrives, that person will probably want to eat it. This is what that event would look like in ActionScript:

```
onLunchArrival = function(){
    eatLunch();
}
```

That looks simple enough, and it is. In Flash, you have events, which we will cover in detail throughout this chapter, that you might want your movie or application to listen for so that it will know when to execute a block of code. But before we cover some of the events of different objects, it's important to know how to handle these events in Flash when they occur.

Handling Events

Knowing how to handle an event is very important. Just the fact that an event occurs doesn't mean anything in itself. In order to do something with that event, you must capture it first. Flash has two basic means of capturing events: the callback and the listener.

The first one we will discuss is the callback.

The Callback

For those who have been programming in Flash for some time, callbacks will seem more familiar and therefore easier to use and implement in your code. *Callbacks*, simply put, are functions tied directly to a particular event.

Because you can create and destroy as well as overwrite any and every variable, function, and method in Flash on the fly, callbacks are basically functions written directly to the event.

For instance, the movie clip object has an event called onMouseDown that is triggered every time the user presses the mouse button on the stage. But if you were to run a blank movie (remember, the main timeline is nothing more than the _root movie clip) and click the mouse on the stage, nothing would happen. This is because no function has been created with the onMouseDown event.

So to handle the event, you need to build a function around the event itself like this:

```
//this refers to the main timeline
this.onMouseDown = function(){
     trace("the mouse is down");
}
```

Usually you would want to do more than simply send a message to the Output panel. Sometimes, you may want the event to interact with other objects, and that's where the downside of callbacks comes in.

Because callbacks are associated directly with events of a specific object, in this case the _root timeline, you cannot always refer directly to other objects on the stage if they are not enclosed in the object of the event being called.

For instance, if you have two movie clips on the stage (movie1_mc and movie2_mc), and you have a onMouseDown event for the movie1_mc movie, you cannot directly access movie2_mc from within that event:

```
movie1_mc.onMouseDown = function(){
     movie2_mc.gotoAndPlay("start");       //this will not work
}
```

The preceding code will not run properly because the onMouseDown event is in the scope of the movie1_mc and not in the scope of movie2_mc. The following code will fix this problem.

```
movie1_mc.onMouseDown = function(){
     _parent.movie2_mc.gotoAndPlay("start");      //this will work
}
```

Just keep in mind the scope of the object you are referring to inside the event.

Another point to note is that some events pass information to the callback. For instance, the onLoad event for the LoadVars object sends the callback a Boolean value based on its success or failure in loading content.

Here's an example of how to get information from events with callbacks:

```
//create the LoadVars object
var myStuff:LoadVars = new LoadVars();
//create the call back
myStuff.onLoad = function(success){
     if(success){
          //it worked
     }else{
          //it didn't work
     }
}
//load the content
myStuff.load("theStuff.txt");
```

Notice that we passed the information coming from the event as a parameter in the function. That's how we get information from events using callbacks. And in this case, the event is a Boolean value that is used in conjunction with conditional statements inside the event.

Now that you see how to create a callback, it is important to know how to destroy them as well.

Removing Callbacks

Sometimes you will want callbacks to stop firing. For instance, if you are using a callback in conjunction with the onEnterFrame event of movie clips, you may only want that event to fire so many times. You can use conditionals to stop the event from affecting anything on the stage, but to regain processor power and virtual memory you need to destroy the callback itself. To do this, you use the delete action.

Here is an example using a loop statement and a delete action:

```
//create a variable we will use in the callback
var i:Number = 0;
//create the callback
this.onEnterFrame = function(){
    //this will trace independant of the conditional
    trace("working");
    if(i < 10){
        trace(i);
    }else{
        delete this.onEnterFrame;
    }
    //increase the variable
    i++;
}
```

The preceding code first creates a variable that is used in the callback. Then it creates the callback and uses a conditional to decide when to destroy itself with the delete action.

Run this code, and you should see an Output panel similar to Figure 14.1. The code runs ten times and then stops completely. To see what would happen if the delete action had not been used, just the conditional, go back and comment out the line containing the delete action. You will see that even though the numbers stop being sent to the Output panel (because of the conditional), the other trace action is still working because the event is still triggering the callback.

Using a callback is just one way of capturing events; the other is using listeners.

FIGURE 14.1   Use the `delete` action to destroy callbacks.

Listeners

If you are new to programming, listeners may appear difficult to use at first, but they are quite powerful when you get used to building them. Listeners take a completely different approach to handling events than callbacks do.

Listeners differ from callbacks in two very important ways. First, listeners do not care where the event is coming from (that is, a movie clip, button, or component)—they only care about who is receiving the event. In the case of the onMouseDown event, the event is coming from the _root timeline, but the Mouse object is actually receiving the event. The other way listeners differ from callbacks is that using a callback with an event will only work with that object, but with listeners, which are objects themselves, you can have several objects "listening" at the same time for the event to fire.

Using listeners is also different from using callbacks. Unlike callbacks, where you just apply a function to that object's event, listeners require you to "subscribe" to the event or object containing the event, or "unsubscribe" from the event or object containing the event. This means that you ask the object to let you know when the event occurs, or you tell it to stop letting you know.

Not all objects support listeners for their events. Those objects that do support listeners have two methods, addListener() and removeListener(). These two methods are how other objects "subscribe" and "unsubscribe" to the events.

Here is an example using the Mouse object's event onMouseDown:

```
//create the object to listen
var listenClick:Object = new Object();
//create the event that looks similar to callback
listenClick.onMouseDown = function(){
    trace("the mouse is down");
```

```
}
//now subscribe the listener
Mouse.addListener(listenClick);
```

All the preceding code does is create a generic object to "listen" for the event. It adds the event to the object (it looks like a callback, but without the listener, it won't work). Then the last line subscribes the object to the Mouse object as a listener.

Now if you test this code, every time the mouse is pressed, the message will be sent to the Output panel.

Also, remember that multiple objects can listen to a single event source. In this next example of code, we will extend the preceding example by creating another object to listen for when the mouse is released:

```
//create the object to listen
var listenClick:Object = new Object();
//create the event that looks similar to callback
listenClick.onMouseDown = function(){
     trace("the mouse is down");
}
//now subscribe the listener
Mouse.addListener(listenClick);
//create another object
var listenUp:Object = new Object();
//create the event similar to before
listenUp.onMouseUp = function(){
     trace("and the mouse is back up again");
}
//now add the new object to the event source as a listener
Mouse.addListener(listenUp);
```

This code merely extends the preceding block of code. It creates another object that will listen to the onMouseUp Mouse event. And then we subscribe it to the Mouse object.

Every time you press and release the mouse button, you will receive two messages in the Output window as shown in Figure 14.2.

You can also have a single listener object listening to several different events like this:

```
//create the object to listen
var mouseListen:Object = new Object();
//create the event that looks similar to callback
mouseListen.onMouseDown = function(){
     trace("the mouse is down");
}
//create the event similar to before
mouseListen.onMouseUp = function(){
```

```
        trace("and the mouse is back up again");
}
//now add the object to the event source as a listener
Mouse.addListener(mouseListen);
```

FIGURE 14.2   Using listeners can increase efficiency for capturing events.

When you test this out, it will work exactly the same way as before.

Now that you know how to subscribe listeners to objects, the next section shows how to unsubscribe them.

Unsubscribing Listeners

Unsubscribing an object uses the method removeListener() in conjunction with the object it is currently listening to. This example shows how to use this method:

```
//create the object to listen
var listenClick:Object = new Object();
//create the event that looks similar to callback
listenClick.onMouseDown = function(){
    //send a message to the output panel
    trace("the mouse is down");
    //remove the listener
    Mouse.removeListener(this);
}
//now subscribe the listener
Mouse.addListener(listenClick);
```

This code starts the same way the preceding code does, but the first time the event fires, the listening object removes itself from the Mouse object. After the first click, no messages will be sent to the Output panel.

Components also use listeners to trigger events associated with them, although the coding is slightly different from what we have used so far.

Components' Special Listeners

Way back in Flash MX, components used a form of callbacks to refer to functions on the timeline of which the component itself resided. However, with the introduction of ActionScript 2.0, components' events are now centered on using listeners.

To add listeners to components, you use the component's instance name and the addEventListener() method.

The generic layout of the addEventListener() method is as follows:

```
component.addEventListener(event, listenerObject);
```

This method has two parameters:

- event—A string literal representing the event you want to listen for
- listenerObject—The object being added as a listener

Here is an example of how to add an event listener to the button component:

1. Create a new Flash document.

2. Drag an instance of the Button component onto the stage.

3. Give the button an instance name of **myButton**.

4. Create a new layer and name it **actions**.

5. In the actions layer, open the Actions panel, and place the following code within it:

```
//create the object
var clickListen:Object = new Object();
//create the event
clickListen.click = function(){
    trace("the button was clicked");
}
//now add the listener
myButton.addEventListener("click", clickListen);
```

The preceding code creates a listener object. Then it creates the event-handling method for that object, which has a trace function in it so it will send a message to the Output panel. Then you add the event listener to the instance of the button.

Now test the movie, and you will see that every time you click the button, the event is triggered, and the listener fires, sending a message to the Output panel.

You can create your own events with components, but that is discussed in more detail in Chapter 16, "Components." And even though component events are centered around listeners, they do have a few hidden callbacks built into them as the next example shows.

Continuing from the previous example, replace the code in the actions layer with the following:

```
//create the callback
myButton.clickHandler = function(){
     trace("the button was clicked, again");
}
```

Run the above example, and again a message will be sent to the Output panel.

But not every listener event in components is as easy as this one, but in general, you can use the event name, in the above case "click," and add "Handler" to it to create a callback. Another example of this is the changeHandler callback for the ComboBox and List component.

And sometimes with callbacks and listeners being triggered all over your code, you might be accidentally duplicating your work.

Duplicating Effort

Some objects will support both callbacks as well as listeners. For instance, you can create a callback with the onMouseDown event and then add a listener to the Mouse object at the same time. Doing this will produce some surprising results, as you will see in the next example of code.

```
//create the callback
this.onMouseDown = function(){
     trace("the mouse is down");
}
//Now add the listener to the Mouse object
Mouse.addListener(this);
```

The code creates the callback that we have been using in this chapter. After that, it adds the _root timeline as a listener to the Mouse object.

Now test the movie, and you will see that every time you press the mouse button on the stage, the message appears twice in the Output panel. Keep this in mind when dealing with both callbacks and listeners.

Now you have seen the two ways Flash handles events, and I bet you are wondering which one you should use.

Callbacks Versus Listeners—The Showdown

We have covered both sides of capturing events, the callbacks and the listeners. Now comes the moment of truth—which one should you use in which situation? Well, if the truth be told, most of the time the choice is already made for you. Most of Flash's built-in object classes support either callbacks or listeners. A few, however, do support both.

The point to keep in mind is that objects that might have other objects wanting to listen for events will support listeners. The `Key` object and the `Mouse` object (which you have already seen) both support listeners because other objects may want to be notified when events occur with these two objects.

Although callbacks are faster to build, it is important to understand listeners, both for better object-oriented programming and because ActionScript 2.0 is more listener-based than ActionScript 1.0.

Throughout the rest of the chapter, we will be going over many of the events for Flash's built-in object classes, starting with the `Button` class.

Button Events

Table 14.1 shows events associated with buttons, but it is important to note that both the `Button` and the `MovieClip` classes of objects support events in frames, as well as in the object actions.

TABLE 14.1   Button Events

Event Handler Object Action	Event Handler Frame Method	Action Description
on (press)	onPress	The event triggered when a user presses a button
on (release)	onRelease	The event triggered when a user releases a button after pressing it
on (releaseOutside)	onReleaseOutside	The event triggered when a user releases the mouse button outside the hit area of a button that has received an onPress event
on (rollOver)	onRollOver	The event triggered when a user's mouse cursor moves over a button without the mouse button being pressed
on (rollOut)	onRollOut	The event triggered when a user moves the mouse cursor outside a button's hit area without the mouse button being suppressed
on (dragOver)	onDragOver	The event triggered when a user moves the mouse cursor over a button's hit area after the button has received an onDragOut event
on (dragOut)	onDragOut	The event triggered when the mouse cursor is moved outside the button's hit area while the mouse button is depressed
on (keyPress"...")	onKeyDown, OnKeyUp	The event triggered when a user presses or releases a key on the keyboard that has been specified in the event
N/A	onSetFocus	The event triggered when a button receives focus from a keyboard interaction (for example, if a user uses the Tab key to gain focus on the button)
N/A	onKillFocus	The event triggered when a button loses keyboard focus

Now that you've seen all the available events for buttons, let's use some of them in the following example:

1. Create a new Flash document.

2. You learned how to create a button in earlier chapters, so we will use one from the common libraries. Choose Window>Common Libraries>Buttons. Choose your favorite button and drag it out to the stage.

3. Give the button on the stage an instance name of **myButton_btn**.

4. Create another layer and name this layer **actions**.

5. In the actions layer, place these actions:

```
//the event for rollover
myButton_btn.onRollOver = function(){
     trace("rollOver occurred");
}
//the event for press
myButton_btn.onPress = function(){
     trace("press occurred");
}
//the event for release
myButton_btn.onRelease = function(){
     trace("release occurred");
}
//the event for release outside
myButton_btn.onReleaseOutside = function(){
     trace("release outside occurred");
}
//the event for rollout
myButton_btn.onRollOut = function(){
     trace("rollOut occurred");
}
//the event for dragOver
myButton_btn.onDragOver = function(){
     trace("dragOver occurred");
}
//the event for dragOut
myButton_btn.onDragOut = function(){
     trace("dragOut occurred");
}
```

The preceding code creates several event callbacks to use with the button we created on the stage.

Test the movie, and do everything you can to the button. You will notice a series of messages in the Output panel depending on what events you trigger with the button. Figure 14.3 shows some of the messages sent to the Output panel.

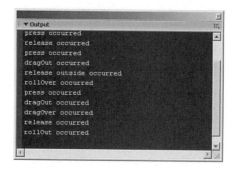

FIGURE 14.3   Use callbacks for button events.

A button is just one of the objects that can handle events on an independent timeline frame or within the object itself. Another object that can do the same is the movie clip object.

Movie Clip Events

Movie clips are another object that uses events regularly. They have several events that may look like duplicates of the button events, but they are independent of them.

Table 14.2 shows the events supported by movie clips.

TABLE 14.2   Movie Clip Events

Event Handler Actions	Event Handler Methods	Action Description
onClipEvent (load)	onLoad	The event that is triggered when a movie clip loads
onClipEvent (unload)	onUnload	The event that is triggered when a movie clip is unloaded
onClipEvent (enterFrame)	onEnterFrame	The event that is triggered as close to the frame rate of a movie clip as possible (the frame rate can be found in the Properties Inspector when the stage has focus)
onClipEvent (mouseDown)	onMouseDown	The event that is triggered whenever the mouse button is pressed anywhere on the stage
onClipEvent (mouseUp)	onMouseUp	The event that is triggered whenever the mouse button is released after an onMouseDown event
onClipEvent (mouseMove)	onMouseMove	The event that is triggered whenever the mouse moves anywhere on the stage
onClipEvent (KeyDown)	onKeyDown	The event that is triggered whenever the user presses a key (after the stage has received focus)

TABLE 14.2 Continued

Event Handler Actions	Event Handler Methods	Action Description
onClipEvent (keyUp)	onKeyUp	The event that is triggered when a user releases a key (after the stage has received focus)
onClipEvent (data)	onData	The event that is triggered when the movie clip receives data

Now that you've seen the events associated with movie clips, here is an example of how to use them:

1. Create a new Flash document.

2. Open the Actions panel in the first frame of the main timeline, and place these actions in it:

```
//create the event for when a user presses the mouse button
this.onMouseDown = function(){
      //create the event for when the user moves the mouse
      this.onMouseMove = function(){
      //send the mouse coordintates to the output panel
      trace("x="+this._xmouse+",y="+this._ymouse);
      }
}
//create the event for when the user releases the mouse
this.onMouseUp = function(){
      //destroy the onMouseMove event
      delete this.onMouseMove;
}
```

The preceding code creates a callback for the onMouseDown event which, when triggered, will create another callback with the onMouseMove event that will continually trace the mouse position while the mouse moves. Then we created a callback for the onMouseUp event that will destroy the onMouseMove callback so that when the user releases the mouse, the trace function will no longer send the mouse position to the Output panel while the mouse moves.

Test the movie, and you will see that if you drag the mouse cursor around the stage, the position will continually be sent to the Output panel. When you release the mouse, the position will no longer be traced.

Even though we listed all the events associated with the movie clip object, those are the events that are associated solely with the movie clip object. The movie clip object itself actually shares other events with the button object.

Movie Clips Handling Button Events

The movie clip object can use all events associated with the button, as well as the movie clip events. Something to note about using button events with movie clips is that if you create a callback for a movie clip object with a button event, the movie clip will display the "button hand" when the mouse cursor is over the top of it.

Here is an example using a movie clip with button events:

1. Create a new Flash document.

2. Draw a square with both width and height of about 100 pixels.

3. Highlight the square you just created, including the stroke, and choose Modify, Convert to Symbol.

4. Give the square a symbol name of **squareMC** and choose Movie Clip for behavior.

5. Back on the stage, give the instance of the square an instance name of **square_mc**.

6. Create another layer and name the layer **actions**.

7. In the actions layer, open the Actions panel, and place these actions in it:

```
//stop the square_mc's playahead
square_mc.stop();
//create the release function
square_mc.onRelease = function(){
    trace("movie clipped released");
}
```

The first thing the preceding code does is to stop the play head of the square_mc movie clip. Normally, this is not necessary because the movie clip only has one frame, but it will become necessary in the next example. The next thing the code does is create a callback event for the square_mc with the button event onRelease.

Now test the movie, and you will see that every time you click the square_mc movie clip, the message will be sent to the Output panel, as you can see in Figure 14.4.

But it's not just the events of buttons that are supported by movie clips—you can also use the special button frames within movie clips. All you have to do is create four keyframes and label each keyframe with these labels:

- _up—This is the frame representing the up state of the button/movie clip.

- _over—This is the frame representing the over state of the button/movie clip.

- _down—This is the frame representing the down state of the button/movie clip.

- _hit—This is the frame representing the hit area of the button/movie clip.

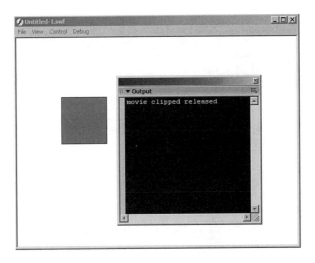

FIGURE 14.4   Button events are supported by movie clips.

Now we are going to continue the preceding example by creating the button states in the movie clip:

1. Close the test movie screen and return to the main timeline.

2. Double-click the instance of the square to enter edit mode.

3. Create three more keyframes, preferably spaced apart a bit so that you can easily read the states.

4. Create a new layer and name it **labels**.

5. Make sure the labels layer has the same keyframes as the other layer in the movie clip.

6. Label each key frame in the labels layer; "_up", "_over", "_down", and "_hit" in that order.

7. Then in each keyframe, change the fill color of the square (your screen should look similar to Figure 14.5).

8. Now test the movie.

Test the movie, and you will see that when you roll your mouse over or press the mouse over the square_mc movie clip, the button changes color to the colors we used in the keyframes.

Now you have seen the events for both buttons and movie clips, but they are not the only objects that have events. Many other objects have events, and here are a few of them starting with the Mouse object.

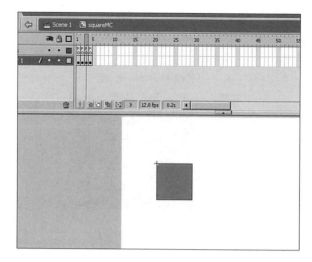

FIGURE 14.5   Using special frame labels, you can create button states within movie clips.

Events of the Mouse Object

The mouse is one of the most frequently used objects for interactive interfaces because the most common ways a user interacts with Flash are with either the mouse or the keyboard.

Table 14.3 shows the events for the Mouse object.

TABLE 14.3   Mouse Events

Event Handler Methods	Action Description
onMouseDown	This event occurs if the user presses the mouse button on the stage.
onMouseUp	This event occurs when the user releases the mouse button over the stage.
onMouseMove	This event occurs when the user moves the mouse over the stage.
onMouseWheel	This event occurs when the user uses the mouse wheel.

Now that you've seen all the events for the Mouse object, here is an example using the addListener() method and the onMouseWheel event.

Here is the code block used to detect the mouse wheel:

```
//create the listener object
var wheelListen:Object = new Object();
//create the event
wheelListen.onMouseWheel = function(amount){
    trace(amount);
}
//add the listener to the Mouse object
Mouse.addListener(wheelListen);
```

In this code block, we create a listener object. Then we create the event-handling method for listening to the mouse wheel. Notice that you pass the event-handling method a parameter. The amount parameter is a numerical value representing which direction the mouse wheel is spinning, and at what speed. We send this numerical value to the Output panel with the trace function. After that, we add the listener to the Mouse object.

Now when you test the movie, if the event doesn't fire when you spin the wheel, click the stage once to make sure it has focus. When the mouse wheel spins, you will see negative and positive numbers in the Output panel.

The other object that is most often used for user interaction is the Key object.

Events of the Key Object

The keyboard is the most important way users interact with applications. It is the only way to enter pertinent information into forms. The Key object is the object that captures events associated with keyboard interaction.

Table 14.4 shows the events for the Key object.

TABLE 14.4 Key Events

Event Handler Methods	Action Description
onKeyDown	This event occurs when the user presses a key on the keyboard.
onKeyUp	This event occurs when the user releases the key that has been pressed.

Now that you've seen the two events associated with the Key object, here is a code example using the onKeyDown event:

```
//create the object to listen to the Key
var keyListen:Object = new Object();
//create the event
keyListen.onKeyDown = function(){
   //trace the character you pressed
   trace(String.fromCharCode(Key.getAscii()));
}
//add the listener
Key.addListener(keyListen);
```

The preceding code creates the listener object. Then it creates the event-handling method that includes the trace function that will send the character the user presses to the Output panel using the String object with the Key object.

Run the code, and if nothing happens at first, give the focus to the stage by clicking on it once. Then, when you use the keyboard, you should begin to see letters appearing in the Output panel.

Another object that uses events is the TextField object.

Events of the `TextField` Object

Flash uses text fields as a means of gathering and displaying information. And because they are objects, they also have events associated with them.

Table 14.5 lists those events.

TABLE 14.5   `TextField` Events

Event Handler Methods	Action Description
onChanged	The event invoked when the text in a text field changes
onScroller	The event triggered when the `scroll` property of a text field changes
onSetFocus	The event called when a text field receives keyboard focus (for example, if a user uses the Tab key to gain focus on the text field)
onKillFocus	The event called when a text field loses keyboard focus

`TextField` objects support listeners and callbacks.

Here are two examples doing the same thing using both means of capturing an event.

First, the callback way:

1. Create a new Flash document.

2. Draw an input text field on the stage.

3. Give the text field an instance name of **input_txt** and make sure the border option is selected (so that you can see it on the stage).

4. Create a new layer and name it **actions**.

5. In the actions layer, open the Actions panel and place these actions in it:

```
//create the callback
input_txt.onChanged = function(){
    trace("changes have been made");
}
```

The preceding code creates a callback such that when a user makes changes to the content in the input_txt text field, a message will be sent to the Output panel.

That example used a callback to capture the onChanged event. This example uses a listener:

1. Create a new Flash document.

2. Draw an input text field on the stage.

3. Give the text field an instance name of **input_txt** and make sure the border option is selected (so that you can see it on the stage).

4. Create a new layer and name it **actions**.

5. In the actions layer, open the Actions panel and place these actions in it:

```
//create the object to listen for the event
var changeListen:Object = new Object();
//create the event method
changeListen.onChanged = function(){
    trace("changes have been made");
}
//add the listener to the TextField
input_txt.addListener(changeListen);
```

The preceding code creates the listener object. Then it creates the event-handling method, which, when triggered, will send a message to the Output panel. Finally, we add the listener object to the text field instance.

Both of these examples accomplish the same tasks, but in different ways. You choose to use the one you feel most comfortable with.

And when dealing with events you do not have to just use certain events with certain objects. In some circumstances, you can use events with objects that they were not meant for.

Cross-Object Events

In HTML forms, when a user has finished entering data, he or she can click the submit button or press the Enter key while in the last text field. Well, Flash, by default, does not have the capability for users to simply press the Enter key and move on through an application or form. So how does a Flash developer overcome this dilemma? Use a Key object listener with the TextField object.

This example will create a text field that will listen for the Enter key to be pressed:

1. Create a new Flash document.

2. Draw an input text field on the stage.

3. Give the text field an instance name of **input_txt** and make sure the border option is selected (so that you can see it on the stage).

4. Create a new layer and name it **actions**.

5. In the actions layer, open the actions panel and place these actions in it:

```
//create the listener with the text field
input_txt.onKeyDown = function(){
//check to make sure its the ENTER key being pressed
    if(Key.isDown(Key.ENTER)){
        //send a message to the output panel
```

```
        trace("I detect an ENTER");
    }
}
//add the text field as a listener
Key.addListener(input_txt);
```

The preceding code uses an event-handling method on a text field with a Key object event. Inside the event, it uses a conditional to check to see which key has been pressed and whether it is in fact the Enter key, and then a message is sent to the Output panel. And finally, it adds the text field as a listener to the Key object.

Test this code and you will see that not only will the event be triggered with the text field as the listener, but the focus must be in the text field itself in order for it to trigger.

That is just one of the many cross-object events that can be accomplished with listeners. Play around with some of the other objects and see if you can build your own custom events.

Summary

This chapter has covered all the basics and even some advanced uses of events. It has covered the major objects that use events, and the different ways to capture those events.

Just remember what events are. They are tattle-tales. They tell Flash exactly when things occur so that as developers, you know when and how to execute certain blocks of code.

CHAPTER 15

Working with Text

Text is one of the earliest forms of media communication, and Flash has not forgotten this. Back in Flash MX, text fields became full-fledged objects with properties, methods, events, and even instance names. In Flash 2004, the ability to load images into HTML text fields was added. This time around, better anti-aliasing in the IDE and the player with FlashType and improved WYSIWYG in the IDE are included.

This chapter explores the many ways to create and manipulate text fields, as well as some new things added to the object with this version of Flash.

Some of the topics to be covered are

- The text field interface
- Creating the three basic types of text fields
- Formatting text fields
- Working with HTML text

Let's start with the interface.

The Text Field Interface

To get to the Text Field interface, you first have to select the Text tool either by going to the large letter *A* on the toolbar, or by pressing the letter *T* on the keyboard. When you have selected the Text tool, the Properties Inspector will look like Figure 15.1.

FIGURE 15.1   The text field interface.

Most of the options are the general variety of font options such as size, font type, font size, alignment, and color. Some of the other options that you may not be familiar with are on the Text Field type drop-down menu, which includes three options:

- **Static Text.** This text is exactly the way it sounds; all the text to be seen in this text field must be placed in it during authoring and cannot be manipulated by ActionScript during runtime.

- **Dynamic Text.** This text field type is as it says, dynamic, meaning that it can be manipulated and adjusted not only during authoring, but also at runtime.

- **Input Text.** This text field is nearly identical to the dynamic text field, except that not only can it be changed at runtime by ActionScript, but the user can also enter text into this type of text field to be used with ActionScript.

All three of these types of text fields will be reviewed in greater detail in the next section.

An upgraded option to text fields is the anti-aliasing options:

- **Use Device Fonts**—This option will make it so the end user must have the selected font on the system for it to render correctly. Although file size is decreased with this option, only use it when using a common font such as Arial.

- **Bitmap Text (No Anti-Alias)**—This option will turn anti-aliasing completely off meaning no smoothing will occur, similar to a pixel font. This option will embed the font into the SWF and increase the file size.

- **Anti-Alias for Animation**—This option will ignore alignment and kerning to create very smooth text for animating. This option will embed the font into the SWF and increase the file size.

- **Anti-Alias for Readability**—This option uses the new FlashType anti-aliasing engine to create crisper text for improved readability. This option will embed the font into the SWF and increase the file size.

- **Custom Anti-Alias**—This Flash Professional 8 only option, when selected, will bring up the Custom Anti-Aliasing dialogue box (Figure 15.2), which will allow you to set the following two options for a custom anti-alis:

  - **Thickness**—Controls the blending between the text edges and the background.

  - **Sharpness**—Transition smoothness between the background and edges of text.

In order to use the *Custom Anti-Aliasing* option, you must publish to the Flash 8 player, and this option will embed the font into the SWF and increase the file size.

And when selecting the *Use Device Fonts* option, remember there are three built-in device fonts that Flash already has:

- **_sans**. Similar to Helvetica or Arial

- **_serif**. Like Times Roman

- **_typewriter**. Like Courier

The important thing to consider when choosing this option is your audience. And play around with the settings before you decide which anti-alias to use, if any.

And when embedding fonts, you can control which glyphs to use by pressing the *Embed* button in the Properties Inspector, which will launch the Character Options as in Figure 15.3. You can specify a range of characters such as Uppercase or Numerals. You can also include only a few select characters you type in, or have the menu select the characters you are already using by clicking the Auto Fill button.

But remember, embedding fonts will increase the file size roughly 100 bytes or more per glyph, so only embed the characters you are sure you will use.

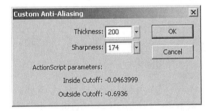

FIGURE 15.2 The Custom Anti-Aliasing dialogue box will allow you to control thickness and sharpness and will also show the ActionScript parameters *Inside Cutoff* and *Outside Cutoff*.

Another option on the text field interface you may not be familiar with is the text direction option that will allow text to be both horizontal and vertical. And when you select text to be vertical, another option becomes available right beside the text direction option. This option is the text rotation option, which will rotate the text field 90 degrees when selected. Text direction and text rotation options are only available to static text fields.

Continuing with the options, there is also the auto kern feature, which will adjust spacing between the letters automatically. There are also three buttons in the middle of the interface that control certain features of text fields:

- **Selectable**. This option controls whether or not a user can select and highlight text in a text field. It is available to static and dynamic text fields only. Input text fields have this set to `true` automatically.

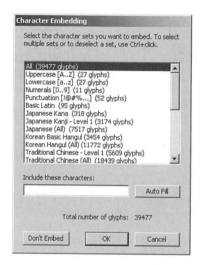

FIGURE 15.3   The Character Options menu for dynamic and input text fields.

- **Render Text as HTML**. This option can turn a normal text field into an HTML text field (more on HTML text in text fields later in this chapter). This option is available to dynamic and input text fields.

- **Show Border Around Text**. This option will create a black rectangle around the text field. It is available to dynamic and input text fields only.

There are also URL options, which allow you to place a link inside the text field as well as choose the URL target type.

And in the properties of dynamic and input text fields, there is also the Var field, which allows you to place a variable name to associate the content of the text field to a variable on the timeline. However, because text fields are now objects, there is a more up-to-date way of doing that, which we will discuss later in this chapter.

Spell Checking Text Fields

One of the hardest things to do from a designer/developer standpoint while building websites and Web applications is to spell check. This had plagued Flash users for some time until the release of Flash 2004, with a built-in spellchecker for text fields.

Before you start using it, you need to make sure it is set up the way you want. To get to the setup, go to Text, Spelling Setup. The Spelling Setup window will pop open as in Figure 15.4. Some of the options include what you want to spell check (it is good practice to have text fields and strings checked), which of the built-in dictionaries you would like to use, and which words to suggest, as well as which words to completely ignore. You can also set up your own personal dictionary and edit it from within Flash.

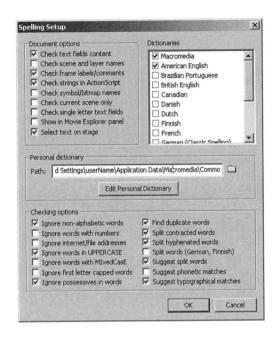

FIGURE 15.4   The Spelling Setup menu.

When you have your setup the way you want it (and it may take some time to get it just right), go ahead and create a static text field on the stage by choosing the Text tool and clicking somewhere on the stage. When the text field has been created, type in the word *thier,* which was meant to be *their,* but is a common spelling mistake (at least by me). Now go to Text and choose Check Spelling, and the Check Spelling dialog box appears as in Figure 15.5. One of the first options should be the correct spelling of the word *their.* Make sure that is selected and click Change. A pop-up will tell you that you're done, and now the word is spelled correctly.

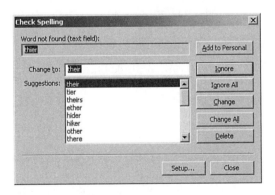

FIGURE 15.5   The Check Spelling dialog box.

So we've covered the text field interface as well as the new Spell Checker. Now let's talk a little more about each type of text field starting with static text fields.

Creating Text Fields

In this section, we'll go over the basic ways to create and use all three types of text fields manually, and then we'll go over how to create a couple of them with ActionScript.

The basic way to manually create a text field is to select the Text tool from the toolbar (T on the keyboard) and click and draw the text fields on the stage.

CAUTION

After a text field has been created, you can still go back and resize it manually using the Text tool. You can also simply select it with the arrow tool, and handles will appear in each corner allowing you to scale it however you wish. You should not, however, use the Free Transform tool to adjust the size of a text field because it will actually stretch and resize the text inside the text field as well.

Static Text

Static text, again, can only be manipulated in the authoring environment. You can, however, do some interesting things with it such as distribute each individual character to its own layer. This can be useful if you want to do some interesting animation with words because each object would have to be on its own layer.

To push letters from a single text field into individual layers, you will first want to create a text field by selecting the Text tool, setting the text type to Static Text, and clicking on the stage. After you have created the text field, you can simply type something in, like your name. When the text field is on the stage, and has some text in it, you can select it with the Selection tool, and either right-click (Mac–control-click) and then select Break Apart, or you can choose Modify>Break Apart. After it has been broken apart, make sure all the text fields are still selected, and choose Modify>Timeline>Distribute to Layers (PC–Ctrl+Shift+D, Mac–Shift+Open Apple+D). Now each letter has its own timeline named for that letter, as you can see in Figure 15.6.

This technique can actually be done with all three types. When dynamic or input text fields are broken apart, they are turned into static text fields, but there isn't really anything special you can do with static text.

Dynamic Text

This type of text field is much more advanced than the static text field because it can be changed and manipulated at any point during authoring or runtime via ActionScript. As a matter of fact, you do not even need to type a single character in the text field itself to have text appear, as you will see in the first example.

For this first example, we are going to put text in a dynamic text field.

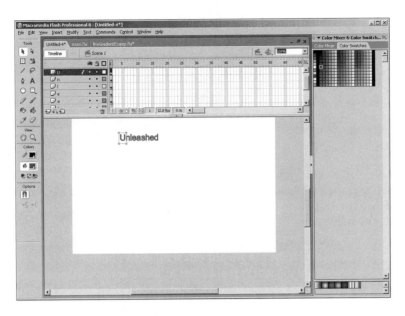

FIGURE 15.6   After you select Distribute to Layers, each letter receives its own layer.

1. Start a new Flash document.

2. Create a second layer, and name the top layer **actions** and the bottom layer **text** (remember from Chapter 8, "Welcome to ActionScript 2.0," that it's good practice to have a layer dedicated to ActionScript).

3. In the text layer, create a dynamic text field, make sure the Show Border option is selected, set the Var property to myText, and give it an instance name of textField_txt.

4. Now we are going to go to the first frame of the actions layer, open the Actions panel (F9), and put these actions in:

```
//this will set the first text field's Var property
var myText = "Testing";
```

Now test the movie (Control>Test Movie) and you will see that the text is now in the text field. It does this by sharing a variable name in ActionScript and the Var property in the text field's properties. This was the way it was done way back in Flash 5. It still works, but now we are going to do it the correct way because text fields are now objects in ActionScript.

1. Using the same example, go to the text field's properties in the Properties Inspector and clear out the Var property box so that it is completely blank.

2. Now go back to the actions in the first frame of the actions layer, delete all of the actions, and place these in instead:

```
//this will create a string to hold our text
var myString_str:String = "Test 2";
//this will set the text field's text property to the string
textField_txt.text = myString_str;
```

Now test the movie again, and you will see that the text field is displaying our text. This way of doing it is much easier to understand because instead of having a blind variable, you actually are setting text to a specific text field. This makes it much easier to go back and read. Because it is good practice to set text to the text field's `text` property, that is the way we will continue to do it.

So far, the two examples we have done using dynamic text were not very dynamic. We could have just written that text in right on the stage. In this next example, you will see why dynamic text fields are so important.

In this example, we are going to build a mouse tracker to show where the mouse is whenever the mouse moves.

1. Start out by creating a new Flash document.

2. As you did before, create two layers, the top one named **actions** and the bottom one **text**.

3. In the text layer, create two dynamic text fields about 100 pixels wide and 20 pixels high. Make sure they both have Show Border turned on, and give them instance names of x_txt and y_txt.

4. Now in the first frame of the actions layer, place these actions:

```
//this event will update everytime the mouse moves
this.onMouseMove=function(){
    x_txt.text="x="+Math.floor(_xmouse);
    y_txt.text="y="+Math.floor(_ymouse);
}
```

Test the movie and you will see that whenever the mouse moves, the text fields will show its position on the main stage.

> **NOTE**
>
> If at first nothing appears in the text fields, click somewhere on the stage. Sometimes the stage must receive focus before mouse events can be detected.

Now that you see how powerful and easy it is to update dynamic text fields, we are going to move on to our last text field type, input text fields.

Input Text

As mentioned earlier, input text fields are exactly like dynamic text fields in how we can set text to them. But unlike dynamic text fields, the user can actually type text in input text fields to interact with our Flash document. Input text fields also have a few extra options that the other two text types do not. The Linetype option can be set to Multiline just like dynamic text fields, but it can also be set to Password, which would make any character in it appear to be an asterisk. That comes in handy when building login systems. Another option is the Maximum Characters field, which you can set to keep the length of what the user can input at a certain length or less.

You will begin to feel comfortable with input text fields as we go through the next example.

In this example, we are going to allow users to input information into one text field, and when they submit it, we will place that exact same string in another field capitalized.

1. Start by creating a new Flash document.

2. Create two more layers so that you have three in total.

3. Name the layers from top to bottom—**actions**, **button**, and **text**.

4. In the **text** layer, create a dynamic text field, make sure the Show Border option is selected, and give it an instance name of `output_txt`.

5. On the same layer, create an input text field, make sure it has Show Border selected, and give it an instance name of `input_txt`.

6. On the **button** layer, create a button, and give it the instance name `submit_btn`.

7. Finally, in the **actions** layer, place these actions:

```
//this event will occur when the submit button is released
submit_btn.onRelease=function(){
    output_txt.text=input_txt.text.toUpperCase();
}
```

Test the movie, type something in the input text field, and then click the submit button to see the same text displayed in our dynamic text field, but in uppercase format. Also, notice in our code that we get text out of text fields using the exact same property we use to set text to text fields, the `text` property.

So far, all we have done when we create a text field is to select the Text tool and draw the field on the stage. Now we are going to go through how to create one dynamically with ActionScript.

Creating Text Fields in ActionScript

One of the nice things about text fields is that now because they are actual objects in ActionScript, you can create and destroy them dynamically. And to create them in AS, we use the `createTextField()` method, which works like this:

```
Movie.createTextField(instanceName, depth, x, y, width, height);
```

Because text fields must be placed within movie clips, `Movie` represents the movie clip that the text field will reside in. The first parameter we set is the instance name; remember to use the suffix "_txt" to activate code hints. The next parameter is the depth, or stacking order, of the text field. The next two parameters are its coordinates, and they represent the top left corner of the text field. The final two parameters are the width and height of the text field.

Let's jump right in and create one in ActionScript.

1. Start off by creating a new Flash document.

2. In the first layer, in the first frame, open the Actions panel and put these actions in:

```
//this will create a text field on the root layer
this.createTextField("myText_txt",1,0,0,120,20);
```

3. Now test the movie and notice that you don't really see anything. This is because even though we have created a text field, we haven't put any text in it. But it is there, and you can see it in the object's list by going to Debug>List Objects while still in the test movie screen. You will see it listed there.

   We already know how to put text in text fields, so let's go back and do that.

4. After we create the text field in the actions, put these actions in:

```
//this will put text in the text field
myText_txt.text = "I created this with code";
```

Now test the movie once more, and you will see the text in the text field at the top left corner of the screen. And because the `createTextField()` method returns a reference to the text field, we could have also written the code like this:

```
//this will create a text field on the root layer
var theText:TextField = this.createTextField("myText_txt",1,0,0,120,20);
//set the text using the reference
theText.text = "I created this with code";
```

Both ways will work the same.

Looking at the text in the test movie screen, notice that the letters are black and appear to be in Times New Roman. That is because when you create text fields in ActionScript they have a few default values:

- `type`—`"dynamic"`
- `border`—`false`
- `borderColor`—`0x000000` (black)
- `background`—`false`
- `backgroundColor`—`0xffffff` (white)

- `textColor`—`0x000000` (black)

- `password`—`false`

- `multiline`—`false`

- `html`—`false`

- `embedFonts`—`false`

- `variable`—`false`

- maxChars—false

- sharpness—0

- thickness—0

- antiAliasType—normal

- gridFitType—pixel

Now you know how to change some of the features, so let's go back into our example and give it a border and a background, as well as change the text color.

1. Building on the preceding example, go back into the actions of the first frame and add these lines at the bottom:

```
//this will add a border around the text field
myText_txt.border = true;
myText_txt.borderColor = 0xff0000;
myText_txt.background = true;
myText_txt.backgroundColor = 0x397dce;
myText_txt.textColor = 0xffffff;
```

When you test the movie again, you will see a border around the text field. And the text field formatting could have been applied before setting the `text` property. But in order to be able to change the color of the border and the background with ActionScript, both properties must be set to `true` or the border will not show.

Now that you've seen how to create text fields manually as well as with ActionScript, and you know how to change properties of the text field itself, let's look at how to change the formatting of the text in the text field.

Formatting the Text in Text Fields

We've already gone over the interface, so you know how to make changes to text manually, but now we will go over how to change the formatting of the text with ActionScript.

We will start out with the built-in object that Flash has for formatting text fields, called the `TextFormat` object.

The `TextFormat` **Object**

Before you can start creating these `TextFormat` objects, you should know that when you create a text field with ActionScript, a default `TextFormat` object is applied to it with these values:

- `font-"Times New Roman"`
- `size-12`
- `color-0x000000` (black)
- `bold-false`
- `italic-false`
- `underline-false`
- `url-""` (empty string)
- `target-""` (empty string)
- `align-"left"`
- `leftMargin-0`
- `rightMargin-0`
- `indent-0`
- `leading-0`
- `bullet-false`
- `letterSpacing-null`
- `tabStops-[]` (an empty array)

Notice that the `textColor` property in the `TextField` object does the same thing as the `color` property of the `TextFormat` object, so if all you want to do is change the color of the text, the `TextFormat` object is overkill; just use the `textColor` property of the `TextField` object.

To create a new `TextFormat` object, you basically create a variable and set it to a new `TextFormat` object like this:

```
var myFormat_fmt:TextFormat = new TextFormat();
```

Now we can start setting properties of this new `TextFormat` object like this:

```
myFormat_fmt.align = "center";
myFormat_fmt.bold = true;
myFormat_fmt.color = 0x00ff00;
```

We still have to apply the format we want to a text field before it can be rendered. There are two options for applying `TextFormats` to text fields. The first one is `setTextFormat()`, which has several different ways of being used:

- `textField.setTextFormat(textFormat)`—This way sets the `textField` to the `textFormat`.

- `textField.setTextFormat(index,textFormat)`—This way sets the `textFormat` to the character at `index`.

- `textField.setTextFormat(startIndex, endIndex, textFormat)`—This way sets the `textFormat` to all characters from `startIndex` to `endIndex`.

It is also important to know that this method can only be applied after the text field has text in it. Also note that indexing strings start at 0, not 1. So the first character in any string has an index of 0.

Let's go over a few examples of how to use this method.

In the first example, we are going to put a small phrase in a text field, and then format that text field to look nice.

1. Star by creating a new Flash document.

2. In the first frame, open the Actions panel, and put these actions in:

```
//this will create the text field
this.createTextField("phrase_txt",1,0,0,100,50);
//this will set the text field to multiline, and wrap words
phrase_txt.wordWrap = true;
//here we put text in the text field
phrase_txt.text = "Every cloud has a silver lining";
//now create the text format object and set some of its properties
var myFormat_fmt:TextFormat = new TextFormat();
myFormat_fmt.color = 0x0000ff;
myFormat_fmt.bold = true;
myFormat_fmt.align = "center";
//now apply the format
phrase_txt.setTextFormat(myFormat_fmt);
```

Now test the movie, and you should see your text formatted similar to Figure 15.7.

In the next example, we are going to use the same method, but change it a bit, and use a loop to gradually change the characters to the format.

1. Using the preceding example, go back into the actions on the first frame and remove the last two lines, including the comment.

2. Now put these actions in at the bottom.

```
//this variable is for our loop
var i:Number = 0;
//this is the looping function that we will use
this.onEnterFrame=function(){
     if(i < phrase_txt.text.length){
```

```
            phrase_txt.setTextFormat(i, myFormat_fmt);
            i++;
        }else{
        //this will get rid of the looping function
            delete this.onEnterFrame;
        }
    }
```

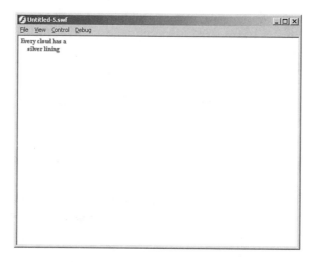

FIGURE 15.7   Using the `TextFormat` object can produce great results.

Now when you test the movie this time, it will gradually change over to the format instead of all at once as it did before.

The final example of using the `setTextFormat()` method will set the text format to just one word.

1. Still building on the preceding example, remove all of the code up to `myFormat_fmt.bold = true`.

2. Now add these actions at the bottom:

    ```
    //this will set the text format to the word "silver"
    phrase_txt.setTextFormat(18,24,myFormat_fmt);
    ```

This time when you test the movie, it will look like Figure 15.8.

As I mentioned earlier, there are two ways to set a `TextFormat` object to a text field, and the second way is using the `setNewTextFormat()` method, which is applied only one way, like this:

```
textField.setNewTextFormat(textFormat);
```

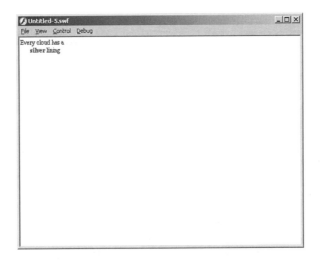

FIGURE 15.8   You can format just certain words in text using the `setTextFormat()` method.

The difference between this method and the preceding one is that this method will work now and forever on text fields. Basically that means that unlike the `setTextFormat()` method where it has to be used only after text has been placed inside a text field, any text put in after that will not only not have the text format, but will also clear the text format back to default values. But if you use the `setNewTextFormat()` method, all text from then on will use that format.

Here is an example to help:

1. Start a new Flash document.

2. In the first frame, open the Actions panel and place these actions in:

```
//create the text field, and put some text in it
this.createTextField("phrase_txt",1,0,0,150,20);
phrase_txt.text = "Every dog has";
//create the text format object and set some properties
var myFormat_fmt:TextFormat = new TextFormat();
myFormat_fmt.color = 0xff0000;
myFormat_fmt.underline = true;
//now set the format to the text field
phrase_txt.setNewTextFormat(myFormat_fmt);
//now add more text to it
phrase_txt.text += " his day";
```

Now when you test it, you won't see anything terrific—it will have just done what you had done before, but this time, you added text to the text field after you applied the format. That would have caused the loss of the format if you had used `setTextFormat` instead of `setNewTextFormat`. To see what it is meant by that, go back to the line that we set the format on, and change it:

```
phrase_txt.setTextFormat(myFormat_fmt);
```

Now when you test, it looks as if the format was never applied, but in actuality it was applied and then it was cleared when you added text.

Now you've seen how to format text inside text fields using the `TextFormat` object, but there are two more ways to format text. One is to use HTML (which we discuss later in this chapter) and the other way is to use Cascading Style Sheets.

Cascading Style Sheets

Cascading Style Sheets (CSS) are not new to the Web, but since Flash can use them, it makes setting formats to text fields completely dynamic because you can actually create the style sheets in a text editor, save them as `.css` files, and load them in at runtime. Another great thing about their being dynamic is that you can have an HTML site and a Flash site all formatted with the same CSS.

For those of you who are new to CSS, it was designed to help keep content and design separate in HTML. What that means is that you can create content, label the type of content it is (title, body, footnote, and so on), and then create a CSS to format those particular types of content and set the CSS to the content. That way, whenever you want to update content, you don't have to worry about it not being in the right format, and if you want to update the format, the content does not have to be touched.

An example of this would be a newspaper. There is tons of content in a newspaper ranging from headlines, text body, writers' names, and even comments. But if there were no way of telling which was which, it would make the newspaper almost impossible to read with the title of the story, the writer's name, and the story itself all the exact same size and format. But the writers do not have time to set up format while they are writing the articles; they simply say this section is a headline, and that section is the body.

Taking that concept over to cascading style sheets, the CSS is the formatter, and all it needs is definitions. So let's take a look at setting up some CSS inside ActionScript.

The first thing you have to do is create a new `StyleSheet` object like this:

```
var myStyle:TextField.StyleSheet = new TextField.StyleSheet();
```

Now that you have your `StyleSheet`, it's time to make some definitions for it using the `setStyle()` method like this:

```
styleSheet.setStyle(styleName, theStyle);
```

In this method, the first parameter is the name of the specific style (which we will go into when we start implementing the style sheets) and the second is an object that has style properties set. There are two ways of implementing this.

The first way is to create the style name and add attributes of that style all in the same method like this:

```
myStyle.setStyle("title", {color: "#ff0000", fontSize: "20px"});
```

And the second way to implement the same method is to create a generic object, set the properties of the object the same way you would set style properties, and then pass the entire object to the style, like this:

```
var tempStyle:Object = new Object();
tempStyle.color = "#ff0000";
tempStyle.fontSize = "20px";
//now pass the object to our already created StyleSheet
myStyle.setStyle("title",tempStyle);
//get rid of the temporary style object
delete tempStyle;
```

Both of these implementations will work with our style sheet, so whichever you feel more comfortable using is what you should go with. Just remember, if you create temporary objects to hold your style properties, get rid of them when you are done to regain memory.

Now that you've seen how to create the style sheet objects and how to set some styles to them, let's look at how to set them to our text, and how our text should be formatted to accept the styles.

There are several different ways of setting text to the StyleSheet. The first one we will cover will use already supported tags such as <p> and <span>. You can use their built-in class attribute to set each class to an already specified style class like this.

```
<p class="title">This is<span class="smaller"> small </span></p>
```

And here is an example pulling the StyleSheet and the text together:

```
//create the text field
this.createTextField("phrase_txt",1,0,0,150,20);
//set the html property to true
phrase_txt.html = true;
//create the StyleSheet object
var myStyle:TextField.StyleSheet = new TextField.StyleSheet();
//create 2 style classes and set them to myStyle
myStyle.setStyle(".title",{color: "#397dce", fontSize: "16px"});
myStyle.setStyle(".body",{color: "#000000", fontSize: "10px"});
//set the text field to the StyleSheet
phrase_txt.styleSheet = myStyle;
//set the text
phrase_txt.htmlText="<p class='title'>This is<span class='body'> small </span>
➥</p>";
```

15

A couple of things to notice in the preceding example; first, "styleSheet" beginning with a lowercase "s" is a property of the text field, and "StyleSheet" beginning with an uppercase "s" is an object class, so don't get those confused. And when we create style classes, we put a "." in front of the name and when we use them in our string, we don't need the period. Also, span tags are used inside the paragraph tag, and therefore must be closed before the paragraph tag.

Here we used classes of styles, but we can also style an entire HTML tag so that anything residing in that tag will inherit the style we apply.

Table 15.1 lists HTML tags in Flash that support having styles applied to them.

TABLE 15.1   Supported HTML Tags in Flash

Style Name	Supported Tag
p	All <p> tags.
body	All <body> tags, but the <p> tag will override this setting.
li	All <li> list item (bullet) tags.
a	All <a> anchor tags.
a:link	All <a> anchor tags, after the a style.
a:hover	All <a> anchor tags when the mouse is hovering over it, after the a and a:link styles have been applied. It will go back when the mouse goes off hover.
a:active	All <a> anchor tags when they are clicked on, after the a and a:link styles have been applied. When the mouse is released, the style will be removed.

Here is an example using the a style name.

```
//create the text field
this.createTextField("link_txt",1,0,0,100,20);
//set the html property to true
link_txt.html = true;
//create the StyleSheet object
linkStyle = new TextField.StyleSheet();
//set the styles of the style sheet
linkStyle.setStyle("a:link",{color: "#ff0000"});
linkStyle.setStyle("a:hover",{color: "#0000ff"});
linkStyle.setStyle("a:active",{color: "#00ff00"});
//set the StyleSheet to the text field
link_txt.styleSheet = linkStyle;
//set the text to the text field
link_txt.htmlText = "<a href='http://www.sams.com' target='_blank'>
➥Sams Publishing</a>";
```

Now you have seen how to format classes of tags as well as how to format the entire class. You can of course mix them together. For instance, you can define the entire <p> tag, and then define classes so that the main <p> tag acts more like a default setting.

You can even create your own tags, and have them formatted to your own style names, as you will see in this next example.

```
//create the text field
this.createTextField("news_txt",1,0,0,200,80);
//set some of the properties
news_txt.html = true;
news_txt.wordWrap = true
//create the StyleSheet object
var myStyle:TextField.StyleSheet = new TextField.StyleSheet();
//define the styles
myStyle.setStyle("title", {color: "#ff0000", fontSize: "20px"});
myStyle.setStyle("body",{color: "#000000", fontSize: "12px"});
//set the StyleSheet to the text field
news_txt.styleSheet = myStyle;
//now set the text
news_txt.htmlText="<title>This just in</title><br><body>
➥Flash supports CSS in text fields</body>";
```

So far in CSS we have talked about creating the styles inside ActionScript, but that really isn't the point. The whole idea is to create the CSS files and store them outside of the Flash file to be loaded in. The method of StyleSheet used to load external files is the load() method, and when the CSS has been loaded, it triggers the onLoad event, which we will also be using in the following example.

1. The first thing you want to do is create a new Flash document, and save it somewhere called CSSTest.fla.

2. After that, open up your favorite text editor, Notepad, or SciTe and put this text in it:

```
title {
    color: #000000
    font-size: 20px;
    display: block;
    textDecoration: italic;
}
body {
    color: #397dce;
    font-size: 12px;
}
emphasized {
    color: #ff0000;
    display: inline;
}
```

3. When the text is in, save the file to the same directory as the Flash file you just saved as myCSS.css.

4. Go back into Flash, and in the first frame open up the Actions panel and place these actions within it:

```
//create the text field
this.createTextField("news_txt",1,0,0,200,80);
//set some of the properties
news_txt.html = true;
news_txt.wordWrap = true
//create the StyleSheet object
var myStyle:TextField.StyleSheet = new TextField.StyleSheet();
//create the event for when the CSS is loaded
myStyle.onLoad = function(done){
     if(done){
          news_txt.styleSheet = myStyle;
          news_txt.htmlText = "<title>Read all about it
➥</title><br><body>Can you <emphasized>believe
➥</emphasized>this<body>";
     }else{
          trace("there was an error");
     }
}
//now load the CSS
myStyle.load("myCSS.css");
```

We have covered a lot of different ways to format a text field (and we will cover one more in the HTML section later in this chapter). We have even covered how to keep content and design separate from one another using Cascading Style Sheets and loading them in from outside our Flash file.

In this next section, we are going to cover how to manipulate the position using scroll properties, and we are going to cover the Mouse event that will make scrolling a lot easier.

Scrolling Text Fields

Many times when you fill text fields with information, the text field just is not large enough to handle it all. You can, of course, make the text field larger, but you can also scroll the text. Scrolling the text will allow you to keep the text field the original size, but still be able to display all of the information.

You can scroll a text field two different sets of directions with two different properties. The first is the scroll property, which controls up and down motion and starts at position 0. The second property is the hscroll property, which controls left and right scrolling and also starts at position 0. And both of these properties have limits, which are maxscroll and maxhscroll oddly enough. With these properties, you can control the positioning of text in text fields.

Let's jump right in with an example of using the `scroll` property.

1. Start a new Flash document.

2. Create two more layers, and name the top layer **actions**, the middle layer **buttons**, and the bottom layer **text**.

3. In the text layer, create a dynamic text field about 200 by 100 with the Show Border option turned on, change the line style to Multiline, and give it an instance name of `info_txt`.

4. Then go into the actions of the first frame of the actions layer and set `info_txt.text` equal to the preceding paragraph (or any large amount of text).

5. Now when you test the movie, you should not be able to see all of the text in the text field because the text field is too small. We are going to fix this by making it scroll.

6. Go into the buttons layer, create two buttons with instance names of up_btn and down_btn, and place them beside the text field as in Figure 15.9.

7. Now go back into the actions layer, and put these actions in under where you set the text to the text field:

```
//this will control the upward motion
up_btn.onPress=function(){
     if(info_txt.scroll != 0){
          info_txt.scroll—;
     }
}
//this will control the downward motion
down_btn.onPress=function(){
     if(info_txt.scroll < info_txt.maxscroll){
          info_txt.scroll++;
     }
}
```

Now test the movie to see that the scroll buttons are working.

Now that you can scroll text, let's take a step further and use the Mouse Wheel Event.

The Mouse Wheel Event

Back in Flash MX, if you wanted to make text fields scrollable by using the wheel mouse, you had to do some fancy JavaScripting. Now it's as easy as hovering over the text field and spinning the mouse wheel.

Going back to our preceding example, save the file somewhere, publish it, and then open up either the .html or the .swf file, hover over the text field, and scroll the text field with your mouse wheel.

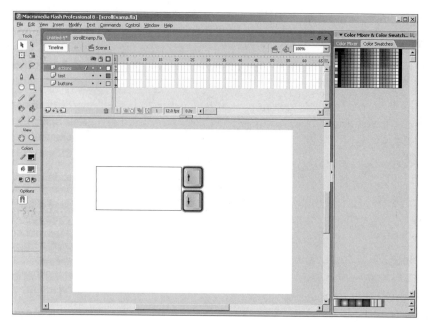

FIGURE 15.9   Position the scroll buttons beside the text field.

But you don't need a text field to get the event. Here is an example that will actually listen for the event, and tell you how fast and which direction the mouse wheel is going.

1. Create a new Flash file.

2. Open up the actions in the first frame and place these actions inside:

```
//create an object to listen for the event
var wheelListen:Object = new Object();
//add the event to the object
wheelListen.onMouseWheel = function(amount) {
//send the speed and direction to the ouptut window
    trace(amount)
}
//add the lisenter to the Mouse Object
Mouse.addListener(wheelListen);
```

Now test the movie (and remember to click on the stage in test mode). When you move the mouse wheel up and down, it will send the speed to the Output window. All positive numbers are scrolling up on the wheel, and all negative numbers are scrolling down on the mouse wheel.

In the next section, we are going to cover HTML text in text fields, which isn't really new because we used some HTML text when we were applying StyleSheet objects.

HTML Text in Text Fields

So far, we have focused on putting raw text directly into text fields and then formatting that text with either a `TextFormat` object or a `StyleSheet` object. With HTML text, you can put content and formatting in one package using supported HTML tags.

Here is a list of the supported HTML tags in Flash:

- Anchor tag—`<a>`—Creates a hyperlink with these attributes:

    `href`—The URL to be loaded

    `target`—The window type to be used when opening a link

    This example creates a link to Macromedia in its own window:

    `<a href="http://www.macromedia.com" target="_blank">click here</a>`

- Bold tag—`<b>`—Creates bold text between the tags:

    `<b>This is what I call bold</b>`

- Line Break tag—`<br>`—This tag creates a new line in HTML text fields.

    This example creates two lines of text:

    `This is one like<br>this is another line.`

- Font tag—`<font>`—This tag can control some properties of text using these attributes:

    `color`—This attribute controls the hexadecimal color of text as in this example:

    `<font color="#0000ff">I am blue</font>`

    `face`—This attribute controls the actual font type of text, and can also handle multiple font names separated by commas. It will choose the first font available on the user's machine.

    This example uses Arial text as our first choice and Courier as our second:

    `<font face="Arial, Courier">I am Arial</font>`

    `size`—This attribute controls the size of the text in pixel points.

    This example sets text to a point size of 20:

    `<font size="20">This is big text</font>`

    `letterSpacing`—This attribute controls the spacing between letters.

    This example sets letter spacing to a point size of 2:

    `<font letterSpacing='2'>This is spaced out</font>`

- Image tag—`<img>`—This tag is new to Flash and allows outside images and SWFs to be brought into HTML text fields as well as internal movie clips with their linkage set. It supports a number of tags:

  `src`—This attribute is the only required attribute and is the URL to the SWF or JPG; it can also be the linkage to an internal movie clip. Both JPGs and SWFs will not display until completely loaded and Flash does not support the loading of progressive JPGs.

  `id`—This attribute gives the movie clip that holds the external image or SWF (which is automatically created by Flash). It is good if you want to be able to manipulate the embedded image with ActionScript.

  `width`—Used to set the width of the JPG, SWF, or internal movie clip you load in.

  `height`—Used to set the height of the JPG, SWF, or internal movie clip you load in.

  `align`—This attribute controls which side the content you load in to the text field will be on. `left` and `right` are the only allowable settings, and the default is `left`.

  `hspace`—This attribute controls the horizontal space in pixels around the loaded content between the content and the text. The default is 8.

  `vspace`—This attribute controls the vertical space in pixels around the loaded content between the content and the text. The default is 8.

  This example places a JPG on the left, with default spacing as well as an id.

  ```
  <img src="local.jpg" width="320" height="240" id="image_mc">
  ```

  For more on embedding images into text fields, look at the section titled "The Image Tag" later in this chapter.

- Italics tag—`<i>`—This tag italicizes text:

  ```
  <i>Here is some italicized text</i>
  ```

- List Item tag—`<li>`—This tag is used to create bulleted lists:

  ```
  Software<li>Flash MX 2004 Pro<li>Dreamweaver<li>Freehand
  ```

  This example would appear like this:

  - Software
  - Flash MX 2004 Pro
  - Dreamweaver
  - Freehand

- Paragraph tag—`<p>`—This tag begins a new paragraph and usually holds a large amount of text. It has two attributes:

align—Controls the horizontal positioning of text between the <p> tags. You can use left, right, center and justify.

class—This attribute is used with the StyleSheet object to control format.

This example creates a new paragraph and sets its alignment to center:

```
<p align="center">New paragraph</p>
```

- Span tag—<span>—This tag is only useful when setting text to StyleSheets. It used to have a different class of style within a <p> tag. It has one attribute:

    class—Used to name the certain style within the StyleSheet to use for formatting.

    In this example we use a span tag to change some text in a <p> tag:

    ```
    <p class="Body">This is <span class="Emphasize">really </span>cool</p>
    ```

- Text format tag—<textformat>—Is used to allow a certain set of the TextFormat object's properties to be used with HTML text. It has many attributes:

    blockindent—This attribute is used to control the block indentation in points.

    indent—This attribute controls the indentation from the left side of the text field in points for the first character in the paragraph.

    leading—This attribute controls line spacing.

    leftmargin—This attribute controls the margin on the left in points.

    rightmargin—This attribute controls the margin on the right in points.

    tabstops—This attribute creates custom tabbing points (creates a mock table). An example using this attribute is provided later in this chapter.

    This example creates some text with 2-point line spacing and a 3-point indentation for paragraphs:

    ```
    <textformat leading="2" indent="3">
    ```

- Underline tag—<u>—This tag underlines text and it has no attributes:

    ```
    <u>I am underlined</u>
    ```

Now that you have seen all the tags HTML text fields will support, let's start using some.

First, if you are creating the text field manually, you must make sure the HTML option in the Properties Inspector is turned on. If you are creating your text fields with ActionScript, make sure you change the html property to true like this:

```
myTextField_txt.html = true;
```

15

Also, we have been using the `text` property to set text to text fields. If we did that with HTML text fields, it would display the actual HTML tags and the text, so instead we set HTML text to text fields using the `htmlText` property like this:

```
myTextField_txt.htmlText = "<b>This is a bold statement.</b>";
```

Okay, now you know some basic rules of HTML text fields. Let's jump right into an example.

In this example, we will create a text field and put some HTML into it.

1. Create a new Flash document.

2. Open the Actions panel in the first frame and place these actions in it:

```
//create the text field
this.createTextField("myText_txt",1,0,0,200,200);
//set of its properties
myText_txt.html = true;
myText_txt.wordWrap = true;
myText_txt.multiline = true;
//create the html string we want to use
var myString:String = "<p align='center'><b>Extra Extra</b>
➥<br> Read <u>all</u> about it</p>";
//now set the text to the text field
myText_txt.htmlText = myString;
```

Test the movie, and it should appear like Figure 15.10. Nothing too spectacular, but you can of course add as much HTML as you want, and play around to see what else you can do.

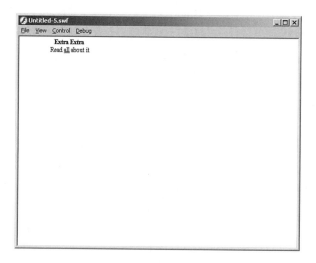

FIGURE 15.10   Use HTML to hold content and format at the same time.

This next example will be a little more advanced. We are going to create a "mock table" with the <textformat> tag to display sets of information. We are going to create three basic field names: name, age, and location. Then we'll add four different people to the table. After that, we will set all of the text to the text field.

1. Create a new Flash document.

2. Open the Actions panel in the first frame and put these actions in:

```
//create the text field
this.createTextField("myText_txt",1,0,0,250,200);
//set its properties
myText_txt.html = true;
myText_txt.multiline=true;
myText_txt.wordWrap = true;
```

This created our text field and set some of the necessary properties.

3. Now we create the string and add all the information we need, so add these actions in:

```
//now create the string to hold the headers
var headers:String = "<u>Name\tAge\tLocation</u>";
//now the string to hold all the rows
var rows:String = "Ben\t25\tVirginia<br>";
rows += "Lesley\t24\tBarcelona<br>";
rows += "Missy\t24\tLondon<br>";
rows += "Jen\t27\tNew Hampshire";
```

4. Finally, create the text format tag and add all the strings to the text field by adding these actions:

```
//add the textformat tag
myText_txt.htmlText = "<textformat tabstops='[70, 120]'>";
//add the headers
myText_txt.htmlText += headers;
//add the rows
myText_txt.htmlText += rows;
//close the text format tag
myText_txt.htmlText += "</textformat>";
```

Now test the movie, and it should appear like Figure 15.11.

That was a pretty powerful example showing how you could display data inside HTML text fields and make it appear to be organized into tables using the <textformat> tag.

Another tag that is very useful is the <img> tag.

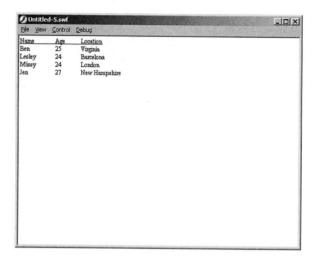

FIGURE 15.11   Use the `<textformat>` tag to create HTML text that appears to have tables.

The Image Tag

The image tag, `<img>`, was introduced in Flash 2004, and it allows the embedding of images as well as SWF files and internal movie clips directly into an HTML text field. This next example will show you how to implement it.

In this example, we are simply going to load in a JPG from the outside and put some text around it. You can use any image because we are going to size it in the tag.

1. Start a new Flash file.

2. Save as `imageLoader.fla`.

3. We are going to load a JPG image into the text field, so make sure there is one in the same directory where you just saved this file.

4. Open the Actions panel in the first frame and put these actions in:

   ```
   //create the text field
   this.createTextField("imageAndText_txt",1,0,0,300,300);
   //set its properties
   imageAndText_txt.html = true;
   imageAndText_txt.wordWrap = true;
   imageAndText_txt.multiline = true;
   imageAndText_txt.border = true;
   ```

   This created our text field and set some necessary properties.

5. Now let's create the string to hold the HTML and insert it into the text field with these actions:

```
//create the string to hold the html
var myString_str:String = "Picture 1<br><img src='platform.jpg'
➥width='200' height='200'>This is a picture of platform 9 3/4 in london."
//set the text in the text field
imageAndText_txt.htmlText = myString_str;
```

Now test the movie, and you should see something similar to Figure 15.12.

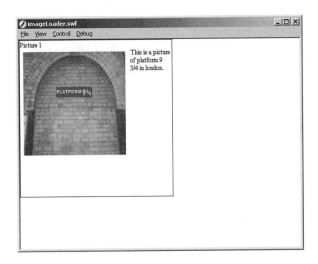

FIGURE 15.12   You can now load images directly into a text field.

That example showed how to load a JPEG from outside the Flash file, and loading SWFs works the exact same way, but now we are going to show how to load a movie clip symbol from the Flash file into the text field.

In this example, we are going to create a rectangle and then load it into the text field we create.

1. Start a new Flash file.

2. Go to Insert>New Symbol.

3. Make sure it is a movie clip you are creating. Give it a Symbol name of `rectangleMC` and check the Export for ActionScript check box (also make sure the Linkage Identifier is the same as the Symbol name).

4. When you're in this new movie clip, draw a rectangle with any stroke and fill color, but make sure it is aligned to the left, and to the top of the movie clip (its top left corner is on the cross hair) or it will not sit correctly in the text field. Make it about 150×150, but again, because we will size it with the <img> tag, it is not that important here (although the closer it is to the actual size, the clearer it will appear).

5. Go back to the main timeline, open the Actions panel in the first frame, and put these actions in:

```
//create the text field
this.createTextField("imageAndText_txt",1,0,0,300,300);
//set its properties
imageAndText_txt.html = true;
imageAndText_txt.wordWrap = true;
imageAndText_txt.multiline = true;
imageAndText_txt.border = true;
```

This will create the text field and set some of its necessary properties.

6. Now that we have our text field, we will create the string and set it to the text field with these actions:

```
//create the string to hold the html
var myString:String = "<img src='rectangleMC' width='150'
➥height='150' align='right'>Now we loaded something from inside of Flash";
//put the text in the text field
imageAndText_txt.htmlText = myString;
```

Now test the movie to see the rectangle load into the text field.

In this example, we embedded the movie clip we created earlier, and set it to the right side of the text box. But let's say we wanted to do something with the rectangle after it has been loaded into the text field. That's where the id attribute of the <img> tag comes in, as you will see as we continue.

Building on our preceding example, we are going to make it so that if a user clicks on the image tag, they will open a link.

1. Go back into the actions, and in the line of code where we create the HTML string, change the image tag to this:

```
<img src='rectangleMC' id='rectangle_btn' width='150' height='150'
➥align='right'>
```

Now we are using the id attribute, so we can interact with the rectangle in ActionScript.

2. Now that we have an id we can use in AS, let's create a function that will open a link when the user clicks on the rectangle, by adding these actions to the bottom:

```
//this will add the event to the rectangle
imageAndText_txt.rectangle_btn.onRelease=function(){
    getURL("http://www.macromedia.com","_blank");
}
```

Now, when you test the movie, you can click on the rectangle, and it will open up a browser window with the link. This example showed how to interact with loaded content in HTML text fields using the id attribute, but if the truth be told, you can also hyperlink these files by using an anchor tag <a> around the image tag <img> like this:

```
<a href="http://www.macromedia.com"> <img src='image.jpg' ></a>
```

We have covered the image tag, and all that can be done with it. Of course, because you can embed outside SWFs as well as movie clips you create inside, you can do a lot of interesting things, such as having a constantly running clock inside a text field. The possibilities are endless.

In the next section, we are going to cover how to interface these HTML text fields with JavaScript, another Web language.

HTML Text Fields and JavaScript

JavaScript, like ActionScript, is an object-oriented programming language, so if you are not familiar with it, it is easy to pick up if you are comfortable with ActionScript. And JavaScript can do many things that ActionScript cannot because it is a browser language. We are going to show two examples of what can be done with JavaScript and HTML text fields in Flash. The first is a simple alert that will pop up when a link is selected. The second is a bit more powerful, and therefore more complicated; we will use JavaScript to open a custom window to load content in.

This first example is fairly simple because we will use the JavaScript inside the ActionScript.

1. Start a new Flash file.

2. Open the Actions panel in the first frame and place these actions within it:

```
//create the text field
this.createTextField("alert_txt",1,0,0,100,20);
//set its properties
alert_txt.html = true;

//now put the text inside the text field
alert_txt.htmlText = "<a href='javascript:
➥alert(&quot;You made an alert!&quot;);'>Alert Me</a>"
```

Before you test your movie, you must load it onto a server, or change the allowScriptAccess attribute in the HTML to "always." (You can of course download the correct HTML from the website.) Once one of these two options has been met, when you test your file in a browser, an alert will pop up when you click the text.

In this next example, we are actually going to publish the HTML and add some JavaScript to it so we can create custom pop-up windows. But we will build the Flash part first.

1. Start a new Flash document.

2. Save the document as **popup.fla**.

3. Open the Actions panel in the first frame, and place these actions in it:

```
//create the text field
this.createTextField("popUp_txt",1,0,0,100,20);
//set some properties
popUp_txt.html = true;
//place the html in the text field
popUp_txt.htmlText = "<a href=\"javascript:
➥popUp('http://www.sams.com',500,500)\">Open POP-UP</a>";
```

Now that we have all the script we need for Flash, we are calling a JavaScript function (that we have yet to build) and passing a few parameters to the function.

4. Go to File, Publish (Shift+F12), which will create the .swf file as well as the .html file.

5. Open the .html file we just created in a text editor (like Notepad or SciTe).

6. The first thing you will want to do is change the line of HTML code that says

```
<param name="allowScriptAccess" value="sameDomain" />
```

to

```
<param name="allowScriptAccess" value="always" />
```

7. Now, between the <head> tags, place this JavaScript:

```
<script language="JAVASCRIPT" type="TEXT/JAVASCRIPT">
<!—
if(screen){
    topPos=0
    leftPos=0
}
function popUp(thePage,wt,ht){
    leftPos= (screen.width-wt)/2
    topPos = (screen.height-ht)/2
    newWin1 = window.open(thePage,'aWin','toolbars=no, resizeable=no,
➥scrollbars=no,left='+leftPos+',top='+topPos+',width='+wt+',height='+ht)
}
// —>
</script>
```

When that text is in the HTML file, you can save the file and close it. Then launch it in a browser and you will see the text we put in the text field. When you click on it, it will open a custom window 500×500 in the center of the screen.

You have seen how to create text fields, add text to them, and style them many different ways. You have also seen how to talk directly to JavaScript from them, which allows even more interaction with the end user. Now we are briefly going to go over how to help make your files multi-lingual.

Multilanguage Text

The Internet has changed how we view the world, how we do business and how we communicate with others. It used to cost a fortune to talk to friends around the globe, or take a long time to correspond with them through the mail. Now with the Internet being the fastest growing means of communication, its nothing to talk to several people in different countries at the same time, all in real time. And even though it is now easier than ever to keep up a conversation with someone with a 12 hour time difference, it still does not necessarily break the language barrier. Flash understands this, and has built in several different methods of communicating your message in different languages.

The first way to do this is to use Unicode-encoded text.

Unicode-encoded Strings

We briefly went over Unicode-encoded strings in Chapter 9, where you used special codes to represent characters. You can use the same technique to have text of different languages. Follow the example below to see how this works:

1. Create a new Flash document.

2. Draw a dynamic text field on the stage with the font being Times New Roman and an instance name of **myText_txt**.

3. Select *Anti-alias for readability* for the anti-aliasing option, and click the embed button.

4. Select Lowercase, Greek and Hebrew from the list and hit OK.

5. Create a second layer called *actions* and open the Actions panel in the first frame of this layer, and add these actions.

   ```
   myText_txt.text = "hello world \u05E2\u03BB\u20AC\u05E3\u03BC\u20AA";
   ```

Now test the movie, and you should see a string that says "hello world."

> **NOTE**
>
> In order to use this technique, you must embed the glyphs you need, and it must be either a dynamic or input text field.

That was one way to make text appear multi language. And to find out more about Unicode-encoding, check out http://www.unicode.org. But that is not the only way to make your text multi-lingual, you can also use the Strings panel.

The Strings Panel

The Strings panel is designed to help you create multi-lingual text and to keep up to date. You can specify several different languages, and have translators actually make the translation for you, but Flash will decide which language to use based on the user's system. Follow these steps to see how it would work:

15

1. Create a new Flash document.

2. Open the Strings panel (Window>Other Panels>Strings) like Figure 15.13 and click the *Settings* button to open the Strings settings like Figure 15.14.

3. Select the languages you want from the list on the left.

4. Select a default language and leave the other options at their default settings and hit OK.

5. Back in the Strings panel, place "1" in the ID field and "This is a test" in the String field and click *Apply*.

   Notice it changes your ID from "1" to "IDS_1".

6. Close the String panel, save your file to the desktop and publish.

   Notice you will have a folder for each language on your desktop now, and inside is an XML document for translators to use and put the translated text in.

7. Once you have the translated text, you will go back into the Strings panel and import the correct XML file for each language. You will notice the grid filling up with the correct information from the XML doc.

   Then your done, you can publish your file again to ensure all the proper XML documents are set, and now your files should be able to support all the languages you selected.

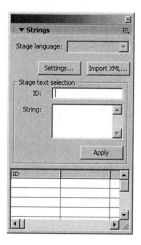

FIGURE 15.13   The Strings panel.

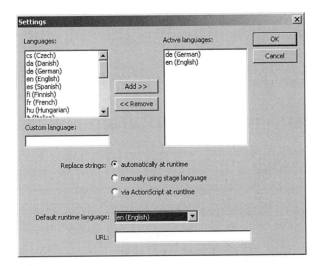

FIGURE 15.14   The Strings panel settings for choosing which languages to support as well as the default language.

Summary

This chapter covered a lot of things you can do with text in Flash from drawing text fields on the stage all the way to creating them in ActionScript with images, tables, and even some JavaScript. We also went over the best ways to format the text. Cascading Style Sheets are the best way to go because they make it easy to update multiple text fields without ever having to open Flash. And we briefly covered how to support text in multiple languages.

The next chapter will go over Components and how they can make your life easier and your development process shorter.

CHAPTER **16**

Components

Components are nothing new to Flash. They were introduced in Flash MX, but version 2.0 was introduced back in Flash 2004 with the introduction of ActionScript 2.0.

This chapter goes over what components are and how to use them, including many of the built-in components in Flash Professional 8. It covers ways to connect components to one another, how to capture component events, and how to skin them. And this chapter will even show you how to create your own component.

What Is a Component?

Even though components were introduced in Flash MX, the idea behind them started back in Flash 5 with smart clips.

Smart clips were the original components—a reusable movie clip that needed only a few parameters set for anyone to customize and use, or such was the plan. In reality, smart clips were not only difficult to use, but were hardly scalable at all. Each time a component needed to be used in a different situation, the designer or developer using them would have to actually go into the code to tweak it slightly so that the smart clip would work. Not only that, but they were tremendous in file size compared to what they were capable of doing.

The next step was Flash MX components; they were scalable, reusable, customizable, and smarter than any smart clip ever created. The components that came with Flash MX were very well-designed and developed to be used in any situation. And building custom components was not a difficult task either.

Then, with Flash MX 2004, components 2.0 were created and included with Flash, and in Flash 8, they have had little change.

Getting Started with Components

Before you start creating applications using components, you need to know where to find them, and how to control them. All components can be found in the Components panel (Window>Components).

The Components Panel

As you can see in Figure 16.1, Flash MX 2004 Professional comes with three distinct sets of components:

- Data components—components for connecting and working with external data sources.

- FLV Playback—Player 8—a fully function component for playing external Flash video files in the Flash player 8.

- FLV Playback Custom UI—these are pieces that can be used to customize the user interface of an FLV Playback component.

- Media Player 6-7—these are components designed to help you work with external Flash video files in the Flash player 6 and 7.

- User Interface—these are, as they state, user interface components for building forms or interactions in your Flash file.

This chapter focuses mainly on the User Interface components, but the other components are covered in other chapters where applicable.

Adding Components to the Stage

Adding components to the stage is as simple as dragging them from the Components panel onto the stage. You can also double-click any one of them, and it will appear on the stage.

> **NOTE**
>
> If you need multiple copies of a single component, drag one instance onto the stage and either copy and paste it, or drag other instances from the library. Do not drag multiple instances of the same component onto the stage from the Components panel because it may increase file size unnecessarily.

After you have brought a component onto the stage, you can also attach more instances to the stage using the `attachMovie()` method.

The `attachMovie()` Method

The `attachMovie` method will use the component's linkage identifier to create a new instance of the component on the stage at runtime.

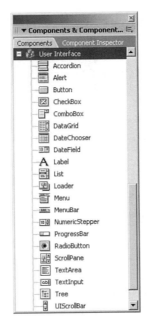

FIGURE 16.1 The Components panel where all components that come with Flash as well as any you create can be found.

The generic template for this method is as follows:

```
movieClip.attachMovie(linkageID, newName, depth, initObj);
```

The `movieClip` in the preceding code represents which movie clip the component will reside in. This method has four parameters:

- `linkageID`—The linkage identifier of the movie clip or component being attached.

- `newName`—A string literal indicating the instance name of the new movie clip or component.

- `depth`—A numerical value representing the depth of the new movie clip or component.

- `initObj`—This optional parameter is an object containing properties, events, and methods with which to initialize the new movie clip or component.

All components, by default, have a linkage identifier that is the same as the component's name. To view it, drag an instance of any component (in this case a `Button` component) onto the stage, open the library and right-click (Mac–Ctrl-Click) the component, and choose Linkage from the menu. You will see the Linkage Properties dialog box as shown in Figure 16.2. You cannot change the linkage identifier of any components.

16

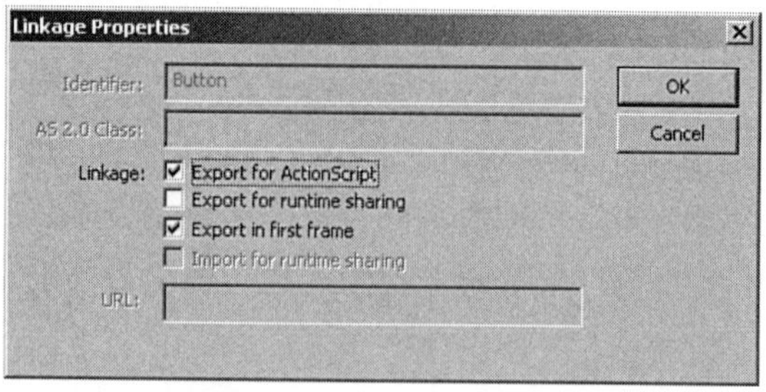

FIGURE 16.2   The Linkage Properties dialog box for a Button component.

Follow these steps to attach a new Button component to the stage:

1. Create a new Flash document.

2. Drag an instance of the Button component to the center of the stage.

   This step will also add the Button component to the library.

3. Create a new layer called **actions**.

4. In the first frame of the actions layer, open up the Actions panel and place this code in it:

```
//attach the Button
this.attachMovie("Button", "myButton_butn", 1);
//give it a label
myButton_butn.label = "Click me";
```

The preceding code first attaches the new Button component and then gives it a label.

If you test the movie, you will see that a second Button component has indeed been brought to the stage. If a label was not assigned to it at runtime, it would be blank, so keep that in mind.

> **TIP**
>
> New to Flash 8 is the ability to drag components directly to the Library from the Components panel. That means you can use the attachMovie() method without ever having placed a component onto the stage.

Now that you know how to add components to the stage, you should know how to control certain aspects of them.

Setting Parameters

Each component has a set of parameters that can be set to adjust the visual aspects of the component, how they operate, or what data they contain. You can set these parameters two different ways: by selecting the Parameters tab in the Properties Inspector, or by using the Component Inspector.

The Properties Inspector

The Properties Inspector will change when you select the Parameters tab for a component, as shown in Figure 16.3 for the Button component.

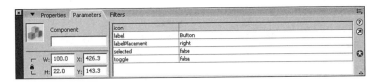

FIGURE 16.3   The Properties Inspector showing the parameters for the Button component.

The following sections list all the parameters with descriptions for all the UI components: Accordion, Alert, Button, CheckBox, ComboBox, DataGrid, DateChooser, DateField, Label, List, Loader, Menu, MenuBar, NumericStepper, ProgressBar, RadioButton, ScrollPane, TextArea, TextInput, Tree, UIScrollbar, and Window.

Accordion Component

- childIcons—An array of linkage identifiers representing symbols to be used as icons in the headers of the Accordion's panels.

- childLabels—An array of text strings to use as headers for the Accordion's panels.

- childNames—An array of text strings used as the instance names of the child symbols for the Accordion component.

- childSymbols—An array of linkage identifiers representing the symbols to be used for the Accordion's children.

Alert Component

The Alert component has no parameters and must be adjusted with ActionScript.

Button Component

- icon—A linkage identifier to the symbol to be used as an icon with the Button component.

- label—A text string representing the text to appear in the Button component.

- labelPlacement—A drop-down menu of choices representing where the text will be placed relative to the icon.

- selected—A Boolean value representing the state of the Button; selected if true, unselected if false.

- toggle—A Boolean value representing whether this Button component is a toggle button (true) or not (false).

CheckBox **Component**

- label—A text string representing the text of the check box.

- labelPlacement—A drop-down menu of choices representing the position of the label to the check box itself.

- selected—A Boolean value representing the initial state of the check box; if this parameter is true, the box is selected; if it is false, the box is unselected.

ComboBox **Component**

- data—An array of data to coincide with each item in the ComboBox. Note that this information will not be displayed in the component itself, but can be accessed via ActionScript.

- editable—A Boolean value indicating whether a user can manually type in the ComboBox or not; editable if true, not editable if false.

- labels—An array of text strings representing the label of each item in the ComboBox.

- rowCount—A numerical value representing the maximum number of rows to be shown when the ComboBox is selected.

DataGrid **Component**

- editable—A Boolean value indicating whether the information in the DataGrid can be edited by a user.

- multipleSelection—A Boolean value indicating whether a user can select more than one row of information at a time. If this parameter is true, selecting multiple rows is allowed; if false, it is not allowed.

- rowHeight—The height in pixels of the rows in a DataGrid.

DateChooser **Component** (Calendar **Component**)

- dayNames—An array of strings representing the name of each day of the week; by default, the letter for each day is already there.

- disabledDays—An array of numerical values (0–6) representing which days to disable, meaning they cannot be selected.

- firstDayOfWeek—A numerical value (0–6) representing which day of the week should be considered the first; by default, the value is 0, Sunday.

- monthNames—An array of text strings representing the names of each month to display (by default, the month names are already there).

- showToday—A Boolean value indicating whether or not to automatically highlight the current date; highlight date if true, do not highlight date if false.

`DateField` **Component**

- `dayNames`—An array of strings representing the name of each day of the week; by default, the names of days are already there.

- `disabledDays`—An array of numerical values (0–6) representing which days to disable, meaning they cannot be selected.

- `firstDayOfWeek`—A numerical value (0–6) representing which day of the week should be considered the first; by default, the value is 0, Sunday.

- `monthNames`—An array of text strings representing the names of each month to display (by default, the month names are already there).

- `showToday`—A Boolean value indicating whether or not to automatically highlight the current date; highlight date if `true`, do not highlight date if `false`.

`Label` **Component**

- `autoSize`—A drop-down menu indicating how the text in the `Label` component will resize. It has these parameters:

  - `none`—The label will not resize at all.

  - `left`—The right and bottom sides of the label resize to fit.

  - `right`—The left and bottom sides of the label resize to fit.

  - `center`—The bottom side of the label resizes to fit.

- `html`—A Boolean value indicating whether the label supports HTML or not.

- `text`—A text string that will appear in the label.

`List` **Component**

- `data`—An array of data to coincide with each item in the `List` component. Note that this information will not be displayed in the component itself, but can be accessed via ActionScript.

- `labels`—An array of text strings representing the label of each item in the `List` component.

- `multipleSelection`—A Boolean value indicating whether a user can select more than one row of information at a time. If this parameter is `true`, selecting multiple rows is allowed; if `false`, it is not allowed.

- `rowHeight`—The height in pixels of the rows in a `List` component.

`Loader` **Component**

- `autoLoad`—A Boolean value indicating whether to automatically load the content or not. If this value is `true`, the content will load automatically. If it is `false`, the `Loader` component will wait until told through ActionScript to load the content.

- contentPath—A text string representing the absolute or relative path to the content being loaded, either a SWF or JPG file.

- scaleContent—A Boolean value indicating whether to scale the content to the size of the Loader component (true), or to scale the Loader component to the size of the content (false).

Menu **Component**
- rowHeight—The height in pixels of the rows in a Menu component.

MenuBar **Component**
- labels—An array of text strings representing the label of each button in the MenuBar component.

NumericStepper **Component**
- maximum—A numerical value representing the maximum allowable value.

- minimum—A numerical value representing the minimum allowable value.

- stepSize—A numerical value representing the amount the value moves up or down.

- value—A numerical value representing the initial value.

ProgressBar **Component**
- conversion—A number to divide the %1 and %2 values of the label being displayed. It is used to display different types of measurements of file sizes such as bytes or kilobytes.

- direction—A drop-down menu indicating which direction the loader should move toward, either right or left.

- label—This is a text string of particular characters used to give feedback to the user as to how much of the content has loaded; here are the special characters to use with the ProgressBar component:

  - %1—The number of bytes loaded

  - %2—The total number of bytes loading

  - %3—The percentage that has been loaded

  - %%—The percentage sign (%)

  The default value of %3%% will show the percentage loaded with a percentage sign (%).

- labelPlacement—A drop-down menu indicating where the label will appear in the ProgressBar component.

- mode—A drop-down menu indicating which mode the ProgressBar will operate in.

- source—A text string representing the source of the download where the loader can get the total file size of the content being loaded, and the current amount loaded (the Loader component for example).

RadioButton **Component**
- data—A text string representing the value associated with the RadioButton. Note that this information will not be displayed in the component itself, but can be accessed via ActionScript.

- groupName—A text string indicating which RadioButton group the individual RadioButton belongs to.

- label—A text string indicating the label of the individual RadioButton.

- labelPlacement—A drop-down menu representing the position of the label in the RadioButton component.

- selected—A Boolean value representing the initial state of the radio button; selected (true), unselected (false).

NOTE

Only one RadioButton in a given group can be selected at a time.

ScrollPane **Component**
- contentPath—A text string representing the relative or absolute path to the content being loaded.

- hLineScrollSize—A numerical value representing the number of units the horizontal scrollbar moves each time a scroll button is clicked.

- hPageScrollSize—A numerical value representing the number of units the horizontal scrollbar moves each time a scroll track is clicked.

- hScrollPolicy—This is a drop-down menu representing whether the horizontal scrollbars will be visible; it will show the bar (on), it will not show the bar (off), or it will decide if it is necessary (auto).

- scrollDrag—A Boolean value indicating whether users can drag the content around (true) or not (false).

- vLineScrollSize—A numerical value representing the number of units the vertical scrollbar moves each time a scroll button is clicked.

- vPageScrollSize—A numerical value representing the number of units the vertical scrollbar moves each time a scroll track is clicked.

- vScrollPolicy—This is a drop-down menu representing whether the vertical scroll-bars will be visible; it will show the bar (on), it will not show the bar (off), or it will decide if it is necessary (auto).

TextArea **Component**

- editable—A Boolean value representing whether the user can edit the TextArea component at runtime (true) or not (false).

- html—A Boolean value indicating whether the TextArea component will display HTML text as HTML (true) or not (false).

- text—A text string that will initially appear in the TextArea component.

- wordWrap—A Boolean value indicating whether to wrap text to the next line when it reaches the border (true) or not (false). Note that you can still create new lines if this parameter is set to false, they will just have to be created manually.

TextInput **Component**

- editable—A Boolean value representing whether the user can edit the TextInput component at runtime (true) or not (false).

- password—A Boolean value indicating whether the text will be legible (false) or just a bunch of asterisks (true).

- text—A text string that will initially appear in the TextInput component.

Tree **Component**

- multipleSelection—A Boolean value indicating whether a user can select more than one node of information at a time; selecting multiple nodes is allowed if true and is not allowed if false.

- rowHeight—The height in pixels of the nodes in a Tree component.

UIScrollBar Component

- _targetInstanceName—The instance name of the text field that the scroll bar will be controlling.

- horizontal—The orientation of the scroll bar to the text field. If true, the scroll bar will control horizontal scrolling of the text field, if false (the default), the scroll bar will control the vertical scrolling of the text field. Note, with this component, you can simply drag and drop it right on the text field you want it to work with, and the parameters will be filled automatically.

Window **Component**

- closeButton—A Boolean value indicating whether the close button at the top right of the Window component will be visible (true) or not (false).

- contentPath—A text string representing either a linkage identifier to a symbol in the library, or a relative or absolute path to external content.

- title—A text string that will appear in the drag bar of the Window component.

Changing the Parameters of a Component

Changing the parameters of a component is easy with the Properties Inspector. Follow these steps to set up the Button component:

1. Create a new Flash document.

2. Drag an instance of the Button component onto the stage.

3. Select the Button component, and change the parameters to the following:

   - icon—leave blank

   - label—"My First Button"

   - labelPlacement—right

   - selected—false

   - toggle—true

Now test the movie, and you will see that you now have a toggle button.

Buttons are pretty easy, but notice that some of the parameters for certain components were arrays, such as the labels parameter for the List component.

Arrays in component parameters have their own special dialog box, as you will see in this next example where we will add some labels to the List box.

1. Create a new Flash document.

2. Drag an instance of the List component onto the stage.

3. Select the List component, and go to the Properties Inspector. Select the labels parameter. Then you will see a small magnifying glass at the end of the field; select it or double click the field.

4. The Values dialog box appears as in Figure 16.4. Click the Add Value button (the plus sign) three times, and you will see three items appear in the dialog box, all labeled "defaultValue".

5. Select each of these three items, and change the text to the following:

   Flash

   Dreamweaver

   Fireworks

6. Click OK, and you will see that the component on the stage shows the new values you just added.

Test the movie, and you will see that the three items are still there.

FIGURE 16.4   The Values dialog box for array parameters in components.

Of course, the Properties Inspector is not the only place to control the parameters of a component; you can also change parameters in the Component Inspector panel.

The Component Inspector Panel

You can find the Component Inspector panel by going to Window>Component Inspector. As you can see in Figure 16.5, the Component Inspector has three tabs; Parameters, Bindings, and Schema. The Bindings tab is used to control data binding between components, and will be covered later in this chapter. The Schema tab controls all the properties of the component and is based on an XML document. In the Parameters tab, you can adjust component parameters as in the following example.

In this example, we are going to use a simple `TextInput` component and change a couple of its parameters using the Component Inspector panel.

1. Create a new Flash document.

2. Drag an instance of the `TextInput` component onto the stage.

3. Select the `TextInput` component and open the Component Inspector. Then choose the Parameters tab.

    Notice in Figure 16.6 that when you use the Component Inspector, you will see many more parameters than you do when using the Properties Inspector. This is because the Component Inspector allows access to more of the component's properties.

FIGURE 16.5 The Component Inspector panel, which is used to control components.

4. Set the parameters of the TextInput component to the following:

   - editable—true

   - password—true

   - text—topSecret

The rest of the parameters we will leave to default values.

As you change the password parameter, and then place text in, notice that the component on the stage again changes before the movie is even tested. Also, the parameters in the Properties Inspector change to match the Component Inspector panel.

Test the movie, and you now have half of a login; all you need is a user name field.

There is a third and final way you can change the parameters of a component, but these changes will not take effect until runtime.

ActionScript

Because component parameters are nothing more than direct links to component properties, we can control them from within ActionScript at runtime.

FIGURE 16.6   The Component Inspector provides direct access to more parameters than does the Properties Inspector.

Follow these steps to create a combo box and fill it with labels all from within ActionScript:

1. Create a new Flash document.

2. Drag an instance of the ComboBox component onto the stage.

3. Give it an instance name of myCombo_cb so that we will be able to access it from ActionScript.

4. Create a new layer called **actions**.

5. In the first frame of the actions layer, open the Actions panel, and place this code in it:

```
//add some data to the ComboBox
myCombo_cb.addItem("ASP");
myCombo_cb.addItem("PHP");
myCombo_cb.addItem("ASP.NET");
myCombo_cb.addItem("ColdFusion");
myCombo_cb.addItem("CGI");
myCombo_cb.addItem("Perl");
//change the width of the drop down
myCombo_cb.dropdownWidth = 200;
```

The preceding code first adds some labels to the ComboBox, and finally changes the width of the ComboBox's drop-down menu to twice its size.

Test the movie, and when you select the ComboBox, you will see that the drop-down is twice its default size.

> **NOTE**
>
> Even if you change a component's parameters manually, because ActionScript runs at runtime, ActionScript will override any manual settings.

Another great way ActionScript interacts with components is when you need to capture a component's event, such as if a user clicks a button. You need to know when that happens to run whatever code is associated with that button.

Capturing Component Events

Way back in Flash MX, component events were easy to control. There was a callback function associated with each instance of a component that would look on the timeline for any function with that name, and then run all the code associated with that function.

Version 2.0 of components is slightly more complicated. In order to capture an event of a component, you must create a listener object. A listener object is a generic object whose sole purpose is to sit around and "listen" for a given event to occur. When this event does occur, it calls its associated callback method.

But first, you have to add the event listener to the component using the addEventListener() method.

The addEventListener() Method

The addEventListener() method is used to add event listener objects to components. Each time it is used, it is basically subscribing the listener object to listen for a component's event.

Here is the generic layout for the addEventListener() method:

```
myComponent.addEventListener(event, listener);
```

One parameter of this method is the *event* parameter, which is a string literal name of the event being listened to. The other parameter is the *listener*, a reference to the event listener object. As you start to build applications with components, you will learn how important it is to be able to capture these events.

For instance, if you wanted to get the label of an item in a List component whenever the user chooses one, you would use code that looks similar to this:

The following code is in a frame on the same timeline where a List component with an instance name of myList_lb resides.

16

```
//create the listener object
var listListen:Object = new Object()
//create the event callback for the event you're listening for
 listListen.change = function(){
    trace(myList_lb.selectedItem.label);
}
//then add the event listener to the instance of the List component
myList_lb.addEventListener("change", listListen);
```

All the preceding code does is create the generic object. Then it creates the callback function for the event it was listening to. Finally, it adds the event listener to the List component.

It is possible to replace the preceding code by putting this code directly into the actions of the component itself:

```
//the event
on(change){
    trace(this.selectedItem.label);
}
```

Even though the preceding code would yield the exact same results, it is bad practice to put code directly in the object actions of components, or any other object for that matter, because it makes it difficult to find code hidden in objects when you need to find it. So throughout the rest of this chapter, we will be using event listeners on the timeline.

You can also use the handleEvent() method, which will allow an event listener to handle multiple events, but you have to pass it the event, and then use conditionals to tell which event was called.

The following is an example of using the handleEvent() to handle multiple events:

```
//create the listener object
var listListen:Object = new Object()
//create the event callback for the event your listening for
listListen.handleEvent = function(eventName){
    if(eventName.type == "change"){
        trace(myList_lb.selectedItem.label);
    }else if(eventName.type == "scroll"){
        trace("scrolling");
    }
}
//then add the event listener to the instance of the List component
myList_lb.addEventListener("change", listListen);
myList_lb.addEventListener("scroll", listListen);
```

As you can see from the preceding code, it is possible to have a single event listener listen to multiple events, but the code is quite messy, and not flexible.

Now that you understand the concepts of capturing events in components, work through the following example to see how to capture the "click" event for a button:

1. Create a new Flash document.

2. Drag an instance of the Button component onto the stage.

3. Give the button an instance name of **myButton_butn** and change the label to "Now".

4. Create a new layer called **actions** and place this code in the first frame of it:

```
//create the event listener object
var clickListen:Object = new Object();
//create the event callback for the click event
clickListen.click = function(){
    trace(getTimer());
}
//now add the event listener to the Button instance
myButton_butn.addEventListener("click", clickListen);
```

The preceding code creates the event listener object, and then creates its event callback method. Every time this event callback is called, it will send the number of milliseconds that have occurred since the beginning of runtime. Finally, we add the event listener to the Button component.

Test this movie out, and every time you click the button, a number will be sent to the Output panel representing the number of milliseconds that have occurred since you tested the file.

There is one more hidden way to capture events from components, and that is to set their own hidden event callbacks.

Hidden Event Callbacks

Components have events, but most look more like properties than events, and there doesn't seem to be any event callbacks for generic movie clips and buttons. However, they are there.

Even though the component event callbacks are hidden, they are easy to guess as they use the word "Handler" in the callback for the event. For example, the Button event click has the event callback of clickHandler. Here is an example that will show it working, and the order in which it fires.

1. Create a new Flash document.

2. Drag an instance of the Button component onto the stage.

3. Give the button an instance name of **myButton_butn**.

4. Create a new layer called **actions** and place this code in the first frame of it:

```
//the event listener
var clickListen:Object = new Object();
```

```
//the event
clickListen.click = function(){
   trace("This is the listener");
}
//add the event listener to the Button component
myButton_butn.addEventListener("click", clickListen);
//the callback
myButton_butn.clickHandler = function(){
   trace("This is the event callback");
}
//output: This is the event callback
//            This is the listener
```

Now test this movie, and you will see that when you click the button, the hidden call-back event will fire first. That is important if you are using listeners in conjunction with the callback. And as you can see, the hidden event callbacks are just a matter of adding the word "Handler" to the event when you set it.

Now you know how to put data into a component, and how to capture events from components. The next step is getting data from components.

Getting Data from Components

Even though we have done some useful examples so far, we haven't really gathered infor-mation from components yet, which is a major point to using components to quickly build applications.

You can access most data by means of either a method, or more likely a property of a component. And in list type components, you can access properties of the selected item.

In the next example, we will use a NumericStepper component to control the _alpha property of a movie clip.

1. Create a new Flash document.

2. Drag an instance of the NumericStepper component onto the top left of the stage; give it an instance name of myStepper and set its parameters to the following:

   • maximum—100

   • minimum—0

   • stepSize—1

   • value—100

3. Now draw a rectangle in the center of the stage.

4. Highlight the entire rectangle including the stroke and choose Modify, Convert to Symbol.

5. Give it a symbol name of **recMC** and make sure the behavior is set to Movie Clip.

6. Give the instance of the rectangle still on the stage an instance name of **rec_mc**.

7. Create a new layer called **actions**.

8. In the first frame of the actions layer, open the Actions panel and place this code in:

```
//create the listener object
var stepListen:Object = new Object();
//add the event callback to the listener
stepListen.change = function(){
    //set the rectangles alpha
    rec_mc._alpha = myStepper.value;
}
//add the listener to the component
myStepper.addEventListener("change", stepListen);
```

The preceding code is nothing new. It creates the event listener. Then it creates the event callback method for the *change* event of the NumericStepper. In that event, every time the user adjusts the NumericStepper component, the _alpha property of the rectangle changes to the value of the NumericStepper. Finally, we add the event listener.

When you test this movie, you will see the transparency of the rectangle change as you change the value in the NumericStepper component.

Now that you have seen how to use components, you need to know how to make them look good.

Skinning Components

Back in Flash MX, skinning components was pretty simple—a lot of work, but simple. When you drag a component onto the stage, the component's skins were added to the library, and you could go in and adjust them any way you wanted. Now in version 2.0 of components, it's not as easy. When you drag a component onto the stage, just the component itself is sent to the library, and you cannot go into it and change it manually. There are, however, a couple of options starting with manually changing the skins.

Manually Skinning a Component

Manually skinning components is not as difficult as it may sound, but it is time-consuming unless you want to keep the default gray colors.

To manually skin components, you have to drag a new "theme" into your current project's library. You get the other theme in the components folder of the configuration directory. Follow these steps to begin manually skinning components:

1. Create a new Flash document.

2. Drag instances of the following components onto the stage:

   • Button

   • TextArea

- RadioButton

- CheckBox

- Window

3. From C:\Program Files\Macromedia\Flash 8\en\Configuration\ComponentFLA, open SampleTheme.fla.

4. In the library of the SampleTheme file, drag the Movie Clip symbol "SampleTheme" into the library of the other file.

5. You will then see a couple of new folders in the library. The themes folder is where all the assets reside, and you can manipulate any visual aspect of the components now.

Notice that when you brought the new theme in, the components on the stage did not change. Only at runtime will the visual aspects of the components change.

Test the movie, and you will see that the components on the stage have changed to an older-looking style.

But that is not the only way to change the visuals of a component; you can also adjust its theme.

Using the style Property

All components support the style property, which allows users to control certain aspects of components ranging from coloring all the way to the speed of the drop-down list in the ComboBox component.

To set a style to a component, you use the setStyle() method like this:

```
component.setStyle(style, value);
```

This method uses two parameters, the style parameter, which is a string literal representing the style property being changed, and the value parameter, which is the value that the style is being changed to.

You can also set global style properties by using the _global identifier, and the keyword style, like this:

```
_global.style.setStyle(style, value);
```

Setting global style properties will affect all components throughout the Flash file. Table 16.1 lists some of the styles that most components will support.

TABLE 16.1 Style Properties That Can Be Used with Components

Style	Description
BackgroundColor	Controls the background color of the component.
BorderColor	Represents the dark corner aspect of three-dimensional objects such as the Button.
borderStyle	Controls the border of components and has four possible values: inset, outset, solid, none.
buttonColor	The color of the Button face, and any component that uses the Button component will inherit this property.
Color	The text color of the Label component. Any component using the Label component (such as the Button or CheckBox) will inherit this value.
disabledColor	The color of text when the component is disabled.
fontFamily	Controls the font used by components.
fontSize	Controls the font size of components.
fontStyle	Controls the style of fonts used by components; it has two values: normal, italic.
fontWeight	Controls the weight of fonts used by components; it has two values: normal, bold.
highlightColor	Controls the highlight portion of the three-dimensional aspects of components.
marginLeft	Controls the left margin of text in components.
marginRight	Controls the right margin of text in components.
scrollTrackColor	Controls the track color of the scrollbar used by components.
shadowColor	Controls the shadow portion of the three-dimensional aspects of components.
symbolBackgroundColor	Controls the background color of both the CheckBox and RadioButton components.
symbolBackgroundDisabledColor	Controls the background color of both the CheckBox and RadioButton components when disabled.
symbolBackgroundPressedColor	Controls the background color of both the CheckBox and RadioButton components when clicked.
symbolColor	Controls the check color of the CheckBox and the dot color of the RadioButton.
symbolDisabledColor	Controls the check color of the CheckBox and the dot color of the RadioButton when disabled.
textAlign	Controls the text alignment of components. Its values can be left, center, or right.
textDecoration	Controls the underlining of text in components. Its values are either none or underline.
TextIndent	Controls the indentation of text in components.

16

And there is one more property to use when using the style property: the themeColor property.

The themeColor property controls the highlighting aspects of components such as the Button component, all at once. You can pass it any hexadecimal color such as 0xff0000 for red or 0x000000 for black. You can also pass it three different prebuilt coloring themes:

- haloBlue

- haloGreen

- haloOrange

To see an example of the themeColor at work, follow the steps in this example:

1. Create a new Flash document.

2. Drag an instance of the Button component onto the stage.

3. Create a new layer called **actions** and place this code in the first frame of that layer:

```
//set the global themeColor to orange
_global.style.setStyle("themeColor","haloOrange");
```

Now test the movie, and you will notice that when you hover your mouse over or click the Button component, the button's color changes to a light orange.

This completes the discussion of the basics of components. The next few sections build on what we have covered so far and take it beyond just fundamentals.

The dataProvider **Property**

So far, we have added data to components that can handle data either manually through their parameters, or by using the addItem method to add individual items. You can also use the dataProvider property.

The dataProvider property is used with some data-ready components such as the List and the ComboBox components. This property can be set to any array, and the component will fill with the array's data.

Here is an example of filling a ComboBox with an array using the dataProvider property:

1. Create a new Flash document.

2. Drag an instance of the ComboBox component onto the stage and give it an instance name of myCombo_cb.

3. Create a new layer called **actions**, and place the following code in the first frame:

```
//create an array full of names
var names:Array = new Array("David","Ben","Eddie","Todd","Doug","Paul");
//now set the dataProvider property to this array
myCombo_cb.dataProvider = names;
```

The preceding code creates an array and fills it with names. Then we set the dataProvider property to the array.

Test the movie and you will see the ComboBox has filled with data. You can also add elements to either the array, or the ComboBox at runtime and it will show up in the ComboBox.

The array we just used is a simple array that just filled the label array property of the ComboBox. To really see what the dataProvider can do, you have to send it an array with objects that have specific properties. The two property names to use for objects are

- label—Elements with this name will go to the labels array.

- data—Elements in this array will be the value of the item.

Let's extend the previous example by adding not only names, but also ages into an array, and then setting that array to the dataProvider. We will also add an event listener to get the age from the ComboBox.

Go back into the actions layer and replace the code with this:

```
//create the necessary arrays
var names:Array = new Array("David","Ben","Eddie","Todd","Jeremy","John");
var ages:Array = new Array(25,25,27,30,26,23);
//create an array to hold all the data
var people:Array = new Array();
//now create a loop statement to combine these two arrays into one
for(var i=0; i < names.length; i++){
    //push the object with the label and data names into the main array
    people.push({label: names[i], data: ages[i]});
}
//now create the event listener for the
var listListen:Object = new Object();
//create the callback event for the listener
listListen.change = function(){
    trace("age - "+myCombo_cb.value);
}
//add the event listener to the ComboBox
myCombo_cb.addEventListener("change", listListen);
//now set the dataProvider property to this array
myCombo_cb.dataProvider = people;
```

Here's what this code does: First, it creates two different arrays to hold the names and ages of people. Then it creates an array to hold all the data at once. After that, it creates a loop statement that will take one element at a time from both the names and the ages arrays and places them in as a single element, as an object, in the main array people. Then we create the listener for our ComboBox. After that, we create the callback function that, when triggered, will pull the selected element's value, in this case the age. Then we add the event listener to the ComboBox and set the dataProvider property to the people array.

16

Test the movie and you will see that not only was the data again successfully placed in the ComboBox, but also when you select an item from the ComboBox, it sends the age of the selected person to the Output panel, not the label.

There is another component that uses the dataProvider property, but in a slightly different way. The DataGrid component will take a dataProvider and create the necessary columns based on the elements provided.

Follow these steps to see how easy it is to fill the DataGrid with data:

1. Create a new Flash document.

2. Drag an instance of the DataGrid component onto the stage.

3. Set its dimensions to about 350×150 and give it an instance name of myDataGrid.

4. Create a new layer called **actions**, and place the following code in the first frame:

```
//create the necessary arrays
var names:Array = new Array("David","Ben","Eddie","Todd","Jeremy","John");
var ages:Array = new Array(25,25,27,30,26,23);
var locations:Array = new Array
➡("Prince George","Sussex","Richmond","Philadelphia","Stafford",
➡"Springfield");
//create an array to hold all the data
var people:Array = new Array();
//now create a loop statement to combine these two arrays into one
for(var i=0; i < names.length; i++){
    //push the object with the label and data names into the main array
    people.push({Name: names[i], Age: ages[i], Location: locations[i]});
}
//now set the dataProvider property to this array
myDataGrid.dataProvider = people;
```

Just like before, we created a few arrays and filled them with data. Then we used a loop statement to fill a main array with one element from each array at a time. Then we set the dataProvider property of the DataGrid to the main array people.

When you test the movie, you should see something like Figure 16.7. This time, the DataGrid used the property names of each person in the main array as column headers.

While on the subject of controlling data and values of components, the next section covers data binding.

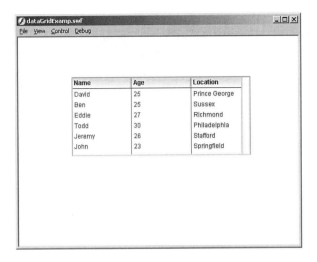

FIGURE 16.7 Use the `DataGrid` component to easily display large amounts of data at a time.

Data Binding

Data binding is one of the nicest features of components. It allows you to link components together without having to use ActionScript.

To data bind one component to another, you use the Bindings tab in the Component Inspector panel, as shown in Figure 16.8. You select the Add Binding button, and the Add Binding dialog box will appear with a list of all the available data binding values (see Figure 16.9). Next, return to the Component Inspector panel, open the Bindings tab, select your new binding, and click the Bound To field where a magnifying glass will appear. Select the magnifying glass, and the Bound To dialog box will appear (see Figure 16.10), which will allow you to choose which component to bind to as well as which of its binding values.

It is difficult to grasp until you do it yourself, so follow these steps to data bind a `List` component to a `TextInput` component:

1. Create a new Flash document.

2. Drag an instance of the `List` component onto the left part of the stage, and give it an instance name of `myList`.

3. Drag an instance of the `TextInput` to the right of the `List` component, and give it an instance name of `myText`.

4. Select the `List` component, open up the Component Inspector, and then select the Bindings tab.

5. Choose the Add Binding button.

16

FIGURE 16.8   The Binding tab in the Component Inspector.

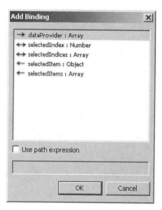

FIGURE 16.9   The Add Binding dialog box for choosing which data binding element you want to bind.

6. From the list in the Binding dialog box, choose `selectedItem : Object` and click OK.

7. Now select the Bound To field in the Component Inspector and click the magnifying glass that appears.

8. Select the `TextInput` component in the left window, and then choose `text : String` in the right window and click OK.

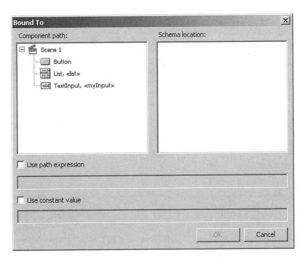

FIGURE 16.10   The Bound To dialog box to choose which data binding element to bind to.

9. Now create a new layer called **actions**, and place this code in the first frame:

```
//create the necessary arrays
var names:Array = new Array("David","Ben","Eddie","Todd","Doug","Paul");
//now set the dataProvider property to this array
myList.dataProvider = names;
```

The code creates an array of names, and fills the List component by means of the dataProvider property.

Test the movie, and you will see that when you select a name from the List component, that name appears in the TextInput component automatically.

Data binding is a great way to quickly and easily link different components together to share data. You will see data binding again in Chapter 25, "Web Services and Flash."

Now that you have seen a great deal about the components that come with Flash, it's time to create one.

Creating a Version 2.0 Component

Creating components with Flash 8 can be difficult, but very rewarding.

Back in Flash MX, to build a component, you placed information in a movie clip, and then converted it to a component. Version 2.0 of components goes a lot further.

In this example, we will create a small component that will have a property specifically designed for data binding. What it will do is allow developers to test information by sending it to this component, which will then automatically send it to the Output panel. Keep in mind that this component will only work in the test mode of the authoring environment and is not meant to be used outside of that.

The first part will be done in Flash, so follow these steps:

1. Create a new Flash document called `Tracer.fla` and save it to the desktop.

2. Using the Text tool, create a letter "T" on the stage and set its size to 16×16.

3. Select the "T" and choose Modify, Convert to Symbol.

4. Give it a symbol name of `tracerG` and make sure the behavior is set for Movie clip, and set its registration point to centered.

5. Right-click (Mac–Ctrl-click) the tracerG movie clip in the library and choose Linkage.

6. Select the Export for ActionScript check box, and uncheck the Export in First Frame check box to save file size. Leave the AS 2.0 Class blank and click OK.

7. Back on the main stage, highlight the movie clip "T" and choose Modify, Convert to Symbol again.

8. Give it a Symbol name of "Tracer," make sure the behavior is set to Movie clip, and set its registration point to centered.

9. Right click (Mac–Ctrl-click) the Tracer in the library and choose linkage.

10. Select the Export for ActionScript check box, and uncheck the Export in First Frame check box to save file size. Set the AS 2.0 Class to "Tracer" and click OK.

11. Now double-click the new movie clip symbol to enter edit mode.

12. Name the layer the "T" is residing on **Bound**.

13. Align the left edge and the top edge to the stage using the Align Panel (Window> Align).

14. Create a second layer under the Bound layer called `assets_mc` and give it an extra keyframe, so there should be two blank key frames on the assets_mc layer.

15. Make a copy of the first frame in the Bound layer, and paste it exactly the same in the second frame on the assets_mc layer.

    This is so that when the component gets dragged onto the stage, the user will be able to see it.

16. In the first frame of the Bound layer, open the Actions panel and place in a `stop` action like this:

    ```
    stop();
    ```

    This will stop the movie clip from looping back and forth, and should always be done in every component you make.

    Your stage should now look like Figure 16.11.

17. Return to the main timeline. We are done with Flash for the time being.

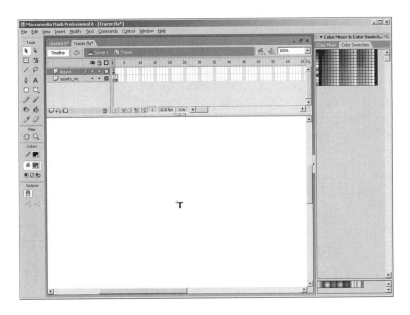

FIGURE 16.11   The stage after step 16 after we have created all the content on the stage needed.

The next section requires us to make a class file. Class files have not been discussed much so far, but you learn more about them in Chapter 18, "External ActionScript." All functionality of components are kept in external class files.

The next step requires the use of a text editor such as Notepad or SciTe. You can also use the AS file builder built into Flash by choosing File, New and choosing ActionScript File.

18. When your new file is open, save it to the same directory as our Flash file as `Tracer.as`.

19. Drop in this code and save the file again:

```
import mx.events.EventDispatcher;

[Event("traced")]
[TagName("Tracer")]
[IconFile("Tracer.png")]
[RequiresDataBinding(true)]

class Tracer extends MovieClip{
   private var tracerInfo:String;
   public var addEventListener:Function;
   public var removeEventListener:Function;
   private var dispatchEvent:Function;
```

```
function Tracer(){
        this._visible = false;
        EventDispatcher.initialize(this);
        super.init(this);
}
[Bindable(param1="writeonly",type="String"))]
[ChangeEvent("traced")]
function set tracerI(t:String):Void{
        this.tracerInfo = t;
        if(tracerInfo.length > 0){
                trace(tracerInfo);
        }
        dispatchEvent({type:"traced"});
}
}
```

Let's break this code into sections so you can see what is happening.

The first section imports the EventDispatcher class, so our component will have events.

The next section uses what are called MetaData tags. These tags are used in processing the component and set certain options. In this case, they are setting the Event we are going to create, the TagName, IconFile, and the fact that this component will need data binding.

```
[Event("traced")]
[TagName("Tracer")]
[IconFile("Tracer.png")]
[RequiresDataBinding(true)]
```

The next section begins our class, which will extend the MovieClip class. Then it creates a private property, tracerInfo, that is the data we are going to trace and then a few methods that we need for the event.

```
class Tracer extends MovieClip{
    private var tracerInfo:String;
    public var addEventListener:Function;
    public var removeEventListener:Function;
    private var dispatchEvent:Function;
```

The section after that creates the constructor function that will be called when the component initializes at runtime. In it, we set the visibility of our component to false. Then we initialize the EventDispatcher class so the component will have an event. After that, we initialize the super class, just as a precaution.

```
function Tracer(){
        this._visible = false;
        EventDispatcher.initialize(this);
        super.init(this);
}
```

After that, we use two more MetaData tags. The first declares the parameter of our component as being data bound. The second declares the event we are going to use.

```
[Bindable(param1="writeonly",type="String"))]
        [ChangeEvent("traced")]
```

Finally, we create two getter/setter methods to control the variable. And we also send the variable to the Output panel here. And finally, we close off the class with a closing curly bracket.

```
    function set tracerI(t:String):Void{
        this.tracerInfo = t;
        if(tracerInfo.length > 0){
            trace(tracerInfo);
        }
    }
}
```

Once that is saved as Tracer.as, you can return to Flash.

> **NOTE**
>
> The PNG file mentioned in the class file is a 16×16 picture of the letter "T," which can be downloaded from the accompanying site, or you can create your own. Just make sure it is residing in the same directory as the FLA and the class file.

16

1. Back in the Flash file, open the Library (Window>Library).

2. Select the Tracer movie clip, right-click, (Mac–Ctrl-click) and choose Component Definition.

   If you have built components before in Flash MX, the dialog screen will be familiar to you (see Figure 16.12).

3. Set the AS 2.0 Class to "Tracer" and check the Display in Components Panel check box.

4. Type **The Tracer Component** in the Tool Tip Text Field and click OK.

5. Now select the component you just made, and right-click again (Mac–Ctrl-click). This time choose Convert to Compiled Clip.

   Converting to a compiled clip will actually return a compiled SWF file to the library, which will be the actual component and will be included in your SWC file. This saves a great deal on file size.

6. Select the component you created again, and right-click again (Mac–Ctrl-click). This time choose Export SWC File, and save it to the desktop as Tracer.swc.

That was it! Now go to the components directory and create a new folder called Unleashed Components, copy the SWC file into it, and restart Flash.

> **NOTE**
>
> If you get a warning telling you that you cannot have two symbols with the same linkage name, ignore it, it just means the component will not work in this file because when we created the compiled clip, it was given the same linkage name as the movie clip.

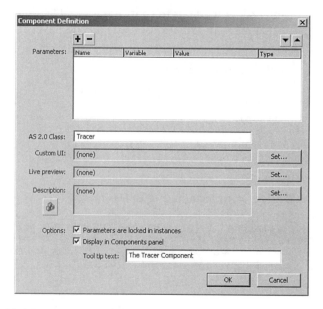

FIGURE 16.12   The Component Definition dialog box where certain parameters of the component are set.

To test the component, follow these steps after you have restarted Flash:

1. Create a new Flash document.

2. Drag an instance of the Tracer component onto the stage and give it an instance name of myTracer.

3. Now drag an instance of the Button component, give it an instance name of myButton, and set the toggle parameter to true.

4. Select the Tracer component, open the Component Inspector, and select the Bindings tab.

5. Click the Add Binding button, choose tracerI:String, and click OK.

6. Select the Bound To field and click the magnifying glass that appears.

7. Choose the Button component in the left window, choose selected : Boolean in the right window, and click OK.

8. Test the movie and every time you toggle the button, it will display a Boolean value in the Output panel.

That was awesome! You have created a component that has data bindings, which will help you test other applications in the future.

Summary

This chapter covered a lot of information about components. We talked about what a component is and when you should use one. We covered the basic fundamentals of components including

- How to set parameters
- How to capture their events
- How to extract data from them

We also went into some more advanced features of components and how to use them including

- The `dataProvider` property
- Data binding

And we finished up by creating a debugger component that can data bind to other components to test data.

You will see components again as you go through the chapters covering external data integration because components make quick work of necessary interface pieces for applications.

16

CHAPTER **17**

Debugging

Throughout this book, we go through many detailed examples of ActionScript, as well as other languages later on in this book. A great deal of effort was made to test the examples to make sure they will work for you as you go through them. But as you begin to create your own projects, you will begin to notice that not every project will work the way you expect, or it may not work at all. This is where debugging becomes invaluable.

In this chapter, you will learn not only how to debug your projects, but you'll also learn some steps to take that may shorten your debugging time as well as how to debug from a remote location. But before we jump into how to debug, it's important to know what debugging is.

What Is Debugging?

Debugging is the process of finding and fixing areas of problematic code. That is basically a dictionary definition of what debugging is, because debugging is much more than finding and fixing errors. You may have to debug an application because certain sections are slow and use too much processor power. You may have to debug a website because certain browsers render your file differently from what you want. You may even have to debug your file because it does not work with some other code (such as PHP or a web service) the way it should, and you can't change the other code because it may not be yours to change.

But the difference between debugging and writing good code is that you can't predict when and where you will have to debug, because you can't possibly know until you test the program. However, you can take some steps that may help you keep debugging to a minimum.

Planning Ahead

This may seem obvious to some, but planning ahead is one of the best ways to avoid errors. When you have clearly defined requirements for your project, begin to map out key points of your project, such as the following:

- What version of the Flash player are you going to use? Because different versions of the Flash player support different objects, this is an important question to answer early. You can check which version of the player is required for the different objects in the Help panel (F1).

- How will the data be handled and stored? Understanding your data before you begin to build the application itself is invaluable because it will define the necessary interface pieces required for the users to work with the data.

- Will there be any Object classes that will have to be created? If you know ahead of time that you need to create your own classes or components, you will have more time to figure out what the properties and function of those classes and components will be.

- What are the basic interactions users will have with this project? It may seem harmless to wait until after everything is done before you begin to work on the interactions, but you would be surprised how often minor adjustments to the timing of how users interact with your project can cause errors.

The list can be much larger than that, and sometimes it may have to be. Just remember, the more planning you do in the beginning, the less guesswork you will have to do at the end. Another great way to help plan your project is to build an application flowchart showing every possible path a user can take with every possible outcome.

After you have well-defined requirements, try not to change them. The more changes you make and the more features you add that are outside the scope of the requirements, the more bugs you will have to fix. And after you start creating your project, you can take other steps to shorten debugging.

Names That Make Sense

This has been touched on in earlier chapters, but it's important enough to mention again. When naming things in Flash, give them names that make sense.

Here is an example: Imagine that you have three rectangle buttons on the stage. One is blue and controls the sound volume of your movie. Another is red and controls where in the movie clip a user is. The last button is green and closes the window. You give them the instance names of `rec1_btn`, `rec2_btn`, and `rec3_btn`. Just from reading this paragraph, do you know what the job of `rec1_btn` is? Of course not, but if they had been named `redRec_btn`, `blueRec_btn`, and `greenRec_btn`, when you code them, or go back to the code at a later time, you would know from the code what the red button does.

And if you are using ActionScript 2.0 in your project, all variable and instance names are case sensitive.

ActionScript 1.0:

```
var myVar = "Test";
trace(myvar);
//output: Test
```

ActionScript 2.0:

```
var myVar = "Test";
trace(myvar);
//output: undefined
```

Documentation

Documenting your code is another great way not only to help prevent unnecessary debugging, but it will also help down the road if you or a colleague needs to revisit the project.

Documenting your code is much harder than it may appear because you don't want to over document your code by putting in comments that are not necessary. For instance, if you set a variable to a specific value, you don't need to document what is being done, but it might be beneficial to document why it is being done. Take the following two pieces of code:

Not helpful:

```
//the next line of code sets the X position of rec_mc to 100
rec_mc._x = 100;
```

Helpful:

```
//the next line of code lines up rec_mc against the picture border
rec_mc._x = 100;
```

With the second snippet of code, you can clearly see what the horizontal position of rec_mc is being set to, but because of the documentation you can also see why. So if you move the picture, you will know to move rec_mc as well. But the first snippet of code basically documents what you can easily tell from the code, so it is redundant.

Documentation becomes even more important when you're working in teams. If, for instance, you are building several object classes for other developers or designers to use, you have to do more than simply document the code. You have to document what the code will be doing because even with good documentation, not everyone who will have to use your code will understand it. It is also a good idea in your documentation of classes to not only document how something works, but also provide examples that can be copied and pasted in so that your teammates can quickly see how the code will work.

Another great thing to document is version changes. As you fix bugs or add features to your project, document the changes you have made and use some form of incrementing identification so that you can backtrack your changes if you need to. A lot of times, what you do to fix one bug can cause bugs in other areas of your code that were working perfectly in previous versions, so it is important to keep a record of changes.

Strict Data Typing

A great way to catch errors early is to set rules for variables and functions using *strict data typing*. Introduced with ActionScript 2.0, strict data typing allows you to set the data types of all variables being created like this:

```
var myString:String = "David";
```

Then, later in the code, if you were to change the data type of the value in the variable like this:

```
myString = 25;
```

you would get an error that would look like Figure 17.1 when you either check the code or when you test the movie. This is helpful because if you happen to change data types while in your project, they can be easily found and fixed.

> **TIP**
>
> Another great feature of strict data typing is that when you data type a variable, code hints for the data type will appear when that variable is used.

FIGURE 17.1   An error message is received when the data type of a variable with strict data typing changes.

You can also use strict data type for functions in two different places. The first is the return value, like this:

```
function myFunc():String{
        return "test";
}
```

If you try to return another data type, or no data type at all, an error will be thrown. If you specifically do not want a return value, you can use Void, like this:

```
function myFunc():Void{
        //do something, but don't return a value
}
```

If a value is returned when using Void, an error will be thrown like before. The next parts of a function that can be strict data typed are the parameters. Each parameter can have a separate strict data type without affecting the others, such as this:

```
function myFunc(age:Number, theName:String):String{
        return theName + " is " + age + " years old.";
}
trace(myFunc(25, "Ben"));
//output: Ben is 25 years old.
```

In the preceding example, a function was created with two parameters, *age* and *theName*. Both have different strict data types, as does the return value of the function. After the function was created, we tested it with the correct data types to see the output. Go back and put quotes around 25 when we call the function and you will see an error like Figure 17.2 because putting quotes around the number converts it to a string, and that is not the correct data type for that parameter.

FIGURE 17.2   An error message is sent to the Output panel when a parameter's value does not match its predefined data type.

Strict data typing is a great way to set stricter guidelines on your data and catch errors early on. Another way to catch errors before they accumulate is by prototyping.

Prototyping and Testing

When your project is finally complete, it may have anywhere from 50 lines to well over 20,000 lines of code in it, or more. If you have waited until this point to begin testing and debugging your application, good luck.

Testing should be done throughout the process of building the project in every major browser and in several versions of the Flash player. (For more on testing for the Flash player, see Chapter 7, "Publishing.") And when you test, don't just test for debugging purposes, but also for usability, scalability, as well as other important factors that go into creating a project, such as memory usage and processor performance. And it's at these times that prototyping becomes a valuable asset.

A prototype is a term you may hear in engineering fields, where people building products will create an unfinished working mockup of the product to make sure all the parts work together and that people can use it. Prototyping is the same with Flash projects. Early on, you can quickly build small-scale working versions of what you believe your project will be. This will give you an opportunity to get feedback early on to see if there are any minor issues that can be avoided now before they become major issues later. And Flash is a great tool for prototyping with its built-in component set and easy-to-use data integration features (which are discussed later in this book). An example of prototyping could be that the project will be a database-driven application. Before you begin to connect Flash to the server, use local data to make sure the internal pieces of your project are functioning well; then when you are satisfied that everything works, connect to the server to make your project truly dynamic.

But no matter how much planning and careful coding you do, sooner or later you will have to debug a project; the next section discusses some of the tools used to get the job done.

Tools of the Trade

When it comes time to debug, Flash has several options that will help you. Some of the simplest options use the Output panel as a means of getting information to you. You can open the Output panel at any time by going to Window, Output (F2), as shown in Figure 17.3. When you test your code or movie, the Output panel is used to display errors in your code, but you will also learn how to manually send information to it.

The first option for sending information to the Output panel that you can use in your own code is the trace function.

The trace Function

The trace function is one of the most widely used tools for debugging in Flash because of its ease of use and capability to be added or removed from your code. The trace function will take any information passed to it and display that information at runtime in the Output panel. You can place trace functions in any part of the code in either frame actions or object actions. Here are a few examples of trace functions:

```
trace("david");          //trace a simple string
trace(129);              //trace simple numbers
trace(1 + 41);           //trace answers to expressions
trace(15 < 35);          //trace results from comparisons
trace(getTimer());       //trace the results of functions
trace(rec_mc._x);        //trace information about objects on the stage
trace(test_array);       //trace entire arrays of information
```

If you were to test the preceding code, the Output panel would appear similar to Figure 17.3, with some exceptions, because a couple of the trace functions refer to objects that may not be present in your file, such as the array and movie clip.

FIGURE 17.3   The Output panel displays information from your movie at runtime.

> **NOTE**
>
> It is important to note that the information being sent to the Output panel will display only from within Flash and Flash's test environment. It will not appear when using your finished file (.swf).

When you are done debugging, you can remove all the `trace` statements manually, or turn them all off at once in the Flash tab of the Publish Settings (File, Publish Settings) and select Omit Trace Actions. This will prevent the `trace` functions from working when you test the movie, but they will still be present in your source file if you need to use them again.

List Options

You can also send other information to the Output panel when debugging. You can list all variables or all objects in your movie during testing. To list this information, test your movie by going to Control, Test Movie (PC—Ctrl+Enter, MAC—Open Apple+Enter). Inside the test movie screen, select either Debug, List Objects (Ctrl+L) or Debug, List Variables (Ctrl+Alt+V). You will see something similar to the following two figures. And when you list the variables, notice a special one that you did not create—$version. This variable is available to you during runtime, and it lists the type of operating system and the version number for the current player running. This can also be helpful if you have content for specific versions of Flash, so make special note of it.

FIGURE 17.4   An example of the output for List Objects.

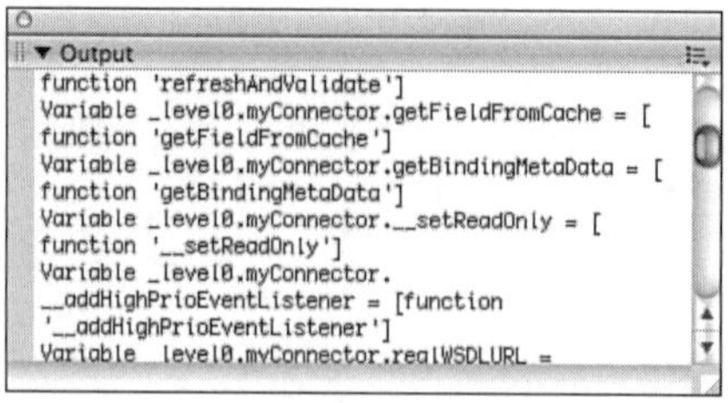

FIGURE 17.5   An example of the output for List Variables.

These options in the test environment can become valuable when you're trying to figure what the value of several variables are during runtime, as well as which objects are available and what some of their properties are.

> **NOTE**
>
> It is important to understand that when you use these listing options, only the objects and variables currently present at the point of the movie you are in will be listed. For instance, if you delete a variable with ActionScript before the point in your movie where you are, that variable will not be listed.

The Error Object

The Error object, introduced back in Flash MX 2004, will probably be familiar to you if you have worked in other programming languages. It is used to hold error messages that can be thrown directly to the Output panel, or they can be caught by either a catch or finally action while inside of a try statement. They are most commonly used with testing functions.

In this example of code, we will create a try statement, and then use conditionals to trigger the error.

```
//create a password
var myPass:String = "testing";
//test the password using a try statement and a conditional
try{
   if(myPass != "password"){
      throw new Error("Incorrect password");
   }
}
//last resort
finally{
   //everything is fine
}
//simple trace action to see if the reader gets this far
trace("test");
```

When you test this code, the error will be thrown to the Output panel. But make special note that the trace function at the end of our code was not sent to the Output panel. This is because when a throw takes place, it stops the ActionScript reader from moving forward. If you change the myPass variable to "password," the error will not be thrown, and the trace function will be run.

In the next example of using the Error object, we will use it inside of a function we build. This time, instead of sending it directly to the Output panel, we will catch it using the try and catch statements, and then send it to the Output panel. You can, of course, catch these errors and do other things with them, but for this example, we will still send it to the Output panel to see immediate results.

```
//create the function
function greaterThan(num1:Number, num2:Number):Void{
//compare the numbers
  if(num1 < num2) {
    throw new Error("The first number is not greater than the second");
  }
}
//try the function
try {
  greaterThan(12,15);
} catch (theError) {
  //trace the error if there is one
  trace(theError.toString());
}
```

Notice that this time we are using the throw statement inside a function. This means that for the error to be shown, it must first be captured with the catch statement.

Those are just two ways the Error object can be used to improve debugging. The Error object is great if you have multiple bugs and want to debug them one at a time, because the Error object can stop the rest of the ActionScript from being run.

Sizing Up Your Project

As mentioned before, not all debugging involves finding and fixing errors. Sometimes you will have to debug the performance and file size of your project. For example, because SWFs are a streaming file type, they will begin playing instantly in your browser. The problem is that sometimes the movie will reach a frame that has not completely loaded yet, and there will be a pause on that frame while the loading catches up. Using a preloader to preload all the content before it moves forward is an easy solution for this, but not always a warranted solution (see Chapter 13, "The Movie Clip Object," for more information on preloaders). Sometimes, you just need to adjust the frame that's slowing up the file, and it will stream fine. And Flash has two tools to help you track down heavy frames.

The Bandwidth Profiler

When testing your movie in Flash's test environment, note that there is a feature that is not turned on by default, called the *Bandwidth Profiler*. This tool displays your file frame by frame in a vertical bar-graph representation, as shown in Figure 17.6, so that you can quickly spot the trouble areas of your file. To open the Bandwidth Profiler, test your movie (Control, Text Movie), and then select View, Bandwidth Profiler (Ctrl+B).

You have two options for viewing this graph: Streaming Graph or Frame by Frame graph. By default, Streaming Graph is selected.

As you can see from Figure 17.6, frame 12 is above the red line, so some work needs to be done in that frame to make it stream correctly. You can also test for streaming in the test environment by selecting View, Simulate Download (Ctrl+Enter) from inside the test environment. There are also bandwidth options under View, Download Settings that simulate different connection speeds.

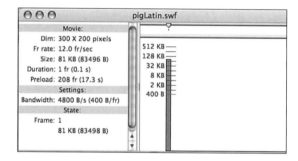

FIGURE 17.6   The Bandwidth Profiler for viewing frame size at runtime.

Generate Size Report

Another tool in Flash for monitoring the size of your file is the Size Report. The size report can be generated automatically by going to the Flash tab of the Publish Settings (File, Publish Settings) and checking the Generate Size Report option. Then when you test your file, information will be sent to the Output panel and a text file will be created right beside the FLA you are working in with the same name plus the word "Report" in it.

Table 17.1 shows an example of what the size report might look like:

TABLE 17.1   Example.swf Movie Report

Frame #	Frame Bytes	Total Bytes	Scene
1	5,492	5,492	Scene 1 (AS 2.0 Classes Export Frame)
2	9,897	15,389	
3	10	15,399	
4	10	15,409	
5	358	15,767	
6	3	15,770	
7	1	15,771	

TABLE 17.1 Continued

Frame #	Frame Bytes	Total Bytes	Scene
8	1	15,772	
9	1	15,773	
10	1	15,774	
11	1	15,775	
12	1	15,776	
13	1	15,777	
14	1	15,778	

Scene	Shape Bytes	Text Bytes	ActionScript Bytes
Scene 1	0	0	6,087

Symbol	Shape Bytes	Text Bytes	ActionScript Bytes
bigT	292	0	0
Symbol 1	0	0	0
PixelFX 4	0	0	0
thumbMC	0	26	1,032
PixelFX 3	0	0	0
PixelFX 1	0	0	0

Font Name	Bytes	Characters
_sans Bold	4742	!"#$%&'()*+,-./0123456789:;<=>?@ABCDEFGHIJKLMN OPQRSTUVWXYZ[\]^_`abcdefghijklmnopqrstuvwxyz{|}~

ActionScript	Bytes	Location
	5,465	Scene 1:actions:1
	599	Scene 1:actions:2
	1,032	thumbMC:actions:1
	23	Scene 1:actions:5

Bitmap	Compressed	Compression	
PixelFX_Element1	2,523	68,264	JPEG Quality=100
PixelFX_Element3	842	7,224	JPEG Quality=100

As you can see from the preceding output, the size report gives much more information about your file than the bandwidth profiler does. Not only does it show the byte size in each frame, it also keeps track of the total running byte size as you move through the frames. You also get information about each symbol in the library and bitmaps. You can even see the file size of just the ActionScript in each frame and symbol.

All of these tools that we have gone over in Flash are great for debugging your project, but sometimes you will need something more directly geared toward finding bugs in your code.

The Debugger

The debugger is a special panel included in Flash that makes it easy to track values and hierarchies in your projects.

In the first example of using the debugger, we will walk through a simple login page that will look for the user's login name and password. You will need debugger1.fla from the website to go through this example.

1. After you have debugger1.fla open, test the movie by going to Control, Test Movie. If you put in "**admin**" for the login and "**letMeIn**" for the password, and then click LOGIN, you will notice it does not move to the next frame. Time to debug.

2. Return to the authoring environment and select Control, Debug Movie. This will test your movie as before, but it will also open the debugger automatically. Notice that the movie is stopped in the first frame; this is to allow you to put breakpoints in your code.

3. On the right side of the debugger, select Actions for Scene 1: Frame 1 of Layer Name As and the ActionScript from that frame will appear.

4. Put a breakpoint at line number 4 by clicking the number 4. This stops the code from running when it reaches this point so we can see what is going on there.

5. Click the Continue button to activate the login screen and put in the same login information as before. Then click LOGIN again. Now your debugger should look like Figure 17.7, with a little golden arrow in the red breakpoint you placed on line 4. This means that the code has stopped here.

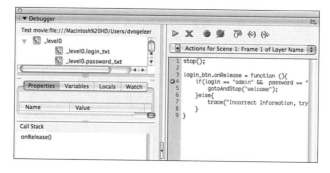

FIGURE 17.7   The debugger is great for finding problems with variable values.

6. Select the _level0 from the top left list, and select the Variables tab. You see that both variables are getting the correct information, but your conditional is looking for the variable *pass* not *password*.

7. Go back into the authoring environment and change your code on line 4 from

```
if(login == "admin" && pass == "letMeIn"){
```

to

```
if(login == "admin" && password == "letMeIn"){
```

and test again. Now when you attempt to log in, you see a message saying you have logged in correctly.

This example was a simple fix, and the debugger will work just as well with huge applications as it did with this little login screen.

The debugger can also be used to adjust visual properties and values of content on the stage at runtime. This next example will have an image that is labeled, but something does not look right with the label. We will adjust its properties in the debugger so we can see what they look like at runtime. You will need debugger2.fla from the website.

1. After you have debugger2.fla open, take a look at the ActionScript in frame 1 of the *as* layer. We create a text field at runtime and then set some text to it to label the image on the stage.

2. Select Control, Debug Movie (Ctrl+Shift+Enter) to debug the movie. The debugger will appear as before, but this time we do not need to add any breakpoints, so click the Continue button to run the file. You can see the label now; it has a background, but no border, and it is in the wrong position.

3. In the top-left list, select level0.label_txt and then select the Properties tab. Your debugger should look similar to Figure 17.8.

FIGURE 17.8   You can use the debugger to fine-tune the visuals of your file.

4. The _x property needs to be set to 0, so double-click in the value field of the _x property, put "**0**" and press Enter. You will note on the stage that the field has moved over to the far left.

5. Do the same to the _y property by setting it to 0 and pressing Enter; now the label is in the top left of the image, but it still needs a border.

6. Select the Values tab and your debugger should look like Figure 17.9. Change the value of border from *false* to *true* and a thin border will appear around the label.

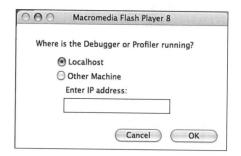

FIGURE 17.9   The Remote Debugging dialog box.

Now that you are satisfied with how the label looks, you can go back to the ActionScript and make the changes, because even though you changed them in the debugger, they do not stay there when you close the test environment. This is so you can make changes to properties of several objects on the stage without fear of messing up your original code. This technique of changing things at runtime will also work on objects created manually.

In this section, you have learned how to debug your projects at your own workstation, but what if you want to debug your project at home and don't have the file, or you want someone else to debug your project and they are not onsite?

Remote Debugging

Debugging from remote locations is a tremendous time-saver when you're working in a team environment where not every team member is at the same site. Remote debugging will allow you to set up your file, with a password, so that users who have Flash in other geographical locations can assist in the debugging process.

The first thing you will have to do is set up your file to allow remote debugging. You can use any of the files mentioned in this chapter, or create your own from scratch.

1. Select File, Publish Settings.

2. In the Flash tab, select the Debugging Permitted option.

3. Give your file a password of **flashUnleashed**.

4. Click Publish. This will create both the SWF file and a SWD file needed for debugging.

5. Post both of those files on a server, in the same directory.

That was the first part; the next part is to actually connect to it using remote debugging.

1. With Flash still open, select Window, Debugger.

2. In the debugger's Options menu (at the top right of the debugger), select Enable Remote Debugging.

3. Now, using a browser or the standalone Flash Player, map to the SWF you have put on the server. This should prompt the Remote Debugging dialog box, as shown in Figure 17.9.

4. Leave the default selection of Localhost selected and click OK. This should prompt you for the password, as in Figure 17.10.

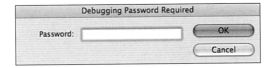

FIGURE 17.10   You can require a password for your file so that only those users you want can debug your file.

5. Enter the correct password and click OK.

After the password is entered, you should be able to debug as if the file were running on your machine.

Summary

Debugging is a part of every developer's job, and hopefully this chapter has shown you the tools and practices to best accomplish the task. The more code you write, and the more debugging you do, the better you will become. Just remember, the more planning and testing you do early on, the less debugging you'll likely have to do at the end. And always document your code.

This concludes this section of the book. The next section shows you how to begin incorporating external data into your projects.

PART III

Outside of Flash

IN THIS PART

CHAPTER **18**

External ActionScript

In earlier chapters, we covered the fundamentals of ActionScript 2.0 and debugging. Now we can begin to start taking ActionScript out of Flash and put it in external `.as` files. Some of the benefits include scalability and reusability; because the ActionScript is outside of Flash, it can be used by several different Flash files without you having to rewrite any of the code.

External `.as` files can be created with any text editor such as Notepad or SciTe and in the Flash authoring environment as well. You can also export directly from the Actions panel by selecting the options drop down and selecting Export script.

To create an external ActionScript file from scratch in Flash, choose File>New and choose ActionScript File. The stage will change to a large version of the Actions panel, which functions in much the same way as the standard Actions panel does in Flash, as you can see in Figure 18.1.

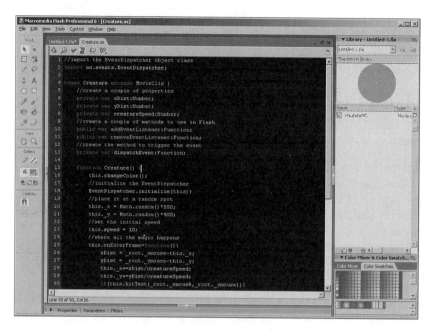

FIGURE 18.1   Create external ActionScript files from within Flash.

Why Use External ActionScript?

Thus far in this book, you have seen that external ActionScript files are not necessary. In fact, creating external AS files would be yet another step in the process of building an application in Flash, so what would be the reason behind it?

ActionScript, as mentioned in previous chapters, is an object-oriented language, meaning that almost every piece of code is based on an object class. But this doesn't directly address the reason behind creating external ActionScript files; it is just the basis behind the reason.

It's no secret that Flash 8 is designed to be used by design and development teams in harmony, and that is where externalizing core ActionScript requirements for a given application comes in handy. A developer can create object classes to be used by designers or other developers easily and quickly at the same time that the designer is creating the visual aspects of the application, thus keeping design, content, and function all separate.

Using external AS files also allows multiple applications to use the same file at the same time. Think of it this way: Imagine having to define the MovieClip object in each file you wanted to use it. It would be very difficult to create the exact same class each time you needed a movie clip, not to mention the repetitiveness of it. But because the MovieClip object is defined already, we can simply use it in Flash and not have to worry about how the movie clip was actually created. Another example might be certain effects or transitions that are prevalent throughout a huge corporate site. It would be difficult to match the effects exactly if you did not create them in the first place. And copying and pasting code from other projects can sometimes be tricky if you are missing a variable. Thankfully, the development team created an external ActionScript file that contains a simple API for all the effects and transitions that you can simply include and use in your files, which is quite a time saver.

As we go through this chapter, all of this will begin to make more sense and you will begin to see the advantages in creating external ActionScript files.

#include **Versus Classpath**

External ActionScript files are not new to Flash, but they were introduced differently in Flash 2004 and are brought in at compile time.

In older versions of Flash, if you wanted to include an external AS file, you would use a pound sign (#) followed by the keyword include, and the path to the AS file as a string literal like this:

```
#include "myFile.as"
```

Notice that this line of code is not followed by a semicolon like most lines in ActionScript. An include statement cannot be followed by a semicolon or errors may occur. Also, do not put code directly below an include statement or errors might occur. Put at least one line of space between include statements and other code.

That was the old way of including external ActionScript in Flash files and it will still work if you want to use it. However, the new way is much simpler and it is called classpath.

The classpath is a path or group of paths to where external ActionScript files can be found. And to include information from within one of the files, you simply call the constructor of the object class and Flash will look for a reference to that object in the classpath.

Here is an example of an external AS file:

```
class MyClass{
    //class definition
}
```

And provided that this external AS file is within the classpath, the ActionScript to use it in Flash would be as follows:

```
    var sampleClass:MyClass = new MyClass();
```

When this action is called, it will look through the classpath to see if there is a class named MyClass in it (which incidentally will be a file named MyClass.as). You can also keep external AS files in the same directory as the Flash file that is trying to use them, and if the class being referred to in Flash cannot be found in the defined paths of the classpath, it will then look in its own directory, which is also controlled by the classpath.

18

> **NOTE**
>
> External ActionScript files are compiled directly into the SWF file when the SWF file is created, so if an external AS file is updated, the Flash file using it must be recompiled before the changes will take effect.

You can set the classpath in your preferences by going to Edit>Preferences and choosing the ActionScript category (see Figure 18.2). Then choose the ActionScript 2.0 Settings button and the ActionScript Settings dialog box pops up as shown in Figure 18.3. Here you can add classpaths, remove them, or edit them. You can also sort the order in which they are checked. Notice that it has two directories by default. The first one listed is the ".", which represents the same directory as the Flash file you are working in. The second classpath is where Flash's built-in classes are kept—in the `Classes` directory of the user's configuration directory.

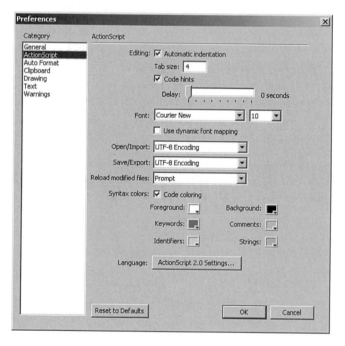

FIGURE 18.2   ActionScript preferences for all Flash documents.

At the top of the ActionScript settings box, there is a field labeled Export Frame for Classes, and it has the number 0 as its value, which means that before the first frame of ActionScript is reached, it will compile the external code that is necessary for that file. But the field is grayed out and cannot be adjusted. This is because there is another spot where you can adjust your classpath settings, in the Publish Settings dialog box, in the Flash section, as shown in Figure 18.4. If you have the ActionScript version set to ActionScript 2.0 (the default), you can click the Settings button, and an ActionScript settings dialog box appears as in Figure 18.5. The difference is that there are no default classpaths, and you can adjust the export frame. This ActionScript setting is for the current file only and will not be kept from file to file (unless you save it as part of your publishing profile). And even though you can adjust the export frame, it will not let you go lower than the number zero.

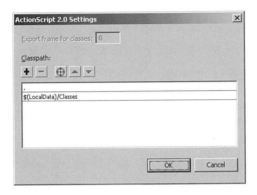

FIGURE 18.3   ActionScript Settings dialog box where you can control your classpaths.

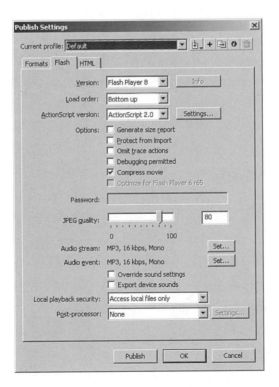

FIGURE 18.4   Publish settings for the Flash tab.

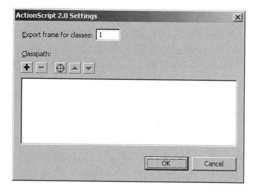

FIGURE 18.5 ActionScript settings for the publish settings.

Now that you have seen where to create external ActionScript, and how to use it, let's start creating these files.

Getting Started with External Class Files

As mentioned earlier, custom class construction is nothing new, but the manner in which it is done is completely new to anything we have gone over so far. In older versions of Flash, you could create classes of objects either externally or internally in the Flash file. But with the introduction of ActionScript 2.0, the only way to correctly build object classes is externally in .as files.

Here are two examples of building the same class, one in ActionScript 1.0 and the other in ActionScript 2.0.

Here's how you would do it in ActionScript 1.0:

```
function Bird (){
    //create an event
    this.onLand=function(){};
    //create a fly method
    this.fly=function(speed, distance){
        //fly
    }
    //create a method to check altitude
    this.checkAltitude=function(){
        if(this.altitude <= 0){
            //call the event for when the bird lands
            onLand();
        }
        return this.altitude
    }
}
```

And this is what you would do in ActionScript 2.0:

```
//get the ability to use listeners
import mx.events.EventDispatcher;

class Bird{
//declare the methods and properties
    public var altitude:Number;
    public var addEventListener:Function;
    public var removeEventListener:Function;
    private var dispatchEvent:Function;
//initialize the ability to have listeners
    function Bird(){
        EventDispatcher.initialize(this);
    }
    //create a fly method
    function fly(speed:Number, distance:Number):Void{
        //fly
    }
    //create a method to check altitude
    function checkAltitude():Number{
        if(this.altitude <= 0){
            //trigger the listener
            dispatchEvent({type:"onLand"});
        }
        return this.altitude;
    }
}
```

You can definitely see the difference in complexity in the ActionScript 2.0 version compared to the ActionScript 1.0 version, but with that complexity comes much more power, flexibility, and scalability than ever before. Don't worry if you do not understand everything in the preceding code; as we move through the chapter, each part will be covered.

Defining a Class

The concept of object-oriented programming was covered back in Chapter 8, "Welcome to ActionScript 2.0," so there is no need to repeat that information here. When creating a class, you are defining what the class has in it, what it can do, and what events are taking place.

Defining a class in ActionScript 2.0 is as simple as using the keyword class, the name of the class, and opening and closing curly brackets like this:

```
class MyClass{
    //class instructions
}
```

Of course this class does not do anything, nor does it have any properties, but we will get to that soon enough.

And when defining a class, you do not always have to start from scratch. If there is a class already made you want to use as a base for your class, you can extend that class with a subclass (child class), like this:

```
class Shape extends MovieClip{
    //extends the MovieClip class
}
```

Now the new class Shape extends the MovieClip class, and therefore has all of the MovieClip properties and methods plus whatever is created within the Shape class itself.

> **NOTE**
>
> Notice that all of the classes we have built thus far are capitalized. This is not necessary, but it is good coding practice to capitalize class names for easy readability. And remember, ActionScript 2.0 is case sensitive, so when you create instances of the new object, use the same case.

> **NOTE**
>
> Another thing of note when building external classes is that the filename must match the class name. For instance, if you have a class called Bird, it must reside in a file named Bird.as.

That covered how to build a class, but so far our classes do not have anything in them. Let's start placing methods and properties in them.

Public, Private, and Static

Before we start creating properties and methods, it's important to know a few keywords that describe how these properties and methods interact in Flash.

When you declare properties and methods, you can use the keywords public or private to set boundaries for their use.

Public means that they can be used within the class itself, or in conjunction with an instance of the object in Flash.

Private means that the property or method can only be used internally in the object class itself.

Here are a few small examples of public and private:

```
class Bird{
    public var birdType:String;
    public var weight:Number;
    private var feathers:Number;
```

```
    public function fly (speed:Number, distance:Number):Void{
        //fly
    }
    private function featherCount():Number{
        return this.feathers;
    }
    public function molt():Void{
        this.feathers = this.featherCount()-25;
    }
}
```

You can see that we create two public properties and one private property for the Bird class of object. We then create a public method to allow the bird to fly. After that, we create a private method that can only be used in this class file. Then we use the private method from within a public method to remove some of the bird's feathers.

The benefit of using public and private is that sometimes in object classes, you don't want certain properties or methods to be accessible directly from the a Flash file: Instead, they are called from within other methods, properties, or events. If you do not declare whether a method or property is either public or private, it will be public by default.

There is another keyword that can be used when creating properties or methods with object classes: the static keyword. Making a property static means that it can only be accessed by using the object's class name, not an instance of that object. Static methods and properties are not new to Flash; in fact, here are a few examples using them with the Math object:

- Math.PI—Approximately 3.1415926

- Math.E—Approximately 2.71828

- Math.tan(0)—Returns tangent of number 0

Notice that when we call either a property or method of the Math object, we use the class name, not an instance of the object.

Most static methods and properties are used with object classes that have just static methods or properties, and they rarely have events. Classes with static elements are used to perform certain tasks where instances of that object class would not be necessary, such as the Math class.

And when creating static properties or methods of objects, they can be either private or public like the following code, which would appear within a class:

```
private static var age:Number = 23;
public static function square(num:Number){
    return num*num;
}
```

Those are the keywords that will help define properties and methods in external ActionScript files.

Declaring Properties with a Constructor Function

Sometimes when you create an instance of an object, you want to set some of the properties of that object right when it is being created. To do so, you need a constructor function inside the class definition.

A constructor function uses the class's name as the function name within itself, so when an instance of that object is created, everything within the constructor function will be done.

Here is an example of using a constructor function to build a House object:

```
class House{
    //declare some properties
    public var houseWidth:Number;
    public var houseHeight:Number;
    public var stories:Number;
    public var houseType:String;
//create the constructor function
    function House(width,height,stories,houseType){
        this.houseWidth = width;
        this.houseHeight = height;
        this.stories = stories;
        this.houseType = houseType;
    }
}
```

And you can then create an instance of the House object in Flash like this:

```
var homeSweetHome:House = new House(50,50,2,"rancher");
```

Now you see not only how to create properties, but also how to create them when an instance of the object is created. Next is how to declare methods.

Creating Methods

If properties are information about an object, methods are what objects do. A method is nothing more than a function directly associated with an object.

When creating a function, it is important to remember to declare whether it is private or public. Otherwise, it will automatically become public, which may not be what you want. It is good practice to always declare which type of method it is no matter which type it will be.

Also note that you cannot declare a blank function and then define it later in the code. Here is an example that will cause an error trying to accomplish this:

```
class Bird{
    public var fly:Function;

    function fly(){
        //fly
    }
}
```

If you attempt to use this code, an error will occur saying that the function cannot be created twice; just something to keep in mind.

Also, when you declare a function, you can set the type of data to be returned. Here is an example of that:

```
class Bird{
    private var altitude:Number;
    public function getAltitude():Number{
        return this.altitude;
    }
}
```

As you can see, in the preceding example, the method getAltitude() will return the current altitude of any instance of the Bird object, and it will always be a number.

But if you are creating a method that will not return a value, you can declare that as well, as you can see in this next example:

```
class Bird{
private var altitude:Number;
private function increaseAltitude(amount:Number):Void{
    this.altitude += amount;
}
}
```

Notice that we used the keyword Void instead of a data type to declare that this method will not return any data. If a method with the Void return type attempts to return data, an error message will appear.

There are also two types of methods that are unique and can be created within external AS files.

Creating Getter/Setter Methods

Getter and setter methods are unique among other methods created in object classes because when they are accessed, they are not accessed in the same way most other methods are. When methods are called, they have a set of parentheses following the name of the method; this is how you can distinguish methods. Getter/setter methods are created in much the same way other methods are created, but they are accessed like properties.

The reason behind this is that it is bad practice for a user to directly access a property of an object, so developers often create methods to both get the information from a property and set information to that property. But getter/setter methods alleviate this problem by creating methods that can be accessed like properties.

Here is an example of creating a getter method using the keyword get:

```
class Bird{
    //declare a property
    private var birdWeight:Number;
    //create the constructor function
    function Bird(weight){
        this.birdWeight = weight;
    }
    //create the getter method
    public function get weight():Number{
        return birdWeight;
    }
}
```

And here is the code that will create a new instance of the Bird object and then get the weight. The code is in a Flash file that resides in the same directory as the Bird.as file:

```
//create a new Bird with a weight of 40
var myBird:Bird = new Bird(40);
//get the birds weight
trace(myBird.weight);
```

As you can see if you test this code, the weight of the bird is returned because we called the getter method, but it looks like a property, not a method.

Here is an example, extending the preceding example to now include a setter method:

```
class Bird{
    //declare a property
    private var birdWeight:Number;
    //create the constructor function
    function Bird(weight){
        this.birdWeight = weight;
    }
    //create the getter method
    public function get weight():Number{
        return birdWeight;
    }
    //create the setter method
    public function set weight(amount:Number):Void{
        this.birdWeight = amount;
    }
}
```

And here is the update to the Flash code that will create an instance of the `Bird` object, get its current weight, then reset it, and finally get the current weight again:

```
//create a new Bird with a weight of 40
var myBird:Bird = new Bird(40);
//get the birds weight
trace(myBird.weight);
//now reset the weight
myBird.weight = 25;
//now get the weight again
trace(myBird.weight);
```

Again, we access the getter and setter methods to control the properties of the `myBird` instance, but they appear to be properties we are calling, not methods.

> **NOTE**
>
> With getter methods, there are never any parameters, just the result being returned. And with setter methods, there is one parameter, and nothing is being returned.

Now we have covered both properties and methods, and the final step is events.

Creating Events

Properties are pieces of information about an object. Methods are what objects do. Events are notifications about objects.

There are two ways to create events so that they can be used in Flash. You can create a callback event or a listener event. In this section, we will go over both.

Creating Callback Events

Callback events are blank methods that can be reassigned to individual instances of objects, but are called from within the object class.

Here is an example of creating a callback event:

```
class Bird{
    //create the callback event method
    public var onLand:Function;
    //create a method that will land the bird
    public function landBird():Void{
        //call the event
        this.onLand();
    }
}
```

18

As you can see, we create a blank function in the beginning of our class. We then create a method that will trigger the event automatically (normally, an event would be triggered within a condition, but in this example, we want it to be triggered no matter what).

Here is the code that will reside in the Flash file that is in the same directory as the preceding .as file:

```
//create a new Bird
var myBird:Bird = new Bird();
//set the callback event for this instance
myBird.onLand=function(){
    trace("the bird has landed");
}
//call the method that will trigger the event automatically
myBird.landBird();
```

In this example, we create an instance of the Bird object. We then set up the callback method for this particular instance for when the onLand event fires. Finally we call the method that will automatically trigger the event. If you test this movie, you will see that the message has been sent to the Output panel.

That was one way to create an event. The other way is a bit more complicated than callbacks, but is much more scalable and flexible to use when you get used to it.

Creating Listener Events

Listeners are another way your objects can have events captured. The difference between listeners and callbacks is that for callbacks, you are creating an event method on the instance of the object. For listeners, you create an object whose sole purpose is to listen to a certain event, and then you add that object to the instance as a listener.

It's a little complicated at first, but after we go through the example, it will be easier to understand.

To create listeners in external object classes, you need to import the EventDispatcher class using the import keyword, like this:

```
import mx.events.EventDispatcher;
```

Importing classes is an important part of creating external AS files. It allows you to use methods from other classes within your own class without having to extend the class you import. You import classes directly from the Classes directory in the First Run directory of Flash 8. You separate subdirectories with dot syntax.

> **TIP**
>
> You can import all external AS class files of a directory by using a wildcard on that directory like this:
>
> ```
> import mx.controls.*;
> ```
>
> Now all class files in the directory mx/controls will be imported.

Now that you know how to import the class we need, let's see how to use it.

This is the code for creating an event that has listener support. We will use the dispatchEvent() method of the EventDispatcher object after we initialize it in our constructor function.

```
//import the object class we need
import mx.events.EventDispatcher;

class Bird {
    //create two methods that will be used in Flash
    public var addEventListener:Function;
    public var removeEventListener:Function;
    //declare the event we will use from the EventDispatcher object
    private var dispatchEvent:Function;
    //declare the constructor function
    function Bird() {
        //initialize the EventDispatcher to work with this object
        EventDispatcher.initialize(this);
    }
    //create the method that will automatically trigger the event
    function landBird():Void {
        dispatchEvent({type:"onLand"});
    }
}
```

The preceding code first imports the object class we need to have listeners. It then declares the object class as Bird. After that, it declares two methods that will be used in the Flash file. Then it declares another method from the EventDispatcher object to be used in the Bird object later on. Then the constructor function is created, initializing the EventDispatcher object to work with the Bird object. Finally, the method that will automatically trigger the event is created and it uses the dispatchEvent() method to send the event name to Flash.

That was the external AS file; here is the code for the Flash file:

```
//create a new Bird
var myBird:Bird = new Bird();
//create an object to listen for the onLand event
var birdListen:Object = new Object();
//create the event for this object
birdListen.onLand = function(){
    trace("the bird has landed");
}
//add the object to the instance of the bird as a listener
myBird.addEventListener("onLand", birdListen);
//now call the method to automically trigger the event
myBird.landBird();
```

This code creates an instance of the `Bird` object. Then it creates a generic object that we will use as the listener. We then create the event with the generic object that will send a message to the Output panel when called. We then add the generic object to our instance of the `Bird` object class as an event listener. Finally we call the method that will automatically trigger the event.

Test the movie, and you will indeed see the message sent to the Output panel.

That ends the basic fundamentals of creating external AS files. Let's move on to an applied example.

Bringing It All Together

In this section, we are going to build an applied example of using external AS files by building a creature that will follow the mouse around wherever it goes.

We will begin with the `Creature` object class.

1. Create a new `.as` file called `Creature.as` and save it to the desktop.

2. Place this code within it:

```
//import the EventDispatcher object class
import mx.events.EventDispatcher;

class Creature extends MovieClip {
    //create a couple of properties
    private var xDist:Number;
    private var yDist:Number;
    private var creatureSpeed:Number;
    //create a couple of methods to use in Flash
    public var addEventListener:Function;
    public var removeEventListener:Function;
    //create the method to trigger the event
    private var dispatchEvent:Function;

    function Creature() {
        this.changeColor();
        //initialize the EventDispatcher
        EventDispatcher.initialize(this);
        //place it at a random spot
        this._x = Math.random()*550;
        this._y = Math.random()*400;
        //set the initial speed
        this.speed = 10;
        //where all the magic happens
        this.onEnterFrame=function(){
            xDist = _root._xmouse-this._x;
            yDist = _root._ymouse-this._y;
```

```
        this._x+=xDist/creatureSpeed;
        this._y+=yDist/creatureSpeed;
        if(this.hitTest(_root._xmouse,_root._ymouse)){
            dispatchEvent({type:"onGotcha"});
        }
    }
}
//create the getter setter methods
public function get speed():Number{
    return this.creatureSpeed;
}
public function set speed(amount:Number):Void{
    this.creatureSpeed = amount;
}
//create the method to change its color
public function changeColor():Void{
    //give it a random color
    var myColor:Color = new Color(this);
    myColor.setRGB(Math.random()*0x10000000);
    delete myColor;
}
}
```

The preceding code may look like a lot, but it really is just all of the things we have covered in this chapter combined. It first imports the EventDispatcher class so that we can have listeners. Then we declare the class, which is an extension of the MovieClip class. After that, we create a few properties that we use within the class. Then we start to create some of the methods we will use in Flash. Then, of course, is the constructor function where we call a method to change the object's color to a random color. Then we initialize the EventDispatcher object so that it will work with our Creature object. We then set the object at a random spot in the stage and using the onEnterFrame event, we move the creature around following the mouse. After that, we declare a couple of getter/setter methods to control the speed, and finally create the method to randomly change the color of the creature.

3. Next comes the Flash part. Create a new Flash document and save it also on the desktop as creatureExample.fla.

4. Draw a circle about 75×75 on the stage.

5. Select the entire circle including the stroke and choose Modify, Convert to Symbol.

6. Give it the same options as in Figure 18.6, which are as follows:

- Name—creatureMC

- Behavior—Movie clip

- Registration—center-center

- Identifier—creatureMC

- AS 2.0 Class—Creature

- Linkage—Export for ActionScript

- Linkage—Export in first frame

Notice that we are setting the class of this movie clip right in its symbol properties. This means that this symbol will now have all of the characteristics of the Creature object.

7. Give the circle an instance name of myCreature.

8. Create a new layer called action.

9. In the action layer, place this code:

```
//create the object to listen for the event
var creatureListen:Object = new Object();
//create the event
creatureListen.onGotcha=function(){
    //we will change the color rapidly
    myCreature.changeColor();
}
//add the listener
myCreature.addEventListener("onGotcha", creatureListen);
```

What the preceding code does is create a new object we will use as a listener for our instance of the Creature object. We then set the event to the listener that, when triggered, will change the color of the creature. Finally, we add the listener to our Creature object.

Now, when you test the movie, the circle will follow your mouse around the stage changing color constantly as long as it is touching the mouse.

There is another way to set the class of our movie clip without having to do it in the linkage box. Select creatureMC in the Library, right click (Mac: CTRL+click) and select Linkage. Uncheck Export for ActionScript and kit OK. Back in your ActionScript, place this line of code above all of the other code:

```
myCreature.__proto__ = new Creature();
```

Now test again, and the results will be the same. This extra line of code will reset the class of object our movie clip will think it is. This means that you can reset the object class of the movie clip anytime you want. A good example of using this technique is in a game where a ally might become an enemy, you can simply reset the class the ally was to enemy, and they will act accordingly while still maintaining separate class files.

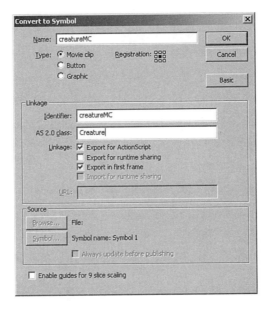

FIGURE 18.6   Set ActionScript 2.0 classes directly to movie clips in the Symbol Properties dialog box so they automatically have all of the specified class's methods and properties.

Summary

This chapter introduced you to the idea of keeping ActionScript outside of Flash for faster, more scalable, and more reusable code. We went over how Flash looks for these files as well as the old way of incorporating external ActionScript. We covered all the fundamentals of creating your own external classes including the differences between `public` and `private` as well as `static`. This chapter also covered the three basic elements each object has:

- Properties
- Methods
- Events

And we finished off with a large example that brought the fundamentals together.

It's important to experiment with external ActionScript and see where you and your team can benefit from using it to achieve greater scalability and reusability.

18

CHAPTER 19

Loading Visual Content

Thus far in the book, we have only dealt with things right on the stage. This chapter goes outside the realm of the stage and shows you how to load external files in at runtime. Not to be confused with importing, which takes place during authoring, loading external files at runtime has many advantages, which will be covered.

Also covered in this chapter is the delicate art of creating preloaders for content, a "must-have" for any heavy Flash content. *Preloaders* are what developers use to keep the user occupied while large amounts of content load in the background. They can also be used to show the progress of content being loaded, as you will see later in this chapter.

Why Load External Content?

Why use external files? Everything we have done so far seems to be working fine with no problems, so what are the benefits of externalizing content?

For starters, file size is a major factor to anyone serious about developing for the Web. With broadband connections crawling to a few new areas every month, dial-up is still the prevalent bandwidth for Internet users. Keeping content external from the Flash movie will speed the process of loading the Flash file itself because the file will be smaller.

Another benefit of externalizing content is user experience. Imagine going to a car dealership for a specific car, and the salesperson starts telling you about every single model they have. You would lose patience with him for wasting your time and go to a different salesperson, or maybe a different dealership. Well, that's what happens when you give users more than they want. With externalizing content, you can load specific content based on the user's choices instead of loading all the content and overloading the user with information.

When you create a Flash file, and you have all your content in that one file, it will take much longer to load than if you only load content that the user wants. This way, the users can come to your site, get the information important to them, and leave knowing that if they need more content, they can always come back.

So think of loading external files as a content-on-demand service.

Another thing to keep in mind is fresh content. Keeping everything inside Flash means that any time you want to update an image or a section of the Flash file, you have to open the entire file. But if you load pieces from external sources, you only have to update those pieces. For instance, if you like to keep an image of yourself somewhere on your site (I know I do), you may want to update it often. Keeping the image in Flash means that you have to upload the new version of your site every time you want to change the image. But if you load the image into Flash with ActionScript, all you have to do is upload the new image every time you want to make a change.

What Content Can Be Loaded and Where?

In Flash 8, you can load PNGs, GIFs, JPEGs and SWFs, but in the 6 and 7 player, you can only load JPEGs and SWFs. You can also load in .flv (Flash Video) files and MP3s, but that is beyond the scope of this chapter. (More on .flv and MP3 loading in Chapter 26, "Streaming Media.")

> **NOTE**
>
> In earlier versions of the Flash player, you could only load nonprogressive JPEG files, but not in the 8 player, they can be progressive download and still work. Just keep this in mind when working on projects with earlier player versions.

You can load .swf files and the three image files into three places:

- **Level Number.** You can load content directly into a level of the Flash player.

- **Movie Clip.** You can load content into any movie clip created manually, or with ActionScript including the _root.

- **Text Fields.** You$I~text fields;loading external content> can load not only images, but also SWF files directly into dynamic text fields.

We will go over each method of loading in external files, but first, let's look at the difference in file size whether we load a file externally or we have it on the stage all the time.

Look at Figures 19.1 and 19.2. There is no difference in image quality, but notice the file size difference. Figure 19.1 was brought into Flash manually, and then the Flash file was compiled at a file size of 165 kilobytes. Now look at Figure 19.2, which shows exactly the same image, but it is being loaded in from an external source. The file size there is 82 bytes, not even one kilobyte in file size.

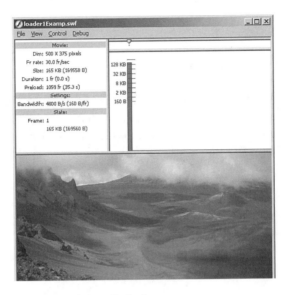

FIGURE 19.1   The image is within the Flash document.

FIGURE 19.2   The image has been loaded in dynamically.

Now, these figures have to be taken with a grain of salt. It is true that the file size of the Flash movie is decreased, but that does not mean that the image is smaller. In fact, the image size may be greater with an external file because Flash can compress JPEGs further.

So what does this mean if the file could have actually been smaller inside the Flash file rather than keeping it on the outside? Simple—the Flash file loaded the image when I told it to, and not before: content-on-demand.

And as far as large files from external sources taking a while to load, later in this chapter we cover preloaders for such an event.

Now you have seen it, but how do you do it?

> **NOTE**
>
> For all examples, you can use your own external files, but for everything to be exactly as it is in the book, you should download the files for this chapter from the website.

Loading Images Dynamically

We will start with images first because they are simpler to work with; they have no "moving parts" so to speak, as Flash files do.

Flash uses certain methods to load content in dynamically, and the first one to cover is the `loadMovie()` method.

The `loadMovie()` Method

The `loadMovie()` method is used to load external files directly into a `MovieClip` object. It can be called either by the ActionScript reader hitting it, or on an event such as a button being clicked.

This method has two layouts; the first is the independent function:

```
loadMovie(URL, movieClip, method);
```

The second is the movie clip method:

```
movieClip.loadMovie(URL, method);
```

Both usages do the exact same thing, and both have the same parameters basically, just arranged differently:

- URL—A string literal representing either a relative or absolute path to an external `.swf` or image file.

- movieClip—This is a reference to the movie clip that will receive the content.

- method—An optional parameter used for sending or receiving variables; it can take either GET or POST as its argument; GET will append variables to the end of the URL, and POST will send the variables in a separate header.

Now that you see the basic usage and parameters, let's do an example:

1. Create a new Flash document.

2. Save this document as `loadImage1.fla` in the same directory as the external images.

3. Name the layer in the main timeline **actions**.

4. Go to the first frame of the actions layer, open the Actions panel, and place this code within it:

```
//load the image
this.loadMovie("bridge.jpg");
```

All this code does is call the `loadMovie()` method.

Run this code, and your screen should look like Figure 19.3. That's it—that's all the code necessary for loading an image into Flash at runtime. You could even take out the comment if you wanted to, but that wouldn't be good coding practice.

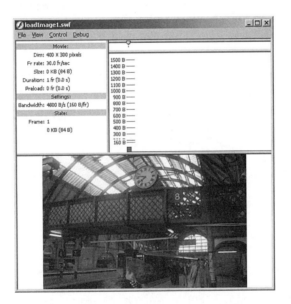

FIGURE 19.3   Loading external files is as easy as adding one line of code.

That was pretty simple. Now let's go back and add a button, and change the way we load the image in.

1. Continuing from the preceding example, close the test movie screen and go back to the main timeline.

2. Create a new layer and name it **button**.

3. Choose Window>Common Libraries>Buttons.

4. Choose your favorite button and drag it from the library to the bottom right of the stage in the button layer.

5. Give the button an instance name of **myButton_btn**.

6. Go back into the actions layer, and replace the code with this:

```
//create the event for the button
myButton_btn.onRelease = function(){
    //load the image
    loadMovie("bridge.jpg",_root);
}
```

This code creates an event for the myButton_btn button on the stage. When triggered, it will accomplish the same thing that the preceding code did—load an image into the _root timeline. Also notice that we used _root this time instead of this because we were calling code from inside a button event. If we had used this, it would have meant we were trying to load the image into the button instead of the _root timeline.

Test the movie; click the button and see what happens. The image still loads, but the button disappears. Welcome to the first limitation of loading external content into movie clips; it replaces everything in that movie clip, which is why the button was removed, because it was on the _root timeline.

Let's fix that by creating an empty movie clip with ActionScript as you learned in Chapter 13, "The Movie Clip Object."

1. Go back into the actions layer, and change the code to this:

```
//create the event for the button
myButton_btn.onRelease = function(){
    //create a movie on the main timeline
    _root.createEmptyMovieClip("target_mc",1);
    //load the image
    loadMovie("bridge.jpg",_root.target_mc);
}
```

This time, we created an empty movie clip on the _root timeline and loaded the image into that. We could have made the empty movie clip outside the button event, but in keeping with the content-on-demand mindset, it was better to create the movie clip when we needed it, and not before.

Test the movie, and as you can see in Figure 19.4, the image loads in when the button is clicked, and the button remains on the stage. As a matter of fact, you can continue to click the button, and it will refresh the image every time.

Now that we are loading content into movie clips other than the _root timeline, it is important to understand inheritance.

FIGURE 19.4   External files should be loaded into empty movie clips, or content within the movie clip being loaded into will be overwritten.

Inheritance

The idea of *inheritance* may be difficult to grasp at first, until you see an example. The idea is that any content loaded into a movie clip will inherit its parent's properties.

For instance, if you load an image into a movie clip that has an alpha of 50, the image in turn will also have an alpha of 50.

Let's take a look at an example of inheritance:

1. Create a new Flash document.

2. Save this document as inheritance1.fla in the same directory as the external images.

3. Go to the first frame of the main timeline, open the Actions panel, and place this code within it:

```
//create the empty movie clip
this.createEmptyMovieClip("holder_mc",1);
//set the position of the holder_mc movie clip
holder_mc._x=400;
holder_mc._y=300;
//rotate the holder_mc movie clip
holder_mc._rotation=180;
//load the image
holder_mc.loadMovie("bridge.jpg");
```

This code creates an empty movie clip on the _root timeline to load the image into. We set a few of its properties including the _rotation set to 180, which will flip the empty movie clip. Then we load the image into the empty movie clip just as before.

Now test the movie, and you will see that the image is completely upside down just like the one in Figure 19.5. This is very useful for aligning images or sizing them before they are even loaded.

FIGURE 19.5   Use inheritance to control external files before they are even loaded.

You are not limited to movie clip properties, however, as you will see in this next example. We will create a color object, change the tint of the empty movie clip, and then load the image into it.

1. Continuing from the preceding example, close the test movie screen and return to the actions on the main timeline.

2. Replace the code in the first frame with the following:

```
//create the empty movie clip
this.createEmptyMovieClip("holder_mc",1);
//create a color object
var myColor:Color = new Color(holder_mc);
//create a transform object
var blueObj:Object = new Object();
//set its blue property to the maximum
blueObj.bb=255;
//change the tint
myColor.setTransform(blueObj);
//load the image
holder_mc.loadMovie("bridge.jpg");
```

The preceding code creates an empty movie clip as it did before. Then it creates an instance of the `Color` object associated with the `holder_mc` movie clip. After that, another object is created that will be used in conjunction with the `Color` object. We set a special property, and then pass the `blueObj` to the `setTransform()` method of the `Color` object, changing the tint of the empty movie clip to a shade of blue. Finally, we load the image into the empty movie clip.

Test the movie again and you will see that the image is right side up again (because we removed the rotation code), but this time the image is a shade of blue.

So far we have loaded images directly into movie clips. Now we will see how to load them into levels of the Flash player directly using the `loadMovieNum()` method.

The `loadMovieNum()` Method

The `loadMovieNum()` method, like the `loadMovie()` method, loads external files into Flash, but unlike the `loadMovie()` method, the `loadMovieNum()` method loads the files into a specific level of the Flash player directly.

This is the generic layout of the `loadMovieNum()` method:

```
loadMovieNum(URL, level, method);
```

This action has three parameters:

- `URL`—A string literal representing either a relative or absolute path to an external `.swf` or image.

- `level`—A numerical value representing the level of the Flash player the content is to be loaded into.

- `method`—An optional parameter used for sending or receiving variables; it can take either `GET` or `POST` as its argument.

Although the `loadMovieNum()` method will not remove everything in a movie clip as the `loadMovie()` method does, it will remove anything on the level number it is being loaded into, so keep that in mind and know that **_level0** is the same as **_root**.

Now that you've seen the parameters and layout of this method, let's start using it.

1. Create a new Flash document.

2. Save this document as `loadMovieNum1.fla` in the same directory as the external images.

3. Go to the first frame of the actions layer, open the Actions panel, and place this code within it:

```
//create an empty movie clip for the background
this.createEmptyMovieClip("holder_mc", 1);
//load the background in
holder_mc.loadMovie("bridge.jpg");
```

19

```
//load the png into the Flash player
loadMovieNum("atSign.png",1);
```

The preceding code first creates an empty movie clip to be the background, then loads an image into it. Next the code loads content into the first level of the Flash player.

Test this code and you will see that both images have loaded into Flash. Also, notice two important things. First, that the second image did not affect the first at all. Second that the second image, because it was a PNG, kept its transparency, even being loaded in at runtime.

Now you know how to load images into Flash, but how do we get rid of them?

The unloadMovie() Method

The unloadMovie() method is designed to clean out movie clips containing any content (but in this case, content that has been loaded into it).

Like the loadMovie() method, the unloadMovie() method has two basic layouts, the first being the independent function:

```
unloadMovie(movieClip);
```

The other use is as a MovieClip method:

```
movieClip.unloadMovie();
```

Both of these actions perform the same thing and have the same basic parameter, movieClip. The movieClip parameter is the movie to be cleaned.

Here is an example of removing a loaded image from the Flash movie:

1. Create a new Flash document.

2. Save this document as unloadMovie1.fla in the same directory as the external images.

3. Name the layer in the main timeline **actions**.

4. Create a new layer and name it **button**.

5. Choose Window, Other Panels, Common Libraries, Buttons.

6. Choose your favorite button and drag it from the library to the bottom right of the stage in the button layer.

7. Give the button an instance name of **myButton_btn**.

8. Go into the first frame of the actions layer, and place this code within it:

```
//create an empty movie clip to house the image
this.createEmptyMovieClip("holder_mc", 1);
//load the image
```

```
holder_mc.loadMovie("bridge.jpg");
//use the button to remove the movie clip
myButton_btn.onRelease = function(){
    //clean the movie clip
    holder_mc.unloadMovie();
    //check to make sure the movie is still there
    trace(holder_mc);
}
```

The preceding code creates an empty movie clip to house the image being loaded into it. Then an event is created to remove the loaded content from that movie, and also to check to see if the movie is still there.

Run this code, and you will see that the image does load in, and when you click the button, the image disappears, and the Output panel shows a reference to the `holder_mc` movie clip that is still present.

There is another way to remove loaded content from movie clips: to remove both the clip and the content. Although it is a little more definite: the `removeMovieClip()` method will accomplish this.

The `removeMovieClip()` Method

The `removeMovieClip()` method can be used to remove loaded content from movie clips, but the difference between it and the `unloadMovie()` method is that the `removeMovieClip()` method will completely remove the movie clip it is referencing, not just the loaded content.

Like the `unloadMovie()` method, the `removeMovieClip()` method has two ways of being written. The first is the independent function:

```
removeMovieClip(movieClip);
```

And the second way is the `MovieClip` method:

```
movieClip.removeMovieClip();
```

Both ways of writing this action accomplish the same task: They both remove the movie clip completely from the Flash player.

We will continue the preceding example by merely changing the code to use the `removeMovieClip()` method.

1. Return to the first frame of the actions layer, and change the code to this:

```
//create an empty movie clip to house the image
this.createEmptyMovieClip("holder_mc", 1);
//load the image
holder_mc.loadMovie("bridge.jpg");
//use the button to remove the movie clip
```

```
myButton_btn.onRelease = function(){
    //remove the movie clip
    removeMovieClip(holder_mc);
    //check to make sure the movie is still there
    trace(holder_mc);
}
```

The only thing changed in the code was that the method unloadMovie() was replaced with removeMovieClip().

Test this movie, and again when the button is clicked, the image is removed. However, this time in the Output panel, there is no reference to the holder_mc movie clip because it was also removed.

Those two methods are used to remove loaded content from movie clips, but to remove content from level numbers you must use the unloadMovieNum() function.

The unloadMovieNum() Function

The unloadMovieNum() method works the same way as the unloadMovie() method except that it cleans levels, not movie clips.

Here is the layout of this method:

```
unloadMovieNum(level);
```

The only parameter this method has is the level parameter representing which level is to be cleaned.

Returning to the same example, we will replace the code to show how the unloadMovieNum() method works.

1. Return to the first frame of the actions layer, and change the code to this:

```
//load the image into level 1
loadMovieNum("bridge.jpg",1);
//use the button to remove the movie clip
myButton_btn.onRelease = function(){
    //clean level 1
    unloadMovieNum(1);
}
```

The preceding code loads the image into level 1 of the Flash player. Then it creates the event for the button so that when the button is clicked, it will clean out that level.

Test this movie, and just like before, the image loads in fine, and when the button is clicked, the image is removed.

After all that work and coding to load images into Flash, now is the perfect time to tell you that there is an easier way.

The `Loader` Component

This is one of the simplest components shipping with Flash 8. The `Loader` component is designed to make it easy for designers and developers to load images and SWF files into Flash dynamically.

It has three parameters:

- `autoLoad`—This is a Boolean value representing whether the component should automatically load the content or wait to be told.

- `contentPath`—The relative or absolute path to the image or SWF file you are loading in. You can also use URLs to load content.

- `scaleContent`—This parameter, if set to `true`, will scale the content being loaded into it to the Loader component's dimensions (which are set during authoring). If this parameter is set to `false`, the component simply acts as a point to load files to.

That's the basics of how these components work. Now let's see them in practice in this next example.

1. Create a new Flash document.

2. Save this document as `loaderComp1.fla` in the same directory as the external images.

3. Drag an instance of the `Loader` component onto the stage.

4. Give it an instance name of **loader**.

5. Set the parameters as follows:

    - `autoLoad`—`true`

    - `contentPath`—`bridge.jpg`

    - `scaleContent`—`true`

Now test the movie, and your screen should look like Figure 19.6. You can go back into the main timeline and change the size of the `Loader` component with the Free Transform tool (Q), retest the movie, and the image will reflect the changes made to the `Loader` component. Also, notice that after you test the movie (or if you click on the stage before you test the movie), the image you have set to it now appears there.

All we have done so far is load images into Flash. Next we begin to load other `.swf` files into Flash.

FIGURE 19.6   The Loader component makes it almost too easy to load dynamic images into Flash.

Loading SWF Files into Flash

The methods used to load images into Flash can also be used to load other Flash-created SWF files. In fact, this is more powerful than loading simple images into Flash because loading other Flash content can help teams of designers and developers to work together more easily. It can allow custom interfaces to be used based on individual tastes. It can even allow objects in the parent timeline to interact with objects in the loaded timeline.

There are a couple of things to consider when loading external Flash content into another Flash movie. First is the frame rate. When Flash content is completely loaded into a new Flash movie, it takes on the root timeline's frame rate whether it's faster or slower than its own, so timing of animations may be off if the two movies are on different frame rates in their individual form.

Another thing to consider is the _root. There can only be one _root to rule them all, so to speak. If code inside the loaded Flash file refers to its _root with absolute identifiers, errors will occur within the code that make it difficult to debug. You can of course use the _lockroot property to bypass this error, but not all previous versions of the Flash player support this property.

Because the methods used in loading images are the very same for loading Flash content, we can go right into examples.

The first one will load a digital clock that you can download from the website.

1. Create a new Flash document.

2. Save this document as loadingSWF1.fla in the same directory as the external files.

3. Go to the first frame of the main timeline, open the Actions panel, and place this code within it:

```
//load the clock in
this.loadMovie("clock.swf");
```

This code is similar to the code we originally used to load an image in except that it uses a different URL.

Test the movie, and on your screen you should see a small digital clock face similar to the one in Figure 19.7.

FIGURE 19.7 Use the loadMovie() method to load external Flash content into your files at runtime.

That was just a simple example of loading Flash content back into Flash. The next section will go over how to manipulate Flash content that has been loaded in.

Manipulating Loaded SWF Files

If you load in Flash content from external sources, you are going to want to know how to control the Flash elements and objects that have been brought in.

Working with loaded content is just as easy as working with content that is created on the stage manually. You simply reference the movie clip the content is residing in, and there you can control variables, manipulate objects, and work with anything in that file.

Here is an example that will load in an external SWF file with a text field in it. When we click a button, it will notify the text field.

1. Create a new Flash document.

2. Save this document as controlSWF1.fla in the same directory as the external files.

3. Name the layer in the main timeline **actions**.

4. Create a new layer and name it **button**.

5. Choose Window, Other Panels, Common Libraries, Buttons.

6. Choose your favorite button and drag it from the library to the bottom right of the stage in the button layer.

7. Give the button an instance name of **myButton_btn**.

19

8. Go into the first frame of the actions layer, and place this code within it:

```
//create an empty movie clip to house the SWF file
this.createEmptyMovieClip("holder_mc",1);
//load the SWF file in
holder_mc.loadMovie("textBox.swf");
//create the event for the button
myButton_btn.onRelease = function(){
     //send text to the text field
     holder_mc.myText_txt.text = "Clicked";
}
```

The preceding code first creates a movie clip for the SWF file to reside in. It then loads the content in. After that, it creates a callback function for the onRelease event of the myButton_btn button so that when the button is released, text will be placed into the text field.

Test the movie and you will see immediately that the SWF file has indeed been brought in because the text field is clearly visible. When you click on the button, the word "Clicked" appears in the text field as in Figure 19.8.

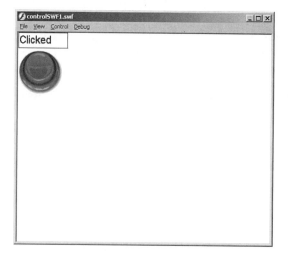

FIGURE 19.8   Accessing content on a loaded SWF file is as easy as if it were made in the host movie clip.

That example loaded a SWF file into an empty movie clip. We will continue the same example by changing the code to put the SWF file in a player level number. We will also change the text sent to the text field.

You access information on a player's level by using the _leveln identifier where n represents the level you are referring to.

1. Continuing from the preceding example, return the first frame of the actions layer, and replace its code with the following:

```
//load the SWF file in
loadMovieNum("textBox.swf",1);
//create the event for the button
myButton_btn.onRelease = function(){
    //send time elapsed to the text field
    _level1.myText_txt.text = getTimer();
}
```

The preceding code loads the SWF file into level 1 of the Flash player. It then creates the callback function, which we have already seen, but this time instead of sending a generic message to the text field, it sends the milliseconds that have elapsed since the movie started playing, using the getTimer() function.

Test the movie, and you will see that once again, the SWF file is loaded successfully, and every time the button is clicked, a number is seen in the text field representing the amount of milliseconds elapsed.

So far we have placed external content in movie clips and levels of the Flash player. Next we will begin to put them in text fields.

Loading External Content into Text Fields

Introduced in the Flash Player 7 is the ability to embed images as well as SWF files right into dynamic text fields. This is accomplished with the use of the <img> tag. And as you can see, because the files are brought in by means of an HTML tag, the text fields must be HTML-enabled.

The <img> tag has several attributes that can be changed and manipulated:

- src—This attribute is the path to the file to be brought in.

- id—The instance name of the movie clip being created by the Flash player to hold the embedded file; it is useful if you want to manipulate the movie clip with ActionScript.

- width—The width of the file being embedded, in pixels.

- height—The height of the file being embedded, in pixels.

- align—Controls the horizontal alignment of the embedded file; left or right are the allowable parameters, and the default is left.

- hspace—Specifies the horizontal space around the embedded file between the file and the text. The default value is 8.

- vspace—Specifies the vertical space around the embedded file between the file and the text. The default value is 8.

19

Those are all the attributes for the <img> tag, so let's go over an example of loading in an image:

1. Create a new Flash document.

2. Save this document as `imageInText1.fla` in the same directory as the external files.

3. Name the layer in the main timeline **actions**.

4. Create a new layer and name it **text**.

5. In the text layer, draw a dynamic text field about 400×400 in the middle of the stage.

6. Give the text field the instance name of **imageText_txt**.

7. Make sure that the Render Text as HTML property is turned on in the Properties Inspector, as well as the border, and that it is set for Multiline.

8. Go into the first frame of the actions layer, and place this code within it:

```
//set the html text to the text field
imageText_txt.htmlText =
➥"<img src='bigBen.jpg' width='200' height='200'>Big Ben!!!";
```

The preceding code simply sets the `htmlText` property of the text field to the text we want to display, plus the image tag that will embed the image.

Test the movie, and you will see a text field with an image and some text in it as shown in Figure 19.9.

FIGURE 19.9   Embedding images into text fields is a great way to liven up boring text.

To continue with this example, we are going to embed the clock SWF file under the image.

1. Return to the actions layer, and add this line of code to what is already there:

```
//add the clock SWF file
imageText_txt.htmlText += "<img src='clock.swf'
➥width='150' height='50' align='right'>What time is it?";
```

This line of code adds the `clock.swf` file to the text field, as well as some more text.

Test the movie again, and now you will see the clock in the text field as well as the image, as in Figure 19.10.

FIGURE 19.10   You can also embed external SWF files right into text fields.

Now we have embedded files into text fields. What if we want to manipulate them?

Manipulating Embedded Content in Text Fields

You can control embedded content in text fields using the *id* attribute within the `<img>` tag. You simply give the movie clip that is containing the embedded content an instance name, and then you can refer to it in ActionScript.

Follow these steps continuing from the preceding example:

1. Close the test screen and return to the main timeline.

2. Go into the first frame of the actions layer, and replace the code with this code:

```
//set the html text to the text field
imageText_txt.htmlText =
➥"<img src='textBox.swf' id='myContent'> _ text field";
//now create the function that will continually run
```

```
this.onEnterFrame = function(){
    //constantly send information to the text field
    imageText_txt.myContent.myText_txt.text = getTimer();
}
```

The preceding code uses the `<img>` tag to place a SWF file in the text field along with some text. Then we create a callback function that will fire continually, thereby sending the result of the `getTimer()` function to the text field constantly.

Test the movie and you will see the text field within the text field constantly being updated by the `getTimer()` method.

We have covered a lot of different ways you can bring content into Flash, but so far, all the examples we have used have brought content into Flash while Flash was running locally on our computer. This means that the transfer has been almost instant. In the real world, this would not be the case because SWFs and images take time to load, and that's where preloaders come in.

Preloaders

Preloaders are movie clips or blocks of code meant to show the user how much content has loaded, and how much there is left to load. It is important to keep the user engaged in something while the content loads in the background. This section will cover several methods of gathering the necessary information to build preloaders, starting with the basic `getBytesLoaded()` and `getBytesTotal()` methods.

The `getBytesTotal()` and `getBytesLoaded()` Methods

The `getBytesTotal()` method returns the total file size of the associated movie clip in bytes. The `getBytesLoaded()` method returns the size of the associated movie clip's file that has been loaded into the Flash player at the time of being called.

Here they both are in their respective forms:

```
MovieClip_mc.getBytesTotal();
MovieClip_mc.getBytesLoaded();
```

Both of these methods return numerical values.

They both seem simple enough, so let's jump right into an example.

In this example, we will place a large image in the timeline, and use the `getBytesLoaded()` and `getBytesTotal()` methods to determine the percentage of content loaded while we wait.

1. Create a new Flash document and name it **preload1.fla**.

2. In the main timeline, create a second keyframe.

3. In the second keyframe, place an image that is of considerable file size, 50 kilobytes or more.

4. Return to the first frame of the main timeline, open the Actions panel, and place these actions in it:

```
//stop right here
stop();
//this gets the total file size
var bT:Number = this.getBytesTotal();
//this event will continually check to see how much has loaded
this.onEnterFrame=function(){
   //create the variable to see how much has loaded
   var bL:Number = this.getBytesLoaded();
   if(bT != bL){
           //send the percentage loaded to the output panel
           trace("Percentage Loaded = "+Math.floor((bL/bT)*100)+"%");
   }else{
           //go to the second frame
           this.gotoAndStop(2);
           //destroy the event we no longer need
           delete this.onEnterFrame;
   }
}
```

The preceding code first stops the play head from moving forward, then gets the total file size of the main movie. After that, it creates a callback that will constantly check to see how much has loaded. It uses a conditional that determines whether the loaded amount is equal to the total amount. If not, it displays a message in the Output panel with the percentage loaded. If they are equal, the play head is moved to frame 2, and the onEnterFrame callback is destroyed because it is no longer necessary.

Test the movie, and you will see that it jumps right to the second frame, so go to View and choose Simulated Download to see the preloader working. We will have to do that each time we test our preloaders because that is the only way to simulate an Internet download.

That example worked well, but it only sent information to the Output panel. And the user will never see the Output panel because it is part of the authoring environment. You can, however, use ActionScript to create a preloader that a user will see.

Creating a Preloader with ActionScript
The idea of a preloader is to give the user something to look at or interact with, while the main chunk of content is being loaded in the background.

We will continue the preceding example by changing the code in the first frame to this:

```
//stop the play head
stop();
//create the movie clip to hold the preloader
this.createEmptyMovieClip("preLoader_mc",1);
```

```
//put the preloader in the right spot
preLoader_mc._x = 200;
preLoader_mc._y = 200;
//create some variables for the preloader
preLoader_mc.tBytes = this.getBytesTotal();
preLoader_mc.startX = 0;
preLoader_mc.startY = 0;
//create the text field to display the information
preLoader_mc.createTextField("loader_txt",10,0,-40,200,40);
//create a text format and set some properties
var loadFormat:TextFormat = new TextFormat();
loadFormat.font="_sans";
loadFormat.bold=true;
loadFormat.size=14;
preLoader_mc.loader_txt.setNewTextFormat(loadFormat);
//this callback will run the preloader
preLoader_mc.onEnterFrame = function(){
     this.clear();
     //create the lineStyle
     preLoader_mc.lineStyle(2,0x000000,100);
     //get the amount of loaded bytes
     lBytes = _root.getBytesLoaded();
     //create the percentage variable
     var percentLoaded:Number = Math.floor((lBytes/this.tBytes)*100);
     if(lBytes != this.tBytes){
          //insert the text into the text field
          this.loader_txt.text="Loaded "+lBytes+" of "
          +this.tBytes+"\nat "+percentLoaded+"%";
          //start the fill
          this.beginFill(0x397dce,60);
          //draw the loader
          this.moveTo(this.startX,this.startY);
          this.lineTo(this.startX,this.startY+25);
          this.lineTo(this.startX+(percentLoaded*2),this.startY+25);
          this.lineTo(this.startX+(percentLoaded*2),this.startY);
          this.lineTo(this.startX,this.startY);
          this.endFill();
     }else{
          //go to the second frame
          _root.gotoAndStop(2);
          //remove this preloader
          this.removeMovieClip();
     }
}
```

This code does a lot of things. First, it stops the play head like before. Then it creates an empty movie clip for the preloader to reside in. After that, it sets some of the positioning properties of the empty movie clip. Next, it sets some variables for the preloader, and then creates a text field within the empty movie clip. After that, a `TextFormat` is created to control the format of our text field. Then the event that will run the preloader for us is created. In the callback, we constantly check the amount loaded, convert it to a percentage, and use a conditional to detect whether the loaded bytes are equal to the total bytes. If not, we put text in the text field and create a rectangle to show the percentage loaded. If the loaded bytes do equal the total bytes, the movie goes to the second frame, and the `preLoader_mc` movie clip is removed.

Test the movie, and then choose View, Simulate Download. Then you should see a preloader similar to the one shown in Figure 19.11.

FIGURE 19.11   Use ActionScript to create visual preloaders.

That was one way to show a preloader, but we had to build it in ActionScript. There is an easier way to have a preloader using the `ProgressBar` component.

The `ProgressBar` **Component**

The `ProgressBar` component can be used in conjunction with the `Loader` component to create a preloader with a dynamic content loader without having to type a single line of ActionScript.

Follow these steps to load in a JPEG image and have it preload:

1. Create a new Flash document.

2. Save this document as `progressBar1.fla` in the same directory as the external files.

3. Drag an instance of the `Loader` component onto the stage and give it an instance name of **loader**.

4. Set its parameters to the following:

   - `autoLoad`—true

   - `contentPath`—bridge.jpg

   - `scaleContent`—true

5. Now drag an instance of the `ProgressBar` above the `Loader` component and set the parameters to the following:

   - `conversion`—1

   - `direction`—right

   - `label`—LOADING %3%%

   - `labelPlacement`—top

   - `mode`—event

   - `source`—loader

The source is the most important parameter; it refers to the `Loader` component we placed on the stage.

Test the movie, and you will see the image and loader on the stage. Choose View, Simulate Download to see the progress bar work as shown in Figure 19.12.

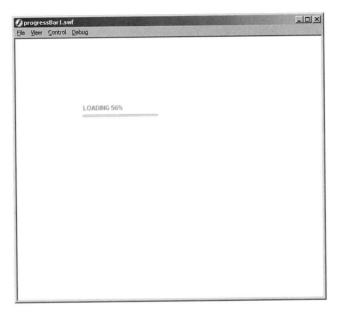

FIGURE 19.12   Use the `ProgressBar` component with the Loader component for a quick and easy dynamic content and preloader combo.

Summary

This chapter went over some of the benefits of using dynamic content including better user experience and smaller file size. We went over the different approaches to loading content, as well as the different file formats, which can be loaded into Flash dynamically.

Then we covered the need for preloaders and the different ways to make them.

We even covered the two components that make it easy to load in content as well as create a preloader without any ActionScript whatsoever.

In later chapters, we cover more on dynamic content including loading in data from external text files and from servers, as well as how to stream video.

CHAPTER **20**

Introduction to Data Integration

We have discussed dynamic content in Chapter 18, "External ActionScript," and Chapter 19, "Loading Visual Content," but this chapter is different. All we have brought into Flash externally are the ActionScript classes we have built, which can be brought in only during compiling of the .swf file. And we have brought in other .swf files as well as a few image formats, which can be brought in during runtime. But that does not do the concept of dynamic content justice.

In this chapter, we talk about the basics of bringing data into Flash and sending data out from Flash, as well as the format the data needs to be in to be successfully interpreted. Then we will go over a new way to communicate to JavaScript and have it communicate back.

Before we go through some of the fundamental ways Flash handles data transfer, it is important to fully understand the benefits of dynamic content.

Why Dynamic Content?

A quick definition of dynamic content could be this: to always have current information or to update regularly. For a better explanation of the importance of dynamic content, here are some of my own experiences with static and dynamic content.

When I first started building applications in Flash, way back in Flash 4, I used to create the interface, all the buttons, text fields, and movie clips right on the stage. All the content would also either be on the stage with the other elements or held in ActionScript waiting to be called.

As clients began to request changes (and they always do), I would have to go into the Flash document (because none of them would have Flash to be able to open the source file), find where the content was, and change it, hoping that I would not have to make another change, which of course I would.

After doing this several times, I decided to start keeping major content in external .txt files or in databases (which is discussed in later chapters). That way, whenever I needed to change content, all I would have to do is change a text file or a database entry. The clients could make changes to text files because they would need only a text editor, and then the application or website would reflect those changes. This way, if I had to make changes, I could do them quickly and would not have to upload the entire application again. Even better, the clients had much more control over their own site (which may or may not be a good thing).

So, as you can see, dynamic content is invaluable in building quality, content-driven sites or applications.

To get started with dynamic content, we will cover the getURL() method, the simplest way to send data out of the Flash environment.

The getURL() Method

Sending data out of Flash is one of the most exciting ways to show interaction. When any user can fill in a form, click a Submit button, and see a web page open with the results, the possibilities are endless. The getURL() method was the earliest means of accomplishing this goal.

Its general usage looks something like this:

```
getURL(URL,window,variables);
```

Let's go over what each part is for:

- URL—This is the path to the web page you would like to go to.
- window—This is an optional parameter specifying the window or frame to load the content; it has four specific keywords:
  - _self—The current frame in the current window the Flash file is residing in.
  - _blank—Creates a new window.
  - _parent—The parent frame of the current frame that the Flash file is residing in.
  - _top—The top-level frame in the window that the Flash file is residing in.
- variables—Optional parameter for sending variables to the URL with either the GET or POST method.

The getURL() method is most often used for links to other pages, but you can use it to send data to other web pages as well. Here is an example of using the getURL() method to accomplish this goal. Place this code in the actions of the first frame on the main timeline:

```
getURL("http://slashdot.org/search.pl?query=apple","_blank");
```

This example, when run, opens up a browser window, and the results from searching slashdot.org display. You can replace the last part, "apple", with something else, and when you rerun the file, it will open up a browser window with the new results.

In the preceding example, we can change what we are looking for in the code itself and then see the results each time the code is run. This is not interactive at all; in fact, the user cannot control what is being searched for. Therefore, the next example will take the preceding one a step further.

In this example, you are going to create an input text field for the user to type in search terms. You will also put a Submit button in the file so that the user can perform different searches.

1. Start a new Flash document.

2. Create a second layer, and name the top layer **actions** and the bottom layer **content**.

3. In the content layer, create an input text field with the border turned on, and give it an instance name of **search_txt**.

4. In the same layer, create a button (or use one from the common libraries by choosing Window, Common Libraries, Buttons). Give it an instance name of **search_btn** and align it to the right of the text field (as in Figure 20.1).

5. Now, in the first frame of the actions layer, open up the Actions panel and place these actions within it:

```
//the event for the button
search_btn.onRelease=function(){
      //call the search URL with the search term
      getURL("http://slashdot.org/search.pl?query="+search_txt.text,
➥      "_blank");
}
```

The actions are calling the getURL() method, and in the URL part we put the path to the search section of slashdot.org and then combined it with the search term that the user will place in the text field.

Test the example, and you will see that when you put a search term in the text field and click the Search button, a browser window opens with the results of the search, as shown in Figure 20.2.

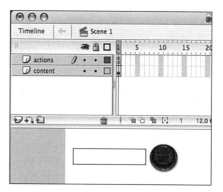

FIGURE 20.1   Place the Search button beside the search field.

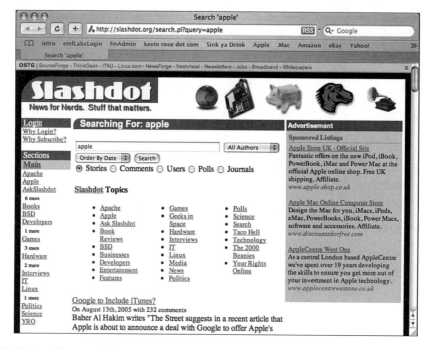

FIGURE 20.2   The results from the search on `slashdot.org`.

That was a good example of how to move data out of Flash with user interaction. The downside is that when you use the `getURL()` method, you are actually going outside of Flash with the results. In the following sections, you will learn how to get data into Flash using several built-in methods as well as the `LoadVars` object class.

Before you start loading data in, however, we need to go over what form the data needs to be in.

The MIME Format

Data being loaded into Flash by means of `loadVariables()`, `loadVariablesNum()`, or the `LoadVars` class must be in standard MIME format. It is in application `/x-www-form-urlencoded` format and is basically a bunch of name/value pairs.

Following is a basic example of a name/value pair in MIME format:

```
name=David
```

Unlike ActionScript, here we do not put the value of the variable `name` in quotes. Also, there is no space after the equal sign; this is because if there were a space, the value would include the space, making `"David"` become `" David"`.

The preceding example had only one name/value pair. To separate multiple name/value pairs, the ampersand (&) is used like this:

```
name=David&age=25
```

You can, of course, put ampersands on either side of the name/value pair just to make sure there are no errors, like this:

```
&name=David&age=25&
```

This way, you can clearly tell where each name/value pair begins and ends.

You can also create URL-encoded strings in Flash for special characters, such as the ampersand, using the `escape()` function.

The `escape()` and `unescape()` functions

Because an ampersand is used to separate individual name/value pairs in URL-encoded content, they cannot be within the content itself or Flash will read it as a separator, which can cause errors. Using the `escape()` function, you can encode the ampersand in a URL-encoded format, as in the following code:

```
//create the string
var myString:String = escape("title=War & Peace");
//send the encoded string to the output panel
trace(myString);
//output: title%3DWar%20%26%20Peace
```

As you can see, the string being created is URL-encoded and stored in a variable. Then the string is sent to the Output panel, where you can see that the ampersand and the spaces in the string have been replaced with special characters. To get the string back to normal, use the `unescape()` function, which will convert URL-encoded strings back to their original format like this:

```
//create the string
var myString:String = escape("title=War & Peace");
```

20

```
//send the encoded string to the output panel
trace(myString);
trace(unescape(myString));
//output: title%3DWar%20%26%20Peace
//         title=War & Peace
```

Now that you have seen the basic format that the data we are going to load needs to be in, let's make a file to hold the information that we will be using in several examples throughout this chapter.

1. Open a text editor such as Notepad or SciTe and put this code in it (you can replace my information with yours if you like):

```
&name=David&
&age=25&
&location=Richmond&
```

Notice that they are on separate lines. This is not necessary; it simply makes it easier to read. Each line begins and ends with an ampersand to make sure that none of the name/value pairs accidentally joins another.

2. Save this file as **sample.txt**.

Now that you have a file you can work with, let's go over some of the methods used to bring in data from external sources, starting with the loadVariables() method.

The loadVariables Method

The loadVariables() method was introduced back in Flash 4, and it has the capability to load data from external files (like the sample.txt file we are going to be using) as well as from middleware such as PHP and ColdFusion, which are discussed in later chapters. It loads the data directly into a movie clip object that must be specified when called. Its general layout looks like this:

```
loadVariables(URL,target,method);
```

Here is what each parameter means:

- URL—This is the string path to either the file holding the data or to the middleware that will send back the data. It can be either an absolute path or a relative path to the file. (The URL must reside on the same domain as the Flash file when on the web.)

- target—This is the name of the movie clip object that will receive the data.

- method—This is an optional parameter for use with middleware that tells how the data will be sent and received from the web server with either GET or POST.

Now that you see what it looks like, let's start using it.

In the next example, we are going to call the text file we have previously created from within Flash using the `loadVariables()` method. We will store the data in the _root timeline by using the keyword `this`.

1. Create a new Flash document.

2. Save this document as **sample-20-1.fla** in the same directory as the text file you have already created.

3. Open the Actions panel in the first frame of the main timeline and place these actions within it:

```
//get the data from the text file
loadVariables("sample.txt",this);
```

We call the text file we have already created that resides in the same directory as the Flash movie, and we place the variables on the main timeline using this. We are not interfacing with middleware, so the `method` parameter is left out.

Now test the movie. You'll see that it appears that nothing has happened, but on the contrary—while still in the test movie screen, select Debug, List Variables, and you will now see the variables that have been brought in displayed in the Output panel, as shown in Figure 20.3.

FIGURE 20.3   The Output panel lists the variables that are available in the movie.

Now that you can see that the variables are being brought in and parsed correctly, we are going to use them. But before we can use them, we have to know when they have loaded in completely. Even though they appear to have loaded in instantly, they did not, and on the web, it is even more important to know when the variables have completed loading because over some dial-up connections, it may take a while.

Fortunately, there is already an event built in to Flash to let us know when data has been fully received in a movie clip: the `onData` event.

The onData Event

The `onData` event is an event that is triggered whenever the associated movie clip receives data using the `loadVariables()` or the `loadVariablesNum()` method. When used in conjunction with the _root timeline, it will receive this event automatically.

We can set a function to this event the same way we have been setting functions to events:

```
movieClip.onData = function(){
    //do something
}
```

The movie clip can be any movie clip created either manually or with ActionScript including the _root timeline.

Now that you see what the event is supposed to do, let's put it into practice with this next example.

1. Start a new Flash document.

2. Save this document as **sample-20-2.fla** in the same directory where the sample.txt file is saved.

3. Name the layer **actions**, and in the first frame of that layer, place these actions:

```
//create the movie clip to hold the data
this.createEmptyMovieClip("holder_mc",1);
//get the data from the text file
loadVariables("sample.txt",holder_mc);
//when the movie receives the data
holder_mc.onData = function(){
    trace("my name is - "+this.name);
    trace("my age is - "+this.age);
    trace("my location is - "+this.location);
}
```

Notice that this time, we create a movie clip object in our code to be the data holder for the data coming in.

Now test the movie, and when the data is received, the Output panel should appear similar to Figure 20.4, with all of the information from the text file.

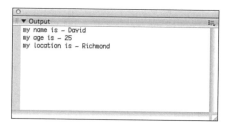

FIGURE 20.4   The onData event is triggered when the movie clip receives data.

That was awesome! We loaded some basic information into Flash and then had an event let us know when the data had been fully loaded.

But what if we want to have multiple pieces of data in a single name/value pair? You cannot use arrays in the text file; they are not supported to be loaded in that way. There is a workaround for this bottleneck.

Even though you cannot store data in arrays in a text file to be loaded in, you can separate data in a single name/value pair with unused characters, such as "~" or "$", and then separate them and store them in an array after they have been received by Flash.

In this example, you will need another text file named `sample2.txt` stored in the same directory as the other text file with this data in it:

```
&names=David~Ben~Doug~Paul~Lesley~Todd~Missy&
```

Notice that we used the tilde (~) character to separate each name in the single name/value pair.

Now that we have the text file we need, we can do another example. This example will have several stop points so that we can see the progression all the way until we fill a `ComboBox` component with the names.

1. Start a new Flash document.

2. Save this document as **sample-20-3.fla** in the same directory as the text file you just created.

3. Create another layer and name the top layer **actions** and the bottom layer **content**.

4. In the first frame of the actions layer, open the Actions panel and place these actions in it:

```
//create the movie clip to hold the data
this.createEmptyMovieClip("holder_mc",1);
//get the data from the text file
loadVariables("sample2.txt",holder_mc);
//when the movie receives the data
holder_mc.onData = function(){
      trace(this.names);
}
```

This code should look familiar; we created the movie clip to handle the data coming in. Then we called the text file with the data within it, and placed the data in the `holder_mc` movie clip. If you test the movie, when data is received, the variable that is brought in, names, is traced, showing all the names in the text file separated by tilde (~) characters.

Now that we know the data is coming in, we can go to the next step, which will separate the names variable and store the information in an array. Then we will trace the array. To do this, we will use the `split()` method.

1. Replace the function for the `onData` event with this one:

```
//when the movie receives the data
holder_mc.onData = function(){
```

```
//create an array to hold the data
var myNames_array:Array = new Array();
//put the data in the array
myNames_array = this.names.split("~");
trace(myNames_array);
```

```
}
```

Now if you test the movie, instead of the names being separated by tilde characters, they are separated by commas showing that they have indeed been placed into the array.

2. The next step is to select the content layer and drag a ComboBox component onto the stage. Give it an instance name of **myCombo_combo**.

3. Finally, replace the trace statement in the onData event with this line of code:

```
myCombo_combo.dataProvider = myNames_array;
```

The preceding line of code takes the array that was filled with the data we brought in and sets it as the dataProvider for the ComboBox component.

Now test the movie, and the end result should look like Figure 20.5, with all the names inside the ComboBox. Now you can really begin to see the benefits of dynamic data. All you have to do is add, change, or remove names from the text file sample2.txt, and the movie, when run, will display the new information without any more work needing to be done in Flash.

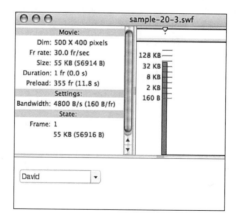

FIGURE 20.5   You can use dynamic content in conjunction with interface pieces quickly and easily.

There is another way to load content into a movie clip from an external source: the loadVariablesNum() method.

The `loadVariablesNum()` **Method**

The `loadVariablesNum()` method is similar to the `loadVariables()` method in that it loads external variables into Flash, but unlike the `loadVariables()` method, the `loadVariablesNum()` method loads the variables into a level instead of directly into a movie clip.

The basic layout of this method looks like this:

```
loadVariablesNum(URL, level, method);
```

Following are the parameters that `loadVariablesNum` will accept:

- URL—The path to either the text file being loaded or the middleware page being called.

- level—The level in the Flash player to receive the variables when they are loaded.

- method—This is an optional parameter used to define the method used when transferring data to and from middleware.

It also supports the `onData` event as a means of announcing when data has been fully loaded.

Here is an example using the `loadVariablesNum()` method:

1. Create a new Flash document.

2. Save this document as **sample-20-4.fla** in the same directory as the text files you have been working with.

3. In the first frame on the main timeline, open the Actions panel and place these actions in it:

```
//get the data from the text file
loadVariablesNum("sample.txt",0);
//when the movie receives the data
this.onData = function(){
    if(init){
        trace("my name is - "+this.name);
        trace("my age is - "+this.age);
        trace("my location is - "+this.location);
    }else{
        init=true;
    }
}
```

Notice that this time, we use a conditional statement to make sure that the event is not accidentally being triggered by the main timeline's initialization. Also notice that we are calling the original text file we created, not the one we used to put in an array.

Now test the movie, and you will see in the Output panel the same text that was in Figure 20.4.

But the two methods we have covered in regard to loading external data are not the end. There is even a built-in object specifically designed for interfacing with external data.

The LoadVars Object

The LoadVars object, introduced back in Flash MX, is an object whose sole purpose is to send and load data in and out of Flash. Because it is its own object with its own events, properties, and methods, you do not have to create a movie clip object to hold the data (which would take up more memory).

Creating a LoadVars object is the same as creating any other object. Create a variable, give it a name, and set it to a new LoadVars() object like this:

```
var myLoader_lv:LoadVars = new LoadVars();
```

There you have it; you have just created your first LoadVars object. Now let's see how to use them.

The LoadVars object has three basic methods for sending and loading data:

- load—This method loads content from either a text file or middleware.
- sendAndLoad—This method sends data out of Flash to middleware and returns the results created by the middleware back to Flash.
- send—This method posts variables to a specified URL and does not return anything.

The last two methods are beyond the scope of this chapter because they deal strictly with middleware, which are scripts that run on web servers designed to create dynamic content when requested. You will be exposed to them in later chapters.

The method that will be covered in this chapter in regard to the LoadVars object is the load() method.

The load() Method

The load() method for the LoadVars object is used to load content into Flash. The format for the content is the same as we have been using, the MIME format.

Here is the load() method's basic usage:

```
loadVars.load(URL);
```

There is only one parameter for this method:

- URL—A path to the text file or middleware to load variables from.

Now that you see what it looks like, let's use it.

1. Create a new Flash document.

2. Save this document as **sample-20-5.fla** in the same directory you have been working in.

3. Open up the Actions panel in the first frame of the main timeline and place these actions within it:

```
//create the LoadVars object
var myLoader_lv:LoadVars = new LoadVars();
//load the content
myLoader_lv.load("sample.txt");
```

Now test the movie and notice that, as before, nothing appears to have happened, but if you select Debug, List Variables, you will see that the variables have been loaded from the original text file you created, as before.

Because LoadVars is its own object, it has its own event for when the variables have completely loaded, the onLoad event.

The onLoad Event

The onLoad event is the only supported event for the LoadVars object. It is triggered when data has been loaded into the LoadVars object that the event is associated with, and the data has been parsed. It is called only when either the load() or the sendAndLoad() methods have finished running.

Its generic layout is

```
LoadVars.onLoad = function(success){
}
```

Notice that unlike the onData event we used earlier, the onLoad event has a parameter that can be passed through the function. This parameter, success, is a Boolean variable, and if the data is loaded correctly, it will be true. If there was an error, success will be false.

The success parameter can be useful, especially when dealing with middleware, which is a bit more complex than the examples we have done in this chapter. You can see its use in the next example, which builds on the preceding one.

After the code that has already been placed in the Actions panel, place this:

```
//the event for when the variables have loaded
myLoader_lv.onLoad = function(success:Boolean){
    if(success){
        trace("my name is - "+this.name);
        trace("my age is - "+this.age);
        trace("my location is - "+this.location);
```

20

```
    }else{
        //there has been an error
        trace("an error has occurred");
    }
}
```

Notice that we used the success parameter to detect whether everything loaded and parsed correctly.

To see an example of what would happen if success had been false, change the line of code that says

```
myLoader_lv.load("sample.txt");
```

to

```
myLoader_lv.load("doesntExist.txt");
```

Now when you test the example, instead of all the variables being displayed in the Output panel, the error message is displayed along with an error message from Flash, as you can see in Figure 20.6.

FIGURE 20.6   Because Flash could not find the file we were looking for, the error message we created is displayed.

The onLoad event is the only supported event for the LoadVars object. However, it is not the only event in general for the LoadVars object.

The Undocumented onData Event

There is an undocumented event for the LoadVars object that is triggered long before the onLoad event is ever triggered: the onData event. This event is called when data is first received by the LoadVars object. It then parses the data into individual properties of the LoadVars object and triggers the onLoad event. You can, however, use this event for your own use, and it can come in quite handy when debugging, especially when working with middleware.

Here is the basic layout of the onData event:

```
        loadVars.onData = function(src){
            //do something
        }
```

Notice in this event, we use a parameter called `src`. This parameter, when used inside the callback function, is all the variables being returned in their raw format, before they are parsed. That means that you will be able to see everything coming back from the text file (or middleware), including all the variable names, the values, equal signs, and ampersands.

Let's do an example using this event.

1. Start a new Flash document.

2. Save this document as **sample-20-6.fla**.

3. In the first frame of the main timeline, open the Actions panel and place these actions in it:

```
//create the LoadVars object
var myLoader_lv:LoadVars = new LoadVars();
//load the content
myLoader_lv.load("sample.txt");
//the event for when the LoadVars object first receives data
myLoader_lv.onData = function(src:String){
    trace(src);
}
```

Now test the movie. This time, instead of getting the usual trace message that you have seen before, you get the entire string of information coming from the text file, as you can see in Figure 20.7.

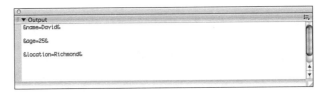

FIGURE 20.7   Using the `onData` event, you can see the entire string coming back to the LoadVars object.

But what if you want to use the `onLoad` event in conjunction with the `onData` event?

Take a look at this next example to see what happens:

1. Start a new Flash document.

2. Save this document as **sample-20-7.fla**.

3. In the first frame of the main timeline, open the Actions panel and place these actions in it:

```
//create the LoadVars object
var myLoader_lv:LoadVars = new LoadVars();
```

```
//load the content
myLoader_lv.load("sample.txt");
//the event for when the LoadVars object first receives data
myLoader_lv.onData = function(src:String){
     trace("onData");
}
//the event for when the variables have loaded
myLoader_lv.onLoad = function(success:Boolean){
     trace("onLoad");
}
```

Now test the movie and notice that only the onData is sent to the Output panel when the onData event is triggered, but the onLoad was not sent to the Output panel because the onLoad event was never triggered. This is because the onData event by default will trigger the onLoad event; however, because we have overwritten the onData event, the onLoad event is never triggered. Like everything else, you can work around this, too.

To trigger the onLoad event from the onData event, two things have to occur. First, the string of information coming to the LoadVars object must be decoded using another undocumented feature of the LoadVars object, the decode() method. The decode() method will take the raw name/value pairs passed to it and change them into properties and values for the LoadVars object receiving the data. It looks like this:

```
loadVars.decode(src);
```

The second thing that needs to be done is the actual triggering of the onLoad event by passing a true Boolean value to it like this:

```
loadVars.onLoad(true); and
```

Now that you've seen the two actions that need to be called within the onData event before the onLoad event can be called, let's take a look at that example again.

1. Start a new Flash document.

2. Save this document as **sample-20-8.fla**.

3. In the first frame of the main timeline, open the Actions panel and place these actions in it:

```
//create the LoadVars object
var myLoader_lv:LoadVars = new LoadVars();
//load the content
myLoader_lv.load("sample.txt");
//the event for when the LoadVars object first receives data
myLoader_lv.onData = function(src:String){
     trace("onData");
     //the two actions that need to be called
     this.decode(src);
```

```
        this.onLoad(true);
    }
    //the event for when the variables have loaded
    myLoader_lv.onLoad = function(success:Boolean){
        trace("onLoad");
    }
```

Now test the movie again, and notice that both `trace` functions are executed and both messages are sent to the Output panel.

Now that you know how the undocumented `onData` event works, you should have no problems debugging your applications when you run into data integration issues.

We have gone over a lot of ways to move data into and out of Flash, and they will be revisited in the next few chapters in conjunction with some server-side scripting. But before we move on to that, let's go over a new feature in Flash 8 that makes integration with JavaScript a breeze.

The ExternalInterface API

One thing that has perplexed Flash developers for years is the lack of a consistent way to communicate between Flash and JavaScript. Calling JavaScript functions from Flash hasn't really been a problem since the `getURL` method because that method can call JavaScript directly, but getting JavaScript to communicate back to Flash has been nearly impossible on a consistent basis across many browsers. Until now.

Here is an example of calling a JavaScript function from Flash with `getURL`:

```
getURL("javascript:alert('hello world!');");
```

The ExternalInterface API is designed for seamless communication calls to JavaScript functions and the capability for JavaScript to be able to call functions that are sitting on the Flash timeline.

Before we jump right in and start using it, we need to make the necessary methods available on the timeline by importing the class like this:

```
import flash.external.*;
```

Now we can work with the first method that will enable us to call JavaScript functions.

The Call Method

The `call` method is a static method of the ExternalInterface object, which means we do not need an instance of the object to call it; we can call it directly on the object class, like this:

```
ExternalInterface.call(functionName:String,Parameters);
```

20

This method has two parameters:

- **functionName**—The name of the JavaScript function you want to call as a string.

- **Parameters**—The parameters you want to pass to the JavaScript function separated by commas. This is an optional parameter.

That's the basic layout, so now let's build an example.

1. Create a new Flash document called **external1.fla.**

2. Create a second layer and call the top layer **actions** and the bottom layer **content**.

3. In the content layer, create a text field and set its type to input, turn on the border so you can see it, give it an instance name of **alert_txt** and put it in the top left of the stage.

4. Still in the content layer, drag a Button component onto the stage and place it to the right of the text field. Set its label to "Alert" and give it an instance name of **alert_butn**.

5. Back in the Actions layer, place this code in the first frame:

```
import flash.external.ExternalInterface;

//call an alert
alert_butn.clickHandler = function() {
    ExternalInterface.call("alert", alert_txt.text);
}
```

The preceding code first imports the ExternalInterface package. Then you set the event for the Button component that, when clicked, calls the JavaScript function alert and passes it the text from the text field all through the ExternalInterface.

Now publish the movie and the HTML and place them on a server. When you test the file on the server, you will see that when you click the button, whatever is in the text field will appear in the alert. But, if you test locally, you will notice that when you click the button, nothing happens. This is a security feature of the Flash player, but there is a workaround.

To be able to run this file locally, you have to open the HTML in a text editor and change the allowScriptAccess parameter from "sameDomain" to "always" in both the object parameter and the embed attribute. After this is done, the file will work locally and the alert message will appear. The final version is available from the website, and it already has this change in place.

That example was a one-way example. You could have done that with the getURL method. The next example, however, will go beyond that and not only send information to JavaScript, but it will also receive data back using the addCallback method.

The addCallback Method

The addCallback method allows JavaScript to call functions sitting on the timeline in Flash. The basic layout is like this:

```
ExternalInterface.addCallback(functionID:String,
➥instance:Object, functionName:Function);
```

As with the call method, this method is a static method and it has these three parameters:

- **functionID**—A string that is the name of the function JavaScript calls that will in turn call the function on your timeline. It does not have to be the same name as the function on the timeline, but it's easier to keep track of them that way.

- **instance**—This represents what "this" will refer to inside the function being called. It does not have to be the same object that the function itself resides in.

- **functionName**—This is the actual function on the Flash timeline that is being called.

That is the basic layout of the addCallback method. Now let's move on to the example. In this example, we will have Flash call a JavaScript prompt to appear that will ask the user to choose a color. After the color is filled in and the user clicks OK, an object back in Flash will change to that color. Follow these steps to see it in action:

1. Create a new Flash document called **external2.fla**.

2. Create a second layer and call the top layer **actions** and the bottom layer **content**.

3. In the content layer, drag a Button component into the top-left corner of the stage and give it a label of **Change** and an instance name of **change_butn**.

4. Still in the content layer, draw a black (0x000000) square directly under the Button about 100×100 in size.

5. Convert the square to a movie clip with the symbol name **recMC** and back on the stage, give it an instance name of **rec_mc**.

6. In the frame of the actions layer, put this code in:

```
import flash.external.ExternalInterface;

//will change the square's color
function onChange(clr:Number) {
    var temp_color:Color = new Color(rec_mc);
    temp_color.setRGB(clr);
}

//allow JS to call onChange
ExternalInterface.addCallback("onChange", this, onChange);
```

20

```
//opents the prompt
change_butn.clickHandler = function() {
    ExternalInterface.call("callPrompt",
➥ "What color would you like it to be? (ex: 0xff0000)");
}
```

The preceding code first imports the `ExternalInterface` package. Then we create the function that will change the color of the square on the stage using the `Color` object. After that, we call the `addCallback` method to make the `onChange` function available to JavaScript. Finally, we create the event for the Button to call the JavaScript prompt.

You need to publish both the SWF and the HTML at this point; then open the HTML file in a text editor. With just calling JavaScript, nothing has to be done to the HTML unless you want to run it locally, but with JavaScript calling functions in Flash, a little more work is required:

Beneath the `title` tag, place the following JavaScript code:

```
<script language=JavaScript>
    var me; //represents the swf id

    //get the correct reference
    function getID(swfID) {
        if (navigator.appName.indexOf("Microsoft") > -1) {
            me = window[swfID];
        } else {
            me = document[swfID];
        }
    }
    //this will call the onChange event back in Flash
    function makeCall(str){
        me.onChange(str);
    }
    //this is the function being called from Flash
    function callPrompt(str){
        makeCall(prompt(str));
    }
</script>
```

First, we create the variable me to hold the reference to the SWF file; without it, we could not make calls to Flash functions. Then the function that will set the reference is created with a conditional that can tell the difference between Microsoft's Internet Explorer and other browsers, because the reference will need to be different for that browser. After that, the function `makeCall` is created, and this is where the Flash function is called. Finally, we create the function that is being called from Flash, which will call the `makeCall` function to send information back to Flash, but not before it receives the data back from the prompt.

In the body tag, add the attribute `onload` and set it equal to the `getID` function like this:

```
<body bgcolor="#ffffff" onload="getID('external2');">
```

Notice that when we set the function to the `onload` event, we pass it the id of the SWF, which can be found where the SWF is embedded. So now, when the page initially loads, the `getID` function will be called, and the `me` variable will set so JavaScript can call the Flash function.

Put the files up on the server to test, or again, change the `allowScriptAccess` parameter and attribute to test locally. When it is run, you should see something similar to Figure 20.8. And when you set the color and click OK (or press the Enter key), the square should change to that color.

> **NOTE**
>
> If the user presses the Cancel button instead of the OK button, `null` would be passed back to JavaScript and consequently to Flash as well, which would make the square black again.

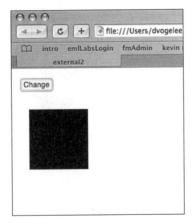

FIGURE 20.8 Communication back and forth between Flash and JavaScript is now a breeze with the ExternalInterface API.

Summary

This chapter was dedicated to showing not only the ways in which you can begin to interact with data, but also the reasons why a developer or designer might want to interact with data, and the benefits of doing so.

We started out with the `getURL()` method, the quickest and easiest way to have user interaction with Flash and data. Then we moved on to some of the fundamental ways to bring in data, and what form that data needs to be in. Next we went over the object that is designed to handle data integration and all of its documented and undocumented events.

20

Finally we finished up the new `ExternalInterface` API to show how easy it is to communicate back and forth to JavaScript.

The next chapter continues with the `LoadVars` object as we move into dealing with different types of middleware languages, starting with ASP.

CHAPTER 21

ASP and Flash

In the previous chapter, we went over how to move dynamic data into Flash. Although we moved the data outside of Flash so that all we have to do is update a simple text file, that text file is now technically static data. For instance, if we have a group of contacts in a text file and wanted to search through them to find a specific contact, we would have to bring in the entire text file and then search it in Flash with ActionScript. This is where middleware comes in.

Middleware is basically logic that takes place on the server between the client-side interface and the data held on the server. Basically, the client sends a request to the middleware. Then the middleware accesses the data, runs any logic functions on it that you require (such as searches or algorithms for math), and sends the data back to the client, as shown in Figure 21.1.

This chapter discusses a specific middleware called ASP to help create truly dynamic content. Although there is now ASP.NET, many people still use classic ASP on their servers. We will also be using an Access database at the end of the chapter to hold some of our data for ASP to work with.

What Is ASP?

ASP, or Active Server Page, is a server-side language developed by Microsoft. However, it really is not a language at all, but more of a "language holder." Because you can use several languages inside of ASP, almost anyone with scripting experience can pick up ASP in a short time. This chapter will be using VBScript as the language of choice, but following is a list of the languages that are available:

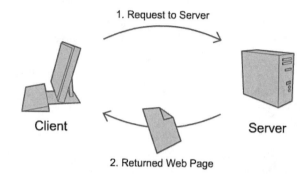

FIGURE 21.1   How middleware works between the client and the data.

- **VBScript**—Based on Visual Basic. This is the language most used in ASP.

- **Jscript**—Based on JavaScript. This is the second most popular choice of language for ASP.

- **Python**—A popular development language.

- **PerlScript**—Based on Perl.

How Does ASP Work?

Pages built with ASP (or any other server-side language) use special tags to tell the server to run some code before sending information back. Code in ASP will fall between <% and %>, like this:

```
<%

ASP code to run here

%>
```

Therefore, if you access the page through a browser, before the page is sent back to the client, whatever is between those two tags must be run first. If those tags were not there, the ASP code would render as if it were plain text.

Before we jump into working with ASP, you must have the server.

Getting the Server

ASP will run on a Windows web server. If you have a web host, check with them to see if you are already on that kind of server and can run ASP. If not, you can run a local version on your PC:

- **Windows XP or Windows 2000**—You will need to install the most up-to-date IIS (Internet Information Services) on your computer. The operating system comes with it, and you can access it by going to Settings, Control Panel, Add/Remove Programs, Add/Remove Windows Components.

- **Windows 98**—You will need to install a PWS (Personal Web Server), which comes with the NT 4 option pack. If you do not have this already, you can get it from http://www.microsoft.com/ntserver/nts/downloads/default.asp.

After you have your server, you can use this script to test it. Simply put the file on your server and call it **aspTest.asp**.

```
<%@Language=VBScript%>
<%Option Explicit%>
 <%
    Response.Write("Your server is running as of " & Now())
 %>
```

Then access the page through a web browser and it should display something similar to the following message:

```
Your server is running as of 2/14/2005 5:15:42 PM.
```

Now that the server is up and running, let's get into some code.

Intro to ASP Scripting

As mentioned earlier, we will be using VBScript in all our examples. With that in mind, the first thing we will be putting in our ASP pages is the Language declaration tag. This tag tells the server, and anyone else who opens the script in a text editor, that we are using VBScript in the page. This is not a necessity in the page, but it is good practice to have it. It looks like this:

```
<%@Language=VBScript%>
```

Notice the @Language at the beginning of the tag, right after the opening server-side language tag. This is a specific property of the ASP page for declaring the coding language.

The next tag that will also be in every one of our ASP pages is the Option Explicit tag. This tag will state that all variables must be declared in the ASP page before they can be instantiated. This tag looks like this:

```
<%Option Explicit%>
```

When the preceding tag is present, variables must be declared with a Dim statement, like this:

```
Dim myVar1, myVar2
```

Again, this tag is not necessary in your ASP pages, but it is good practice to have it.

Because ASP is a server-side language, it will not simply display the information (or send the information back to Flash, which is our ultimate goal). For this reason, we will be using the Write method of the Response object, like this:

```
Response.Write("text here")
```

Your First ASP Page

The following example is the "Hello World" example. We will be sending a simple string to display in Flash. The first step is to create the ASP page, so here is the code:

```
<%@Language=VBScript%>
<%Option Explicit%>
<%
  Response.Write("Hello World!!")
%>
```

If you were to test this script right now in a browser, it would display the text as it is, but from the previous chapter you learned that Flash will need this data in name/value pair format. So change the Response.Write line to the following:

```
Response.Write("message=Hello World!!")
```

Save the script as **helloWorld.asp** and put it on the server. Next up is the Flash part, so open Flash and follow these steps:

1. Create a new Flash document and save it as **helloWorld.fla**.

2. In the Actions panel of the first frame, place this code:

```
//create the text field
this.createTextField("display_txt",1,0,0,100,20);
//the LoadVars object for loading the data
var hello_lv:LoadVars = new LoadVars();
//when the LoadVars object receives the data
hello_lv.onLoad = function(success){
    if(success){
        display_txt.text = this.message;
    }else{
        trace("An error has occurred.");
    }
}
//load the asp
hello_lv.load("http://MYSERVER/helloWorld.asp");
```

The first thing that happens in the preceding code is that a text field is created to display the message being returned. Next up is the LoadVars object, which will connect to the

ASP page to get the message. After that, we set up the onLoad event callback for when the data is received. In it, we pass the parameter success to make sure there were no problems connecting to the ASP page. If success is true, the message is displayed in the text field we created; if not, an error is sent to the Output panel. Finally, we call the load method to get the data by passing it the full path to ASP page. If you were to put this on a server, you would not need the full path to the script, just a relative path.

Test the movie, and you should see a result similar to Figure 21.2.

> **NOTE**
>
> Wherever you see MYSERVER in the script, it is referring to the path to your server where the ASP pages reside.

FIGURE 21.2   The results of your first integration between Flash and ASP.

That was a good example of connecting to an ASP page on a server and getting data back to Flash, but it is still not truly dynamic because we hard-coded the string to be sent back. The next example uses the built-in Now function in ASP to send back the date and time on the server.

> **NOTE**
>
> When something is referred to as *hard-coded*, it means that the particular piece of code being referred to cannot be changed by outside forces, such as interaction with users or database information. It will stay exactly as the programmer coded it.

For this example, you need a new ASP page, so here is the code:

```
<%@Language=VBScript%>
<%Option Explicit%>
<%
  Response.Write("stamp=" & Now())
%>
```

Similar to the previous example, this example sends back a single name/value pair to Flash. This time, however, it uses the Now function to get the current time and date on the server. Also notice that an ampersand (&) is used to combine strings in VBScript. Save this script as **getDateStamp.asp** and put it on your server. If you like, you can test the page to see what is being returned by simply mapping to it with a browser.

Now for the Flash part:

1. Create a new Flash document called **getServerDate.fla**.

2. Select the first frame, open the Actions panel, and then place these actions in it:

```
//create the text field
this.createTextField("display_txt", 1, 0,0,200,40);
//set a few properties of text field
display_txt.html = true;
display_txt.multiline = true;
//the LoadVars object for getting the data
var stamp_lv:LoadVars = new LoadVars();
//for when the LoadVars object receives data
stamp_lv.onLoad = function(success){
    if(success){
        display_txt.htmlText = "The time on the server is:<br>";
        display_txt.htmlText += "<b>" + this.stamp + "</b>";
    }else{
        trace("There was an error connecting, try again.");
    }
}
//get the data
stamp_lv.load("http://MYSERVER/getDateStamp.asp");
```

This code is very similar to the previous example, except we mixed it up a bit by setting the html property to true and the multiline property to true so it will display a little differently. Test it out and it should appear like Figure 21.3 but with a different date and time.

FIGURE 21.3   The first example of using ASP and Flash to create truly dynamic content.

It was not a lot of data, but it was dynamic, and you can tell because every time you test the Flash file, it will display different information.

Sending and Receiving Data

The most dynamic content you can have comes from interaction with the user. When users interact with your project, either through search engines, forum boards, or even comments found in most blogs, they are not just receiving content—they are requesting content, and in some cases, even adding content. Some of the most popular sites rely on "content-on-demand" principles to keep users coming back. They do not just give information; they ask the user what they want to see and provide it.

So far we have only loaded content from our ASP pages, but in this section, you'll learn how to make it truly dynamic by sending data to the ASP page and then receiving data back.

The first step in this process is setting up the ASP page to receive data from the user.

Receiving Data in ASP

To receive data in ASP, we will use the Request object like this:

```
Dim myVar
myVar = Request("whatWasSent")
```

The preceding code sets the variable `myVar` equal to the value of `whatWasSent`.

We will also be using the `Trim` function to get rid of any unnecessary spaces. This function works like this:

```
Dim myVar
myVar = Trim(Request("whatWasSent"))
```

The preceding code produces the exact same result, except that all extra spaces are removed. This is very important when working with data coming from the client side, especially when searching for items in a database. An extra space can be the difference between getting all the search results and getting none.

That was the basics; now let's look at a working example. This next example will create a small ASP page that will receive a number, square it, and send it back to the user.

This is the code for the ASP page:

```
<%@Language=VBScript%>
<%Option Explicit%>
<%
  Dim inNum, answer
  inNum = Trim(Request("sentNum"))
  '''CREATE THE ANSWER
  answer = inNum*inNum

  Response.Write("answer=" & answer)
%>
```

This script will take a number sent to it through the Request object, multiply it by itself, and then send it back out as a name/value pair. Save this file as `squareNum.asp` and post it to your server.

If you want to test this page right now, you can, by passing the `sentNum` through the URL:

```
http://MYSERVER/squareNum.asp?sentNum=10
```

You should see something like this in your browser:

```
answer=100
```

And you can change the number in the URL to see more results.

> **TIP**
>
> You can always test your ASP pages by passing information through the URL in the browser. The first variable after the path to the page must follow a question mark (?) like the preceding example, but the rest of the name/value pairs must be separated by ampersands (&) like this:
>
> ```
> http://MYSERVER/example.asp?var1=sample&var2=anotherSample
> ```

That will do it for the ASP part of this example; next up is the Flash part.

Sending and Receiving in Flash

When sending and then receiving information in Flash, the LoadVars object will still be used. However, there are a couple new things we need to go over. The first is how to set the data being sent out.

Setting data for an instance of the LoadVars object to send out is like setting a property. Here is an example setting two variables to be sent out:

```
var test_lv:LoadVars = new LoadVars();
test_lv.sentName = "David";   //Sending a string
test_lv.sentAge = 25;      //Sending an integer
```

In the preceding code, two variables are ready to be sent to an awaiting ASP page.

> **TIP**
>
> As a personal practice, I usually name variables that are being sent out to middleware pages starting with "sent." This way, I don't get them confused with the data being returned that may have a similar name.

That was setting up the data to be sent out; now we need to actually send it using the sendAndLoad method of the LoadVars object. It looks something like this:

```
test_lv.sendAndLoad(URL, returnToObj, method);
```

The preceding line of code has the following parameters:

- **URL**—The path where your server-side script is. It can be absolute or relative.

- **returnToObj**—The LoadVars object where the return data is being returned to. Most often, this will be the same object calling the sendAndLoad method.

- **method**—Either the GET or POST method for sending information through HTTP.

Those were the two new features of the LoadVars object we are using. Now let's get back to the example:

1. Create a new Flash document and save it as **squareNum.fla**.

2. Create a new layer in the timeline (so you have two in total) and call the top layer **actions** and the bottom layer **content**.

3. In the first frame of the Actions layer, place this code in the Actions panel:

```
//The object for communicating with the ASP page
var sNum_lv:LoadVars = new LoadVars();
//When the object receives data back from the ASP page
sNum_lv.onLoad = function(success){
  if(success){
   trace(this.answer);
  }else{
   trace("There was an error connecting");
  }
}
//set the number we are sending
sNum_lv.sentNum = 15;
//send and receive the data
sNum_lv.sendAndLoad("http://MYSERVER/squareNum.asp", sNum_lv, "POST");
```

Most of the preceding code is not new, as we have used it throughout this chapter. First, the LoadVars object is instantiated. Then the callback event onLoad is created for when data is received. After that is what may appear new, we set the variable we are sending to our ASP script to 15 and finally call the sendAndLoad method. Test your movie at this point by choosing Control, Test Movie.

Close down the test screen after you see how the data is being sent from Flash, and then the answer is received back.

Next up is the interface so we can change the data being sent (and consequently, the answer being returned) as often as we like without having to alter the code.

1. Back on the timeline, in the Content layer, draw two text fields, one on top of the other (with some spacing so we can place a button between them), both about 40×20 in size. Here are the properties for the top field:

   - **Type**—Input
   - **Show Border Around Text**—True
   - **Font Size**—14
   - **Instance Name**—num_txt

   The rest you can leave at default settings. Next are the properties of the bottom field:

   - **Type**—Dynamic
   - **Show Border Around Text**—True

- **Font Size**—14

- **Instance Name**—answer_txt

You can use static fields to label each of the fields as "Number" and "Answer" if you like.

2. Now you will need a button to trigger the call to the ASP page. You can make your own or use one from Window, Common Libraries, Buttons. Just place it between the two fields and give it an instance name of **square_btn**. Your screen should now look like Figure 21.4.

Now that we have the fields and the button on the stage, we need to change the ActionScript a little bit to be able to grab the info from the first field and place the answer in the second field.

1. The first thing to change is what happens to the answer when it returns. Right now it is being sent to the Output panel through the *trace* function. Remove that line and put this line in its place:

```
answer_txt.text = this.answer;
```

Now the answer will appear in the bottom text field when it is returned.

2. Now we want to send the information to the ASP page when we release the button we put on the stage, so remove the last two lines of code (plus their comments) and put this in its place:

```
square_btn.onRelease = function(){
  //set the number we are sending
  sNum_lv.sentNum = num_txt.text;
  //send and receive the data
  sNum_lv.sendAndLoad("http://MYSERVER/squareNum.asp", sNum_lv, "POST");
}
```

The only difference between this code and the code we just cut (besides this code now residing in the onRelease event of the button) is that instead of hard-coding the number we are sending, we grab it from the top text field. Now you can test the movie again, place a number in the top field, click the button, and see the result. And now you do not have to change the ActionScript to see a different result; just change the top field and click the button again.

Could this have been done in Flash? Yes, but it is a good example of sending information to the server and letting the server do the work and send you the answer back. As you work more and more with the server, you will see that when it comes to mathematical functions, servers are much faster than Flash is, especially with very complicated algorithms. It's another reason why server-side scripting and Flash work so well together.

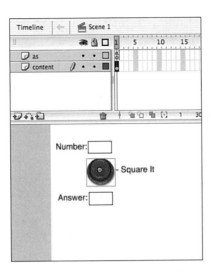

FIGURE 21.4   The stage is now set to work with the ASP page.

Accessing Access

We have gone over how to load data in from ASP pages as well as how to send data to them with results being returned. This section is going to build on what we have covered so far and add database integration into the mix by means of an Access database.

Integrating Flash projects with databases is a great way to separate content from design. Because the content is stored in a very raw form of pure data, it can be placed into more than one setting. This is how many sites offer different versions of their site, because all they have to do is build the different front-ends and then connect to the data source through ASP or another middleware language.

But before we start integrating with a database, we need to have one. We will use Microsoft's Access database format (.mdb). If you have Microsoft Office, you should have a copy of Access, but if you don't, it's not a big deal; you can grab the database from the book's website and upload it to your web server. The database itself holds close to 20 DVDs in a table called "dvds," as you can see in Figure 21.5. If you want to set up the database yourself, the table has the following fields:

- **id**—This field is an AutoNumber type field, which means that as you add data to the database, this field will automatically be filled for you with an incrementing number. This field is also the unique key for our database, so the values will never duplicate.

- **title**—This is the title of the movie.

- **director**—This is the director of the movie.

- **rating**—This is the "5-star" rating it received from Amazon.com at the time it was added to the database. It will be a number from 0 to 5.

- **rated**—This is the MPAA rating the movie was given.
- **type**—This is the type of a movie it is (Drama, Comedy, Action).

id	title	director	rating	rated	type
1	A Beautiful Mind	Ron Howard	4.13	PG-13	Drama
2	Antitrust	Peter Howitt (II)	3.71	PG-13	Suspense
3	Caddyshack	Harold Ramis	4.23	R	Comedy
4	Catch Me If You Can	Steven Spielber	4.1	PG-13	Drama
5	Clerks	KevinSmith	4.38	R	Comedy
6	Fletch	Michael Ritchie	4.66	PG	Comedy
7	Good Will Hunting	Gus Van Sant	4.09	R	Drama
8	Hackers	Iain Softley	4.11	PG-13	Action
9	Harry Potter and The Chamber of Secrets	Chris Columbus	4.28	PG	Family
10	High Fidelity	Stephen Frears	3.91	R	Comedy
11	Mallrats	Kevin Smith	4.41	R	Comedy
12	Sneakers	Phil Alden Robi	4.4	PG-13	Suspense
13	The Animatrix	Takeshi Koike	3.94	PG-13	Anime
14	The Net	Irwin Winkler	4.15	PG-13	Action
15	The Odyssey	Andrei Konchal	3.75	PG-13	Action
16	The Sting	George Roy Hill	3.59	PG	Comedy
17	The Burbs	Joe Dante	4.4	PG	Comedy
18	Witness for the Prosecution	Billy Wilder	4.8	NR	Suspense
(AutoNumber)					

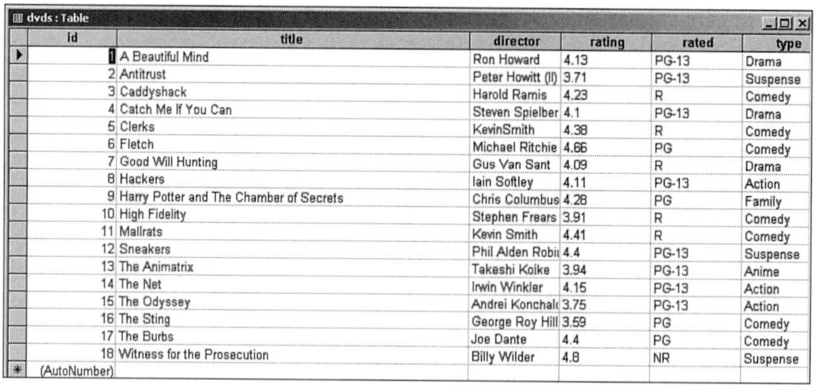

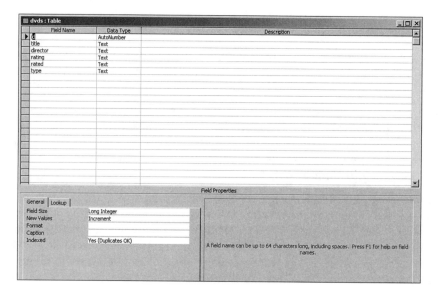

FIGURE 21.5 The data that is held in the dvds table in Access.

FIGURE 21.6 The Design view of the dvds table in Access.

TIP

It is not always necessary to have an id field in your tables with AutoNumber turned on, but it is good practice because you will not repeat a value in this field. However, you could possibly have an identical value in the other fields. For instance, if you had both the original version and the new version of the *Manchurian Candidate*, the easiest way to tell the difference between the two is the id field.

Now that the table is up on the server, we can go over how to connect to it in ASP.

To connect to a database with VBScript, you have to use the ADODB object to make the connection. This object enables you to connect, query, and return information from databases. With four lines of code like the following, you will create an instance of the ADODB.Connection object, create the ConnectionString, and finally open the connection:

```
Dim myConnection
  Set myConnection=Server.CreateObject("ADODB.Connection")
  myConnection.ConnectionString="DRIVER={Microsoft Access Driver (*.mdb)};" &
"DBQ=" & Server.MapPath("movies.mdb")
  myConnection.Open
```

Notice that when we create the ConnectionString, we use a function called Server.MapPath. This is because when you pass the path of the database in the ConnectionString, you have to have the full path, but this function will create the full path for you.

The next step is to create the SQL string we are going to use to "talk" directly to the database. SQL syntax is basically a list of commands set up a certain way so that the database will understand the request. With SQL strings, you can get, add, edit, and delete the data in the database. Here are a couple examples of basic SQL strings with the keywords in bold:

```
SELECT fieldName1, fieldName2 FROM tableName WHERE fieldName1 = value
INSERT INTO tableName (fieldName1, fieldName1,) VALUES ('value1', 'value2')
DELETE FROM tableName WHERE fieldName = value
```

In the first one, the SQL string will get all the data from fieldName1 and fieldName2 where the value in fieldName1 matches value. The second one will create a new row in tableName and put value1 in fieldName1 and value2 in fieldName2. And the final one will delete all rows from tableName where the value in field fieldName is equal to value. SQL strings are difficult at first because they are unlike any code we have covered in this book, but the more you use them, the more familiar they will become.

TIP

In the first SQL string, we select two different fields to get data from. If you want all the fields, you can type them in one by one, or use the asterisk (*) to select all fields, like this:

```
SELECT * FROM tableName WHERE fieldName1 = value
```

Now every field will be returned from rows matching the condition.

After you have your SQL string, you would instantiate an ADODB.Recordset object to capture the data and then open it like this:

```
Dim myRS
  Set myRS=Server.CreateObject("ADODB.Recordset")
  myRS.Open mySQLString, myConnection
```

After that is run, you would have some code to handle all the information being returned in the recordset. After that, the recordset and connection would have to be closed, or errors could occur if the database is getting a lot of requests. The code for that would look something like this:

```
myRS.Close
Set myRS=Nothing
myConnection.Close
Set myConnection=Nothing
```

Notice that not only did we close both the recordset and the connection, but the references were set to Nothing as an extra precaution.

Those were just some of the basic pieces for interacting with a database, so now let's build a page to actually interact with the movies.mdb database.

The project we are building in the example is an application that can view all the DVDs in the database. Then the user can select a specific one to see all of that DVDs data as well as be able to search the titles for keywords.

The first ASP page to build is the one that will return the title and id of every DVD in the table. You will see why we need the id later. The page will look like this:

```
<%@Language=VBScript%>
<%Option Explicit%>
<%
    ''''''''Make the connection
    Dim myConnection
        Set myConnection=Server.CreateObject("ADODB.Connection")
        myConnection.ConnectionString="DRIVER={Microsoft Access Driver (*.mdb)};" &
➥"DBQ=" & Server.MapPath("movies.mdb")
        myConnection.Open
    ''''''''Create the SQL statement we need and set it to a variable
    Dim getAllDVDS
        getAllDVDS = "SELECT title, id FROM dvds"
    ''''''''Make the record set object
    Dim myRS
        Set myRS=Server.CreateObject("ADODB.Recordset")
        myRS.Open getAllDVDS, myConnection
    Dim allDVDs, ids, mainMessage
        Do While Not (myRS.EOF)
            allDVDs = allDVDs& myRS("title") & "~"
            ids = ids & myRS("id") & "~"
            myRS.MoveNext
```

```
      Loop
''''''''Create the message we are sending to Flash
      mainMessage = "dvds=" & allDVDs & "&ids=" & ids

''''''''Clean up...MUST HAVE!!!
      myRS.Close
      Set myRS=Nothing
      myConnection.Close
      Set myConnection=Nothing
''''''''Send that data to Flash
      Response.Write(mainMessage)
%>
```

The top section does what it has done in the entire chapter—it sets the language and the Option Explicit. After that, the connection to the database is opened. Then we create the recordset and open it with our SQL string. Next, a couple of variables we need are created, and then the recordset being returned is parsed with the data being thrown into the variables we just created, separated by "~". Then we set the mainMessage variable to the data we are sending back to Flash. Finally, the connection and recordset are closed, and the data is sent out. Save this page as **getAllDVDs.asp**, upload it to your server, and test it to see the information being returned. It should look like Figure 21.7.

FIGURE 21.7   This is the data being returned in its raw format, before Flash parses it.

Next up is the Flash part. This Flash file will be the one we use throughout the whole example; we will add new pieces to it as we go forward. Follow these steps to get started:

1. Create a new Flash document and save it as **dvdList.fla**.

2. Create a second layer, and call the bottom layer **content** and the top layer **actions**.

3. In the Content layer, drag an instance of the List component onto the stage at coordinate x20, y50, and size it to 175×200. Also, give it an instance name of **dvds_list**.

4. Now for some ActionScript. Select the first frame in the Actions layer, and place this code:

```
function getAllDVDs():Void{
  var getAll_lv:LoadVars = new LoadVars();
  getAll_lv.onLoad = function (success){
   if(success){
     //get the data being returned
```

```
        var titles_array = this.dvds.split("~");
        var ids_array = this.ids.split("~");
        //temporary array to hold the data before it goes to the list
        var temp_array = new Array();
        //because of the extra "~", there is an extra element
        //so we only need every element, but the last one
        var tempLength = titles_array.length - 1;
        var i = 0;
        while(i < tempLength){
         temp_array.push({label: titles_array[i], data: ids_array[i]});
         i++;
        }
        //set the list component
        dvds_list.dataProvider = temp_array;
        }else{
         trace("An error occurred with the connection");
        }
      }
     //get the data
     getAll_lv.load("http://MYSERVER/getAllDVDs.asp");
   }
  //call the function
  getAllDVDs();
```

The preceding code does a lot. First, we create a function to get all the DVDs (this could have been done without it being in a function, but later you will see why a function was used). In the function, a new LoadVars object is created, and the onLoad event is set. When data is received back, it will go through it element by element and store the info in another array that eventually gets set to the `dataProvider` of the List component. At the end of the function, we load the ASP page with all the data. Then, after the function is complete, we call it to get all the DVDs. Test it out, and you should see something like Figure 21.8.

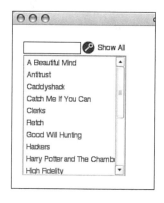

FIGURE 21.8   All the DVDs in the database are now in the List.

Next up is the ASP page that will receive some data from Flash and return all the information on a given DVD. The page will look like this:

```
<%@Language=VBScript%>
<%Option Explicit%>
<%
  ''the data coming from Flash
  Dim dvdID
  dvdID = Trim(Request("sentID"))
  ''''''Make the connection
  Dim myConnection
   Set myConnection=Server.CreateObject("ADODB.Connection")
   myConnection.ConnectionString="DRIVER=
{Microsoft Access Driver (*.mdb)};" & "DBQ=" & Server.MapPath("movies.mdb")
   myConnection.Open
  ''''''Create the SQL statement we need and set it to a variable
  Dim getDVDInfo
   getDVDInfo = "SELECT * FROM dvds WHERE id=" & dvdID
  ''''''Make the record set object
  Dim myRS
   Set myRS=Server.CreateObject("ADODB.Recordset")
   myRS.Open getDVDInfo, myConnection
  Dim mainMessage
   IF NOT(myRS.EOF)THEN
     MainMessage = "title=" & myRS("title")
     mainMessage = mainMessage & "&director=" & myRS("director")
     mainMessage = mainMessage & "&rating=" & myRS("rating")
     mainMessage = mainMessage & "&rated=" & myRS("rated")
     mainMessage = mainMessage & "&type=" & myRS("type")
   ELSE
     mainMessage="error=none returned"
   END IF
''''''Clean up...MUST HAVE!!!
  myRS.Close
  Set myRS=Nothing
  myConnection.Close
  Set myConnection=Nothing
''''''Send that data to Flash
  Response.Write(mainMessage)
%>
```

There are a few differences between this ASP page and the last one. First, this page is accepting some data being sent to it from Flash (the id of the DVD, so now you see why we grabbed the ids in the first ASP page). Next, the SQL string is a little different; all the fields in the row matching the id are returned. We then check to make sure some data was returned and put it in mainMessage to be sent back to Flash. If no rows are returned, an error is sent back to Flash saying none was returned. And just like before, at the bottom we close the connection and recordset and send the data to Flash.

Save this file as **getDVDInfo.asp** and put it up on your server. If you want to see the results being returned, try this URL: http://MYSERVER/getDVDInfo.asp?sentID=1.

Now we'll go back to Flash to add a few fields and some more ActionScript.

1. Before we get to the ActionScript, we need to create a few text fields on the stage. They will all be dynamic text with the border turned on and on the Content layer. The instance names will be the following: title_txt, director_txt, rating_txt, rated_txt, type_txt. You can see their layout and how they are labeled in Figure 21.9 (which also shows results being returned).

2. After that, it's back to ActionScript. Add these lines of code to the first frame of the Actions layer:

```
//The listener object for when a user selects a DVD
var dvd_obj:Object = new Object();
dvd_obj.change = function(){
  var dvdID = dvds_list.value;
  var dvdInfo_lv:LoadVars = new LoadVars();
  dvdInfo_lv.onLoad = function(success){
    if(success){
      if(!this.error){
        title_txt.text = this.title;
        director_txt.text = this.director;
        rating_txt.text = this.rating;
        rated_txt.text = this.rated;
        type_txt.text = this.type;
      }else{
        trace(this.error);
      }
    }else{
      trace("An error occurred with the connection");
    }
  }
  dvdInfo_lv.sentId = dvdID;
  //send and receive the data
  dvdInfo_lv.sendAndLoad("http://MYSERVER/getDVDInfo.asp",dvdInfo_lv, "POST");
}
//add the event listener to the List component
dvds_list.addEventListener("change", dvd_obj);
```

Part of this code was covered back in Chapter 16, "Components 2.0." A listener object is built, and then the event is set to it for when a user selects a DVD from the list. When this event is triggered, another LoadVars object is created that handles sending the correct id to the ASP page and handles the data being returned. If, for some reason, no DVD information is returned, an error is sent to the Output panel. But if data is returned, it is sent to the text fields we just made. After the event, we add the event listener to the List component holding the DVDs. Test it out and you will see, as in Figure 21.9, when you click on a DVD, the information is returned to Flash and the fields are filled.

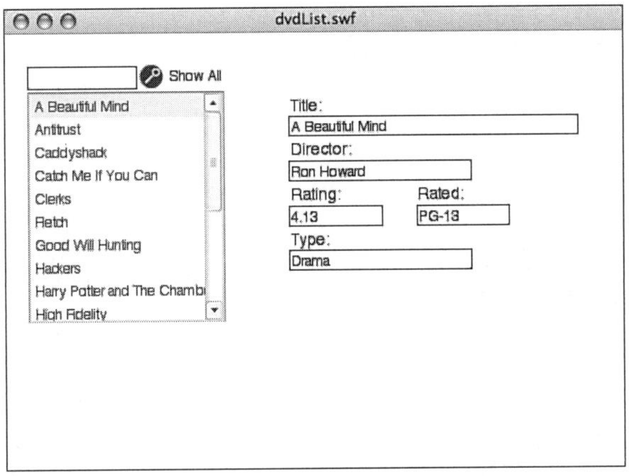

FIGURE 21.9 Using another ASP page, you can return specific data about a selected DVD and fill the fields in Flash.

The final piece of this example is the capability to search through the titles and return results based on the keyword. Again, we will start with the ASP page.

```
<%@Language=VBScript%>
<%Option Explicit%>
<%
  ''the data coming from Flash
  Dim keyWord
   keyWord = Trim(Request("keyWord"))

  '''''''Make the connection
  Dim myConnection
   Set myConnection=Server.CreateObject("ADODB.Connection")
   myConnection.ConnectionString="DRIVER={Microsoft Access Driver (*.mdb)};" &
➡"DBQ=" & Server.MapPath("movies.mdb")
   myConnection.Open
  '''''''Create the SQL statement we need and set it to a variable
  Dim searchDVDs
   searchDVDs = "SELECT title, id FROM dvds WHERE title LIKE '%" & keyWord & "%'"
  '''''''Make the record set object
  Dim myRS
   Set myRS=Server.CreateObject("ADODB.Recordset")
   myRS.Open searchDVDs, myConnection
   Dim allDVDs, ids, mainMessage
```

```
   Do While Not (myRS.EOF)
    allDVDs = allDVDs& myRS("title") & "~"
    ids = ids & myRS("id") & "~"
    myRS.MoveNext
   Loop
 ''''''Create the message we are sending to Flash
 mainMessage = "dvds=" & allDVDs & "&ids=" & ids
 ''''''Clean up...MUST HAVE!!!
 myRS.Close
 Set myRS=Nothing
 myConnection.Close
 Set myConnection=Nothing
 ''''''Send that data to Flash
 Response.Write(mainMessage)
%>
```

This file builds on the original getAllDVDs.asp page we started with, but the difference is we collect a keyword being sent from Flash, and search the database using a special SQL string that has the keyword LIKE in it. This keyword does comparisons combined with the wildcard % on either side of the string we are looking for. This means it will look both at the beginning and the end of the value of title in each row. That means it will return any title that has the keyword anywhere in it. After that, the rest is just like getAllDVDs.asp.

Save this file as **searchDVDs.asp**. If you want to see it work, try this URL: http://MYSERVER/searchDVDs.asp?keyWord=can

Now, we'll go back to Flash for the final few interface pieces and a little more ActionScript:

1. The first thing is to create an input text field above the List component in the content layer for the search keyword. It has an instance name of search_txt and the border is enabled.

2. After that, we will need two buttons, both on the Content layer. One should have an instance name of search_btn for searching, and the other with an instance name of showAll_btn for returning all the DVDs again. You can see the layout of the field and the two buttons in Figure 21.10.

3. Now for the ActionScript: back in frame 1 of the *actions* layer, we will add a few more things starting with a function to clear all the fields and the List component. This is because when we search for results, we want to clear everything out. The code looks like this:

```
//clear the fields and the List
function clearForm():Void{
  dvds_list.removeAll();
  title_txt.text = "";
  director_txt.text = "";
```

```
  rating_txt.text = "";
  rated_txt.text = "";
  type_txt.text = "";
}
```

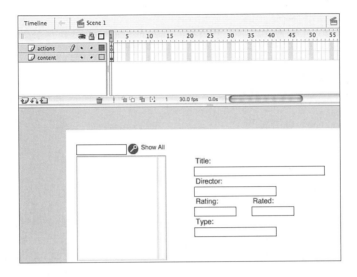

FIGURE 21.10   The final layout of the application in the Flash authoring environment.

4. The next piece of code is the event when a user clicks on the Search button:

```
search_btn.onRelease = function(){
  //make sure there is a term to search for
  if(search_txt.text.length>0){
   //clear the fields
   clearForm();
   var search_lv:LoadVars = new LoadVars();
   search_lv.onLoad = function(success){
     if(success){
       //get the data being returned
       var titles_array = this.dvds.split("~");
       var ids_array = this.ids.split("~");
       //temporary array
       var temp_array = new Array();
       //because of the extra "~", there is a blank element
       var tempLength = titles_array.length - 1;
       if(tempLength>0){
         var i = 0;
         while(i < tempLength){
         temp_array.push({label: titles_array[i], data: ids_array[i]});
         i++;
```

```
    }
    //set the list component
    dvds_list.dataProvider = temp_array;
   }else{
    trace("None Returned");
   }
  }else{
   trace("An error occurred with the connection");
  }
 }
//send the keyword
search_lv.keyWord = search_txt.text;
//go get the results
search_lv.sendAndLoad
➡("http://www.playgroupfinder.com/searchDVDs.asp", search_lv, "POST");
 }
}
```

This code does a lot. First it checks whether there is a term to search for. If not, it just ignores the request. If there is a keyword in the field, the form is cleared with the function we just created, and a new LoadVars object is created. This LoadVars is very similar to the first one we made in this example, except that when results are returned, it makes sure at least one DVD is returned, or it sends a message to the Output panel saying no results are returned. If there are results, they are parsed and placed in the List component just like when we get all the DVDs. And when you click on the DVDs in the List component, the info for that DVD is returned.

5. There is just one more thing to add to the ActionScript—the code for the showAll_btn:

```
//Go get all DVDs
showAll_btn.onRelease = function(){
  clearForm();
  search_txt.text = "";
  getAllDVDs();
}
```

This final piece of code clears the form (as well as the search text field) and calls the first function we made in this example to go get all the DVDs in the database. Now test the movie out, and it will be able to do everything it has done so far, as well as search through the movie titles for keywords and return their results.

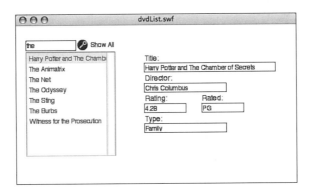

FIGURE 21.11 Flash and ASP combined with Access make a great team for storing, organizing, and displaying data.

Summary

This chapter has gone over a lot about Flash and ASP: how to write some basic ASP code with VBScript, how to write ActionScript to communicate with ASP pages, and how to write more VBScript to communicate to a database. This chapter could not cover all there is to know about ASP and interacting with databases, but it is a good start. For more information about ASP, check out http://safari.sampspublishing.com/?XmlId=0-672-31863-6 as well as http://aspalliance.com.

The next chapter is going to go over some similar things with Flash dealing with middleware; however, instead of ASP pages, Flash will be communicating with PHP, an opensource standard for dynamic content.

CHAPTER 22

PHP and Flash

In this chapter, we discuss how to integrate Flash with the server-side scripting language PHP. Flash, as you may already know, has some amazing capabilities as an application development medium. Still, to create some truly dynamic applications—working with real, changing data— you are going to need to extend to other technologies. As you learned in the previous chapter, Flash works well with other server-side languages, such as ASP. Now we'll show you the amazing capabilities of Flash when working with PHP.

> **NOTE**
>
> This chapter is written under the assumption that the reader is familiar with and has basic knowledge of Flash ActionScript, the ability to create and edit HTML files, and at least a beginner-level understanding of PHP scripting.

We'll begin with some simple examples of Flash receiving data from PHP. After you have an understanding of how this works, you can then take it a step further, having Flash "speak" back to PHP. That's right, a two-way conversation! This "conversation" is where the power of your future applications begins to take shape. After you have a good understanding of this, we can then integrate the final step in any well-rounded application: integrating a database.

Setting Up Your Server

Because this chapter is written under the assumption that you have a beginner-level understanding of PHP scripting, it may be safe to also assume that you have a server environment to develop on. But because it's never safe to make such assumption, we have provided the necessary information to create a server environment in which you can duplicate the examples in this chapter.

The server setup that we are using for the examples in this chapter runs on a Microsoft Windows server. The environment works the same on other servers (Unix, for example), but you will need to download the appropriate files and follow the instruction for the particular server you are working with. To duplicate the examples in this chapter, you will need a server environment with three components:

- Apache Server
- PHP
- MYSQL Database

If you are not familiar with any or all of these components, it may seem like a daunting task to set it all up yourself. Don't fear. It is much easier than you think and there is a world of support out there to help you understand the technology behind it all. The best thing to do is to find a friend or colleague who is familiar with setting up the above-mentioned environment, and have them help you. Each component's website is also jammed packed with tutorials, and the best thing to do is just follow the readme.txt (or install.txt, or setup.txt) files that come with each component's installation files.

> **NOTE**
>
> We almost forgot to tell you the best part about APACHE/PHP/MYSQL development—it's free! That's right, all three of the components needed are open-source projects with years of development and support. Thought that you might like that!

Installing Apache Server

The Apache server is the "environment" that PHP and MYSQL run in. The Apache server can be downloaded from http://httpd.apache.org/download.cgi. The current version at the time of this writing is 2.0, but we will be using 1.3 because it has been in use for some time and will be the version most hosting companies are currently running on their servers (2.0 also does not offer us any features needed over 1.3; the choice is yours).

The Windows download is a self-extracting installation file. Follow the instructions and refer to the documentation at http://httpd.apache.org/docs/install.html if needed.

Installing PHP

PHP can be downloaded from http://www.php.net/downloads.php. The current version at the time of this writing is 5.0, but we require that you use 4.3 because it has been in use for some time and will be the version most hosting companies are currently running on their servers. PHP 5.0 is not just an upgrade, but a reconstruction of PHP and will not be widely supported for some time. (Hosting companies are starting to offer special servers with PHP 5.0 support, but at the time of this writing support for and development with PHP 5.0 is very limited).

After you download and extract the files, open the `install.txt` for installation instruction. The installation and configuration for PHP is mostly manual, compared to APACHE being a program installation, but the instructions are simple enough and should be easy to follow.

Installing MySQL

MYSQL is the database that is used mostly when you're working with PHP. MySQL can be downloaded from http://dev.mysql.com/downloads/index.html. The current recommended version at the time of this writing is 4.1; 5.0 is currently in development, but we recommend sticking with 4.1 because it has been in use for some time and will be the version most hosting companies are currently running on their servers.

The Windows download is a self-extracting installation file. Follow the instructions and refer to the documentation at http://dev.mysql.com/doc/mysql/en/windows-installation.html if needed.

Having MySQL installed and working with MySQL are two different things. You can work with MySQL through the command prompt (Windows) or the console (Unix), but we prefer to use a web-based alternative that is much more user friendly, PhpMyAdmin. PhpMyAdmin can be downloaded from http://www.phpmyadmin.net and is very easy to set up. After you download the appropriate files and extract them, open up `Documentation.txt` (on Windows you will need to open this up in WordPad instead of Notepad because of some rich-text formatting) to find the installation instruction.

> **NOTE**
>
> We recommend that you install each of these components yourself, simply because the education you gain will help you in the future, as well as make you more comfortable with setting up server environments. As mentioned before, it is not as daunting a task as it may seem, and the World Wide Web is chock full of help. Fear not!

Now That It's All Installed

After you have your server set up, you'll want to make sure it works properly.

1. Create a new PHP document, save it as **test.php**, and place the following script inside:

```php
<?php
echo "Your server is running as of " . date("l dS of F Y h:i:s A");
?>
```

2. Put test.php in your server's root directory and then view it through your browser (the default address for a local server is http://localhost/). If you did this correctly, your browser should display something like the following:

```
Your server is running as of Wednesday 13th of April 2005 03:07:34
PM
```

Learning More About PHP

You may already have a pretty good understanding of working with PHP, but the language has as many functions as the day is long. If you want to learn more about PHP scripting, we recommend that you go straight to the source at http://www.php.net.

PHP is a very powerful language and the more you work with PHP and Flash, the more you will want to do with PHP. Whenever working with PHP I always have php.net open in a browser window to do quick searches. You would be amazed how many times you will learn something new that makes working with PHP easier.

PHP and Flash—Receiving Data

As stated before, integrating Flash with PHP will allow us to create some pretty dynamic applications. We aren't quite there yet, so let's start with some simple examples of how Flash can receive data from PHP.

Example 1—Hello World

In our first example we will use the most common of examples, displaying the text Hello World. Here our PHP file will already contain the variable and send it to Flash to be displayed. Create a new PHP file, save it as **helloWorld.php**, and paste the following script inside:

```php
<?php
echo "myVariable=Hello World";
?>
```

See a difference? In this example, not only are we displaying "Hello World," but we are saying that it is the value of "myVariable." The reason for this is that Flash will understand only the data in the name/value pair format. Now that we have the PHP script created, let's move on to our Flash file.

1. Create a new Flash file, save it as **helloWorld.fla**, and save it to the same directory as helloWorld.php on your server.

2. In the Actions panel of the first frame, place this code inside:

```
//Create a text field
this.createTextField("display_txt",1,0,0,100,20);
//The LoadVars object for loading the data
var hello_lv:LoadVars = new LoadVars();
//When the LoadVars object receives the data
hello_lv.onLoad = function(success){
    if(success){
        display_txt.text = this.myVariable;
    }else{
        trace("An error has occurred.");
    }
}
```

```
//Load the PHP
hello_lv.load("http://PATH_TO_YOUR_SERVER/helloWorld.php");
```

Walking through the ActionScript, we can see that we have created a dynamic text field in the top-left corner of the canvas. We then create an instance of the LoadVars object, which will be used to connect to the PHP page and receive the data. The onLoad event is then created to tell Flash what to do when the requested data is returned. In it we test the value of success to see if there were any issues connecting to our PHP page. If success returns true, it will write the myVariable value to our text field, and if not it will display "An error has occurred" in the Output panel. Now all we have to do is make the request using the load method by passing it the full path to your helloWorld.php file.

Publish your movie, and if you run the generated SWF you should see the following result, as shown in Figure 22.1:

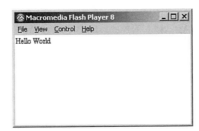

FIGURE 22.1 The result of our "Hello World" example.

NOTE

When you are using PHP with Flash, we recommend using an absolute path to access your PHP files. This ensures that no matter where your Flash files are on the server, you can still access the PHP files. In the preceding example, as well as in the following examples, you will need to change "PATH_TO_YOUR_SERVER" to the actual path to your PHP scripts. You may be working from the root of your server or within a directory, so customize the paths respectively.

Example 2—Hello, Goodbye World

In this example we will be passing two variables instead of one. These variables will be displayed in different text fields.

1. Create a new PHP file, save it as **helloGoodbye.php**, and paste the following script inside:

```
<?php
echo "myVariable1=Hello World&myVariable2=Goodbye World";
?>
```

As you can see, the PHP script is identical to example1 except for one small thing: We are now passing two variables instead of one. To pass numerous variables, we place an ampersand (&) between the name/value pairs.

2. Create a new Flash file, save it as **helloGoodbye.fla**, and save it to the same directory as helloGoodbye.php on your server.

3. In the Actions panel of the first frame, place this code:

```
//Create a text field
this.createTextField("displayHello_txt",1,0,0,100,20);
this.createTextField("displayGoodBye_txt",2,0,40,100,20);
//The LoadVars object for loading the data
var hello_lv:LoadVars = new LoadVars();
//When the LoadVars object receives the data
hello_lv.onLoad = function(success){
    if(success){
        displayHello_txt.text = this.myVariable;
displayGoodBye_txt.text = this.myVariable;
    }else{
        trace("An error has occurred.");
    }
}
//Load the PHP
hello_lv.load("http://PATH_TO_YOUR_SERVER/helloGoodbye.php");
```

Walking through the ActionScript, you can see that we are now creating two dynamic text fields in the top-left corner of the canvas, 20 pixels apart. Notice that we place them on separate levels; otherwise, the next field will wipe out the preceding field. After success returns true, we will write the two variables we have received to their respective fields. Now all we have to do is make the request using the load method by passing it the full path to your helloGoodbye.php file.

Publish your movie, and if you run the generated SWF, you should see the result shown in Figure 22.2:

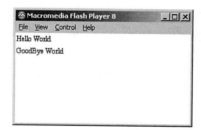

FIGURE 22.2   The result of our "Hello, Goodbye World" example.

Example 3—Multiple Values and Multiple Variables

In this example, we will work with multiple variables, like example 2. The difference is that the variables in this example will have multiple values. Instead of using a name/value pair for each variable, we can place multiple values into one variable.

In this example we have three people. Each person has a name, age, and weight. If we did this with individual variables it would take a total of nine variables. Instead we pass three variables, one for name, one for age, and one for weight, and let Flash do the work of parsing the values. Create a new PHP file, save it as **multipleValues.php**, and paste the following script inside:

```php
<?php
//Arrays that hold the values
$personName = array("Rick", "Jane", "Andy");
$personAge = array("12", "13", "11");
$personWeight = array("115", "103", "105");
//Loop through the array and store the values in new variables
for($i=0;$i<count($personName);$i++){
    $sentName .= $personName[$i] . "~";
    $sentAge .= $personAge[$i] . "~";
    $sentWeight .= $personWeight[$i] . "~";
}
//Write the results to the screen
echo "sentName=$sentName&sentAge=$sentAge&sentWeight=$sentWeight";
?>
```

Because we are working without a database, our information is currently stored in arrays. We cannot pass these arrays directly to Flash, so we loop through them and store the data as a string into new variables, separated by the tilde (~) character. Finally, we write the information to the browser. If you test this page alone on your server, you should see what is shown in Figure 22.3:

Now we can move on to the Flash component of this example. We need to create a file that will draw this data in, parse it back into arrays, and then write it to the text fields we create.

1. Create a new Flash file, save it as **multipleValues.fla**, and save it to the same directory as multipleValues.php on your server.

2. In the Actions panel of the first frame, place this code:

```
//Create the text fields
this.createTextField("name_txt",1,20,20,100,100);
this.name_txt.multiline = true;
this.name_txt.border = true;
this.createTextField("age_txt",2,130,20,100,100);
this.age_txt.multiline = true;
this.age_txt.border = true;
```

```
this.createTextField("weight_txt",3,240,20,100,100);
this.weight_txt.multiline = true;
this.weight_txt.border = true;
//The LoadVars object for loading the data
var multipleValues_lv:LoadVars = new LoadVars();
//When the LoadVars object receives the data
multipleValues_lv.onLoad = function(success){
    if(success){
        var name_array = this.sentName.split("~");
        var age_array = this.sentAge.split("~");
        var weight_array = this.sentWeight.split("~");
        //Because of the extra "~", there is an extra element
        //so we only need every element, but the last one
        var tempLength = name_array.length - 1;
        for(i=0;i<tempLength;i++){
            name_txt.text += name_array[i] + newline;
            age_txt.text += age_array[i] + newline;
            weight_txt.text += weight_array[i] + newline;
        }
    }else{
        trace("An error has occurred.");
    }
}
//Load the PHP
multipleValues_lv.load("http://PATH_TO_YOUR_SERVER/multipleValues.php");
```

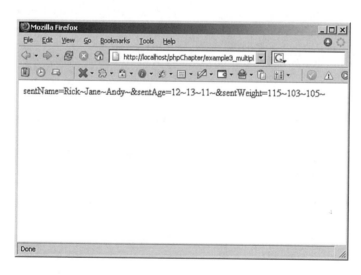

FIGURE 22.3   Data written to the browser.

The ActionScript for this example is slightly different from the previous examples. First, we create the text fields, but because they are going to be holding multiple strings, we make them multiline. We also give them a border so we can see their size and placement. Next we use the LoadVars object, but the difference is how we handle the data that is returned. First we create three arrays and store the incoming data into those arrays by splitting the values based on the ~ character. Then we look through the arrays and populate the text fields with the values returned. Finally, we call the PHP page to get the process going. If you test the movie, you should see the results shown in Figure 22.4:

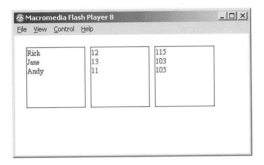

FIGURE 22.4   The text fields populated with the parsed data.

As you can see, it's easier to store multiple values into a single variable and allow Flash to parse that data, instead of handling individual variables for each value.

Example 4—Sending Mail with Flash and PHP

The first three examples have no real-world application, but they give you a basis for understanding how to integrate Flash and PHP. This next example will show you how to send a simple email using Flash as the interface and using PHP to process the email. Create a new PHP file, save it as **sendMail.php**, and paste the following script inside:

```
<?php
//Get the external variable
$destMail = $_REQUEST["destMail"];
$senderName = $_REQUEST["senderName"];
$senderMail = $_REQUEST["senderMail"];
$senderSubject = $_REQUEST["senderSubject"];
$senderBody = $_REQUEST["senderBody"];
//Add header information
$header = "From: $senderName <$senderMail>\n";
$header .= "Reply-To: $senderName <$senderMail>\n";
//Send Email (to, subject, body, header)
mail($destMail, $senderSubject, $senderBody, $header);
?>
```

As you can see, the script is very straightforward. This page will first accept the five variables passed to it:

- **destMail**—Destination email address
- **senderName**—Name of the sender
- **senderMail**—Email address of the sender
- **senderSubject**—Subject of the email
- **senderBody**—Body of the email

Then we format the header information for the email (the sender's name and email address) and use the `mail` function to send the email. Now we can move on to the Flash part of this example. We need to create a file that will allow a user to enter in the five pieces of information and submit them to the page we just created.

1. Create a new Flash file, save it as **sendMail.fla** and save it to the same directory as sendMail.php on your server. Create five text fields and place them on the canvas, aligned vertically.

   The first field should have the following properties:

   - **Type**—Input
   - **Show border around text**—true
   - **Font size**—12
   - **Instance name**—destEmail_txt

   The second field should have the following properties:

   - **Type**—Input
   - **Show border around text**—true
   - **Font size**—12
   - **Instance name**—senderName_txt

   The third field should have the following properties:

   - **Type**—Input
   - **Show border around text**—true
   - **Font size**—12
   - **Instance name**—senderEmail_txt

   The fourth field should have the following properties:

   - **Type**—Input
   - **Show border around text**—true

- **Font size**—12

- **Instance name**—senderSubject_txt

The fifth field should have the following properties:

- **Type**—Input

- **Show border around text**—true

- **Font size**—12

- **Instance name**—senderBody_txt

2. Create a button symbol and place it below the text fields. The button should have the following properties:

- **Instance name**—send_btn

You may format, label, and color your file however you like. Your basic layout should look, in some way, like Figure 22.5 :

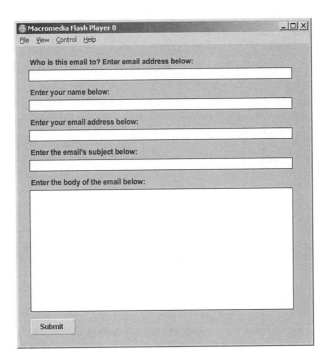

FIGURE 22.5   The mail interface laid out and labeled.

Now that we have our interface laid out, we need to do two things. First, we need to create a way that the Submit button will not pass the variables unless all the text fields are filled out. Second, we need to write the actual script to pass the information from these text fields to the PHP script. In the Actions panel of the first frame, place this code:

```
//Add a listener to make sure fields are filled
//If all fields are filled enable button
fieldsFilled = new Object();
fieldsFilled.onKeyUp = function(){
        if(destMail_txt.text != '' && senderName_txt.text != '' &&
senderMail_txt.text != '' && senderSubject_txt.text != '' &&
senderBody_txt.text != ''){
                send_btn.enabled = true;
            } else {
                send_btn.enabled = false;
            }
}
//Apply the listener, and disable the button on init
Key.addListener(fieldsFilled);
send_btn.enabled = false;

//The object for communicating with the PHP page
var sendMail_lv:LoadVars = new LoadVars();
send_btn.onRelease = function(){
    //set the variables we are sending
    sendMail_lv.destMail = destMail_txt.text;
    sendMail_lv.senderName = senderName_txt.text;
    sendMail_lv.senderMail = senderMail_txt.text;
    sendMail_lv.senderSubject = senderSubject_txt.text;
    sendMail_lv.senderBody = senderBody_txt.text;
    //send and receive the data
    sendMail_lv.sendAndLoad("http://PATH_TO_YOUR_SERVER/sendMail.php",
➥ sendMail_lv, "POST");
}
```

In the preceding code, we start with the field requirements. Because we need all five pieces of the information, we create a listener (`fieldsFilled`) that checks to see whether all field fields are not empty. If they all contain some sort of text, then `send_btn` is enabled. We then create the LoadVars object (`sendMail_lv`) that we will use to pass the variables. Then we create a function and attach it to the `onRelease` event of `send_btn`. This function grabs the values of the five text fields, places them in the LoadVars object, and then calls the sendAndLoad event to pass the data to our PHP page.

Now that you have a good understanding of how to send data to PHP from Flash, let's work on PHP sending some data back to Flash.

PHP and Flash—Sending and Receiving Data

As you can see, receiving data can open up a lot of doors to the capabilities of your Flash projects. Still, this only touches on the extent of integrating server-side scripting. When users interact with a web page or an application they often enter data to get certain results. The most common example of this interaction is a search engine: users enter their request, the request is sent to the server, and the server provides the users with data based on the specific information they requested.

Example 5—Confirming `sentMail`

Example 4 showed you a real-world application of sending variables from Flash to PHP by creating and sending a basic email. In this example, we take that a step further by having PHP confirm that the email was sent. This confirmation will be sent to and displayed by Flash. By doing this we can show how to send data back and forth between Flash and PHP.

1. Duplicate the files you have for our `sendMail` example and rename each of them `confirmMail`.

2. Open up `confirmMail.php` and replace the last line of the script, the mail function call, with the following code:

```
if(@mail($destMail, $senderSubject, $senderBody, $header)){
    echo "confirmStatus=success&confirmName=$senderName&confirmMessage
=The email was sent successfully.";
}else{
    echo "confirmStatus=failed&confirmName=$senderName&confirmMessage
=There was an error in sending your email.";
}
```

This script modification does a few things. First, when it calls the mail function, it tests the variables being passed to it. Then, based on the success of the mail function call, it echoes a multiple variable string back to the browser. This string contains three variables:

- **confirmStatus**—Either "success" or "failed" to let Flash know whether the function call was completed

- **confirmName**—The senderName variable

- **confirmMessage**—A generic message stating the status of the action executed

Now we move on to the modification to our Flash file.

1. Open up `confirmMail.fla` and create a text field next to your send_btn with the following properties:

- **Type**—Dynamic

- **Font size**—12

- **Bold Style**—true

- **Instance name**—confirm_txt

2. In the Actions panel of the first frame, add this code to the bottom:

```
//When the object receives data back from the PHP page
sendMail_lv.onLoad = function(success){
    if(success){
        if(this.confirmStatus == "success"){
            confirm_txt.textColor = 0x006600;
            confirm_txt.text = "Congratulations " + this.confirmName + "." +
➥newline;
            confirm_txt.text += this.confirmMessage;
        }else{
            confirm_txt.textColor = 0x990000;
            confirm_txt.text = "Sorry " + this.confirmName + "." + newline;
            confirm_txt.text += this.confirmMessage;
        }
    }
}
```

The preceding addition uses the `onLoad` event of the LoadVars object to test whether the data from PHP has been received. If so, based on the value of `confirmStatus`, the script formats the variables `confirmName`, `confirmMessage` and places them in the `confirm_txt` text field. It also sets the field's text color to add emphasis.

We now have a good example of Flash and PHP sending data to each other. This should give you an idea of how powerful Flash and server-side scripting can be. It also gives us a good basis for our next example—drawing data from a MySQL database to be displayed in Flash.

Incorporating a MySQL Database

If you have made it this far and are still up for more—congrats! You have learned how to load data from your server-side PHP scripts and how to send and receive data back from them. Up to this point, you have provided the data for our examples, either through hard coding or manually entering it in Flash.

Example 6—Address Book

In the following example, we will create a very simple address book and store our data in a MySQL database.

Building the Database

Before we get into our example, we will need to build the database that is going to hold our content. You can download the SQL file from the book's website or build it on your own. If you want to build it yourself, follow these steps:

1. Create a new database and name it **addressBook**.

2. Create a new table in this database and name it **contacts**.

3. Add the following fields to the new table:

- **contactId**—This field is a unique identifier of the record in the database. This field should have the following properties:
    - Type: INT
    - Length: 11
    - Extra: auto_increment
    - Primary Key: true
- **firstName**—The contact's first name. This field should have the following properties:
    - Type: VARCHAR
    - Length: 255
- **lastName**—The contact's last name. This field should have the following properties:
    - Type: VARCHAR
    - Length: 255
- **phoneNum**—The contact's phone number. This field should have the following properties:
    - Type: VARCHAR
    - Length: 255
- **email**—The contact's email address. This field should have the following properties:
    - Type: VARCHAR
    - Length: 255

If you built the database on your own, you will also have to populate it with some records. Table 22.1 is a table of the data we will be using for this example.

TABLE 22.1   Sample Data Table

Firstname	Lastname	Phonenum	email
Tom	Hanks	(555) 555-1234	tom.hanks@hanks.com
Dale	Gordon	(444) 444-1234	dale.gordon@gordon.com
Christopher	Walken	(333) 333-1234	chris.walken@walken.com
Julia	Roberts	(222) 222-1234	julia.roberts@roberts.com
Ashley	Judd	(111) 111-1234	ashley.judd@judd.com

Getting the Data from the Database

Now that our database is created, and populated with some test data, let's move on to creating the PHP script that will grab this data and pass it to Flash. Create a new PHP file, save it as **contactList.php**, and paste the following script inside. Don't forget to put in your username and password:

```php
<?php
//Database Information
$dbHost = "localhost";
$dbUser = "YOUR_USERNAME";
$dbPass = "YOUR_PASSWORD";
$dbName = "addressBook";
//Open database connection
function openConn() {
    global $dbHost;
    global $dbUser;
    global $dbPass;
    global $dbName;
    $curConn = mysql_connect($dbHost, $dbUser, $dbPass);
    if (!$curConn) {
        echo "<p>Could not connect to the database.</p>";
    }
    if (!@mysql_select_db($dbName)) {
        echo "<p>Couldn't find database $dbName.</p>";
    }
    return $curConn;
}
openConn();
//Open database connection, and request the data
$tempConn = openConn();
$listQ = "SELECT contactId, firstName, lastName FROM contacts";
$listR =  mysql_query($listQ);
$listN = mysql_num_rows($listR);
//Write the returned data to the screen
if ($listN != 0){
    for ($count = 1; $count <= $listN; $count++){
        $aResult = mysql_fetch_array($listR);
            $allContacts .= $aResult["lastName"] . ", " .
➥$aResult["firstName"] . "~";
            $allIds .= $aResult["contactId"] . "~";
    }
    echo "contacts=" . $allContacts . "&ids=" . $allIds;
}else{
    echo "No records were returned, sorry.";
}
//Close the database connection
mysql_close($tempConn);
?>
```

This file will connect to the database, grab the contactId field, the firstName field, the lastName field, and write them to the browser in the name/value pair format that Flash can understand.

Now let's move on to the Flash file:

1. Create a new Flash document and save it as **addressBook.fla**.

2. Create a new layer in the timeline. Rename the top layer **actions** and rename the bottom layer **content**.

3. In the Content layer, drag an instance of the List component onto the stage and place it at X 20, Y 20. Set its size to 175×200. Give it an instance name of **contacts_list**.

4. In the first frame of the Actions layer, paste the following code into the Actions panel:

```
function getAllContacts(){
    var getAll_lv:LoadVars = new LoadVars();
    getAll_lv.onLoad = function (success){
        if(success){
            //get the data being returned
            var name_array = this.contacts.split("~");
            var ids_array = this.ids.split("~");
            //temporary array to hold the data before it goes to the list
            var temp_array = new Array();
            //because of the extra "~", there is an extra element
            //so we only need every element, but the last one
            var tempLength = name_array.length - 1;
            var i = 0;
            while(i < tempLength){
                temp_array.push({label: name_array[i], data: ids_array[i]});
                i++;
            }
            //set the list component
            contacts_list.dataProvider = temp_array;
        }else{
            trace("An error occurred with the connection");
        }
    }
    //get the data
    getAll_lv.load("http://PATH_TO_YOUR_SERVER/contactList.php");
}
//call the function
getAllContacts();
```

22

First we create a function called getAllContacts. This function holds all the data-loading code. Inside, we create an instance of the LoadVars object, set the onLoad event to take the returned data and put it into arrays, and after we have the data in Flash, we hand it over to the dataProvider object of the List component.

NOTE

As you can see, we like to make just about anything a function. In the Address Book example we did not have to do this, but it is a good practice to get into. Having the code run on the frame puts you in a position of having to line everything up right on the timeline. If you put your code into function, it gives you the capability to call it when and wherever you need it, giving you a little bit more freedom in how you build your projects.

If everything went well, when you test your movie you should be presented with the List component, populated with the Last Name, First Name of every contact in your database, as you can see in Figure 22.6.

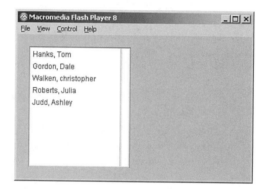

FIGURE 22.6   Your List component populated with the contact names.

Now this is great, but what happened to the rest of the data? All that information is still in the database, so we have to do some more work to get it displayed in Flash. Let's start with the PHP page that we will use to request the rest of that data for a specific contact. Create a new PHP file, save it as **contactInfo.php**, and paste the following script inside. Don't forget to put in your username and password:

```php
<?php
// Database Information
/////////////////////////
$dbHost = "localhost";
$dbUser = "YOUR_USERNAME";
$dbPass = "YOUR_PASSWORD";
$dbName = "addressBook";
// Open database connection
/////////////////////////////
```

```
    function openConn() {
        global $dbHost;
        global $dbUser;
        global $dbPass;
        global $dbName;
        $curConn = mysql_connect($dbHost, $dbUser, $dbPass);
        if (!$curConn) {
            echo "<p>Could not connect to the database.</p>";
        }
        if (!@mysql_select_db($dbName)) {
            echo "<p>Couldn't find database $dbName.</p>";
        }
        return $curConn;
    }
    openConn();
    //Connect to the database
    $tempConn = openConn();
    //Make our request, store it in an array, and count it
    $listQ = "SELECT * FROM contacts where contactId = '" .
➥$_REQUEST["contactId"] . "'";
    $listR =  mysql_query($listQ);
    $listN = mysql_num_rows($listR);
    //Write the returned data to the screen
    if ($listN != 0){
        $aResult = mysql_fetch_array($listR);
        $contactInfo = "firstName=" . $aResult["firstName"];
        $contactInfo .= "&lastName=" . $aResult["lastName"];
        $contactInfo .= "&phoneNum=" . $aResult["phoneNum"];
        $contactInfo .= "&email=" . $aResult["email"];
        echo $contactInfo;
    }else{
        echo "No records were returned, sorry.";
    }
    //Close the database connection
    mysql_close($tempConn);
    ?>
```

contactInfo.php is very similar to contactList.php, but there are three differences. First of all, in this page we are expecting a variable from Flash, contactId. This variable will tell us what contact's data to grab. We use that variable in the SQL query to grab all the fields (*) from the record whose contactId field is equal to the contactId variable this page received. After we get the information, we create a string that has all the contact's data in the name/value pair format and write it to the browser. You can test this page in your browser by passing it a variable in the URL like so:

```
http://PATH_TO_YOUR_SERVER/contactInfo.php?contactId=1
```

You should be presented with a page that looks like Figure 22.7.

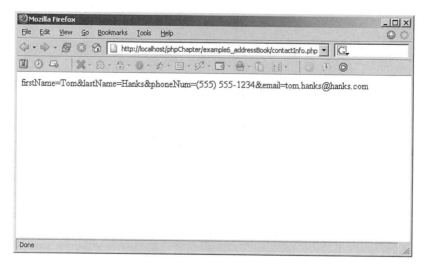

FIGURE 22.7   The requested contact's data written to the browser.

Now we need to get back to the Flash file and set it up to display the data that
`contactInfo.php` will return.

1. Open up `addressBook.fla`.

2. Create four text fields on the Content layer with the following properties:

    -   **Type**—Dynamic

    -   **Show border around text**—true

    -   **Font size**—14

3. Give these text fields the following instance names: **firstName_txt**, **lastName_txt**,
    phoneNum_txt, and **email_txt**. You can place and label them however you want, or
    refer to Figure 22.8 to see how we placed them.

4. Place the following code in the first frame of the Actions layer below the code
    already there:

```
//The listener object for when a user selects a contact
var contact_obj:Object = new Object();
contact_obj.change = function(){
    var contactId = contacts_list.value;
    var contactInfo_lv:LoadVars = new LoadVars();
    contactInfo_lv.onLoad = function(success){
        if(success){
            if(!this.error){
                firstName_txt.text = this.firstName;
```

```
          lastName_txt.text = this.lastName;
          phoneNum_txt.text = this.phoneNum;
          email_txt.text = this.email;
      }else{
          trace(this.error);
      }
   }else{
      trace("An error occurred with the connection");
   }
}
contactInfo_lv.contactId = contactId;
//send and receive the data
contactInfo_lv.sendAndLoad(
➥"http://localhost/phpChapter/example6_addressBook/contactInfo.php",
➥contactInfo_lv, "POST");
}
//add the event listener to the List component
contacts_list.addEventListener("change", contact_obj);
```

Test your movie and select a movie in the list. You should see something similar to Figure 22.8:

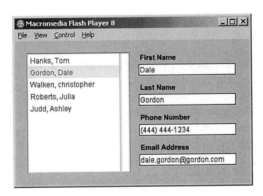

FIGURE 22.8   Our example now gets all the info for the selected contact.

File Uploads—Flash 8 Specific

One of the largest demands from the Flash development community was a file system object that could be used for file uploading. When Macromedia developed Flash 8, they incorporated the fileReference object, which allows SWF files to access the file system of the user's machine. We will use this new object in our next, and final, example.

Example 7—File Upload

In the following example, we will create a simple file upload utility. This utility will be composed of two parts: one Flash file that will access the file system and grab the file and one PHP page that will do the work of uploading said file. Create a new PHP file, save it as **upload.php**, and paste the following script inside:

```php
<?php
if ($_FILES['Filedata']['name']) {
    $uploadDir = "images/";
    $uploadFile = $uploadDir . basename($_FILES['Filedata']['name']);
    move_uploaded_file($_FILES['Filedata']['tmp_name'], $uploadFile);
}
?>
```

This page is called under the pretense that we are passing it a file to upload that has been stored in the browser's temp directory. First it checks to see whether the file is there by testing the Boolean value of Filedata. Then we define the directory to upload to and define the file to upload. Finally, we move the file from the browser's temp directory to our directory on the server.

Now we can move on to the Flash.

1. Create a new Flash file and save it as **fileUpload.fla**.

2. Create a new layer in the timeline. Rename the top layer **actions** and rename the bottom layer **content**.

3. In the Content layer, create a new rectangle, make it a movie clip named **rect_mc**, and be sure that it is big enough to hold the following:

   - Textfield
   - Instance name—**name_txt**
   - Button Component
   - Instance name—**browse_butn**
   - Label—Browse
   - Button Component
   - Instance name—**upload_butn**
   - Label—Upload

4. In the Actions layer, in frame 1, paste the following code:

```actionscript
//import the FileReference Object
import flash.net.FileReference;
//initial settings
upload_butn.enabled = false;
//the FileReference object
```

```
var file_fr:FileReference = new FileReference();
//object for listening to for FileReference events
var list_obj:Object = new Object();
list_obj.onSelect = function(){
    upload_butn.enabled = true;
    name_txt.text = file_fr.name;
}
list_obj.onComplete = function(){
    name_txt.text = "All Done";
    rec_mc.clear();
    upload_butn.enabled = false;
}
list_obj.onProgress = function (bytesTotal, bytesLoaded){
    var percent = bytesLoaded/file_fr.size;
    drawRec(percent);
}
//if a user selects cancel
list_obj.onCancel = function(){
    name_txt.text = "Cancel was selected";
}
//if there is an IO error
list_obj.onIOError = function(fileRef){
    name_txt.text = "IO error with " + fileRef.name;
}
//security error problem
list_obj.onSecurityError = function(fileRef, error){
    name_txt.text = "Security error with " + fileRef.name + ":" + error;
}
//httpError
list_obj.onHTTPError = function(fileRef:FileReference, error:Number){
    name_txt.text += "HTTP error: with " + fileRef.name + ":error #" + error;
}
//attach the listener
file_fr.addListener(list_obj);
//the event for the browse button
browse_butn.clickHandler = function(){
    file_fr.browse([{description: "JPEGs", extension: "*.JPG;*.jpg"}]);
}
//the event for the upload button
upload_butn.clickHandler = function(){
    file_fr.upload("upload.php");
    rec_mc.fillColor = Math.random()*0x1000000;
}
//drawing the rectangle
function drawRec (per){
```

22

```
    rec_mc.clear();
    rec_mc.lineStyle(0);
    rec_mc.beginFill(rec_mc.fillColor, 70);
    rec_mc.lineTo(per*rec_mc._width, 0);
    rec_mc.lineT o(per*rec_mc._width, rec_mc._height);
    rec_mc.lineTo(0, 30);
    rec_mc.lineTo(0,0);
    rec_mc.endFill();
}
```

In the preceding code we do quite a few things. First we import the fileReference object so that we can access the file system. Then we create a new instance of this object named **file_fr**. Then we create list_obj, which we will use as a listener for file_fr. Now the majority of the events (onSelect, onComplete, and so on) should be self-explanatory, but some that you may not recognize are the error-checking events. These are built-in events and allow for error checking against Security, IO, and HTTP errors that may arise. Then we attach the click handlers to the browser button, and limit the filetypes to JPEGs. The upload button click handler used the upload method to pass our file_fr object to the upload.php page. Finally, we added a little progress bar animation that used the drawing API to fill the rectangle.

5. In the same directory as your published files, create a directory named images with full read and write permissions for public users.

If you followed the instructions correctly, your file should allow you to access JPGs and upload them to the images directory on your server.

Summary

As you can see, integrating PHP with Flash can lead to some pretty powerful application development. If you followed through the lessons and examples in this chapter, you should pat yourself on the back. You now have an understanding of setting up an Apache/PHP/MySQL server, a beginner-level skill set of working with PHP scripts, and the knowledge on how to integrate PHP (or other server-side language) with Macromedia Flash. The examples we have shown here, although simple, should give you a good stepping-stone for further development. Best of luck!

CHAPTER **23**

Flash Remoting with ColdFusion

Fast-food restaurants have become a part of everyone's lives, and the driving force of most fast-food restaurants is the drive-through window. The drive-through window allows you (the client) to interact with the restaurant (the server). You drive up to the intercom, place your order to the server, the server processes your order, and by the time you drive around to the next window, your order is ready to go.

We have all heard the term *client/server* and we are familiar with the definition, but over time there has been a constant introduction of new methods to communicate between the client and server. It does not matter if it is technology or fast-food related; new methods are always being introduced to increase productivity. Macromedia also has seen the need to increase productivity by creating Flash Remoting.

Flash Remoting allows a Flash movie/application (the client) to interact with the host computer (the server). This may not sound exciting, but if you already understand the power of Flash, after you learn Flash Remoting, there is no turning back. The combination of the rich media (animation, sound, and video) that Flash allows us to integrate into our projects and dynamic data that resides on servers or web services creates an unparalleled user experience.

Can you picture your favorite fast-food restaurant without a drive-through window? After learning this technology, it will be difficult to picture Flash without Flash Remoting.

> **NOTE**
>
> You will need to have a basic knowledge of Flash ActionScript, web server administration, and at least a beginner-level understanding of scripting to understand this chapter.

What Is Flash Remoting?

Macromedia Flash Remoting, in technical terms, is an application server gateway that provides communications between Flash and remote services. I will revisit the definition throughout this chapter to bring more clarity to the meaning. In practical terms, Flash Remoting is a tunnel that allows data to flow between an external data source and the Flash Player within your web browser.

Although many other methods exist for connecting Flash to external data—built-in functions such as getURL, loadVariables, loadVars, and XMLSocket—Flash Remoting is becoming the recommended method to connect to databases and web services. What makes Flash Remoting so different?

- The Macromedia AMF (Action Message Format) protocol used to provide a lightweight means to transport data
- Performance
- Ease of use versus other methods such as XMLSocket
- Client-side data management

Flash Remoting is one of the most essential components within the Macromedia family of products and the Flash Platform. The Flash Platform has taken Flash from a lightweight animation tool to an application and communication tool with the capability to incorporate various types of rich media.

The Application Server

As the definition states, Flash Remoting is an application server gateway. So, what is the application server? In our fast-food example, the application server would be the cook. When the cook receives your order, he or she processes it and prepares your "fast" cooked meal.

The application server is the application that holds the information that you request; it processes functions that require more than the client can handle, and many other tasks.

Currently, the only supported application servers are ColdFusion MX, JRun4, and ASP.NET. Macromedia ColdFusion MX is the application server that is most commonly used with the Flash Remoting gateway. One reason for this is that Flash Remoting comes bundled with ColdFusion MX or later and is also part of the Macromedia family, which makes the integration seamless. Flash Remoting is available as a standalone application for purchase and requires installation for ASP.NET. This chapter will focus only on Flash Remoting via ColdFusion. For more information, on Flash Remoting for Java and ASP.NET, visit http://www.macromedia.com/software/flashremoting.

Many people have asked me about Flash Remoting, and when I mention ColdFusion, they say, "I don't know ColdFusion." My usual response is, "I don't either! I am a Flash Developer, not a ColdFusion Developer."

The great thing about Flash Remoting with ColdFusion is that you do not really have to learn a great deal about ColdFusion. Now, I am not an advocate of learning only what is needed to get by, because the more you know, the more you can accomplish! But if you are a Flash designer or developer, you may want to just stick to what you are good at. I come from an ASP (Active Server Pages) background and I knew the learning curve for ColdFusion was not a major one, but I also did not have a great deal of time to learn an entirely new server-side language. As you will see later in this chapter, the ColdFusion elements of Flash Remoting are fairly straightforward.

There is more than one way to skin a cat, as we see with the different types of application servers, but within Flash Remoting via ColdFusion, there are three main server-side methods to communicate with Flash:

- ColdFusion Components (CFC)

- ColdFusion pages

- Server-side ActionScript

ColdFusion Components (CFC) is the preferred method for Flash interaction with ColdFusion; thus, this chapter will focus on CFCs. More information about the other methods can be found by visiting http://www.macromedia.com/software/flashremoting.

Technical Requirements

The technical requirements for Macromedia Flash Remoting differ for each application server. This unit will focus on the technical requirements needed to complete the exercise in the chapter. For a complete list of technical requirements for your platform, visit http://www.macromedia.com/software/flashremoting.

To successfully complete the exercise in this chapter, you will need all of the following:

- Macromedia Flash MX or later

- Macromedia Flash Player 6 or later

- Macromedia Flash Remoting Components

- ActionScript 2.0

- Knowledge of ActionScript

- ColdFusion MX or later

- A ColdFusion compatible database, such as MS Access

- Knowledge of SQL (Structured Query Language)

- A web server that can run ColdFusion, such as IIS

ColdFusion and Flash Flowchart

When creating Flash Remoting applications, it is recommended that you follow a series of tasks. Although there is no standard order or starting point, I have found that creating a Flash Remoting application to connect to an external database in the order given in the following section can mean less debugging.

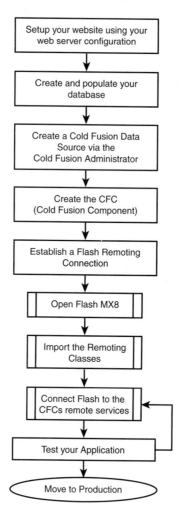

FIGURE 23.1   Flash Remoting flowchart.

Flash Remoting Setup Process

1. Create a directory on your hard drive for your files.

2. Set up your website using your web server configuration.

3. Create and populate your database.

4. Create a data source in ColdFusion via the ColdFusion Administrator.

5. Create the CFC.

6. Establish a Flash Remoting Connection.

7. Open Flash Professional MX8.

8. Import `RemotingClasses`.

9. Connect to the remote service(s) using ActionScript.

10. Set up your Flash Interface.

11. Test your application.

12. Move your application to production.

Setting Up the Server

If you do not have the pleasure of testing on a ColdFusion machine, don't worry. Macromedia ColdFusion has a fully functional Developer Edition that will allow you to test and run ColdFusion applications and pages before you move them to production.

Also, if you do not have Microsoft Internet Information Services (IIS), don't worry. ColdFusion can be configured to run as a standalone web server. This is a very useful feature that will allow you to test your scripts and ColdFusion applications. Because the ColdFusion's web server is not recommended for production, for the purposes of "real world" experience, we will configure ColdFusion to run with IIS.

Installing IIS

IIS is Microsoft's web server product. It is used on many Windows-based servers. It allows you to set up and configure websites that can be viewed on the World Wide Web.

First, you need to create a directory for your files to reside on. Name the directory **unleashedCafe** and place it on your C: drive:

```
C:\unleashedCafe
```

Now that you have your directory created, you can create a virtual directory in IIS. In Windows, IIS is usually found under Administrative Tools, Internet Information Services.

If you cannot find the icon or you do not have it installed, you can install IIS by going to Control Panel, Add or Remove Programs, Add/Remove Windows Components and place a check beside Internet Information Services IIS. Click Next and follow the instructions on the screen.

After IIS is installed, create your website by following these steps:

1. Open IIS under Administrative Tools, Internet Information Services.

2. Expand the tree until you see Default Web Site.

3. Right-click Default Web Site.

4. Select New, Virtual Directory.

5. Click Next.

6. Under Alias, type `unleashedCafeSite`.

7. Click Next.

8. Under Directory, type `C:\unleashedCafe`.

9. Click Next.

10. Under Access Permissions, leave the default settings.

11. Click Next.

12. Click Finish.

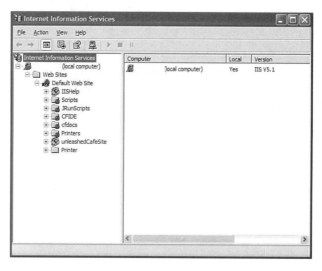

FIGURE 23.2   Installing Internet Information Services (IIS).

That's it—you have just set up a website. To test to see if your web server is running, follow these steps:

1. Open your default browser.

2. In the URL field, type in `http://localhost.`

The preceding URL is used as the default web address. An IIS welcome and setup page should be displayed. If you do not see this page, consult your IIS documentation.

Installing ColdFusion MX7

The installation of ColdFusion MX or later is fairly straightforward. After installation has started, follow the instructions in the wizard until installation is complete. During the installation process, you will be prompted to configure a web server for IIS. If you did not configure IIS during the installation process, you can manually configure IIS using the Web Server Configuration tool. To configure ColdFusion for IIS, select Start, Programs, Macromedia, ColdFusion MX7, Web Server Configuration Tool.

After the installation of ColdFusion, your server and Flash Remoting Gateway are ready for action!

Setting Up Your Database

There are many external data methods that you can connect to using Flash Remoting. This unit focuses on connecting to a Microsoft Access database. You can also connect to many other databases, such as Oracle, SQL Server, and MySQL.

> **NOTE**
>
> This unit is written under the assumption that the reader is familiar with and has basic knowledge of creating a database, tables, and populating the database.

Copy the Access database (`cafedata.mdb`) from the enclosed CD to the following directory:

`C:\unleashedCafe`

Creating a ColdFusion Data Source

1. Open ColdFusion MX7 Administrator.
2. In the ColdFusion MX7 Administrator, select Data and Services, Data Sources.
3. In the Data Source Name box, enter **unleashedMenuData**.
4. In the Driver list, select Microsoft Access with Unicode.
5. Click Add.
6. Click Browse Server and navigate to the `c:\unleashedCafe\ cafedata.mdb` file.
7. Click Apply.
8. Click Submit to complete the data source setup.
9. Ensure that OK appears in the Status column for `unleashedMenuData`.

For more information on setting up a ColdFusion Data Source, visit www.macromedia.com/devnet/mx/coldfusion.

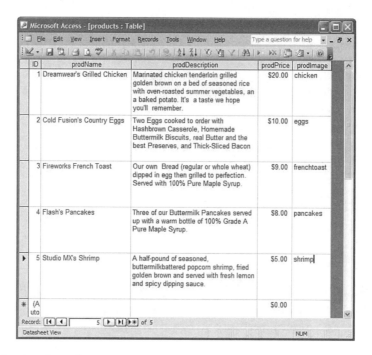

FIGURE 23.3   Database design and data.

Reviewing the Application

The files used in this chapter are included on the enclosed CD. The directory structure for the unleashedCafeSite website is displayed in Figure 23.4.

To test the application, you can copy all the files from the CD to the following location:

```
C:\unleashedCafe
```

In the previous exercises, we have already established the following:

- The web server—IIS
- A website—unleashedCafeSite
- The application server—ColdFusion

If all of the preceding items have been installed successfully, you should be able to open your default browser and type in the following:

```
http://localhost/unleashedCafeSite/unleashedCafeMain.html
```

The home page for the unleashedCafeSite should be displayed in your browser. (Refer to Figure 23.5.) You should see a listing of delectable food; if you select an item, you can view the details and an image of the plate. All this data is stored in the database! It is not local nor built into the .swf file. This is dynamic data—the beauty of Flash Remoting.

FIGURE 23.4 Directory structure for `unleashedCafe`.

After successfully reviewing the application, delete all files in
`C:\unleashedCafe` *except* `cafedata.mdb` and `\images` (the `images` directory).

FIGURE 23.5 The home page for http://localhost/unleashedCafeSite/unleashedCafeMain.html.

Let's Begin: ColdFusion Components (CFCs)

Now the fun begins. We have established the structure for our website. We have created a ColdFusion data source. Next, we will discuss how to communicate with ColdFusion. ColdFusion Components (CFCs) are the preferred method to bridge the gap between Flash and ColdFusion.

The filename of the extension .cfc will be used as the service name in ActionScript. In other words, if we name our CFC **myCFC.cfc**, within Flash our service name will be myCFC. Think of your CFC as a container that holds a lot of tasks (functions). To communicate with any of the functions, you need to call the container name—in this example, myCFC.

CFCs are composed of ColdFusion tags that allow you to create functions and return the results to Flash. The main ColdFusion tags that we will be using in this chapter are cfcomponent, cffunction, cfargument, cfquery, and cfreturn.

- **cfcomponent**—Used only once; it defines a block of code as one CFC. They are a lot like objects in that they can have their own methods and properties.

- **cffunction**—This tag is used to define one function or method. The functions we will create will be used to interact with your data source.

- **cfargument**—This tag is used to define an argument in a function.

- **cfquery**—This tag is used to define a query. This enables you to use SQL statements to query the database.

- **cfreturn**—Returns a value from the function to Flash. In this chapter, the tag will return the results of a query.

The structure of a CFC is as follows:

```
<cfcomponent displayName="componentFileName">
<cffunction name="function1" access="remote" returnType="string">
<cfquery name="myQueryName" datasource="myDataSource">
/// your statements go here
</cfquery>
<cfreturn myQueryName>
</cffunction>
<cffunction name="function2" access="remote" returnType="string">
<cfreturn "PUT SOME TEXT HERE">
</cffunction>
</cfcomponent>
```

Macromedia Dreamweaver MX or later has a built-in editor that will assist in the creation of CFCs. To take advantage of this feature, create a new file and save the file as C:\unleasedCafe\unleashedCom.cfc.

If you do not have Dreamweaver MX or later, you can simply open a text editor of your choice and save the file as C:\unleasedCafe\unleashedCom.cfc.

After your CFC has been saved, you can start creating your component. The first CFC that we will create will be used to test our Flash Remoting connection.

Type the following:

```
<cfcomponent displayName="unleashedCom">
<!— Establish a Flash Remoting Connection —>
<cffunction name="getTestConn" access="remote" returnType="string">
<cfreturn ". . . connection successful">
</cffunction>
</cfcomponent>
```

Save your file.

That's it! You now have a component with one function called getTestConn. Next, you will learn how to call this function from Flash.

Flash Remoting and ActionScript 2.0

"Learn the true power of ActionScript and you can become more powerful than any..."—sorry, wrong book. But in reality, if you do learn ActionScript, your skills and abilities with Flash will increase. In my opinion, ActionScript is the heart of Flash. Pretty much everything you can do within the Flash GUI, you can accomplish using ActionScript, but more! This unit will cover the basic ActionScript commands that are used in Flash Remoting.

> **NOTE**
>
> Make sure you have the Macromedia Flash Remoting for ActionScript 2.0 components installed on your machine. This download includes:
>
> - The Flash Remoting ActionScript API
> - The RemotingConnector component
>
> To download Macromedia Flash Remoting for ActionScript 2.0 components, visit http://www.macromedia.com/software/flashremoting.

Macromedia created the Flash Remoting ActionScript classes to assist in the configuration of Flash Remoting, to communicate with remote services (CFCs), and to control client data. To use these classes within your project, you must place the Remoting library on your stage. The Remoting.fla library contains two items: RemotingClasses and RemotingDebugClasses. They enable you to utilize some of the following classes: Connection, DataGlue, FaultEvent, Log, NetDebug, PendingCall, RecordSet, RelayResponder, ResultEvent, and Service.

The following is an overview of the steps to follow to create Flash Remoting using ActionScript 2.0:

1. Drag the RemotingClasses to the stage. You can leave the RemotingDebugClasses alone.

2. Import your required Flash Remoting ActionScript classes.

3. Establish a gateway connection and service object (CFC).

4. Communicate with the CFC (functions and methods).

5. Handle the results in Flash.

So, let's get started:

1. Open Flash 8. You now should have a new document.

2. Change the size of the stage to 550×500 pixels.

3. Save this document as **unleashedCafeMain** in
   `C:\unleasedCafe\unleashedCafeMain.fla`.

4. Rename Layer1 to **RemotingClasses**.

5. Create a new layer and name it **remotingActions**.

6. Drag the RemotingClasses to the stage. To open the Remoting library, select
   Window, Common Libraries, Remoting, and then select the remotingClasses layer.

7. Drag the clip RemotingClasses to the stage on the remotingClasses layer. Place the
   object off the stage on the upper-left side.

8. Lock the remotingClasses layer.

When RemotingClasses is placed on your stage, it also places a copy of it in your library
(F11). The RemotingClasses are exported in your SWF when you publish your movie. For
this reason, the clip can actually be deleted from the stage, but for the purposes of this
chapter we will keep it on the stage.

Import Flash Remoting ActionScript Classes

Use the import keyword to access the Flash Remoting classes without needing to use the
fully qualified name.

1. Select the remotingActions layer.

2. Open the Actions panel by selecting Window, Actions, or press F9.

The following directives need to be implemented: type the following into the Actions
panel:

```
// Import the Flash Remoting Classes
import mx.remoting.Service;
import mx.services.Log;
import mx.rpc.RelayResponder;
import mx.rpc.FaultEvent;
import mx.rpc.ResultEvent;
```

```
import mx.remoting.PendingCall;
import mx.remoting.RecordSet;
import mx.remoting.DataGlue;
```

The preceding lines of code allow us to access all the methods and properties for each of the preceding classes. Each will be explained as we move along. For more information on the import keyword and a full list of directives, visit www.macromedia.com.

Establish a Gateway Connection and Service

Now that we have access to the Service class, we can create a new Service object. The Service class allows us to establish a gateway connection while creating a link to the CFC and its functions.

The constructor for the Service class is as follows:

- **Service** (gatewayURI, logger, serviceName, conn, resp).

- **gatewayURI**—A reference to the gateway on the application server.

- **logger**—Creates a log object using the Log class; it is used to send debugging messages.

- **serviceName**—The name of the CFC, which is now considered "the service."

- **conn**—The Connection object used to connect to the service. This replaces the NetConnection class in ActionScript 1.0. If used, it will take precedence over the gatewayURI. If this object is not used, you must enter a null value.

- **Resp**—The Responder object used to handle the results from the server. If this object is not used, you must enter a null value.

Create a new Service object:

Return to the Actions panel and type the following under the last import directive.

```
// Connect to the Gateway
// Establish the Service
var unleashedService : Service = new Service(
➥"http://localhost/flashservices/gateway",
➥new Log (Log.DEBUG),
➥"unleashedCafeSite.unleashedCom",
➥null,
➥null);
```

This will allow us to link to the Flash Remoting gateway, create a log for debugging in the Output window, and establish a link to the remote service (CFC).

The URI (http://localhost/flashservices/gateway) is only a reference to a virtual directory. There is no physical directory on your server named flashservices/gateway. The gateway is considered a servlet mapping, and flashservices is a Java application context.

The new Log (Log.DEBUG) sends events and error information to the Output window within the Flash environment. This object is an optional parameter to the Service class.

The `unleashedCafeSite.unleashedCom` refers to the directory where your CFC is located. The name of our CFC is unleashedCom and it is located in `C:\unleashedCafeSite`, hence `unleashedCafeSite.unleashedCom`. In some cases it may not be necessary to include the directory name. If you are having some problems with your Flash Remoting application connecting to the CFC, this may be the first area that you attempt to debug.

Communicate with the CFC and Handle the Results

Imagine walking into your boss's office and asking for a day off. Your boss answers your request and regardless of the outcome, yes or no, you process the answer. Also, in some cases, your boss may act as if he never heard your request. This most definitely is an error! You then process this error and either ask again or fix the error.

The preceding example is a demonstration of how Flash communicates with the CFC. Flash asks the CFC for a request, the CFC processes the request and either returns the success or failure.

> **NOTE**
>
> For the sake of understanding, the terminology used in this chapter is as follows:
>
> - Method—Refers to an `ActionScript` function
> - Function—Refers to a `CFC` function

First, we need to create a ActionScript function (method). A method is simply a group of statements that perform actions. Methods allow you to consolidate many similar actions and use a single identifier to execute them.

Next, we will establish the service named unleashedService with a call to our CFC function named getTestConn(). To call this function from Flash, we need to create a PendingCall object.

To do so, open your Actions panel and type the following under the Service declaration:

```
// Test the Connection
function getTestConn(){
//Create a PendingCall objects
var testConn_pc:PendingCall = unleashedService.getTestConn();
//Use the responder property to handle the success for failure
testConn_pc.responder = new RelayResponder(this, "getTestConn_Result",
➥ "getTestConn_Fault");
}
```

There are a few ways of communicating or calling functions within the CFC from Flash. The recommended method is to utilize the PendingCall class. The PendingCall object has a responder property that provides access to an associated RelayResponder object. The

`RelayResponder` class provides a means of relaying messages to predefined methods that execute various actions based on the success or failure of the call to the `service` function. In our example, we create a new `RelayResponder` object and assign a `result` method (getTestConn_Result) and a `fault` method (getTestConn_Fault) and assign access to these methods to our `PendingCall` object (testConn_pc.responder).

Next, we will create the Result function and the `Fault` function. To do so, type the following code after the closing brace (}) of our `getTestConn()` method:

```
//Handle the Success
function getTestConn_Result(re:ResultEvent){
trace(re.result);
}
//Handle the Failure
function getTestConn_Fault(fault:FaultEvent):Void{
trace("error");
}
```

The preceding code creates two methods that handle the results. Let's look at the getTestConn_Result() method. The service function unleashedCom.getTestConn() returns a simple string "....connection successful". Take another look at our CFC:

```
<cfcomponent displayName="unleashedCom">
<!— Establish a Flash Remoting Connection —>
<cffunction name="getTestConn" access="remote" returnType="string">
<cfreturn ". . . connection successful">
</cffunction>
</cfcomponent>
```

This string is passed as an argument to the getTestConn_Result method as a `ResultEvent` object. The `ResultEvent` object has a property called `result`. The result property provides access to the returned result. So, to access this string in Flash we simply would reference the result property of the `ResultEvent` object—that is, `re.result`. Since we do not have any components or text field objects on our stage to apply the results, the quickest way for us to view the results would be to send the results to the Output window using the trace command, trace (`re.result`).

The next method, getTestConn_Fault, handles errors. In our example, if Flash Remoting returns `fault`, the method would send "error" to the Output window. The `FaultEvent` class is a very helpful means of debugging your application along with the `Log` class.

For more information on the `ResultEvent`, `FaultEvent`, and `Log` objects, refer to the Flash Remoting ActionScript Dictionary Help.

Type the following line of code to execute the `getTestConn()` method:

```
//Start the Application
getTestConn();
```

The Preceding line of code executes everything that is within the `getTestConn()` method. Now test your movie. From the main menu, select Control, Test Movie.

Your Output window should appear and look as shown in Figure 23.6:

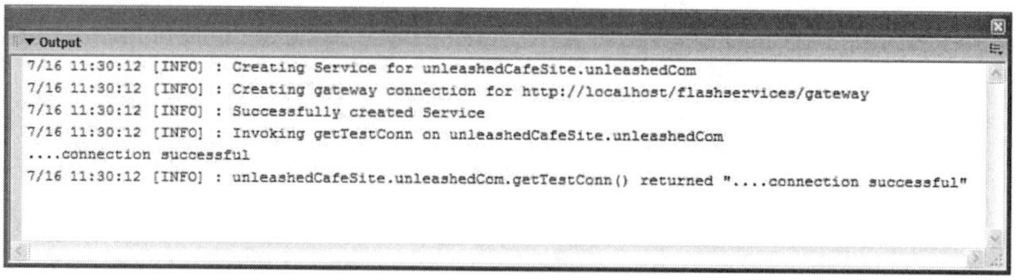

```
▼ Output
7/16 11:30:12 [INFO] : Creating Service for unleashedCafeSite.unleashedCom
7/16 11:30:12 [INFO] : Creating gateway connection for http://localhost/flashservices/gateway
7/16 11:30:12 [INFO] : Successfully created Service
7/16 11:30:12 [INFO] : Invoking getTestConn on unleashedCafeSite.unleashedCom
....connection successful
7/16 11:30:12 [INFO] : unleashedCafeSite.unleashedCom.getTestConn() returned "....connection successful"
```

FIGURE 23.6   The Output window.

That's it; you now have completed your first Flash Remoting application. You can use this script along with the CFC in each of your Flash Remoting applications to test your connection. As you build more Flash Remoting applications, you will find that connecting to your remote service can be your biggest headache. Your code should look as follows:

```
// Import the Flash Remoting Classes
import mx.remoting.Service;
import mx.services.Log;
import mx.rpc.RelayResponder;
import mx.rpc.FaultEvent;
import mx.rpc.ResultEvent;
import mx.remoting.PendingCall;
import mx.remoting.RecordSet;
import mx.remoting.DataGlue;
// Connect to the Gateway
// Establish the Service
var unleashedService : Service = new Service(
 "http://localhost/flashservices/gateway",
 new Log (Log.DEBUG),
 "unleashedCafeSite.unleashedCom",
 null,
 null);
// Test the Connection
function getTestConn(){
//Create a PendingCall objects
var testConn_pc:PendingCall = unleashedService.getTestConn();
//Use the responder property to handle the success for failure
testConn_pc.responder = new RelayResponder(this, "getTestConn_Result",
➡ "getTestConn_Fault");
```

```
}
//Handle the Success
function getTestConn_Result(re:ResultEvent){
trace(re.result);
}
//Handle the Failure
function getTestConn_Fault(fault:FaultEvent):Void{
trace("error");
}
//Start the Application
getTestConn();
```

Building Your Application

Now that we have established a connection with our remote service, we can start to create other remote services to interact with our database. CFCs can be used many ways to return data to Flash. In our next example, we will use the `<cfquery>` tag to submit SQL (Structured Query Language) statements to communicate with the database and return the results of the query to Flash. In our getTestConn function, we only returned a string. Our returnType property in our `<cffunction>` tag was set to string. When returning values from a query, our returnType property needs to be set to query.

Return to your CFC unleashedCom.cfc, and type the following after the getTestConn function and above the closing `</cfcomponent>` tag:

```
<!— Get the ID and product name —>
    <cffunction name="getProducts" access="remote"
➥ returnType="query" output="true">
    <cfquery name="productQuery" datasource="unleashedMenuData">
    SELECT ID,prodName FROM products ORDER BY prodName ASC
    </cfquery>
 <cfreturn productQuery >
    </cffunction>

<!— get all records associated with the selected product ID —>
    <cffunction name="getProductsDetails" access="remote"
➥ returnType="query" output="true">
    <cfargument name="prodID" type="numeric">
    <cfquery name="productDetailQuery" datasource="unleashedMenuData">
    SELECT * FROM products WHERE ID = #prodID#
    </cfquery>
 <cfreturn productDetailQuery >
    </cffunction>
```

We now have added two more functions, also known as remote services, to our CFC:

- getProducts—Retrieves the ID and product name from the products table in the database
- getProductsDetails—Retrieves all associated records based on the selected product ID

We now have completed our CFC. Next, we will add our elements to our Flash document. To do so, follow these steps:

> **NOTE**
>
> To save time from building the interface, you can open unleashedCafeMain_shell.fla and save it as **unleashedCafeMain.fla**.

1. Return to Flash 8.
2. Create two new layers and name them **text** and **components**.
3. Select the Components layer.
4. Open the Components panel.
5. Drag a ListBox Component to the stage.
6. Drag the Loader Component to the stage.
7. Select the ListBox component, open the Properties panel, and enter the following values:
   - instanceName—productsList
   - Width—200
   - Height—130
   - X—10
   - Y—45
8. Select the Loader Component, open the Properties panel, and enter the following values:
   - instanceName—imageHolder
   - Width—300
   - Height—300
   - X—10
   - Y—185
9. Lock the Components layer.

10. Select the Text layer.

11. From the Tools menu, select the Text tool.

12. Create three dynamic text fields and give each an instance name: **prodTitle**, **prodDesc**, and **prodPrice**. Make sure your prodDesc text field is mutiline.

13. Create two static text fields and populate them with **Description:** and **Price:**

14. Create two static text fields: Description and Price. Place them on the stage as pictured in Figure 23.7.

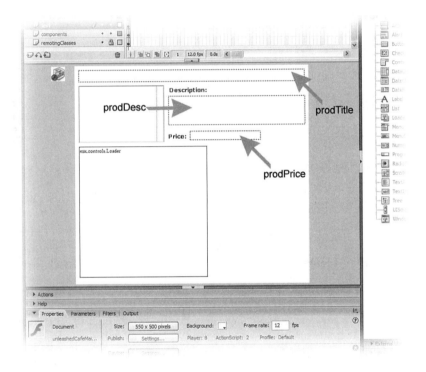

FIGURE 23.7   The Flash interface.

Now we have our interface set up and ready to go! Next, we can use ActionScript to apply the Flash Remoting results to some of our components and text fields. The great thing about Flash's capability to Test Movie is that you can view your progress as you build your movies and applications. During the following exercise, I encourage you to use Test Movie frequently to view your progress.

Comment the trace statement and add the following line:

```
//trace(re.result);
prodTitle.text = re.result;
```

The preceding code populates the prodTitle dynamic text field with the string returned from our getTestConn() function. To view the outcome, Test Movie.

In our next task, we will use ActionScript to create a new method called getProducts(), which will call the getProducts function in our CFC. We will also create a ResultEvent and FaultEvent for the getProducts() call. This task is very similar to how we created the getTestConn() procedure.

Open your Actions panel and type the following after the closing brace (}) in the getTestConn_Fault() method:

```
//Get the Products
function getProducts(){
var products_pc:PendingCall = unleashedService.getProducts();
products_pc.responder = new RelayResponder(this,"getProducts_Result",
➥"getProducts_Fault");
}
function getProducts_Result (re : ResultEvent){
    DataGlue.bindFormatStrings (productsList, re.result, "#prodName#", "#ID#")

}
function getProducts_Fault (fault:FaultEvent):Void{
    trace ("error");
}
```

The getProducts method creates a new PendingCall object for our getProducts service. It also creates a new RelayResponder object that redirects the results to either getProducts_Result or getProducts_Fault.

The getProducts_Result method handles the results from the SQL statement executed from the remote service. It receives the query results as a ResultEvent object. There are many ways to handle and manipulate data after it is returned to Flash. The DataGlue class is one method—it formats data to be used in many of the UI components, such as ListBox and ComboBox. The DataGlue parameters are as follows:

- **dataConsumer**—The UI component that will hold the data.
- **dataProvider**—The RecordSet(data) to populate the dataConsumer.
- **labelString**—The actual contents that the user will see in the UI component.
- **dataString**—The data that is associated with the labelString, hidden from the user.

The dataString parameter is vital in completing our application. It will be used to retrieve the rest of the data associated with that record. Refer to Figure 23.8.

Product ListBox

label = product name   data = product ID

Cold Fusion's Country Eggs	2
Dreamwear's Grilled Chicken	1
Fireworks French Toast	3
Flash's Pancakes	4
Studio MX's Shrimp	5

FIGURE 23.8   Products—Label and Data values.

So, what does all of this mean? When the getProducts() method is called, it executes the following SQL statement from the CFC: SELECT ID,prodName FROM products ORDER BY prodName ASC. The data that is returned from this query is sent back to Flash and is caught by the getProducts_Result() method. The data is then treated as a ResultEvent object. The result property of the ResultEvent object, re.result, actually holds all the data in the form of a RecordSet. Using the DataGlue class, we can bind fields from the re.result to the productsList ListBox.

For our application to work, we need to add a line of code to our getTestConn_Result() method to see if the connection to Flash Remoting is successful. We want the application to execute the getProducts() method. Add the following line of code under prodTitle.text = re.result;:

```
// Call the Products method
getProducts();
```

At this point your code should look as follows:

```
import mx.remoting.Service;
import mx.services.Log;
import mx.rpc.RelayResponder;
import mx.rpc.FaultEvent;
import mx.rpc.ResultEvent;
import mx.remoting.PendingCall;
import mx.remoting.RecordSet;
import mx.remoting.DataGlue;
// Connect to the Gateway
// Establish the Service
var unleashedService : Service = new Service(
```

23

```
 "http://localhost/flashservices/gateway",
 new Log (Log.DEBUG),
 "unleashedCafeSite.unleashedCom",
 null,
 null);
//Test the Connection
function getTestConn ()
{
    //Create a PendingCall object
    var testConn_pc : PendingCall = unleashedService.getTestConn ();
    //Use the responder property to handle the success or failure
    testConn_pc.responder = new RelayResponder (this,
➡ "getTestConn_Result", "getTestConn_Fault");
}
//Handle the Success
function getTestConn_Result (re : ResultEvent)
{
    //trace(re.result);
    prodTitle.text = re.result
    // Call the Products component
    getProducts();
}
//Handle the Failure
function getTestConn_Fault (fault:FaultEvent):Void
{
    trace ("error");
}
//Get the Products
function getProducts ()
{
    var products_pc : PendingCall = unleashedService.getProducts ();
    products_pc.responder = new RelayResponder
➡ (this, "getProducts_Result", "getProducts_Fault");
}
function getProducts_Result (re : ResultEvent)
{
    DataGlue.bindFormatStrings (productsList, re.result, "#prodName#", "#ID#")

}
function getProducts_Fault (fault:FaultEvent):Void
{
    trace ("error");
}
//Start the Application
getTestConn();
```

Test your movie; your application checks to see if the Flash Remoting connection is successful and then retrieves all the product names from the database and populates the ListBox (productsList). This is great, we are on our way! Next, we need to apply an event handler. When a user selects an item from the menu, we want to view the details about that particular item.

Type the following code above the //Start the Application comment:

```
// Create an Event Handler for the ListBox
var listBoxListener : Object = new Object ();
this. listBoxListener.change = function ()
{
    var prodID:Number = productsList.selectedItem.data;
    getProductsDetails(prodID);
}
this.productsList.addEventListener ("change", listBoxListener);
```

The preceding code listens for a change event for the ListBox and executes the statement within the function. The first line of code in the function retrieves the data that corresponds to the selected label and places it in a variable named prodID. (Remember, by using the DataGlue class, we are able to set the labelstring and datastring for the ListBox component.) Then it passes the value of prodID to a new method (that we have not created yet) called getProductsDetails(). For more information on the listenerObject, refer to the ActionScript Dictionary.

Next, we will create a new method called getProductsDetails(). This method will do the following:

1. Create a new PendingCall object.

2. Call our CFC unleashedCafeCom.getProductsDetails.

3. The function within our CFC executes a query in the following SQL statement:

   ```
   SELECT * FROM products WHERE ID = #prodID#
   ```

4. The query returns the records to Flash. Flash will show the details within the interface.

5. Now type the following code under the closing brace (}) of the getProducts_Fault() method:

   ```
   //Get the Products Details
   function getProductsDetails (prodID)
   {
       var productsDetails_pc : PendingCall =
   ➥ unleashedService.getProductsDetails (prodID);➥
       productsDetails_pc.responder = new RelayResponder
   ➥ (this, "getProductsDetails_Result", "getProductsDetails_Fault");
   }
   ```

```
function getProductsDetails_Result (re : ResultEvent)
{
    this.prodTitle.text = re.result.items[0].prodName;
    this.prodPrice.text = "$ " + re.result.items[0].prodPrice;
    this.prodDesc.text = re.result.items[0].prodDescription;
    var myImage:String = "images/" + re.result.items[0].prodImage + ".jpg";
    this.imageHolder.contentPath = myImage;
}
function getProductsDetails_Fault (fault:FaultEvent):Void
{
    trace ("error");
}
```

Now, let's look over the steps up to this point:

1. Remote call to getTestConn.

2. Success returned to getTestConn_Result().

3. getTestConn_Result() makes a remote call to getProducts().

4. Results returned to getProducts_Result().

5. getProducts_Result() populates the ListBox.

6. The ListBox event handler makes a remote call to getProductsDetails().

7. getProductsDetails_Result() populates the Flash interface objects with data.

In the preceding code, the prodID parameter is made when a user selects a item in the ListBox. That prodID is then passed as a parameter to the function in our remote service, unleashedService.getProductsDetails(prodID). Now, the other functions in our CFC did not take any arguments, but this function must. Let's take a look at the function in the CFC:

```
<!— get all records associated with the selected product ID —>
    <cffunction name="getProductsDetails" access="remote"
➥ returnType="query" output="true">
    <cfargument name="prodID" type="numeric">
    <cfquery name="productDetailQuery" datasource="unleashedMenuData">
    SELECT * FROM products WHERE ID = #prodID#
    </cfquery>
<cfreturn productDetailQuery >
    </cffunction>
```

This CFC uses the <cfargument> tag. This tag passes the prodID to the SQL statement. If you look at the SQL statement SELECT * FROM products WHERE ID = #prodID#, you will notice that we are selecting everything from the products table that matches the ID that was selected from the ListBox. Refer to Figure 23.8.

If you take a look at our database design (refer to Figure 23.3), if a user selects Flash's Pancakes, which has an ID of four (4), the following items are returned, just for this one record: ID, prodName, prodDescription, prodPrice, and prodImage. This query is returned to Flash and is caught by the getProductsDetails_Result() method. This method takes the query, returns it as a RecordSet object, and places it in a ResultEvent object. Because re.result is a RecordSet object, to access these records individually, we need to utilize the items property of the RecordSet object. The items property is an array that contains all the data that was returned from the server. (For more information on arrays, refer to the ActionScript Dictionary.) So we could access all the items returned by using the following syntax:

```
re.result.items[0].DATABASE FIELD NAME
re.result.items[0].prodName;
re.result.items[0].prodPrice;
```

So the following lines of code:

```
this.prodTitle.text = re.result.items[0].prodName;
    this.prodPrice.text = "$ " + re.result.items[0].prodPrice;
    this.prodDesc.text = re.result.items[0].prodDescription;
    var myImage:String = "images/" + re.result.items[0].prodImage + ".jpg";
    this.imageHolder.contentPath = myImage;
```

take the values received from the database and place them into the relating text fields and Loader component.

This may seem like a lot, but after you get the hang of it, it will be a breeze. Now if you select Test Movie, you will find that your ListBox is populated with data, but there is not a default description that is displayed with the first entry, ColdFusion's Country Eggs.

Add a line of code that will return the description for the first item in the ListBox. Put the following line of code inside the getProducts_Resut() method and under DataGlue.bindFormatStrings (productsList, re.result, "#prodName#", "#ID#").

```
getProductsDetails(re.result.items[0].ID);
```

This line will return the description and populate the Flash interface with data after the products are populated in the ListBox. That's it! Now, that wasn't so bad. All of your code in your Actions panel should look as follows:

```
import mx.remoting.Service;
import mx.services.Log;
import mx.rpc.RelayResponder;
import mx.rpc.FaultEvent;
import mx.rpc.ResultEvent;
import mx.remoting.PendingCall;
import mx.remoting.RecordSet;
import mx.remoting.DataGlue;
// Connect to the Gateway
```

```
// Establish the Service
var unleashedService : Service = new Service(
 "http://localhost/flashservices/gateway",
 new Log (Log.DEBUG),
 "unleashedCafeSite.unleashedCom",
 null,
 null);
//Test the Connection
function getTestConn ()
{
    //Create a PendingCall object
    var testConn_pc : PendingCall = unleashedService.getTestConn ();
    //Use the responder property to handle the success or failure
    testConn_pc.responder = new RelayResponder
➥ (this, "getTestConn_Result", "getTestConn_Fault");
}
//Handle the Success
function getTestConn_Result (re : ResultEvent)
{
    //trace(re.result);
    prodTitle.text = re.result
    // Call the Products component
    getProducts();
}
//Handle the Failure
function getTestConn_Fault (fault:FaultEvent):Void
{
    trace ("error");
}
//Get the Products
function getProducts ()
{
    var products_pc : PendingCall = unleashedService.getProducts ();
    products_pc.responder = new RelayResponder
➥ (this, "getProducts_Result", "getProducts_Fault");
}
function getProducts_Result (re : ResultEvent)
{
    DataGlue.bindFormatStrings (productsList, re.result, "#prodName#", "#ID#")
        getProductsDetails(re.result.items[0].ID);
}
function getProducts_Fault (fault:FaultEvent):Void
{
    trace ("error");
}
```

```
//Get the Products Details
function getProductsDetails (prodID)
{
    var productsDetails_pc : PendingCall = unleashedService.getProductsDetails
(prodID);
➡productsDetails_pc.responder = new RelayResponder
➡(this, "getProductsDetails_Result", "getProductsDetails_Fault");
}
function getProductsDetails_Result (re : ResultEvent)
{
    this.prodTitle.text = re.result.items[0].prodName;
    this.prodPrice.text = "$ " + re.result.items[0].prodPrice;
    this.prodDesc.text = re.result.items[0].prodDescription;
    var myImage:String = "images/" + re.result.items[0].prodImage + ".jpg";
    this.imageHolder.contentPath = myImage;
}
function getProductsDetails_Fault (fault:FaultEvent):Void
{
    trace ("error");
}
// Create an Event Handler for the ListBox
var listBoxListener : Object = new Object ();
this. listBoxListener.change = function ()
{
    var prodID:Number = productsList.selectedItem.data;
    getProductsDetails(prodID);
}
this.productsList.addEventListener ("change", listBoxListener);
//Start the Application
getTestConn();
```

Summary

That's it—you've done it! You have created your first Flash Remoting application. Select Test Movie and click away! Upon testing your application, you should notice the following events:

- "….connection successful" should display in the title text field for a few seconds.

- "ColdFusion's Country Eggs" should display in the title text field.

- "ColdFusion's Country Eggs" description, price, and image should display in the text fields and loader.

- Selecting a new menu item should display its description and image.

Some important things to remember:

- Plan carefully.

- Import the Remoting classes.

- Test for a connection before writing a lot of code.

- Use the FaultEvent class; this can help if problems occur.

- If you create a "site" in Dreamweaver MX or later, you can easily connect to your ColdFusion datasource and create a CFC.

Flash Remoting is a dynamic product that can enhance your Flash movies and applications. This chapter is a brief overview on Flash Remoting. I recommend that you visit http://www.macromedia.com/software/flashremoting for more documentation, tutorials, and articles.

CHAPTER **24**

XML and Flash

The preceding chapters introduced you to data integration. They used name/value pairs to keep data in text files and databases that would be brought into Flash with most likely the LoadVars object and possibly some middle ware.

This chapter introduces another way to keep data separate from Flash in an external file: XML.

XML is a buzzword on the Internet, a W3C standard, and more importantly, another language that Flash can work with and understand natively. But what is XML really?

What Is XML?

XML stands for Extensible Markup Language. I know what you're thinking; extensible starts with an "e," not an "x." Well, the reason behind using the "x" instead of "e" is that XML sounds important and "techie."

Now that we have established that the name does not really use the correct letters, we can begin to go over what exactly *extensible* means.

The extensible part of XML is the fact that XML is much more of a format and set of rules than a language. By that I mean it is a metalanguage. XML is meant to be written in such a way that there are no boundaries for what it can be—it just has simple rules. This is because XML is actually a simple form of SGML that allows you to create your own set of tags for different situations, as you will see while you move through the chapter.

Many languages used today are based on XML, such as Extensible HyperText Markup Language (XHTML), Scalable Vector Graphics (SVG), RDF Site Summary (RSS), and Wireless Markup Language (WML).

XML, in its most raw form, does not have conditionals and loop statements like some other languages; it is merely a very strict data holder.

So now you know what its definition is, but how does it work?

Formatting XML

Before we go over the basic rules and formatting of XML, you should know that you will want to use a text editor such as Notepad for building the XML files. Also, XML files can be opened in a browser such as Internet Explorer 5 (or better) of FireFox and will show errors in the form, so it is good to test your XML in browsers first to make sure it is well formed.

Here is a basic snippet of XML:

```
<root>
     <sample>
          the stuff
     </sample>
</root>
```

The first thing you will notice in this XML is that XML uses tags. If you are familiar with HTML, you know what tags are. If you are not familiar with HTML, *tags* describe the data held between them. If the data in between the tags is supposed to be a title, you would use the tags `<title>` and `</title>` on either end of the data. And in XML lingo, these tags with their data are called *elements* and that is how we will be referring to them. So you see, elements are data holders and the data they hold.

In the preceding snippet of code, you see that the first element, `<root>` has a sub-element, `<sample>`, which then contains some data. And that's XML really, just a bunch of tags and data. Of course, it can get more complicated, and we will be going over how to extend the elements and data later in the chapter.

Notice that the structure of the XML is very tree-like with its hierarchy. As we continue to move forward in building out the XML documents, you will begin to see the structure more easily.

That small example showed you the basic layout. Now we will create a larger XML document, and then discuss some of the rules for XML.

Here is the code that you should type into a text editor such as Notepad or SciTe. (Or you could get it from the website.) Save this code as `team1.xml`.

```
<team>
   <player>
        <name>Paul</name>
        <number>15</number>
        <position>Point Guard</position>
   </player>
   <player>
```

```
        <name>Matt</name>
        <number>21</number>
        <position>Small Forward</position>
    </player>
    <player>
        <name>Doug</name>
        <number>33</number>
        <position>Center</position>
    </player>
    <player>
        <name>Todd</name>
        <number>51</number>
        <position>Power Forward</position>
    </player>
    <player>
        <name>Eddie</name>
        <number>11</number>
        <position>Shooting Guard</position>
    </player>
</team>
```

And to make sure everything is fine with your XML file, open it in a browser, and you should see a layout similar to Figure 24.1.

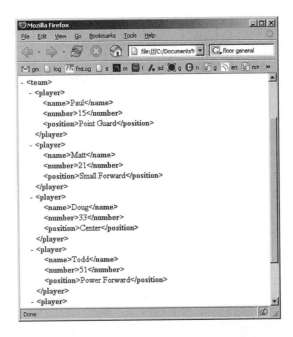

FIGURE 24.1   XML viewed in FireFox will help weed out possible bugs or typos in making sure your document is well formed.

You can use the handles on the left side of the elements to collapse or expand their substructure.

Now that you have a better idea of the structure of XML, it's time to go over some basic rules.

Rules of XML

There are several rules to creating well-structured XML. And it is very important that your XML be as perfect as possible when bringing it into Flash. The first rule concerns the first line in the document.

XML Declaration

Although we have not yet done so in our XML, it is good practice to put a line of code in the beginning that declares what the document is, and what version the document is in.

The declaration line looks like this:

```
<?xml version="1.0"?>
```

Notice that the line may look like an XML element, but in fact, it is not; it is a processing instruction because of the <? ?> surrounding it. It is used to tell the browser or parser that the content is XML, and should be viewed that way.

From here on out, all of our XML documents will have this line in it.

Open-and-Shut Case

Another rule that you may have noticed we are already implementing is that all elements that open must also close. Notice in our last example each new element started with a <team> tag and ended with a </team> tag.

Here is an example of an element:

```
<name>David</name>
```

There are elements that open and close in one single tag, and they are called empty elements, meaning they do not have any data, or sub-elements.

Here is an example of an empty element:

```
<empty/>
```

The difference is that instead of the closing slash being at the front, it is at the end of the element name.

No Overlapping

HTML is pretty soft when it comes to elements being within other elements, and the order in which they close. XML, however, is not. If you open a child element within a parent element, the child element must be closed before the parent element is closed.

Here are two examples of what I mean:

```
<parent><child>this is legal</child></parent>
<parent><child>this is not legal</parent></child>
```

The latter of the two lines of code will produce an error because it is not permitted.

Those are a couple of rules about how the elements work; there are also naming convention rules associated with elements.

Element-Naming Conventions

The elements themselves do have some rules and guidelines to follow when creating them.

- Element names, much like variables in Flash, are case sensitive, meaning that element, ELEMENT, and Element are completely different elements.

- Element names must begin with a letter or an underscore.

- Element names cannot begin with a number or a special character (@,#).

- Element names cannot begin with "xml" in upper- or lowercase.

- Element names cannot have spaces in them (you will see why when we discuss attributes).

Commenting XML

Not all information in an XML document has to be elements or data within elements: XML does support the use of comments. Comments in XML have the same syntax as comments in HTML.

Here is an example of a comment found in an XML document

```
<!—here lies a comment—>
```

They are not allowed to be within tags, however, so the following code is illegal:

```
<team <!—this won't work—> >data</team>
```

The preceding code will cause errors.

There is another part of XML we have yet to cover: attributes.

Attributes

Those familiar with HTML know what attributes are. They are snippets of data stored within tags (or in this case, within elements). They are used to distinguish between elements of the same name. After the element name, use a space, then the attribute name followed by equal signs "=" and the attribute value in quotes.

Here is an example of using attributes:

```
<root>
    <element number="1">stuff</element>
```

```
        <element number="2">more stuff</element>
    </root>
```

Notice that you still close the element with the element name only.

You can also put multiple attributes in a single element separated by spaces like this:

```
<element number="1" name="David" type="author">stuff</element>
```

And empty elements can also have attributes.

```
<element style="none" color="blue"/>
```

No Duplicating Attributes

There is one strict rule for attributes; they cannot be duplicated in the same element.

Here is an example of an illegal use of attributes:

```
<element number="1" number="2">stuff</element>
```

The preceding code cannot be used in well-formed XML documents.

Now that you understand attributes, we can revisit the XML document we created earlier.

Here is the first of two new versions of the team XML document. Save this one as team2.xml.

```
<?xml version="1.0"?>
<team>
    <player name="Paul">
        <number>15</number>
        <position>Point Guard</position>
    </player>
    <player name="Matt">
        <number>21</number>
        <position>Small Forward</position>
    </player>
    <player name="Doug">
        <number>33</number>
        <position>Center</position>
    </player>
    <player name="Todd">
        <number>51</number>
        <position>Power Forward</position>
    </player>
    <player name="Eddie">
        <number>11</number>
        <position>Shooting Guard</position>
    </player>
</team>
```

The preceding code removes the child element <name> and creates a name attribute in the player element. You can immediately see the benefits of using attributes: Now when you look through the player elements, you can see which one is which immediately without having to look to its child node. Also notice that we now include the XML declaration line in the beginning. You can see the output of this XML document in the browser in Figure 24.2.

Here is another version of the team XML document. Save it as `team3.xml`.

```
<?xml version="1.0"?>
<team>
    <player name="Paul" number="15" position="Point Guard"/>
    <player name="Matt" number="21" position="Small Forward"/>
    <player name="Doug" number="33" position="Center"/>
    <player name="Todd" number="51" position="Power Forward"/>
    <player name="Eddie" number="11" position="Shooting Guard"/>
</team>
```

In this version, we removed all the child elements and replaced them with attributes in the player elements. Also notice that all of the player elements are empty elements. You can see the output of this document in the browser in Figure 24.3.

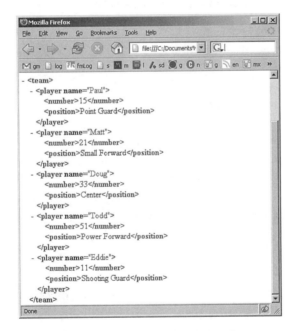

FIGURE 24.2   Use attributes to help identify multiple elements.

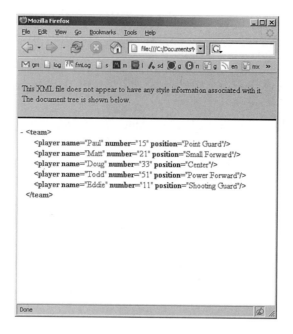

FIGURE 24.3   You can have all attributes and no child elements, and the document is still well-formed.

Now you have seen elements and attributes, but you might be confused as to which to use when.

Elements Versus Attributes

Because attributes can handle data and so can elements, the question often arises: Which one should be used for which situation? Back in Flash 5, the built-in XML parser would cycle through attributes faster than data held in elements. But with the Flash 8 Player, they parse at virtually the same speed, so now it is a matter of preference.

Personally, I tend to use attributes only to keep track of which element is which. I keep most data as element data. And, in the Web services chapter, you will see that Web services format their XML in a similar fashion.

XML and Flash

Now that you have seen the structure of the XML document, and how to create elements and attributes, it's time to go over what Flash can do with it.

Before we start loading XML into Flash, it is important to understand the XML class of object in Flash as well as some of its methods, properties, and events.

The XML **Object**

Introduced back in Flash 5, the XML object is Flash's means of loading, parsing, and handling XML data. You create XML objects the same way you create any other object.

Here is the generic code for creating XML objects:

```
var myXML_xml:XML = new XML();
```

Now that you have a new XML object, you will need to know the methods, events, and properties that make it work. And the first thing you will want to know is how to get XML into Flash with the load() method.

The load() **Method**

Similar to the LoadVars load() method, the XML load() method goes to an assigned URL and brings the entire XML document back into Flash using HTTP. When the method is called, it sets the property loaded in the XML object to false until the document is completely loaded. Any XML data held within the XML object prior to the load() method being called will be disregarded completely.

The generic layout of the code for the load() method is as follows:

```
myXML_xml.load(URL);
```

The URL parameter is a string literal path that is either relative or absolute to the XML document you want to load.

When the data has completely loaded, the onLoad event will be triggered.

The onLoad **Event**

The onLoad event is triggered when the entire XML document has been loaded. It is best used as a callback for the XML object.

Here is the generic layout of the onLoad event:

```
myXML_xml.onLoad = function(success){
    //do something
}
```

This event has a single parameter that it passes into the function, the success parameter. The success parameter is a Boolean value that represents whether the XML document loaded without errors (true) or with errors (false).

When the onLoad event fires, several properties of the XML object data is being loaded into change.

The loaded **Property**

Although it is obvious that when the onLoad event triggers, the loaded property will change, it is still important to know that this property can be monitored. The value of this property will always be a Boolean value. When the `load()` method is called, the property is set to `false`; when the content has loaded, it is changed to `true`.

```
myXML_xml.loaded;
```

The `hasChildNodes()` Method

When called, the `hasChildNodes()` method will return a Boolean value stating whether or not the loaded XML content has child nodes.

A *node* is another name for element.

```
myXML_xml.hasChildNodes();
```

This method is good for determining whether you have loaded a blank XML document.

The `status` Property

The `status` property is very important when debugging XML-driven applications in Flash. This property returns a numerical value indicating whether the XML document loaded successfully. If it does not load successfully, it will return a number representing the error that occurred.

This is the generic layout of the property:

```
myXML_xml.status;
```

And here is the list of the possible values it will return:

- `0`—No error has occurred; the information was parsed successfully.
- `-2`—Termination error with CDATA.
- `-3`—Termination error with the XML declaration.
- `-4`—Termination error with the DOCTYPE declaration.
- `-5`—Termination error with a comment in the XML document.
- `-6`—An ill-formed XML element was detected.
- `-7`—Not enough memory is available.
- `-8`—Termination error with an attribute in the XML document.
- `-9`—There is an opening element without a matching closing element.
- `-10`—There is a closing element without a matching opening element.

Now you have seen a few of the properties, methods, and events associated with the XML class (we will go over more as we continue through the chapter). Here is an example that will load an XML document that has been previously created into Flash, and then send messages about its loading success (or failure, but we hope not) to the Output panel.

1. Create a new Flash document.

2. Save the document in the same directory as the `team1.xml` file you created earlier, as **`sample1.fla`**.

3. In the first frame of the main timeline, open the Actions panel, and place this code in it:

```
//create the XML object
var myXML_xml:XML = new XML();
//create the event for when it loads content
myXML_xml.onLoad=function(success){
     if(success){
          trace("loaded - "+this.loaded);
          trace("has child nodes - "+this.hasChildNodes());
          trace("status - "+this.status);
     }else{
          trace("there was a major error");
     }
}
//now load the content
myXML_xml.load("team1.xml");
```

The preceding code does a great deal. First, it creates the XML object that will be doing all the work and holding all the data. Then it creates a callback event for when the data is loaded. In that callback function, it checks to make sure the load went successfully, and if so, it sends the properties of `loaded` and `status` as well as the result from the `hasChildNodes()` method to the Output panel. If there was a major error, it will send an error message to the Output panel. After the callback is complete, it calls the `load()` method to bring in the content.

Test the movie, and as long as you have the XML file and the Flash file in the same directory, you should have an Output panel similar to Figure 24.4.

FIGURE 24.4   Use the `onLoad` event to alert your code when the XML has loaded.

When you have successfully brought XML data into Flash, you will want to do something with the data. And the first thing you will want to get out of the XML document you are loading is the `firstChild`.

The `firstChild` Property
The `firstChild` property in the XML object represents the root node (element) in the XML document. This property not only contains the root node, but also all other nodes and their data as well. Basically, the `firstChild` property is the entire XML document.

Let's look back at our preceding example, and this time, we will send the `firstChildNode` to the Output panel.

1. Create a new Flash document.

2. Save the document in the same directory as the `team1.xml` file you created earlier, as **sample2.fla**.

3. In the first frame of the main timeline, open the Actions panel, and place this code in it:

```
//create the XML object
var myXML_xml:XML = new XML();
//create the event for when it loads content
myXML_xml.onLoad=function(success){
    if(success){
        trace(this.firstChild);
    }else{
        trace("there was a major error");
    }
}
//now load the content
myXML_xml.load("team1.xml");
```

This code is nearly identical to the preceding, except that this time, we send the XML object's `firstChild` property to the Output panel.

When this code is run, you will see all the XML data displayed in the Output panel.

The next step is to go through the other nodes and get the data you need out of them. This is referred to as "walking the tree."

Walking the tree means that we will go through each node and pull out the data or child nodes of that node, and then continue until we have walked the entire XML document. To do this, we use the `childNodes` property.

The `childNodes` Property
We use the `childNodes` property in the XML object to walk the tree of our XML data. It returns an array of the current node's children nodes. That's a little confusing; what this means is that the property will return an array of every node (element) held within a

specific node. Each element in the array is in fact an XML element and can be manipulated as such.

Before we start using this property, it is important to look at the XML we are working with again.

```
<team>
<player>
      <name>Paul</name>
      <number>15</number>
      <position>Point Guard</position>
</player>
<player>
      <name>Matt</name>
      <number>21</number>
      <position>Small Forward</position>
</player>
<player>
      <name>Doug</name>
      <number>33</number>
      <position>Center</position>
</player>
<player>
      <name>Todd</name>
      <number>51</number>
      <position>Power Forward</position>
</player>
<player>
      <name>Eddie</name>
      <number>11</number>
      <position>Shooting Guard</position>
</player>
</player>
</team>
```

This is the XML file we created and used in previous examples. And as mentioned, using the `childNodes` property, it converts this information into arrays of information, so let's take a look at what that might look like if we kept our data in arrays instead of XML.

Here is the exact same information (minus the data itself) in array format:

```
team[0]
team[0].player[0]
team[0].player[0].name[0]
team[0].player[0].number[0]
team[0].player[0].position[0]
team[0].player[1]
team[0].player[1].name[0]
```

```
team[0].player[1].number[0]
team[0].player[1].position[0]
team[0].player[2]
team[0].player[2].name[0]
team[0].player[2].number[0]
team[0].player[2].position[0]
team[0].player[3]
team[0].player[3].name[0]
team[0].player[3].number[0]
team[0].player[3].position[0]
team[0].player[4]
team[0].player[4].name[0]
team[0].player[4].number[0]
team[0].player[4].position[0]
```

I'm just glad we can use XML instead of having to create the array structure like that. Although this setup is difficult to read, you can easily see the tree-like structure our XML documents have.

So now that you've seen the structure, there is one more thing to cover before we start walking the tree: white space.

White Space

Even though we can tell just by looking at the XML structure where one node ends and the other begins, the computer has more difficulty. It uses white space, the empty space between each node, as its own node value. If we were to attempt to walk the tree without taking white space into consideration, we would receive many hard-to-find bugs.

Thankfully, Flash's XML object does have a solution, the ignoreWhite property. By default, this property is set to false, meaning the parser takes the white space into consideration. We will want to ignore that white space by setting this property to true like this:

```
myXML_xml.ignoreWhite = true;
```

Put this with the code that creates the XML object, and you do not have to worry about white space any longer.

> **NOTE**
>
> If you are compiling to the Flash 5 Player, be careful; the ignoreWhite property sometimes does not work properly. Just make sure to test carefully when using it in that version of the player. However, it works fine in the Flash 6 Player and up.

That's everything we need to know to begin walking the tree. Let's begin using the childNodes property in the following example.

1. Create a new Flash document.

2. Save this document as **sample3.fla** in the same directory as the XML files we created.

3. Open the Actions panel in the first frame of the main timeline and place these actions in it:

```
//create the XML object
var myXML_xml:XML = new XML();
//ignore the white space
myXML_xml.ignoreWhite = true;
//create the event for when it loads content
myXML_xml.onLoad=function(success){
     if(success){
           //trace the first player's stuff
           trace(this.firstChild.childNodes[0]);
           //trace the first player's name element
           trace(this.firstChild.childNodes[0].childNodes[0]);
     }else{
           trace("there was a major error");
     }
}
//now load the content
myXML_xml.load("team1.xml");
```

This code works the same as previous examples, but this time when the XML has finished loading, if there are no errors, the first player node is sent to the Output panel along with the first player's name node.

Now when you test the movie, the entire first player's node was traced along with the entire first player's name node. We will extend this example by pulling the data itself out with the nodeValue property of the node. The nodeValue property is a text node containing the actual data of the element.

Each individual node has its own set of properties:

- nodeName—This is the element name, for example, the nodeName of <team> is "team", but if the node is a text type node, the value is null.

- nodeType—This is a numerical value representing the type of node:

  - 1—An XML node containing an XML element

  - 3—A text node containing data

- nodeValue—This property returns the data held between nodes, for example, the nodeValue of <name>Paul</name> is "Paul".

So now we will go back into the code in the main timeline and replace what is there with this:

```
//create the XML object
var myXML_xml:XML = new XML();
//ignore the white space
myXML_xml.ignoreWhite = true;
//create the event for when it loads content
myXML_xml.onLoad=function(success){
     if(success){
     //trace the first player's, first elements value, name and type
          trace(this.firstChild.childNodes[0].childNodes[0].childNodes[0].node-
Value);
          trace(this.firstChild.childNodes[0].childNodes[0].nodeName);
          trace(this.firstChild.childNodes[0].childNodes[0].nodeType);
     }else{
          trace("there was a major error");
     }
}
//now load the content
myXML_xml.load("team1.xml");
```

The preceding code should look familiar by now except that we have changed what is being sent to the Output panel. This time we are sending the name of the node we are looking at, its value, and the type.

Run this code, and you should see in the Output panel the name "Paul," the node name "name," and the node type "1" meaning that it is an XML node.

Now we will go a step further and incorporate a loop statement to walk the entire tree and return all of its values.

Still in the same example, replace the code in the main timeline with the following:

```
//create the XML object
var myXML_xml:XML = new XML();
//ignore the white space
myXML_xml.ignoreWhite = true;
//create the event for when it loads content
myXML_xml.onLoad=function(success){
   if(success){
   //this will search through the players
      for(var i:Number = 0; i<this.firstChild.childNodes.length; i++){
      //this will search through the players' nodes
         for(var j:Number = 0;
      j<this.firstChild.childNodes[i].childNodes.length; j++){
            var nodeName:String =
      this.firstChild.childNodes[i].childNodes[j].nodeName;
```

```
                var nodeValue:String = this.firstChild.childNodes[i].
➡    childNodes[j].childNodes[0].nodeValue;
             trace(nodeName+"="+nodeValue);
         }
      }
   }else{
      trace("there was a major error");
   }
}
//now load the content
myXML_xml.load("team1.xml");
```

This code takes a giant step forward from what we have done so far. Now instead of hard-coding the function to walk through each node, we use two looping statements to go through each node and return not only the node's value, but also the node's name. This has tremendous implications because now we can extend our XML document not only by adding players, but also by adding information about each of those players. For instance, if you were to return to the XML document we are using in this example, give each player a new child node that represents the height of the player, and place a value for the nodes, you could still go back to Flash and run the identical code to get all the information.

Run this code and you will see all the players and their information in the Output panel.

But using childNodes is not the only way to walk an XML tree, there is also the nextSibling property.

The nextSibling Property

The nextSibling property allows you to move to the next available node in a certain level of hierarchy. For instance, if the selected node is the first player node, the nextSibling property of that node would be the next player node. If there is no nextSibling available, then null is returned.

Here is the same example we just went through, but now using the nextSibling property.

Replace the current ActionScript with this:

```
//create the XML object
var myXML_xml:XML = new XML();
//ignore the white space
myXML_xml.ignoreWhite = true;
//create the event for when it loads content
myXML_xml.onLoad=function(success){
    if(success){
     //the first player node
     var playerNode = this.firstChild.firstChild
     //this will search through the players
     while(playerNode){
            //the first property node of a player
```

```
            var propNode = playerNode.firstChild;
        //this will search through the players' nodes
            while(propNode){
                var nodeName:String = propNode.nodeName;
                var nodeValue:String = propNode.firstChild.nodeValue;
                trace(nodeName+"="+nodeValue);
                propNode = propNode.nextSibling;
            }
            playerNode = playerNode.nextSibling;
        }
    }else{
        trace("there was a major error");
    }
}
//now load the content
myXML_xml.load("team1.xml");
```

This code looks very similar to the previous version, except this time instead of using the childNodes property, we use the nextSibling property to go through the actual nodes of the XML object. We first create a variable to hold the first player node. Then we use a while loop to walk through each of the player nodes. Because the nextSibling property will return null when there are no more sibling nodes, the loop will end with the last player node. And at the end of that loop, we set the variable to its own nextSibling. Inside the main loop, we do basically the same thing with the individual player property nodes. Notice that in order to grab the data within the node using nextSibling, we call the firstChild property again.

Walking the tree this way may seem odd at first, but the more you work with it, the more you will see it is much faster than using childNodes.

So far, all we have done is use information in the nodes. Now let's go over how to get attributes out of the nodes.

The attributes **Property**
The attributes property of the XML object is used to get all known attributes of a single node, and return them in the form of an array with named elements.

For example, the following node has three different attributes:

```
<player name="Paul" number="15" position="Point Guard"/>
```

The attributes property of this node would return an array with three elements: name, number, and position.

Before we continue with the example, we should look at the XML we will be working with. You have already created it and called it team3.xml:

```
<?xml version="1.0"?>
<team>
     <player name="Paul" number="15" position="Point Guard"/>
     <player name="Matt" number="21" position="Small Forward"/>
     <player name="Doug" number="33" position="Center"/>
     <player name="Todd" number="51" position="Power Forward"/>
     <player name="Eddie" number="11" position="Shooting Guard"/>
</team>
```

Notice that this XML has no data in the nodes, only attributes. We will be working with this file in a similar fashion as the previous one.

In this example, we will grab the information from a single attribute:

1. Create a new Flash document.

2. Save this document as **sample4.fla** in the same directory as the XML files we created.

3. Open the Actions panel in the first frame of the main timeline and place these actions in it:

```
//create the XML object
var myXML_xml:XML = new XML();
//ignore the white space
myXML_xml.ignoreWhite = true;
//create the event for when it loads content
myXML_xml.onLoad=function(success){
     if(success){
          //trace each attribute individually
          trace("name="+this.firstChild.firstChild.attributes.name);
          trace("number="+this.firstChild.firstChild.attributes.number);
          trace("position="+ this.firstChild.firstChild.attributes.position);
     }else{
          trace("there was a major error");
     }
}
//now load the content
myXML_xml.load("team3.xml");
```

This code creates the XML object as before. And as before, it creates the callback for the onLoad event, but this time, we send the attributes in the nodes to the Output panel.

Run this code and you will see the same information we have covered before, but this time it was derived from attributes, not node values.

You can also get all the attributes with a specific node using the following example.

Go back into the main timeline and replace the code with this:

```
//create the XML object
var myXML_xml:XML = new XML();
//ignore the white space
myXML_xml.ignoreWhite = true;
//create the event for when it loads content
myXML_xml.onLoad=function(success){
    if(success){
       //first player node
       var playerNode = this.firstChild.firstChild;
       //create the loop statement to look through the players' attributes
       for(attribute in playerNode.attributes){
             trace(attribute);
       }
    }else{
         trace("there was a major error");
    }
}
//now load the content
myXML_xmlA.load("team3.xml");
```

What this code does is use a `for in` loop to look through the array of attributes, and it sends each attribute name to the Output panel.

Run this code and you will see all three attributes in the Output panel.

Now that we have seen how to create the XML, load the XML, and walk the tree, the next example will use some visual elements on the stage and bring it all together.

In this example, we will still be using the `team3.xml` file we created before:

1. Create a new Flash document.

2. Save the document as **teamStats.fla** in the same directory where the `team2.xml` file resides.

3. Drag a `List` component onto the stage and place it in the top left corner. Give it an instance name of **myList_list**, and leave the parameters with their default settings.

4. Drag an instance of the `TextArea` component and place it to the right of the `List` component, give it an instance name of **number_ta**, and change its properties to the following:

    - editable—false

    - html—false

    - text—Number

    - wordWrap—false

5. Copy the `TextArea` component, paste a copy under the `number_ta` TextArea component, give it an instance name of **`position_ta`**, and change the text parameter to "position."

6. Your screen should look similar to Figure 24.5.

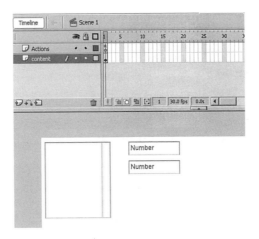

FIGURE 24.5   Components are used to speed production of the project.

7. Create another layer and call it **actions**.

8. In the actions layer, open the Actions panel and place this code in it:

```
//create the XML object
var myXML_xml:XML = new XML();
//ignore the white space
myXML_xml.ignoreWhite = true;
//create the event for when it loads content
myXML_xml.onLoad=function(success){
    //create the main array
    var myArray_array:Array = new Array();
    if(success){
            //the first player node
            var playerNode = this.firstChild.firstChild;
            //this will search through the players
            while(playerNode){
                    //create the temporary array to be placed in the main array
                    var tempArray_array:Array = new Array();
                    var atts_array = playerNode.attributes;
                    tempArray_array.label = atts_array.name;
                    tempArray_array.number = atts_array.number;
                    tempArray_array.position = atts_array.position;
```

```
                    myArray_array.push(tempArray_array);
                    playerNode = playerNode.nextSibling;
            }
    }else{
            trace("there was a major error");
    }
    //now set the data provider for the List component
    myList_list.dataProvider = myArray_array;
}
//now load the content
myXML_xml.load("team3.xml");
//now create the object to listen to the List
var listListen:Object = new Object();
//now the event for when a user selects an item
listListen.change=function(){
    number_ta.text = myList_list.selectedItem.number;
    position_ta.text = myList_list.selectedItem.position;
}
//add the event listener to the List component
myList_list.addEventListener("change",listListen);
```

The preceding code creates the XML object to handle the XML data. It creates the callback for when the XML is completely loaded, and within this callback, it creates an array, which we use later in the code. It loops through the XML placing information into a temporary array that is then added to the end of the main array. At the end of the loop, we set the dataProvider property of the myList_list List component. After that, it loads the XML into the XML object.

Then it creates a generic object to listen for the event that is triggered when a user selects a player from the List component. When a user makes a selection, the TextArea components receive the information, and the number and position of the selected player is shown. After that, the code sets the event listener to our List component, myList_list.

Run this code, and you will see that every time you click a player's name, his information is shown in the TextArea components, as shown in Figure 24.6. You can go out and change the XML file to have more players, and this application will still work. That's the benefit of using XML data and Flash; you can build rich, engaging interfaces that will always run with the newest information.

So far we have covered how to work with XML manually. Now with Flash Professional 8, you can use the XMLConnector component to help speed up production.

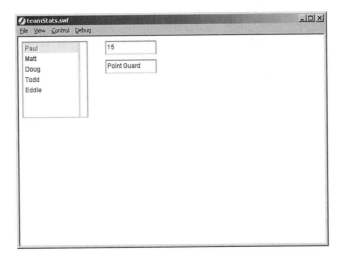

FIGURE 24.6   Every time a player's name is selected, his information is displayed in the application.

The XMLConnector **Component**

The Professional edition of the new Flash 8 comes with a set of data components. These components are meant to help Flash developers and designers to quickly and efficiently hook their applications into external data sources. The one we are focusing on in this chapter is the XMLConnector component.

This component will assist you in connecting to outside XML documents. It has five parameters:

- URL—The path either relative or absolute to the XML document.

- direction—This parameter is for either sending or receiving XML information or both.

- ignoreWhite—This parameter is similar to the ignoreWhite property of the XML object; it will set whether or not Flash should take into account the white space of the XML document when parsing.

- multipleSimultaneousAllowed—This parameter sets whether the connector can make several calls to the XML document at once.

- suppressInvalidCalls—If true, this parameter will halt the trigger() method being called if data bound parameters are invalid.

Those are the parameters of the XMLConnector component. The next step is to know how it works.

The `trigger()` Method

The `trigger()` method is called on an instance of the `XMLConnector` component to go out and either send data to an XML document, or receive data from an XML document. It has no parameters.

Its generic layout is as follows:

```
myConnector.trigger();
```

Now what do we do with the data when it comes back?

The `result` Event

The `result` event is the event we use when the XMLConnector receives data. This event uses a special component event listener.

Here is the generic layout of how to use the `result` event:

```
listener.result=function(result){
    trace(result.target.results);
}
```

This event has one parameter, the `result` parameter. The `result` parameter is the XML being received, and to use it, use `result.target.results`, which will be the actual XML that has been returned.

Enough talking about what it does. Let's do an example:

1. Create a new Flash document.

2. Save this document as **xmlConnector.fla** in the same directory as the `team1.xml` file.

3. Drag an instance of the `XMLConnector` component onto the stage, give it an instance name of **xmlCon**, and use these settings for the parameters:

   - URL—team1.xml

   - direction—receive

   - ignoreWhite—true

   - multipleSimultaneousAllowed—false

   - suppressInvalidCalls—false

4. Now create a new layer and call it **actions**.

5. In the actions layer, open the Actions panel, and place these actions in it:

```
//create the listener object
var xmlListen:Object=new Object();
//create the event
xmlListen.result=function(result){
```

```
    var playerNode = result.target.results.firstChild.firstChild;
    //this will search through the players
      while(playerNode){
        //the first property node
        var propNode = playerNode.firstChild;
          //this will search through the players' nodes
          while(propNode){
             var nodeName:String = propNode.nodeName;
             var nodeValue:String = propNode.firstChild.nodeValue;
             trace(nodeName+"="+nodeValue);
           propNode = propNode.nextSibling;
           }
        playerNode = playerNode.nextSibling;
        }
}
//add the event listener
xmlCon.addEventListener("result", xmlListen);
//trigger the XML Connector to get the XML
xmlCon.trigger();
```

Some of the preceding code should look familiar. We created a listener for the result event, and then created the event. In the event, we capture the first player node of the XML data coming back to the connector. We walk the tree the same way we would any other XML object, and send the results to the Output panel. Then we add the event listener to the XMLConnector component, and finally trigger the component to go out and get the XML.

Run this movie, and you should see a screen similar to Figure 24.7. Notice that the information is sent to the Output panel just as it was before, and the component we dragged out onto the stage is now invisible.

FIGURE 24.7   Using the XMLConnector can have the same results as the XML object with a faster implementation for the developer.

There is another component that can make quick work of an XML document, and that is the `Tree` component.

The `Tree` **Component**

The `Tree` component is a Flash Professional only component that can be tied directly to an `XMLConnector` component so that you can have your data brought in, parsed, and set to an interface component with only one line of ActionScript.

The `Tree` component looks for a specific attribute in the XML document to display, namely the `label` attribute. So before we go into the example, we will need another XML document like the one below.

Create a new XML document and save it as **teamTree.xml** with this data:

```
<?xml version="1.0"?>
<node label="Starting 5">
  <node label="Paul">
          <node label="15"/>
          <node label="Point Guard"/>
  </node>
  <node label="Matt">
          <node label="21"/>
          <node label="Small Forward"/>
  </node>
  <node label="Doug">
          <node label="33"/>
          <node label="Center"/>
  </node>
  <node label="Todd">
          <node label="51"/>
          <node label="Power Forward"/>
  </node>
  <node label="Eddie">
          <node label="11"/>
          <node label="Shooting Guard"/>
  </node>
</node>
```

Notice that we name every node "node" because those names do not matter, only what we set as the label attribute. Now we have our XML, let's go through the final example.

1. Create a new Flash document.

2. Save this document as **treeExamp.fla** in the same directory as the teamTree.xml file.

3. Drag an instance of the XMLConnector component onto the stage, give it an instance name of **xmlCon**, and use these settings for the parameters:

   - URL—teamTree.xml
   - direction—receive
   - ignoreWhite—true
   - multipleSimultaneousAllowed—false
   - suppressInvalidCalls—false

4. Drag an instance of the Tree component onto the stage and give it an instance name of **treeComp** and make it about 200x200 in size.

5. Create a second layer and name it "actions," then put the following code in the first frame of that layer:

```
//create the listener object
var xmlListen:Object=new Object();
//create the event
xmlListen.result=function(result){
    treeComp.dataProvider = result.target.results;
}
//add the event listener
xmlCon.addEventListener("result", xmlListen);
//trigger the XML Connector to get the XML
xmlCon.trigger();//
```

This code does basically what the code in the previous example did, but this time it sets the XML being returned directly to the dataProvider property of the Tree component. This could have been done with even less code if we were using Data Binding, but that will be discussed in the next chapter.

Test the movie, and you will be able to select the team, as well as the individual players to see more data like Figure 24.8.

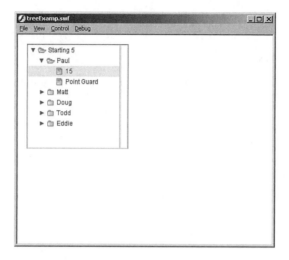

FIGURE 24.8   Combining the `Tree` component with the `XMLConnector` component can make quick work of an XML driven interface.

Summary

This chapter has taken the idea of dynamic content a different direction than what we have seen so far. XML is much more than a simple buzzword on the Internet; it is well-formed and structured data that nearly all applications on the Web can run on, including any you build in Flash.

We not only covered how to use it in Flash, but also how to create well-formed XML, a good asset to have. We even covered the `XMLConnector` and Tree component, the easiest way to connect and work with your XML documents.

The next few chapters build on XML as they go into Web Services and how to bring them into Flash.

CHAPTER **25**

Web Services and Flash

So far, we have been moving data with name/value pairs, static XML documents, or with server-side programming and LoadVars. This chapter will change all that by opening your eyes to the world of web services.

We will go over what web services are and why you use them, as well as how to create them and how to tie into them using Flash 8. We will finish up by creating an application to search the web for DVDs using the Amazon.com API.

What Is a Web Service?

A web service is exactly what it says; it's a service on the web. So what "service" do web services provide?

A web service's goal is to provide raw data in XML format to any application that makes a request to it. That may not make sense by itself, so here is exactly what a web service does.

A web service sits on a server much like any server-side page, and when a request is made to it, the web service will perform a desired task and return data in the form of XML. XML, as you learned in the previous chapter, is a language that nearly any application can read because it is in fact a meta-language made up of customized tags containing well-formed and structured data.

That is what a web service is and does, but that doesn't explain why anyone should use them.

Why Use Web Services?

Some time ago, I was working on a sales force application that managed all the retail outlets for a client's sales force. I made all the Flash pieces and the objects necessary for it to work, but when I started testing it with live data, it wouldn't return all the correct information. I looked through the database itself at the point where it was getting hung up, and lo and behold, there was an ampersand in not only one, but a few of the store names. Remember back in Chapter 20, "Introduction to Data Integration," where you were introduced to data integration with Flash? You learned that name/value pairs are separated by ampersands. This means that when the parser reached the store name with the ampersand, it would think that part of the name was data, and the other part was the beginning of the next name/value pair, like this:

The original store name: `A&B Grocery`

Was thought to be: `name=A&B Grocery=`. You can see how frustrated I was after checking everything else first.

This is a very common problem for developers working with middleware, having to check individual data pieces to make sure each one fits exactly. And then you have to make sure the data cannot be put back in with an ampersand so that the problem won't happen again. Even worse, what if I can't see the data and the middleware page? I would be stuck with no idea of what is causing the strange error with my data.

This is where web services really fit in. Because web services send back XML data, all I have to do is create a parser to parse XML, and then it does not matter what data is coming back because the XML has self-describing tags.

Web services can be written in several languages, but in this chapter, we will use ASP.NET. Each web service written will have a WSDL (Web Services Description Language) file that will describe our web service to anyone who intends to use it. More on that later in this chapter.

To use .NET you must have a personal web server (or a web server on the web with .NET installed) and you must install .NET. You can get .NET from this link:

```
http://www.microsoft.com/downloads/details.aspx?
➥familyid=9B3A2CA6-3647-4070-9F41-A333C6B9181D&displaylang=en
```

Not all examples will require you to have .NET or a personal web server installed, but to re-create some of the web services from this chapter, you will need it.

Creating a Web Service

To create a web service, open your favorite text editor, such as Notepad or SciTe (http://www.scintilla.org/) for PC or TextEdit for Mac users. ASP.NET supports several languages for web services, but we will be using the C# language because it closely mimics ActionScript.

The first line of a web service will declare that we are in fact creating a web service, which language we are using, whether to allow debugging, and any web service classes we will be creating.

Here is a generic template for the first line:

```
<%@ WebService Language="c#" debug="true" class="MyClass" %>
```

In the preceding code, we declare that we are creating a web service in the C# language, that we will allow debugging (very important in case you make minor errors), and that we will be creating a web service class called MyClass.

> **NOTE**
>
> Notice that the first line of the web service falls within the <% %> tags. This is because we want the browser to recognize anything between these two tags as a server-side script. The rest of the web service itself does not require them, but the first line does.

After that, you need to provide a few web service namespaces that we will need to produce the correct results:

```
using System.IO;
using System.Web.Services;
```

In this code, we used the keyword using to signify that we will be using the System.IO and the System.Web.Services namespaces.

After that, we begin to create the web service methods. These are the methods that will be called from the web service itself; they describe what the service does.

First, declare the class of web service:

```
public class MyClass: System.Web.Services.WebService{
```

Notice that this class is public, which means it can be called from outside the service itself. After that, we use the class keyword and name our class MyClass. Then we begin to create the service with the System.Web.Services.WebService class.

The next step is to begin declaring the web methods. To do this, you use the keyword WebMethod in brackets, along with a description, if desired, that will help anyone looking at the web service tell what each web method is doing.

```
[WebMethod(Description="Description of the Web method")]
```

Then create the web method itself declaring whether it is private or public. Before you name the web method, you have to declare what data type will be returned. For example, the following will return an integer data type, so we use the keyword int:

```
public  int myMethod(){
        return 15;
    }
}
```

Now that you have seen the basic parts of a web service, we can begin to create them.

The first web service will simply return a string saying "hello world". So open your favorite text editor and place this code in it:

```
<%@ WebService Language="c#" debug="true" class="Hello" %>
using System.IO;
using System.Web.Services;

public class Hello: System.Web.Services.WebService{

  [WebMethod(Description="Say hello")]
  public  string sayHello() {
       return "hello world";
    }
  }
```

The preceding code does everything we have discussed so far. It declares that we are creating a web service in C#. It then gets the classes we need to use. After that, it creates the `Hello` class and then the method `sayHello`, which will send the string literal "hello world" back to us.

Now save as `hello.asmx` in either your web server or PWS (personal web server). The directory on most web servers including PWSs is at `c:\inetpub\wwwroot\` or one of its subdirectories. The .asmx extension is the extension for web services on .NET.

Map to the new file using the browser, using `http://` not `file://`, and you should see a screen similar to Figure 25.1.

NOTE

You must browse to web services to view them in action. Otherwise, the browser will attempt to open them up in an application.

This screen is created automatically to help test the web service without an application. You can see all the web methods listed (in this case, just the `sayHello` method) and their description if it was declared. Select the `sayHello` method, and you will be taken to a screen that looks like Figure 25.2. Here you can invoke (run) the method to see its results. Also, you can see all the information about the method, including its return value, and if we had any parameters, they would be shown here as well. Choose the Invoke button, and another browser window will pop up with XML data as shown in Figure 25.3. This is the result of the web service. Now in this case, it's not all that impressive, but as we move forward it will become so.

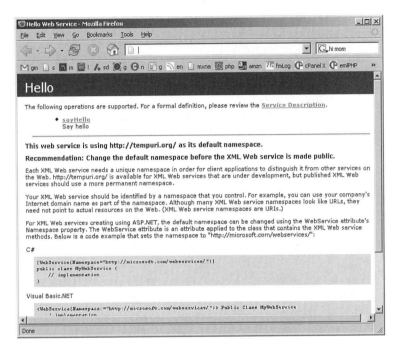

FIGURE 25.1   You can test your web methods without an application.

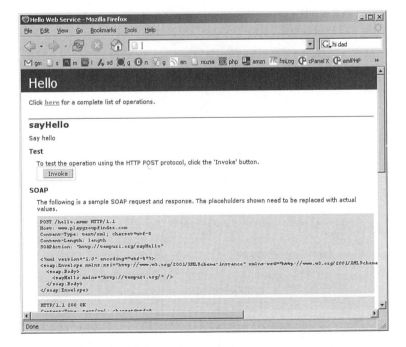

FIGURE 25.2   The web method information.

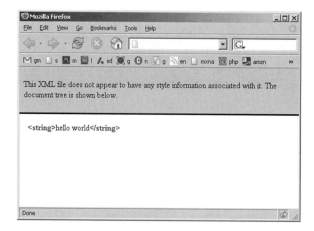

FIGURE 25.3   The results from the web service.

And the final page to look at is the WSDL, so return to the original page, and at the top, choose the Service Description link; the window will fill with more XML data, as shown in Figure 25.4. This tells any user of the web service everything they need to know to use it. It shows all the methods, their return values, and their parameters.

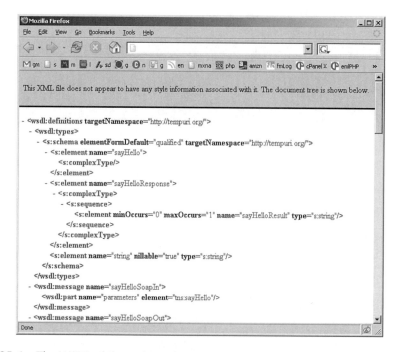

FIGURE 25.4   The WSDL of the web service.

Consuming Web Services with Flash

Now that you see how to make a basic web service and how to test it, let's take it a step further and bring the data into Flash.

We will begin working with the XML object to bring the data in, and finally move over to using the WebServiceConnector component.

Using the XML Object

We went over the basics of the XML object back in Chapter 24, "XML and Flash." Now we are going to use it to consume the web service that we have created.

To absorb a web service with the XML object, when you load it in, use the path to the web service, followed by a slash, and then the name of the web method being called, like this:

```
myXML.load("http://localhost/myWebService.asmx/myWebMethod");
```

And after it is loaded, you will have to parse the data as an XML document.

This example uses the web service we have already created to bring in the phrase "hello world" and put it in a dynamic text field on the stage.

1. Create a new Flash document.

2. Draw a dynamic text field on the stage, give it an instance name of **myText_txt**, and make sure the border setting is turned on.

3. Create a new layer called **actions**.

4. In the Actions layer, open the Actions panel, and place this code in it:

```
//create the XML object
var myXML_xml:XML = new XML();
//ignore white space
myXML_xml.ignoreWhite = true;
//create the event for when data is loaded
myXML_xml.onLoad=function(success){
    if(success){
        myText_txt.text = this.firstChild.firstChild.nodeValue;
    }else{
        myText_txt.text = "An error has occurred";
    }
}
//load the web method result
myXML_xml.load("http://localhost/hello.asmx/sayHello");
```

The preceding code first creates an XML object to absorb the web service. It then sets the ignoreWhite property to true. After that, it creates the event callback for the XML object, so that when it receives data back, it will send the result to the text field. Finally, it loads the web method.

Test the movie and you will see that the phrase "hello world" has appeared in the text field.

NOTE

If you are running certain versions of the .NET framework, the preceding code may not work correctly by default. If this is the case, add this to the `web.config` file located on `c:\`:

```
<webServices>
            <protocols>
              <add name="HttpGet"/>
            </protocols>
</webServices>
```

Add the preceding code before the `</system.web>` closing tag, and then restart your computer.

That example demonstrated how to absorb a web service with the XML object, but there is a much better way to do it using Flash Remoting.

Flash Remoting

Because it was mentioned back in Chapter 23, "Flash Remoting with ColdFusion," we won't go over it in great detail here, but it is important to mention Flash Remoting again. Flash Remoting is a way of interacting with web services in a whole new light. Instead of receiving XML back from the web service, Flash Remoting returns objects that are easier to use and parse.

If you do not have Flash Remoting, you can download the free developer edition here:

`http://www.macromedia.com/software/flashremoting/downloads/components/`

Also, for Flash Remoting to work with the web services we create in this chapter, you will need the .NET Framework Redistributable installed, which can be found here:

`http://www.microsoft.com/downloads/details.aspx?FamilyId=262D25E3-F589-4842-8157-034D1E7CF3A3&displaylang=en`

When you complete the download, a new directory in your local host directory will be created called `flashremoting`. This directory is important because it will hold the gateway we need to go through to use Flash Remoting. Now you will be able to absorb web services with it instead of using the XML object.

Again, for more on Flash Remoting, check out Chapter 23.

Another great way to connect to web services is through the WebServiceConnector component. But before we can use it, we have to set up our web services in the Web Services panel.

The Web Services Panel

The Web Services panel is an easy way to keep track of all of the web services you are working or experimenting with. To open it, go to Window, Other Panels, Web Services.

The window that opens up will look like Figure 25.5. You will see two buttons at the top, the Define Web Services and the Refresh Web Services buttons. The Refresh Web Services button refreshes all the information with regard to the current web services in the panel. The Define Web Services button adds web services.

Click the Define Web Services button to see the Define Web Services dialog box, as shown in Figure 25.6. Add the web service you have just created using the path to its WSDL:

http://localhost/hello.asmx?WSDL

After it has been entered, click OK and you will be taken back to the Web Services panel, where your newly added web service will appear. Notice that if you click the little plus sign beside the web service, it will show all the available methods (just one in this case), and you can dig down further to see all the parameters that need to be sent (in this case, zero) and everything being returned. This is very helpful when working with web services, and it makes tying components together much easier, as you will see later.

FIGURE 25.5   The Web Services panel.

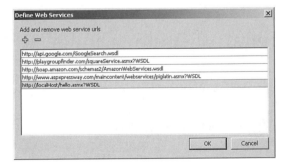

FIGURE 25.6   The Define Web Services dialog box.

Now you have a web service defined, we can go over how to use the WebServiceConnector component.

The `WebServiceConnector` Component

The `webServiceConnector` component is designed to easily and quickly connect to web services on the web. To use it, drag it onto the stage, set the URL for the web service's WSDL, select the web method you are going to call, and trigger it.

Data from the `webServiceConnector` comes back as an object, as you will see in the following example.

1. Create a new Flash document.

2. Drag an instance of the `WebServiceConnector` component onto the stage; give it an instance name of `myConnector`, set its WSDLURL parameter to `http://localhost/hello.asmx?WSDL` (because you put it in the Web Services panel, you can use the drop-down menu and choose it), and then set the operation parameter to `sayHello` (it will be the only choice in the drop-down).

3. Drag an instance of the `TextInput` component onto the stage and give it an instance name of **results_ti**.

4. Create a new layer called **actions**.

5. In the first frame of the Actions layer, open the Actions panel and place this code in it:

```
//create an object to listen for when the WebServiceConnector receives data
var resultListen:Object = new Object();
//create the event for the listener
resultListen.result=function (myResults) {
    results_ti.text = myResults.target.results;
}
//add the event listener to the WebServiceConnector
myConnector.addEventListener("result", resultListen);
//connect to the web service
myConnector.trigger();
```

The preceding code creates a listener object for the `webServiceConnector` component. It then creates an event callback, passing it one parameter, the `myResults` parameter, which will be the results coming back from the web service. We then add the event listener to the `webServiceConnector` and finally call the `trigger()` method, which will activate the `webServiceConnector`.

When you test the movie, you will get the same result as before using this web service. This example just shows how simple it is to connect to web services using the `webServiceConnector`.

But what if it were simpler?

Data Binding

Data binding is a feature introduced back in Flash MX 2004 Professional. It allows you to tie properties of components to one another that will automatically update when certain component events fire. It makes creating web-service-driven applications that much easier because there is very little code required. In fact, you will see that the preceding example can be done in a single line of code.

1. Return to the stage and open up the Actions panel in the first frame of the actions layer. Remove all but the last line, so the code should now read like this:

   ```
   myConnector.trigger();
   ```

2. Now select the `WebServiceConnector` component, go to the Component Inspector panel (Window, Component Inspector), and select the Binding tab.

3. Select the Add Binding button, and the panel should then look like Figure 25.7. Choose `results:String` and click OK.

4. Now you will see the "results" data binding in the Component Inspector panel. Select it and click in the `bound to` field.

5. When you do this, a magnifying glass will appear at the end of the field. Select it, and the Bound To dialog box appears as shown in Figure 25.8. (You can also double-click this field to get the same result.)

6. Select the `TextInput` component in the left window and click OK.

Now test the movie again.

Again, you get the same results as before, but the difference is that the only ActionScript in this file is the line that activates the `webServiceConnector` component.

FIGURE 25.7 The Add Binding dialog box used to add data bindings between components for fast development.

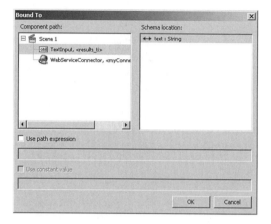

FIGURE 25.8   The Bound To dialog box.

Now that we are interacting successfully with our web service and have found the easiest way to work with them, let's actually make a useful web service.

In the following example, you will create a web service that accepts a parameter, then squares it, and returns the results.

Open a text editor, create a new file and enter the following code, and then save the file to your web root directory as squareService.asmx.

```
<%@ WebService Language="c#" debug="true" class="Square" %>
using System.IO;
using System.Web.Services;

public class Square: System.Web.Services.WebService{

  [WebMethod(Description="Square the number")]
  public  int squareNum(int sentNum) {
      int myReturn = sentNum*sentNum;
      return myReturn;
  }
}
```

Much like our previous web service, this one starts off by declaring that it is a web service written in C#. It then grabs the object classes we need. Next, it declares the web service class. After that, we declare the web method and set its description. Then we create the web method. Notice we declare that the result being returned will be an integer. And the parameter being sent will also be an integer.

Save this file and then browse to it and choose the squareNum web method. You will see a screen like Figure 25.9. As you can see, the web service has provided a field where we can place a number to test, so enter the number **8** and click Invoke. You should then see another browser screen like Figure 25.10, indicating that it worked.

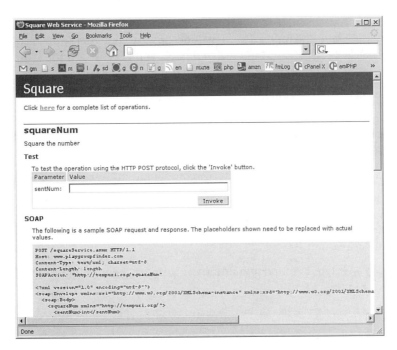

FIGURE 25.9 The web service provides a field to test the web method.

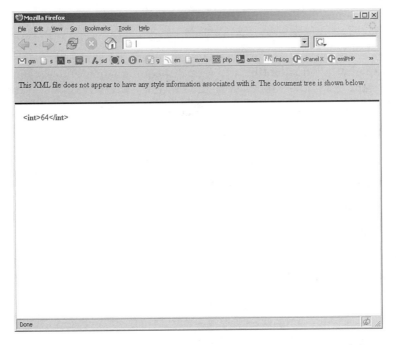

FIGURE 25.10 Use parameters in web methods to make web services work for you.

Now we will use the webServiceConnector component to create a small app that will use this web service. Again, the only code we will need is the code that will activate the connection. But before you can use the web service, you have to add the WSDL to the Web Services panel, so do that first (http://localhost/squareService.asmx?WSDL).

1. Create a new Flash document.

2. Drag an instance of the WebServiceConnector component onto the stage and give it an instance name of **myConnector**; set the WSDLURL parameter to http://localhost/ squareService.asmx?WSDL, and set the operation parameter to squareNum.

3. Now drag an instance of the TextInput component onto the stage and give it an instance name of **num_ti**.

4. Drag an instance of the Button component onto the stage under the num_ti TextInput component; give it an instance name of **square_butn**, and change its label to square.

5. Copy the TextInput component and paste it under the button; change its instance name to **results_ti**.

6. Select the myConnector, WebServiceConnector and open the Component Inspector panel.

7. As you did before, choose the Binding tab and select Add Binding; select sentNum: Integer and click OK.

8. Select the Bound To field, bind it to the num_ti TextInput component, and click OK.

9. This time, we will be do something a little different. Select the Formatter field and choose Number Formatter (this will format the information of the TextInput component to a number so it can be used with the web service).

10. Select Add Binding again and choose results:Integer.

11. Select the Bound To field and bind it to the results_ti TextInput component.

12. Create a new layer called **actions**.

13. Place the following code in the first frame of the Actions layer:

```
//create the listener object
var clickListen:Object = new Object();
//add the event to the listener
clickListen.click = function(){
    myConnector.trigger();
}
//finally add the event listener to the button
square_pb.addEventListener("click", clickListen);
```

The preceding code is nothing new; we create the event listener object. Then we set the event to the listener that will trigger the `webServiceConnector` to activate. And finally, we add the event listener to the `Button` component.

Now that you have seen how to create and consume web services, let's create an application that will use a web service that we did not create.

Consuming Outside Web Services

So far, the only web services we have worked with are the ones we built ourselves. That's not the idea behind web services. The idea is that anyone can build them, and anyone can use them as long as they know how to work with them.

There are a couple of great sites on the web that store references to web services for people to work with:

```
http://www.webservicex.net/WS/default.aspx
```

```
http://www.xmethods.com/
```

The one we will be using can be found at

```
http://www.aspxpressway.com/maincontent/webservices/piglatin.asmx
```

This web service will translate a string of text we send it to pig Latin and return it.

For those not familiar with pig Latin, it's a language that moves the first letter from the front of certain words to the end and then adds an "ay" to it.

So if you have a sentence just like this, it would read like this:

So if you avehay a entencesay ustjay ikelay isthay, it ouldway eadray ikelay isthay.

The following example will build an application to do just that. But before you jump in to the example, add the WSDL to the Web Services panel (http://www.aspxpressway.com/maincontent/webservices/piglatin.asmx?WSDL).

1. Create a new Flash document.

2. Drag the `TextArea` component onto the stage, give it an instance name of **text_ta**, and change its dimensions to 250×130.

3. Drag an instance of the `Button` component onto the stage under the `TextArea` component; give it an instance name of **translate_butn**, and change its label parameter to Translate.

4. Then drag an instance of the WebServiceConnector component onto the stage and give it an instance name of **myConnector**.

5. With the WebServiceConnector component selected, open the Component Inspector to the Bindings tab and click the Add Binding button. Select the **textToTranslate:String** option and click OK. Then bind it to the TextArea

component. Add another binding and this time select the **results:String**, click OK, and bind that to the TextArea component as well. (This will make it so the text being translated will come from and be returned to the TextArea component.)

6. Create a new layer called `actions`.

7. In the first frame of the Actions layer, open the Actions panel and place this code in it:

```
//create the listener object
var tranObj:Object = new Object();
//the event
tranObj.click = function(){
    myConnector.trigger();
}
//add the event listener to the Button component
translate_butn.addEventListener("click", tranObj);
```

Now test the movie, place this paragraph in (or one of your own), and click the Translate button. When the results are returned, you should see something like Figure 25.11.

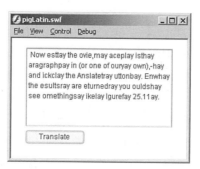

FIGURE 25.11   Using external web services with Flash is fun and easy with the WebServiceConnector and Data Binding.

Now that you have seen how to absorb web services created by other people, you might want to start working on some of the major web services on the web, such as the Google.com web service found at

http://www.google.com/apis/

Or you might want to experiment with the web service API of the mother of all web apps—Amazon.

Absorbing the Amazon Web Service

Amazon is one of the most well-known Internet storefronts on the planet, and they have opened up their product database to the public for free.

With the Amazon web service, you can search their database web for books, DVDs, and more, and have the results sent back to an application you design and build.

The first thing you will have to do is get your key from Amazon by signing up at

http://www.amazon.com/gp/browse.html/103-7710202-8564650?%5Fencoding= UTF8&node=3435361

The key lets Amazon know who is using the search engine.

When you have gotten your personal key, you will need to download the sample file for this application from the accompanying website. The application itself has everything but the key.

The purpose of this application is to see the power of web services. This example allows you to search Amazon's DVD collection at will, and it returns 10 results each time. When one of those results is selected, it displays an image of that DVD. When you have downloaded the sample application from the website and have gotten your key from amazon.com, open the file `amazonFinal.fla` and follow these steps to make it work:

1. Select the `WebServiceConnector` component in the top left of the stage.

2. Open the Component Inspector panel (Window, Component Inspector).

3. Select the Binding tab, where you will see a list of all the bindings that have already been set.

4. Choose the last binding, the `params.keyWordSearchRequest.devtag` binding.

5. Select the Bound To field and click the magnifying glass that appears.

6. When the Bound To dialog box appears, select the bottom check box, Use a Constant Value.

7. Then in the accompanying field, type in your key.

8. Click OK, and test the application, which should look like Figure 25.12.

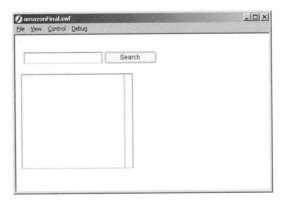

FIGURE 25.12   The Amazon DVD application using web services.

25

Let's go over the code in the first frame of the Actions layer.

The first section creates the object to listen to the search button. We then assign the event to it that, when triggered, activates the `webServiceConnector` component. Finally, we add the event listener to the Search button.

```
//the listener object
var amzObj:Object = new Object();
//the event
amzObj.click=function(){
    myConnector.trigger();
}
//add the event listener to the button
search_butn.addEventListener("click",amzObj);
```

This application is not using all the results that are returned. Use the Web Services panel to see what else is available (http://soap.amazon.com/schemas2/ AmazonwebServices.wsdl). You can also see all the different web methods we did not use, such as author search. The possibilities are endless, and this application is merely a good start.

Summary

This chapter covered a lot of material pertaining to web services and their integration into Flash. If web services are the future in middleware, and Flash is the future of application front ends, it's a perfect match.

Follow the links to other web services provided earlier in this chapter, and add them to the Web Services panel to see how to use and experiment with them.

This section ends the data integration part of the book, but the next chapter goes in a different direction with dynamic content, covering Flash's new streaming technologies.

CHAPTER **26**

Streaming Media

Earlier in this book, in Chapter 6, "Working with Sound and Video," you discovered how Flash can import and work with video. This chapter takes that a step further by showing not only how to import video, but also how to convert it to Flash's proprietary video format, Flash Video. You will also learn how to work with this video format, along with other media formats, to create a more media-centric application.

Why Stream Media?

Flash is not just a web application tool or a vector animation application; it is also a media-creation tool. Even though it is possible to import video and sound into Flash and then use it, that process creates large file sizes in most instances. This is where streaming comes in.

Streaming is the capability to load a file, and as soon as it begins loading, it can begin playing. This process requires a streaming server (such as the Flash Communication Server), but you can still test everything locally or on a nonstreaming server. If you are testing locally, you will notice very little difference because using progressive download, the video will begin playing shortly after loading begins.

So what does this mean? It means that anyone can take nearly any video they create, and with a few clicks of a button, have it streaming on the web.

A great benefit of streaming technology is the capability to keep the video outside the main file, thereby making the main file size that much smaller.

But before you can stream video, you need to know how to manually create video in the format Flash will be able to stream.

Creating a Flash Video

There are several programs that will allow the conversion of normal video directly to Flash Video format (.flv). A plug-in is also available that will work with most video-editing programs, allowing you to save as Flash Video. And of course, the Flash Communication Server has the capability to record video from Flash directly into Flash Video (FLV). But, if you don't feel like paying for any of these, Flash has a way of converting video to FLV as well.

When you bring video into Flash, depending on the option you select in the beginning, it can automatically create an FLV file for you. However, for this example, we will go through each piece step-by-step so that you can then export directly from the video's property dialog box to FLV from the library.

Follow these steps to create your first Flash video:

1. Create a new Flash document.

2. Choose File, Import, Import to Library, which will pop open the Import to Library dialog box and allow you to choose a video.

   Flash can import most video formats, including

   - .wmv

   - .avi

   - .mov

   - .asf

   - .flv

   - .mpg

   - .mpeg

   - .dv

   - .dvi

   It does not, however, support Real Player video.

3. After you have chosen your favorite video to import and have clicked Next, the Video Import Wizard will look like Figure 26.1. For this example, we will embed the video; choose that option and click Next. Your screen should then look like Figure 26.2.

4. We will import the entire video, so make sure that option is selected and then uncheck the Place Instance on Stage option and click Next.

5. The next screen enables you to choose the quality of the video and make minor adjustments to the cropping and encoding of the video (if you have the Advanced

Settings turned on), as you can see in Figure 26.3. Keep the default settings for the time being, and choose Next. In the next screen, choose Finish.

6. When the video has finished importing, open up your library (Window, Library) and you will see the video. Select it and click the Info button at the bottom of the library (or right-click it and choose Properties), and you will see the Properties dialog box for the video. Here you can update the video by choosing Update. You can also import FLV files directly, and finally, you can export.

7. After you click Export, the Export FLV window will appear, allowing you to choose where you want to save this FLV. So give it a name, choose the desktop, and click Save.

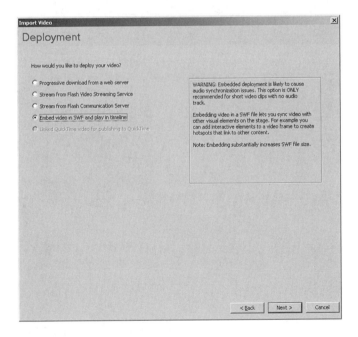

FIGURE 26.1   The Video Import Wizard.

That was it; you have now made your first manual Flash video. Not only was it easy, but it was free (provided you already own Flash, of course). Now that you have the video, let's go over what is necessary to stream into Flash.

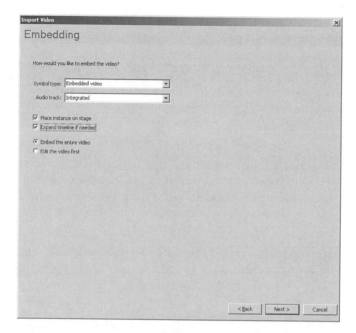

FIGURE 26.2   Options for importing external video.

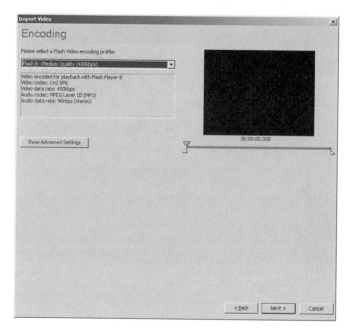

FIGURE 26.3   More options for importing external video.

The NetConnection Object

The NetConnection object allows users of the Flash 7 Player or later to stream video or audio directly into Flash. If NetConnection is used in the Flash 6 Player, it must be in conjunction with the Flash Communication Server.

It has a single method, the connect() method, and here is its general layout:

```
myConn_nc.connect(null);
```

When you call the connect method, you pass the parameter null so that it will create a local connection.

This object by itself is useless, but in conjunction with the NetStream object, it is very important.

The NetStream Object

The NetStream object allows the control of streaming video through the NetConnection object. The NetStream object has several properties, methods, and an event to assist in controlling the playing of video as well as monitoring its progress.

When instantiating a new NetStream object, you pass it the NetConnection object that the video will go through, like this:

```
//first create an instance of the object
var netCon_nc:NetConnection = new NetConnection();
//now call the connect method
netCon_nc.connect(null);
//Create the NetStream object
var myStream_ns:NetStream = new NetStream(netCon_nc);
```

Notice that we created a NetConnection object, called the connect() method, and then created an instance of the NetStream object, passing it the NetConnection.

Following are some of the methods and properties for the NetStream object that we will be using throughout this chapter.

The play() Method

The play() method for the NetStream object is used to begin the streaming of a certain Flash Video. You pass the string literal path of the FLV as a parameter in this method like this:

```
myNetStream_ns.play("myVideo.flv");
```

When this method is called, if the video is found it will begin to stream. If the video is not found, the onStatus event is invoked.

26

NOTE

Just calling the `NetStream.play()` method will not display the video. The video must be attached to a `Video` object first. However, the audio from the Flash Video will begin to start playing automatically.

The `pause()` Method

The `pause()` method can be misleading if used incorrectly. It not only pauses an incoming video, but it can also resume play.

Its generic layout is as follows:

```
myNetStream_ns.pause(pauseResume);
```

The only parameter is the `pauseResume` parameter, which is a Boolean value passed to the method saying whether to pause or resume the video feed:

- `true`—Pauses the video
- `false`—Resumes the video from its current position

If the parameter is left out, the `pause()` method will switch back and forth automatically between resuming and pausing, like a toggle switch.

The `close()` Method

The `close` method will stop all streaming media coming into the `NetStream` instance and will reset the `NetStream` itself to be used for another video.

Its generic layout looks like this:

```
myNetStream_ns.close();
```

The `seek()` Method

The `seek()` method allows users to move to a certain point in the stream. It does this by going to the closest keyframe that matches the number of seconds passed into the `seek()` method. When the stream reaches that point, it resumes playing.

Its generic layout is as follows:

```
myNetStream_ns.seek(seconds);
```

The seconds parameter is the number of seconds since the beginning of the video, where playback would preferably begin. You can use this method in several ways:

```
myStream_ns.seek(20);   //moves to the 20 seconds spot
myStream_ns.seek(0);   //moves to the beginning of the stream
myStream_ns.seek(myStream.time - 10);
//moves to the current position minus 10 seconds
```

The setBufferTime() Method

The setBufferTime() method is an important one because it controls how many seconds must be in the buffer before the stream can begin playing. Use this method to control playback of the stream, especially on slow connections.

Its generic layout is like this:

```
myStream_ns.setBufferTime(seconds);
```

The only parameter is the seconds parameter specifying how many seconds to have in the buffer before playing. The default value is 0.1 (one-tenth of a second).

The onStatus Event

The onStatus event is the only event for the NetStream object, and it is triggered often. Whenever any aspect of a NetStream instance changes, the event is triggered and can pass information about what caused the event.

The generic layout for this event is in a callback like this:

```
myStream_ns.onStatus = function(infoObj){
    //code to run
}
```

The one parameter associated with this event is the infoObj parameter. This parameter is a reference to an object that will store information about the triggering event.

The infoObj parameter has two properties: the code property giving information on what caused the status change, and the level property showing whether it was a simple status change or an error.

Table 26.1 shows the different values for the code property and their meanings.

TABLE 26.1 Possible Values for the Code Property

Code	Level	Description
NetStream.Play.Start	Status	The stream has begun playing.
NetStream.Play.Stop	Status	The stream has stopped playing.
NetStream.Buffer.Full	Status	The buffer has reached its defined point in seconds, and the stream will begin to play.
NetStream.Buffer.Empty	Status	Data from the stream is not filling the buffer fast enough, and playback will stop until the buffer is full again.
NetStream.Play.StreamNotFound	Error	Flash cannot find the FLV.

All of these properties can be received by being called on the infoObj parameter within the onStatus event like this:

```
myStream_ns.onStatus = function(infoObj){
    trace(infoObj.code);
    trace(infoObj.level);
}
```

Those were the methods and event for the `NetStream` object; it also has a few properties.

Properties of the `NetStream` Object

Following are just a few of the properties of the `NetStream` object that you might use when working with streaming video:

- `bufferLength`—The number of seconds currently in the buffer
- `time`—The position in the stream where the play head is in seconds
- `currentFps`—The current frames per second the stream is displaying
- `bufferTime`—The number of seconds that must be in the buffer before it is full

Now you know how to get the video in, but before you can see anything, you have to attach the stream coming in to a video object.

The `Video` Object

Although you may not have known it, we already created one video object when we imported the video into Flash. Video objects do more than that, though; they allow developers to display video streaming from external sources. To do this, you have to create a blank video object.

Follow these steps to create a new blank video object:

1. Start a new Flash document.
2. Open the library (Window, Library).
3. Select the Options drop-down in the top right of the library and choose New Video.
4. Select Video (ActionScript-controlled) and click OK.

Now if you want to use it, just drag it out onto the stage and give it an instance name so that you can refer to it in ActionScript.

> **TIP**
>
> "video" is the suffix for video object instances that will automatically open code hints.

And that was it—you now have a blank video object on the stage.

The `Video` object has a few methods and properties, but the one we will be using is the `attachVideo()` method.

The `attachVideo()` Method

The `attachVideo()` method allows video being streamed to a `NetStream` object to be viewed on the stage. You can also set a `Camera` object to it (more on the `Camera` object later in this chapter).

The generic layout to attach a `NetStream` to a `Video` object is as follows:

```
myVideo_video.attachVideo(myStream_ns);
```

The only parameter passed is the `NetStream` object being displayed.

We have covered a lot of code that shows how to create a video stream. Now let's put it all together.

Streaming Video

This section will bring together all the steps we have gone over so far into a media streaming application.

The first step is to either create your own Flash Video using the steps we went over earlier or download the one from the companion website.

When you have the Flash video, follow these steps to build a simple video streaming application:

1. Create a new Flash document.

2. Save it as **videoStream.fla** in the same directory as the Flash Video `cats.flv`.

3. Create a new blank video object the same way you did earlier.

4. Drag the blank video object out of the library and onto the stage. Give it an instance name of **myVideo_video**, and change its dimensions to 200×160.

5. Drag an instance of the `Button` component onto the stage and place it under the instance of the `Video` object.

6. Give the button an instance name of **play_butn** and change its label to "Play."

7. Create a dynamic text field, give it an instance name of `status_txt`, turn the border on, and set it beside the Play button.

8. Create a new layer called **actions**.

9. In the first frame of the Actions layer, open the Actions panel, and place this code in:

```
//Create the NetConnection object:
var myConn_nc:NetConnection = new NetConnection();
//Create the connection
myConn_nc.connect(null);
//Create the NetStream object
var myStream_ns:NetStream = new NetStream(myConn_nc);
```

```
//Set the onStatus event for the NetStream object
myStream_ns.onStatus = function(infoObject){
    status_txt.text=infoObject.code;
}
//Attach the NetStream video to the Video object
myVideo_video.attachVideo(myStream_ns);
//Set the buffer time to 5 seconds
myStream_ns.setBufferTime(5);
//create a variable to see if we have played the video yet
var played:Boolean = false;
//create an object to listen to our play button
var clickListen:Object = new Object();
//create the event for the listener
clickListen.click = function(){
    if(!played){
        myStream_ns.play("cats.flv");
        played = true;
        play_butn.label = "Pause";
    }else{
        if(play_butn.label == "Play"){
            play_butn.label = "Pause";
        }else{
            play_butn.label = "Play";
        }
        myStream_ns.pause();
    }
}
//now add the listener to the button
play_butn.addEventListener("click", clickListen);
```

This code accomplishes several things; let's break it into sections so that it can be more easily analyzed.

The first section creates a NetConnection object and then calls the connect() method to make a local connection:

```
//Create the NetConnection object:
var myConn_nc:NetConnection = new NetConnection();
//Create the connection
myConn_nc.connect(null);
```

The next section creates the NetStream object and sets its onStatus event to send what caused the event to the text field we created.

```
//Create the NetStream object
var myStream_ns:NetStream = new NetStream(myConn_nc);
//Set the onStatus event for the NetStream object
```

```
myStream_ns.onStatus = function(infoObject){
    status_txt.text=infoObject.code;


}
```

The next section attaches the `NetStream` video to the video object. Then it sets the buffer time (but because we are running locally, it really doesn't matter). Finally, it creates a variable we will use to see whether the video has started streaming yet.

```
//Attach the NetStream video to the Video object
myVideo_video.attachVideo(myStream_ns);
//Set the buffer time to 5 seconds
myStream_ns.setBufferTime(5);
//create a variable to see if we have played the video yet
var played:Boolean = false;
```

In the final section, we create a listener to listen to the Play button component. We create the event for the listener that checks to see whether the user has started streaming the video yet. If the video has not started streaming yet, it will start; set the variable to `true` so that it won't try to start it again, and set the label for the Play button to "Pause" so that the user will know it is playing. After that, if the user clicks the button again, it checks the label to see what the user is trying to do, and it either plays or pauses the movie accordingly. Finally, we add the event listener to the `Button` component.

```
//create an object to listen to our play button
var clickListen:Object = new Object();
//create the event for the listener
clickListen.click = function(){
    if(!played){
        myStream_ns.play("cats.flv");
        played = true;
        play_butn.label = "Pause";
    }else{
        if(play_butn.label == "Play"){
            play_butn.label = "Pause";
        }else{
            play_butn.label = "Play";
        }
        myStream_ns.pause();
    }
}
//now add the listener to the button
play_butn.addEventListener("click", clickListen);
```

Test the movie and click the Play button; you will see something similar to Figure 26.4. You can then pause and resume play, and the text field shows you when the `onStatus` event fires.

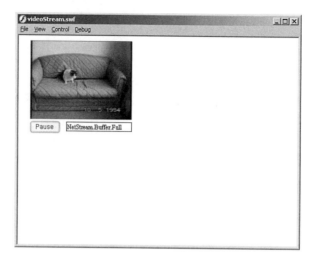

FIGURE 26.4   Streaming video is a snap with the `NetStream` and `NetConnection` objects.

Now that you have coded all of that and built the video streaming application, we move on to the easy way to do it using the FLVPlayback component.

The FLVPlayback Component

With Flash Professional 8 come a lot of components, including the FLVPlayback component that will help speed application development of streaming media applications.

With the FLVPlayback component, you can drag it onto the stage, set a single parameter, and you now have a streaming media application. It is really that easy, as you will see. To further increase its usefulness, you can also automatically create an instance of it, with the selected skin you want, when you import the video. But for this example, we will go step-by-step.

> **NOTE**
>
> The FLVPlayback component is for the Flash Player 8 only, and if FLVPlayback component is published in a lower version, it will throw an error. For Flash player 6 and 7, use the Media Components that are also included with Flash Professional 8.

Before we start using the FLVPlayback component, we should look at its parameters. Drag an instance of the FLVPlayback onto the stage, select it, and open the Properties Inspector (Window, Properties, Parameters). Following are the properties for the FLVPlayback component and a short definition:

- **autoPlay**—If set to `true`, the FLV will play immediately when it is loaded. Otherwise, it will wait for ActionScript or user interaction to begin playing. The default value is `true`.

- **autoRewind**—If set to `true` will automatically take the FLV back to the beginning once it has either reached the end of the video, or a user hits the stop button. The default value is `true`.

- **autoSize**—If set to `true`, the FLVPlayback component will resize itself at runtime to the dimensions of the FLV. The default value is `false`.

- **bufferTime**—The number of seconds to hold in the buffer before it will start playing (similar to the `bufferLength` of the `NetStream` object). The default value is 0 seconds.

- **contentPath**—A string path (relative or absolute) to the FLV player, or an XML document (for streaming services only) describing how to play the FLV. Double-clicking this parameter (or clicking the little magnifying glass on the right side of it) will open the Content Path dialog box, as shown in Figure 26.5, which will allow you to browse to your file or type it in manually. The default value is an empty string.

FIGURE 26.5   The Content Path dialog box.

- **cuePoints**—A list of cue points in a string. Cue points allow you to sync other media in your Flash file to the playing FLV file. You can double-click this parameter, and the Flash Video Cue Points dialog box will appear, as shown in Figure 26.6, allowing you to set the different cue points in your video. The default value is None or an empty string.

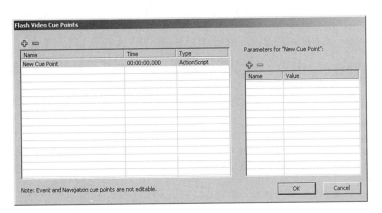

FIGURE 26.6   The Flash Video Cue Points dialog box.

- **isLive**—If set to `true`, it indicates the file is coming from a streaming server and should be treated as such. The default value is `false`.

- **maintainAspectRatio**—If set to `true`, the FLVPlayback component will resize itself at runtime to match the aspect ratio of the FLV file. The default value is `true`.

- **skin**—This parameter allows you to select from several premade skins for the FLVPlayback from the Select Skin dialog box shown in Figure 26.7. The default choice is your previously selected skin.

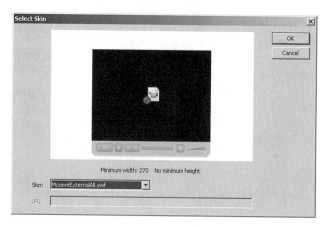

FIGURE 26.7   The Select Skin dialog box.

- **skinAutoHide**—If set to `true`, the interface for the player will disapear when not in use and reappear when the user moves the mouse over or near the FLVPlayback component at runtime. The default value is `false`.

- **totalTime**—The total amount of seconds in the FLV file. If the FLVPlayback component is set for progressive download, this parameter will be used if the value is greater than 0. If the component is set for streaming, it will attempt to grab the totalTime from the metadata of the FLV itself. The default value is 0.

- **volume**—The initial value of the volume for the FLV. The default value is 100.

Now that you have seen the parameters, let's see how easy it is to create a media application with this component:

1. Create a new Flash document.

2. Save it in the same directory as the Flash Video as `flvPlaybackExample.fla`.

3. Drag an instance of the `FLVPlayback` component onto the stage.

4. Set its contentPath parameter to `cats.flv`.

5. Test the movie.

FIGURE 26.8   Use the FLVPlayback component to build media applications quickly.

That's it! That is all it took to build a media application.

You just learned how to play video, but there is another object you can send to the Video object: the Camera object.

The Camera **Object**

The Camera object, which is available in the Flash 6 Player and later (but is undocumented in the 6 Player), is a way to work with web cams running on local machines. It isn't really streaming, but it is a lot of fun to work with, and it can be placed in the Video object, so I put it in this chapter.

The Camera object has a lot of methods, properties, and events, but the two we are going to focus on are the get() method and the activityLevel property.

The get() **Method**

The get() method for the Camera object is used to get the web cam. If more than one web cam is attached to your computer, you can choose which one you want to work with; otherwise, the get() method will use the default camera.

The generic layout for the get() method is as follows:

```
myCamera_cam.get(index);
```

The parameter index is used in case there is more than one camera attached to the computer. It is a numerical value representing each camera, starting at zero.

The `activityLevel` **Property**

The `activityLevel` property returns the amount of visual activity the camera is detecting, ranging from zero to 100.

This property will work only when you have created an `onActivity` event callback.

Now let's see the `Camera` object at work:

1. Create a new Flash document.

2. Create a blank video object as you did before.

3. Drag the blank video object onto the stage and give it an instance name of **myVideo_video**.

4. Create a dynamic text field under the blank video object.

5. Give the text field an instance name of **activity_txt** and make sure the border property is turned on.

6. Create a new layer called **actions**.

7. In the first frame of the Actions layer, open the Actions panel and place this code in:

```
//get the web cam
var myCam_cam:Camera = Camera.get();
//create the function to monitor the activity
this.onEnterFrame = function(){
    activity_txt.text = myCam_cam.activityLevel;
}
//create a blank event handler to kick-start the activityLevel property
myCam_cam.onActivity=function(){};
//attach the cam to the video object
myVideo_video.attachVideo(myCam_cam);
```

The preceding code creates a reference to the web cam we are getting. Then it creates a constantly repeating event that will send the `activityLevel` of the web cam to the text field. After that, we create a blank event callback for the `onActivity` event to initialize the `activityLevel` property. Finally, we attach the video from the web cam to the `Video` object.

Test the movie, and you will see something like Figure 26.9. If you get a pop-up asking to allow local access to your web cam or microphone, go ahead and allow it so that it will work.

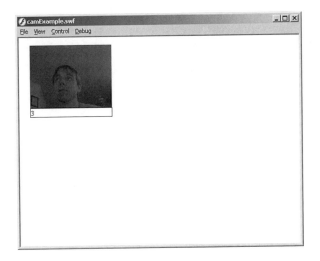

FIGURE 26.9   Use a web cam as another means of sending video to the `Video` object.

Summary

This chapter covered the basics of streaming media into Flash as well as some of the reasons behind it, including smaller file size. We went over all the major objects required to stream media, including the `NetConnection`, `NetStream`, and the `Video` objects, as well as a component that makes building streaming video applications a breeze. We finished up with another approach to putting video into Flash by means of a web cam using the `Camera` object.

Streaming video in Flash is a major step forward for making Flash a central application development tool for a rich Internet experience.

26

CHAPTER **27**

Extending Flash

Back in Flash MX 2004, Macromedia was not satisfied with just creating a better IDE and leaving it at that. They introduced the capability for any user to extend the authoring environment using the Extensibility layer.

The Extensibility layer allows users to create custom tools and panels as well as personalized commands, behaviors, and effects. Most of this is accomplished with either the JavaScript Flash Language (JSFL) or using XML-driven GUI interfaces.

To go over every individual piece of code that JSFL has and every way to use it is beyond the scope of this chapter. But this chapter does cover each item that can be built in the Extensibility layer, and goes over some basic uses of JSFL and the XML-to-UI interface.

Why Extend Flash?

I remember in older versions of Flash always wanting some tool that didn't exist or a panel to take care of something that hadn't been made yet. Now I can do more than just want them, I can make them.

When Macromedia gave the capability to extend the Flash authoring environment to all users, it gave us the power to make Flash our own. You can create your own panel sets to do certain things. You can create your own custom tools to draw more shapes than just circles and squares. You can create custom commands to do repetitive tasks and then link them to shortcuts. You can even create your own *behaviors*, which are small, reusable pieces of code, and *effects*, which are reusable visual controls for objects.

The first extendable item covered in this chapter is the command.

Commands

JSFL commands are reusable pieces of JSFL code that control any aspect of the Flash's DOM (Document Object Model). This means that commands can be written to do almost anything that you do manually in the Flash authoring environment, plus a lot more. They can do just about anything ranging from drawing a simple line on the stage all the way to saving the document with custom settings.

Not only can they be written manually in JSFL, but they can also be created directly from the History panel.

The History Panel

The History panel was introduced with JSFL. It records each step taking place in the authoring environment. You can open the History panel by choosing Window, Other Panels, History (Ctrl+F10). Figure 27.1 shows the History panel.

FIGURE 27.1   The History panel.

The History panel has several control features, including the slide bar, which enables you to go back to a certain point or record up to that point into a command. You can also replay a selected step by selecting the step and clicking the Replay button. The two options on the bottom right of the History panel are used in creating commands. The first copies a selected step or steps in JSFL to the Clipboard, and the second button saves those steps as a command.

Before we go over how to create a command, you should learn about a few options for the History panel; one in particular is the view. The default view for the History panel shows the names of the steps being taken, as you can see in Figure 27.1. To get used to JSFL, you should switch the view to JavaScript in Panel by choosing View, JavaScript in Panel. This will show the JSFL commands being called, as shown in Figure 27.2. After this option is changed, you will be able to view the JSFL commands that are being run, as well as any parameters being passed to the commands.

FIGURE 27.2   The names of the commands are replaced with the actual JSFL commands.

To see the process of replaying a command, follow these steps:

1. Create a new Flash document.

2. Open the History panel by choosing Window, Other Panels, History.

3. Make sure the History panel's view setting is set to JavaScript in Panel.

4. Draw a square on the stage and a command will appear in the History panel similar to this:

```
fl.getDocumentDOM().addNewRectangle(
➥{left:107.0, top:105, right:203.0, bottom:201}, 0);
```

This command creates a rectangle with several parameters showing position and size of the square.

5. Now highlight the entire square, including its stroke, and delete it. Another command should appear in the History panel similar to this:

```
fl.getDocumentDOM().setSelectionRect(
➥{left:1, top:69, right:322.0, bottom:287.9});
fl.getDocumentDOM().deleteSelection();
```

These commands create a selection rectangle to highlight the rectangle shape we created and then delete it.

6. Now that your stage is blank, select the command that created the rectangle and click the Replay button.

You will see the rectangle reappear. If you moved or deleted the rectangle and then selected the same command and clicked Replay again, it would still work.

That example demonstrates how to replay a step in the History panel. Now we are going to see how to save a step or groups of steps as commands.

27

Saving Commands from the History Panel

Creating commands from the History panel is the quickest and simplest way to create commands. You highlight the steps that you want to become a command and click the Save Selected Steps as a Command button.

Follow these steps to create your first command in the History panel:

1. Create a new Flash document.

2. Make sure the History panel is open and you can see the JSFL commands in the view.

3. Draw a square on the stage.

4. Choose Edit, Select All, and this command should appear in the History panel.

   ```
   fl.getDocumentDOM().selectAll();
   ```

   This command selects everything on the stage.

5. Now press the Delete key, which will delete the square, as well as put the Delete command in the History panel again.

6. Highlight the selection command and the Delete command in the History panel and click the Save Selected Steps as a Command button, which will pop up the Save as Command dialog box, as shown in Figure 27.3.

7. Give the command the name **Delete All** and click OK.

8. Now on the stage, draw several different shapes, lines, or curves.

9. Go to Commands in the menu bar, and you will see the new command you just created. Select it and everything on the stage will be deleted.

FIGURE 27.3   The Save as Command dialog box, where you name your commands.

That was a good example of a useable command, but you have to go to Commands to get to it every time, which takes two clicks more than necessary. So now let's add a shortcut key combination to this new command.

1. Choose Edit, Keyboard Shortcuts from the menu bar, which will pop up the Keyboard Shortcuts dialog box.

2. To create your own shortcut keys, you must make a copy of the default Keyboard Shortcuts by choosing the Duplicate Set button; give the new set the name **Flash Unleashed**.

3. Select Drawing Menu Commands from the Commands drop-down menu as in Figure 27.4. Then select the plus sign beside the Commands option and select Delete All (the command you just made).

4. Select the Add Shortcut button (the large plus sign by Shortcuts). In the Press Key field, press Ctrl+Alt+D at the same time, click Change, which will show the shortcut in the Shortcuts field and beside the command in the large field. Finally, click OK and you're done.

Now you will be able to use that keyboard combination as a shortcut for the command, and if you select Commands from the menu bar, you will see that the command you just created now has a shortcut associated with it.

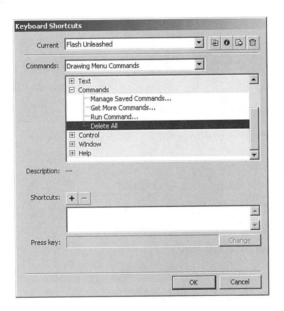

FIGURE 27.4 Create custom shortcut key combinations for your new commands.

You just learned how to make a command with the History panel. It was quick and easy, but not all that powerful because we could not customize it to the exact way we want. In the next section, we will cover how to create commands in a more hands-on kind of way.

Creating Commands Manually with JSFL

Building commands from scratch is a little more difficult and requires correct coding of JSFL or errors will appear. However, it's more powerful than creating commands from the History panel because there are more commands available.

To create a JSFL file, select File, New and choose Flash JavaScript File. This will change the entire authoring environment to look like Figure 27.5. The stage will disappear, an actions window will fill up most of the authoring environment, and the surrounding area will be grayed out for the most part.

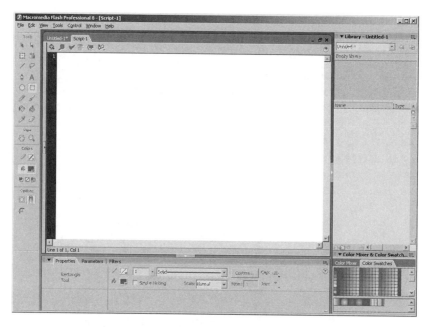

FIGURE 27.5   The authoring environment for creating JSFL files.

This Actions window acts in much the same way the Actions panel does. You can type in code manually, or use the Add New Script button.

Let's jump right in and create a very basic command that will send a string to the Output panel while still in the authoring environment.

1. Create a new Flash JavaScript file.

2. Place this code within the file:

   ```
   fl.trace("my first manual command");
   ```

3. Now save this command to your desktop as `traceMe.jsfl`.

4. Create a new Flash document.

5. Choose Commands, Run Command to open the Open File dialog box. Choose the `traceMe.jsfl` command and the Output panel should then look like Figure 27.6.

That was a pretty basic example, and we will return to it in a later section.

In this situation, we use the Run Command option from the Commands menu, but if you wanted it to appear with the other commands, you would have to place the JSFL file into the Commands directory located at `C:\Program Files\Macromedia\Flash 8\en\First Run\Commands` for Windows and `Applications\Macromedia\Flash 8\en\First Run\Commands` for Macs. Then reboot Flash for the new command to be visible in the Commands menu.

FIGURE 27.6   Create manual commands to accomplish tasks in the authoring environment.

Now that you know how to create commands two ways, we can go over how to manage those commands.

Managing Commands

Managing commands is pretty easy. Select Commands, Manage Saved Commands. The Manage Saved Commands window opens as shown in Figure 27.7. You can rename or delete each command from there.

FIGURE 27.7   Use the Manage Saved Commands window to control all saved commands created manually or with the History panel.

The preceding example did in fact send a string of text to the Output panel in the authoring environment, but every time you run the command, it will keep sending the same message, which is not very useful. In the next section, you will learn one of the ways to add dynamic content and customization to commands, as well as other extensible objects.

XML-to-UI Controls

You can create an interface between extendable JSFL files and Flash in two ways. One, which we will discuss later in this chapter, you build directly in Flash itself. The other involves a specific way of coding XML.

Using specific XML tags (elements), we can describe and define a user interface for controlling any of our JSFL files. Listing every single tag is beyond the scope of this chapter, but Tables 27.1 and 27.2 show a few of the major tags. Table 27.1 lists layout tags, and Table 27.2 lists UI element tags.

27

TABLE 27.1   Layout Tags

Tag	Description	Attributes	Child Tags
`<dialog>`	This tag will hold the entire UI.	buttons (Accept, Cancel, Help) `title`	`<hbox>`, `<vbox>`, `<grid>`
`<hbox>`	Contains horizontally aligned UI elements.	N/A	`<hbox>`, `<vbox>`, controls
`<vbox>`	Contains vertically aligned UI elements.	N/A	`<hbox>`, `<vbox>`, controls
`<spacer>`	Invisible bumper for arranging UI elements.	N/A	N/A
`<separator>`	Visible bar aligned with parent `<vbox>` or `<hbox>`.	N/A	N/A
`<grid>`	Used to lay out tabular elements.	N/A	`<columns>`,`<rows>`
`<columns>`	Holds individual `<column>` tags.	N/A	`<column>`
`<column>`	Specifies column in grid.	N/A	controls
`<rows>`	Holds individual `<row>` tags.	N/A	`<row>`
`<row>`	Controls to be placed within these tags.	`align` (start, center, end, baseline)	controls

TABLE 27.2   UI Element Tags (Controls)

Tag	Description	Attributes	Child Tags
`<button>`	Clickable buttons	`id` `label` `accesskey` `tabindex` `oncommand`	N/A
`<checkbox>`	Element for selecting Boolean values (true/false, yes/no)	`id` `label` `accesskey` `tabindex`	checked (true, false) N/A
`<colorchip>`	Color grid where a user can choose a certain color	`id` color (default color)	N/A
`<listbox>`	Holds `<listitem>` tags in a list box	`id` `tabindex` rows (rows to display)	`<listitem>`
`<listitem>`	A single element in a list box	`label` `value`	N/A

TABLE 27.2   Continued

Tag	Description	Attributes	Child Tags
`<menulist>`	A drop-down list or combo box	`id` `tabindex`	`<menupop>`
`<menupop>`	Part of the `<menulist>` drop-down box	N/A	`<menuitem>`

`<menuitem>`	Item in the `<menulist>` drop-down box	`label`
		`value`
		`selected (true, false)`
			N/A

`<radiogroup>`	Holds radio button objects	`id` `tabindex`	`<radio>`
`<radio>`	Individual choice in a `<radiogroup>`	`label` `selected (true, false)`	
`accesskey`	N/A		

`<popupslider>`	A slider with a movable slide bar to control the value	`id`
		`tabindex`
		`minvalue`
		`maxvalue`
			N/A

`<textbox>`	Simple text field	`id`
		`maxlength`
		`value` (default text)
		`tabindex`
		`size` (in characters)
		`literal` (puts quote marks around text)
			N/A

`<label>`	Text label for UI elements	`control` (id of control being labeled)
		`accesskey`
		`value`
			N/A

`<flash>`	Embedded Flash movie (`.swf`)	`id`
		`width`
		`height`
		`src` (source file)
			N/A

`<targetlist>`	Used to sort through and choose instances of objects on the stage	`id`
		`class`
		`tabindex`
		`required (true, false)`
			N/A

27

So now that you've seen the basic code being used, let's return to the `myTrace.jsfl` example and make it more dynamic:

1. Open a text editor such as Notepad or SciTe.

2. Save the file on the desktop as `traceMe.xml`.

3. Place the following code within it.

```
<dialog buttons="accept, cancel" title="Trace What?">
    <hbox>
        <label value="String: "/>
        <textbox id="string" value="Sample Text" size="40"/>
    </hbox>
</dialog>
```

The preceding code creates a UI box with the title "Trace What?" and two buttons. It then creates the type of UI box (<hbox>) and within that, it labels the text field, which is created 40 characters wide with the default text "Sample Text." And as in all XML documents, when a tag is opened, it must be closed.

4. Now return to Flash and open myTrace.jsfl.

5. Change the code that is already present to the following:

```
myResult = fl.getDocumentDOM().xmlPanel(fl.configURI +
➥ "/Commands/traceMe.xml");
if(myResult.dismiss == "accept"){
    fl.trace(myResult.string);
}
```

This code does the following: First, it maps to the XML file that describes the UI for this command and sets it to a variable myResult. Then, using a conditional statement, it checks whether the user has clicked the Accept button or the Cancel button, because we want the command to run only if the user clicks Accept. If the Accept (OK) button is clicked, it sends the message that is in the text field to the Output panel.

6. Now save the JSFL file to the desktop.

7. Copy both the JSFL file and the XML document to the Commands folder in the Flash 8 directory and restart Flash.

After you have restarted Flash, you can go to Commands in the menu bar, and you should see traceMe as a listed command. Select it and Figure 27.8 should appear. You can type in anything or keep the default text, and when you click OK (the Accept button), the message is sent to the Output panel. Also, if you select Cancel, nothing will happen except that the UI box will close.

NOTE

It is not necessary to have buttons in the UI (although you would normally want to). If a user cannot close the dialog box by clicking a button, the Escape key will always close the UI box.

FIGURE 27.8   Enter some text to have the traceMe command trace the text.

That was one way to use the XML-to-UI API. Another way is with behaviors.

Creating Behaviors

Behaviors, as discussed in Chapter 8, "Welcome to ActionScript 2.0," are small blocks of code that can be adjusted to fit individual needs. Some of the behaviors that come with Flash can be used to control movie clips, screens (Flash PRO only), and to open new web pages. Those are okay, but for more intermediate to advanced developers, you will want more. Building behaviors is a simple process provided that you familiarized yourself with the XML-to-UI API. Table 27.3 shows a few other tags for behaviors that you should make yourself aware of.

TABLE 27.3   XML Tags for Behaviors

Tag	Description	Attributes	Child Tags
<flash_behavior>	Tells Flash that this XML is for a behavior	version	N/A
<behavior_definition>	Defines certain aspects of the behavior	dialogID category name class	N/A
<properties>	Holds the declared properties <property>	N/A	<property>
<property>	Declares a property of the behavior	id default	N/A
<actionscript>	Holds the ActionScript being placed	N/A	N/A

27

Now that you have seen the new tags for behaviors, you can go ahead and create them. In the following example, you will create a behavior to color components:

1. Open up your favorite text editor.

2. Save the file to the `C:\Program Files\Macromedia\Flash 8\en\First Run\Behaviors` directory as **componentColor.xml**.

3. Place this code in; then we can go over each part:

```
<?xml version="1.0"?>
<flash_behavior version="1.0">
<behavior_definition dialogID="Style-component"
➥category="Flash Unleashed" name ="Style a component" >
<properties>
    <property id="TARGET" default=""/>
    <property id="COLOR" default="#000000"/>
</properties>
  <dialog id="Style-component"
➥title="Style a component" buttons="accept, cancel">
    <vbox>
        <hbox>
            <label value="Select a component:"
➥control="TARGET" required="true"/>
            <targetlist id="TARGET"/>
        </hbox>
        <seperator/>
        <hbox>
            <label value="Select a color:" control="COLOR" required="true"/>
            <colorchip id="COLOR" color="#000000"/>
        </hbox>
    </vbox>
  </dialog>
<actionscript>
<![CDATA[
// Color a component
// Flash Unleashed
var htmlColor:String = "$COLOR$";
$TARGET$.setStyle("themeColor", "0x"+htmlColor.slice(1));
//end component color
]]>
</actionscript>
</behavior_definition>
</flash_behavior>
```

This code does a lot of things, so let's break it apart and talk about each piece.

The first piece declares that it is an XML document, and then that it is a Flash behavior.

```
<?xml version="1.0"?>
        <flash_behavior version="1.0">
```

The next section sets some of the behavior's attributes and declares a couple of properties.

```
<behavior_definition dialogID="Style component"
➥category="Flash Unleashed" name ="Style a component" >
<properties>
    <property id="TARGET" default=""/>
    <property id="COLOR" default="#000000"/>
</properties>
```

After that comes the dialog box construction with all of the elements.

```
  <dialog id="Style-component" title="Style a component" buttons="accept,
➥ cancel">
    <vbox>
        <hbox>
            <label value="Select a component:" control="TARGET" required="true"/>
            <targetlist id="TARGET"/>
        </hbox>
        <separator/>
        <hbox>
            <label value="Select a color:" control="COLOR" required="true"/>
            <colorchip id="COLOR" color="#000000"/>
        </hbox>
    </vbox>
  </dialog>
```

Then the ActionScript is created. Following are some things to know about sending ActionScript out of the behavior: In addition to the fact that it must be between <actionscript> tags, it must also follow <![CDATA[and end with]]>. Getting information from the UI elements in the dialog box is as easy as wrapping the *id* attribute of that element in dollar signs ($*id*$).

```
<actionscript>
    <![CDATA[
    // Color a component
    //Flash Unleashed
    var htmlColor:String = "$COLOR$";
    $TARGET$.setStyle("themeColor", "0x"+htmlColor.slice(1));
    //end of code
    ]]>
</actionscript>
```

27

And finally, the other open tags are closed as well.

```
</behavior_definition>
</flash_behavior>
```

Now that you understand the fundamentals behind the behavior we just built, let's use it.

1. Make sure the `componentColor.xml` document is in the `behaviors` directory of the Flash 8 directory.

2. Restart Flash.

3. Create a new Flash document.

4. Drag the `Button` component onto the stage.

5. Create another layer called **actions**.

6. Select the first frame of the Actions layer, and open the Behaviors panel by choosing Window, Behaviors.

7. Click the Add Behavior button and choose Flash Unleashed, Style a Component, which will pop up the dialog box shown in Figure 27.9.

8. Choose the `Button` component that was placed on the stage, and because it wasn't given an instance name, another dialog box will pop up that is built in to the `targetlist` UI element, as you can see in Figure 27.10. Give the `Button` component the instance name of **myButton_butn** and choose your favorite color.

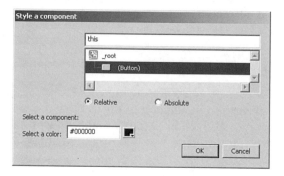

FIGURE 27.9   The User Interface for your first custom behavior.

FIGURE 27.10   The Instance Name dialog box.

9. Now test the movie, and you will see that the button has taken on the color characteristics of the color you have chosen (sometimes it's hard to see until the button is actually clicked).

That was how to make a behavior. To see more about behaviors, look at the ones that come with Flash. Because they are made in XML, they are open source, so learn from their creators.

Behaviors can save you development time, and so does the topic of the next section—panels.

Creating Your Own Panels

Flash comes with a lot of panels, but you might not need or want every one. No worries—you can create your own panels, which isn't really new, but now you can use the MMExecute() function, which will execute any JSFL command within the authoring environment. When the Flash file (.swf) has been created, you can drop it in the WindowSWF directory in the Flash 8 directory and restart the Flash authoring environment. Then you can find it under Windows, Other Panels in the menu bar.

The basic layout of the MMExecute() method is as follows:

```
MMExecute(command);
```

The difficult aspect of using the MMExecute() method is that the command must be passed as a string, but the dynamic content cannot. For instance, if you were to send the current date and time to the Output panel, it would look something like this:

```
MMExecute("fl.trace('" + new Date() + "');");
```

Notice the abundance of quotation marks to make it work right, just something to keep in mind when using the MMExecute() function.

Now that you have seen the basic usage of the function we are going to use to create our first panel, let's get started.

1. Create a new Flash document.

2. Set its dimensions to 200×100.

3. Drag three components onto the stage and place them as follows:

   - TextInput component—Set its width to about 180, give it an instance name of **myText_ti**, and place it in the top half of the stage.

   - Button component—Give it an instance name of **myButton_butn**, set its label parameter to **Send**, change its width to about 48, and place it in the bottom left of the stage.

   - ComboBox component—Give it an instance name of myCombo_combo, place it at the bottom right of the stage, and give it two labels:

27

```
"to output"
"to alert"
```

Your stage should now look like Figure 27.11.

4. Create a new layer called **actions**.

5. Open the Actions panel in the first frame of the Actions layer and place this code in:

```
//event listener object
var clickListen:Object = new Object();
//create the event
clickListen.click = function(){
    if(myCombo.value == "to output"){
        MMExecute("fl.trace('" + myText.text + "');");
    }else{
        MMExecute("alert('"+myText.text + "');");
    }
}
//add the listener
myButton.addEventListener("click",clickListen);
```

The preceding code first creates an event listener object. Then it creates an event callback method for that object that checks where the string from the TextInput component is supposed to go—either to the Output panel or to an alert message. Then finally we add the event listener to the Button component.

6. Now save the file as Send Out.fla and test the movie.

7. Copy the .swf file created to the WindowSWF directory of the Flash 8 first-run directory and restart Flash.

8. When Flash has been restarted, choose Window, Other Panels, Send Out. Now you have the capability to send messages to the Output panel as well as in the form of alert messages, as in Figure 27.12.

This example does not have the most practical uses, but it does show what is possible by combining Flash developing, JSFL, and the MMExecute() function. As you become more comfortable with JSFL, you will begin to create many of your own panels.

But panels are not the end of customizing the authoring environment of Flash. You can also create your own tools with JSFL and place them in the toolbar.

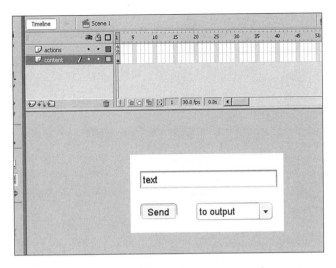

FIGURE 27.11   Use components to quickly create custom panels.

FIGURE 27.12   You can see that the panel created can send messages both to the Output panel and as an alert message.

Creating Custom Tools

Other great objects that you can create on the Extensibility layer are custom tools. Custom tools can be used to do a lot of things, including drawing shapes, adjusting elements on the stage, and even creating new instances of objects.

There are certain aspects of JSFL that are used specifically for tools, but we will go over them as we build our tool.

The tool being built in the following example is a drawing tool designed for drawing heart shapes just as quickly and easily as drawing squares in Flash.

1. Create a new JavaScript Flash file.

2. Save the document in the tools directory of the Flash MX 2004 directory as **heart.jsfl**.

3. Place this code in:

```
function configureTool(){
    myTool = fl.tools.activeTool;
    myTool.setToolName("Heart");
```

```
        myTool.setIcon("Heart.png");
        myTool.setMenuString("Heart Tool");
        myTool.setToolTip("Heart Tool");
    }

    function drawHeart(startX,startY,theWidth,theHeight){
        if(fl.tools.shiftIsDown){
            if(Math.abs(theWidth) > Math.abs(theHeight)){
                if(theWidth<0 && theHeight<0){
                    theHeight = theWidth;
                }else if(theWidth<0){
                    theHeight = -theWidth;
                }else if(theHeight<0){
                    theHeight = -theWidth;
                }else{
                    theHeight = theWidth;
                }
            }else if(Math.abs(theHeight) > Math.abs(theWidth)){
                if(theHeight<0 && theWidth<0){
                    theWidth = theHeight;
                }else if(theHeight<0){
                    theWidth = -theHeight;
                }else if(theWidth<0){
                    theWidth = -theHeight;
                }else{
                    theWidth = theHeight;
                }
            }
        }
        thePath.addCurve(startX+(theWidth/2),startY+(theHeight*.3),
➥startX+(theWidth/2),startY,startX+(theWidth/4),startY);
        thePath.addCurve(startX+(theWidth/4),startY,startX,
➥startY,startX,startY+(theHeight*.3));
        thePath.addCurve(startX,startY+(theHeight*.3),startX+(theWidth/100),
➥startY+(theHeight*.75),startX+(theWidth/2),startY+theHeight);
        thePath.addCurve(startX+(theWidth/2),startY+theHeight,startX+(theWidth-
(theWidth/100)),startY+(theHeight*.75),startX+theWidth,startY+(theHeight*.3));
        thePath.addCurve(startX+theWidth,startY+(theHeight*.3),startX+theWidth,
➥startY,startX+(theWidth*.75),startY);
        thePath.addCurve(startX+(theWidth*.75),startY,startX+(theWidth/2),
➥startY,startX+(theWidth/2),startY+(theHeight*.3));
    }

    function activate(){
        myTool = fl.tools.activeTool;
    }
```

```
function mouseDown(){
    fl.drawingLayer.beginDraw();
}
function mouseMove(){
    if(fl.tools.mouseIsDown){
        var difX=fl.tools.penLoc.x-fl.tools.penDownLoc.x;
        var difY=fl.tools.penLoc.y-fl.tools.penDownLoc.y;
        fl.drawingLayer.beginFrame();
        drawLayer = fl.drawingLayer;
        thePath = drawLayer.newPath();
        drawHeart(fl.tools.penDownLoc.x,fl.tools.penDownLoc.y,difX,difY);
        drawLayer.drawPath(thePath);
        fl.drawingLayer.endFrame();
    }
}

function mouseUp(){
    fl.drawingLayer.endDraw();
    thePath.makeShape();
}
```

This code may look like a lot, but it isn't, as you will see as it is broken apart into sections.

The first section appears to create a function, but in fact, it creates a function specific to tools, the configureTool() function. Within this function, we set the active tool to a variable for easy reference. We then set the tool's name along with its icon (which we will build later). After that, the menu string is set as well as the ToolTip, which will appear when the tool is hovered over in the toolbar.

```
function configureTool(){
    myTool = fl.tools.activeTool;
    myTool.setToolName("Heart");
    myTool.setIcon("Heart.png");
    myTool.setMenuString("Heart Tool");
    myTool.setToolTip("Heart Tool");
}
```

After that, we create a function that we use later in the code. The drawHeart() function does all the hard work and the math for drawing the actual heart shape. Also, notice that we check to see whether the Shift key is down. This is to make it work like the oval and rectangle tool already in Flash, in that when the Shift key is down, it constrains proportions to make a perfect shape.

```
function drawHeart(startX,startY,theWidth,theHeight){
    if(fl.tools.shiftIsDown){
        if(Math.abs(theWidth) > Math.abs(theHeight)){
```

27

```
            if(theWidth<0 && theHeight<0){
                theHeight = theWidth;
            }else if(theWidth<0){
                theHeight = -theWidth;
            }else if(theHeight<0){
                theHeight = -theWidth;
            }else{
                theHeight = theWidth;
            }
        }else if(Math.abs(theHeight) > Math.abs(theWidth)){
            if(theHeight<0 && theWidth<0){
                theWidth = theHeight;
            }else if(theHeight<0){
                theWidth = -theHeight;
            }else if(theWidth<0){
                theWidth = -theHeight;
            }else{
                theWidth = theHeight;
            }
        }
    }
    thePath.addCurve(startX+(theWidth/2),startY+(theHeight*.3),startX+(theWidth/2),
➥startY,startX+(theWidth/4),startY);
    thePath.addCurve(startX+(theWidth/4),startY,startX,startY,
➥startX,startY+(theHeight*.3));
    thePath.addCurve(startX,startY+(theHeight*.3),startX+(theWidth/100),
➥startY+(theHeight*.75),startX+(theWidth/2),startY+theHeight);
    thePath.addCurve(startX+(theWidth/2),startY+theHeight,startX+(theWidth-
(theWidth/100)),startY+(theHeight*.75),startX+theWidth,startY+(theHeight*.3));
    thePath.addCurve(startX+theWidth,startY+(theHeight*.3),startX+theWidth,
➥startY,startX+(theWidth*.75),startY);
    thePath.addCurve(startX+(theWidth*.75),startY,startX+(theWidth/2),startY,
➥startX+(theWidth/2),startY+(theHeight*.3));
}
```

After that comes another specific function for the tool object, the `activate()` function, which is called when the specific tool is activated.

```
function activate(){
    myTool = fl.tools.activeTool;
}
```

Then the `mouseDown()` function is created, which will be called after the tool is selected and the user presses the mouse button on the stage.

```
function mouseDown(){
    fl.drawingLayer.beginDraw();
}
```

Next, the `mouseMove()` function is created. This function first checks to make sure that the user is still clicking the mouse button; otherwise, it will draw a single check mark as long as the mouse moves around on the stage. If the mouse is down (meaning that the user is in fact trying to draw something), it gets the most recent position of when the user clicked the mouse, using the `penDownLoc` property. It then activates the Drawing layer and creates a new path in the Drawing layer. After that, the `drawHeart()` function is called, which will draw the heart on the stage. Then we set the drawing path and end the drawing frame.

```
function mouseMove(){
    if(fl.tools.mouseIsDown){
        var difX=fl.tools.penLoc.x-fl.tools.penDownLoc.x;
        var difY=fl.tools.penLoc.y-fl.tools.penDownLoc.y;
        fl.drawingLayer.beginFrame();
        drawLayer = fl.drawingLayer;
        thePath = drawLayer.newPath();
        drawHeart(fl.tools.penDownLoc.x,fl.tools.penDownLoc.y,difX,difY);
        drawLayer.drawPath(thePath);
        fl.drawingLayer.endFrame();
    }
}
```

The final function is created for when the user releases the mouse. When this occurs, we stop drawing on the Drawing layer and create the shape with the fill color and stroke already set in the authoring environment.

```
function mouseUp(){
    fl.drawingLayer.endDraw();
    thePath.makeShape();
}
```

Now that you see what the code is doing, the next step is to create the icon for our tool. Still in Flash, or any other drawing program you use such as Fireworks, draw a basic heart, about 16×16, and save it as **Heart.png** in the same directory as the JSFL file.

There is one final step before we have to reboot Flash; we have to add the tool to the toolbar. In the tools directory, open `toolConfig.xml` and change its content (add the line shown in bold):

> **NOTE**
>
> Before you start changing this file, or any other file in the Flash 8 directory, be sure to make a backup of it, just in case.

```
<group name="selection">
    <tool name="arrow" />
    <tool name="bezierSelect" />
    <tool name="line" />
    <tool name="lasso" />
    <tool name="pen" />
    <tool name="text" />
    <tool name="oval" />
    <tool name="rect">
        <tool name="polystar" />
        <tool name="Heart"/>
    </tool>
    <tool name="pencil" />
    <tool name="brush" />
    <tool name="freeXform" />
    <tool name="fillXform" />
    <tool name="inkBottle" />
    <tool name="bucket" />
    <tool name="eyeDropper" />
    <tool name="eraser" />
    <tool name="hand" />
    <tool name="magnifier" />
</group>
```

All we did here is add the Heart tool after the PolyStar tool.

Now restart Flash, create a new Flash document, select the Rectangle tool in the toolbar, hold it down, and you will see the heart tool, which makes it easy to draw heart shapes, as shown in Figure 27.13.

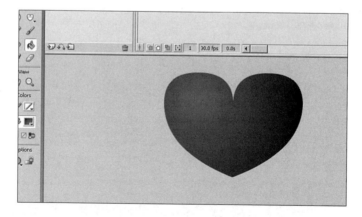

FIGURE 27.13   Create custom tools for your own needs and preferences.

Even after everything we have gone over that can be created with the Extensibility layer, JSFL, and the XML-to-UI API, there is one more: effects.

Creating Custom Effects

Effects are reusable and customizable ways to create visual effects with objects on the stage, such as movie clips or static text fields. There are several built-in effects, but it's important to understand how to make your own.

Much like tools, effects have certain functions that are specific for them, and as before, we will go over them as we build our effect.

The effect we are going to create will fade a movie clip to a certain point in a certain number of frames that we will set using XML to UI.

1. Open your favorite text editor and save a file in the effects directory of the Flash 8 first run directory as **fade.xml**.

2. Place this code within it:

```
<group name="Flash Unleashed">
    <effect name="Fade">
    <source file="fade.jsfl">
    <allow types="all">
</group>
<properties>
    <property name="Fade To" variable="alpha" defaultValue="0"
➡type="Number"/>
    <property name="Frame Amount" variable="frameAmount"
➡ defaultValue="10" type="Number"/>
</properties>
```

The preceding code creates the group name and the effect's name. It also declares the source JSFL file for the effect and declares what type of objects can use this. Then we declare the two properties we will use: the fade to point and the frame amount with some default values.

3. Now create a new JSFL file and save it as **fade.jsfl** in the same directory as the XML file.

4. Place this code within it:

```
function executeEffect(){
    var myEffect = fl.activeEffect;
    var myDoc = fl.getDocumentDOM();
    var myTimeline = myDoc.getTimeline();
    var theFrame = myTimeline.currentFrame;
    myTimeline.insertFrames(myEffect.frameAmount-1);
    myDoc.enterEditMode();
```

27

```
    myTimeline = myDoc.getTimeline();
    myTimeline.insertFrames(myEffect.frameAmount-1);
    myTimeline.createMotionTween(0, myEffect.frameAmount-1);
    myTimeline.convertToKeyframes(myEffect.frameAmount-1);
    myTimeline.currentFrame = myEffect.frameAmount-1;
    myDoc.selectAll();
    myDoc.setInstanceAlpha(myEffect.alpha);
    myDoc.exitEditMode();
    myTimeline = myDoc.getTimeline();
    myTimeline.currentFrame = theFrame;
}
function removeEffect(){
    var myDoc = fl.getDocumentDOM();
    myDoc.enterEditMode();
    var myTimeline = myDoc.getTimeline();
    var totalFrames = myTimeline.layers[0].frameCount;
    myTimeline.removeFrames(1, totalFrames);
    myTimeline.setFrameProperty('tweenType', 'none', 0);
    myTimeline.currentFrame = 0;
    myDoc.selectAll();
      myDoc.exitEditMode();
    myTimeline = myDoc.getTimeline();
    var selFrames = myTimeline.getSelectedFrames();
    myTimeline.removeFrames(selFrames[1]+1, selFrames[2]);
    myTimeline.setSelectedFrames(selFrames[1], selFrames[1]);
}
```

The preceding code creates two functions, both specific for effects. The first is the executeEffect() function, which will be called when the user creates the effect. The second function is the removeEffect() function for when a user wants to remove an effect.

The first function, executeEffect(), sets the active effect and places it in the myEffect variable. It then gets the Flash DOM and sets that to the myDoc variable. Then it grabs the current timeline and that timeline's currentFrame. After it has that, it can begin adding the correct number of frames to the timeline, and because it already has a frame, we subtract one from the total frames given by the user and add the new amount to the current timeline. We then enter Edit mode, which will allow us to create the tween. We enter the Edit mode, create the total frames there, and then we create the motion tween, grab the content in the final frame, and reset its alpha. After that, we exit the Edit mode and select the current frame in the current timeline.

```
function executeEffect(){
    var myEffect = fl.activeEffect;
    var myDoc = fl.getDocumentDOM();
    var myTimeline = myDoc.getTimeline();
    var theFrame = myTimeline.currentFrame;
```

```
    myTimeline.insertFrames(myEffect.frameAmount-1);
    myDoc.enterEditMode();
    myTimeline = myDoc.getTimeline();
    myTimeline.insertFrames(myEffect.frameAmount-1);
    myTimeline.createMotionTween(0, myEffect.frameAmount-1);
    myTimeline.convertToKeyframes(myEffect.frameAmount-1);
    myTimeline.currentFrame = myEffect.frameAmount-1;
    myDoc.selectAll();
    myDoc.setInstanceAlpha(myEffect.alpha);
    myDoc.exitEditMode();
    myTimeline = myDoc.getTimeline();
    myTimeline.currentFrame = theFrame;
}
```

The second function created will remove the effect if the user wants. It first grabs the DOM and then enters Edit mode. In edit mode, it removes the frames and the tween setting. Then it goes back to the previous timeline and removes the excess frames there as well.

```
function removeEffect(){
    var myDoc = fl.getDocumentDOM();
    myDoc.enterEditMode();
    var myTimeline = myDoc.getTimeline();
    var totalFrames = myTimeline.layers[0].frameCount;
    myTimeline.removeFrames(1, totalFrames);
    myTimeline.setFrameProperty('tweenType', 'none', 0);
    myTimeline.currentFrame = 0;
    myDoc.selectAll();
      myDoc.exitEditMode();
    myTimeline = myDoc.getTimeline();
    var selFrames = myTimeline.getSelectedFrames();
    myTimeline.removeFrames(selFrames[1]+1, selFrames[2]);
    myTimeline.setSelectedFrames(selFrames[1], selFrames[1]);
}
```

Make sure both the XML document and the JSFL file are in the effects directory in the Flash 8 directory and restart Flash. Then create a square, convert it to a movie clip, select it, and choose Insert, Timeline Effects, Flash Unleashed, Fade. The dialog box shown in Figure 27.14 will pop up. You can use the default settings and then test the movie and watch the square fade out over and over.

Now you have seen the Extensibility layer and some of the things that can be created within it, but you do not necessarily have to create them yourself. There is one more command we want to make, and it involves something that was only introduced well after Flash MX 2004 was introduced.

27

FIGURE 27.14   Custom effects make visual eye candy quickly and easily.

File I/O in JSFL

Introduced after the launch of Flash MX 2004, File I/O was one of the most requested features to be added to JSFL. A specific class, called `Flfile`, was created to handle this new feature. `Flfile` has several methods, but we are going to be using three for our example, the `exists` method, the `remove` method, and the `write` method. Here are those three methods with some explanation:

- `exists` (fullPath)—This method checks to see if the file in the `fullPath` parameter exists; it returns a Boolean value `true` if the file does exist and `false` if the file does not exist.

- `remove` (fullPath)—This method completely removes the file at `fullPath` and returns a Boolean value based on its success.

- `write` (fullPath, stringContent)—This method creates a file at `fullPath` and fills it with the `stringContent`.

Remember, all these methods require a full, absolute path to the file you are referencing.

The example we are going to create, when run from within a Flash document, will create an Excel file that lists every single item in the library with some pertinent information about each one.

We will first go over the command step-by-step and then show the code in its entirety.

First, create a new JSFL file called **createLibraryListXLS.jsfl** and paste this first bit of code in it:

```
//get the path of the doc
var tPath = fl.getDocumentDOM().path;
var fileName = tPath.slice(tPath.lastIndexOf("\\")+1,tPath.lastIndexOf("."));
tPath = tPath.slice(0,tPath.lastIndexOf("\\"));
var filePath = "file:///"+tPath.split("\\").join("/")+"/"+fileName+"_library.xls";
```

This bit of code first gets the path to the open file you are calling the command on (FLA). It then extrapolates the filename from the full path to use as part of the Excel filename. Finally, it creates the new absolute file path of the file you are going to create at the end. After that bit of code, paste this small piece:

```
//if the file already exists.. get rid of it
if(FLfile.exists(filePath)){
    FLfile.remove(filePath);
}
```

These three lines of code do a lot. They look to see if the file has already been made. If the file has been made before, it is destroyed so that later we can re-create it. The next section begins the content variable we are going to use to store everything we want put in the file.

```
//start of the content
var content="";
content+="<html>\n\t<body>\n";
content+="\t\t<table border='1'>\n";
content+="\t\t\t<tr>\n";
content+="\t\t\t\t<th nowrap>id</th>\n";
content+="\t\t\t\t<th nowrap>type</th>\n";
content+="\t\t\t\t<th nowrap>linkageClassName</th>\n";
content+="\t\t\t\t<th nowrap>linkageURL</th>\n";
content+="\t\t\t\t<th nowrap>linkageIdentifier</th>\n";
content+="\t\t\t\t<th nowrap>libraryPath</th>\n";
```

The preceding code creates the beginning of our file by creating all the header fields we will need in Excel. Next up is all the information in the library:

```
//now its time to run through the array of library items
var itemArray= fl.getDocumentDOM().library.items;
itemArray.sort();
var tLength = itemArray.length;
var i=0;
while(i<tLength){
    var tItem = itemArray[i];
    if(tItem.itemType != "folder"){
        content+="\t\t\t<tr>\n";
        content+="\t\t\t\t<td align='right'>";
        content+=i;
        content+="</td>\n";
        content+="\t\t\t\t<td align='right'><b>";
        switch (tItem.itemType){
            case "movie clip":
                content+="<font color='ff0000'>movie clip</font>";
                break;
            case "bitmap":
                content+="<font color='006600'>bitmap</font>";
                break;
```

```
                    case "sound":
                        content+="<font color='cc9900'>sound</font>";
                        break;
                    case "graphic":
                        content+="<font color='9933cc'>graphic</font>";
                        break;
                    case "button":
                        content+="<font color='0000ff'>button</font>";
                        break;
                    case "compiled clip":
                        content+="<font color='333300'>compiled clip</font>";
                        break;
                    case "font":
                        content+="<font color='cc9900'>button</font>";
                        break;
                    case "video":
                        content+="<font color='996600'>compiled clip</font>";
                        break;
                    default:
                        content+=tItem.itemType;
            }


        content+="</b></td>\n";
        content+="\t\t\t\t<td align='right'>";
        (tItem.linkageClassName)? content+="<i>"+
➥tItem.linkageClassName+"</i>":content+="N/A";
        content+="</td>\n";
        content+="\t\t\t\t<td align='right'>";
        (tItem.linkageURL)? content+="<i>"+tItem.linkageURL+"</i>":content+="N/A";
        content+="</td>\n";
        content+="\t\t\t\t<td align='right'>";
        (tItem.linkageIdentifier)? content+="<b>"+
➥tItem.linkageIdentifier+"</b>":content+="N/A";
        content+="</td>\n";
        content+="\t\t\t\t<td align='right'>";
        content +=tItem.name;
        content+="</td>\n";
        content+="\t\t\t</tr>\n";
    }
    i++;
}
content+="\t\t</table>\n\t</body>\n</html>";
```

The preceding code looks like a lot, but it's mostly the switch statement (more on switch statements in Chapter 11, "Statements and Expressions"). We first grab a copy of all the items in the library as an array. Then we begin to go through them one by one, setting each row of our Excel spreadsheet with properties of each item; using the `switch` statement, we even color code each type of library item. When the loop is over, we close off the Excel spreadsheet and are ready to create the file with the next piece of code:

```
//write the file
FLfile.write(filePath,content);
```

And that's the last line where we create the Excel file at `filePath` and write `content` to it. All together, the code looks like this:

```
//get the path of the doc
var tPath = fl.getDocumentDOM().path;
var fileName = tPath.slice(tPath.lastIndexOf("\\")+1,tPath.lastIndexOf("."));
tPath = tPath.slice(0,tPath.lastIndexOf("\\"));
var filePath = "file:///"+tPath.split("\\").join("/")+"/"+fileName+"_library.xls";

//if the file already exists.. get rid of it
if(FLfile.exists(filePath)){
    FLfile.remove(filePath);
}
//start of the content
var content="";
content+="<html>\n\t<body>\n";
content+="\t\t<table border='1'>\n";
content+="\t\t\t<tr>\n";
content+="\t\t\t\t<th nowrap>id</th>\n";
content+="\t\t\t\t<th nowrap>type</th>\n";
content+="\t\t\t\t<th nowrap>linkageClassName</th>\n";
content+="\t\t\t\t<th nowrap>linkageURL</th>\n";
content+="\t\t\t\t<th nowrap>linkageIdentifier</th>\n";
content+="\t\t\t\t<th nowrap>libraryPath</th>\n";

//now its time to run through the array of library items
var itemArray= fl.getDocumentDOM().library.items;
itemArray.sort();
var tLength = itemArray.length;
var i=0;
while(i<tLength){
    var tItem = itemArray[i];
    if(tItem.itemType != "folder"){
        content+="\t\t\t<tr>\n";
        content+="\t\t\t\t<td align='right'>";
        content+=i;
        content+="</td>\n";
        content+="\t\t\t\t<td align='right'><b>";
        switch (tItem.itemType){
```

```
            case "movie clip":
                content+="<font color='ff0000'>movie clip</font>";
                break;
            case "bitmap":
                content+="<font color='006600'>bitmap</font>";
                break;
            case "sound":
                content+="<font color='cc9900'>sound</font>";
                break;
            case "graphic":
                content+="<font color='9933cc'>graphic</font>";
                break;
            case "button":
                content+="<font color='0000ff'>button</font>";
                break;
            case "compiled clip":
                content+="<font color='333300'>compiled clip</font>";
                break;
            case "font":
                content+="<font color='cc9900'>button</font>";
                break;
            case "video":
                content+="<font color='996600'>compiled clip</font>";
                break;
            default:
                content+=tItem.itemType;
        }

        content+="</b></td>\n";
        content+="\t\t\t\t<td align='right'>";
        (tItem.linkageClassName)? content+="<i>"+
➥tItem.linkageClassName+"</i>":content+="N/A";
        content+="</td>\n";
        content+="\t\t\t\t<td align='right'>";
        (tItem.linkageURL)? content+="<i>"+tItem.linkageURL+"</i>":content+="N/A";
        content+="</td>\n";
        content+="\t\t\t\t<td align='right'>";
        (tItem.linkageIdentifier)? content+="<b>"+
➥tItem.linkageIdentifier+"</b>":content+="N/A";
        content+="</td>\n";
        content+="\t\t\t\t<td align='right'>";
        content +=tItem.name;
        content+="</td>\n";
        content+="\t\t\t</tr>\n";
    }
```

```
    i++;
}
content+="\t\t</table>\n\t</body>\n</html>";

//write the file
FLfile.write(filePath,content);
```

Now you can test this file by opening any Flash document that has items in its library and running the command, as shown in Figure 27.15.

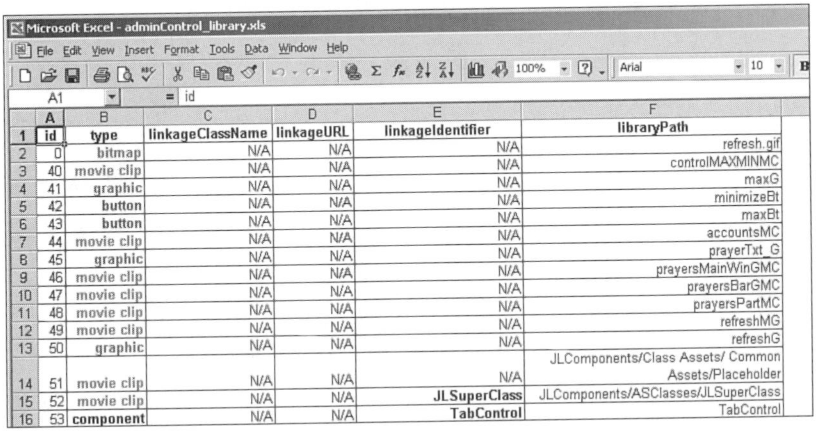

	A	B	C	D	E	F
1	id	type	linkageClassName	linkageURL	linkageIdentifier	libraryPath
2	0	bitmap	N/A	N/A	N/A	refresh.gif
3	40	movie clip	N/A	N/A	N/A	controlMAXMINMC
4	41	graphic	N/A	N/A	N/A	maxG
5	42	button	N/A	N/A	N/A	minimizeBt
6	43	button	N/A	N/A	N/A	maxBt
7	44	movie clip	N/A	N/A	N/A	accountsMC
8	45	graphic	N/A	N/A	N/A	prayerTxt_G
9	46	movie clip	N/A	N/A	N/A	prayersMainWinGMC
10	47	movie clip	N/A	N/A	N/A	prayersBarGMC
11	48	movie clip	N/A	N/A	N/A	prayersPartMC
12	49	movie clip	N/A	N/A	N/A	refreshMG
13	50	graphic	N/A	N/A	N/A	refreshG
14	51	movie clip	N/A	N/A	N/A	JLComponents/Class Assets/ Common Assets/Placeholder
15	52	movie clip	N/A	N/A	JLSuperClass	JLComponents/ASClasses/JLSuperClass
16	53	component	N/A	N/A	TabControl	TabControl

FIGURE 27.15 File I/O in JSFL opens up a lot of avenues for interesting and time-saving commands.

CAUTION

It is important to understand that although File I/O is very powerful and fun to work with, it is also dangerous because it can in fact destroy and overwrite files. This is even more important to remember when installing and running commands from unknown third parties. Always check the code if it is not from a trusted source. And even if it is from a trusted source, check it anyway.

TIP

If you want to turn off the capability to have File I/O running completely, you can change the name of the file. PC users will find the file here: `C:\Program Files\Macromedia\Flash 8\en\First Run\External Libraries\FLfile.dll` and Mac users can find the file here: `Mac:HardDrive\Applications\Macromedia Flash 8\en\First Run\External Libraries\FLfile`.

Summary

This chapter covered a lot of the Extensibility layer in Flash, including JSFL and the XML-to-UI API. With these technologies, you can extend the Flash authoring environment as far as you like to increase efficiency and speed in creating, managing, and organizing Flash content. The most important things to take away from this chapter are the fundamentals and the desire to experiment. Try taking what you have seen in this chapter and combining certain steps into your own panel, command, or tool.

You can also find some great extensions here:

http://www.macromedia.com/go/flash_exchange/.

CHAPTER **28**

Beyond Flash

Throughout this book, we have covered nearly all aspects of Flash and creating Flash content. I say "nearly" because Flash is not the only tool on the block that can create Flash content, but it is the best. There are, however, several alternatives for creating Flash content as well as third-party applications for enriching content.

This chapter covers many other applications that can create the now-famous Swiff (.swf) format. We also go over some applications that can help you with creating and even securing your Flash files.

Flash Alternatives

There are several alternatives to using Flash to create Flash content quickly; the first is SWiSHmax.

SWiSHmax

Swish has been around for several years starting out as a general text animator that can export in the form of .swf files. It has blossomed into a full-blown Flash content creator while maintaining its roots in text animation with over 200 individual effects. The stage has the same feel as Swish 2.0, as you can see in Figure 28.1, but the effects are now limitless.

SWiSHmax can be found at http://www.swishzone.com and it costs about $100. You can also find even more applications at swishzone.com that will create Flash content, but SWiSHmax is their premiere product.

FIGURE 28.1   The SWiSHmax stage where you can create elements to be animated.

Building files in SWiSHmax is fast and easy.

1. After closing the pop-up dialog box that will appear by default, create a new Swish file.

2. Select the Text tool and draw a text field on the stage.

3. Select the Text tab in the options menu on the right of the stage, and in the window, type `Flash 8 Professional Unleashed`.

   Notice that when you create a text field, a layer is created automatically in the timeline.

4. Now select the first frame in the new layer and click the Add Effect button.

5. Move down and select Looping Continuously>Flapping Wave.

6. Now the timeline has 20 frames in it. Click the Play Effect button to see the effect at work.

7. You can also customize the effect by selecting the effect and choosing Edit, Properties as you can see in Figure 28.2

Play with the different effects and customize them to get your own. From the properties dialog box of the effects, you can even save your own effects to distribute to your friends.

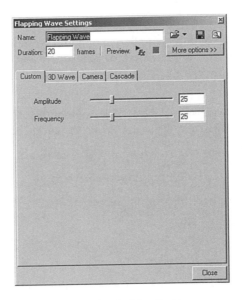

FIGURE 28.2   The properties dialog box for Swish effects.

Another great application from Swish that will make creating online photo albums a breeze is SWiSHpix.

SWiSHpix

SWiSHpix allows users to quickly create digital photo albums, which you can animate and even put to music. After that, you can either burn to a CD or quickly upload to a Web server via FTP.

The program has five simple steps:

1. **Get Pictures.** You gather the pictures and make minor edits to their layout and title.

2. **Edit Pictures.** You crop and adjust brightness and contrast of the images.

3. **Create Album.** You set options for the album such as music, time delays, and theme.

4. **Decorate Pictures.** You add text bubbles or clip art to individual images.

5. **Publish Album.** You make choices for the form that the album will be published in, such as on a CD or published directly to the Web.

SWiSHpix is a great tool to quickly create online content for photo albums, screen savers, or CD albums. It is available at `swishzone.com`.

But SWiSH isn't the only great software for people to quickly and easily create Flash files. PowerCONVERTER from PresentationPro is another one.

28

PowerCONVERTER

PowerCONVERTER is great for users who like to build presentations in PowerPoint, but want to move to the Web. PowerCONVERTER will take any and all PowerPoint presentations (.ppt) and convert them to either a Swiff file (.swf) for the Web, or a projector file (.exe) for CD content.

You can get a trial version of PowerCONVERTER from PresentationPro at http://www.presentationpro.com/products/PowerCONVERTER.asp.

Some of the features PresentationPro says PowerCONVERTER has are

- File size reduction up to 97% from PowerPoint to Swiff (.swf)

- Retains all sounds, transactions, and graphics

- Secure file conversion free of viruses

And it currently retails for about $400.

If you are interested in converting video to Flash, but do not need the entire Flash suite, there are two very good options available.

Wildform FlixPro

FlixPro is a product that makes turning video into a Swiff file very easy and fast. It also has a great compression ratio and several built-in players.

The software is available at http://www.wildform.com and retails for about $99. It does have a trial version.

With FlixPro, you can import and convert the following formats:

- .avi

- .dv

- .mov/.qt

- .mpeg

- .mp4

- .3gp

- .asf/.wmv

With the ability to export as a raw Swiff file, or as a Swiff file with a built-in video player, if all you are interested in is converting video to .swf, FlixPro is definitely an option, but not the only option.

Sorenson Squeeze

Sorenson Squeeze is another good choice for converting video to Flash. It has many settings for controlling quality output and has a great compression package.

Sorenson Squeeze can be found at `http://www.sorensonmedia.com/` and has a trial version. The retail price on the full suite of Sorenson Squeeze Compression is about $450.

Here are the formats Sorenson Squeeze supports for importing:

- `.aif/.aiff`
- `.asf`
- `.avi`
- `DV`
- `.mov`
- `.wmv`
- `.wma`
- `.wav`

It supports most of the same video formats, but it can export to some of them as well as `.swf` and `.flv` (Flash Video).

But if video is not what you are looking for, there are other products that can produce high-end 3D vector graphics and animations that can be exported into .SWF format.

Swift 3D

Swift 3D, from Electric Rain, is the premier product for creating 3D vector animations. It can export in a variety of popular formats including `.swf` and `.svg`. Some of its features include

- Enhanced vector realism
- Full preview system
- Sophisticated cameras and lighting
- High level of object control
- Advanced modeling

You can see in Figures 28.3 and 28.4 some of the interface features of Swift 3D. Swift 3D can be found at `http://www.swift3d.com` for about $229.

28

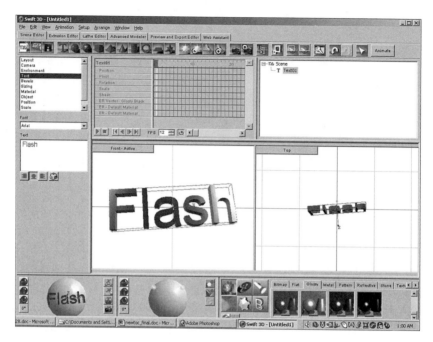

FIGURE 28.3   The Scene Editor in Swift 3d.

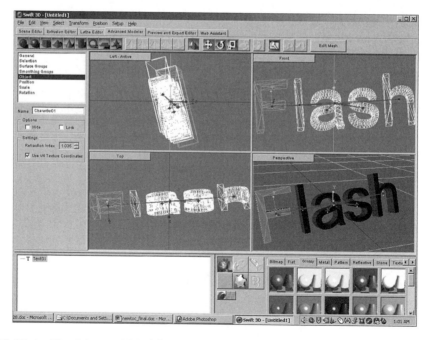

FIGURE 28.4   The Advanced Modeler, a new feature in Swift 3D 4.

And if screen capture is what you are after, there are several products out there that fit the bill, even one from Macromedia.

Captivate

Captivate, formerly known as RoboDemo, is a screen recording application that allows you to demonstrate software usage or present walkthroughs and have the data be exported into a .swf file. Easily add audio, video, captions, and interactions to your walkthroughs without ever opening anything in Flash.

And because Captivate is both SCORM 1.2 and 2004 compliant, you can deploy your projects, with scoring mechanisms built right in, to most major Learning Management Systems. You can find captivate at http://www.macromedia.com/software/captivate/ and it retails for about $499.

You can see a screen shot of Captivate in Figure 28.5.

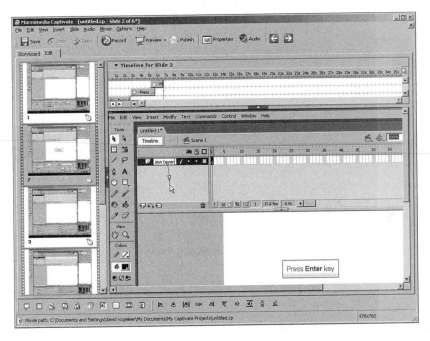

FIGURE 28.5 Captivate will record mouse movement as you work through your demonstration.

So far, we have talked about the different ways to make Flash content without necessarily using Flash. There are many more examples such as Flex, Macromedia's presentation server, and even PHP can create Flash content with the Ming library: http://us3.php.net/manual/en/ref.ming.php. Next we will go over some third-party applications that will significantly improve certain aspects of what can be accomplished using Flash.

Enhancing Flash Files

These next few applications will take different approaches in how they help developers to improve aspects of their Flash file and to be able to retrieve lost information.

The first application will help users drastically reduce the file size of their work.

Optimize

Optimaze is a vector-crunching machine. It can compress vector graphics up to 60% better than Flash itself can while maintaining the same crisp, tight lines that it was originally created in.

It has a very familiar and Flash-based interface for controlling the compression, and it imports .swf files directly, so the original .fla file is not necessary.

Optimaze can be found at http://www.optimaze.biz. It does not have a trial version, but at about $130, if you are into animation in Flash, or you use a lot of vector graphics in your sites or applications, Optimaze is a good tool to keep on hand.

The next software doesn't necessarily help in the design or development stage itself, but if you are like me and are constantly accidentally overwriting the newest version of your Flash file with an older one, this next tool is for you.

Action Script Viewer 4.0

Sometimes, you might lose the original source code, or accidentally overwrite a newer version of the .fla file with an older one, and then realize that your last 10 hours of coding have been lost. In steps Action Script Viewer.

Now in version 4.0, Action Script Viewer from Manitu Group can decompile compiled .swf files into readable format. After you have decompiled the file, you can view any and all ActionScript within the file as well as export certain resources from within the file such as bitmaps, sounds, and movies. The new version of Action Script Viewer has gone even further by allowing the resources and a JSFL command to be created to assist in reconstructing an original FLA file.

At the time of this writing, there was no demo version of version 4 available (but there is a demo for version 3, which has most of the same features). Version 4 is available to purchase for about $60 at http://www.buraks.com/asv/index.html.

Also available on their site are many tools, which complement the Action Script Viewer application, and they are free of charge.

Now that you know Flash files can be decompiled, read and in some cases, can even be turned back into an original source file, you might be wondering what you can do to keep someone else from doing this to your files.

SWF Encrypt™

Even though for the most part, the Flash community is an open-source community, sometimes you might not want prying eyes looking at how your application works. Or worse yet, they could find the server-side pages you are using, and corrupt the data on the back end. Not to worry—SWF Encrypt is here to help.

Mostly, ActionScript is written in plain English (or whatever other language you choose to write it in) for anyone to be able to read, as oppose to Binary, which is unreadable.

SWF Encrypt takes ActionScript and encrypts it with a unique fingerprint key. This means that the same SWF can be used twice and have two unique fingerprint keys. The computer can still understand exactly what the ActionScript is saying, but it is very difficult for anyone looking at it to see what it says.

There is a free trial version of SWF Encrypt at `http://www.amayeta.com/software/swfencrypt/` and the full version is about $99.

Now you have seen several ways to create Flash content and to improve Flash content. You have even seen how to decompile Flash content if you want, but what if you want to take the Flash content itself beyond the Web?

Beyond the Web

Flash does come bundled with the ability to export its content in the form of a projector file, which means it can be placed on a CD and distributed without the need for the player because the projector file has its own built-in player. You can also export in the form of a QuickTime movie (`.mov`) if you have the required plug-in, which costs about $30. But both of these formats have their shortcomings. Even though projector files can be easily created, they are not very powerful and have difficulty interacting with the user's computer.

This section focuses on three applications that will help take your Flash content to places you might never have imagined, starting with screen savers.

ScreenTime

ScreenTime is an application built to allow users to quickly build screen savers for both Windows and Macintosh platforms with their Flash movies.

How easy is it to use? These are the directions from their website:

1. Drop a SWF on the ScreenTime window.

2. Click Build.

And that is it.

Of course, you can do more steps if you like to further customize your screen saver, and you can even create another Flash file to be the control panel for your screen saver for other users to make adjustments to variables.

ScreenTime can be found at `http://www.screentime.com/software/stf/`; it does have a trial version, and the commercial version is about $200.

Another format you might want to put your Flash content in is video, and as mentioned before, with the correct plug-in you can export your Flash files in QuickTime (`.mov`) format. But what if you want to export in another video format?

SWF2Video

SWF2Video allows Flash designers and developers to convert their SWF files to AVI video files while maintaining ActionScript and interactivity. It can even do batch jobs converting several compiled Flash files to AVI.

You can find SWF2Video at `http://www.flashants.com/root/swf2video.shtml`. It does have a trial version available for download, and to purchase the full version will set you back about $80.

Also available on their site is an SWF2Video plug-in for Adobe Premier. This plug-in will allow Adobe Premier users to import SWF files directly into Premier for editing.

The final third-party application that can help take your Flash content beyond the Web is SWF Studio 3.0.

SWF Studio 3.0

SWF Studio 3.0 is the last third-party application in this chapter for a reason. It can take your Flash file and convert it to a full-blown desktop application. It accomplishes this by wrapping the compiled SWF file with several plug-ins that can be accessed by using the ActionScript objects that are installed with the application.

Here is an example that will send a message to a pop-up window when it has been wrapped with SWF Studio:

```
ssCore.App.showMsgBox({icon:"question",buttons:"YesNoCancel",defaultButton:
"button1",prompt:"Isn't this cool?",title:"Simple Question"});
```

Of course, that is a very generic example of what can be done. Using SWF Studio, you can interact with an FTP server, the user's local computer file system, as well as the registry, and even create your own browser. For an example with all source code, go to the companion site for a simple MP3 player.

SWF Studio has a very easy-to-use interface, as you can see in Figures 28.6.

In addition, you can download another app called Code Builder, which will help you get started writing code for SWF Studio.

SWF Studio is not limited to creating desktop applications; it can also create screensavers.

SWF Studio can be found at `http://www.northcode.com` and it does have a free trial download. The purchase price for the full version is about $299.

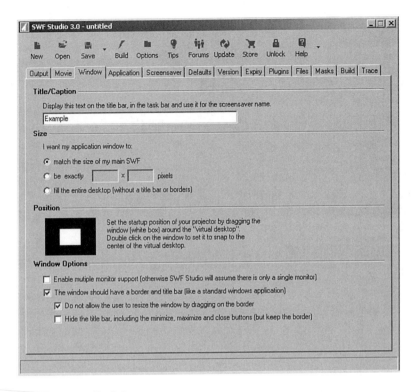

FIGURE 28.6   SWF Studio 3.0.

SWF Studio is not the only application that can create desktop apps from your Flash files, for a full list of reviews, try this link: http://www.flashmagazine.com/1100.htm.

And although SWF Studio is the last application we cover in this chapter, there is still one place we have not taken Flash, into the real world.

MakingThings

MakingThings is a company out of San Francisco, California, that produces teleo modules. Teleo modules are small calculator size circuit boards that can send information to, or receive information from Flash by means of an XML socket server and USB connection. You can see a picture of a teleo module in Figure 28.7.

And these circuit boards can receive data from buttons, switches, and photocells, anything that can send a digital or analog signal. They can also control any electronic device including lights, motors, and buzzers.

The software required to run these modules is free and will run on both Mac and PC. The modules themselves range around $150 or more, depending on what you are trying to accomplish. The introductory module, a good module to start with, is $159. They can all be found at http://www.makingthings.com.

28

FIGURE 28.7   The introductory module from MakingThings.

Summary

This chapter has covered many third-party applications to help you not only create SWF files without Flash itself, but to also improve your content either by lowering its file size or taking it beyond the web altogether.

If you are planning to purchase any of these third-party applications, if they have a free trial download, download it, play with it, and then make a decision.

PART IV

Appendix

IN THIS PART

ActionScript Reference

This appendix covers some of the new Flash classes that come with Flash 8.

It is important to note that in the availability of each action, you will see two acronyms, FP (Flash Player) and AS (ActionScript). They are there to show the minimum requirement for that script.

The BitmapData Class

The BitmapData class is designed to be able to load and manipulate bitmaps at runtime.

It is important that when using this class to import it first at the beginning of your script, like this:

```
import flash.display.BitmapData;
```

To instantiate a new instance of the BitmapData class, use this code as a template:

```
var myBitmapData:BitmapData = new
BitmapData(width,height,transparent,fillColor);
```

- width—The width of the bitmap in pixels.

- height—The height of the bitmap in pixels.

- transparent—A Boolean value representing transparency of the bitmap.

- fillColor—The hex color value representing the fill color of the bitmap.

Properties

`height`
Availability: FP:8, AS:1.0

Generic Template: `myBitmapData.height;`

Description:

A numerical value representing the height of the bitmap in pixels.

Example:

This example will trace the height of a bitmap:

```
import flash.display.BitmapData;
var myBitmapData:BitmapData = new BitmapData(20,30);
trace(myBitmapData.height);
//output: 30
```

`rectangle`
Availability: FP:8, AS:1.0

Generic Template: `myBitmapData.rectangle;`

Description:

A Rectangle object holding position and dimension data about a given bitmap. The top (y) and left (x) are zero.

Example:

This example will trace the information stored in the rectangle property:

```
import flash.display.BitmapData;
var myBitmapData:BitmapData = new BitmapData(20,30);
trace(myB.rectangle);
//output: (x=0, y=0, w=20, h=30)
```

`transparent`
Availability: FP:8, AS:1.0

Generic Template: `myBitmapData.transparent;`

Description:

A Boolean value representing the state of transparency in a bitmap.

Example:

This example will trace transparency in a given bitmap:

```
import flash.display.BitmapData;
var myBitmapData:BitmapData = new BitmapData(20,30,true);
```

```
trace(myBitmapData.transparent);
//output: true
```

width
Availability: FP:8, AS:1.0

Generic Template: `myBitmapData.height;`

Description:

A numerical value representing the width of the bitmap in pixels.

Example:

This example will trace the width of a bitmap:

```
import flash.display.BitmapData;
var myBitmapData:BitmapData = new BitmapData(20,30);
trace(myBitmapData.width);
//output: 20
```

Methods

applyFilter
Availability: FP:8, AS:1.0

Generic Template: `myBitmapData.applyFilter(bitmap, rec, point, filter);`

Parameters:

bitmap—The source bitmap image having the filter applied to it. It can be either the current bitmap instance or a different bitmap.

rec—A Rectangle object that will define the area to apply the filter to.

point—A Point object that represents the top-left point of the applied area.

filter—A Filter object representing the type of filter to be applied to the bitmap.

Returns: Number

If the filter has been applied successfully, the number 0 will be returned; otherwise a negative number will be returned.

Description:

This method will apply a defined filter to the designated bitmap.

Example:

This example will attach an image residing in the library and apply a Blur filter to it:

```
import flash.display.BitmapData;
import flash.geom.Point;
import flash.filters.BlurFilter;
```

```
var point:Point = new flash.geom.Point(0,0);
var blur:BlurFilter = new flash.filters.BlurFilter(5, 5, 100);
var myBitmapData:BitmapData =
➥BitmapData.loadBitmap("bigBen");//an image in the library
//apply the filter
myBitmapData.applyFilter(myBitmapData, myBitmapData.rectangle, point, blur);
//attach the image
this.attachBitmap(myBitmapData, 1);
```

clone

Availability: FP:8, AS:1.0

Generic Template: `myBitmapData.clone();`

Returns: BitmapData

This method will return an exact duplicate of the BitmapData object it is being called on.

Description:

This method will create an exact copy of the bitmap image it is being called on.

Example:

This example will create a generic bitmap image, create a copy, and attach that copy:

```
import flash.display.BitmapData;
var myBitmapData:BitmapData = new BitmapData(100,100,false,0xff0000);
//create the copy
var copyBitmap:BitmapData = myBitmapData.clone();
//attach the bitmap
this.attachBitmap(copyBitmap,1);
```

colorTransform

Availability: FP:8, AS:1.0

Generic Template: `myBitmapData.colorTransform(rec, transformObj);`

Parameters:

> *rec*—A Rectangle object that will define the area to apply the color transform to.
>
> *transformObj*—A ColorTransform object used to adjust the color of the bitmap.

Description:

This method will apply a defined ColorTransform object to the designated bitmap.

Example:

This example will create a red rectangle that we will convert to a green rectangle with a ColorTransform object:

```
import flash.display.BitmapData;
import flash.geom.ColorTransform;
//create a red rectangle
var myBitmapData:BitmapData = new BitmapData(100,100,false,0xff0000);
//create the color transform
var myTransform:ColorTransform = new ColorTransform(100,100,100,1,255,150,100,1);
//apply the transform
myBitmapData.colorTransform(myBitmapData.rectangle,myTransform);
//attach the bitmap
this.attachBitmap(myBitmapData,1);
```

copyChannel
Availability: FP:8, AS:1.0

Generic Template: `myBitmapData.copyChannel(bitmap, rec, point, sourceChannel, destChannel);`

Parameters:

> *bitmap*—The source BitmapData object where the channel will be copied from.
>
> *rec*—A Rectangle object that will define the area the new channel will be applied to.
>
> *point*—A Point object that represents the top left point of the applied area.
>
> *sourceChannel*—The source channel that is being copied from *bitmap*.
>
> *destChannel*—The destination channel where the *sourceChannel* will be copied to.

Description:

This method will copy a channel from one BitmapData instance to another. Here are the available channels:

- 1—red
- 2—green
- 4—blue
- 8—alpha

Example:

This example will create a red rectangle and then create a blue rectangle. After that, the blue channel will be copied from the second rectangle into the first, making it a purple rectangle. Then the rectangle will be displayed using the `attachBitmap` method:

```
import flash.display.BitmapData;
import flash.geom.Point;
//create the point
var point:Point = new Point(0,0);
//create a red rectangle
```

```
var myBitmapData:BitmapData = new BitmapData(100,100,false,0xff0000);
//create a second BitmapData object
var myBitmapData2:BitmapData = new BitmapData(100,100,false,0x0000ff);
//copy the blue channel over
myBitmapData.copyChannel(myBitmapData2,myBitmapData.rectangle, point, 4, 4);
//attach the bitmap
this.attachBitmap(myBitmapData,1);
```

copyPixels
Availability: FP:8, AS:1.0

Generic Template: `myBitmapData.copyPixels(bitmap, rec, point, aBitmap, aPoint, merge);`

Parameters:

> *bitmap*—The source BitmapData object where the pixels will be copied from.
>
> *rec*—A Rectangle object that will define the area the new pixels will be applied to.
>
> *point*—A Point object that represents the top left point of the applied area.
>
> *aBitmap*—An optional second BitmapData object to use as the alpha source.
>
> *aPoint*—An optional Point object parameter representing the top left of the *aBitmap* parameter to use on the *rec* parameter.
>
> *merge*—An optional Boolean value that states to use the alpha channel (`true`) or not (`false`).

Description:

This method will copy over a selection of pixels from one BitmapData object to another:

Example:

This example will load two bitmaps that currently reside in the library (both 400×300 in size) and copy the one on the top half into the other to display:

```
import flash.display.BitmapData;
import flash.geom.*;
//create the rectangle to only grab the top half
var rec:Rectangle = new Rectangle(0,0,400,150);
//top left
var point:Point = new Point(0,0);
//create the first bitmap object
var myBitmapData:BitmapData = BitmapData.loadBitmap("bridge");
//create a second BitmapData object
var myBitmapData2:BitmapData = BitmapData.loadBitmap("bigBen");
//copy the top half of the second rectangle over
myBitmapData.copyPixels(myBitmapData2, rec, point);
//attach the bitmap
this.attachBitmap(myBitmapData,1);
```

dispose
Availability: FP:8, AS:1.0

Generic Template: `myBitmapData.dispose();`

Description:

This method will free up all memory in the instance of the BitmapData object.

Example:

This example will create a generic bitmap image, attach it to the root timeline so it is visible, and then set up an onMouseDown event so that when a user clicks the stage, the rectangle will be gone, and the memory will have been freed:

```
import flash.display.BitmapData;
//create the bitmap object
var myBitmapData:BitmapData = new BitmapData(100,100,false,0xff0000);
//attach the bitmap
this.attachBitmap(myBitmapData,1);
//when the user clicks the mouse, clear the memory
this.onMouseDown = function():Void{
    myBitmapData.dispose();
}
```

draw
Availability: FP:8, AS:1.0

Generic Template: `myBitmapData.draw(bitmap, matrix, transformObj, blendMode, clipRec, smooth);`

Parameters:

> *bitmap*—The BitmapData object that will be drawn.
>
> *matrix*—A Matrix object used to control visual aspects of the bitmap (that is, rotation and scaling).
>
> *transformObj*—A ColorTransform object used to adjust the color of the bitmap.
>
> *blendMode*—A BlendMode object used to control the blend properties of the bitmap.
>
> *clipRec*—An optional Rectangle object parameter representing the clipping region.
>
> *smooth*—An optional Boolean value that states to smooth the bitmap if it scales (`true`) or not (`false`). The default is `false`.

Description:

Using vector rendering, this method will draw an image based on *bitmap* and other parameters you pass it.

Example:

This example will create a red square as the first bitmap. Then it will load in a bitmap from the library. The first bitmap will automatically display when tested, and when a user clicks the mouse, the second bitmap will be drawn in its place.

```
import flash.display.BitmapData;
//create the first BitmapData as a red square
var myBitmapData:BitmapData = new BitmapData(100,100,false,0xff0000);
//load the second bitmap from the Library
var myBitmapData2:BitmapData = BitmapData.loadBitmap("bigBen");
//display the first bitmap
this.attachBitmap(myBitmapData,1);
//when a user clicks the stage, draw the second one
this.onMouseDown = function(){
    myBitmapData.draw(myBitmapData2);
}
```

fillRect
Availability: FP:8, AS:1.0

Generic Template: `myBitmapData.fillRect(rec, color);`

Parameters:

> *rec*—The Rectangle object that defines the area of the bitmap to be filled.
>
> *color*—An ARGB value that represents the color the rectangle will be filled with.

Description:

This method will fill a defined Rectangle with the ARGB (0xAARRGGBB) color passed to it.

Example:

This example will create a generic bitmap image with no defined color. It will then fill the entire rectangle with a semitransparent red color. Then the bitmap will be attached to the main timeline:

```
import flash.display.BitmapData;
//create the bitmap object
var myBitmapData:BitmapData = new BitmapData(100,100);
//fill the rectangle
myBitmapData.fillRect(myBitmapData.rectangle, 0x88ff0000);
//attach the bitmap
this.attachBitmap(myBitmapData,1);
```

floodFill
Availability: FP:8, AS:1.0

Generic Template: `myBitmapData.floodFill(x, y, color);`

Parameters:

x—The horizontal coordinate of the bitmap.

y—The vertical coordinate of the bitmap.

color—An ARGB (0xAARRGGBB) value that represents the color the rectangle will be filled with.

Description:

This method will carry out a flood-fill operation beginning at the designated coordinates.

Example:

This example will first import the necessary class file. Then we will create an initial color to work with later in the example. After that, we create a new bitmap, set its color to a light gray, and then attach it to the root timeline. Finally, we create an event that is triggered each time the user clicks the stage and that will incrementally increase the startColor variable; then, using the floodFill method, it changes the color of the rectangle to gradually appear more red:

```
import flash.display.BitmapData;
//create the initial color
var startColor:Number = 0x00110000;
//create the bitmap
var myBitmapData:BitmapData = new BitmapData(100, 100, false, 0x00bbbbbb);
//attach the bitmap
this.attachBitmap(myBitmapData, 1);
//incrament the color and fill the rectangle
this.onMouseDown = function():Void{
        startColor += 0x00100000;
        myBitmapData.floodFill(0, 0, startColor);
}
```

generateFilterRect
Availability: FP:8, AS:1.0

Generic Template: myBitmapData.generateFilterRect(rec, filter);

Parameters:

rec—The Rectangle object used to define the designated area to have the filter applied to it.

filter—The Filter object that will be applied.

Returns: Rectangle

The Rectangle object returned will represent the necessary dimensions and placement to fully display the bitmap when the given filter is applied.

Description:

This method will generate the Rectangle necessary to accommodate the bitmap if it is applied to the given filter.

Example:

This example will generate the necessary `Rectangle` to use if a BlurFilter is applied to a 400×300 image:

```
import flash.display.BitmapData;
import flash.filters.BlurFilter;
//create the filter
var blur:BlurFilter = new flash.filters.BlurFilter(5, 5, 100);
//load the bitmap
var myBitmapData:BitmapData =
BitmapData.loadBitmap("bigBen");//an image in the library
//generate the rectangle
trace(myBitmapData.generateFilterRect(myBitmapData.rectangle, blur));
//output: (x=-18, y=-18, w=436, h=336)
```

getColorBoundsRect
Availability: FP:8, AS:1.0

Generic Template: `myBitmapData.getColorBoundsRect(maskColor, color, findColor, filter);`

Parameters:

maskColor—An ARGB hexadecimal color.

color—An ARGB hexadecimal color.

findColor—A Boolean value that if `true`, returns the bounding Rectangle where *color* exists; if `false`, will return the bounding Rectangle where *color* does not exist.

Returns: Rectangle

The `Rectangle` object returned will represent the minimum size rectangle to encompass all pixels of the bitmap that contain the given color.

Description:

This method will search the bitmap image for the given hexadecimal color and return a bounding rectangle capable of encompassing all pixels with that color.

Example:

This example will generate the necessary `Rectangle` to encompass a color at a given pixel (10,10):

```
import flash.display.BitmapData;
//load the bitmap
var myBitmapData:BitmapData =
BitmapData.loadBitmap("bigBen");//an image in the library
//generate the rectangle
```

```
trace(myBitmapData.getColorBoundsRect
➡(0xffffffff, myBitmapData.getPixel32(10,10), true));
//output: (x=8, y=10, w=32, h=34)
```

getPixel
Availability: FP:8, AS:1.0

Generic Template: `myBitmapData.getPixel(x, y);`

Returns: Number

The RGB value of a given pixel.

Parameters:

> x—The horizontal coordinate of the bitmap.
>
> y—The vertical coordinate of the bitmap.

Description:

This method will return the RGB value of a pixel at coordinate (x,y).

Example:

This example will load a bitmap from the library, then return the color of the pixel at coordinate (100,100). After that, we will use the `fillRect` method to completely color the bitmap with the selected color. And finally, the block of color will be displayed.

```
import flash.display.BitmapData;
//load the bitmap
var myBitmapData:BitmapData =
➡BitmapData.loadBitmap("bigBen");//an image in the library
//grab the color of the pixel at (100,100)
var tempColor:Number = myBitmapData.getPixel(100,100);
//fill the rectangle with that color
myBitmapData.fillRect(myBitmapData.rectangle, tempColor);
//display the color block
this.attachBitmap(myBitmapData, 1);
```

getPixel32
Availability: FP:8, AS:1.0

Generic Template: `myBitmapData.getPixel32(x, y);`

Returns: Number

The ARGB value of a given pixel.

Parameters:

> x—The horizontal coordinate of the bitmap.
>
> y—The vertical coordinate of the bitmap.

Description:

This method will return the ARGB value of a pixel at coordinate (x,y).

Example:

This example will load a bitmap from the library, then return the color of the pixel at coordinate (100,100). After that, we use the `fillRect` method to completely color the bitmap with the selected color. And finally, the block of color will be displayed.

```
import flash.display.BitmapData;
//load the bitmap
var myBitmapData:BitmapData =
➡BitmapData.loadBitmap("bigBen");//an image in the library
//grab the color of the pixel at (100,100)
var tempColor:Number = myBitmapData.getPixel32(100,100);
//fill the rectangle with that color
myBitmapData.fillRect(myBitmapData.rectangle, tempColor);
//display the color block
this.attachBitmap(myBitmapData, 1);
```

hitTest
Availability: FP:8, AS:1.0

Generic Template: `myBitmapData.hitTest(point, alpha, obj, bitmapPoint, alphaThreshhold);`

Parameters:

> *point*—A `Point` object representing a point in the bitmap.
>
> *alpha*—The maximum alpha that is still considered opaque.
>
> *obj*—A `Rectangle, Point,` or `BitmapData` object.
>
> *bitmapPoint*—An optional parameter representing the `Point` in the second bitmap image, if BitmapData is the *obj* data type.
>
> *alphaThreshold*—The maximum alpha that is still considered opaque in the second bitmap image, if BitmapData is the *obj* data type.

Returns: Boolean `true` if the hit is within designated area, otherwise `false`.

Description:

This method will return a Boolean value answering whether a hit has occurred in a designated area of a bitmap.

Example:

This example will first get the necessary classes we need. Then a bitmap will be created with a red square being drawn. Next, the bitmap will be attached to the root timeline. And finally, we use the `onMouseMove` event to monitor whether the user moves the mouse over the rectangle:

```
import flash.display.BitmapData;
import flash.geom.Point;
//create the bitmap
var myBitmapData:BitmapData = new BitmapData(100, 100, false, 0x00FF0000);
//attach the bitmap
this.attachBitmap(myBitmapData, 1);
//monitor the mouse position
this.onMouseMove = function():Void{
   if(myBitmapData.hitTest(new Point(), 255, new Point(_xmouse, _ymouse))) {
      trace("x - " + _xmouse + " y - " + _ymouse);
   }
}
```

loadBitmap
Availability: FP:8, AS:1.0

Generic Template: `myBitmapData.loadBitmap(id);`

Parameters:

  id—The linkage identifier of a bitmap in the library.

Returns: BitmapData

The `BitmapData` information for the loading bitmap.

Description:

This method will load a bitmap from the library into a `BitmapData` object at runtime.

Example:

This example will load a bitmap from the library and display it in the root timeline.

```
import flash.display.BitmapData;
//load the bitmap
var myBitmapData:BitmapData =
➡BitmapData.loadBitmap("bigBen");//an image in the library
this.attachBitmap(myBitmapData, 1);
```

merge
Availability: FP:8, AS:1.0

Generic Template: `myBitmapData.merge(bitmap, rec, point, red, green, blue, alpha);`

Parameters:

  bitmap—The bitmap image that will have the merge applied to it. It does not have to be the
  BitmapData object calling the method.

  rec—The Rectangle that defines the area where the merge will take effect.

point—The Point object representing the top left of the current BitmapData object that corresponds to the top left of *rec*.

red—The number to multiply the red channel by.

green—The number to multiply the green channel by.

blue—The number to multiply the blue channel by.

alpha—The number to multiply the alpha channel by.

Description:

This method will join two `BitmapData` objects and combine their channels based on the amount of multiplication given.

Example:

This example will create a red and a blue bitmap, then combine them and increase the blue by 255. Then the bitmap will be displayed as purple:

```
import flash.display.BitmapData;
import flash.geom.Point;
//create the point
var point:Point = new Point(0,0);
//create both bitmaps
var myBitmapData:BitmapData = new BitmapData(100,100,false, 0xff0000);
var myBitmapData2:BitmapData = new BitmapData(100,100,false, 0x0000ff);
//merge the 2 and increase the blue
myBitmapData.merge(myBitmapData2, myBitmapData.rectangle, point, 0, 0, 255, 0);
//display the bitmap
this.attachBitmap(myBitmapData, 1);
```

noise
Availability: FP:8, AS:1.0

Generic Template: `myBitmapData.noise(seed, low, high, channels, grayScale);`

Parameters:

seed—A random number to create a random feeling noise.

low—The minimum value per channel between 0–255. Default value is 0.

high—The maximum value per channel between 0–255. Default value is 255.

channels—This represents which channels to use; 1, 2, 4, or 8. You can also combine them using the *logical OR* operator (|) like this (1|4|8). The default value is (1|2|4).

grayScale—A Boolean value determining whether to use a grayscale image. The default value is `false`.

Description:

This method will fill a bitmap with pixels representing random noise (static).

Example:

This example will create a small rectangle of constantly changing static:

```
import flash.display.BitmapData;
//create the bitmap
var myBitmapData:BitmapData = new BitmapData(100,100);
//constantly update the noise
this.onEnterFrame = function(){
    myBitmapData.noise(Math.random()*100, 1, 255, 1, true);
}
//display the static
this.attachBitmap(myBitmapData,1);
```

paletteMap
Availability: FP:8, AS:1.0

Generic Template: myBitmapData.paletteMap(bitmap, rec, point, redArray, greenArray, blueArray, alphaArray);

Parameters:

bitmap—The bitmap image that will have the paletteMap applied to it. It does not have to be the BitmapData object calling the method.

rec—The Rectangle that defines the area where the paletteMap will take affect.

point—The Point object representing the top left of the current BitmapData object that corresponds to the top left of *rec*.

redArray—The array of values to use with the red channel.

greenArray—The array of values to use with the green channel.

blueArray—The array of values to use with the blue channel.

alphaArray—The array of values to use with the alpha channel.

Description:

This method will re-map each of the four channels in a given bitmap using four arrays each containing 256 values.

Example:

This example will first import the necessary class files. Then we will create a variable to hold an initial height that we will use later. Next, we create the bitmap as a 100×100 red square. Then the bitmap is attached to the root timeline. Finally, we use the onMouseDown event to create blue, horizontal stripes down the red square:

```
import flash.display.BitmapData;
import flash.geom.Rectangle;
import flash.geom.Point;
//create the start height variable
```

A

```
var startHeight = 2;
//create the bitmap
var myBitmapData:BitmapData = new BitmapData(100, 100, false, 0x00FF0000);
//attach the bitmap
this.attachBitmap(myBitmapData, 1);
//make some stripes
this.onMouseDown = function():Void{
   var red_array:Array = new Array();
   red_array[255] = 0x000000FF;
   var blue_array:Array = new Array();
   blue_array[255] = 0x00FF0000;
   myBitmapData.paletteMap(myBitmapData, new Rectangle(0, 0, 100, startHeight),
➡ new Point(), red_array, undefined, blue_array);
   startHeight+=2;
}
```

perlinNoise
Availability: FP:8, AS:1.0

Generic Template: myBitmapData.perlinNoise(baseX, baseY, octaves, seed, stitch, fractal, channels, grayscale, offSet);

Parameters:

>   *baseX*—The horizontal frequency.
>
>   *baseY*—The vertical frequency.
>
>   *octaves*—The total number of individual noise functions. The higher this number, the more detailed and the more processor-intensive the bitmap will become.
>
>   *seed*—A random number used to create a realistic noise effect.
>
>   *stitch*—A Boolean value that if true will attempt to smooth the transition edges in the bitmap image.
>
>   *fractal*—A Boolean value that if true will generate fractal noise, but if false will create turbulence.
>
>   *channels*—This represents which channels to use; 1, 2, 4, or 8. You can also combine them using the *logical OR* operator (|) like this (1|4|8). The default value is (1|2|4).
>
>   *grayScale*—A Boolean value determining whether to use a grayscale image. The default value is false.
>
>   *offSet*—The array of values that correspond to x, y coordinates that can smoothly scroll the layers.

Description:

This method will create a more advanced form of noise than the noise method does. Images made with perlinNoise are often used for things such as fire or water.

Example:

This example will create a small lightning effect in a BitmapData object:

```
import flash.display.BitmapData;
//create the bitmap
var myBitmapData:BitmapData = new BitmapData(200, 200);
//make lightning
this.onEnterFrame = function(){
    myBitmapData.perlinNoise(50, 50, 5, Math.random()*100,
➥ false, false, 8, false);
}
//display the lightning
this.attachBitmap(myBitmapData,1);
```

pixelDissolve
Availability: FP:8, AS:1.0

Generic Template: `myBitmapData.pixelDissolve(bitmap, rec, point, seed, numPixels, fillColor);`

Returns: Number

This number represents the next random seed that should be used.

Parameters:

> *bitmap*—The bitmap image that will have the pixelDissolve applied to it. It does not have to be the BitmapData object calling the method.
>
> *rec*—The `Rectangle` that defines the area where the pixelDissolve will take effect.
>
> *point*—The `Point` object representing the top left of the current BitmapData object that corresponds to the top left of *rec*.
>
> *seed*—A random number used to begin the dissolve. The default value is 0.
>
> *numPixels*—The number of pixels to dissolve. The default value is 1/30 of the overall area.
>
> *fillColor*—An ARGB color used to fill pixels.

Description:

This method will render a pixel dissolve effect on the given bitmap using a second bitmap.

Example:

This example will load two bitmaps from the library, display the first, then continually dissolve in the second one.

```
import flash.display.BitmapData;
import flash.geom.Point;
//create the point
var point:Point = new Point(0,0);
//create the first BitmapData as a red square
var myBitmapData:BitmapData = BitmapData.loadBitmap("bridge");
```

```
//load the second bitmap from the Library
var myBitmapData2:BitmapData = BitmapData.loadBitmap("bigBen");
//display the first bitmap
this.attachBitmap(myBitmapData,1);
//randome seed
var nextNum:Number = 0;
//run this continually
this.onEnterFrame = function():Void{
    nextNum = myBitmapData.pixelDissolve(myBitmapData2, myBitmapData.rectangle,
➥point,nextNum,500,0x000000);
}
```

scroll
Availability: FP:8, AS:1.0

Generic Template: `myBitmapData.scroll(x, y);`

Parameters:

> x—The horizontal amount to scroll of the bitmap.
>
> y—The vertical amount to scroll of the bitmap.

Description:

This method will scroll an image by the pixel amount given.

Example:

This example will load a bitmap from the library, display that bitmap, and finally scroll it by (1,1) continually creating a color stream effect.

```
import flash.display.BitmapData;
//create the first BitmapData as a red square
var myBitmapData:BitmapData = BitmapData.loadBitmap("bridge");
//display the first bitmap
this.attachBitmap(myBitmapData,1);
//continually scroll the image
this.onEnterFrame = function():Void{
    myBitmapData.scroll(1,1);
}
```

setPixel
Availability: FP:8, AS:1.0

Generic Template: `myBitmapData.setPixel(x, y, color);`

Parameters:

> *x*—The horizontal position of the pixel to color.
>
> *y*—The vertical position of the pixel to color.
>
> *color*—The RGB value to set the given pixel to.

Description:

This method will set the RGB value of a given pixel.

Example:

This example will load a bitmap from the library, display that bitmap, and create an event that allows the user to color every pixel the mouse touches to a random color.

```
import flash.display.BitmapData;
//create the first BitmapData as a red square
var myBitmapData:BitmapData = BitmapData.loadBitmap("bridge");
//display the first bitmap
this.attachBitmap(myBitmapData,1);
//continually scroll the image
this.onMouseMove = function():Void{
    myBitmapData.setPixel(_xmouse, _ymouse, Math.random()*0x1000000);
}
```

setPixel32
Availability: FP:8, AS:1.0

Generic Template: `myBitmapData.setPixel32(x, y, color);`

Parameters:

> *x*—The horizontal position of the pixel to color.
>
> *y*—The vertical position of the pixel to color.
>
> *color*—The ARGB (0xAARRGGBB) value to set the given pixel to.

Description:

This method will set the ARGB value of a given pixel.

Example:

This example will load a bitmap from the library and make a copy in a second `BitmapData` object. Then two variables will be created to hold the height and width of the bitmap. After that, the bitmap will be displayed. Then two more variables will be created to help walk through the image. And finally, an `onEnterFrame` event will be used to completely flip the bitmap both vertically and horizontally, pixel by pixel.

```
import flash.display.BitmapData;
//create the first BitmapData as a red square
var myBitmapData:BitmapData = BitmapData.loadBitmap("bridge");
```

A

```
var myBitmapData2:BitmapData = myBitmapData.clone()
var w:Number = myBitmapData.width;
var h:Number = myBitmapData.height;
//display the first bitmap
this.attachBitmap(myBitmapData,1);
var column:Number = 0;
var row:Number = 0;
//continually scroll the image
this.onEnterFrame = function():Void{
    if(column>w){
        column=0;
        row++;
    }
    myBitmapData.setPixel32(column, row,
➡ myBitmapData2.getPixel32(w-column,h-row));
    column++;
}
```

threshold
Availability: FP:8, AS:1.0

Generic Template: `myBitmapData.threshold (bitmap, rec, point, operation, threshold, color, mask, copy);`

Returns: Number

This number is the number of pixels that were changed.

Parameters:

bitmap—The bitmap image that will have the threshold applied to it. It does not have to be the BitmapData object calling the method.

rec—The `Rectangle` that defines the area where the threshold will take effect.

point—The `Point` object representing the top left of the current BitmapData object that corresponds to the top left of *rec*.

operation—A comparison operator used to compare different colors.

threshold—The color value that each pixel will be tested against to see if it meets or goes beyond the threshold.

color—An ARGB color used to fill pixels where the threshold test succeeds. The default is 0x00000000.

mask—An ARGB color used to isolate color components. The default value is 0xffffffff.

copy—If this value is `true`, pixels will be copied from the source bitmap to the destination bitmap when the threshold is not met. If `false`, no copies are made. The default value is `false`.

Description:

This method will test different pixel values in a given bitmap and decide whether to swap them out with a given ARGB color.

Example:

This example loads a bitmap image from the library and then displays it. After that, an event will be set up so that when a user selects a pixel by clicking it, every pixel in the bitmap will be compared to that pixel and colored blue if the threshold test succeeds.

```
import flash.display.BitmapData;
import flash.geom.Point;
var point:Point = new Point(0,0);
//create the first BitmapData as a red square
var myBitmapData:BitmapData = BitmapData.loadBitmap("bigBen");
//display the first bitmap
this.attachBitmap(myBitmapData, 1);
//select a pixel
this.onMouseDown = function(){
    myBitmapData.threshold(myBitmapData, myBitmapData.rectangle, point, "<=",
➡myBitmapData.getPixel32(_xmouse,_ymouse), 0x00397dce, 0xffffffff, false);
}
```

The ExternalInterface Class

The ExternalInterface class is designed to be able to communicate with external functionality such as JavaScript.

It is important that when using this class to import it first at the beginning of your script, like this:

```
import flash.external.ExternalInterface;
```

Properties

available
Availability: FP:8, AS:1.0

Generic Template: ExternalInterface.available;

Description:

The property indicates whether the player it is residing in is capable of offering an external interface; true if yes and false if no.

Example:

This example will send to the Output panel the availability status of an external interface:

```
import flash.external.ExternalInterface;
trace(ExternalInterface.available);
```

Methods

```
addCallback
```
Availability: FP:8, AS:1.0

Generic Template: `ExternalInterface.addCallback(nickName, instance, function);`

Returns: Boolean

This will indicate if the call succeeded. If it did not, check the *allScriptAccess* attribute in both the OBJECT and EMBED tags to make sure you are not in a security violation.

Parameters:

> *nickName*—This string is what the external interface will call the method with. It does not have to be the same name as the function in the timeline.
>
> *instance*—This object represents what "this" will represent in the function being called.
>
> *function*—This is the actual function being called on the timeline.

Description:

This method will add the capability for an external interface to be able to call a function on the Flash timeline.

Example:

This example will send to the Output panel the availability status of an external interface:

```
import flash.external.ExternalInterface;
//the function
function visitSams() {
    getURL("http://www.sams.com", "_blank");
}
//add the callback
ExternalInterface.addCallback("visitSams", this, visitSams);
```

And then in the HTML, you might have something like this:

```
<script>
function goOut() {
   document.getElementById("visitSams").flash.visitSams();
}
}
</script>
```

```
<form>
<input type="button" onclick="goOut()" value="Go to Sams" />
</form>
```

> **NOTE**
>
> When setting up the JavaScript to call the Flash function, you must make sure the id attribute of the object tag and the name attribute of the embed tag are set to the same thing.

call
Availability: FP:8, AS:1.0

Generic Template: ExternalInterface.call(function, parameters);

Returns: Object

This will be the response from the external function being called if there is one. If there is no return value, or the method failed, null will be returned.

Parameters:

function—This string is the name of the function in the external interface.

parameters—These are the parameters that are passed to the external function, each separated by a comma. This is an optional parameter.

Description:

This method will allow Flash to call functions in the external interface as well as pass parameters to them.

Example:

This example will call the alert function in JavaScript, passing it a simple string:

```
import flash.external.ExternalInterface;
//send an alert
ExternalInterface.call("alert", "there is an alert");
```

Again, if this does not work at first, check the *allowScriptAccess* attribute in your HTML.

The BevelFilter Class

The BevelFilter class is designed to create bevel-image effects on objects.

It is important when using this class to import it first at the beginning of your script, like this:

```
import flash.filters.BevelFilter;
```

To instantiate a new instance of the `BevelFilter` class, use this code as a template:

```
var myFilter:BevelFilter = new BevelFilter(dist, angle, highlightColor,
➥ highlightAlpha, shadowColor, shadowAlpha, blurX, blurY,
➥ strength, quality, type, knockout);
```

- *dist*—The distance in pixels for the bevel to be offset. Default value of 4.0.

- *angle*—The bevel's angle between 0 and 360. Default value of 45.

- *highlightColor*—The highlight ARGB color of the bevel. Default value of 0x00ffffff.

- *highlightAlpha*—The alpha of the highlight color in the bevel from 0 to 1. Default value of 1.0.

- *shadowColor*—The shadow ARGB color of the bevel. Default value of 0x00000000.

- *shadowAlpha*—The alpha of the shadow color in the bevel from 0 to 1. Default value of 1.0.

- *blurX*—The total amount of horizontal blur from 0–255. Default value of 4.0.

- *blurY*—The total amount of vertical blur from 0–255. Default value of 4.0.

- *strength*—This number represents the strength of the bevel's imprint. From 0–255, the higher this number, the more contrast there will be. Default value of 1.

- *quality*—This number represents the number of times to apply the filter, ranging from 0–15. Default value of 1.

- *type*—This string represents the type of bevel to apply: "inner," "outer," or "full." Default value of "inner."

- *knockout*—The Boolean value controls whether the object having the filter applied to it will be transparent, `true`, or not, `false`.

Example:

This example will create a small blue square using the drawing API and apply the filter to it:

```
import flash.filters.BevelFilter;
//create the movie clip to display the filter
var rec_mc:MovieClip = this.createEmptyMovieClip("rec_mc", 1);
//move the rectangle towards the center of the stage
rec_mc._x = rec_mc._y = 200;
//draw a squar inside the movie clip
rec_mc.lineStyle(0,0x000000,0);
rec_mc.beginFill(0x397dce, 100);
rec_mc.lineTo(100,0);
rec_mc.lineTo(100,100);
rec_mc.lineTo(0,100);
rec_mc.lineTo(0,0);
rec_mc.endFill();
```

```
//create the filter
var myFilter:BevelFilter = new BevelFilter(5, 45, 0x00ccff, 1,
➥0x000033, 1, 5, 5, 2, 3, "inner", false);
//apply the filter
rec_mc.filters = new Array(myFilter);
```

Because the properties of this object match the parameters identically, they will be skipped.

Methods

```
clone
```
Availability: FP:8, AS:1.0

Generic Template: `myFilter.clone()`

Returns: `BevelFilter`

An exact copy of the `BevelFilter` will be returned.

Description:

This method will create a duplicate copy of the `BevelFilter` it is called on.

Example:

This example will create a filter, clone it, and then walk through all the properties to see that they match:

```
import flash.filters.BevelFilter;
//create the filter
var myFilter:BevelFilter = new BevelFilter(5, 45, 0x00ccff, 1,
➥0x000033, 1, 5, 5, 2, 3, "inner", false);
//create a copy
var myNewFilter:BevelFilter = myFilter.clone();
//walk through and display each property
for(each in myNewFilter){
    trace(each + ": " + myNewFilter[each]);
}
//output:clone: [type Function]
//type: inner
//blurY: 5
//blurX: 5
//knockout: false
//strength: 2
//quality: 3
//shadowAlpha: 1
//shadowColor: 51
//highlightAlpha: 1
//highlightColor: 52479
```

A

```
//angle: 45
//distance: 5
```

The BlurFilter **Class**

The BlurFilter class is designed to create blurred image effects on objects.

It is important when using this class to import it first at the beginning of your script, like this:

```
import flash.filters.BlurFilter;
```

To instantiate a new instance of the BlurFilter class, use this code as a template:

```
var myFilter:BlurFilter = new BlurFilter(blurX, blurY, quality);
```

- *blurX*—The total amount of horizontal blur from 0–255. Default value of 4.0.
- *blurY*—The total amount of vertical blur from 0–255. Default value of 4.0.
- *quality*—This number represents the number of times to apply the filter ranging from 0–15. Default value of 1.

Example:

This example will create a small blue square using the drawing API and apply the filter to it:

```
import flash.filters.BlurFilter;
//create the movie clip to display the filter
var rec_mc:MovieClip = this.createEmptyMovieClip("rec_mc", 1);
//move the rectangle towards the center of the stage
rec_mc._x = rec_mc._y = 200;
//draw a squar inside the movie clip
rec_mc.lineStyle(0,0x000000,0);
rec_mc.beginFill(0x397dce, 100);
rec_mc.lineTo(100,0);
rec_mc.lineTo(100,100);
rec_mc.lineTo(0,100);
rec_mc.lineTo(0,0);
rec_mc.endFill();
//create the filter
var myFilter:BlurFilter = new BlurFilter(10, 10, 3);
//apply the filter
rec_mc.filters = new Array(myFilter);
```

Because the properties of this object match the parameters identically, they will be skipped.

Methods

```
clone
```
Availability: FP:8, AS:1.0

Generic Template: `myFilter.clone()`

Returns: `BevelFilter`

An exact copy of the `BlurFilter` will be returned.

Description:

This method will create a duplicate copy of the `BlurFilter` it is called on.

Example:

This example will create a filter, clone it, then walk through all the properties to see that they match:

```
import flash.filters.BlurFilter;
//create the filter
var myFilter:BlurFilter = new BlurFilter(10, 10, 3);
//create a copy
var myNewFilter:BlurFilter = myFilter.clone();
//walk through and display each property
for(each in myNewFilter){
    trace(each + ": " + myNewFilter[each]);
}
//output:clone: [type Function]
//quality: 3
//blurY: 10
//blurX: 10
```

The `ColorMatrixFilter` Class

The `ColorMatrixFilter` class lets you apply a 4×5 matrix object to the RGBA of every pixel in an object.

It is important when using this class to import it first at the beginning of your script, like this:

```
import flash.filters.ColorMatrixFilter;
```

To instantiate a new instance of the `ColorMatrixFilter` class, use this code as a template:

```
var myFilter:ColorMatrixFilter = new ColorMatrixFilter(matrix);
```

- *matrix*—An Array with 20 elements for a 4×5 matrix.

Example:

This example will create a small blue square using the drawing API and apply the ColorMatrixFilter filter to it to make it pink:

```
import flash.filters.ColorMatrixFilter;
//create the movie clip to display the filter
var rec_mc:MovieClip = this.createEmptyMovieClip("rec_mc", 1);
//move the rectangle towards the center of the stage
rec_mc._x = rec_mc._y = 200;
//draw a squar inside the movie clip
rec_mc.lineStyle(0,0x000000,0);
rec_mc.beginFill(0x397dce, 100);
rec_mc.lineTo(100,0);
rec_mc.lineTo(100,100);
rec_mc.lineTo(0,100);
rec_mc.lineTo(0,0);
rec_mc.endFill();
//create the matrix
var matrix:Array = new Array(0, 0, 0, 3, 3, 1, 1, 0, 0,
➡ 1, 1, 1, 1, 0, 0, 0, 0, 0, .5, 2);
//create the filter
var myFilter:ColorMatrixFilter = new ColorMatrixFilter(matrix);
//apply the filter
rec_mc.filters = new Array(myFilter);
```

Because the properties of this object match the parameters identically, they will be skipped.

Methods

```
clone
```
Availability: FP:8, AS:1.0

Generic Template: `myFilter.clone()`

Returns: `ColorMatrixFilter`

An exact copy of the ColorMatrixFilter will be returned.

Description:

This method will create a duplicate copy of the ColorMatrixFilter it is called on.

Example:

This example will create a filter, clone it, and then walk through all the properties to see that they match:

```
import flash.filters.ColorMatrixFilter;
//create the matrix
var matrix:Array = new Array(0, 0, 0, 3, 3, 1, 1, 0, 0, 1,
```

```
➡1, 1, 1, 0, 0, 0, 0, 0, .5, 2);
//create the filter
var myFilter:ColorMatrixFilter = new ColorMatrixFilter(matrix);
//create a copy
var myNewFilter:ColorMatrixFilter = myFilter.clone();
//walk through and display each property
for(each in myNewFilter){
    trace(each + ": " + myNewFilter[each]);
}
//output:clone: [type Function]
//matrix: 0,0,0,3,3,1,1,0,0,1,1,1,1,0,0,0,0,0,0.5,2
```

The ConvolutionFilter Class

The ConvolutionFilter class is designed to apply matrix convolution effects on objects.

It is important when using this class to import it first at the beginning of your script, like this:

```
import flash.filters.ConvolutionFilter;
```

To instantiate a new instance of the ConvolutionFilter class, use this code as a template:

```
var myFilter:ConvolutionFilter = new ConvolutionFilter(matrix, matrixY,
➡ matrix, divisor, bias, preserveAlpha, clamp, color, alpha);
```

- *matrixX*—The number of columns in the matrix. Default value of 0.

- *matrixY*—The number of rows in the matrix. Default value of 0.

- *matrix*—An Array with (matrixX × matrixY) elements for the transformation.

- *divisor*—The divisor used for the matrix transformation. Default value of 1.

- *bias*—The bias that is added to the matrix transformation result. Default value of 0.

- *preserveAlpha*—A Boolean value that if true will make it so the convolution filter will not affect the alpha channel. Default value of true.

- *clamp*—A Boolean value that if set to true will extend the bitmap along its edge and duplicate the existing colors; if false, *color* will be used.

- *color*—A substitute color for pixels outside the bitmap.

- *alpha*—The alpha value of *color*.

Example:

This example will create a small blue square using the drawing API and apply the convolution filter to it to make it a semitransparent gray square:

```
import flash.filters.ConvolutionFilter;
//create the movie clip to display the filter
```

```
var rec_mc:MovieClip = this.createEmptyMovieClip("rec_mc", 1);
//move the rectangle towards the center of the stage
rec_mc._x = rec_mc._y = 200;
//draw a squar inside the movie clip
rec_mc.lineStyle(0,0x000000,0);
rec_mc.beginFill(0x397dce, 100);
rec_mc.lineTo(100,0);
rec_mc.lineTo(100,100);
rec_mc.lineTo(0,100);
rec_mc.lineTo(0,0);
rec_mc.endFill();
//create the matrix
var matrix:Array = [0, 1, 0, 0, 1, 0, 0, 1, 0];

//create the filter
var myFilter:ConvolutionFilter = new ConvolutionFilter(3, 3, matrix, 18, 1, false);
//apply the filter
rec_mc.filters = new Array(myFilter);
```

Because the properties of this object match the parameters identically, they will be skipped.

Methods

clone
Availability: FP:8, AS:1.0

Generic Template: myFilter.clone()

Returns: ConvolutionFilter

An exact copy of the ConvolutionFilter will be returned.

Description:

This method will create a duplicate copy of the ConvolutionFilter it is called on.

Example:

This example will create a filter, clone it, and then walk through all the properties to see that they match:

```
import flash.filters.ConvolutionFilter;
//create the matrix
var matrix:Array = [0, 1, 0, 0, 1, 0, 0, 1, 0];

//create the filter
var myFilter:ConvolutionFilter = new ConvolutionFilter(3, 3, matrix, 18, 1, false);
//create a copy
var myNewFilter:ConvolutionFilter = myFilter.clone();
```

```
//walk through and display each property
for(each in myNewFilter){
    trace(each + ": " + myNewFilter[each]);
}
//output:clone: [type Function]
//alpha: 0
//color: 0
//clamp: true
//preserveAlpha: false
//bias: 1
//divisor: 18
//matrix: 0,1,0,0,1,0,0,1,0
//matrixY: 3
//matrixX: 3
```

The DisplacementMapFilter Class

The DisplacementMapFilter in conjunction with the BitmapData class creates a mapped displacement with an image.

It is important when using this class to import it first at the beginning of your script, like this:

```
import flash.filters.DisplacementMapFilters;
```

And to instantiate a new instance of the DisplacementMapFilter class, use this code as a template:

```
var myFilter:DisplacementMapFilter = new DisplacementMapFilter(bitmap, point,
↪compX, compY, scaleX, scaleY, mode, color, alpha);
```

- *bitmap*—The BitmapData object containing the displacement information.
- *point*—The top-left corner of the bitmap in comparison to the image being displaced.
- *compX*—The color to use on the horizontal displacement. Values: 1, 2, 4, 8.
- *compY*—The color to use on the vertical displacement. Values: 1, 2, 4, 8.
- *scaleX*—The multiplier used to scale the horizontal displacement.
- *scaleY*—The multiplier used to scale the vertical displacement.
- *mode*—A string value representing the filter mode that has these possible values:
  - *clamp*—locks the displacement value to the edge of the bitmap.
  - *color*—if the displacement value is beyond the bitmap, *color* will be used as a substitute.

- *ignore*—if the displacement is beyond the bitmap, it will be ignored.

- *wrap*—when the displacement value goes beyond the bitmap, it will be wrapped around.

- *color*—A substitute color for pixels outside the bitmap. This parameter is only used when *mode* is set to "color."

- *alpha*—The alpha value of *color*. Range is between 0 and 1 with the default being 1. This parameter is used only when *mode* is set to "color."

Example:

This example already has an image on the stage called img_mc. The code imports all the classes we need. Then it creates a point at (0,0). After that, it creates an instance of the BitmapData object to use as the displacement map. It sets the dimensions to the dimensions of the image. And finally, it creates an event that will constantly update the filter.

```
import flash.filters.DisplacementMapFilter;
import flash.display.BitmapData;
import flash.geom.Point;
//create a point
var pint:Point = new Point(0,0);
//create the map displacement bitmap with the images dimensions
var myBitmapData:BitmapData = new BitmapData(img_mc._width, img_mc._height);
//constantly update
this.onEnterFrame = function(){
    myBitmapData.noise(Math.random()*20, 1, 200, 1, true);
    //create the filter
    var myFilter:DisplacementMapFilter = new DisplacementMapFilter
➥ (myBitmapData, point, 1,1,10,10,"wrap");
    //apply the filter
    img_mc.filters = new Array(myFilter);
}
```

Because the properties of this object match the parameters identically, they will be skipped.

Methods

```
clone
```
Availability: FP:8, AS:1.0

Generic Template: `myFilter.clone()`

Returns: `DisplacementMapFilter`

An exact copy of the `DisplacementMapFilter` will be returned.

Description:

This method will create a duplicate copy of the `DisplacementMapFilter` it is called on.

Example:

This example will create a filter, clone it, then walk through all the properties to see that they match:

```
import flash.filters.DisplacementMapFilter;
import flash.display.BitmapData;
import flash.geom.Point;
//create a point
var pint:Point = new Point(0,0);
//create the map displacement bitmap with the images dimensions
var myBitmapData:BitmapData = new BitmapData(100, 100);
//create some noise
myBitmapData.noise(Math.random()*20, 1, 200, 1, true);
//create the filter
var myFilter:DisplacementMapFilter = new DisplacementMapFilter
➥ (myBitmapData, point, 1,1,10,10,"wrap");
//apply the filter
img_mc.filters = new Array(myFilter);
//create a copy
var myNewFilter:DisplacementMapFilter = myFilter.clone();
//walk through and display each property
for(each in myNewFilter){
    trace(each + ": " + myNewFilter[each]);
}
//output:clone: [type Function]
//alpha: 0
//color: 0
//mode: wrap
//scaleY: 10
//scaleX: 10
//componentY: 1
//componentX: 1
//mapPoint: (x=0, y=0)
//mapBitmap: [object Object]
```

The DropShadowFilter **Class**

The `DropShadowFilter` class is designed to create drop shadows on objects at runtime.

It is important that when using this class to import it first at the beginning of your script, like this:

```
import flash.filters.DropShadowFilter;
```

To instantiate a new instance of the `DropShadowFilter` class, use this code as a template:

```
var myFilter:DropShadowFilter = new DropShadowFilter(dist, angle,
➥ color, alpha, blurX, blurY, strength, quality, inner, knockout, hideObj);
```

- *dist*—The distance in pixels for the shadow to be offset. Default value of 4.0.

- *angle*—The shadow angle between 0 and 360. Default value of 45.

- *color*—The color of the shadow in RGB. Default value of 0x000000.

- *alpha*—The alpha of the shadow from 0–1. Default value of 1.0.

- *blurX*—The total amount of horizontal blur from 0–255. Default value of 4.0.

- *blurY*—The total amount of vertical blur from 0–255. Default value of 4.0.

- *strength*—This number represents the strength of the shadows imprint. From 0–255, the higher this number, the more contrast there will be. Default value of 1.

- *quality*—This number represents the number of times to apply the filter ranging from 0–15. Default value of 1.

- *inner*—If true, the shadow will become an inner shadow. Default value of `false`, creating an outer shadow.

- *knockout*—The Boolean value controls whether the object having the filter applied to will be transparent `true` or not `false`.

- *hiddenObj*—Similar to the *knockout* parameter, but if this is set to `true`, the entire drop shadow will be visible, not just what is outside the edge of the object.

Example:

This example will create a small blue square using the drawing API and apply the filter to it:

```
import flash.filters.DropShadowFilter;
//create the movie clip to display the filter
var rec_mc:MovieClip = this.createEmptyMovieClip("rec_mc", 1);
//move the rectangle towards the center of the stage
rec_mc._x = rec_mc._y = 200;
//draw a squar inside the movie clip
rec_mc.lineStyle(0,0x000000,0);
rec_mc.beginFill(0x397dce, 100);
rec_mc.lineTo(100,0);
rec_mc.lineTo(100,100);
rec_mc.lineTo(0,100);
rec_mc.lineTo(0,0);
rec_mc.endFill();
//create the filter
var myFilter:DropShadowFilter = new DropShadowFilter
➥ (10, 45, 0x000033, 50, 10, 10, 2, 3);
```

```
//apply the filter
rec_mc.filters = new Array(myFilter);
```

Because the properties of this object match the parameters identically, they will be skipped.

Methods

```
clone
```
Availability: FP:8, AS:1.0

Generic Template: `myFilter.clone()`

Returns: `DropShadowFilter`

An exact copy of the `DropShadowFilter` will be returned.

Description:

This method will create a duplicate copy of the `DropShadowFilter` it is called on.

Example:

This example will create a filter, clone it, then walk through all the properties to see that they match:

```
import flash.filters.DropShadowFilter;
//create the filter
var myFilter:DropShadowFilter = new DropShadowFilter
➥ (10, 45, 0x000033, 50, 10, 10, 2, 3);
//apply the filter
img_mc.filters = new Array(myFilter);
//create a copy
var myNewFilter:DropShadowFilter = myFilter.clone();
//walk through and display each property
for(each in myNewFilter){
    trace(each + ": " + myNewFilter[each]);
}
//output:clone: [type Function]
//hideObject: false
//strength: 2
//blurY: 10
//blurX: 10
//knockout: false
//inner: false
//quality: 3
//alpha: 1
//color: 51
//angle: 45
//distance: 10
```

A

The GlowFilter **Class**

The GlowFilter class is designed to create glow effects on objects at runtime, both inner and outer.

It is important when using this class to import it first at the beginning of your script, like this:

```
import flash.filters.GlowFilter;
```

To instantiate a new instance of the GlowFilter class, use this code as a template:

```
var myFilter:GlowFilter = new GlowFilter(color, alpha,
➥ blurX, blurY, strength, quality, inner, knockout);
```

- *color*—The color of the glow in RGB. Default value of 0xFF0000.

- *alpha*—The alpha of the glow from 0–1. Default value of 1.0.

- *blurX*—The total amount of horizontal blur from 0–255. Default value of 4.0.

- *blurY*—The total amount of vertical blur from 0–255. Default value of 4.0.

- *strength*—This number represents the strength of the shadow's imprint. From 0–255, the higher this number, the more contrast there will be. Default value of 2.0.

- *quality*—This number represents the number of times to apply the filter ranging from 0–15. Default value of 1.

- *inner*—If true, the glow will become an inner glow. Default value of false, creating an outer glow.

- *knockout*—The Boolean value controls whether the object having the filter applied to it will be transparent, true, or not, false.

Example:

This example will create a small blue square using the drawing API and apply the filter to it:

```
import flash.filters.GlowFilter;
//create the movie clip to display the filter
var rec_mc:MovieClip = this.createEmptyMovieClip("rec_mc", 1);
//move the rectangle towards the center of the stage
rec_mc._x = rec_mc._y = 200;
//draw a squar inside the movie clip
rec_mc.lineStyle(0,0x000000,0);
rec_mc.beginFill(0x397dce, 100);
rec_mc.lineTo(100,0);
rec_mc.lineTo(100,100);
rec_mc.lineTo(0,100);
rec_mc.lineTo(0,0);
rec_mc.endFill();
```

```
//create the filter
var myFilter:GlowFilter = new GlowFilter(0x000033, 75, 20, 20, 2, 3);
//apply the filter
rec_mc.filters = new Array(myFilter);
```

Because the properties of this object match the parameters identically, they will be skipped.

Methods

```
clone
```
Availability: FP:8, AS:1.0

Generic Template: `myFilter.clone()`

Returns: `GlowFilter`

An exact copy of the `GlowFilter` will be returned.

Description:

This method will create a duplicate copy of the `GlowFilter` it is called on.

Example:

This example will create a filter, clone it, then walk through all the properties to see that they match:

```
import flash.filters.GlowFilter;
//create the filter
var myFilter:GlowFilter = new GlowFilter(0x000033, 75, 20, 20, 2, 3);
//apply the filter
img_mc.filters = new Array(myFilter);
//create a copy
var myNewFilter:GlowFilter = myFilter.clone();
//walk through and display each property
for(each in myNewFilter){
    trace(each + ": " + myNewFilter[each]);
}
//output:clone: [type Function]
//strength: 2
//blurY: 20
//blurX: 20
//knockout: false
//inner: false
//quality: 3
//alpha: 1
//color: 51
```

A

The GradientBevelFilter **Class**

The GradientBevelFilter class is designed to create beveled gradient effects on objects at runtime, both inner and outer.

It is important when using this class to import it first at the beginning of your script, like this:

```
import flash.filters.GradientBevelFilter;
```

To instantiate a new instance of the GradientBevelFilter class, use this code as a template:

```
var myFilter:GradientBevelFilter = new GradientBevelFilter(dist, angle,
➥ colors, alphas, ratios, blurX, blurY, strength, quality, type, knockout);
```

- *dist*—The distance in pixels for the bevel to be offset between 0–8. Default value of 4.0.

- *colors*—An array of colors to use in the gradient.

- *alphas*—An array of alphas to use in the gradient.

- *ratios*—An array of ratios to use in the gradient.

- *blurX*—The total amount of horizontal blur from 0–255. Default value of 4.0.

- *blurY*—The total amount of vertical blur from 0–255. Default value of 4.0.

- *strength*[d]This number represents the strength of the bevel imprint. From 0–5, the higher this number, the more contrast. Default value of 1.0.

- *quality*—This number represents the number of times to apply the filter ranging from 0–15. Default value of 1.

- *type*—This string represents the type of bevel to apply: inner, outer, or full. Default value of inner.

- *knockout*—The Boolean value controls whether the object having the filter applied to will be transparent, true, or not, false.

Example:

This example will create a small blue square using the drawing API and apply the filter to it:

```
import flash.filters.GradientBevelFilter;
//the arrays we need
var colors:Array = [0x00ccff, 0x397dce, 0x000033];
var alphas:Array = [1, 0, 1];
var ratios:Array = [0, 125, 255];
//create the movie clip to display the filter
var rec_mc:MovieClip = this.createEmptyMovieClip("rec_mc", 1);
//move the rectangle towards the center of the stage
```

```
rec_mc._x = rec_mc._y = 200;
//draw a squar inside the movie clip
rec_mc.lineStyle(0,0x000000,0);
rec_mc.beginFill(0x397dce, 100);
rec_mc.lineTo(100,0);
rec_mc.lineTo(100,100);
rec_mc.lineTo(0,100);
rec_mc.lineTo(0,0);
rec_mc.endFill();
//create the filter
var myFilter:GradientBevelFilter = new GradientBevelFilter
➡ (5, 45, colors, alphas, ratios, 10, 10, 2, 3, "inner");
//apply the filter
rec_mc.filters = new Array(myFilter);
```

Because the properties of this object match the parameters identically, they will be skipped.

Methods

```
clone
```
Availability: FP:8, AS:1.0

Generic Template: `myFilter.clone()`

Returns: `GradientBevelFilter`

An exact copy of the `GradientBevelFilter` will be returned.

Description:

This method will create a duplicate copy of the `GradientBevelFilter` it is called on.

Example:

This example will create a filter, clone it, then walk through all the properties to see that they match:

```
import flash.filters.GradientBevelFilter;
//the arrays we need
var colors:Array = [0xFFFFFF, 0xCCCCCC, 0x000000];
var alphas:Array = [1, 0, 1];
var ratios:Array = [0, 128, 255];
//create the filter
var myFilter:GradientBevelFilter = new GradientBevelFilter
➡ (5, 45, colors, alphas, ratios, 10, 10, 2, 3, "inner");
//apply the filter
img_mc.filters = new Array(myFilter);
//create a copy
var myNewFilter:GradientBevelFilter = myFilter.clone();
```

A

```
//walk through and display each property
for(each in myNewFilter){
    trace(each + ": " + myNewFilter[each]);
}
//output:clone: [type Function]
//type: inner
//knockout: false
//strength: 2
//quality: 3
//blurY: 10
//blurX: 10
//ratios: 0,128,255
//alphas: 1,0,1
//colors: 16777215,13421772,0
//angle: 45
//distance: 5
```

The GradientGlowFilter Class

The GradientGlowFilter class is designed to create beveled gradient effects on objects at runtime, both inner and outer.

It is important when using this class to import it first at the beginning of your script, like this:

```
import flash.filters.GradientGlowFilter;
```

To instantiate a new instance of the GradientGlowFilter class, use this code as a template:

```
var myFilter:GradientGlowFilter = new GradientGlowFilter(dist, angle, colors,
➥alphas, ratios, blurX, blurY, strength, quality, type, knockout);
```

- *dist*—The distance in pixels for the glow to be offset between 0–8. Default value of 4.0.

- *colors*—An array of colors to use in the gradient.

- *alphas*—An array of alphas to use in the gradient.

- *ratios*—An array of ratios to use in the gradient.

- *blurX*—The total amount of horizontal blur from 0–255. Default value of 4.0.

- *blurY*—The total amount of vertical blur from 0–255. Default value of 4.0.

- *strength*—This number represents the strength of the glow imprint. From 0–5, the higher this number, the more contrast. Default value of 1.0.

- *quality*—This number represents the number of times to apply the filter ranging from 0–15. Default value of 1.

- *type*—This string represents the type of bevel to apply: inner, outer, or full. Default value of inner.

- *knockout*—The Boolean value controls whether the object having the filter applied to will be transparent, true, or not, false.

Example:

This example will create a small blue square using the drawing API and apply the filter to it:

```
import flash.filters.GradientGlowFilter;
//the arrays we need
var colors:Array = [0xFFFFFF, 0x000033, 0x397dce, 0x00CCFF];
var alphas:Array = [0, .25, .5, 1];
var ratios:Array = [0, 60, 125, 255];
//create the movie clip to display the filter
var rec_mc:MovieClip = this.createEmptyMovieClip("rec_mc", 1);
//move the rectangle towards the center of the stage
rec_mc._x = rec_mc._y = 200;
//draw a squar inside the movie clip
rec_mc.lineStyle(0,0x000000,0);
rec_mc.beginFill(0x397dce, 100);
rec_mc.lineTo(100,0);
rec_mc.lineTo(100,100);
rec_mc.lineTo(0,100);
rec_mc.lineTo(0,0);
rec_mc.endFill();
//create the filter
var myFilter:GradientGlowFilter = new GradientGlowFilter
➥ (5, 45, colors, alphas, ratios, 30, 30, 2, 3, "outer");
//apply the filter
rec_mc.filters = new Array(myFilter);
```

Because the properties of this object match the parameters identically, they will be skipped.

Methods

clone
Availability: FP:8, AS:1.0

Generic Template: myFilter.clone()

Returns: `GradientGlowFilter`

An exact copy of the `GradientGlowFilter` will be returned.

Description:

This method will create a duplicate copy of the `GradientGlowFilter` it is called on.

Example:

This example will create a filter, clone it, then walk through all the properties to see that they match:

```
import flash.filters.GradientGlowFilter;
//the arrays we need
var colors:Array = [0xFFFFFF, 0xCCCCCC, 0x000000];
var alphas:Array = [1, 0, 1];
var ratios:Array = [0, 128, 255];
//create the filter
var myFilter:GradientGlowFilter = new GradientGlowFilter
➥ (5, 45, colors, alphas, ratios, 30, 30, 2, 3, "outer");
//apply the filter
img_mc.filters = new Array(myFilter);
//create a copy
var myNewFilter:GradientGlowFilter = myFilter.clone();
//walk through and display each property
for(each in myNewFilter){
    trace(each + ": " + myNewFilter[each]);
}
//output:clone: [type Function]
//type: outer
//knockout: false
//strength: 2
//quality: 3
//blurY: 30
//blurX: 30
//ratios: 0,128,255
//alphas: 1,0,1
//colors: 16777215,13421772,0
//angle: 45
//distance: 5
```

The `ColorTransform` **Class**

The `ColorTransform` class is an object containing specific RGB and alpha properties.

It is important when using this class to import it first at the beginning of your script, like this:

```
import flash.geom.ColorTransform;
```

To instantiate a new instance of the `GradientGlowFilter` class, use this code as a template:

```
var myTransform:ColorTransform = new ColorTransform(redMult, greenMult,
➥blueMult, alphaMult, redOff, greenOff, blueOff, alphaOff);
```

- *redMult*—Numerical value of red multiplier from 0–1.
- *greenMult*—Numerical value of green multiplier from 0–1.
- *blueMult*—Numerical value of blue multiplier from 0–1.
- *alphaMult*—Numerical value of alpha multiplier from 0–1.
- *redOff*—The offset of the red channel from –255 to 255.
- *greenOff*—The offset of the green channel from –255 to 255.
- *blueOff*—The offset of the blue channel from –255 to 255.
- *alphaOff*—The offset of the alpha channel from –255 to 255.

Example:

This example will create an instance of the `ColorTransform` class:

```
import flash.geom.ColorTransform;
var myTransform:ColorTransform = new flash.geom.ColorTransform
➥ (1, .7, .8, 1, 5, 15, 25, 0);
```

Because all but one of the properties of this object match the parameters identically, they will be skipped.

Properties

rgb
Availability: FP:8, AS:1.0

Generic Template: `myTransform.rgb`

Description:

This property contains the RGB value of a `ColorTransform` object.

Example:

This example will create a `ColorTransform` object and send the `rgb` property to the Output panel:

```
import flash.geom.ColorTransform;
var myTransform:ColorTransform = new flash.geom.ColorTransform
➥ (1, .7, .8, 1, 5, 15, 25, 0);
trace(myTransform.rgb);
//output: 331545
```

Methods

concat
Availability: FP:8, AS:1.0

Generic Template: `myTransform.concat(colorTransform);`

Parameters:

- *colorTransform*—A second `ColorTransform` object.

Description:

This method will add a second color transformation to a movie clip.

Example:

This example will import the necessary class file. Then we create the first instance of the `ColorTransform` object we need and trace its `redOffset` property. Next, the second `ColorTransform` object is created and concatenated to the first. Finally, the `redOffset` property of the first object is traced again to reveal it has changed:

```
import flash.geom.ColorTransform;

//first ColorTransform object
var myTrans:ColorTransform = new ColorTransform(1, 1, 1, 1, 200, 0, 0, 0);
trace(myTrans.redOffset);
//second ColorTransform object
var myTrans2:ColorTransform = new ColorTransform(1, 1, 1, .5, 55, 0, 0, 0);
//concat the color transforms
myTrans.concat(myTrans2);
trace(myTrans.redOffset);
//output: 200
//        255
```

toString
Availability: FP:8, AS:1.0

Generic Template: `myTransform.toString();`

Returns: String

This method will return a formatted string containing all the `ColorTransform` properties.

Description:

This method will return a formatted string with each individual property labeled and defined.

Example:

This example will create a ColorTransform object and trace all of its properties using the toString method:

```
var myTransform:ColorTransform = new flash.geom.ColorTransform
➥ (1, .7, .8, 1, 5, 15, 25, 0);
trace(myTransform.toString());
//output: (redMultiplier=1, greenMultiplier=0.7, blueMultiplier=0.8,
➥alphaMultiplier=1, redOffset=5, greenOffset=15, blueOffset=25, alphaOffset=0)
```

The Matrix Class

The Matrix class allows you to perform a transformation by manipulating coordinates.

It is important when using this class to import it first at the beginning of your script, like this:

```
import flash.geom.Matrix;
```

To instantiate a new instance of the Matrix class, use this code as a template:

```
var myMatrix:Matrix = new Matrix(a,b,c,d,tx,ty);
```

- *a*—Numerical value of the first row, first column.
- *b*—Numerical value of the first row, second column.
- *c*—Numerical value of the second row, first column.
- *d*—Numerical value of the second row, second column.
- *tx*—Numerical value of the third row, first column.
- *ty*—Numerical value of the third row, second column.

Example:

This example will create an instance of the Matrix class and send it to the Output panel:

```
import flash.geom.Matrix;
var myMatrix:Matrix = new Matrix(1,2,3,4,5,6);
trace(myMatrix);
//output: (a=1, b=2, c=3, d=4, tx=5, ty=6)
```

Because all the properties of this object match the parameters identically, they will be skipped.

A

Methods

clone
Availability: FP:8, AS:1.0

Generic Template: `myMatrix.clone();`

Returns: `Matrix`

This method will return an exact duplicate of the `Matrix` object it is being called on.

Description:

This method will create an exact copy of the `Matrix` object it is being called on.

Example:

This example will create a `Matrix` object, create a copy, and output that copy:

```
import flash.geom.Matrix;
var myMatrix:Matrix = new Matrix(1,2,3,4,5,6);
var myMatrix2:Matrix = myMatrix.clone();
trace(myMatrix2);
//output: (a=1, b=2, c=3, d=4, tx=5, ty=6)
```

concat
Availability: FP:8, AS:1.0

Generic Template: `myMatrix.concat(matrix);`

Parameters:

- *matrix*—Another `Matrix` object concatenated to the one calling the method.

Description:

This method will combine one `matrix` with another. This may seem like the values will be added, but instead a `matrix` multiplication will occur.

Example:

This example will create two `Matrix` objects and combine them:

```
import flash.geom.Matrix;
var myMatrix:Matrix = new Matrix(1,2,3,4,5,6);
var myMatrix2:Matrix = myMatrix.clone();
myMatrix.concat(myMatrix2);
trace(myMatrix);
//output: (a=7, b=10, c=15, d=22, tx=28, ty=40)
```

createBox
Availability: FP:8, AS:1.0

Generic Template: `myMatrix.createBox(scaleX, scaleY, rot, x, y);`

Parameters:

- *scaleX*—Horizontal scaling value.

- *scaleY*—Vertical scaling value.

- *rot*—A numerical value to rotate the `Matrix` by, in radians. Default value of 0.

- *x*—The amount in pixels of horizontal movement. Default value of 0.

- *y*—The amount in pixels of vertical movement. Default value of 0.

Description:

This method will transform the matrix values based on given information such as scaling and rotation. This one method will accomplish in a single task what it would take several other of the Matrix methods to accomplish in a row.

Example:

This example will create a `Matrix` object, use the `createBox` method to transform it, and then output the results:

```
import flash.geom.Matrix;
var myMatrix:Matrix = new Matrix(1,2,3,4,5,6);
myMatrix.createBox(2, 2, 45, 10, 10);
trace(myMatrix);
//output: (a=1.05064397763546, b=1.70180704906824,
➥c=-1.70180704906824, d=1.05064397763546, tx=10, ty=10)
```

createGradientMatrix
Availability: FP:8, AS:1.0

Generic Template: `myMatrix.createGradientMatrix(w, h, rot, x, y);`

Parameters:

- *w*—Width of the gradient box.

- *h*—Height of the gradient box.

- *rot*—A numerical value to rotate the `Matrix` by, in radians. Default value of 0.

- *x*—The amount in pixels of horizontal movement. Default value of 0. It will be offset by half of *w*. Default value of 0.

- *y*—The amount in pixels of vertical movement. Default value of 0. It will be offset by half of *h*. Default value of 0.

Description:

This method will create a very specific type of matrix, the gradient matrix.

Example:

This example will use the `createGradientMatrix` method to create the gradient for a square that will be drawn with the drawing API:

```
import flash.geom.Matrix;
//create the arrays we need
var colors:Array = [0x397dce, 0x000033];
var alphas:Array = [75, 100];
var ratios:Array = [0, 255];
//create the matrix
var myMatrix:Matrix = new Matrix();
//create the gradient
myMatrix.createGradientBox(200, 200, 0, 50, 50);
//draw the square
this.beginGradientFill("linear", colors, alphas, ratios, myMatrix);
this.lineTo(0, 300);
this.lineTo(300, 300);
this.lineTo(300, 0);
this.lineTo(0, 0);
this.endFill();
```

`deltaTransformPoint`
Availability: FP:8, AS:1.0

Generic Template: `myMatrix.deltaTransformPoint(point);`

Parameters:

- *point*—A Point object.

Returns: Point

A new Point object.

Description:

This method will create a new Point object based on the transformation. This method differs from the `transformPoint` method in that it does not use `tx` or `ty` when the transformation occurs.

Example:

This example will use the `deltaTransformPoint` to transform a point from one coordinate to another:

```
import flash.geom.Matrix;
import flash.geom.Point;
//create the point
var point:Point = new Point(25, 15);
//create the matrix
```

```
var myMatrix:Matrix = new Matrix(1,2,3,4,5,6);
//trace the point after delta transformation
trace(myMatrix.deltaTransformPoint(point));
//output: (x=70, y=110)
```

identity
Availability: FP:8, AS:1.0

Generic Template: `myMatrix.identity();`

Description:

This method will cause the matrix calling it to revert back to a default matrix.

Example:

This example will create a defined matrix and send its information to the Output panel.
Then it will call the `identity` method and send the information again:

```
import flash.geom.Matrix;
var myMatrix:Matrix = new Matrix(4,5,6,7,8,9);
trace(myMatrix);
myMatrix.identity();
trace(myMatrix);
//output:(a=4, b=5, c=6, d=7, tx=8, ty=9)
//(a=1, b=0, c=0, d=1, tx=0, ty=0)
```

invert
Availability: FP:8, AS:1.0

Generic Template: `myMatrix.invert();`

Description:

This method will completely reverse the matrix if, for instance, you want to undo a transformation.

Example:

This example will create a defined matrix and send its information to the Output panel.
Then it will call the `invert` method and send the information again:

```
import flash.geom.Matrix;
var myMatrix:Matrix = new Matrix(1,2,3,4,5,6);
trace(myMatrix);
myMatrix.invert();
trace(myMatrix);
//output:(a=1, b=2, c=3, d=4, tx=5, ty=6)
//(a=-2, b=1, c=1.5, d=-0.5, tx=1, ty=-2)
```

A

rotate
Availability: FP:8, AS:1.0

Generic Template: `myMatrix.rotate(rot);`

Parameters:

- *rot*—The amount to rotate the matrix by, in radians.

Description:

This method will alter the *a* and *d* properties of the matrix so it can be used to apply rotation.

Example:

This example will create a defined matrix and send its information to the Output panel. Then it will be rotated 45 degrees and sent back to the Output panel:

```
import flash.geom.Matrix;
var myMatrix:Matrix = new Matrix(1,2,3,4,5,6);
trace(myMatrix);
myMatrix.rotate(45);
trace(myMatrix);
//output:(a=1, b=2, c=3, d=4, tx=5, ty=6)
//(a=-1.17648506025051, b=1.90154750216958, c=-1.82764813168328,
➥d=4.65399852887327, tx=-2.47881120311606, ty=7.40644955557697)
```

scale
Availability: FP:8, AS:1.0

Generic Template: `myMatrix.scale(x,y);`

Parameters:

- *x*—The horizontal scaling amount.
- *y*—The vertical scaling amount.

Description:

This method will alter the *a* and *d* properties of the matrix so it can be used to apply scaling.

Example:

This example will create a defined matrix and send its information to the Output panel. Then it will be scaled and sent back to the Output panel:

```
import flash.geom.Matrix;
var myMatrix:Matrix = new Matrix();
trace(myMatrix);
myMatrix.scale(2,2);
trace(myMatrix);
```

```
//output:(a=1, b=0, c=0, d=1, tx=0, ty=0)
//(a=2, b=0, c=0, d=2, tx=0, ty=0)
```

toString
Availability: FP:8, AS:1.0

Generic Template: myMatrix.toString();

Returns: String

The string will contain all the properties of the matrix.

Description:

This method will return a string with every property of the matrix fully defined.

Example:

This example will create a defined matrix and send the output of the toString method to the Output panel:

```
import flash.geom.Matrix;
var myMatrix:Matrix = new Matrix();
trace(myMatrix.toString());
//output:(a=1, b=0, c=0, d=1, tx=0, ty=0)
```

transformPoint
Availability: FP:8, AS:1.0

Generic Template: myMatrix.transformPoint(point);

Parameters:

- *point*—The Point object that will be transformed.

Returns: Point

A new Point object.

Description:

This method will apply a transformation on the defined point based on the given matrix.

Example:

This example will create a Point at (10,10) and run it with the matrix using the transformPoint method:

```
import flash.geom.Matrix;
import flash.geom.Point;
var point:Point = new Point(10,10);
var myMatrix:Matrix = new Matrix(1,1,1,1,1,1);
trace(myMatrix.transformPoint(point));
//output:(x=21, y=21)
```

translate
Availability: FP:8, AS:1.0

Generic Template: `myMatrix.translate(x,y);`

Parameters:

- *x*—The amount of horizontal movement.
- *y*—The amount of vertical movement.

Description:

This method will modify a matrix by adjusting it along the horizontal and vertical axes.

Example:

This example will create a default matrix and adjust it by (10,10):

```
import flash.geom.Matrix;
var myMatrix:Matrix = new Matrix();
trace(myMatrix);
myMatrix.translate(10,10);
trace(myMatrix);
//output:(a=1, b=0, c=0, d=1, tx=0, ty=0)
//(a=1, b=0, c=0, d=1, tx=10, ty=10)
```

The `Point` Class

The `Point` class allows you to create two-dimensional points along the horizontal (x) and vertical (y) axes.

It is important when using this class to import it first at the beginning of your script, like this:

```
import flash.geom.Point;
```

To instantiate a new instance of the Point class, use this code as a template:

```
var myPoint:Point = new Point(x, y);
```

- *x*—The two-dimensional point on the horizontal axis.
- *y*—The two-dimensional point on the vertical axis.

Example:

This example will create an instance of the `Point` class at coordinate (5,5) and send it to the Output panel:

```
import flash.geom.Point;
var myPoint:Point = new Point(5,5);
trace(myPoint);
//output: (x=5, y=5)
```

One other property is not a parameter.

Properties

`length`
Availability: FP:8, AS:1.0

Generic Template: `myPoint.length;`

Description:

This property will return the length of the line from coordinate (0,0) to the given point.

Example:

This example will create an instance of the `Point` class at coordinate (5,5) and send the length from (0,0) to the Output panel:

```
import flash.geom.Point;
var myPoint:Point = new Point(5,5);
trace(myPoint.length);
//output: 7.07106781186548
```

Methods

`add`
Availability: FP:8, AS:1.0

Generic Template: `myPoint.add(point);`

Parameters:

- *point*—Another `Point` object to be added to given point.

Returns: `Point`

The new point will be a combination of the `Point` object calling the method and *point*.

Description:

This method will add another point to the given point to create a new point.

Example:

This example will create an instance of the `Point` class at coordinate (5,5), add the point (4,4), and `trace` the result:

```
import flash.geom.Point;
var myPoint:Point = new Point(5,5);
var myPoint2:Point = new Point(4,4);
trace(myPoint.add(myPoint2));
//output: (x=9, y=9)
```

```
clone
```
Availability: FP:8, AS:1.0

Generic Template: `myPoint.clone();`

Returns: `Point`

This method will return an exact duplicate of the `Point` object it is being called on.

Description:

This method will create an exact copy of the `Point` object it is being called upon.

Example:

This example will create a `Point` object, create a copy, and output that copy:

```
import flash.geom.Point;
var myPoint:Point = new Point(5,5);
var myPoint2:Point = myPoint.clone();
trace(myPoint2);
//output: (x=5, y=5)
```

```
distance
```
Availability: FP:8, AS:1.0

Generic Template: `Point.distance(point1, point2);`

Parameters:

- *point1*—The first point.
- *point2*—The second point.

Returns: Number

The distance between the two points in pixels.

Description:

This method will calculate the distance between two points in two-dimensional space and return it in pixels.

Example:

This example will create two points and `trace` the distance between them:

```
import flash.geom.Point;
var myPoint:Point = new Point(5,5);
var myPoint2:Point = new Point(15,20);
trace(Point.distance(myPoint, myPoint2));
//output: 18.0277563773199
```

equals
Availability: FP:8, AS:1.0

Generic Template: `myPoint.equals(point);`

Parameters:

- *point*—The second `Point` that *myPoint* is being compared to.

Returns: Boolean

If the two points are equal, `true`; otherwise, `false`.

Description:

This method will determine if the two points are equal to one another (that is, have the same coordinates) and return a Boolean value.

Example:

This example will create three points and `trace` whether or not they are equal:

```
import flash.geom.Point;
var myPoint:Point = new Point(5,5);
var myPoint2:Point = new Point(15,20);
var myPoint3:Point = myPoint.clone();
trace(myPoint.equals(myPoint2));
trace(myPoint.equals(myPoint3));
//output: false
//        true
```

interpolate
Availability: FP:8, AS:1.0

Generic Template: `Point.interpolate(point1, point2, lvl);`

Parameters:

- *point1*—The first Point.

- *point2*—The second.

- *lvl*—A floating point number between 0–1 where if 1 is used, *point2* will be returned, and if 0 is used, *point1* will be returned.

Returns: `Point`

A point between the two points.

Description:

This method will determine a `Point` object that resides between the two points. You can use the *lvl* parameter to control how near to either point the new point should be.

Example:

This example will create a point directly between two points:

```
import flash.geom.Point;
var myPoint:Point = new Point(5,5);
var myPoint2:Point = new Point(15,20);
trace(Point.interpolate(myPoint, myPoint2, .5));
//output: (x=10, y=12.5)
```

```
normalize
```
Availability: FP:8, AS:1.0

Generic Template: `myPoint.normalize(length);`

Parameters:

- *length*—The amount to scale the point by.

Description:

This method will normalize a point based on the given *length*.

Example:

This example will create a normalized point based on the length of 2:

```
import flash.geom.Point;
var myPoint:Point = new Point(4,10);
myPoint.normalize(2);
trace(myPoint);
//output: (x=0.742781352708207, y=1.85695338177052)
```

```
offset
```
Availability: FP:8, AS:1.0

Generic Template: `myPoint.offset(x, y);`

Parameters:

- *x*—The horizontal amount to offset the point by.
- *y*—The vertical amount to offset the point by.

Description:

This method will offset a point by the given (x,y) amounts.

Example:

This example will create a Point and then offset it by (4,4):

```
import flash.geom.Point;
var myPoint:Point = new Point(5,10);
```

```
myPoint.offset(4,4);
trace(myPoint);
//output: (x=9, y=14)
```

polar
Availability: FP:8, AS:1.0

Generic Template: `Point.polar(length, angle);`

Parameters:

- *length*—The length coordinate from the polar pair.

- *angle*—The angle of the polar pair, in radians.

Returns: `Point`

The Cartesian point from the polar coordinates.

Description:

This method will convert polar coordinates to a Cartesian point.

Example:

This example will create a Cartesian point based on the polar coordinates.

```
import flash.geom.Point;
var myPoint:Point = Point.polar(10, 45);
trace(myPoint);
//output: (x=5.2532198881773, y=8.50903524534118)
```

subtract
Availability: FP:8, AS:1.0

Generic Template: myPoint.subtract(point);

Parameters:

- *point*—The second point to subtract from *myPoint*.

Returns: `Point`

The newly created point based on the difference between the two given points.

Description:

This method will subtract the second point from the `Point` calling the method and return a new point.

Example:

This example will create a Point and subtract a second point (4,4) from it:

```
import flash.geom.Point;
var myPoint:Point = new Point(5,5);
var myPoint2:Point = new Point(4,4);
trace(myPoint.subtract(myPoint2));
//output: (x=1, y=1)
```

toString
Availability: FP:8, AS:1.0

Generic Template: `myPoint.toString();`

Returns: String

The coordinates in the form of a string.

Description:

This method will convert the coordinates into a defined string for output.

Example:

This example will create a Point and send the coordinates to the Output panel:

```
import flash.geom.Point;
var myPoint:Point = new Point(5,5);
trace(myPoint.toString());
//output: (x=5, y=5)
```

The Rectangle **Class**

The `Rectangle` class allows you to create rectangles at runtime.

It is important when using this class to import it first at the beginning of your script, like this:

```
import flash.geom.Rectangle;
```

To instantiate a new instance of the `Rectangle` class, use this code as a template:

```
var myRectangle:Rectangle = new Rectangle(x, y, width, height);
```

- *x*—The x coordinate at the top-left corner.
- *y*—The y coordinate at the top-left corner.
- *width*—The width of the rectangle.
- *height*—The height of the rectangle.

Example:

This example will create an instance of the Rectangle class and send its information to the Output panel:

```
import flash.geom.Rectangle;
var myRectangle:Rectangle = new Rectangle(10,10,100,100);
trace(myRectangle);
//output: (x=10, y=10, w=100, h=100)
```

There are a few more properties, which were not in the parameters.

Properties

bottom
Availability: FP:8, AS:1.0

Generic Template: myRectangle.bottom;

Description:

This numeric property is the sum of the y property and the height property.

bottomRight
Availability: FP:8, AS:1.0

Generic Template: myRectangle.bottomRight;

Description:

This property is a Point object with the (x,y) coordinate being the bottom-right corner of the rectangle.

left
Availability: FP:8, AS:1.0

Generic Template: myRectangle.left;

Description:

This numeric property is the x property representing the left side of the rectangle.

right
Availability: FP:8, AS:1.0

Generic Template: myRectangle.right;

Description:

This numeric property is the sum of the x property and width property representing the right side of the rectangle.

`size`
Availability: FP:8, AS:1.0

Generic Template: `myRectangle.size;`

Description:

This property is a `Point` object, but the values (x,y) stand for (width, height).

`top`
Availability: FP:8, AS:1.0

Generic Template: `myRectangle.top;`

Description:

This numeric property is the y property representing the top side of the rectangle.

`topLeft`
Availability: FP:8, AS:1.0

Generic Template: `myRectangle.topLeft;`

Description:

This property is expressed as a `Point` object containing the coordinates for the top left corner of the rectangle.

Example:

This example will create a rectangle and `trace` every property it has:

```
import flash.geom.Rectangle;
var myRectangle:Rectangle = new Rectangle(10,10,100,100);
trace("x - "+myRectangle.x);
trace("y - "+myRectangle.y);
trace("width - "+myRectangle.width);
trace("height - "+myRectangle.height);
trace("left - "+myRectangle.left);
trace("topLeft - "+myRectangle.topLeft);
trace("top - "+myRectangle.top);
trace("right - "+myRectangle.right);
trace("bottomRight - "+myRectangle.bottomRight);
trace("bottom - "+myRectangle.bottom);
trace("size - "+myRectangle.size);
//output: x - 10
//y - 10
//width - 100
//height - 100
//left - 10
//topLeft - (x=10, y=10)
//top - 10
```

```
//right - 110
//bottomRight - (x=110, y=110)
//bottom - 110
//size - (x=100, y=100)
```

Methods

```
clone
```
Availability: FP:8, AS:1.0

Generic Template: `myRectangle.clone();`

Returns: `Rectangle`

This method will return an exact duplicate of the `Rectangle` object it is being called on.

Description:

This method will create an exact copy of the `Rectangle` object it is being called on.

Example:

This example will create a `Rectangle` object, create a copy, and output that copy:

```
import flash.geom.Rectangle;
var myRectangle:Rectangle = new Rectangle(10,10,100,100);
var myRec2:Rectangle = myRectangle.clone();
trace(myRec2);
//output: (x=10, y=10, w=100, h=100)
```

```
contains
```
Availability: FP:8, AS:1.0

Generic Template: `myRectangle.contains(x, y);`

Parameters:

- *x*—The horizontal position of the point being checked.
- *y*—The vertical position of the point being checked.

Returns: Boolean

If the coordinate falls within the rectangle, `true` will be returned. Otherwise, `false` will be returned.

Description:

This method will check to see if a coordinate (x,y) falls within a rectangle.

Example:

This example will check to see if two coordinates are within a rectangle:

```
import flash.geom.Rectangle;
var myRectangle:Rectangle = new Rectangle(10,10,100,100);
trace(myRectangle.contains(5,5));
trace(myRectangle.contains(20,20));
//output: false
//       true
```

containsPoint
Availability: FP:8, AS:1.0

Generic Template: `myRectangle.containsPoint(point);`

Parameters:

- *point*—A Point object containing the (x,y) coordinate to check.

Returns: Boolean

If the Point falls within the rectangle, `true` will be returned. Otherwise, `false` will be returned.

Description:

This method will check to see if a Point falls within a rectangle.

Example:

This example will check to see if two Points are within a rectangle:

```
import flash.geom.Rectangle;
import flash.geom.Point;
//the points
var point1:Point = new Point(5,5);
var point2:Point = new Point(20,20);
var myRectangle:Rectangle = new Rectangle(10,10,100,100);
trace(myRectangle.containsPoint(point1));
trace(myRectangle.containsPoint(point2));
//output: false
//       true
```

containsRectangle
Availability: FP:8, AS:1.0

Generic Template: `myRectangle.containsRectangle(rec);`

Parameters:

- *rec*—A Rectangle object.

Returns: Boolean

If the Rectangle falls entirely within the first rectangle, true will be returned. Otherwise, false will be returned.

Description:

This method will check to see if a Rectangle falls entirely within the first rectangle.

Example:

This example will check to see if a couple of Rectangles fall entirely within the first rectangle:

```
import flash.geom.Rectangle;
var myRectangle:Rectangle = new Rectangle(10,10,100,100);
var myRec2:Rectangle = new Rectangle (20,20,20,20);
var myRec3:Rectangle = new Rectangle (0,20,20,20);
trace(myRectangle.containsRectangle(myRec2));
trace(myRectangle.containsRectangle(myRec3));
//output: true
//        false
```

equals
Availability: FP:8, AS:1.0

Generic Template: myRectangle.equals(rec);

Parameters:

- *rec*—A Rectangle object to compare to *myRectangle*.

Returns: Boolean

If *rec* is equal to *myRectangle* in the properties x, y, width and height, true will be returned. Otherwise, false will be returned.

Description:

This method will check the four main properties of two rectangles to see if they are equal.

Example:

This example will check to see if a couple of Rectangles are equal to one another:

```
import flash.geom.Rectangle;
var myRectangle:Rectangle = new Rectangle(10,10,100,100);
var myRec2:Rectangle = new Rectangle (20,20,20,20);
var myRec3:Rectangle = myRectangle.clone();
trace(myRectangle.equals(myRec2));
trace(myRectangle.equals(myRec3));
//output: false
//        true
```

inflatePoint
Availability: FP:8, AS:1.0

Generic Template: `myRectangle.inflatePoint(point);`

Parameters:

- *point*—The `Point` object used to inflate the rectangle.

Description:

This method will increase the size of the rectangle as well as adjust the x and y properties using a `Point` object.

Example:

This example will create a rectangle and then increase its dimensions:

```
import flash.geom.Rectangle;
import flash.geom.Point;
//create the point
var point:Point = new Point(5,5);
var myRectangle:Rectangle = new Rectangle(10,10,100,100);
trace(myRectangle);
myRectangle.inflatePoint(point);
trace(myRectangle);
//output: (x=10, y=10, w=100, h=100)
//(x=5, y=5, w=110, h=110)
```

intersection
Availability: FP:8, AS:1.0

Generic Template: `myRectangle.intersection(rec);`

Parameters:

- *rec*—The Rectangle object being used to see if it intersects *myRectangle*.

Returns: `Rectangle`

The area of intersection is returned as a `Rectangle`.

Description:

This method will check to see if two `Rectangles` intersect, and if they do, a `Rectangle` object containing the intersection data is returned.

Example:

This example will create two `Rectangles` and see if they intersect:

```
import flash.geom.Rectangle;
var myRectangle:Rectangle = new Rectangle(10,10,100,100);
var myRec2:Rectangle = new Rectangle(20,0,50,30);
```

```
trace(myRectangle.intersection(myRec2));
//output: (x=20, y=10, w=50, h=20)
```

intersects
Availability: FP:8, AS:1.0

Generic Template: `myRectangle.intersects(rec);`

Parameters:

- *rec*—The Rectangle object being used to see if it intersects *myRectangle*.

Returns: Boolean

`true` if the rectangles intersect; `false` if they do not.

Description:

This method will check to see if two `Rectangles` intersect and returns a Boolean response.

Example:

This example will create two `Rectangles` and see if they intersect:

```
import flash.geom.Rectangle;
var myRectangle:Rectangle = new Rectangle(10,10,100,100);
var myRec2:Rectangle = new Rectangle(20,0,50,30);
trace(myRectangle.intersects(myRec2));
//output: true
```

isEmpty
Availability: FP:8, AS:1.0

Generic Template: `myRectangle.isEmpty();`

Returns: Boolean

If the rectangle has neither width nor height, `true` is returned. Otherwise, `false` is returned.

Description:

This method will check to see if a rectangle is empty (absent width and height).

Example:

This example will check to see if either of the two `Rectangles` are empty:

```
import flash.geom.Rectangle;
var myRectangle:Rectangle = new Rectangle(10,10,100,100);
var myRec2:Rectangle = new Rectangle();
trace(myRectangle.isEmpty());
trace(myRec2.isEmpty());
```

A

```
//output: false
//        true
```

offset
Availability: FP:8, AS:1.0

Generic Template: `myRectangle.offset(dx,dy);`

Parameters:

- *dx*—The horizontal adjustment in pixels.

- *dy*—The vertical adjustment in pixels.

Description:

This method will adjust the x and y positions of the rectangle.

Example:

This example will create a `Rectangle`, output the information, adjust the position, and output the information again:

```
import flash.geom.Rectangle;
var myRectangle:Rectangle = new Rectangle(10,10,100,100);
trace(myRectangle);
myRectangle.offset(5,5);
trace(myRectangle);
//output: (x=10, y=10, w=100, h=100)
//(x=15, y=15, w=100, h=100)
```

offsetPoint
Availability: FP:8, AS:1.0

Generic Template: `myRectangle.offsetPoint(point);`

Parameters:

- *point*—The `Point` object that contains the horizontal and vertical adjustments being applied to the rectangle.

Description:

This method will adjust the x and y positions of the rectangle using a `Point` object.

Example:

This example will create a `Rectangle`, output the information, adjust the position, and output the information again:

```
import flash.geom.Rectangle;
import flash.geom.Point;
//create the point
```

```
var point:Point = new Point(5,5);
var myRectangle:Rectangle = new Rectangle(10,10,100,100);
trace(myRectangle);
myRectangle.offsetPoint(point);
trace(myRectangle);
//output: (x=10, y=10, w=100, h=100)
//(x=15, y=15, w=100, h=100)
```

setEmpty
Availability: FP:8, AS:1.0

Generic Template: myRectangle.setEmpty();

Description:

This method will set all Rectangle options to 0.

Example:

This example will create a Rectangle, output the information, set it to empty, and output the information again:

```
import flash.geom.Rectangle;
var myRectangle:Rectangle = new Rectangle(10,10,100,100);
trace(myRectangle);
myRectangle.setEmpty();
trace(myRectangle);
//output: (x=10, y=10, w=100, h=100)
//(x=0, y=0, w=0, h=0)
```

toString
Availability: FP:8, AS:1.0

Generic Template: myRectangle.toString();

Results: String

The Rectangles information.

Description:

This method will return the Rectangles information in the form of a string.

Example:

This example will create a Rectangle and output the information:

```
import flash.geom.Rectangle;
var myRectangle:Rectangle = new Rectangle(10,10,100,100);
trace(myRectangle);
//output: (x=10, y=10, w=100, h=100)
```

```
union
```
Availability: FP:8, AS:1.0

Generic Template: `myRectangle.union(rec);`

Parameters:

- *rec*—The `Rectangle` object being joined.

Results: `Rectangle`

The combined dimensions of both `Rectangles`.

Description:

This method will combine both `Rectangles` at their absolute highest points.

Example:

This example will create two `Rectangles` and combine them to form one big `Rectangle`:

```
import flash.geom.Rectangle;
var myRectangle:Rectangle = new Rectangle(10,10,100,100);
var myRec2:Rectangle = new Rectangle(50,50,80,80);
trace(myRectangle.union(myRec2));
//output: (x=10, y=10, w=120, h=120)
```

The `Transform` **Class**

The `Transform` class allows you to collect information about color transformations and matrixes applied to movie clips.

It is important that when using this class to import it first at the beginning of your script like this:

```
import flash.geom.Transform;
```

To instantiate a new instance of the `Transform` class, use this code as a template:

```
var myTrans:Transform = new Transform(mc);
```

- *mc*—The movie clip that the `Transform` is being applied to.

Properties

```
colorTransform
```
Availability: FP:8, AS:1.0

Generic Template: `myTrans.colorTransform;`

Description:

This property is a `ColorTransform` object used to adjust colors of movie clips.

Example:

This example will create a new instance of the Transform object and send it to the Output panel:

```
import flash.geom.Transform;
var trans:Transform = new Transform(this);
trace(trans.colorTransform);
//output: (redMultiplier=1, greenMultiplier=1, blueMultiplier=1,
➥alphaMultiplier=1, redOffset=0, greenOffset=0, blueOffset=0, alphaOffset=0)
```

concatenatedColorTransform
Availability: FP:8, AS:1.0

Generic Template: myTrans.concatenatedColorTransform;

Description:

This property is the combined ColorTransform objects used to adjust colors of movie clips.

Example:

This example will create a new instance of the Transform object, set its color transform, and output it:

```
import flash.geom.Transform;
import flash.geom.ColorTransform;
var trans:Transform = new Transform(this);
trace(trans.colorTransform);
var myColorTrans:ColorTransform = new ColorTransform(1, 3, 6, 1, 0, 0, 255, 0);
trans.colorTransform = myColorTrans;
trace(trans.concatenatedColorTransform);
//output: (redMultiplier=1, greenMultiplier=1, blueMultiplier=1,
➥alphaMultiplier=1, redOffset=0, greenOffset=0, blueOffset=0, alphaOffset=0)
//(redMultiplier=1, greenMultiplier=3, blueMultiplier=6, alphaMultiplier=1,
➥redOffset=0, greenOffset=0, blueOffset=255, alphaOffset=0)
```

concatenatedMatrix
Availability: FP:8, AS:1.0

Generic Template: myTrans.concatenatedMatrix;

Description:

This property is the combined Matrix objects used to adjust positions of movie clips.

Example:

This example will create a new instance of the Transform object, set its matrix, and output it:

```
import flash.geom.Transform;
import flash.geom.Matrix;
//create the matrix
var myMatrix:Matrix = new Matrix();
myMatrix.rotate(45);
var trans:Transform = new Transform(this);
trace(trans.matrix);
trans.matrix = myMatrix;
trace(trans.concatenatedMatrix);
//output: (a=1, b=0, c=0, d=1, tx=0, ty=0)
//(a=0.525321960449219, b=0.850903511047363, c=-0.850903511047363,
➡d=0.525321960449219, tx=0, ty=0)
```

matrix
Availability: FP:8, AS:1.0

Generic Template: `myTrans.matrix;`

Description:

This property is the `Matrix` object used to adjust positions of movie clips.

Example:

This example will create a new instance of the `Transform` object and output its `matrix` property:

```
import flash.geom.Transform;
var trans:Transform = new Transform(this);
trace(trans.matrix);
//output: (a=1, b=0, c=0, d=1, tx=0, ty=0)
```

pixelBounds
Availability: FP:8, AS:1.0

Generic Template: `myTrans.pixelBounds;`

Description:

Defines the bounding rectangle of the movie clip being used.

Example:

This example will create a new instance of the `Transform` object and output its `pixelBounds` property:

```
import flash.geom.Transform;
var trans:Transform = new Transform(this);
trace(trans.pixelBounds);
//output: (x=33554431, y=33554431, w=0, h=0)
```

The FileReference **Class**

The FileReference class was created to allow users to browse for, upload, and download single files.

It is important when using this class to import it first at the beginning of your script, like this:

```
import flash.net.FileReferece;
```

And to instantiate a new instance of the FileReference object, use this code as a template:

```
var myFile_fr:FileReference = new FileReference();
```

Properties

creationDate
Availability: FP:8, AS:1.0

Generic Template: myFile_fr.creationData;

Description:

This Date property represents the creation date of the file on the end user's computer.

creator
Availability: FP:8, AS:1.0

Generic Template: myFile_fr.creator;

Description:

This string property represents the Macintosh creator file type of the file on the end user's computer.

modificationDate
Availability: FP:8, AS:1.0

Generic Template: myFile_fr.modificationDate;

Description:

This Date property represents the last modification date of the file on the end user's computer.

name
Availability: FP:8, AS:1.0

Generic Template: myFile_fr.name;

Description:

This string property is the name of the file on the end user's computer. Note that this will not return the path to the file, because that is a security risk.

size
Availability: FP:8, AS:1.0

Generic Template: `myFile_fr.size;`

Description:

This property represents the total size of the file in bytes.

type
Availability: FP:8, AS:1.0

Generic Template: `myFile_fr.type;`

Description:

This string property represents the file type date of the file on the end user's computer.

Methods

addListener
Availability: FP:8, AS:1.0

Generic Template: `myFile_fr.addListener(listener);`

Parameter:

- *listener*—This is the object that listens for the events of a `FileReference` object.

Description:

This method will add an event listener to an instance of the `FileReference` object.

Example:

This example will create a `FileReference` object and automatically call the browse method when you test it. After you select a file and click Open, all the properties of that file will be sent to the Output panel:

```
//import the FileReference Object
import flash.net.FileReference;
//the file reference object
var file_fr:FileReference = new FileReference();
//object for listening to for FileReference events
var list_obj:Object = new Object();
//the event for when a user selects a file and hits open
list_obj.onSelect = function(){
    trace("name: "+file_fr.name);
    trace("creation date: "+file_fr.creationDate);
    trace("modification date: "+file_fr.modificationDate);
    trace("type: "+file_fr.type);
    trace("size in bytes: "+file_fr.size);
    trace("creator: "+file_fr.creator);
```

```
}
//add the listener to the FileReference object
file_fr.addListener(list_obj);
//browse
file_fr.browse();
```

browse
Availability: FP:8, AS:1.0

Generic Template: `myFile_fr.browse(types);`

Parameter:

- *types*—This array is an optional parameter that will allow you to set certain file types to be able to be selected. Inside this array are objects that have three properties:

    - *description*—This is what appears to the user in the file type drop-down.

    - *extensions*—These are the different file type extensions you want to allow, each separated by a semicolon, like this: `"*.jpg;*.png;*.gif"`.

    - *macType*—This a Macintosh-specific property that will allow you to limit files to macType.

Description:

This method will allow end users to browse for files on their local system and have them returned to Flash.

Example:

This example will create a `FileReference` object and automatically call the `browse` method when you test it. And it will limit the files to just a few image types. After you select a file and select Open, all the properties of that file will be sent to the Output panel:

```
//import the FileReference Object
import flash.net.FileReference;
//the file reference object
var file_fr:FileReference = new FileReference();
//object for listening to for FileReference events
var list_obj:Object = new Object();
//the event for when a user selects a file and hits open
list_obj.onSelect = function(){
    trace("name: "+file_fr.name);
    trace("creation date: "+file_fr.creationDate);
    trace("modification date: "+file_fr.modificationDate);
    trace("type: "+file_fr.type);
    trace("size in bytes: "+file_fr.size);
    trace("creator: "+file_fr.creator);
}
//add the listener to the FileReference object
```

```
file_fr.addListener(list_obj);
//the file types you want
var fileTypes:Array = new Array({description:
➥"Images - .jpg, .gif, .png", extension: " *.jpg;*.gif;*.png"});
//browse
file_fr.browse(fileTypes);
```

cancel
Availability: FP:8, AS:1.0

Generic Template: `myFile_fr.cancel();`

Description:

This method will cancel any download or upload currently active.

Example:

This example will allow someone to download about 90% of the file and then cancel on
them:

```
import flash.net.FileReference;
//the file reference object
var file_fr:FileReference = new FileReference();
//the listener
var list_obj:Object = new Object();
list_obj.onProgress = function(file:FileReference,
bytesLoaded:Number, bytesTotal:Number):Void  {
    if ((bytesLoaded/bytesTotal/2) >= .9) {
        //almost completed, but not quite
        file_fr.cancel();
    }
}
//add the listener
file_fr.addListener(list_obj);
var path:String = "http://localHost.com/bigImage.jpg";
file_fr.download(path,"myImage.jpg");
```

download
Availability: FP:8, AS:1.0

Generic Template: `myFile_fr.download(path, fileName);`

Parameters:

- *path*—This is a string holding the path to the file on the server you want to download.

- *fileName*—This string is the default filename displayed in the window that allows
  you to map to where you want to save the file.

Returns: Boolean

If the window pops up allowing you to map where the file should be saved, it returns `true`; otherwise, `false` is returned.

Description:

This method will allow end users to download files from a server directly to their computer.

Example:

This example will allow someone to download a file from the local server:

```
import flash.net.FileReference;
//the file reference object
var file_fr:FileReference = new FileReference();
//the listener
var list_obj:Object = new Object();
list_obj.onComplete = function(file:FileReference):Void  {
    trace("ALL DONE!");
}
//add the listener
file_fr.addListener(list_obj);
var path:String = "http://localHost.com/bigImage.jpg";
file_fr.download(path,"myImage.jpg");
```

```
removeListener
```
Availability: FP:8, AS:1.0

Generic Template: `myFile_fr.removeListener(listener);`

Parameter:

- *listener*—This is the object that listens for the events of a `FileReference` object.

Returns: Boolean

If the listener is removed successfully, `true` is returned; otherwise, `false` is returned.

Description:

This method will remove an event listener from an instance of the `FileReference` object.

Example:

This example will create a `FileReference` object and automatically call the `browse` method when you test it. After you select a file and click Open, the name property will be sent to the Output panel, and the listener will be removed:

```
//import the FileReference Object
import flash.net.FileReference;
//the file reference object
```

```
var file_fr:FileReference = new FileReference();
//object for listening to for FileReference events
var list_obj:Object = new Object();
//the event for when a user selects a file and hits open
list_obj.onSelect = function(){
    trace("name: "+file_fr.name);
    trace(file_fr.removeListener(this));
}
//add the listener to the FileReference object
file_fr.addListener(list_obj);
//browse
file_fr.browse();
```

upload
Availability: FP:8, AS:1.0

Generic Template: `myFile_fr.upload(path);`

Parameter:

- *path*—This is the path to the server-side script where the upload will take place.

Returns: Boolean

If there was no problem with calling this method (that is, no file in the `FileReference` yet), then `true` is returned; otherwise, `false` is returned.

Description:

This method will allow end users to upload files directly from Flash to a server.

Example:

This example will create a `FileReference` object and automatically call the `browse` method when you test it. After you have selected a file, it will call the upload method that will send the information to a server-side page.

```
//import the FileReference Object
import flash.net.FileReference;
//the file reference object
var file_fr:FileReference = new FileReference();
//object for listening to for FileReference events
var list_obj:Object = new Object();
//the event for when a user selects a file and hits open
list_obj.onSelect = function(){
    file_fr.upload("http://localHost/upload.php");
}
//add the listener to the FileReference object
file_fr.addListener(list_obj);
```

```
//browse
file_fr.browse();
For a real working example, see Chapter 22, "PHP and Flash."
```

Events

`onCancel`
Availability: FP:8, AS:1.0

Generic Template: `Listener.onCancel = function(fileRef);`

Parameter:

- *fileRef*—This is a reference to the FileReference object that initiated the dialog window opening.

Description:

This event is triggered when the dialog window is open, and the user chooses Cancel.

Example:

This example will open a dialog box for a user to choose a file, and then it listens for the Cancel button:

```
//import the FileReference Object
import flash.net.FileReference;
//the file reference object
var file_fr:FileReference = new FileReference();
//object for listening to for FileReference events
var list_obj:Object = new Object();
//the event for when a user selects a file and hits cancel
list_obj.onCancel = function(fileRef:FileReference){
    trace("Cancel Hit");
}
//add the listener to the FileReference object
file_fr.addListener(list_obj);
//browse
file_fr.browse();
```

`onComplete`
Availability: FP:8, AS:1.0

Generic Template: `Listener.onComplete = function(fileRef);`

Parameter:

- *fileRef*—This is a reference to the `FileReference` object that initiated the dialog window opening.

Description:

This event is triggered when a file upload or download completes successfully.

Example:

This example will allow a user to upload a file to a PHP page; then it listens for when the upload is complete:

```
//import the FileReference Object
import flash.net.FileReference;
//the file reference object
var file_fr:FileReference = new FileReference();
//object for listening to for FileReference events
var list_obj:Object = new Object();
//the event for when a user selects a file and hits open
list_obj.onCancel = function(fileRef:FileReference){
    fileRef.upload("http://localHost/upload.php");
}
//the event for when the file is finished uploading
list_obj.onComplete = function(fileRef:FileReference){
    trace("ALL DONE!!");
}
//add the listener to the FileReference object
file_fr.addListener(list_obj);
//browse
file_fr.browse();
For a real working example, see Chapter 22, "PHP and Flash."
```

onHTTPError
Availability: FP:8, AS:1.0

Generic Template: `Listener.onHTTPError = function(fileRef, error){`

Parameter:

- *fileRef*—This is a reference to the `FileReference` object that initiated the dialog window opening.

- *error*—A numerical value representing the error returned. For a complete list of errors, try ftp://ftp.isi.edu/in-notes/rfc2616.txt.

Description:

This event is triggered when an HTTP error occurs during uploading.

Example:

This example will allow a user to upload a file to a PHP page; then it listens for an HTTP error:

```
//import the FileReference Object
import flash.net.FileReference;
//the file reference object
var file_fr:FileReference = new FileReference();
//object for listening to for FileReference events
var list_obj:Object = new Object();
//the event for when a user selects a file and hits open
list_obj.onCancel = function(fileRef:FileReference){
    fileRef.upload("http://localHost/upload.php");
}
//the event for HTTP errors
list_obj.onHTTPError = function(fileRef:FileReference, error:Number){
    trace("HTTP error: with " + fileRef.name + ":error #" + error);
}
//the event for when the file is finished uploading
list_obj.onComplete = function(fileRef:FileReference){
    trace("ALL DONE!!");
}
//add the listener to the FileReference object
file_fr.addListener(list_obj);
//browse
file_fr.browse();
```

For a real working example, see Chapter 22, "PHP and Flash".

onIOError

Availability: FP:8, AS:1.0

Generic Template: `Listener.onIOError = function(fileRef){`

Parameter:

- *fileRef*—This is a reference to the FileReference object that initiated the dialog window opening.

Description:

This event is triggered when any input or output errors occur. You will see these errors most often when servers require authentication, and because there are no means for this to be accomplished with Flash, an error will occur.

Example:

This example will allow a user to upload a file to a PHP page; then it listens for an IO error:

```
//import the FileReference Object
import flash.net.FileReference;
//the file reference object
var file_fr:FileReference = new FileReference();
```

```
//object for listening to for FileReference events
var list_obj:Object = new Object();
//the event for when a user selects a file and hits open
list_obj.onCancel = function(fileRef:FileReference){
    fileRef.upload("http://localHost/upload.php");
}
//the event for IO errors
list_obj.onIOError = function(fileRef:FileReference){
    trace("Input/Output error occured");
}
//the event for when the file is finished uploading
list_obj.onComplete = function(fileRef:FileReference){
    trace("ALL DONE!!");
}
//add the listener to the FileReference object
file_fr.addListener(list_obj);
//browse
file_fr.browse();
For a real working example, see Chapter 22, "PHP and Flash."
```

onOpen

Availability: FP:8, AS:1.0

Generic Template: `Listener.onOpen = function(fileRef){`

Parameter:

- *fileRef*—This is a reference to the `FileReference` object that initiated the dialog window opening.

Description:

This event is triggered when an `upload` or `download` method is called.

Example:

This example will allow a user to upload a file to a PHP page; then it listens for when the upload starts:

```
//import the FileReference Object
import flash.net.FileReference;
//the file reference object
var file_fr:FileReference = new FileReference();
//object for listening to for FileReference events
var list_obj:Object = new Object();
//the event for when a user selects a file and hits open
list_obj.onCancel = function(fileRef:FileReference){
    fileRef.upload("http://localHost/upload.php");
}
```

```
//the event for when the upload starts
list_obj.onOpen = function(fileRef:FileReference){
    trace("Upload has started");
}
//the event for when the file is finished uploading
list_obj.onComplete = function(fileRef:FileReference){
    trace("ALL DONE!!");
}
//add the listener to the FileReference object
file_fr.addListener(list_obj);
//browse
file_fr.browse();
```

For a real working example, see Chapter 22, "PHP and Flash."

onProgress

Availability: FP:8, AS:1.0

Generic Template: `Listener.onProgress = function(fileRef, bytesLoaded, bytesTotal){`

Parameter:

- *fileRef*—This is a reference to the `FileReference` object that initiated the dialog window opening.

- *bytesLoaded*—This is a reference to amount of bytes that have been downloaded or uploaded, depending on the method called.

- *bytesTotal*—This is a reference to total amount of bytes being downloaded or uploaded, depending on the method called.

Description:

This event is triggered periodically during either upload or download.

Example:

This example will download a file and trace the percentage downloaded as it progresses:

```
import flash.net.FileReference;
//the file reference object
var file_fr:FileReference = new FileReference();
//the listener
var list_obj:Object = new Object();
//the event that monitors download progress
list_obj.onProgress = function(file:FileReference,
➥bytesLoaded:Number, bytesTotal:Number):Void  {
    var per = bytesLoaded/bytesTotal;
    trace(Math.floor(per*100)+"%");
}
```

A

```
//add the listener
file_fr.addListener(list_obj);
var path:String = "http://localHost.com/bigImage.jpg";
file_fr.download(path,"myImage.jpg");
```

onSecurityError
Availability: FP:8, AS:1.0

Generic Template: `Listener.onSecurityError = function(fileRef, error){`

Parameter:

- *fileRef*—This is a reference to the `FileReference` object that initiated the dialog window opening.

- *error*—This is a string describing the security error that occurred.

Description:

This event is triggered when a security error occurs during either upload or download.

Example:

This example will attempt to download a file from the server, and if a security error occurs, it will be sent to the Output panel:

```
import flash.net.FileReference;
//the file reference object
var file_fr:FileReference = new FileReference();
//the listener
var list_obj:Object = new Object();
//the event that is triggered when a security error occurs
list_obj.onSecurityError = function(file:FileReference, error:String):Void  {
    trace("Security error: " + error);
}
//add the listener
file_fr.addListener(list_obj);
var path:String = "http://localHost.com/bigImage.jpg";
file_fr.download(path,"myImage.jpg");
```

onSelect
Availability: FP:8, AS:1.0

Generic Template: `Listener.onSelect = function(fileRef){`

Parameter:

- *fileRef*—This is a reference to the `FileReference` object that initiated the dialog window opening.

Description:

This event is triggered when a user selects a file and either clicks Open or double-clicks the file.

Example:

This example will allow the user to select a file, and when the user clicks open, all the file properties will be sent to the Output panel:

```
//import the FileReference Object
import flash.net.FileReference;
//the file reference object
var file_fr:FileReference = new FileReference();
//object for listening to for FileReference events
var list_obj:Object = new Object();
//the event for when a user selects a file and hits open
list_obj.onSelect = function(){
    trace("name: "+file_fr.name);
    trace("creation date: "+file_fr.creationDate);
    trace("modification date: "+file_fr.modificationDate);
    trace("type: "+file_fr.type);
    trace("size in bytes: "+file_fr.size);
    trace("creator: "+file_fr.creator);
}
//add the listener to the FileReference object
file_fr.addListener(list_obj);
//browse
file_fr.browse();
```

The FileReferenceList Class

The FileReferenceList class was created to allow users to browse for and upload multiple files. It is important to note that even though you can use this object to select and upload multiple files, the files themselves must still be uploaded individually.

It is important when using this class to import it first at the beginning of your script, like this:

```
import flash.net.FileReferenceList;
```

To instantiate a new instance of the FileReference object, use this code as a template:

```
var myFile_frl:FileReferenceList = new FileReferenceList();
```

A

Properties

fileList
Availability: FP:8, AS:1.0

Generic Template: myFile_frl.fileList;

Description:

This property is an array file of different FileReference objects.

Example:

This example will allow the user to select multiple files, and when the user clicks Open, all the properties of each FileReference will be sent to the Output panel:

```
import flash.net.FileReferenceList;
//the listener object
var list_obj:Object = new Object();
//when the user has finished selecting the files
list_obj.onSelect = function(fileRefList:FileReferenceList){
    var list_array = fileRefList.fileList;
    var tLength:Number = list_array.length;
    var i = 0;
    while(i<tLength){
        var file = list_array[i];
        for(prop in file){
            trace(prop + " - " + file[prop]);
        }
        i++;
    }
}
//FileReferenceList object
var file_frl:FileReferenceList = new FileReferenceList();
//add the listener
file_frl.addListener(list_obj);
//browse
file_frl.browse();
```

Methods

addListener
Availability: FP:8, AS:1.0

Generic Template: myFile_frl.addListener(listener);

Parameter:

- *listener*—This is the object that listens for the events of a FileReference object.

Description:

This method will add an event listener to an instance of the `FileReferenceList` object.

Example:

This example will create a `FileReferenceList` object, and automatically call the `browse` method when you test it. After you select a file and click Open, all the properties from the first file will be sent to the Output panel:

```
import flash.net.FileReferenceList;
//the FileReferenceList object
var file_frl:FileReferenceList = new FileReferenceList();
//object for listening to for FileReference events
var list_obj:Object = new Object();
//the event for when a user selects the file(s) and hits open
list_obj.onSelect =function(fileRefList:FileReferenceList){
    trace("name: "+fileRefList.fileList[0].name);
    trace("creation date: "+fileRefList.fileList[0].creationDate);
    trace("modification date: "+fileRefList.fileList[0].modificationDate);
    trace("type: "+fileRefList.fileList[0].type);
    trace("size in bytes: "+fileRefList.fileList[0].size);
    trace("creator: "+fileRefList.fileList[0].creator);
}
//add the listener to the FileReference object
file_frl.addListener(list_obj);
//browse
file_frl.browse();
```

browse
Availability: FP:8, AS:1.0

Generic Template: `myFile_frl.browse(types);`

Parameter:

- *types*—This array is an optional parameter that will allow you to set certain file types to be able to be selected. Inside this array are objects that have three properties:

  - *description*—This is what appears to the user in the file type drop-down.

  - *extensions*—These are the different file type extensions you want to allow, each separated by a semicolon, like this: `"*.jpg;*.png;*.gif"`.

  - *macType*—This a Macintosh-specific property that will allow you to limit files to `macType`.

Description:

This method will allow end users to browse for files on their local system and have them returned to Flash.

Example:

This example will create a `FileReferenceList` object and automatically call the `browse` method when you test it. It will limit the files to just a few image types. After you select the file(s) and click Open, all the properties of the first file will be sent to the Output panel:

```
import flash.net.FileReferenceList;
//the FileReferenceList object
var file_frl:FileReferenceList = new FileReferenceList();
//object for listening to for FileReference events
var list_obj:Object = new Object();
//the event for when a user selects the file(s) and hits open
list_obj.onSelect =function(fileRefList:FileReferenceList){
    trace("name: "+fileRefList.fileList[0].name);
    trace("creation date: "+fileRefList.fileList[0].creationDate);
    trace("modification date: "+fileRefList.fileList[0].modificationDate);
    trace("type: "+fileRefList.fileList[0].type);
    trace("size in bytes: "+fileRefList.fileList[0].size);
    trace("creator: "+fileRefList.fileList[0].creator);
}
//add the listener to the FileReference object
file_frl.addListener(list_obj);
//the file types you want
var fileTypes:Array = new Array({description:
➥"Images - .jpg, .gif, .png", extension: " *.jpg;*.gif;*.png"});
//browse
file_frl.browse(fileTypes);
```

`removeListener`
Availability: FP:8, AS:1.0

Generic Template: `myFile_frs.removeListener(listener);`

Parameter:

• *listener*—This is the object that listens for the events of a `FileReferenceList` object.

Returns: Boolean

If the listener is removed successfully, `true` is returned; otherwise, `false` is returned.

Description:

This method will remove an event listener from an instance of the `FileReferenceList` object.

Example:

This example will create a FileReferenceList object and automatically call the browse method when you test it. After you select the file(s) and click Open, the name property of the first file will be sent to the Output panel, and the listener will be removed:

```
import flash.net.FileReferenceList;
//the FileReferenceList object
var file_frl:FileReferenceList = new FileReferenceList();
//object for listening to for FileReference events
var list_obj:Object = new Object();
//the event for when a user selects a file and hits open
list_obj.onSelect = function(fileRefList:FileReferenceList){
    trace("name: "+fileRefList.fileList[0].name);
    trace(file_frl.removeListener(this));
}
//add the listener to the FileReference object
file_frl.addListener(list_obj);
//browse
file_frl.browse();
```

Events

onCancel
Availability: FP:8, AS:1.0

Generic Template: Listener.onCancel = function(fileRefList);

Parameter:

- *fileRefList*—This is a reference to the FileReferenceList object that initiated the dialog window opening.

Description:

This event is triggered when the dialog window is open, and the user chooses Cancel.

Example:

This example will open a dialog box for a user to choose a file; then it listens for the Cancel button:

```
import flash.net.FileReferenceList;
//the FileReferenceList object
var file_frl:FileReferenceList = new FileReferenceList();
//object for listening to for FileReference events
var list_obj:Object = new Object();
//the event for when a user selects a file and hits cancel
list_obj.onCancel = function(fileRefList:FileReferenceList){
    trace("Cancel Hit");
```

```
}
//add the listener to the FileReference object
file_frl.addListener(list_obj);
//browse
file_frl.browse();
```

onSelect
Availability: FP:8, AS:1.0

Generic Template: `Listener.onSelect = function(fileRefList){`

Parameter:

- *fileRefList*—This is a reference to the `FileReferenceList` object that initiated the dialog window opening.

Description:

This event is triggered when a user selects a file and either clicks Open or double-clicks the file.

Example:

This example will allow the user to select multiple files, and when the user clicks Open, all the properties of each `FileReference` will be sent to the Ouput panel:

```
import flash.net.FileReferenceList;
//the listener object
var list_obj:Object = new Object();
//when the user has finished selecting the files
list_obj.onSelect = function(fileRefList:FileReferenceList){
    var list_array = fileRefList.fileList;
    var tLength:Number = list_array.length;
    var i = 0;
    while(i<tLength){
        var file = list_array[i];
        for(prop in file){
            trace(prop + " - " + file[prop]);
        }
        i++;
    }
}
//FileReferenceList object
var file_frl:FileReferenceList = new FileReferenceList();
//add the listener
file_frl.addListener(list_obj);
//browse
file_frl.browse();
```

The TextRenderer Class

The TextRenderer class was created to provide more control over the advanced anti-aliasing capabilities of embedded fonts.

It is important when using this class to import it first at the beginning of your script, like this:

```
import flash.text.TextRenderer;
```

Properties

antiAliasType
Availability: FP:8, AS:1.0

Generic Template: TextRenderer.antiAliasType;

Description:

This string literal property controls the specific anti-aliasing type for the movie. Available options are

- *default*—Using this option will restore anti-aliasing controls back to individual text fields.

- *off*—This option will set all text fields' anti-aliasing to normal, overriding any individual settings.

- *on*—This option will set all text fields' anti-aliasing to advanced, overriding any individual settings.

Example:

This example will set anti-aliasing for all text fields to normal:

```
import flash.text.TextRenderer;
TextRenderer.antiAliasType = "off";
```

maxLevel
Availability: FP:8, AS:1.0

Generic Template: TextRenderer.maxLevel;

Description:

This numerical value controls the level of ADF (Advanced Distance Fields) for all text fields in a movie; it can accept 3, 4, or 7, with 7 being of the highest quality.

Example:

```
This example will set ADF level to the maximum setting:
import flash.text.TextRenderer;
TextRenderer.maxLevel = 7;
```

Methods

setAdvancedAntialiasingTable
Availability: FP:8, AS:1.0

Generic Template: TextRenderer.setAdvancedAntialiasingTable(font, style, color, advancedTable);

Parameters:

- *font*—The name of the font to be used as a string literal.

- *style*—The style being used as a string literal. Possible values are "bold," "bolditalic," "italic," and "none."

- *color*—This string literal can either be "dark" or "light."

- *advancedTable*—An array of object elements representing GSM settings for *font*.

  - *fontSize*—Pixel size of *font*.

  - *insideCutOff*—Affects stroke weight; is usually a positive number.

  - *outsideCutOff*—Affects stroke weight; is usually a negative number.

Description:

This method will set up a custom CSM lookup table for a given font.

Example:

This example will create a lookup table for the Arial font:

```
import flash.text.TextRenderer;
//items to add to the arrau
var item_obj:Object = {fontSize:12, insideCutoff:.5, outsideCutoff:-.5};
var item_obj2:Object = {fontSize:15, insideCutoff:.9, outsideCutoff:-.91};
//create the array
var lookup_array:Array = new Array(item_obj, item_obj2);
//setup the lookout table
TextRenderer.setAdvancedAntialiasingTable("Arial", "bold", "dark", lookup_array);
```

Index

Symbols

& (ampersand), 523

\ (backslash), 182

?: (conditional statement), 260

" (double quotes), 181

== (equality operator), 252

// (forward slashes), 169

> (greater than operator), 253

>= (greater than or equal to operator), 253

++ (increment operator), 203

!= (inequality operator), 252

< (less than operator), 252

<= (less than or equal to operator), 253

! (logical NOT operator), 256

|| (logical OR operator), 258-260

+ (plus) operator, 183

&& (short-circuit AND operator), 257-258

' (single quotes), 181

=== (strict equality) operator, 253-254

!== (strict inequality) operator, 254

~ (tilde), 549

A

<a> tag (HTML), 385

aa property (transformObject object), 315

ab property (transformObject object), 315

How can we make this index more useful? Email us at indexes@samspublishing.com

I

NumericStepper component, 406

RadioButton component, 407

label tag (XML), 667

labelPlacement parameter

Button component, 403

CheckBox component, 404

NumericStepper component, 406

RadioButton component, 407

labels, 356

labels parameter

ComboBox component, 404

List component, 405

MenuBar component, 406

labelString parameter (DataGlue class), 586

Lasso tool, 55-56

lastIndexOf method, 188

layer option

Blend mode, 13

QuickTime Publish Settings, 139

layers

creating, 72

Layer folder, 72

locking, 72

mask layer, 100-101

removing, 72

showing as outline, 72

showing/hiding, 72

layout tags (XML), 666-669

Left Channel option (sound), 107

left property (Rectangle class), 763

length function, 301

length operator, 231

length property, 221-222

arguments object, 288-291

indexing string characters, 185-186

Point class, 757

less than operator (<), 252

less than or equal to operator (<=), 253

Level Number option, 472

level parameter (loadVariablesNum method), 507

<li> tag (HTML), 386

library, 6-7, 94-96

Library command (Window menu), 94

lighten option (Blend mode), 13

Line Break tag, 385

Line tool, 52-55

lineGradientStyle method, 334-335

lines

drawing

Line tool, 52-55

Pen tool, 56-57

Pencil tool, 60-61

scaling, 15

stroke improvements, 15

stroke properties, 53-55

lineStyle method, 330-331

lineTo method, 332-334

Linkage Properties dialog box, 402

linkageID parameter (attachMovie method), 401

List component, 405

List Item tag, 386

List Objects, 439-440

List Variables, 439-440

listbox tag (XML), 666

listeners, 347-351

adding to component events, 413-415

compared to callbacks, 351-352

components, 350-351

creating, 464-466

unsubscribing, 349

listitem tag (XML), 666

How can we make this index more useful? Email us at indexes@samspublishing.com

onRollOver event handler, 352

onScroller event handler, 360

onSecurityError event handler, 786

onSelect event handler, 786-787, 792

onSetFocus event handler, 352, 360

onStatus event handler, 647-648

onUnload event handler, 354

OOP (object-oriented programming), 143-144

Open/Import option (ActionScript), 165

operators

    comparison, 251-252

        equality operator (==), 252

        greater than operator (>), 253

        greater than or equal to operator (>=), 253

        inequality operator (!=), 252

        less than operator (<), 252

        less than or equal to operator (<=), 253

        strict equality (===) operator, 253-254

        strict inequality (!==) operator, 254

    converting variables, 209

    delete, 230-231

    increment (++), 203

    Logical NOT (!), 256

    logical OR operator (||), 258-260

    new, 218-219

    short-circuit AND (&&), 257-258

Optimize, 698

Optimize Colors option (GIF Publish Settings), 135

Optimize for Flash Player 6 r65 option (Publish Settings), 130

ord function, 303

Output panel, 27, 438, 503

Oval tool, 58

ovals, drawing, 58

Over state (buttons), 88

overlay option (Blend mode), 13

P

<p> tag (HTML), 386

pages (ASP), 521-522

    Access databases, accessing, 529-540

        ConnectionString, 531

        dvdList.fla file, 533-534

        getAllDVDs.asp page, 532-533

        getDVDInfo.asp page, 535-536

        searchDVDs.asp page, 537-540

        SQL strings, 531

    Hello World example, 522-524

    sending and receiving data

        in ASP, 525-526

        in Flash, 526-528

Paint Bucket tool, 63

Palette option (GIF Publish Settings), 136

Palette Type option (GIF Publish Settings), 136

paletteMap method, 719-720

panels, 26. *See also* dialog boxes; windows

    Accessibility, 27

    Actions, 27, 160-164

        buttons, 161

        conversion functions, 298-299

        mathematical functions, 299-300

        preferences, 164-166

    Align, 26-31

    Behaviors, 27, 167-169

    collapsing, 28

    Color Mixer, 27, 65-66

    Color Swatches, 27, 65

    Common Libraries, 27

    Component Inspector, 27, 410-412

    Components, 27, 400-401

    creating, 673-674

    Debugger, 27

    design, 26-32

How can we make this index more useful? Email us at indexes@samspublishing.com

S

How can we make this index more useful? Email us at indexes@samspublishing.com

Oval tool, 58

Paint Bucket tool, 63

Pen tool, 56-57

Pencil tool, 60-61

PolyStar tool, 59-60

Rectangle tool, 59

Subselection tool, 51

Text tool, 57-58

Zoom tool, 50

top property (Rectangle class), 764

topLeft property (Rectangle class), 764-765

toString method, 208, 235, 748-749, 755, 762, 771

Total Items option (library), 94

totals array, 234

totalTime property (FLVPlayback component), 654

toUpperCase function, 191

Trace Bitmap command (Bitmap menu), 69

trace function, 218, 291, 438-439

tracing bitmaps, 69

Transform class

colorTransform property, 772-773

concatenatedColorTransform property, 773

concatenatedMatrix property, 773-774

matrix property, 774

pixelBounds property, 774

Transform panel, 27, 30-31

transformObject object, 314-315

transformPoint method, 755

translate method, 756

Transparent option (GIF Publish Settings), 135

transparent property (BitmapData class), 706

Tree component, 408, 620-621

trigger method, 618

Trim function, 525

tween editor, 96-97

tweening

Motion Tweening

creating, 96

mask layer, 100-101

Motion Guides, 98, 100

nested animations, 97-98

tween editor, 96-97

Shape Tweening

creating, 78-80

moveCircle.fla example, 78-80

shape hints, 80-82

Type option (Clipboard Preferences), 38

type property (FileReference class), 19, 776

typeof function, 206

types. *See* **data types**

typewriter font, 365

typing, strict, 157-160, 173, 436-437

U

<u> tag (HTML), 387

UI tags (XML), 666-669

UIScrollBar component, 408

Undefined data type, 180, 199

Underline tag, 387

Undo Levels option (General Preferences), 35

Undo option, 7, 35

undoing mistakes, 7

unescape function, 501-502

Unicode

escape sequences, 193

Unicode-encoded strings, 395

union method, 772

unleashedCafeSite sample application, 583-593

code listing, 591-593

DataGlue class, 586

How can we make this index more useful? Email us at indexes@samspublishing.com

How can we make this index more useful? Email us at indexes@samspublishing.com